OTHER BOOKS BY TR1

"Ida's Ride," a novel.

"Behind These Walls," an anthology in which Schiesser's works appeared.

"In the Company of Women," an anthology, Women's Studies.

"Pieces . . . of Our Lives," an anthology.

"These Guys: Cold War Stories Told by Cold War Warriors," a collection of stories about those who served in intelligence communications, and/or during the Vietnam era.

The color of the cover for "These Guys: Cold War Stories Told by Cold War Warriors" has been scanned into the computer by use of a patch cut from a 1950's USAF Blue Uniform, color number 86. The silver letters stand for the silver buttons. The Editor and Publisher have strived to make the cover as accurate as possible in order to truly honor the cold war warriors who have made this book what it is.

Trish Schiesser,
Editor/2009

To Don, Best Wishes, Trish 5/09

THESE GUYS

COLD WAR STORIES

TOLD BY

COLD WAR WARRIORS

1945-1991

Trish Schiesser

COLLECTED AND EDITED

BY

TRISH SCHIESSER

OLD LIEUTENANT PRESS
PORTSMOUTH VA

Published by Old Lieutenant Press

Copyright 2009 Trish Schiesser

Printed in the United States of America

All rights reserved including the right to reproduce this book or portions thereof in any form without permission from the Editor.

Editor: Trish Schiesser

Cover: Trish Schiesser, Bob Schiesser

ISBN: 0-9670169-4-0

DEDICATION

I dedicate this book to my late brother, SSGT Phillip C. Noland, AF12392047, USAFSS (Ret), who was a Radio Intercept Analyst, 20270, during the cold war from 1951 through 1968. He was Honorably discharged from the USAFSS in 1965. It was his life, and honor to serve in the USAFSS, which he did in excellence on the job and off the job, that inspired me to begin this book.

A few months after beginning research about him, I met so many fine ex-USAFSS men that I decided to open the book up to submissions from "These Guys," and so, this book is in remembrance of my brother, and all his brothers in arms.

ACKNOWLEDGMENTS

I would like to express my thanks to all of the writers in this book for their stories and assistance when I most needed it, also for their love and appreciation for what I have done in researching and collecting and editing this book, "These Guys: Cold War Stories Told by Cold War Warriors." It is YOUR book, guys, because without you it couldn't have happened.

Also, I would like to acknowledge my husband, Bob's support and work he has done for this book - it is because of him that this book has come to fruition. And, Bob, you are the best damned Port Engineer on the waterfront, Norfolk, Virginia as you do your fine work and give all your heart to the USNS GRASP,(T-ARS 51) rescue/salvage ship.

John Oberg, thank you for the magnificent Foreword you have written for this book. Everyone will know what the Cold War is all about after reading your work.

Capt. Bill Person, USAFSS (Ret) my thanks and love go out to you for your help during my research and for writing CODEBREAKERS and allowing me to print it on the back of this book.

Ed Leonard, ex-USAFSS, thank you for your quote in the front pages of THESE GUYS . . . and for your support early on when my research began.

Last but not least, Vince Wuwert, Sgt. ex-USAFSS for your lovely quote on the front pages of THESE GUYS and for all of your support during these years of research and plugging in stories, one by one, on my computer.

And, to Andrea Robin (Schiesser) Rose, bless her soul, for her help when this book was just a gleam in my eye. I love you.

My love goes out to 'Maverick' as he sat under my desk throughout the years and does so, today.

If I have forgotten anyone, please know that your support and writings are well received.

T.S. - 2009

FOREWORD

"Cold War" is a term that deceptively limits one's understanding of the substance and dynamics of international affairs in the Post-World War II era when humankind came very close to causing its own extinction. Some people have forgotten or may simply be too young to know the seriousness of the worldwide impact of the Cold War. To be sure, not being aware of the genesis of the Cold War and its implications for the present and future constitutes accidental or willful ignorance of a dangerous kind.

On the surface, "Cold War" seems to imply just major non-shooting hostilities between combatants, a remote event possibly deserving little serious examination. And actually choosing not to acquire this knowledge provides no immunity from almost certain worldwide suffering that will be experienced if any new outbreak of an international struggle resembling the Cold War occurs. The biggest challenge facing curious people, though, may be that Cold War as a concept even obscures events and issues amazingly vast in scope, sweeping in time and serious in their implications for the future.

Indeed, in just the first few years of the 21st Century, Vladimir Putin's Russian Federation ominously signals a resurgent xenophobic and aggressive Russian nationalism similar to what the world has already experienced for roughly half of the 20th Century. The case can be made that a robust and acquisitive Russian foreign policy has existed for several centuries. And if past performance is the best predictor of future performance, freedom-loving people in Western democracies may well be obliged to relive the long trauma of the Cold War if we fail to learn from the lessons of the past. For good reason, the humanist philosopher George Santayana counseled, "Those who cannot remember the past are condemned to repeat it." That the vast majority of people have little awareness of international affairs is well-known. But imagine the serious implications of general worldwide ignorance! Even the wisest mind has something yet to learn from history's lessons.

Conventional practice suggests we begin the story of the Cold War on Wednesday, 20 April 1945: Torgau, is a small German town on the Elbe River some 70 miles south of the Nazi capital in Berlin; American Army and Soviet Army combat patrols achieve their first unit-level contact as allies, and exchange protocols commonly known among soldiers. They recognize the significance of their meeting: the end of World War II, the most destructive and costly war in terms of lives lost in history, is close at hand.

In an ironically fitting way, these soldiers are but small cogs in two immense war machines allied only temporarily out of mutual necessity to effect the defeat of Nazi Germany, their common enemy. A display of official and superficial friendship is shown between these American and Soviet soldiers and, by extension, the governments they represent. With well-founded suspicion and even some foreboding, these soldiers are keenly aware of the major differences between the two societies each group of soldiers represents.

At the time of this meeting at Torgau, Hitler had not yet committed suicide and Nazi Germany had not yet unconditionally surrendered, events which would occur in the ensuing two weeks. The defeat of the Nazis forces on 08 May 1945 gave great cause for joy and celebration for victims and victors, but the maelstrom of events in those closing days of the war was also the occasion and the setting for a terribly tragic scene of anguish for millions of people who suffered grievously during the war. Amid their fear, hopelessness and hunger, though, was to be found a palpable yearning for peace. Unfortunately, that yearning could hardly be embraced intellectually and emotionally because those convoluted times also obscured for many some ominous realities with far-reaching ramifications for the entire world for at least the next half century. Hunger almost always trumps preoccupations with international relations!

In the smoking ruins of Germany, the United States and the Soviet Union stood tall and strong as the primary actors in the opening scenes of an intense half-century drama leading to confrontations and hostilities commonly referred to as the Cold War. To be sure, the destruction and killing of World War II had officially ended, but the immense and dark shadow over human affairs in which most of the world lived at that time obscured the fact that a new era of peace was not at hand.

Long before Nazi Germany unconditionally surrendered, the basic factors leading up to the Cold War was already in place, ready for their interaction on the world stage. Essentially, the close of World War II was the opening of the Cold War which proved to be an intense and sustained period of international discord between the two major victors of World War

II, with far-reaching implications for all of humankind.

Any useful explanation of the genesis of the Cold War necessarily involves the interplay of three complex factors:

- Long-standing and irreconcilable differences between philosophies of the democratic Western Allies and the totalitarian Soviet Union;
- Lessons learned by the Western democracies about the consolidation of Soviet power in Russia when the Communist Party of the Soviet Union (CPSU) systematically used executions, torture, deportations and starvation as tools to impose its ideology on its own people and, via the Comintern, spread its influence worldwide;

- The legacy of several World War II agreements from several Allied war planning conferences to coordinate Allied military operations against Nazi Germany and to deal with the after-effects of the war.

In Shakespeare's, "The Tempest," the conceptual tool exists for acquiring a useful understanding of one of the longest, most expensive, most tension-filled struggles fraught with the most unthinkable consequences between international adversaries that the world has ever known. "What's past is prologue," the Bard tells us. So, with Shakespeare's permission, how do these three essential interwoven strands promote a useful understanding of the origins of the Cold War and, by extension, the Cold War's implications for the future?

Cold War Genesis: Philosophical Considerations:

The fundamental distrust between American and Soviet soldiers meeting at Torgau in 1945 stems from profoundly different philosophical underpinnings of the political systems represented by these forces. Western democratic political traditions can be easily traced to numerous references to Greek city-states, including selected portions of Plato's, "The Republic" Out of the 16th Century Protestant Christian Reformation concepts arose of individual liberty where people would be free to construct their own well-lived lives in accordance with clear, yet demanding ethical standards. Significantly, the Peace of Westphalia (1648) ending the Hundred Years War gave further momentum to the rise of the modern nation-state system so central to evolving precepts in Western democratic political philosophy.

From the 18th Century European Age of Enlightenment, Americans read several expositions on political, social and economic order pertinent to the emerging thesis on American governance, in general, these views centered on how best to develop the full humanity of citizens. Specific topics included the revolutionary idea that a nation's sovereignty lies naturally and inalienably with the people - NOT with any sort of autocratic leader ruling by divine right. Also, inspiring ideas of human equality; personal liberty; free speech, freedom of religion, due process of law; freedom of assembly; and the separation of governmental powers are advanced by several writers of this era. Most notably, these beliefs came from treatises in political philosophy notably by John Locke of England and both Montesquieu and Jean-Jacques Rousseau of France.

As well, several well-read and politically active Americans before and after American independence from Great Britain in 1776 contributed substantially to the growing body of uniquely American orienting principles of American political philosophy. These contributors include: Thomas Jefferson, Benjamin Franklin, James Madison and John Adams.

In large measure, the impetus in European minds and, by extension, the minds of early American political philosophers for this philosophical awakening was the generation-by-generation growth of resistance by millions of people to centuries of aristocratic and autocratic forms of social order characterized by class privilege and exploitation. By the late 1760's, an American ideal extolling the virtue of the individual person and the role of government facilitating the best development of individual human potential clearly emerges. From and because of its inception, America is unique in human history because it is intentionally created on the basis of an idea: that all people are created equal with inalienable rights to life, liberty and the pursuit of happiness.

A clear and succinct summary of the differences in political philosophies of the United States and the Soviet Union begins by examining a motto, the Great Seal of the United States:

NOVUS ORDO SECLORUM

(A new order of the ages)

Even though both the United States and the Soviet Union promised a "new order for the ages," a quick and careful look of the nature of the two visions reveals just how different the two visions of "new order," are.

Consider the essence of America's uniqueness expressed on a motto of the Great Seal of the United States:

E PLURIBUS UNUM
(Out of many, one)

The idea contained in the phrase, "Out of many, one," is the story and the promise of immigrants and citizens freely associating in one united country. At the heart of the American system is the idea that the people themselves form and guide governments at all levels – NOT monarchs by divine right or tyrannical autocrats coming to power by force of arms and subversion. The goal of American self-government is to create conditions where people decide how governments shall reasonably manage and to protect residents so that equality of opportunity and reasonable justice for all exist in a well-run nation.

The cherished and logical extension of the idea that, 'the people decide', is that tyrannical and autocratic political behavior by anyone is antithetical to the American ideal and is despised and rejected. Right here is the nexus of the conflict between
American democratic ideals and revolutionary socialist (i.e., Communist) ideals. Fundamentally and irreconcilably, these two visions are diametrically opposed to one another, and a more profound conceptual difference is difficult to imagine.

This latter view of the "citizen-State" relationship -- where the State decides political priorities and process -- is what existed in absolute monarchies, military dictatorships and some theocratic states. And to put a fine point this statement, is what existed in the Soviet Union and the few remaining Communist nation-states around the world, including Communist China; North Korea; Laos and Vietnam. Yes, both the American and the Russian Revolutions brought about a 'new order', but the Communist 'new order' has usually been forced onto people by military force and subversion and maintained by totalitarian repression.

Presenting a realistic yet fictional motto for the Soviet Union clearly shows the differences between American and Communist political systems. In the former, the people are central and paramount, but in the latter, the Communist Party-led government is central and paramount.

In contrast to the American motto "E PLURIBUS UNUM" (Out of many, one), consider this proposal for a Soviet motto:

PLURES IN UNUM COMMIXTI
(Many forced into one)

. . . Offered for consideration as an effective and, admittedly, fictional encapsulation of the Soviet Union's practice of the implementing of its political philosophy. Semantics are important!

The source of this phrase is the *Aeneid*, written over 2,000 years ago by the Roman classical poet Virgil. With admiration, Virgil describes what Greek soldiers did to the people of Troy in and after the battle there in the 12th Century BCE. In the classical Roman style, Virgil subscribes to the myth that the earliest Romans were descendants of Troy. By inference, Virgil identifies with the Greeks and implies that Roman soldiers and administrations did, and would proudly do to opponents of the Roman imperial system what the Greeks did to the Trojans.

Just as in the Battle of Troy where conquered Trojans were slain by victorious Greeks, so in the Carthaginian Wars conquered Carthaginians were slain by victorious Romans. The 'oneness or uniformity' of the Greek and Roman examples is the 'oneness or uniformity' of a new society ruthlessly imposed on the victims by lethal coercion, and intimidation fueled by an absence of regard for the humanity of the victims.

The historical record is replete with identical examples of ideologically committed conquerors (State sponsored and non-State sponsored) using mass killings and terror against their victims to achieve the dominance of the conquerors. Shocking evidence of this include from Roman subjugation of the Celts in Britain; early Islamic practices in North Africa and Spain against anyone whom they deemed to be infidels; Genghis Khan's rampages throughout Asia; and Spanish ruthless imperialism in Central and South America.

This process has continued from the turn of the 20th Century onward, including the Ottomans' 20-year genocidal treatment of Armenians; from the days of the Bolshevik Revolution and subsequent decades when tens of millions of Russian citizens were murdered, starved, imprisoned, deported and otherwise terrorized in the process of erecting and solidifying the Soviet Union; and from Nazi extermination of Jews and Slav minorities during World War II.

After World War II and continuing for some 40-odd years, millions of people in Eastern Europe became the victims of brutal and oppressive Soviet military occupation and subsequent installation of Soviet-puppet governments that ruled in totalitarian ways, while coercing and exploiting others economically, to expand Soviet-style revolutionary Communism beyond Russia's borders. The written and filmed record of the outrageous tragedies experienced by people in the Ukraine; Poland; the Czech Republic; Slovakia; eastern Germany Hungary; Romania and Bulgaria provide stark lessons to Western democracies about what can happen when people do not inform and defend themselves against invidious subversions of revolutionary Communism.

This ruthless, diabolical disregard for human life occurred on the mainland of China when Mao Dze Dong came to power in 1949 and his totalitarian policies were pursued with murderous effect on countless Chinese people who simply disagreed with his goals and methods. These Communist Party policies continued in the 1940's and 1950's in Vietnam when Vietnamese Communists systematically murdered tens of thousands and terrorized countless others in their process of imposing a totalitarian revolutionary Communist social order in Vietnam. In the name of a revolutionary socialist ideology, the same goals and strategies were employed in Cuba where, from March, 1962 onward, the Communist Party of Cuba imposed the Marxist-Leninist model of social revolution on the people of Cuba. Between 1970 and 1998, Cambodia was repulsively yet accurately described as "the killing fields" when Khmer Rouge Communists initiated their systematic culling of nearly 2.4 million (34%) of their fellow countrymen in the interests of creating a Marxist-Leninist version of a 'purer'

Communist state. By whatever means necessary, these 'new order' forces have used murder, torture and various forms of terror against 'old order' adherents to achieve the victory of their revolutionary Communist utopian visions – just as Greeks and Romans did in centuries past.

Virgil's stated vision of "many being forced by any means necessary into one new uniform" accurately captures the essence of how Lenin's and Stalin's revolutionary Communism was, by traditional Western standards, inhumanly imposed on others in Russia and elsewhere. People themselves do not choose the 'new order' of revolutionary Communism; Communist zealots choose for their victims, rationalizing their societal conversions both inside and outside of Russia with philosophical arguments showing a blatant disregard for the personal dignity and worth of now countless millions of people. Once again, the utter contrast between American and revolutionary Communist political philosophies is apparent.

In contrast to philosophical underpinnings associated with American political traditions, Communist political traditions also have a unique pedigree. These traditions can also be traced from ancient Greek sources, including Plato's *The Republic*, but more specifically to references where group identity and group cohesiveness were regarded as primary and essential for group preservation. Some of St. Paul's writings in the early Christian Church even extolled the virtues of a Christian sort of communalism, themes used and developed in the early 16th Century by Thomas More in his *Utopia*. The early 17th Century European Age of Reason was also intellectually fertile ground for further discussion of idealized societies advocating the pre-eminence of group and collective social organization as essential for protecting the welfare of the group.

By the 18th Century Age of Enlightenment, various writings - famously including those of Voltaire and Rousseau – advocated visions of utopian societies where commonly shared values brought people together for the greater well-being of all concerned. Writers promoted ideas critical of existing class structures and extolled the equal worth of people; promoted concepts of public property ownership, while being highly critical of private property ownership rights; and even promoted the merit of an "enlightened despotism" (echoing political views advanced by Plato in *The Republic*) to bring about social justice.

With not a little inspiration from both Voltaire and Rousseau, Robespierre during part of the French Revolution claimed (in 1793) the general will of the people demanding social justice was of such absolute necessity that he could justify his formation of the Committee of Public Safety in 1793, which set loose a lethal reign of terror over all opposition, causing the executions of thousands of French counter-revolutionaries, priests, nobles and the king and queen of France! To suggest that Robespierre's reign of terror in France foreshadowed Lenin's terror-filled and ruthless imposition of revolutionary Communism in Russia 114 years later is not an original thought: Lenin himself reflected on the parallels! For one example, the entire Romanov family (the royal family of Czarist Russia) and their servants were murdered by a Bolshevik execution squad in the early morning hours of 17 July 1918.

In the early 19th Century, secret and non-secret utopian socialist groups in Western Europe; England; Scandinavia and even Latin America promoted visions of egalitarian social order generally characterized by intense contempt for private property ownership rights and distinct rejection of what they termed a 'bourgeois' vision of society. Generally, these groups held the view that the well-being of society as a whole, as a general group, should be the pre-eminent societal vision. At this time, the German philosopher Georg Hegel advanced positions (including dialectics, 'the end justifies the means' and the dominant role of the State) which were seminal to later development of revolutionary socialist views.

However, decades of debate in these socialist groups revolved around questions of methods for achieving a new and dominate socialist order. Should the change occur in an evolutionary and relatively peaceful manner, working with and within established political structures OR should the change occur in a revolutionary, forceful and violent manner? Without broad consensus to answer this question, advocates of the violent, revolutionary model of social change were left to sporadic, anarchistic struggles often producing discouragement and failures. Perhaps the most notable though temporary example of an anarchistic socialist overthrow of existing government was the short-lived Paris Commune of 1871 when Parisian Communards overthrew the existing municipal government of Paris and declared, among other things, the beginning of the establishment of a world republic based on their utopian socialist beliefs.

From the Communist League in 1847 to the present-day, violence costing the lives of several hundred millions of people to achieve societal change is the chief characteristic of Communist efforts to establish their concept of a 'new social order'. Examine carefully the harsh rallying cry from the *Communist Manifesto* (1848) in the name of which hundreds of thousands of revolutionary socialists – i.e., Communists – have passionately dedicated themselves. Stirringly and aggressively, this *Manifesto* is the spark energizing Communist movements around the world:

> Communists disdain to conceal their views and aims. They openly declare that their ends can be attained only by the forcible overthrow of all existing social conditions. Let the ruling classes tremble at a Communistic revolution. The proletarians have nothing to lose but their chains. They have a world to win. Workers of the world, Unite!

In the mid- and late 19th Century, a few prominent writers advanced principles forming the seedbed out of which grew increasingly refined political views favoring the resolution of class struggles by violent overthrow and subversion of established Western democratic governments because those governments were, allegedly, anathema to the interests of workers. Most famously, these writers include Karl Marx and Friedrich Engels.

By 1903, a resolution of the general socialist squabbling over how to achieve the new socialist order came about when, surprisingly from the agrarian periphery of Europe, a young radicalized Russian lawyer named Vladimir Ilyich Lenin succeeded in getting his Russian Social Democratic Labor Party to adopt two central ideas contained in his political treatise, "What is to be Done?" Effectively, Lenin answered questions raised in the *Communist Manifesto* (1848) on how economic class struggles were to be won; how Western democratic systems were to be overthrown; and how the workers of the world were to be united. Lenin's primary contribution to Marxist visions of societal change calls for:

- Revolutionary means (violent if necessary; subversive if possible) NOT evolutionary and peaceful means or sporadically anarchistic means;
- Formation of a cadre of professional revolutionaries to lead, speak and act on behalf of the workers of Russia by assigning the

paramount leadership role for societal change to Communist Parties in countries ripe for change.

Lenin's 'cadre of professional revolutionaries' became an expanded vision of Robespierre's 12-person Committee of Public Safety, but now in 1903 Lenin was a beneficiary of the Hegelian view that the State arrogates to itself a supreme position in relation to the individual whose supreme duty is to subordinate 'self' to the State. Logically, Lenin (and his successors) as the head of the Russian Social Democratic Labor Party would be the head of the new Soviet state leading Russians to the 'new order' of a Socialist Utopia. Lenin had formulated a vision of a totalitarian dictatorship over the people ... for the people. In Russian, Lenin used the preposition "za" referring to "for" in the rather patronizing sense of "over" the people. Dare Virgil's "PLURES IN UNUM COMMIXTI" be reintroduced here?

With the adoption of Lenin's new Party-centered leadership introducing social change, Russian revolutionary Communism was born, and that caused a spiritual break with the West that has never been healed. In 1917, Lenin launched the Great October Socialist Revolution (**Великая Октябрьская Социалистическая Революция**) ruthlessly and violently installing revolutionary Communism in Russia. And in early 1919 in the midst of a violent and destructive civil war, Lenin significantly increased Communist hazards to Western democracies when he created the Comintern, a Soviet-sponsored organization designed to defend and spread the tenets of revolutionary Communism wherever opportunities could be created or exploited around the world. The Comintern was Lenin's deadly and insidiously effective political tool elevating the revolutionary Communist ideology he was forcing domestically onto the people of Russia onto a new international adversarial stage affecting the people of the world.

Once again, Virgil's PLURES IN UNUM COMMIXTI (Many forced into one) is used to succinctly illustrate how Lenin's revolutionary socialist views forcibly won the struggle between growing Western democratic traditions and revolutionary Communism in Russia. From the Bolshevik Revolution onward, though, the United States and her allies stood resolutely and vigilantly in defense of Western democratic values and traditions. They had more than enough evidence to recognize the challenges posed by Marxist-Leninist Communism.

Overall, highlighting just these few basic philosophical considerations illustrates the major difference between the American and Soviet systems and helps one understand the superficial displays of friendship and the underlying distrust exhibited by American and Soviet soldiers at Torgau in April, 1945.

The competing philosophical visions energizing their respective societies were viewed as potentially threatening both to American and her Western Allied partners and to Communist forces and their governmental superiors. These visions were and are irreconcilable because each is based on different assumptions causing, among other things, the direction of flow of political power to proceed in diametrically different directions. In these two societies, the theoretical nature of the relationship of citizens to their governments is completely different: in the Western democratic and American traditions, the citizen is paramount; in the revolutionary Communist tradition, the State led by the 'professional cadre' of Communist Party *apparatchiks* is paramount.

In reflection, hundreds of millions of people in Communist countries have had to experience a heroically tragic fate. One of the distinguishing characteristics of societies the Communists wanted to overthrow (the existence of a class structure) actually became one of the characteristics of the society they created in Russia – and in the several Eastern European countries from the end of World War II through to the end of the Cold War. Communist societies too have class divisions with upward social mobility virtually assured if one belongs to the Communist Party, but the average citizen in Communist countries traditionally did not have the freedoms and liberties or the hope and incentives enjoyed by most people in Western democracies.

Consider the general life experiences of hundreds of millions of people in the former Soviet Union and in former Soviet-dominated Eastern European countries where totalitarian Communist Parties ruthlessly imposed their rule over others. Based on several flagrant outbursts of popular reaction to the imposition of totalitarian Communist regimes in Eastern Europe during the Cold War, the hollow ring of Communist promises for a 'new socialist world order' became so raucous, incredulous, angering and resented that Communist governments in Eastern Europe, puppets all of the Soviet Union, successively fell to the clamor of millions of repressed people yearning for a change to social systems reflecting Western democratic traditions offering hope and reasonable means for life-improving opportunities and self-determination.

Basically, the 74-year long Communist experiment in Marxism-Leninism in the Soviet Union, proved that political utopias cannot really survive without strong, violent and systematic coercion and that visions of political utopias cannot be sustained without the free-will informed support of the people affected by that vision.

Though the Soviet Union failed as a nation-state and was officially dissolved in 1991, a good case can be made that Russia's centuries-old tendencies for intolerant and imperialistic expansion remain a challenge for Western democracies. Because recent Russian Federation activities in the early years of the 21st Century reveal disturbing patterns of traditional Russian international behavior, Western needs for vigilance and verification of Russian intentions and actions continue. America and her allies are properly concerned that another protracted Cold War-type struggle between the same two protagonists who confronted one another for nearly five decades is a very real possibility.

Consider the People's Republic of China, long known in the West as Communist China (to distinguish it from the Republic of China). For at least 23 years, Mao Dze Dong struggled to bring Marxist-Leninist revolutionary ideology to China, and he succeeded in doing that in 1949 in the early years of the Cold War. The violent history of establishing Communism in China and continuing the use of violence to consolidate that rule is a lurid tale rivaling that found in the Soviet Union. Unlike the Soviet Union, though, mainland China is the world's most populous nation, has the fastest growing economy in the world and is projecting its political, military and economic interests world-wide in places where it has never gone before. Any reasons Westerners have had for concern about Communism in Russia are reasons that generally apply to the Communist government in China. Those in the intelligence services of the Western democracies who have been vigilant about Communism in Russia have equal reason to be vigilant about Communism in China.

Most people in the United States and other Western democracies preoccupied with making ends meet, getting kids to school and paying down mortgages have little opportunity to develop a well-informed awareness of the philosophical implications of the inherent rivalry between American democratic and Communist totalitarian systems. This goes far to explain why many people have been so surprised by events during the Cold War and why so many have been anxious for their own survival - economically, politically, personally - during the 46-year period of the Cold War. This also explains why Western reaction to the use of violence in building the Communist Chinese state and Western reaction to the burgeoning presence of Communist China in the past decade or two necessarily involves apprehension and vigilance on the part of the Western democracies.

Western governments have been aware of the theory and practice of revolutionary Communist philosophy, as well as the future implications of that philosophy, regardless of where in the world the Communist challenge comes from. The men and women of the intelligence services of the United States and the Western democracies also have been well aware of these concerns. Yet, not surprisingly, simple prudence understandably requires silence from the people tasked with conducting the vigilance on the potential and actual adversaries of the United States. Suffice it to say that knowledge informs, reveals truths, and sets one free to better maintain their freedoms regardless of the nature of all challenges.

There are no short-cuts and no easy solutions in the defense of Western democratic traditions. Only rewards accrue to the countries where knowledgeable people work diligently to inform themselves in the defense of the liberties and cultural traditions whose protection the United States undertook to accomplish when leading the Allies in both World War II and the Cold War. American men and women by the tens of millions have served and hundreds of thousands have paid with their lives to resist and defend against Nazi and Communist challenges to our way of life.

Thoughtful and informed people would never willingly give up their freedoms by choosing to become another ghastly statistic on a list of Communist or even non-State sponsored terrorist victims. Fortunately, citizens of the Western democracies can be confident that at the forefront of our defensive capabilities will be the intelligence services of the United States and her allies, ordinary guys performing in extraordinary situations.

U.S. President Ronald Reagan's reminder that we must verify the intentions and actions of our adversaries, before deciding on whether to trust them indirectly, acknowledges the critical role that people in the intelligence services of our country have to protect and enhance our nation's ability to meet and prevail over any challenge to our nation's well-being. They do this out of patriotic duty in fulfillment of the promise made by another US President, John Kennedy, who in his Inaugural Address on 20 January 1961 said, "Let every nation know, whether it wishes us well or ill, that we shall pay any price, bear any burden, meet any hardship, support any friend, oppose any foe, in order to assure the survival and success of liberty."

Cold War Genesis: Russia's Toll for Imposing Communism

From a focus on philosophical issues associated with American and Soviet Communist societies, a new focus now concentrates on what Russian Communists actually did to impose their ideology on Russia. Just how far would Communists in Russia go and at what human costs to impose their totalitarian ideology? For present purposes, only a synopsis of selected events in the roughly two-decade era before World War II ensues, dealing with Joseph Stalin's devastating collectivization programs and his purges of competing Communist Party members from the Communist Party. This will further clarify why the veneer of superficial friendliness barely disguised underlying suspicions manifest between American and Soviet soldiers on that spring morning in April of 1945 just before the end of the war.

To set the scene, it is helpful here to recall that:

• Vladimir Ilyich Lenin led the Bolsheviks in the Great October Socialist Revolution (Великая Октябрьская Социалистическая Революция) in 1917 through to the conclusion of the Russian Civil War in 1923;

• After Lenin's death in January, 1924, Joseph Stalin promoted himself as Lenin's successor, effectively becoming the dictator of the Soviet Union in the late-1920's and continuing in that role until his death in March, 1953;

• The utility of the fictional motto proposed earlier succinctly and effectively describes methods Lenin and Stalin used to establish and solidify the new Communist state in Russia.

PLURES IN UNUM COMMIXTI
(Many forced into one)

Virgil's words from long ago serve particularly well as the over-arching theme of how Russian Communists established and consolidated their power in Russia, a process with goals completely antithetical to American political ideals.

From the days of the Bolshevik Revolution through to the end of the Russian Civil War, Lenin's use of police-state terror has shocked many Russians and vast numbers of informed people in the West. In the name of steadfast (some say pathological) adherence to ideological principle, Lenin and Stalin used, without regard to the human costs, executions; mock trials; spying on their own people; deportations to Siberian labor camps; and religious persecution with lethal effect on many tens of millions of Russians. Tragically for vast numbers of people in Russia, ruthless and autocratic treatment by the Communists was explained as necessary because, inspired by the Hegelian view that "the end justifies the means," they were being taken, whether they wanted to or not, to the 'new social order' promised by Marx and Lenin.

Resistance to Bolshevik revolutionary change was widespread, not surprisingly; human resistance to change is a common phenomenon. The Bolshevik suppression was savage, (without implying any justification of it), the hypocrisy of Bolshevik action demands recognition. Yes, many Bolshevik victims were non-peasants, but many more were the peasants and poor workers who were the very people whose interests the Bolsheviks claimed to represent. In the years following the Russian Civil War, the revolutionary leadership of this Bolshevik 'professional cadre of social change agents' continued their lethal campaigns to impose Soviet ideology on those who remained.

As grotesque as it is to contemplate, it is one thing to be a revolutionary party initiating cataclysmic social change and triggering a devastating Civil War in the name of creating a new Soviet State. But doing this at a cost of over 20,000,000 civilian and military fatalities, (three quarters of whom were civilians, one quarter of whom were soldiers or, stated differently, roughly 11% of one's total national population), is shockingly quite something else! Maybe a defense of sorts is possible by Soviet apologists if one starts with the premise that non-peasants are non-human class enemies given an outlaw status which denies them human rights.

Moral people choose whether such crushing and dehumanizing application of revolutionary ardor is rational and justifiable. Allowing people to make informed choices according to ethical standards promotes the best of humankind and protecting the weakest among us is what humane societies do. Lenin and Stalin gave no choice to Russian citizens in the first six or seven years after the October Revolution, unless one accepts the idea that 'adapt or die' is a valid, reasonable and morally defensible choice. The millions who were killed and deported into 'internal' exile at Soviet prison camps never to be heard from again were allowed no choice and did not choose to die.

If from the mid-19th Century onward more Socialists and more Russians had examined carefully the horrific implications of Marxist principles of violent overthrow of existing national institutions (Communist Manifesto of 1848), then the immense upheaval in Russian society by Communists in the 20th Century -- applying the idea of 'many being forced into one' may not have happened. Instead, social justice could have been achieved in Russia, as has happened elsewhere when evolutionary socialists have brought about significant social and economic change without the violent destruction associated with the totalitarian dictatorship Lenin and Stalin imposed on Russia. But rarely does retrospective speculation produce useful contemporary answers to problems. The realities of what Russian Communists did to their own people for the 74 year period they were in power presents Russians and non-Russians alike with immensely complex questions whose answers have far-reaching implications.

After the end of the Russian Civil War and Lenin's death, the merciless and violent imposition of Soviet ideology continued as tens of millions more Russians - as much as another 10% of the then existing Russian population - paid with their lives for Stalin's plans to solidify his control of the Communist Party over every facet of Russian life. Taken together, Lenin's and Stalin's ruthless, capricious, sustained and systematic use of violence against their own people, constitutes the most extreme abuse of many tens of millions of people in the name of erecting a utopian Soviet society. Many Russians then and now have characterized Lenin's and Stalin's zealous pursuit of ideology as fanatically maniacal.

Between 1928 and 1940, three topics associated with Stalin's continuing process of imposing revolutionary socialism in Russia are essential to addressing the question of how far Communists in Russia would go to impose their totalitarian ideology: Soviet collectivization of farms and factories; Stalin's purge of competitors from the Communist Party; and religious persecution.

In the late-1920's, Stalin pursued policies throughout Russia where individually owned farm land and manufacturing plants were taken over by the State and managed as collectives. From a strictly Soviet legal perspective, these measures amounted to government fulfillment of the constitutional promise made by the Bolsheviks in the 1918 Soviet Constitution which called for: ". . . the complete transfer of factories, works, shops, mines, railways, and other means of production . . . to the ownership of the workers' and peasants' Soviet Republic, and in order to insure the supremacy of the laboring masses over the exploiters . . ."

Since the Revolution in 1917, private land ownership had been tolerated, but Stalin significantly sped up this collectivization process. Stalin's approach to collectivizing poor or landless peasants began with targeting 'selfish kulaks' (middle-class land owners since 1906) as class enemies to win over poorer peasants and redirect their antipathy toward forced collectivization: the classic 'divide-and-conquer' strategy when attacking one's opponent. Because of the Bolshevik goal of eliminating private property ownership, Stalin justified kulak repression on more promises from the 1918 Soviet Constitution: ". . . the establishment of the dictatorship of the urban and rural proletariat and the poorest peasantry [to secure] the complete suppression of the bourgeoisie [and] the abolition of the exploitation of man by man . . ."

Forced collectivization simply sparked widespread and intense resistance by poor peasants and kulaks. No records exist indicating exactly how many kulaks, along with their families, were executed or deported to Siberian and Central Asian agricultural labor camps penal institutions, but some reports cite 10 - 12 million were involved up to 1935. At least 5 million 'non-kulak' Russian peasants also died through systematic starvation and executions, while others formed armed groups to resist Communist organizers. Many slaughtered their own cattle for food rather than turn over their animals to government authorities. Many hoarded their own grain, burying it for surreptitious retrieval when Communist agents were unaware, while others simply burned their crops or dumped product into nearby rivers to foil Communist agents. And none of that reaction deterred Stalin's implementation of collectivization!

In Ukraine alone, Stalin's collectivization policies included the intentional famine against uncooperative peasants causing deaths by starvation to nearly 7,000,000 people to crush their resistance to collectivization. For other Ukrainians, Stalin ordered the use of numerous trains to deport innumerable train loads of peasants from their homes and farms to 'internal' exile in Russia's North, far-off Siberia and Central Asia. Soviet soldiers and Communist Party agents often shot resisting peasants, burned communities and arrested peasants to form forced labor battalions. For these deported peasants, expansions were made to the Soviet prison system and an extensive slave labor camp system (the GULAG) was developed from which many hundreds of thousands of Russians, minorities and dissidents were never heard from again. Even the immense human costs to Ukrainians had no deterrent effect on Stalin's implementation of collectivization!

The sheer inhumane use of force and complete disregard for human life, justified in the Communist mind by their ideological right and duty to force the 'new Communist social order' onto Russians, is why many consider Soviet steps to establish and consolidate their political power has absolute pathological dimensions.

The scale of repressive totalitarian social engineering brought by the Communist Russian government staggers the imagination of both Westerners and Russians. Several thousands of Ukrainians managed to flee the Soviet Union and resettle in Canada and the United States, where archival material tells the tragic tale of their experiences during Stalin's collectivization programs. Even Soviet government accounts before the fall of the Soviet Union in 1991 mention the disappearance of roughly 24 million people from rural areas during the collectivization programs, with barely over half of these ultimately working for State-run organizations. The other half, by Soviet accounts, died directly or indirectly due to social upheavals encountered during collectivization. And post-Soviet sources confirm earlier reports. All of Stalin's restructuring of Russian society, in Stalin's mind, was simply a justifiable government program in the name of building the new Soviet Utopia! After all, the Bolsheviks wrote their own constitution giving themselves *a priori* legitimacy for their future activities. Ukrainians were given no voice in Russian collectivization programs, and dead Ukrainians have no voice. But Ukrainians who fled have spoken eloquently, with damning and exhaustive detail!

Then, also in the 1930's, Stalin's desire to preserve his own vision of how Communism would be maintained in Russia took an unusually worrisome turn, for his fellow Communists! Stalin's insistence on total control of the Communist Party led to his purge of allegedly undesirable Communists from Party ranks. His ruthless and intolerant elimination of anyone known or suspected of not following exactly his dictates created a hysteria within Communist Party ranks and elsewhere in Russian society.

Some Communists and intellectuals had expressed varying degrees of disagreement with Stalin's harsh and lethal repression of peasants and kulaks during the early years of collectivization. In 1930, the intellectuals' reward was show trials alleging anti-Party and counter-revolutionary; the Menshevik wing of the Communist movement were prosecuted for the same charges in 1931. Imprisonment and executions followed these trials. Generally, Stalin's concerns that his ideological goals and tactics could be thwarted by any opposition triggered a progressively lethal culling of potential adversaries. And the hysteria only grew!

Stalin's views on Marxist-Leninist dogma are one thing; the ruthlessness with which he applied those views on Russian society is another. The proverb that 'actions speak louder than words' applies here: Stalin had a crushing disdain for the common person, despite (or because of?) Marxist-Leninist teachings. To his brutally destructive views of the common man, for whom he claimed to be their leader, Stalin added his paranoid views on anybody in the Party expressing views differing from his own.

When H.G. Wells, the famed English author, historian and socialist, visited Stalin in 1934, Wells expressed admiration for Stalin's progress in building a new Soviet society, but he also expressed concern for Stalin's suppression of divergent views with the Communist Party. To that, Stalin rationalized his use of brutality on any sort of opposition by saying, "I do not forget that many people are evil."

Such a response reveals his strident, moralistic and paranoid views toward opposition and, by extension, toward truly democratic principles.

Perhaps those sentiments stem from his Russian Orthodox upbringing and seminary studies, or perhaps it reveals his vision of himself as the sole leader of the 'professional cadre of revolutionary socialists' bringing the Communist order promised in the 1848 *Communist Manifesto*. Probably, Stalin's response reflects both his orthodox religious heritage which he had disavowed prior to the Bolshevik Revolution and his perceived mandate as leader of the cadre of professional revolutionaries. Little wonder, then, that authorities on 20th Century Communism in Russia (even some Communists!) describe Stalin's character traits as megalomaniacal; capricious; strangely both puritanical and lascivious; obsessive; diabolically controlling; and paranoid.

In any case, late in 1934 Stalin engineered the collaboration of his secret police (NKVD, the precursor to the KGB) in the murder Sergei Kirov, one of his chief rivals within the Party. And his paranoid ruthlessness only escalated, for before that year ended Stalin decreed that anybody accused of anti-Party and therefore anti-State terrorism was to be summarily executed, with the result that more Communists fell victim to Stalin's whims. Over the next two years, this pattern of sham secret trials, executions and imprisonments in the GULAG continued.

By 1936, Stalin initiated a series of sensational show trials against fellow Communists. His drive for total control of the Communist Party and therefore the State was such that millions of people died, either in summary executions or in banishment to the barbaric conditions of the GULAG. At one point, Stalin even decreed that the Comintern could hunt down and execute 'enemies of the State' wherever in the world those could be found. That is what led to Leon Trotsky's murder with an ice axe in Mexico City in 1940!

A truly bizarre example of Stalin's paranoid character occurred in 1937. Double-crossed by Nazi German intelligence agents, Stalin and the NKVD were tricked into believing that numerous Soviet Army marshals; other senior officers; and all of the Soviet Navy's admirals were conspiring against Stalin. On Stalin's orders, some 35,000 officers were imprisoned or executed by the time Stalin's purge of military ranks ended.

The net effect of Stalin's purges of Party and military ranks was that Stalin's opponents within his own system whom he termed "enemies of the people" had been effectively silenced. Anyone even contemplating anything

Stalin could construe as anti-Stalin and therefore counter-revolutionary would think long and hard about before actually doing anything. The widespread hysteria in reaction to Stalin's paranoid behavior even led millions of Russians to falsely report fellow Russians to the secret police in hopes of protecting themselves from Stalin's wrath. Reports exist indicating between 500,000 and 2,000,000 of his own 'professional cadre of political and military leaders" had been executed as "enemies of the people" in his efforts to impose on Russia his vision of totalitarian control. Reports exist of Stalin himself often signing death warrants at the rate of 1,000 per day!

A critical sub-set of Stalin's harsh treatment policies of so-called counter-revolutionary people and institutions he considered to be "enemies of the people" briefly examines his persecution of religious people and institutions. Though both the United States and the Soviet Union have constitutional provisions for freedom of religion, only have Soviet constitutions provided justified Soviet government activities euphemistically categorized as "freedom . . . of anti-religious propaganda."

From 1917 to at least the fall of the Soviet Union in 1991, Soviet governments have used the constitutional clause of "freedom . . . of anti-religious propaganda" to justify religious persecution. Most of the religious persecution was aimed at the Russian Orthodox Church because of its previous relationship with the monarchy (who was considered the titular head of the Russian Orthodox Church) and its strong and spiritual influence over most Russians. During the Russian Civil War, Bolshevik "anti-religious propaganda" activity included widespread bureaucratic restrictions, such as barring priests, along with capitalists, imbeciles, ex-Czarist police and criminals, from voting, holding elected office and teaching positions. Tragically, an intense lethal State-run campaign against prominent religious leaders resulted in at least 28 bishops and thousands of priests being murdered. Not surprisingly, such action had a dramatically terrifying effect on millions of Russians and sparked numerous instances of violent resistance on the part of faithful Orthodox Christians.

With anti-religious activities largely delegated to provincial and local Communist authorities, an irregular and inconsistent anti-church campaign by the Bolsheviks resulted in some churches losing rights to have schools and other churches losing rights to own property. Some churches and monasteries were confiscated and destroyed or were set aside for any sort of non-religious activity, including stabling animals and storing grain. Naturally, the Communist degradation of people and buildings simply inflamed Orthodox Christian attitudes toward Marxist-Leninist-Stalinist atheism. Shortly after Lenin's death, the Bolshevik government created the League of the Militant Godless to promote atheism and agitate against religious activities of established churches at all levels of Soviet society. By 1933, one hundred churches operated in Moscow, compared to over 600 in the early days of the Civil War. At the outbreak of World War II, nearly 95% of the churches in all of Russia ceased functioning as churches!

By 1941, of over 25,000 mosques operating in Russia, State-sponsored anti-religious campaigns succeeded in reducing the number of mosques to roughly 1,500, a reduction of over 95%. Buddhists, too, eventually became victims of Soviet anti-religious propaganda activities, resulting in most Buddhist churches and monasteries being closed and then destroyed in the 1930's. Finally, Protestant Christian churches in Russia, though initially tolerated in the early years of Bolshevik rule in a policy to weaken the influence of the Russian Orthodox Church, were also persecuted with church closures, arrests, executions and deportations into 'internal' exile in Siberia. In short, occurring at approximately the same time as Stalin's purges against fellow Communists, various religious bodies in Russia suffered through a starkly repressive constitutionally sanctioned and State-sponsored campaign "in the name of the people" against perceived counter-revolutionaries.

In general, this pattern of State-sanctioned and State-run collectivization of farms and factories and repression against perceived political, military and religious counter-revolutionaries demonstrates that no grounds existed for Western trust of Communism in Russia. None!

In the 20th Century, hundreds of millions of people who experienced the establishment and consolidation of an attempted Soviet Utopia in Russia would respond with affirming alacrity to a rhetorical paraphrase of a comment made by H.G. Wells at a 1902 lecture in London: "It is possible to believe that all the Communist mind accomplished up to the start of the Great Patriotic War (the Russian term for their portion of World War II) is but a nightmarish dystopia."

By 1941 when Hitler unilaterally abrogated the Treaty of Non-Aggression between Germany and the USSR, western academics and government people were aware of many aspects of the immensity of Soviet brutality inflicted on the people of Russia by the totalitarian and dictatorial leadership of Lenin, Stalin and their "professional cadre of revolutionary socialists." However, the effects of the Great Depression in the West severely limited general awareness of the costly human toll Russians were paying to satisfy the Communist drive to create the Soviet Utopia.

Western military intelligence personnel accompanying Allied forces in Germany in 1945 would certainly have been fairly well informed about the scope of Soviet social re-engineering, and this knowledge would have been shared, as necessary, with appropriate ground troops. Indeed, Nazi German intelligence was also aware of and alarmed by Soviet government practices to construct a new Communist Utopia and was one additional source of information about the Soviet Union.

One particularly important question demands a clear answer: Why would the United States and the Soviet Union ally themselves during World War II, if these two countries were so dissimilar? The answer is that they had a common threat - Nazi Germany - that, at the time, was a far more serious and imminent threat to survival than either the United States or the Soviet Union was to each other. Western Allies needed the Soviet Union to create an Eastern Front to engage Hitler's war machine in a far more complicated war strategy with far fewer prospects of success. And the Soviet Union needed vital and massive amounts of help to survive Hitler's (Operation Barbarossa) invasion of Russia. Clearly, the alliance of the United States and the Soviet Union was only a temporary alliance based simply on mutual necessity in the face of a common enemy.

Thus, the underlying American distrust of Soviet soldiers and Soviet governmental aims again becomes understandable. If Communists in Russia would treat their own people as they had been for the previous 40 years, American military and civilian personnel had good cause to be alert to the worldwide implications of the spread of Communism outside the borders of Russia. Soviet behavior toward their own people would certainly cool the ardor of any greetings between American and Soviet soldiers at Torgau on that spring morning in April, 1945, when for the sake of convenience it is said that the Cold War began.

In short, consider this faithful and rhetorical paraphrase of a comment by H.G. Wells as a summation of what Russian Communists actually did to their fellow countrymen while imposing their ideology on Russians: "It may be possible to believe that all the Marxist-Leninist-Stalinist mind ever accomplished is but the nightmare experienced by the people of Russia, Eastern Europe and elsewhere before all of them had the chance to throw off the chains of Soviet oppression."

Cold War Genesis: Legacy of WWII Conference Agreements

The third strand in the story about why the United States and the Soviet Union ended up as the two primary actors on the world's stage immediately after the end of the World War II involves a cluster of issues emanating from a series of planning conferences held by members of the Western Alliance throughout the course of the war.

The unintended postwar effects of some of these conferences had profound consequences for hundreds of millions of people in Central Europe, the United States, the Soviet Union, and for the populations of various countries affiliating with each other in the North Atlantic Treaty Organization (NATO) and its political and military opposite, the Warsaw Pact. These consequences became the basis for many of the Cold War antagonisms for the 46-year period after World War II.

Twenty-three planning conferences were held by the Western Allies during the war to strategically coordinate their war effort. In broad stroke, the Western Allies generally cooperated well on their war aims, but the devil was in the details, so to speak, regarding a small set of specific issues emanating from five of these conferences: the first and third Moscow Conferences; the Teheran Conference; the Yalta Conference; and the Potsdam Conference.

- 1941 Moscow Conference:

Stalin and the Soviet Union were formally acknowledged as co-equals of the Western Allies at the first Moscow Conference (29 September – 01 October 1941). In exchange for Allied aid to the Soviet Union, Stalin's agreed to open an Eastern Front to divide Hitler's forces and complicate Hitler's war efforts. Germany had invaded the Soviet Union in June of that year, prompting Stalin to join the Allies primarily as a means of protecting his Communist state from the Nazi onslaught.

- 1943 Moscow Conference:

At the third Moscow Conference (18 October – 11 November 1943), the Western Allies, now with the Soviet Union as an equal partner, agreed to create a European Advisory Commission to collaborate on a study of anticipated postwar political problems with the study's findings going to each Allied government. At this point, the Soviet Union became intimately involved with the process of finding solutions to postwar issues in Eastern and Central Europe. Stalin negotiated and threatened whenever necessary to ensure that postwar Eastern European affairs would be solved consistent with his view of Communist and national interests of the Soviet Union. As was to become evident, Stalin was not interested in dealing fairly and respectfully with the affairs of the people in countries on the western borders of the Soviet Union. He wanted to expand Soviet influence into Eastern Europe while simultaneously creating a protective ring of puppet Communist states on his western border. As Winston Churchill famously said in his "Iron Curtain" speech after the war, "[The Soviets] desire . . . the fruits of war and the indefinite expansion of their power and doctrines."

- 1943 Cairo Conference:

On the heels of the third Moscow Conference came the Cairo Conference (22 – 26 November 1943), producing one particular agreement relating unintentionally to future Cold War difficulties between the United States and the Soviet Union, the Korean War. This Cairo Conference agreement stated that "in due course Korea shall become free and independent." How and according to what specific criteria were not addressed.

The Korean Peninsula was simply a time-bomb waiting to go off. An intense, 'hot' proxy war, began in June, 1950, between Communist forces (ably supported by China and the Soviet Union) and Western countries (under the aegis of the United Nations, led by the United States) vying for the installation of a non-Communist government hopefully sympathetic to Western interests. Due to heavy costs in lives and destruction stemming from the war (nearly 500,000 killed and wounded on the United Nations' side and nearly 1,600,000 killed and wounded on the Communist side, along with over 2,000,000 killed and wounded Korean civilians), an armistice calling for a cease fire with forces remaining 'in place' was reached in July, 1953.

The concept of 'a final peace settlement' on the Korean Peninsula meant two different things to opposing ground forces in the Korean War. From the 1953 armistice to the end of the Cold War in 1991, the status quo between the two Koreas as defined in the armistice remained unchanged and served as a sensitive flash point in relations between Communist and non-Communist countries. Indeed, as of the end of 2008, still no change, no move toward a final peace settlement between the two Koreas has occurred.

- 1943 Teheran Conference:

Within a month of the Cairo Conference, the Western Allies met for the Teheran Conference (28 November - 01 December 1943). A European Advisory Commission was established to deal with postwar political problems in Europe. Again, Stalin proved to be an astute and persistent negotiator with his Western Allies. At this time, though, Stalin clearly held the upper hand in negotiations on postwar settlements due to the steady westward progress his Red Army had been having since the Battle of Stalingrad (17 July 1942 - 02 February 1943).

The United States and the United Kingdom obtained full support from Stalin for war policies, but in return Stalin obtained American and British agreement that they must formally recognize him as leader of the Soviet Union and must permit him to establish his own Communist sphere of influence in Eastern Europe.

Initially, the United States and Britain believed the western border of Soviet influence would be the Soviet Union's own western border as of 1937, but by the time the Teheran Conference was held, Soviet forces had quickly and steadily pushed back Nazi forces and the new *de facto* western border of the Soviet sphere of influence was taken to mean the western border of the most westerly advance of Soviet forces. In fact, those concessions eventually resulted in Stalin establishing puppet Communist governments in Poland; Czechoslovakia; Hungary; Romania; Bulgaria; and the Baltic states of Estonia; Latvia; and Lithuania forcing between 80 and 90 million people of those Eastern European countries to a loss for over 45 years of their independence and freedom and resulting in some of the most awkward and tense confrontations between East and West in the Cold War.

- 1945 Yalta Conference:

In February the Western Allies met at Yalta in the Crimea. The British worked hard for free elections and democratic governments in Eastern European countries, all of which had formerly been under Nazi German occupation but by this time were under Soviet occupation. Stalin's actions on the subject of free elections, though, spoke more eloquently than his words: he had indicated his support for free elections in Eastern Europe, but his talk obscured unilateral developments he had initiated. He had begun to create Communist puppet governments in Eastern European countries because the Red Army already occupied these countries, and this fact freed him from risks of having opposition to his plans from his Western partners. Stalin claimed that security needs of the Soviet Union trumped Polish wishes for freely elected national governments because the plains of Northern Europe had regularly been a major route through which foreign armies invaded Russia. To protect Russia, Stalin again claimed he needed to establish a Soviet sphere of military and political influence at least in Poland. He even let it be known that a strong Polish government could be a dependable protector of sorts for Russian security interests. However, mouthing support for free elections while acting *sub rosa* for his view of Soviet borderlands security, Stalin ensured that Communism would thrive in Poland. With a Communist puppet government in Warsaw and the Soviet Red Army controlling Poland, Stalin then moved the Soviet Union's western border further west into Polish territory.

Eventually, each of the Eastern European countries freed from Nazi occupation but subjugated immediately by Stalin's Red Army succumbed to indefinite Soviet control in direct and unchallenged opposition to the West's position of free elections and independent countries in Eastern Europe. Many citizens in Eastern European countries freely speak to this day of Western unwillingness to check the spread of permanent Soviet influence into Eastern Europe. They characterize Western behavior as spineless acquiescence and regard toleration of Soviet expansionism as merely the early steps of a betrayal of Eastern European countries by the West.

When people in the Eastern European countries are asked whether they believe Western initiatives against the Soviet Union to restore the national independence of these countries would have been justified even if those initiatives had led to World War III, a bitter resignation and acceptance usually ensues that the Soviet sphere of influence had to be accepted. All in all, the situation for Eastern Europeans stemming from the Yalta Conference constitutes a "no-win" situation for the millions of Eastern European people who, because of this, ended up being occupied by unwanted foreign forces (first Nazi, then Soviet) for roughly half a century. In the end, these Eastern Europeans frustratingly allege that American toleration of Soviet expansionism is just an example of American hypocrisy relative to America's own traditional ideals. Thus, the tragic complexity of the situation facing Eastern Europeans after World War II becomes apparent.

- 1945 Potsdam Conference:

This was the last and only postwar conference of the Western Allies; it was held in the Berlin suburb of Potsdam (July 16 to August 2). Their task was to deal with a complex list of postwar issues, including border alignments, occupation of Germany and the rebuilding of nations ravaged by the effects of war.

Polish borders on the east and the west were moved to the west, and German borders were reset to their position at the end of 1937. The Soviets had already created a Communist puppet government in Lublin as early as 1944, demonstrating Soviet intent to formalize in a *de facto* sense their sphere of influence in Poland and serving somewhat as a model for subsequent creation of Communist puppet governments in other Eastern European countries.

As well, the idea of four occupation zones in Germany was ratified. Implemented by the Allied Control Commission for Germany (ACC), the four victorious Allies agreed to several terms giving each of the four Allies full control of internal affairs in the four German zones of occupation. Berlin, too, was divided into four zones, with one zone controlled by each of the Allied victors. According to ground rules also agreed to by the four Allied victors, administrative decisions of the Allied Control Commission for Germany were to be made by consensus. Unfortunately, the Soviet Union refused to agree to consensus on the length and nature of occupation of Allied zones, effectively neutralizing the possibility of joint-Allied cooperation in the postwar occupation of Germany.

Citing the ACC's inability to reach consensus, the Soviets unilaterally withdrew from the ACC in March, 1948, a rupture of ACC operations that led directly to the creation of two German states: the Federal Republic of Germany (aka West Germany) and the German Democratic Republic (aka East Germany). West Germany was founded on Western capitalistic and democratic principles, while East Germany was formed under Soviet direction according to the totalitarian and dictatorial model demanded by Stalin. Essentially, the building blocks of the most formidable area of confrontation during the Cold War were in place, and that presented the entire world with implications of the most far-reaching sort for the next nearly 50 years!

The legacy of World War II conference issues also requires a brief glimpse at some of unintended conference outcomes and their significant implications international relations in the Cold War era and beyond.

The ACC reconvened twice during the Cold War, once in 1971 to deal with transportation problems in Berlin and again in 1989 to assist in German re-unification efforts. The ACC was permanently terminated in 1991, nine months before the Soviet Union itself was dissolved (25 December), the date commonly considered the end of the Cold War.

The Potsdam Proclamation also announced on 26 July the unconditional surrender terms for Imperial Japan, including the warning that a failure to comply with ultimatum terms would initiate "prompt and utter destruction" on Japan. The Japanese government publicly announced their rejection of surrender terms in a press conference using phraseology consistent with its desire to avoid humiliation by using the term *mokusatsu* which in English means variously "take no notice," "treat with silent contempt," "ignore" or "kill [it] with silence."

The wording of the ultimatum did not reveal what President Truman already knew: that the 'Trinity' test explosion of America's first nuclear device had been successful and that the United States could deliver on its promise if Japan failed to accept the ultimatum.

With no acceptance of the ultimatum arriving in Western hands as late as 05 August, flight preparations were finished for the *Enola Gay*, the B-29 of the American's 509th Composite Group of the Second Air Force that would soon depart the island of Tinian in the Northern Marianas in fulfillment of the Potsdam Proclamation to bring "prompt and utter destruction" to Japan. And, at 2:45 a.m. in the morning darkness of August 6th, the *Enola Gay* began its six-hour flight to Hiroshima, where, for operational combat purposes, the first nuclear weapon was dropped . . . thus, ushering in the nuclear age, at least in terms of military weapons!

But Stalin at Potsdam also knew what Truman knew about American progress toward a deliverable nuclear weapon! The Americans had learned (Venona Project) that a German-born British physicist named Klaus Fuchs had been regularly funnelling back to Moscow information on progress within the American nuclear program! Not complicity in an activity one associates with an ally! But this illustrates once again the perfidious behavior of Stalin and the Soviet Union in relation to their allies during the prosecution of World War II.

The link between the Potsdam Conference and the Cuban Missile Crisis is now clear. On 29 August 1945 (three days before Japan's surrender), the Soviet Union detonated its first nuclear weapon (detected by an American B-29) and, because of the fast-paced development of nuclear weapons technology, the two main victors of World War II now could use nuclear weapons, if they so chose, in pursuit of their respective foreign policy goals. Thus, perhaps the single most worrisome and transcending issue of the Cold War was born, with lingering effects to this day.

Significantly, perhaps one reason why the Japanese cabinet rejected the Potsdam surrender ultimatum is related information retrieved from American archives in the 1980's: by mid-1945 Japan's nuclear program was but weeks behind the American program, and they succeeded with a rarely publicized test of a small, low-yield nuclear bomb in Japanese occupied Korea on 09 August 1945, the same day that Americans dropped their second nuclear weapon on Nagasaki!

The putative 'start' date for the Cold War of 25 April 1945 has been set forth, but that date can now more precisely be said to apply only in a naively positive light and only for the European Theatre of World War II.

In a much more startling and usefully realistic manner, the 'start' date of the Cold War may said to be 29 July 1944 or 20, 27 or 29 August 1945 based on Soviet activity against five American B-29's and their crew in the Pacific Theatre of World War II.

On these four occasions, forces of the Soviet Union - nominally an ally of the United States - engaged in hostile activity against aircraft and crews of American B-29's engaged in routine missions over China; Japan; Korea and Russian regions of East Asia. With the exception of the 27 August incident, B-29 crews and aircraft were detained when their aircraft landed under emergency situations in Vladivostok. One of these B-29's had crashed. Four B-29's remained for future use!

From the four intact and detained B-29's, the Soviets used them to clone their own long-range bomber, the Tupolev-4 (NATO codename "Bull"). On 03 August 1947, at Aviation Day festivities in Moscow, four four-engined aircraft thought to be from the group of captured B-29's conducted a low-altitude fly-by. They were just four of an eventual 1,200 of these aircraft produced by the Soviets!

The 27 August 1945 B-29 incident vividly demonstrates the absence of mutuality of interests and earnest collaboration as allies by the Soviets. On this occasion, one B-29 clearly marked "P.W.MISSION" painted in six-foot long white letters on the wings was shot down over Japanese-occupied Korea while delivering relief supplies to Allied prisoners-of-war! Even though the aircrew was eventually returned, Soviet actions in this set of B-29 incidents spoke much more clearly about their antipathy and duplicity toward the United States! All the potential for the very unpleasant and periodically lethal relationship between the United States and the Soviet Union during the Cold War became brutally clear on those days in late July and late August, 1945!

On 05 March 1946, the former British Prime Minister Winston Churchill warned America and her Allies that:

> From Stettin in the Baltic to Trieste in the Adriatic an iron curtain has descended across the Continent . . . Warsaw; Berlin; Prague; Vienna; Budapest; Belgrade; Bucharest and Sofia; all these famous cities and the populations around them lie in what I must call the Soviet sphere, and all are

subject, in one form or another, not only to Soviet influence but to a very high and in some cases increasing measure of control from Moscow.

With somber precision, Churchill described the state of affairs between the two most potent adversaries the world has ever known – potent in terms of their different philosophical origins and aspirations and potent in terms of their military might. That description was valid through to late 1991 when the Cold War ended.

This overview of issues emanating from World War II allied conferences, issues having direct impact on postwar affairs between the United States and the Soviet Union serves to highlight how critical these issues were to become for relations between the United States and the Soviet Union for decades to follow. Whether these issues re-emerge as contentious issues for the United States and the Russian Federation in the early 21st Century remains to be seen.

To conclude, the significant antecedents leading up to the Cold War have been woven together to assist in understanding what the Cold War became and to shed light on implications of these issues for the future. The three strands of this overview are:

- Philosophical heritages of competing American and Soviet societies.

- Actual behavior of the "professional cadre of revolutionary socialists" when imprinting their Communist ideology on the Russian people.

- An examination of issues intended primarily for dealing with the successful prosecution of World War II but also having unexpected and profound ramifications for the ensuing Cold War.

This understanding also shows that underlying basic suspicions mutually held by many in both American and Russian societies at the start of the Cold War were, and remain, well-founded.

In the 1950's through the 1990's, the choice between a world order in the totalitarian, repressive Communist model and a world in the tradition of the Western democracies really existed! [The choice facing the world in the early 21st Century is one where Western democracies are challenged by authoritarian and repressive non-State terrorist movements.] During the Cold War, both the Soviet Union and the United States pursued nuclear dimensions to their respective foreign policies. The fitting and disturbing acronym for these nuclear policies - MAD - referred to Mutual Assured Destruction, an allusion to the idea that the threatened use of nuclear weapons on an enemy also armed with those weapons might prevent the use of those weapons by that enemy.

At an excruciatingly slow pace, these two adversaries began to accept the ultimate madness of such policy, and slow progress toward the non-use of nuclear was made. The prospects of a nuclear holocaust, one legacy of World War II, were the over-arching theme of Cold War relations, and such a holocaust never happened due in no small way to the non-stop vigilance of the men and women in the intelligence services of the Western democracies. So quickly had the nightmarish fear of nuclear destruction emerged and for so many decades had that fear reigned in the minds of people in all countries that the relief in the surprise for all when the Soviet Union was dissolved in 1991 was that the dissolution was done by the Russians themselves – NOT by destruction from American nuclear weapons! Russians themselves invalidated Marxist-Leninist precepts and consigned them to the dustbin of history!

The geographical scope of the Cold War was the entire earth and outer space, not mere regions or continents. Realistically, the Cold War was comprised of both terribly "hot" wars (the Korean War, Vietnam War, several proxy wars, and numerous fatal incidents for both American and Soviet forces) interspersed with periods of a "cold" confrontational stance filled with almost unnerving stress waiting for the next outbreak of 'hot' altercations.

Throughout the 46-year period of the so-called Cold War, it was not wishful thinking that saved the world from a nuclear holocaust. No! An informed suspicion and distrust of Communism wherever it has existed justifiably caused Western democracies to allocate trillions of dollars and millions of people to protect themselves in the face of the worldwide Communist challenge.

Now, seventeen years after the generally accepted 'end' of the Cold War, geopolitical posturing by the Russian Federation raises continuing concerns over whether the current Russian government has just repackaged Soviet ambitions. If so, President Kennedy's inaugural alert still applies!

The basic inspiration underlying the activities of the intelligence gathering agencies of the Western democracies: "Eternal vigilance is the price of liberty!" focuses attention on what energizes people in the first line of defense of Western ideals.

The United States has developed an extensive, multi-faceted, intelligence community in both its civilian and military governmental agencies. The people in these agencies are the front-line eyes and ears informing the United States on the nature of the world order so that, hopefully, the United States can function effectively within the community of nations of the world and continue to be the country our forefathers set up well over two centuries ago. America's allies have done the same because the practice has become a simple but challenging fact of life in the modern world.

No country would be so foolish as to avoid reality and leave themselves vulnerable by pursuing foreign policies based on wishful thinking. The men and women in the service of our country's intelligence community are on the front lines . . . and behind the front lines, if needed, because it is very difficult to obtain good quality useful information from within closed societies. These people in our nation's intelligence service are ordinary people, performing extraordinary tasks in defense of our country and its values. These people, who for present purposes may be called 'these guys', are just like the rest of us. Their character, abilities, training, commitment and performance are first-class! Yes, we are vigilant. And, yes, we remember our fallen friends who have given their all to defend our country's interests.

Because of their mission's national security needs, no member of the intelligence community receives public or military acclaim for acts of service and bravery above and beyond the call of duty – no acclaim, in fact, for even the very ordinary work they do. These guys in the intelligence service of our country usually perform their work completely out of the public eye, and they do so out of necessity. On rare occasions, a name or a success or an incident appear in the media, but rarely do they receive public recognition for their service.

These are the reasons why Trish Schiesser's: **THESE GUYS: Cold War Stories Told by Cold War Warriors** is such an exceptional collection of writings by former United States intelligence community personnel. This overview of events leading up to the start of the Cold War is designed to provide valuable insights into the philosophical and military context of the Cold War so the reader can better appreciate what the contributors to THESE GUYS have to share. These guys share memories and other thoughts about harrowing and life-altering experiences. Sometimes for counter-point and comic relief they write about very mundane experiences providing intimate insights into their humanity when they were young. Schiesser has assembled this collection of writings as a tribute to the courageous and unsung patriots in the service of our country. In a personal and poignant way, she has also dedicated this collection in loving memory of her brother who served with distinction in the United States Security Service.

John C. Oberg
USAFSS, 2009

EDITOR'S NOTE:

WHILE THE COLD WAR WAS GOING ON
By Trish Schiesser

I played with my friends, Carol, Karen, Liz, Chris, Lynne and Carolyn. We formed a club and called ourselves The Seven Dots. We'd known each other since at least second grade and throughout high school and to this day in the year 2008!

Oh, we were buddies! We supported each other with the toils and troubles of teachers who disliked us one day and couldn't be sweeter to us the next. We sat in classrooms side by side squeamish and holding our breath while our eighth grade teacher, Ms. Rudtke, lifted up her leg, showing her long john underwear while cracking her raw egg on her knee and then slurping the entire mess with nary a drop on her clothes or the floor. We were disgusted. What a hag she was, why her dresses of black and hair like a witches looked as if she'd flown into school via broom! She'd pick on my boyfriend, (today a great writer), David Denby, and every other Friday she'd have me or my friend, Karen, going home crying, consoling each other, as both of us were timid young things and Rudtke had the knack, all right! One day some of the students got together and let all the air out of the tires on her car. O, we loved that and wished we'd all been in on it. However, we were lucky because all hell broke loose when the culprits were discovered.

All of this was going on including air raid drills, back in the 1940's and 1950's, where we were to hide under our desks in case a bomb was dropped on our school. Nothing ever happened. When the all-clear sirens sounded, we thanked God, except for the boys teasing the girls about having seen their underwear while under the desks. Boy, we wanted to pop them one!

None of us knew then and are just discovering now, that a Cold War was going on between the United States and Russia and that many of the men (and some women) in our families were in that Cold War defending our country and giving their lives to spying on the Russkies and other countries; listening, with their headgear, spinnin' and a grinnin' on their radio frequencies, wherever they were stationed: Japan, Korea, Turkey, W. Germany, Greece, Peshawar, Vietnam, and other places from: 5 September 1945 through 21 August 1991.

Our loved ones were in the Navy, Air Force, Army, Marines. My brother, SSGT Phillip C. Noland, among many in this book, became chosen for an elite group, unknown to the public, the United States Air Force

Security Service. I'm not talking about AP's (Air Police), I'm talking about something so secret that those who served in that group, and the Naval Security Group, among other secret groups, were not aware of WHAT they were doing and WHY they were doing it, nor did they speak to one another about it. To this day, we are only now discovering some of what really went on behind special closed steel doors of special dilapidated buildings during the Cold War era. Many, mostly enlisted people, were required to take an oath of silence for thirty years, and if they spoke of their work and their oath, they were promised they'd spend many, many years in Leavenworth at hard labor.

    My brother took this oath, at least I suppose he did, because he never uttered a word about what he was doing - utter silence - was what we got from him, so after awhile, we knew not to ask questions. Now, he rests, dead, in a National Cemetery located in Bourne, Cape Cod, Massachusetts in utter cold and silence, with so many of those like him, where the seagulls shit on the markers of those who were known as Silent Warriors; Spooks; The Prop Wash Gang; and sites like Berlin; Karamursel, Turkey; Alaska; Hawaii; Elemendorf; Tempelhof; Wiesbaden; Zweibrucken where the infamous, "didn't exist, doesn't exist," according to the record keepers, and the 6901st SCG (Security Communications Group) did their work, but the government won't say. I could name more places, but why not go to the Internet and search for "USAFSS" and find out some history you don't know, didn't know was happening to protect America, and probably some history you don't want to know. Maybe you'll be lucky enough to find a loved one who served. I did. None of the information you'll find today was on the Internet when I started my research for this book. Strange, isn't it, how it's all opening up now - almost all of it.

    The center in St. Louis, MO neglected to tell me that my brother was a spy; it took me four months of calling, writing, then contacting the Pentagon, where some nice woman put in an order for me and I received my brother's papers in just a few days . . . I guess she didn't like the fact that I had threatened her with "going to my Congressman." Phil's papers, strangely enough, came from Randolph Air Force Base; why, I don't know and I don't care. None of Phil's papers contained all of his assignments. Among the papers were no TDY's (Temporary Duty Stations), I don't know whether the rumor is true that he flew in a bomber or some little plane they used back then; I don't know if he went on "ferret missions;" I don't know if he went to Chicksands, England, or Menwith Hill; or if he was a "double plant" as one person suggested; or if he was a courier or assassin.

He worked for the USAFSS and did what the USAFSS and NSA (National Security Agency) told him to do. Those who were 'agents' came, not from the CIA, FBI, NSA, they were hand picked by those agencies, from each service, and told where to go and what to do, and to whom to report and to keep their mouths shut.

Phil was ultimately (in the end) a 20270 - Intercept Radio Analyst Technician or Specialist. I should tell you this point last, but will say it now - he was a Temporary Tech Sgt. before the end, the AF just didn't give me the papers telling me that. I found it on a piece of scratch paper they had sent along with some of his documents.

I love my nation. I am a patriot, but some of what Phil and others had to undergo, of which there ARE no records (many records weren't written down) is what led a sweet, highly intelligent, gentle man, to go absolutely from completely sane, to what the AF diagnosed as Paranoid/Schizophrenic, after his last three day TDY to London. Something happened there, I know not what, but he was a changed man upon return. He complained, 10 June 1963, that he had lost several good male friends at that point in time. Some suggest that he'd lost them on duty and some say there was a car accident, and some say that he and his buddies had disappeared and one day Phil came back to base. Some say he was exchanged for another Russian agent. At any rate, Phil had become, strange, unlike himself, according to his wife, during her interview by people at the 6901st SCG, Zweibrucken, revealed (on 13 January 1964), that she had last seen her husband on 9 January 1964. She also reported that she first noticed a change in the character and behavior of her husband following a TDY trip, which he made to England 10 June 1963. Finally, it was a Master Sergeant Thaddeus Szychowski, AF 133112147, on 25 October who first noticed and reported Phil's "erratic behavior," and related, "Sgt. Noland had become increasingly nervous during the previous weeks. This had interfered with his work." Then, the papers I have, reveal, "Sgt. Noland was interviewed on 24 September 1963 by his supervisors as to observations of the change in his personality." Phil had stated that he had "no personal grudges with any of the co-workers or supervisors, but just felt dejected because he was not making the progress that he felt he should be making in his job."

Phil's normal duties at that time required access to SENSITIVE CLASSIFIED INFORMATION, THE UNAUTHORIZED DISCLOSURE OF WHICH WOULD BE PREJUDICIAL TO THE DEFENSE INTERESTS OF THE UNITED STATES OF AMERICA.

Here I was, his sister, graduated and working and then, married and one child by 1963, never knowing where he was located, exactly, and receiving only a few letters from his family from time to time. So, while the cold war was going on, I knew in my heart that my brother was into something deep, and he never spoke of anything when on leave visiting the family. What a guy! His wife and two children (his son was born in Turkey) were real troupers! Whether they knew things or not, I didn't know at that point in time.

Now, I hear from some family, for most will not speak of Phil and his friends and their duties that he was in intelligence. That's it! Intelligence! Who knew, back then - who the hell knew what was really going on with this damned thing we called the cold war.

And now, all the veterans of that cold war from 5 September to 21 August 1991 have received nothing but a cheap piece of paper that is white with a bunch of red lines. What does that paper, that cheap paper say - that we recognize that - NAME - served, and a few other dumb words. That's it! Congress, to this day, still won't approve a medal for these courageous men (and women!).

You may think that I have a beef with Congress, but I don't, for I am a loyal American and I visit my brother's grave as often as possible - living in California and now Virginia, it isn't easy to get there, but my husband made sure he took me there three times. Our mother is buried there too, right down the hill from her son.

While I was playing "jacks" and going to school with the Seven Dots, Phil's comrades were out there listening for the Russian chatter, trying to break their code, as the Russians were doing to us, laying his life on the line as an Analyst of that traffic.

Phil, his papers state, was, "In the military, [and] he has been an analyst in Communications for twelve years." Our family thought he'd been doing some type of intelligence work for just a few years, so he must have been in intelligence since he entered the Air Force 21 November 1951! And that is why he earned the Korean Service Medal. Not only that, but, there's a scribbled note in his files from the Surgeon General, who was interested in "this case;" this case of my ol' bros, Phil, cracking up at the 690wurst, Zweibrucken. Strange. Yes. Why? Because "they" knew something had happened to him, and wanted to check out the reasons that made him go south, to cover their asses.

A lot of the guys went mental. Some took guns and shot themselves because they couldn't stand the pressure put upon them by the USAFSS; not being able to talk to anyone about what they were doing.

Some were helped by their buddies, keeping what they were going through from the public, until "these guys" came around and felt better.

The stress of the work they did and the fear of the Russian bounties on their heads, plus being utter silent, was too much for some of these intelligent, young, honorable men, who worked in their jobs under extreme conditions so Americans could sleep better at night. They gave their best, they gave their all, and I am proud to be an honorary member of the 6901st SCG Zweibrucken, online.

I love you guys and I thank you for your stories. You are welcome in my life.

Now, I present to you, your book, THESE GUYS: Cold War Stories Told by Cold War Warriors.

T.S. 2009

And what is so wrong about working the black side,
gleaning vital intelligence data in the cause of giving
ones own comrades a vital edge in battle
I'll not hide in shame when someone points and says,
He is a spy.
He seeks out my secrets and shares them
with those who would defend freedom against tyranny.

        E. Leonard
        USAFSS
        COLD WAR

Your late brother
was one of our USAFSS guys who took the terms
Duty, Honor, Country very seriously.
What more can one ask of an American Military man
and then tell him to keep his mouth shut
all his remaining years on earth?
He was one of my guys . . . and I am proud
to be in his lineage.

                                                                V. Wuwert

IN MEMORY OF PHILLIP C. NOLAND, USAFSS-SSGT-(Ret.) 20270
1931 - 1986
By his sister Trish (Noland) Schiesser

Phillip Clarence Noland was born in the year 1931.
He was an August child.
He was a first child.
He was the brother who sang me to sleep every night, (Brahms' Lullaby),
and
wakened me in the mornings.

Some children grew up on Dr. Seuss' Green Eggs and Ham.
I grew up eating Phil's cold spaghetti, or scrambled eggs and toast in the chill of the predawn hours, before I dressed
and
walked to school. He filled me with warmth, sharing his coffee. I was ready.

He shadow-walked me to school. I'd turn and look, but he was too silent, too quick,
and
so I thought of myself as an adult-child.

I'm sure you remember the albums we received upon graduating eighth grade:
"Go little album, far and near, to all my friends I hold so dear, and ask them each to write a page that I may read in my old age."
That's what I am doing right now. I am sixty-five. Phil would have been seventy-five.
He died at fifty-five. Allow me to acquaint you with my brother's words written into my album on a sunny, yellow page on 06 Jun 55:
"To Sis: Forever Kid: It's really hard to write a line, especially if it doesn't rhyme.
But you know what I'm trying to say, you're the best and a little OK.
Good luck! Love, Your bros., Sgt. Noland."

Phil was my first hero who showed me the way towards independence and love for my fellow man.

His contribution to the Cold War was valuable. As a SSGT of the USAFSS he gave his all with kindness and understanding and passed on his wisdom in his 202 capacity.

Years ago, while at "Mudsite" Phil received high praise on his Airman Performance Reports, some of which I will include: "SSGT Noland does all of his own reporting. His ability to identify and put out the proper end product report has resulted in numerous citations from higher headquarters. He has changed many operating procedures to make more timely reporting a reality. He has set up a new and efficient system, which cuts down on the time needed to identify certain classified entities. He has on his own initiative tracked down seemingly unrelated bits of information and put out an excellent tip-off and end product reports. He has rendered timely and accurate assistance to subordinate units resulting in a well-coordinated interchange of information. He has increased the efficiency and coordination between two separate entities through his effective leadership qualities as an NCO. His high degree of interest in his career field, his ability to analyze and digest facts quickly and accurately, combined with his extensive job knowledge of his particular entity qualify SSGT Noland as one of the better analysts at this station."

Dorothy Aspell, Captain, OIC "C" Flight, TUSLOG Det. 3, said of Phil: "His off duty conduct is above reproach and he has been an exemplary NCO and I believe that he possesses all the qualities desired of an NCO. Plans for him include supervisory duties."

My brother died Valentine's Day of 1986 from surgical complications due to being struck down by a New York City Taxi as he stepped off a curb into the streets of a city he loved. He left behind numerous relatives, and his daughter, Sherry, and a son, Billy, who was born in Istanbul.

Phil has never left me - in the silent hours at the close of day he inspires my writing and spirituality. Buried with full military honors, he resides in the National Cemetery located in Bourne, Cape Cod, Mass., just up the hill from our mother.

At this time I would like to write the three verses of TAPS in not only SSGT Noland's honor, but in memory of all the dedicated men and women who serve in the military, yesterday, today, and tomorrow.

TAPS

Day is done
Gone the sun
From the Lakes
From the hills
From the sky.
All is well,
Safely rest.
God is nigh.

Fading light
Dims the sight
And a star
Gems the sky,
Gleaming bright
From afar,
Drawing nigh,
Falls the night.

Thanks and praise,
For our days,
Neath the sun,
Neath the stars,
Neath the sky,
As we go,
This we know,
God is nigh.

This Preface and Acknowledgment, is a partial Brief History of the Air Intelligence Agency and its Predecessor Organizations from A Continuing Legacy: USAFSS to AIA, 1948- 2000, by Dr. Dennis F. Casey and MSgt Gabriel G. Marshall and published by the Air Intelligence Agency History Office, San Antonio, TX. This came to me via http://www.Silent.Warriors.com/Wheelock.htm, to each, I give credit. I feel that their words describe, best, the continuing legacy of the USAFSS - AIA, 1948- 2000.

USAFSS to AIA - 1948 - 2000
By Dr. Casey and MSgt Marshall

The Air Intelligence Agency's rich and colorful heritage began nearly fifty-two years ago and encompasses much of the Cold War. Indeed, the activities and many accomplishments of the United States Air Force Security Service, later the Electronic Security Command, and for a brief time the Air Force Intelligence Command contributed importantly to the history of the United States during this period which was replete with the threat of nuclear confrontation with our primary opponent, the Soviet Union. As scholars look back on this period and try to explain its major trends and developments, as well as its frustrations and the chasm that separated the two super powers, the role of air intelligence will surely be seen as a defining influence.

As the Air Intelligence Agency steps forward into the 21st century and carries out its mission of information operations it is worth a moment to reflect on where the command was, where it has been and what it has achieved. This publication outlines briefly the command's first 52 years as the Air Force's air intelligence arm and chronicles many of the important contributions which have provided for the continued security of the United States. We wish to recognize the superb support provided by the 690th Information Systems Squadron Visual Production Flight and the Headquarters Air Intelligence Agency Public Affairs Office. To Jim Pierson and Mary Holub and the others who endeavored tirelessly over the years to record this exciting and important story, and to Juan Jimenz whose assistance and advice were invaluable, we express our special thanks.

The Foreword: In this fast-paced environment of the 21st century, driven as it often is by seemingly constantly changing information age technologies, it is fundamentally important to pause occasionally and reflect on where the Air Intelligence Agency (AIA) has been. Even in the autumn of 1947, when Colonel Richard P. Klocko began laying the groundwork for a separate Air

Force organization devoted to special information, change was everywhere. Unprecedented accuracy and speed in communications, the unleashing of the atomic age, and the advent of a bipolar world heralded much of this change. The Air Force Security Group established on 23 June 1948, underwent a significant metamorphosis and became the United States Air Force Security Service (USAFSS) on 20 October 1948, before even five months had passed. Not quite two years later USAFSS personnel found themselves headed into a new conflict when on 25 June 1950 North Korean ground forces crossed the 38th parallel into South Korea. The Cold War had suddenly heated up. Today's AIA is a fused intelligence organization serving as a critical part of the air operations arm of the United States. Its mission continues to change as it endeavors to provide its many customers with current, readily usable and focused information products and services. AIA's personnel accomplish this complex mission of information operations with a high degree of professionalism and effectiveness. They participate directly in combat operations and capitalize upon new and promising technologies, adapting them to current as well as perceived needs. In so doing AIA defines and sharpens the Air Force Core Competency of information operations. Today's AIA warriors, backed by a rich 52-year heritage, look forward to the challenges of the future and stand ready to defend the United States and its people, its interests and its allies in the 21st century.

This Foreword signed by: Bruce A. Wright, Major General, USAF
Commander, Air Intelligence Agency

The bulk of the information presented here has been extracted from Wikipedia.com on November 19, 2006. Information on the Cold War has also been extracted from World Book Encyclopedia and Learning Resources with approval.

UNITED STATES AIR FORCE SECURITY SERVICE AND THE COLD WAR.
Submitted by Trish Schiesser

On the USAFSS emblem the globe symbolizes worldwide influence, the lightning bolt symbolizes transmissions, the wind symbolizes the Air Force itself, and the sword symbolizes protection and security.

The "United States Air Force Security Service" (often abbreviated "USAFSS") was essentially the United States Air Force's intelligence branch; its motto was "Freedom through Vigilance." It was created in October of 1948 and operated until 1979, when the branch was redesignated the Electronic Security Command (now the Air Intelligence Agency).

Composed primarily of airmen culled from the cream of the Air Force's enlisted recruits, the USAFSS was a secretive and tight-knit branch of Air Force cold warriors tasked with monitoring and interpreting military voice and electronic signals of countries of interest (which often were Eastern bloc countries). USAFSS intelligence was often analyzed in the field, and the results transmitted to the National Security Agency for further analysis and distribution to other intelligence recipients.

Individual airmen stationed at locations scattered across the globe, ranging from Alaska to Pacific Islands to The Far East to Mediterranean Countries to the Middle East to Western Europe to North Africa did a variety of jobs, almost all of them related to listening to and interpreting Eastern Bloc, Communist Chinese, and North Vietnamese military communications. Some airmen were linguists who listened to voice communications. Others monitored Soviet and other nations' military Morse code broadcasts. Some were engaged in monitoring other types of radio signals such as facsimile transmissions. The information collected in the field was usually sent to a co-located group of USAFSS analysts who would interpret the data, format reports, and send them on to National Security Agency or other recipients.

These jobs, which required top secret clearances, were extremely high pressure and were considered essential to U.S. cold war efforts. Members of the USAFSS were not allowed to discuss their jobs with outsiders. In fact, USAFSS members could not talk amongst themselves about their jobs unless they were in a secure location. Because of their value as targets (in Cold War Berlin, the capture of a USAFSS member was worth several thousand dollars), while stationed overseas, their off-base travel was severely restricted. Many adopted "cover jobs" to more easily conceal their real work.

The USAFSS had two major areas of operations: ground based and airborne. Ground based units were scattered across the globe, and collected information from fixed sites with large antenna arrays and from mobile units equipped with electronic gear and antennas that skirted sensitive areas collecting data. Airborne units were associated with the strategic reconnaissance units of Strategic Air Command, and flew aboard SAC reconnaissance flights to collect data from shorter range communication systems and other types of signals. A primary job of USAFSS airborne linguists aboard SAC reconnaissance aircraft was to provide self-protection early warning of impending fighter or missile response by a target nation's air defense system.

The activities of the USAFSS have only recently been declassified.

Country music icon Johnny Cash was a USAFSS member while stationed in Germany in the early 1950s.

TABLE OF CONTENTS

Levesque, Don (Freedom Through Vigilance)	1
Anonymous	2,7,8,13,15,19
Anonymous	27,31,32,33,36
Bravenet	18
Brun, Dick (Phil at Karamursel)	36
Conrad, Phil (Management, AFSS Security Service, Re: Blessed Christmas)	37,109,110
Conrad, Phil (Oberauerbach)	114
Anderson, Gary (Mike, Cold War Recollections, Ten Months, Eleven Days. . . .)	40,41,45
Anderson, Gary (Sere, 2T Program)	56,68
Person, Bill (Re Sere)	56,59
Wuwert, Vince (Sere)	59
Sadler, Deryl (Sere)	59,60,63
Sadler, Spencer (Sere)	61,65
Ashcroft, Bruce (Brain Wasting Disease Kills Area Soldier)	73
Babb, Wayne (Blitz of Whip Decoux, Best Damned 202 Ever)	79,84
Barker, Ted (The Day Testosterone Ruled the Waves)	86
Baxter, Addis Titus (Brooks AFB, USAFSS 1950)	90

TABLE OF CONTENTS

Benjamin, Jack (Funny Story about Courage and Polar Bears) — 91

Benjamin, Jack (St Lawrence Island in the Spring Of 1954) — 92

Bergman, Dick (136th Css Hqs at Brooks AFB, USAFSS - The Good, The Bad, the Ugly) — 95,99

Bergman, Dick (USAFSS-Excitement, Excitement, Sadness, NATO Maneuvers) — 101,102,103

Bristol, Dave (Re Little Toy Dog) — 104

Brown, Colonel Charles V, USAFR (Ret) (No Sleeping in the Ashtrays) — 105

Cox, Dale (Morale Caps, Sailboat for Sale) — 111,115

Fehrs (Us Electronic Espionage, Zweibrucken) — 117,152

Fortin, J (6900th Anecdotes) — 155

Galt, John (E-mail re Yahoo Site) — 157

Giere, John (E-mail, re Phil Noland) — 159,163

Gray, Captain Paul N., USN, (Ret) (Bridges at Toko-ri) — 165

Grayson, William C. (President Visits Troops in Combat Zone, Ear on Vietnam War) — 171,174

Grimsley, Daniel (Third Squadron Mobile-Alaska-on St Lawrence Island) — 180

Dodd, Keith (Responding to Grimsley) — 182

Olson, Ed (Responding to Grimsley) — 185

TABLE OF CONTENTS

Bush, David (Responding to Grimsley) — 187

Baert, Bob (Freedom Through Vigilance Association) — 191

Schiesser, Trish (Responding to Grimsley) — 192

Guest, Bob (Notes re Phil Noland, Karamursel) — 194

Hall, Honorable Ralph, of Texas (Recognition Of Pappy Hicks) — 197

Hamann, Rog (Rustic Yankee - OV-10 GIB) — 199

Hicks, Pappy via Bill Person (S & W 38') — 211

Hazlett, Bob (I Was a Sergeant Pilot, My Second (And Only Other) Crash Landing) — 212, 214

Hazlett, Bob (Korean Stories, Cold War Stories) — 217, 226

Hicks, D.L. "Pappy" (Letters) — 242

Horton, Jon (The Return of the Teuton Hordes, Epitaph) — 244, 248

Huffman, George (A Very Moving Story) — 251

Levesque, Don (E-mail re These Guys) — 254

Jamison, Joe (Misty Report) — 256

Roth, Jim (Bat Cat (EC-121R) Mission) — 261

Kaptur, Honorable Mary, Ohio (Letter to Vince Wuwert) — 262

Kilthau, Gus (SAFB) — 264

TABLE OF CONTENTS

King, David and Special Services Libraries (Zweibrucken - A Short History) — 266

Lafitte, Paul (Thanks for the Invite to Write Something for Your Book) — 269

Lally, Dave (Cuban Missile Crises New Info) — 270

Lally, Tim (On the Indy, Sea Duty, 206) — 271, 273, 276

Hall, Robert A. via Tim Lally (Women, Whiskey And War) — 278

Leonard, Ed (USAFSS Lite, Don't Ask Why, Emails, Re These Guys, Welfare Case) — 280, 281, 285, 288

Leonard, Ed (E-mails, The Real World, My War Was Psywar, Memories) — 290, 292, 295, 302

Levesque, Don (Veteran's Day November 2002, The 6901st Zweibrucken) — 306, 307

Levesque, Don (Ferret Missions, Don Levesque Sounds Off) — 308, 309

Levesque, Don (German Shepherd Dogs, At Francis Warren AFB) — 311, 313

Levesque, Don (For Your Eyes Only, E-mails) — 325, 321

Mayer, Donny for John McCain (One Nation, Under God) — 323

Leinweber, Dr Al (An Earlier Time, Rosemary, Letter from Chau N Lam, D. MD.) — 325, 331, 333

TABLE OF CONTENTS

Levine, Irv (P-51, Another Remembrance . .,Ta-Ra-Boom-Dee-AAAA)   335,337,338

Levine, Irv (Objective Look at the War We're In, Downtown, Thunderthud, Thud Ridge)   339,496 493,497

Mower, Patrick (Short Term Separations)   341

Global Spy Magazine (NSA Abandons Wondrous Stuff)   343

NSARCHIVE (Havana Conference, Cuban Missile Crisis after 40 Years)   348,351

Neeland, Herb (E-mail, the Young Pilot, Medic, Boys in the Mist)   352,354,361 364

Neeland, Herb (Brave Thai Soldier, Babysan, Date of Separation)   367,368,370

Nishio, Renate (Do You Remember Me)   372

Oberg, John (E-mail, Ride in a C 124, John Oberg And the Captain)   374,380,385

Person, Bill (Zoomies/Tests, Ejection and Other Things Important, Turkey Stuff)   387,388,392

Person, Bill (Weapons, Planes, a Trip to Neverland, Short Round)   396,399,401 404

Person, Bill (Blondes, Avatar Dawn, Shithot Pilot, 'Thailand, Burma')   406,408,410 412

Person, Bill (Cambodia, Sensors Go to War, Batcats: Sensors Go to War)   417,418,425

TABLE OF CONTENTS

Person, Bill (S & W 38' Special, A Scary Time, CIA And Other Intelligence Stuff)	427,439,440
Person, Bill- Jarrett, Richard (I Drove a Truck)	433
Person, Bill- Eaker, Gen Ira (Army Flier)	435
Person, Bill (Not Allowed to Keep Notes, Very Unique Status Board)	448,450
Person, Bill (War up Too Close and Personal: My Story)	451
Person, Bill-Crittenden, Stephen (Air CIA)	472
Person, Bill (Queen Bee Delta Project, Intelligence Matters, Turtleneck)	478,479,486
Person, Bill (Reflections of Honor, .45 ACP, Red River Valley, Life's Clock)	488,489,491 717
Red (Okay Guys, Lets Hear Your Stories!)	498
Reed, William with Reed, Craig (Some Interesting Cryptologic History from the Past)	499
Rose, Ray (Re: Bye Bye, USAFSS Lite, Bravenet Hansen Affair)	515,518,521
Sadler, Deryl (Do You Believe This?, Yarns, ECI Course Intelligence Fundamentals, F-106 Tactical Employment Evaluation ADC/ADWC Project 68-12 USAF Interceptor Weapons School 1968)	524,526,527 530
Sadler, Deryl (Top Secret-"Need to Know", Survival Schools, My Plan for Desert Storm II)	535,541 543

TABLE OF CONTENTS

Scanlon . . . (Your Brother at Samson AFB)	544
Schiesser, Bob (Christmas Ops Tempo, How to Bake A Chicken}	545,547
Schiesser, Trish (Hi this Is Trish Schiesser, Surreal Or Tongue in Cheek, Rangers Words, Johnny Cash)	548,550,552 553
Wood, Jack (Karamusel, Turkey)	549
Schiesser, Trish (Dugway-Bender Gestalt Tests, Fulda Gap, USAFSS Command Emblem)	554,555,557
Stallings, Jim (From an Ex-USAFSS Guy (#1), #2, #3, #4, #5, #6, #7)	560,564,565 567,571,572
Steve, (Zweibrucken Pictures)	579
Swain, James F (Happier Young Men	581
Tarin, Bill (Re: 6901st SCG Zweibrucken, Knew of Phil)	585,587
Thomson, Ray (Our Secret Cold War)	590
EW or Anonymous (Low Visibility TDY Assignments)	595
Walzak, Keith (A Little Note from the USNS Spica's Final Voyage)	597
Watts, Ed (Elitists, School Gives "No Comment" To Moscow Spy Charge)	599,601
Weaver, Bill (SR-71 Breakup)	602

TABLE OF CONTENTS

Wheatley, Bob (Listening to the Red Chinese Pilots at Ramasun Station, Capture of the Pueblo, No Hero's Welcome, Sitting Ducks, Sappers, and Artificial Boundaries) 609,615 618 629

Casey, Dr. Dennis F and Marshall, Msgt Gabriel G. (USAFSS to AIA-1949-2000) 641

Wuwert, Vince (The Good and the Bad, Those Dits and Dahs, Typing 101, Check Out Reconnaissance Flights and Sino-American Relations, China) 643,647 648 649,650

Wuwert, Vince (Go to Hell, From My Days at Chicksands, Re: Phil, Ramasun Station, Thailand) 653,656,658 659

Wuwert, Vince (A Part of an E-mail from Vince Wuwert, About England, Thank You for Your Service, Re: a Little Help, Re: These Guys-Mao's Words) 660,661 662 666

Wuwert, Vince (If You Have Any Questions, Re: USAF Security Service-Plaine De Jars Area, Gen Custer, Email to Trish) 667,669,670 671

Wuwert, Vince (Security Breach at Chicksands, Surmises about Phil, Re: Bill's (Person) Book, Radio Caroline) 673,675,678 679

Wuwert, Vince (Keesler AFB, Laos: Quiet and Laos: AA Flak, USS Pueblo, USS Pueblo II) 681,683,685 687

Wuwert, Vince (Honorable Servicemen, When The Roll Is Called up Yonder I'll Be There, The Russians Are Coming, Remembrances of a Ditty Bopper) 688,690 691 695

Wuwert, Vince (The Secret War Weapon in Thailand, NCO's, NCO's-continued, True Russian Story from Chicksands) 696,698 702,705

TABLE OF CONTENTS

Wuwert, Vince (The Battlefield) — 707

Xieques, Jeri (Elmendorf AFB, Anchorage) — 710

An Air Force Reservist by Bill Person (Battle of Today) — 712

Person, Bill (Life's Clock) — 717

THESE GUYS

COLD WAR STORIES

TOLD BY

COLD WAR WARRIORS

1945-1991

COLLECTED AND EDITED

BY

TRISH SCHIESSER

These Guys

These words were told to me by Don Levesque, a former USAFSS man.

The United States Air Force Security Service (often abbreviated USAFSS) was essentially the United States Air Force's intelligence branch; its motto was *Freedom Through Vigilance*. It was created in October of 1948 and operated until 1979, when the branch was re-designated the Electronic Security Command (now the Air Intelligence Agency).

Composed primarily of airmen culled from the cream of the Air Force's enlisted recruits, the USAFSS was a secretive and tight-knit branch of Air Force cold warriors tasked with monitoring and interpreting military voice and electronic signals broadcast by former Eastern Bloc countries, primarily the Soviet Union, Poland and Czechoslovakia. Often, USAFSS intelligence was funneled to agents at the National Security Agency.

Individual airmen -- stationed at locations scattered across the globe, ranging from Alaska to Pacific Islands to The Far East to Mediterranean Countries to The Middle East to Western Europe to North Africa -- did a variety of jobs, almost all of them related to listening to and interpreting Eastern Bloc military communications. Some airmen were linguists who listened to Russian and Polish radio broadcasts, then translated them and evaluated from for their intelligence value. Others monitored Russian and Polish military Morse code broadcasts. Still others were cryptographers.

These jobs, which required top secret clearance, were extremely high pressure and were considered essential to U.S. cold war efforts. Members of the USAFSS were not allowed to discuss their jobs with outsiders -- in fact, USAFSS members could not talk amongst themselves about their jobs unless they were in a secure location. Because of their value as targets (in Cold War Berlin, the capture of a USAFSS member was worth several thousand dollars), while stationed overseas their off-base travel was severely restricted. Many adopted "cover jobs" to more easily conceal their real work.

The activities of the USAFSS have only recently been declassified.

These Guys

I thought this story would be appropriate to begin THESE GUYS. It was sent to me by Anonymous and everything has been done to find the author, to no avail. This takes place in January 1944 - just before the Cold War began in 1945. The story is so overpowering that I felt I might begin the cold war stories with a bit of WWII.

ACCOUNT OF MANEUVERS: B-17 (42-39957) Halberstadt, Germany 01-11-44 - 11 JANUARY 1944 AIRCRAFT NO. 42-39957 HALBERSTADT, GERMANY

Took off at 0745 o'clock with a load of 2300 gallons of gasoline, 6000 pounds of bombs, full load of ammunition, and the usual weight of men and equipment. Everything on plane was in perfect working order. Joined the group formation at 1010 o'clock and flew into target without incident but was forced to use 2400 R.P.M. and 40" at times. Dropped our bombs at 1152 o'clock, everything still in good shape. At 12 o'clock we were hit by fighters which stayed with us for one hour and fifty minutes. They attacked us from 5-7 o'clock position at first and gradually as more enemy fighters joined they attacked us from 3-9 o'clock positions. We were flying "Tail End Charlie," #7 position. The fighters created much excitement among the squadron, resulting in more power being applied to the engines. We were forced to use 2500 R.P.M. and 40"-46" almost continuously. About 1245 o'clock more enemy fighters joined the attack and finally we were being attacked from all positions on the clock, high and low. The plane was vibrating and pitching unbelievably, as a result of all guns firing, fighting prop-wash, and evading collision with our own as well as enemy planes. Enemy fighters would come through our formation from 12 o'clock positions, level in groups of 20-40 at one time, all shooting. The sky in front of us was a solid mass of exploding 20 M.M. shells, flak, rockets, burning aircraft, and more enemy fighters. B-17's were going down in flames every 15 minutes and enemy fighters seemed to explode or go down in smoke like flies dropping out of the sky. The "Luftwaffe" attacked us in ME 109's, ME 210's, FW 190's JU 88's, and some we couldn't identify. The enemy fighters made suicidal attacks at us continuously, coming into about fifty feet before turning away. It seemed that the greater part of the attack was aimed at our ship, perhaps for the following reason. Our ship was the only one in the group that was not firing tracer bullets and they apparently thought we had no guns or were out of ammunition.

The heaviest assault and the one that damaged us happened as follows. At approximately 1330 o'clock we were attacked by another group of enemy fighters numbering about forty which came at us again from 12 o'clock position, level in formation pattern. Again, we saw that solid wall of exploding shells and fighters. This time we were flying #3 position in the second element of the lead squadron. As they came in the top turret gunner of our ship nailed a FW 190 which burst into flames, nosed up and to its left, thus colliding with the B-1-7 flying #2 position of the second element on our right. Immediately upon colliding this B-17 burst into flames, started into a loop but fell off on its left wing and across our tail. We were really hit and we had "Had it." At the time we were thus stricken we were using a full power setting of 2500 R.P.M. and 40"- 46" Hg. Our I.A.S. was approximately 165 MPH, and our altitude was 19,000 feet. Immediately upon being hit by the falling B-17 we were nosed up and went into a loop, confusion, no less, and embarrassment. Pilot called crew at once and ordered them to prepare to bail out. Response was instantaneous and miraculously proficient. Not one crew member grew frantic or lost his head, so to speak. All stood ready at their stations to abandon the ship. The action of the Pilot regarding the handling of the ship was as follows. As quickly as we were hit we engaged the A.F.C.E. which was set up for level flying. Full power was applied with throttle and both Pilot and C-Pilot began the struggle with the manual controls.

It was noted at once that the rudder control was out because the rudder pedals could not be moved. In only a fraction of a second the ship had completed a beautiful loop and was now merrily spinning toward the ground, with five enemy fighters following on the tail. Although the spin seemed flat and rather slow it was vicious and we were losing altitude fast. As soon as we had completed the loop and had fallen into a spin the Pilot, having full confidence in a prayer, recalled the crew members and ordered them to stand by for a little while longer.

"Guts" discipline, and confidence in their Pilot was certainly displayed by the crew by the fact that they stayed with the ship, to return to the spin and its final recovery. When the ship fell into a spin the Pilot after determining its direction applied full inside throttle, retarded the other two, used only aileron A.F.C.E. control, and applied it in full opposite position, rolled elevator trim-tab fully forward, and in addition both pilots applied full forward position on control column, plus full opposite aileron. After making at least two or three complete 360-degree turns, the ship finally swept into a clean dive at an angle of approximately 45 degrees from level.

The I.A.S. at this time was approximately 280 M.P.H. The altitude was approximately 12,000 feet. Power setting was reduced to about 2/3. At this point it was noted that one enemy fighter was still following on our tail, therefore seeing a solid undercast below we nosed the ship down and applied additional power. We were heading for cloud cover at an angle of approximately 75 degrees to 80 degrees from the level at a speed of about 400 M.P.H. indicated. All this while the aileron was clutched into A.F.C.E. and was holding wings level. The elevators were controlled entirely by the trim tab.

At 6000 feet we began easing back the elevator trim tab and slowly started to level out. Finally leveled off in the clouds at 4000 feet, trimmed the ship, and engaged elevator clutch of A.F.C.E. Disengaged this every few seconds to re-trim ship, kept it perfectly level and flying smoothly. The I.A.S. after leveling off in the clouds was still around 340 M.P.H. But was dropping off quite rapidly until it reached 200 M.P.H. Maintained an I.A.S. of 190-200 M.P.H. from then on with a power setting of 2100 R.P.M. and 31" Hg.

Checked all engine instruments immediately after leveling off and found everything functioning normally, except the Pilot's directional gyro which apparently had tumbled. Flew in the cloud cover for about ten (10) minutes then came out above to check for more enemy fighters. Saw one fighter after several minutes at five (5) o'clock position came out above to check for more enemy fighters. Saw one fighter after several minutes at five (5) o'clock position high so we ducked back into the clouds for about ten minutes longer. Came out again and found everything clear.

Rode the top of the clouds all the way back across the North Sea. The point where we first entered the cloud cover was about thirty (30) minutes flying time (at our speed) from the enemy sea coast. An interesting point which occurred was that we came out of our spin and dive on a heading of 270 degrees which fortunately was our heading home. Immediately after we had leveled off in the clouds each crew member reported into the Co-Pilot that he was back at his station and manning his guns. No particular excitement or scare was apparent for the crew members started a merry chatter over the interphone.

During the violent maneuvers of the loop the left waist gunner, S/Sgt. Warren Carson, was thrown about in the waist of the ship resulting in a fractured leg. However, he did remain at his guns until the chances of more enemy attacks was nil. After we were well out over the North Sea the injured waist gunner was moved to the radio room where he was treated and made comfortable by the Bombardier who went back to assist.

At this time also the Co-Pilot went to the rear of the ship to examine the Control cables and make a general survey of the damage to the tail section. He reported that about 1/3 of the left horizontal stabilizer and elevator were off and that almost the entire vertical stabilizer and rudder had been sheared off but that all control cables were O.K. However, the ship was functioning quite normally except for the fact that we had to make turns with aileron only. It also seemed to fly quite smoothly in spite of the missing vertical stabilizer and rudder. It was therefore decided by the pilot that a normal landing could be attempted.

Reaching the English coast we headed for our home field but the weather had closed in and the ceiling was getting lower as we neared our field. Finally, we were forced to fly at tree-top heights in order to stay out of the clouds, thus getting lost. All radio equipment was out and we were not sure where the field was. Finally it began to rain, besides our other trouble, so we decided to land at the first field we found. Pilot ordered all crew members to radio room to prepare for crash landing. However, the Navigator volunteered to remain in the nose of the ship to direct the Pilot and Co-Pilot in their approach to the field and a final landing.

The landing was accomplished in the normal manner, taking advantage of a slightly longer approach. Picked the longest runway which suited the wind direction but still had to contend with a cross wind. With the aid of the Navigator's directions we made a low approach to the runway, correcting for draft by holding the windward wing low and holding it straight by jockeying the throttles. "No, you're wrong," we greased it on. Made a perfect landing. After setting it on the ground it was noted that the right tire was flat. However, this did not trouble us because the ship was stalled out at low speed and slowed down immediately by use of brakes. It was noted that the ship was almost dry of fuel. Positively no stress was placed on the ship in landing. It was a landing as any normal landing would be.

We now know from experience that a B-17 will loop, spin, pull out of a dive when indicating 400 M.P.H., fly without a rudder and very little horizontal stabilizer, and will land normally without a rudder and a flat tire added. The "guts," courage, and confidence displayed by the crew of this mission is highly commendable. The navigator displayed extreme courage when he volunteered to remain in the nose to direct the Pilot in landing in almost zero weather. The Co-Pilot deserves special commendation for his capable assistance in maneuvering this ship, guarding the engine, his careful survey of the damage, his assistance in determining the possibility of a safe landing and finally his reassuring words to the crew over the interphone during the homeward journey.

The gunners shot down nine (9) enemy aircraft and claimed to have damaged at least ten (10) more.

PILOT 1st Lt. JOHN W. RAEDEKE CO-PILOT 2nd Lt. JOHN E. URBAN, (wherever you are.)

From: airforcesecurityservice@yahoogroups.com

AIR FORCE SECURITY SERVICE (OLD MEMORIES)
By Anonymous (Every effort has been made to find "Anonymous" to no avail - but "he" is given credit for what is written below.

Old Memories: a few nights ago on the tonight show, Jay Leno had the 'Jay-Walking' segment: How much do you know about USA history. Who was the first female astronaut? Sally Ride. Who can remember the first female in space? Valentina Teriscova, June 1963. I was on Shemya at the time, and one of the missions was downrange soviet missile activity. We had the first voice copy of this mission. This was a two soyouz mission, two space craft up at the same time. Valentina was supposed to be up 5 days, curtailed to 3 days. Seems like Valentina went bonkers locked up in small capsule and was ready to crawl out, even while in orbit.

This is an e-mail which I received from a former USAFSS person. I shall, at his request, refer to him as anonymous.

CLASSIFIED ADVENTURES
By Anonymous
Trish: Below are two stories: one I know of personally and the other I got second hand from a very reliable source who was involved in the first. I am an unidentified source. Use them if you wish.

In 1955 intercept operators began recording an aircraft with an unidentifiable call number. The aircraft was landing at a nearby air base. An analyst became very curious about this aircraft as we were supposed to know all ID numbers and call signs.

This analyst took it upon himself to drive to the airbase and see if he could identify the aircraft. He took his camera along. The rest you can guess. He was arrested by the Air Police and placed in secure lockup until the commanding officer of the USAFSS wing showed up. The aircraft was the U2. This occurred in Europe.

This one verifies what you may have gleaned from Silent Warriors or the online encyclopedia. A group of USAFSS people were on an aircraft that had a layover in Turkey. They decided to take a holiday to an island off the coast where there were ancient ruins and night life and of course BABES. A storm came up the first night and they were unable to return to the mainland as the ferry would not sail. Unfortunately, they had not informed their commander as to where they were going.

Given the known fact that there was a reward offered by the USSR and its satellites the USAF issued a worldwide alert for the missing airmen. Needless to say there were some very sorry NCO's when they were finally found, and they had to explain why they had not reported their destination.

Today is my birthday. I am now officially 74 but as you may have concluded, I don't feel like it. Shot a rabbit this morning. He was eating my broccoli. Will make a nice evening meal next week.

Stay well and say hello to Bob. He has my respect.
Anonymous

This story was sent to me by someone I don't recall - however, I give credit to J.D. Wetterling and the person who thought this story was remarkable - and it is.

STILL the NOBLEST CALLING
By J.D. Wetterling

I visited with three old friends recently at a park near my town. It seemed like only yesterday that we were all together, but actually it had been twenty-eight years. There was a crowd at the park that day, and it took us a while to connect, but with the aid of a computer we made it. I found Lance at panel 54W, line 037, Lynn over at panel 51W, line 032, and Vince down at panel 27W, line 103.

In 1968 we were gung-ho young fighter pilots in Vietnam, the cream of the crop of the U.S. Air Force pilot training system, and now their names are on that 250-foot-long, half-size model of Washington's Vietnam War Memorial that moves around the country. I had intentionally avoided visiting the wall when it came to town in years past because I did not trust myself to keep my composure. But after nearly three decades it was time to try for some closure on this issue. I told my wife that I preferred to go alone, if that was all right.

Truth be known, I nearly backed out at that.

Dancing the Wild Blue standing in front of that somber wall, I tried to keep it light, reminiscing about how things were back then. We used to joke about our passionate love affair with an inanimate flying object - we flew F-100s - and we marveled at the thought that we actually got paid to do it. We were not draftees but college graduates in Vietnam by choice, opting for the cramped confines of a jet fighter cockpit over the comfort of corporate America. In all my life, I've not been so passionate about any other work. If that sounds like an exaggeration, then you've never danced the wild blue with a supersonic angel.

I vividly remember the Sunday afternoon, in the summer of '68, when we flew out of Travis Air Force Base, California, on a troop transport headed for Vietnam. Lynn, Lance and I crowded around the same porthole and watched the Golden Gate Bridge disappear below broken clouds. We had gone through fighter pilot school together and had done some serious bonding. In an exceedingly rare moment of youthful fighter pilot humility, I wondered if I would live to see that bridge again.

For reasons I still don't understand, I was the only one of the three of us who did.

Once in Vietnam, we passed the long, lonely off-duty hours at Dusty's Pub, a lounge that we lieutenants built on the beach of the South China Sea at Tuy Hoa Airbase. The roof at Dusty's doubled as a sun deck and the walls were nonexistent. The complaint heard most often around the bar, in the standard gallows humor of a combat squadron, was, "It's a lousy war, but it's the only one we have." (I've cleaned up the language a bit.) We sang mostly raunchy songs that never seemed to end - someone was always writing new verses - and , as an antidote to loneliness, fear in the night and the sadness over dead friends, we often drank too much. ("Knee-walking drunk" was the term that got us through many nights.)

Vince joined us at Dusty's Pub halfway through my tour of duty, and since he was a like-minded country kid from Montana, we hit it off. He had a wide grin, slightly stooped shoulders and his own way of walking - he just stooped shoulders and just threw his feet out and stepped on them. But what he lacked in military bearing he made up for with the heart of a tiger. He often flew as my wingman, and we volunteered for the night missions on the Ho Chi Minh Trail. One starless night, the longest, saddest night of my life, we got into a nasty gun duel with some antiaircraft artillery batteries. I watched Vince die in a mushroom-shaped fireball that for a moment turned night into day.

Lance - a New York boy who took unmerciful grief from us because he talked like a New Yawker - crashed into the side of a mountain (karst) in the central Vietnamese highlands while attacking a target. Lynn, a happy-go-lucky jock from Pennsylvania's Slippery Rock College with a hound name John the Basset, returned to his base on a stormy night in July after weather aborted his mission. Two miles of wet runway weren't enough to stop an F-100 landing at 160 knots with all its bombs still on board. He ran off the end, flipped over, and slid through the minefield at the perimeter fence, setting off a gruesome sound and light show.

These Guys

At the wall, I told the guys only about the good parts of the last twenty-eight years.

Lacy, one of our associates from Dusty's Pub, became an astronaut, and a few summers ago I watched from my backyard, near Tampa, as he blasted off. His voice over the radio from space was at least an octave lower than it was the day I heard him radio for help while swinging from his parachute hung in a tree in Laos.

Another Dusty's patron, Rick, is now a two-star general, and I reminded them what we used to say about the military promotion system - it's like a septic tank, only the really big chunks float to the top.

I didn't tell them about how ostracized Vietnam vets still are, that during that same week, one of the nation's leading newspapers had run an article that implied us Vietnam vets were, to quote one syndicated columnist, "either, suckers or psychos, victims or monsters." I didn't tell them that the secretary of defense they fought for back then has now declared that he was not a believer in the cause for which he assigned them all to their destiny. I didn't tell them that a draft-age kid from Arkansas who hid out in England to dodge his duty while they were fighting and dying is now the commander-in-chief.

One more over that even went to Moscow to decry our involvement in that war. And I didn't tell them we lost that lousy war, (or were ordered out before we had a chance to win it.)

I gave them the same story I've used since the Nixon administration: We were winning when I left. (But he also quit before the Hanoi leaders ever gave up in the "enemy friendly war." Hell, they even pot-shotted us as we were pulling out.)

I relived that final day as I stared at the black onyx wall. The dawn came up like thunder after 268 combat missions in 360 days in the valley of the shadow. The ground trembled as 33 F-100s roared off the runway, across the beach and out over the South China Sea, climbing into the rising sun. On the eastern horizon, a line of towering deep-purple clouds stood shoulder-to-shoulder before a brilliant orange sky that slowly turned powder blue from the top down.

From somewhere on that stage, above the whine of spinning turbine blades, I could hear a choir singing Handel's "Hallelujah Chorus" in fortissimo: "The Lord God omnipotent reigneth," and He was bringing me home, while Lance and Lynn and Vince will remain as part of the dust of Southeast Asia until the end of time. I was not the only one talking to the wall through tears. A leather-vested, bare-chested biker two panels to my left was in even worse shape. I backed about 25 yards away from the wall and sat down on the grass under a clear blue sky and midday sun that perfectly matched the tropical weather of the war zone. The wall, with all 58,200 names, consumed my field of vision. I tried to wrap my mind around the megatonnage of violence, carnage and ruined lives that it represented. Then I thought of how Vietnam was only one small war in the history of the human race. I was overwhelmed with a sense of mankind's wickedness.

God, Duty, Honor, Country. My heart felt like wax in the blazing sun and I was on the verge of becoming a spectacle in the park. I arose and walked back up to the wall to say good-bye and ran my fingers over the engraved names - Lance and Lynn and Vince-as if I could communicate with them in some kind of spiritual Braille.

I wanted them to know that God, Duty, Honor and Country will always remain the noblest calling. Revisionist histories from elite draft dodgers trying to justify their own cowardly actions will never change that.

I have been a productive member of society since the day I left Vietnam. I am proud of what I did there, and I am especially proud of my friends - heroes who voluntarily, enthusiastically gave their all. They demonstrated no greater love to a nation whose highbrow opinion makers are still trying to disavow them. May their names, indelibly engraved on that memorial wall, likewise be found in the Book of Life.

These Guys

I don't know if this is a true story or not, but it has come to my attention and sounds as if it could be true. If any of you reading this story know of the truth of the matter please don't hesitate to contact me by e-mail. I thank ANONYMOUS who wishes his/her name to be withheld, for this story. I have tried to establish the authenticity of this story, but to no avail.

TEMPLEHOF
By Anonymous

Trish Schiesser wrote:

Were you in Berlin? I cannot remember.
I saw a photo of Gary Anderson, and Al Leinweber - who are both in THESE GUYS. I've seen this site before, while researching for my brother, Phil. He wasn't in Berlin, though.
Thanks,
Trish . . . A guy named Ed Leonard was in Berlin, do you know of him?

Anonymous wrote:

Only periodically on business, never on their duty roster.
No, I don't recall anyone named Ed Leonard. I did have some buddies at the Berlin unit I got to know when we attended Indiana U (Bloomington) - Ed Kirstein, Ray Gonczy, David Baker and one or two more whose names I can't remember at this late hour.

You might want to contact somebody you know who was stationed there, and ask what he knows about the rusted, steel doors in one of the basements of Templehof. I do remember one of my friends showing me the doors and telling me that the doors had been shut since March or April of 1945 by the Soviet Army. They had come into the building and the resident SS or some other Nazi unit refused to surrender. So, the Soviets just shut the doors and flooded the basement - drowning all the Nazi soldiers inside, where (I was told) their bodies remained and were supposed to be behind those macabre doors when I visited once in 1964 - nineteen years after the war ended! My suggestion about contacting somebody you might know is that you could get corroboration of what I have just written. What I have written is based solely on what I was told on one of my visits, but corroboration would be a good idea. In fact, maybe other sources on the internet might shed some light on what the Soviet Army did inside Templehof when they assaulted Berlin.

Anonymous

I reached out to some of the "buddies" I've made since researching for THESE GUYS and most of them knew the basements of Templehof, but had not heard the story above. There is a site about Templehof where it is said that, "not all the doors and such have been opened, to this day, so who knows, maybe this story is true." So far, extensive research has been done on the basements at Templehof, but to no avail on this story.

Subj: Re: Update: Spy Agencies Abuse Freedom of Information Exemptions
Date: 6/12/03 5:31:15 AM Pacific Daylight Time
From: Anonymous
To: IdaReedBlanford

Trish,

When I talk, on rare occasions, about England and the phenomenal Flare-9 antenna and how it could hear radio short wave signals ten time zones away and virtually clear as a bell, few people are impressed. They think "inside the box" so to speak. They are thinking that their portable AM radio in their back pack can only pick up an AM signal a few hundred miles and that is in the dark of night, so I must be just "telling war stories". They will never know the technology America had back in the 60s and I for one was extremely happy that WE had it and not the Rooskies.

There is still stuff we knew and kept it locked up, even today, we do that because if our enemies knew "we knew" they would change everything drastically and then we'd be on page one and starting all over again, a very exasperating thing to have confronting you.

We learned our lessons (American and western nations) in WWII. We were batting our heads into a brick wall trying to figure out the German Enigma code . . . we just couldn't break it. We could copy the messages with no problem, but discerning what the messages said was another question.

The British Y service - Wireless intercept ops, my guys, from the British side - did outstanding work during WWII and for the most part were never recognized because of the secrecy involved. But we finally, as history records obtained one of the German Enigma coding boxes . . . looks like a typewriter . . . but was the small machine that would scramble letters and make it virtually impossible to read them. We simply (actually the blokes did it but I use the term "we" because we were on the same side) reversed the process and examined the wiring and BINGO. Soon we were reading German Luftwaffe messages right and left; biggest secret of all; we never allowed the Krauts to know "we knew." Lots of sons of Adolph Hitler went to their demise because the British were waiting for them.

As I have always contended, I am a succeeding generation of guys who recovered radio intelligence. The tools I used like the AN-FLR-9 antenna were marvelous. Guys like Phil [the editor's brother] . . . gad zooks, what a wonderful guy he must have been . . . he did so much for his country . . . and as they say, he was an unsung hero and as I have said many times, I am proud to be accounted for as being one of his "guys" in the over all mission. A couple of other things: When I got to England in April of 1966 I think I grew up very fast. When I walked into the ops building and saw all that classified stuff all over the place . . . paper work, equipment, conversations, the entire operation; I knew then, my country needed my skills, and like it or not, I had a job to do, it was my turn and damn it, I did the best I could and my country benefitted and exists today because of my efforts and the efforts of everyone in operations like at Chicksands.

On a personal note, the Russians . . . I hated them; Godless wretches. They have butchered more of their own people in the last 100 years than Adolph Hitler did in WWII to the entire world. Feel even less sympathy for the Chinks. As far as Asians are concerned, I look at them today as untrustworthy wretches, most of them.

The Thai's I can be comfortable around . . . but pretty much everyone else over there . . . if you told me to shoot them in the back, I'd do it, without hesitation. Barbarous butchers, especially Ho Chi Minh, and he is dead thankfully, but he has left a legacy of death and enslavement that makes modern day tyrants look like panty wastes.

Speaking of Ho Chi Minh . . . at this time of my life . . . I am proud to march with Vietnam Vets who have been "in country" and who have seen combat. We have a few in my Chapter who have the CIB - Combat Infantry Badge - you get that for several months in the "shit" . . . combat . . . I always feel a bit awed by those guys, but highly respectful of them . . . to this day they are still sacrificing for their country and remembering guys who never came back, and whose names are on that long black wall in Washington, D.C.

I consider it a privilege, not a duty, to be around them.

Like Phil, I am in a piece of history in defense of our nation, and proud of it and for all those who read this, and say, "You were never in battle. You never got shot. You never saw a guy get his brains blown out while lying next to you," I simply respond, "perhaps so, but I saved a hell of a lot of guys from that type of horrible death by the intelligence I gathered, so kiss my ass!"

Trish, you have a unique way with writing a few words and bingo . . . you turn on my feelings . . . and get me talking. I don't mind. Sometimes I think, hey, maybe some of the stuff I am telling Trish . . . I could tell you stuff that would make the hairs under your arms go stiff, and scare the hell out of you. Hey . . . wear your Cold War Medal, proudly, far as I'm concerned, you are one of "us."

You know something else? I suffer from a type of PTSD . . . Post traumatic stress dysfunction syndrome . . . that type of stuff, only that doesn't come from being in combat . . . it comes from the stress we worked under. Lots of guys have it and never report it or are never treated by the VA or just get it treated privately at their own expense, like I've done. I had a break down back in 1973 - ended up in a "psych" ward for a month - I never talk about it, but I am convinced, with my sensitive personality and what I saw and did, it finally caused me to crack, but I am not ashamed, some people handle it differently than others. Some are able to keep it inside forever, others, like myself, we bust open and we need a bit of help. No shame in that, and I have never been back to "the zoo" as I say . . .
God love ya,

Anonymous

These Guys

This is taken from the old Bravenet Internet Site for the USAFSS-Lite site.

Bravenet Web Services

Date: 11/2/02 02:02:29 AM
Name: Anonymous
Subj: Re:Re:Re:Re: Cuban Missile Crises new infor.

At the time I had volunteered for a "Special Assignment" and 5 months later I had orders for the 6901st Special Communications Group. What the hell would a "Comm Group" do with a computer operator/programmer. When I got to Zwei I found out what "Special" meant.

Phil

Replying to:

Over at that place in Germany that never existed, the one with about 500 pounders from VII Corps. Logistics and about 600 guys reputed to have got learnt to be spies at Monterey and Skytop, the weather was cold, wet, and foggier than hell. Everybody was on alert, whatever that was supposed to mean. The P's were doing 12-on, 12-off, and were issued live rounds, although they had to recheck the manuals to figure out which end of the piece the slugs went in. With the Empire fleet only 4-5 days from Kyuber, things seemed to be going to hell. The comm. center crowd might as well have been on Mars for all they knew. It seemed the best source of information was shortwave BBC or Radio Luxembourg or them offshore pirate radio outfits. The animals in the pinochle game that ran non-stop on the third floor of the barracks (later to adopt the name 'Bay of Pigs') became irate when their beer runner go-fer of the evening tried to crawl through a chain link fence shortcut to the cantina at the adjacent German paratroop Kaserne, was challenged by a P ("You want a round up your ass?"), and retreated back to the barracks without any beer. They decided then and there, if it came to war, they'd take up a collection and bribe their Warsaw foes to stay the hell away from the pinochle game.
Man's got to get his priorities straight, right?

EW

These Guys

SPYPLANE AND SATELLITE WARFARE -*Credit given to anonymous who gave me this information from the Internet. These spyplanes and satellites were used during the Cold War, including and up to the Afghanistan Campaign. Today, much is known about what is in this article. This article was last updated on the internet on 1/09/02.*

Aircraft have been used in spying ever since their invention. The Wright Brothers intended the airplane for photo reconnaissance use. Unfortunately, the U.S. Military was not initially impressed, and the Wright Brothers traveled to Europe where their invention was put to use by several nations as intended during World War I. Some of the most popular spyplanes during this period were the British de Havillands and the American Curtis Jenny biplanes, modified specifically for photo reconnaissance. The French also developed an excellent air camera system. They took photos of enemy troops on the move, the trench system, and important towns and cities. Some countries never caught onto the idea of spyplanes – Russia, for example, which would occasionally attach cameras to their bombers, but never send in a plane loaded only with cameras.

It was during WWI with these air reconnaissance missions that the terms "tactical" and "strategic" were first invented. TACTICAL INTELLIGENCE came to refer to photos of the front lines -- where the action was on the battlefield, and STRATEGIC INTELLIGENCE referred to photos of supply dumps, etc., far behind the front lines.

In 1939, the Germans launched their famous airships, the Graf Zeppelins. To most of the world, the Zeppelins were thought of as passenger ships, and everybody who could afford it wanted to ride in the big balloons. To the German Luftwaffe, however, these were ingenious intelligence gathering ships, and the first example of airborne ELECTRONIC INTELLIGENCE. You see, only the large zeppelins could spread enough antennae wire inside of them to pick up Allied radio broadcasts.

The Zeppelins became the first airships to engage in FERRET MISSIONS. The word "ferret" refers to a vehicle, usually an aircraft, used to investigate foreign radar systems by approaching them so as to cause them to be turned on. The Allies learned quickly during WWII about the importance of ferret missions to locate enemy radar sites and coverage from the frequent prewar testing of English defenses by German flyovers with their zeppelins. America experimented with sending balloons aloft -- outfitted with cameras -- but generally abandoned the whole approach until 1982 when the Israelis shared their technology for unmanned Scout drones. The Gulf War of 1991 saw the first action of these drones, called Pioneer drones, and of course, slightly modified from the Israeli version. They have the size and looks of a model airplane; they have stealth capability; and they broadcast real-time television pictures with a remote controlled telephoto lens. Drones were also experimented with during the Vietnam War.

The millionaire, Howard Hughes, during WW II, developed special spyplanes (the XF-11 prototypes) for the U.S. military. These prototypes (powered gliders) eventually became the model for spyplanes after the war, particularly the famous U-2 aircraft which were used to spy on the Soviet Union starting in 1956. One of our U-2 planes got shot down in 1960. Lockheed Aircraft (at their secret Skunk Works plant in Burbank, CA) was where the U-2, the SR-71 Blackbird, and the F-117A Stealth Fighter were developed. The SR-71 Blackbird was America's premiere spyplane from 1960 to 1990, replacing the U-2s which America graciously donated to Taiwan.

AURORA PROJECT

The Blackbird spyplane was touted as the fastest plane on the planet. It could go as fast as Mac 2 (1,385 mph) which is about as fast as you need to avoid enemy antiaircraft weaponry. (The U-2, by comparison, could only go about 466 mph). However, a Pentagon budget report in 1985 slipped out the code name "Aurora" in reference to a super-secret plane that could go as fast as Mach 8 (5,300 mph). The U.S. defense department has always denied the existence of such a plane, what with that kind of power, could travel into outer space and back or circle the globe in about two and a half hours. The plane is said to look like our B-2 Stealth Bomber (a delta shape with no tail surfaces), and there have been several sightings. NASA admits to a joint project, called the X-30, a plane that can go Mach 6.

The Soviet Union never really developed any high-speed, high-altitude spyplanes like our U-2s or Blackbirds. For over 40 years, the Soviets have relied upon their "Bear" long-range bombers-unmistakably large, four engine turboprops that were originally designed to deliver nuclear weapons. Soviet "Bear" are planes with the longest production run in history. There's never been a single case of the U.S. shooting down a Russian spyplane. The Israelis have shot down several, but they shoot at anyone or anything spying on them. On the other hand, the Russians have shot down at least 20 of our spyplanes and captured or killed at least 200 of their crew personnel. The most famous one of these was Francis Gary Powers who was captured and put on display as a CIA operative after the Russians shot his U-2 down in 1960.

Satellite launchings indicate that a nation is up to something. Military satellites are usually launched in secrecy. However, you can often infer some information from the direction the missile goes after launch. If it goes east or west, it's probably an electronic eavesdropping satellite headed for a geostationary, equatorial orbit. If it goes north or south, it's most likely a photo-reconnaissance satellite headed for a geostationary, equatorial orbit. If it goes north or south, it's most likely a photo-reconnaissance satellite headed for a polar or figure-eight orbit. Satellites are designed for STRATEGIC than TACTICAL intelligence. They are also useful for gathering SCIENTIFIC and TECHNICAL intelligence, such as evidence of any new weapons program or military-industrial buildup.

In 1954, the RAND Corporation released a study suggesting the feasibility of conducting surveillance from satellites in space, and in 1956, the Air Force initiated project development. It's well known that the Russians beat us first in the space race with the launch of their Sputnik satellite in 1957, but the United States beat them to the launching of the first spy satellite.

CORONA PROJECT

Corona was the code name for the U.S. surveillance satellite program (cover name Discoverer with accompanying story as research satellites). The U.S. began to develop Corona in 1957; eight weeks after the Soviets launched Sputnik. Corona was to have a fixed camera that would turn on and off automatically as it passed over preselected targets (Russia, China, and the Middle East). A film canister would then be dropped from space which would be picked up by airplanes trolling a big net. After thirteen failures, the first one was called "Keyhole" or KH-1, launched in 1960. The final Corona mission was flown in 1972, for a total of 95 successful and 26 unsuccessful missions. The results provided more photographic coverage of the Soviet Union than all the 24 U-2 spyplane flights that had been done. In all, over 1.6 million miles of Soviet territory was photographed. This led to an explosion in the number of people with careers as photographic interpreter. Two years later, in 1962, Russia launched its Zenit series of spy satellites (cover name Cosmos). In many ways, the Zenit was a superior satellite, some ten times the size of a Corona, with four cameras instead of one, and possessing signals intelligence or ferret capability.

During 1961, the Air Force launched its first military intelligence satellite, the SAMOS, which contained a television-like data link, but the video reception was bad in comparison to the photos that Corona parachuted back to earth. The CIA and Air Force fought over who controlled the satellites, and the National Reconnaissance Office (NRO) was created to settle the matter. The U.S. never perfected the real-time video downlink technology until 1976 with the KH-11 series. The Soviets placed the MIR space station in orbit in 1986, and it had extensive intelligence gathering capabilities.

Radar ocean-reconnaissance satellites (RORS) are Russia's primary means of keeping tabs on the West's naval forces. Russian RORS are nuclear powered satellites which, because of their small fuel supply, generally only last about a year in space. A country needs to have two or three satellites in orbit at any one time in order to obtain militarily useful information, so satellite-capable nations (Russia, China, and the U.S.) make at least this many launches per year (often as many as two or three a week in times of crisis). The U.S. doesn't use nuclear-powered satellites because there's already enough radioactive debris in orbit, and sometimes it comes crashing down, usually over Canada. The U.S. uses self-powering satellites with solar panels and on-board booster rockets to maintain permanent orbit.

A typical launch would use a three-stage Delta rocket. Delta rockets have been around since 1960, and have a success rate of 98%. Their primary advantage over space shuttle delivery is that space shuttles only have a weightlifting capacity of about 2,000 pounds, and some military satellites weigh up to eighteen tons. The preferred orbit is high geostationary transit orbit (GTO), sometimes called geosynchronous orbit. By matching the speed of earth's rotation (22,300 mps), the satellite essentially hovers above a given point. It takes about twenty minutes for a rocket to reach 300 miles up, where it is largely free of Earth's gravity. Most satellites orbit from 400 (low altitude Lacrosse system) to 800 (high altitude RORS system) miles up.

From 1985-1986, the U.S. committed to exclusive use of the space shuttle to launch its satellites, but the *Challenger* disaster in 1986 brought an end to that commitment. The shuttle program died until 1989, and between 1986 and 1989, the U.S. only had one of its normally two KH-11 recon satellites available, and this single KH-11 was short on fuel and thus unable to move around a lot. The U.S. intelligence community was almost blind during this period. The 1989 launch of KH-12 birds proved to be worth the wait, as the photo reconnaissance was so sharp as to be able to count the rivets on equipment coming out of Russian factories, and due to improvements in sensor development, KH-12 and post KH-12 satellites can see through darkness and clouds (using radar).

The Lacrosse system (as it is called), once associated with the Star Wars initiative, enables the U.S. to see all parts of Russia at the same time.

Many nations sell their low-resolution LANDSAT photos, and occasionally a high-resolution photo is seen on the open market. The U.S. does not provide high-resolution photos (the ability to detect objects as small as a meter), but France (SPOT satellite photography) and Russia do. The same is true with the satellite-based Global Positioning System (GPS). Normally, military uses of GPS are capable of accuracy to within 30 meters, but most of what is available to the public is only 100-meter accuracy.

Starting in 1990, the MILSTAR (Military Strategic Tactical, And Relay) satellite system was deployed. Most satellites broadcast a very wide signal that can be picked up in areas hundred of miles wide (the basis of TV satellite reception), but military satellites need to broadcast a narrow beam (as well as use encryption and frequency hopping). Broadcasting a narrow beam is the purpose of the MILSTAR system. The military now uses a JSTARS system to obtain "dominant battlespace awareness," mapping every square inch of ground.

Satellites are excellent for picking up telemetry. Telemetry signals are the signals radioed back to earth every time a missile is tested or launched. Data such as missile characteristics, throw weight, number of warheads, and targeting can all be interpreted from telemetry data. It's important to know where a missile is headed as soon as it's launched.

Satellites are also intimately involved in ECM (electronic countermeasures) warfare. Complicated electronics gear and sophisticated computer systems are used in confusing the enemy, jamming the enemy's signal, or revealing (or pretending) to be revealing enemy activities that are intended to be undetectable. Special, low-flying "ferret" satellites pick up ECM gear as it is being tested or used. More advanced systems switch between jamming and listening fast enough to allow both nearly simultaneously. Some of the most valuable information in espionage involves the frequencies and what kind of transmitters the enemy is using for its ECM equipment.

Satellites are also good surveillance devices. The ECHELON system captures and records virtually every phone call, fax, or Internet transmission worldwide. It is controlled by the NSA and is a fairly simple design of spy satellites in equatorial orbit with a number of intercept stations. Computers flag messages for recording when keywords are picked up. Intelligence analysts maintain the keyword lists.

Space Warfare is the latest thing in conventional warfare. The military call it RMA, or Revolution in Military Affairs and much of it is imaginative, involving autonomous machines battling it out in space. All the various RMA schemes involve advanced, special satellites as well as regular observation, navigation, and communications satellites. Current U.S. policy considers satellite attacks an act of war.

The earth is an imperfect sphere with a somewhat higher concentration of mass around the equator. This anomaly produces a 1 degree per day degradation in the orbit of any satellite, especially those that are equatorial (zero inclination) and polar (90 degrees). The effect is partially cancelled out by a 63.4 degree inclination (figure-eight orbit).

There are four (4) basic orbital patterns: (1) high-resolution photography satellites are usually in low-altitude polar orbits to take advantage of angle to the sun; (2) navigation satellites use mid altitude (20,000 kilometers) orbits of 63.4 degree inclinations; (3) surveillance satellites use equatorial orbits or zero inclination, and are maintained geo-synchronously by matching the speed of earth's rotation; (4) communication satellites use elliptical orbits (a perigee, or low point of 500 kilometers, and an apogee, or high altitude of 40,000 kilometers).

At any given time, there are about 550 operational satellites in orbit, but the number is growing. There are about 120 satellite launches a year, but only about half of these are successful. Many things go wrong with satellite launches. The most common problem is that the equipment explodes or falls apart. Currently, there are about 10,000 objects of trackable debris floating around the earth. It takes a lot of energy to put a satellite in orbit -- enough rocket fuel to achieve a speed of 8 kilometers a second. In addition, some geosynchronous satellites need to carry their own fuel to maintain orbit.

DRONES

The latest in U.S. unmanned surveillance drones, named Global Hawk, began their first flights over Afghanistan in mid-November, 2001. The 44-foot-long Global Hawk is particularly used for its ability to remain on station during winter weather at over 12 miles in altitude for over 24 hours per patrol. According to press accounts based on statements of its Air Force developers, its radar takes one-foot ground images 100 miles away -- through all weather. Its heat-seeking cameras also can pick up images of an individual about 35 miles away in most weather. Flown over Afghanistan by operators at a ground station at an undisclosed Gulf State, the images are sent to an intelligence center for the beginning of the fusion process. Reportedly, Air Force hopes to accelerate Global Hawk purchases from two per year to six annually for a total of 51. The Global Hawk drone, or UAV, is considered inferior to the manned U-2 but may eventually subsume the high-altitude role following some sensor upgrades.

The Global hawk is expected to enjoy eventual success comparable to that of the small RQ-1A Predator, which has been fitted out variously with electro-optical, infrared and synthetic radar to fly at about three-mile altitude. The Predator has become an intelligence/surveillance/reconnaissance workhorse since its advent in the early 1990s despite some reliability limitations. Successfully equipped with the laser-guided anti-tank Hellfire missile by the Air Force in early 2001, the armed Predator was reportedly introduced into Afghanistan by CIA, firing a claimed dozens of times "very successfully." The Air Force plans to acquire 12 Predator systems, with each system consisting of a ground control station and related spares and satellite communications equipment.

Designed about 50 years ago and largely unmentioned by the media in current reporting of the Afghanistan struggle, the backbone of the aerial reconnaissance effort over Afghanistan is the venerable U-2. According to the Congressional Research Service in 2000, the Air Force has a fleet of 30 U-2 for reconnaissance and surveillance, and the fleet is relatively young, having been delivered in the late 1980s. Current planning is to keep them in service until at least 2020; while U-2 were lost in the 1960s and 1970s; none have been shot down in the post-Cold War era. Statistics for surveillance and targeting for the Afghanistan campaign are not yet available for any of the reconnaissance platforms.

INTERNET RESOURCES
http://faculty.ncwc.edu/toconnor/392/spy/satellite.htm

PRINTED RESOURCES
MacGregor, C & L Livinston (1977) Space Handbook. AL: Air Univ. Press.
Polman, N& T Allen (1999) Spybook: The Encyclopedia of Espionage. Gramercy.
RAND Corp. (1998) In Athena's Camp: Preparing for Conflict in the Information Age. Santa Monica: RAND.
Steinbruner, J. (2000) Principles of Global Security. Washington DC: Brookings Inst.

These Guys

From Bravenet Web Services - USAFSS Lite - the early days when the "Editor" was accepted. I give you some interesting writings back and forth from those who wrote with publication in mind. Therefore I give them all credit for their interesting, sometimes hilarious stories.

11/15/02 3:01:23 am
Name: Anonymous

Subject: Re: Re: AN-2 (Ve Need Only ODIN Dvigatel" Capitalist DC-3's Need DVA!)

The C46 was used by the CIA in the Far East in the 50-60's. I was transported to Korea in a CIA C46 in 1960. I will never forget getting on the unmarked aircraft and two pilots came on board with 45's in their shoulder holsters and I thought what the hell did I get into.

Replying to:

You're right, Bill. The AN-2 was post-war. As a killer of the Boeing-247. Douglas cranked out the DC-1 in late 1933, the enlarged (by two seats) DC-2 in 1934 and the DC-3 in late 1935. More than 10,000 C-47's were built for the USAAF, RAF Canucks, and - of all people - the Russians. The Russians used them for freight and paratroops, although I don't think the chutists climbed out on the wings and slid off the trailing edge as they did from the old Maxim Gorky aircraft. I used to bounce around the Rockies on N'west AL DC-3's in the late 50's, by which time a standard 21-passenger config had been adopted. Weather and avionics being what they were then, arrival at the desired destination was never guaranteed; the plane drivers subbed as baggage handlers and ticket agents for Trailways, Greyhound, and the Milwaukee, Great Northern, Union Pacific, and Northern Pacific RR's. Still see the occasional DC-3 motoring around here, but have never had the good fortune to see an AN-2. I would get in the heap and drive to see one of those suckers!

Replying to:

Interesting data on the AN-2 "Kukuruznik"

These Guys

I have always thought that the C-47 Gooneybird was the longest-lived transport aircraft. Am I wrong? I believe some C-47's are still in operation in several South American countries.

As the Russians often say, the AN-2 is the only aircraft in service that takes bird strikes from the rear.

Regards,
BB

Replying to:

From Alex Panchenko's site of design-bureau metal and resin models, all scale, all for sale:
AN-2 (Many models and national liveries available)
"... ORIGINALLY HAND MADE BY ANTONOV DESIGN BUREAU MODEL DEPARTMENT IN SCALE 1/150 FROM HEAVY RESIN AND METAL PRESENTATION DESK TOP DISPLAY MODELS TO BE PRESENTED TO VETERANS OF FACTORY IN 50 YEARS ANNIVERSARY (1946-1996) OF FIRST AN-2 AIRCRAFT BUILT. ON THE PICTURES DEPICTED AN-2 AIRCRAFT SERVED IN AEROFLOT (SOVIET AIRLINES), POLAR ARCTIC, SOVIET AIRFORCES, AMBULANCE, AGRICULTURE, VIETNAMESE AIR FORCES, CUBAN AIRLINES. MODELS CAN BE DISPLAYED ON OWN WHEELS OR ON CHROME ASHTRAY STANDS WITH ENGRAVED AEROFLOT LOGO OR ANTONOV DESIGN BUREAU LOGO.
AIRCRAFT DESCRIPTION: IF EVER AN AIRPLANE WAS BORN STRUGGLING FOR SURVIVAL, IT WAS THE ANTONOV AN-2, EVEN IN 1946. THIS TAIL-DRAGGING SINGLE ENGINE BIPLANE WAS AN ANACHRONISM IN A WORLD OF INCREASINGLY SLEEK, TRICYCLE GEAR MONOPLANES, SURVIVE IT DID, HOWEVER, TO BECOME THE BIGGEST SELLING, LONGEST-LIVED TRANSPORT IN THE WORLD. PRODUCTION BEGAN IN THE USSR BUT THE 14-SEAT MINI AIRLINER 30 YEARS AFTER CONTINUED IN PRODUCTION IN POLAND AS THE PZL MIELEC. AN-2 ANTEC PRODUCTION CONTINUES TODAY IN CHINA WHERE THE AN-2 BECAME THE SAMC-5B, AN AGRICULTURE MODEL. MORE THAN 40,000 OF THESE AERONAUTICAL

ODDITIES HAVE BEEN BUILT AND THEY'VE BEEN USED FOR JUST ABOUT EVERYTHING, MILITARY AND COMMERCIAL PASSENGER TRANSPORT, CARGO HAULING, MARINE BIOLOGY RESEARCH, PARATROOPER OPERATIONS, AG-PLANE, AIRSHOW ATTRACTION. THE AN-2 HAS DONE IT ALL, ON LAND AND ON WATER. IN RECENT YEARS SOME PLANES HAVE EVEN COME TO THE UNITED STATES, MOSTLY AS CURIOSITIES WITH ITS BRUISING 1000-HP RADIAL ENGINE, WIDEBODY (ALMOST THE SAME WIDTH AS A DC-3), AND STOL CHARACTERISTICS, AN-2 IS FOR ALL
ALL SEASONS, FROM MONGOLIA TO NORTH AMERICA."

http://www.ussr-airspace.com/Site/new_site_frames.htm

As graceful as an adobe brick, ugly as my wife's mum, the An-2 remains at once a throwback to design and one hell of a fine airplane. Just wish Panchanko the borned-agin capitalist didn't charge so much for the models. A year, or so, ago, they tended to run between $350-$550 each, ge-nyu-wine Commie ashtray thrown in.

Replying to:

Ray, 50 years is about right. According to my super duper encyclopedia of world's aircraft the first prototype flew 31 August 1947.
Talking about memories, I have nothing like yours but do remember our Sino friends had some AN-2's and I can still remember some of the tail numbers from 1965.

Regards,
the other Leonard

Replying to:

God, you just brought me back to 1967 with the An-2. While I was at Trab about 10 Soviets tried to defect to Trab. They came out of the Transcaucacus and at less than 50 feet over the Black Sea. We suspect that when the mountains got smaller, they decided to come up, which triggered the MIGs to come out; first the MIG-23s, then the 21s and the SU27s, but nothing could shoot them down. The AN-2 was flying too slow. Finally a MIG-17 came out and shot the aircraft down. I was amazed listening to the Soviet pilots talk about the bodies of their own fellow citizens floating in the water. They flew around the bodies for about 15 minutes, proud of the shoot down, and describing the bodies floating in the water. Never made the papers. The An-2 must be 50 years old by now. Too bad we can't find a place for these Haitians. If they are desperate enough to risk drowning coming to America, too bad we can't just find a place in Miami to keep them. I mean, we find places for generals, colonels, congressmen, lawyers and other thieves to live. Why not Haitians? Send the lawyers, generals and congressman to Haiti. Even swap!

G'Night,
Ray

P.S. Happy Veterans Day. To all those that served, and never asked for the "thank you," I say thank you. For all those that went to Canada, I use a similar sentence, but I remove the "thank" and put in another word.

Replying to:

Ok, everyone that wants to see a live AN-2, make a run to Key West and see the one that landed today with a bunch of Cubans on it.
Hmm, a couple of weeks ago Miami Beach was invaded by a boat load of Haitians on a wooden freighter and now today an AN-2 comes in to Key West

These Guys

This is from anonymous, but I thought I'd bring a little levity to this book, and show the reader that the USAFSS guys were humorous too.

Sent: Wednesday, November 20, 2002 9:16 AM
Subj: Analytical Model

It was autumn, and the Indians on the remote reservation asked their new Chief if the winter was going to be cold or mild. Since he was an Indian Chief in a modern society, he had never been taught the old secrets, and when he looked at the sky he couldn't tell what the hell the weather was going to be. Nevertheless, to be on the safe side, he replied to his tribe that the winter was indeed going to be cold and that the members of the village should collect wood to be prepared.

Being a practical leader, after several days he got an idea. He went to the phone booth, called the National Weather Service and asked, "Is the coming winter going to be cold?"

"It looks like this winter is going to be quite cold indeed," the Meteorologist at the weather service responded. So the Chief went back to his people and told them to collect even more wood in order to be prepared.

One week later he called the National Weather Service again. "Is it going to be a very cold winter?" he asked. "Yes," the man at the National Weather Service again replied, "It's going to be a very cold winter." The Chief again went back to his people and ordered them to collect every scrap of wood they could find.

Two weeks later he called the National Weather Service again. "Are you absolutely sure that the winter is going to be very cold?"

"Absolutely," the man replied. "It looks like it's going to be one of the coldest winters ever."

"How can you be so sure?" the Chief asked. The weatherman replied, "The Indians are collecting firewood like crazy."

Whoever sent this, thank you for your sense of humor and forwarding it to the Editor.

Note: This is a true story, but in the interest of the person who served, I have chosen to withhold the person's name.

CUBAN MISSILE CRISIS - by Anonymous

I was stationed at McGuire AFB during the time of the Cuban Missile Crisis. One night, about 0200 hours, the NCOIC from the computer room came through the barracks and rounded five or six of us up and told us to report to the computer center.

When we arrived a couple of Operations Officers were there and told us we were going to run the War Plans for the invasion of Cuba.

One problem, none of us had Top Secret clearances.
The answer was, we will downgrade the data to Secret and when it comes off the printers it will be Top Secret and we were not to look at it.
Man, we were all EYES.

If I remember, the invasion was to take place in two days with the 101st and 82nd Airborne taking the lead after the Air Force and Navy bombed the shit out of it.

These Guys

An e-mail story sent to [the editor] by Bill Person who received it from anonymous..

FROM A TOP SECRET SPECIAL INTELLIGENCE GUY
By Anonymous

(An answer to Bill Person from anonymous and his story that follows.)

Your book arrived in good shape! Just getting started, but some of the things hit home in your intro. Spent five years (less two weeks) in Germany at Allied Sector Three at Ramstein as a Sector Controller. As a result of job requirements I had a TS-SI, as did all five of the sector controllers who rotated in the job.

What that meant was that if one of us was sick or on leave, the other four had to fill in. If one guy was on leave and one went sick, then the other three filled in. We covered the slot 24/7 and no one from the office could fill in for us. It was a peculiar job. Due to the shrinks having gotten involved early on, the work schedule was two nights, a sleep day, then two days and five and a half days off. "Off" meant completely off. No paperwork, no extra duties, no nothing. We each had ONE super-qualified MSgt. assistant that we had to write an ER on once a year. That was it. No IGs, no tac evals, no getting anyone out of jail, no letters to write to congressmen. Maybe an aggravated wife once in a while but that was all.

If for some reason the officer OR the Sgt. didn't care for each other, they were split and a new crew pairing came into effect. Damnedest job I ever had.

Physically you took a beating as well as mentally. The night shift was thirteen hours long, the day shift was eleven. Because of so many psychosomatic illnesses . . . shingles, polyps and the like . . . the shrinks (somewhere) considered abbreviating the three year tour to eighteen to twenty-four months. Once they tried putting rated guys in, either as a career boost similar to a command slot, or as punishment . . . never knew which. The rated guys almost went bonkers from stress. So they dropped them completely and went back to the GCI controller field for the cannon fodder.

Getting in the job to begin with was some wild process that involved not only being tapped and the lengthy SI clearance but also being signed off by a shrink. One of our replacements got fed up with waiting and called the shrink somewhere at Pentagon level and told him to either hire him or fire him, but to do something. They fired him. Can't have aberrant behavior like that, now can we? And it took forever to get another replacement tagged, then an SI, and finally get him there. I could have killed him!

Most people left the job like all the devils in hell were after them. I stayed in for five full years and ate it up. Somewhere on the other side of the fence was a Russian doing the same thing I was doing. If the intel dudes were correct, I'd gotten three of them fired during my tour.

The Sector Controller (then, at least . . . 1970-75) was G*O*D in the air defense world over there. When we sat down in the chair we literally owned all the USAF and GAF resources, radars and planes from north of Frankfurt to the Swiss border. We reported to one guy, usually a major general on a rotating roster. Since he knew squat about what was going on he tended to let us do what needed to be done and trusted us with his job. Only one ever got fired and that was because he ordered the sector controller to do something against the NATO ROE. Then he denied doing it. Wrong thing to do. His tour was cut short and he vanished back to the States.

If you were on shift and an event happened just before the replacement controller got there, you stayed until it was over. Neither he nor the rest of the crew could sign on. I did a 24 hour stint that way one time. The crew consisted of liaison people mostly and was small. Had two intel reps in the SI booth, a wx-man, my personal tech (who was God in my absence), a Luxembourg liaison, a French liaison, a GAF fighter liaison, a SAM liaison, and two electronic maintenance Sgts.

If war started, we were to lock the bunker down and continue ops until we felt like opening it up for replacements. The sector controller owned the bunker when he was on duty . . . mess hall, latrines, MP guards and all; like I said, strange job.

Stranger still were the events we got involved in. Some days/nights nothing would happen. Other times all hell broke loose. Whatever we did was virtually on our own and our careers hung by a very fine thread because no one was going to cover for us. Or could. Several times I had to go see someone up at AFCE and explain in person. Gen. Davy Jones requested my audience one time and gave me his full attention while I was explaining the event. USA-Heidelberg had me as a guest speaker several times when their choppers screwed things up, rather nicely. I got to know those people personally! Couldn't believe the lack of air discipline they exercised! I made it down to Stuttgart as a guest speaker as well.

It was amazing how little our leadership knew about what was going on over there and who was in charge. Any USAFE general just KNEW he was in charge and one of our biggest problems was keeping them from exercising power beyond their chatter. Here's a motley group of majors and LC's telling generals that they can't do this or that . . . and naturally this resulted in more guest appearances of which I seemed to be the speaker of choice by my management.

I was the senior troop amongst the sector controllers and I swore that the commies held off doing things until I came on shift.

One of the drills was to thoroughly write the event up, even if it took another whole shift to do it. Then make a checklist of what to do if it ever happened again. NOTHING, but nothing, ever happened twice. If it seemed to be similar, then it was in name only. We had a shelf about six feet long of three ring binders of event logs and checklists, none of which were worth the match to burn them. Since each event was virtually original, you can see how there was little to fall back on by saying, 'I followed the checklist'. Further which you had no time to go find a checklist. You were suddenly immersed in whatever was ruining your day and just hoped you didn't have to take a leak (one latrine was clear across the bunker and the other was up three flights of stairs.)

Ah yes, it was an interesting tour! One of the few jobs where you had the power, resources and authority to do the task.

An answer to a question asked about the KGB during the cold war.

KGB
By Anonymous

What I know was that the KGB often had personnel and/or 'listening' and observing vehicles parked at various places such as at Indiana and Syracuse Universities; in San Angelo, Texas where Goodfellow AB is located; around Ramstein AB (just 35 or so kms north of the 6901st), and we operated on the assumption that such activity was common around all USAFSS installations and, probably, around all NATO installations. Tended to keep you on your toes! One temptation, though, was German beer, especially German beer with high-powered chasers (vodka, etc) which was a common practice at gasthauses and bars. One had to be very careful! And this one was! To nobody's surprise, the US, Britain and the West Germans (probably other NATO members, too) did whatever they could in East Germany and in the other Warsaw Pact countries. Why not? Knowledge is power and power is essential in the successful prosecution of military and political objectives. And, you surely have heard about how the US has planted huge numbers of listening devices on the floors of all the Earth's oceans, haven't you? I would expect that the USSR and the current formulation of Russia has done something similar. And what about all the military satellites the US has in orbit? Surely, the USSR/Russia has something similar. Thus, the concern when Communist China successfully launched one of its own missiles to destroy one of their own weather satellites this past year. If they can do that, they could shoot down anybody's satellites. Isn't there an old English axiom about how unwise it is to put all of your eggs in one basket? So, what are the mandarins at NSA doing about that? Hope you all sleep well tonight!

Dick Brun, a very nice guy, saw my message about my brother, Phil, on a website and answered me. We e-mailed back and forth and telephoned each other, once. Then he moved and I don't have any more contact with him, but here is the essence of what he told me.

PHIL AT KARAMURSEL
By Dick Brun

Hi Trish . . . No, you did not leave anything out of the message. I was going to write you a reply indicating that I had received the photos which you sent. The telephone rang and my little finger hit the Enter key and away went my first on-message of the day. Sorry. I did appreciate your response however.

Well I can tell you this about Phil. I do remember him. He was a hi! How are you doing? acquaintance. He went to the NCO club but he was not a regular (night after night) kind of guy. He was fairly non-descript and quiet per my recollection. A lot of USAF guys were . . . the Army guys were more boisterous and feisty. I remember passing by Phil in the hallway between the two security service buildings that were located in the secure area.
The '01st had two fences around the two buildings. The inner fence could be electrified, the outer fence was just a barrier fence. All windows were painted white and covered with cheesecloth so any peeping Toms or other folks could NOT see through the windows at any time . . . the windows were also barred with jail type bars. The two buildings were to the right and the far away building was the 7th Army Stock Control HQ.

The fence on the left bordered the road that separated the barracks (on the left side of the road) from the '01st work area that was on the right side of the road and to the right of a little road separation. Zweibrucken was beautiful but in the winter it was nigh near intolerable . . . cold, wet . . . colder and wetter. Not a picturesque Bavarian locale . . . but being that close to France . . . it had to be the pits.

Looking forward to our future photo swaps and information exchange. I will be writing to some of the Sgt's. this weekend and forwarding Phil's photo to them.
Best regards to you Trish and to your husband.
 Dick Brun.

These Guys

Subj. Management
Date: 12/22/02 11:27:30 AM Pacific Standard Time
From: Philconrad
To: IdaReedBlanford

We should have used this in USAFSS.

Retired Spook
Phil

Parable Number 1:
A crow was sitting on a tree, doing nothing all day.
A small rabbit saw the crow, and asked him,
"Can I also sit like you and do nothing all day long?"
The crow answered: "Sure, why not."
So, the rabbit sat on the ground below the crow, and rested.
All of a sudden, a fox appeared, jumped on the rabbit and ate it.
Management Lesson:
To be sitting and doing nothing, you must be sitting very, very high up.

Parable Number 2:
A turkey was chatting with a bull.
"I would love to be able to get to the top of that tree," sighed the turkey, "but I haven't got the energy."
"Well, why don't you nibble on some of my droppings?" replied the bull. "They're packed with nutrients."
The turkey pecked at a lump of dung and found that it actually gave him enough strength to reach the first branch of the tree.
Then after eating some more dung, he reached the second branch. Finally after a fourth night, there he was proudly perched at the top of the tree. Soon he was promptly spotted by a farmer, who shot the turkey out of the tree.
Management Lesson:
Bullshit might get you to the top, but it won't keep you there.

Parable Number 3:
A little bird was flying south for the winter.
It was so cold the bird froze and fell to the ground in a large field. While it was lying there, a cow came by and dropped some dung on it. As the frozen bird lay there in the pile of cow dung, it began to realize how warm it was. The dung was actually thawing him out!
He lay there all warm and happy, and soon began to sing for joy.
A passing cat heard the bird singing and came to investigate.
Following the sound, the cat discovered the bird under the pile of cow dung, and promptly dug him out and ate him!
Management Lesson:
1: Not everyone who shits on you is your enemy.
2: Not everyone who gets you out of the shit is your friend.
3: And when you're warm & happy in a pile of shit, keep your mouth shut?

Parable Number 4:
The boy rode on the donkey and the old man walked.
As they went along, they passed some people who remarked "it was a shame the old man was walking and the boy was riding."
The man and boy thought maybe the critics were right, so they changed positions. Later, they passed some people that remarked, "What a shame, he makes that little boy walk."
They decided they both would walk!
Soon they passed some more people who thought they were stupid to walk when they had a decent donkey to ride.
So they both rode the donkey!
Now they passed some people that shamed them by saying "how awful to put such a load on a poor donkey."
The boy and man said they were probably right so they decided to carry the donkey. As they crossed a bridge, they lost their grip on the animal and he fell into the river and drowned.
Management Lesson:
If you try to please everyone, you will eventually lose your ass.

These Guys

Hi Phil:
I'd like to invite you to allow me to use your "Management" piece in my book. The piece is very good. Is it original? (by you).
Please let me know via e-mail.
Hope your Christmas was a blessed one.
Trish

Phil: No, I am not the author. I received it in an e-mail. U could put author unknown (haha).
CUL

Phil

Management piece is credited to "unknown."

MIKE - a poem By Gary Anderson

Not with teaching and proud words
But with curses, ignorance and dirt
They strip away civilization
And leave only the will to hurt.

You are torn up from your country
To a backward, stinking place
To crawl through the ooze and slime
to kill an enemy without a face.

The cravens, resistors and dodgers
they allow to languish at home.
Only the best of you are taken
to be maimed or to die alone.

And when they've taken the best that you've got
and left you an empty shell.
They bring you back to your family and friends and say,
"You take him and make him well!"

This was written on July 2, 1968. Gary had never written a poem in his life. He had just gotten home from the hospital where his first daughter was born when his brother, Ron, came to visit him and informed him that his wife's brother, Mike, had been severely wounded in Viet Nam. Thank you for sharing this once in a lifetime poem with us, Gary.

COLD WAR RECOLLECTIONS - By Gary Anderson

My family was living in Oregon in 1950 when the war ended. I was 12 years old at the time.

My father was a farm laborer. We lived in a ladder shed that my father's boss converted into a house with lumber from a barracks at Camp Adair, Oregon that was purchased for one dollar. I can remember pulling the nails from the lumber and straightening them for use on the lean-to-kitchen and bedrooms that were added to the shed.

We had running water, a telephone and electricity but no indoor plumbing. We considered ourselves fortunate.

Like most families after the war, we had a radio but television was unheard of. Any news we got was from the newspapers, the radio or the RKO newsreels at the Saturday matinee movies that we attended when we could afford the 10 cent admission.

The cold war, from my perspective, started with the cessation of WWII. In retrospect, General George Patton may have been correct when he wanted to fight the Russians when the peace treaty with Germany was signed.

The Marshall Plan was implemented to help rebuild Europe and our allies and restore democracy to the counties annexed to Germany. Russia, in the meantime was stripping all of the manufacturing facilities of the countries they controlled as a result of the WWII peace treaty. Those facilities were used to rebuild the Russian economy and their war machine.

Rather than a war of fighting and killing, the cold war was one of production of weapons of war and diplomatic maneuvering between the US and their allies and the members of the Warsaw pact led by Russia and her captive satellite states.

The Cold war turned hot in June of 1950 when North Korea crossed over the 38th parallel and invaded South Korea. I was 12 at the time and was dealing with many difficulties in my own life. I had two cousins who were recalled to active duty by the military. They were heroes to me because of their military service.

Information was very sketchy at the time; I do remember the furor that was caused when communist China entered the war and attacked the United Nations forces led by the United States and the many battles that were fought. Newsreel movies and stories of the retreat of the US forces in Korea remain fresh in my mind. The winters were bitterly cold and our soldiers were ill equipped for that kind of weather.

When I was 14, one of my friends from the little grade school I attended, quit high school and joined the army by lying about his age. He was 16 and an orphan taken in by an old couple in our little community. He survived the war but never returned to our area. I think he had what we call post-traumatic stress. Then it was called shell shock. Years later, I heard that he was a desk clerk in a cheap hotel in San Francisco . . . Sad.

When the Red Chinese entered the war things got brutal. One of my friends told me that when his outfit was in danger of being overrun by the Chinese, he fired his rifle so much that the wood of the stock charred and crumbled to the touch. The firing mechanism was so hot that the cartridges ignited from the heat when they entered the chamber from the clip of his M-1. His company crammed 50-gallon drums full of napalm and whatever scrap metal they could find and rolled them down hill into the Chinese and detonated them with dynamite. The anti aircraft guns were also turned down and fired point blank into the massed Chinese army. It was war at its worst.

Later in life, one of my friends was one of the replacement troops who were put in the front lines at Heartbreak Ridge directly from basic training. He lasted 15 minutes in battle before a Chinese hand grenade forever changed his life. He was horribly scarred, crippled and legally blind. He was not treated kindly when the Viet Nam war became unpopular.

During the Korean War period of time, Eugene McCarthy, a senator from Wisconsin, started a lengthy witch-hunt to oust communists, real or imagined, from American life and positions of authority. Lives were forever changed and many were ruined when they were labeled as commies or commie sympathizers. Even the preacher who led our Young Life group in high school was suspect. Thankfully, Senator McCarthy fell from grace, was not re-elected and faded into a well-deserved obscurity. The Red scare continued all through the 50s and intensified with the arrest and convictions of many Russian Spies. The cold war heated up.

These Guys

I really don't remember much about the Russian spies system: I do remember the Rosenbergs and several other Americans who sold nuclear secrets to the Russians but coverage during the 50s was not as widespread or intense as it is now.

In February 1961, I ran out of college money and job prospects at the same time so I joined the USAF. Immediately out of basic training, I was selected for the Russian language program at Syracuse University in New York. This was the same course as given to the diplomatic corps and consisted of 3 years of college Russian and history condensed into a one year, total immersion course with native Russian speakers. We had classes 8 hours a day with several hours of memorizing dialogue in the evening.

After completing that course, I was sent to Texas for a 3 month course in radiotelephone procedures.

After that training, I was sent to Berlin, Germany in July 1962 where I became a voice intercept specialist.

In October 1962, the Russians built a base and started shipping nuclear warhead missiles to Cuba, 90 miles from the US mainland. The US retaliated by blockading Cuba with the US Navy fleet. Every B-52 bomber in the USAF was either in the air with nuclear bombs on board or on the ground refueling. One of them crashed in North Carolina but little information was leaked to the public about that mishap.

My outfit was put on Class A alert, the highest possible and confined to base. We had to wear a steel helmet and carry a musette bag with a mess kit in it and a gas mask to our duty station. My mask was dated 1943.

At the same time, my organization in Berlin received a telegram from the White House, which stated, "Continue sending all messages yy. (Top secret, Top Priority) If further messages are not forthcoming, we will consider you no longer viable."

In the end, Khrushchev blinked, the missiles left Cuba, all the B52's landed and I put away my steel pot, the mess kit and the gas mask until the next crisis.

In the 18 months I was in Berlin we had the Cuban missile crisis, the completion of the Berlin wall, the continued harassment of military troops through the Berlin Corridor leading to the Western Zone of Germany and the assassination of John F. Kennedy. During my 3 years overseas in the Security Service, 13 of my friends and acquaintances suffered nervous breakdowns due to the pressures of the job.

The Cold War continued well past the ending of the Viet Nam war well into the 1980s when the Russian government and their economy collapsed.

The free world had won, I feel, because we had concentrated on the civilian population, which supported the military rather than the other way around.

These Guys

TEN MONTHS, ELEVEN DAYS AND EIGHT HOURS
By Gary Anderson

The following is taken from the sixty-four letters I wrote from NE Cape Air Force Station on St. Lawrence Island, Alaska to the lady who later became my wife.

My introduction to Alaska on February 5, 1964 came very close to being a disaster. We left McChord AFB in Washington at 7:00 PM and were to arrive at Anchorage International Airport at 9:30 PM. The Northwest Airlines 727 was on the final approach at about 1000 feet when we hit a wind shear of about 60-70 miles an hour which created severe air currents and deep pockets of turbulence. At three different times in about that many minutes the aircraft dropped over 500 feet. Luggage from the overhead storage bins was floating all over the passenger compartment. The only thing I remember was telling my friend to "Hang on!" The last thing I remember was trying to pull myself back down into the seat.

The pilot started to pull out of the approach and was gaining altitude when we hit more turbulence and dropped nearly 1000 feet. We were told later that we were about 50 feet off the runway when the pilot was able to gain control, abort the landing and head for Fairbanks.

On the last drop, an entire bank of seats were torn from the floor of the aircraft, four people were very badly hurt, two of them had broken backs and two other passengers were taken to the hospital in shock.

I was knocked out by a camera bag and don't remember the trip to Fairbanks. I did have a large goose egg on my forehead when I came to. I really was shook when it was all over.

I talked to one colonel who had been a military pilot for 20 years who said he didn't "give us a chance in Hell when we hit that last pocket."

After spending the night in the transient barracks in Ellison AFB at Fairbanks, we boarded the same aircraft to return to Anchorage. One person refused to take the flight and caught a bus back to Anchorage. Fortunately, the return flight was without incident.

I spent the next two weeks at the 6981 Security Group at Elmendorf AFB getting briefed on the mission at St. Lawrence Island. We were also issued nearly 100 pounds of cold weather gear; white insulated, Mickey Mouse: boots, a heavy parka and fatboy pants along with wool underwear, socks and a stocking cap.

All of us attended mandatory classes on arctic survival and nuclear attack survival. Several things about those classes stick out in my mind.

A person's survival time in the Arctic Ocean surrounding St. Lawrence Island would be from three to twelve minutes depending on the time of year and the survival gear one was wearing at the time you were immersed. An individual could not survive on a diet of arctic hares as there was no fat on them.

In the event of a nuclear attack, the best bet was to grab your ankles, bend over and kiss your fanny goodbye! If you did survive the explosion and the radioactive fallout and you could find a vegetable food source in the arctic, you could safely eat it provided you peeled it first. If you could find an animal that the explosion or radioactivity had killed, it was also safe to eat provided you "peeled it first" in the words of our instructor. Altogether the classes were not terribly encouraging with respect to survival.

I arrived at NE Cape AFS on 17 February, 1964 at 11:30 in the morning. It was 18 below zero and the sun was shining. The entire site was completely covered with snow.

There was a little excitement the very first night I spent on the island. Apparently, the pilot of the civilian aircraft that brought us out also smuggled some whiskey out to the Eskimo village about 2 miles from the site. Two natives got pretty intoxicated and got into a fight over something. One of them cut the other one up pretty bad with a uulu, the native skinning knife. The medic on the site sewed up his face and neck without any anesthetic. The two left the site as if nothing had happened between them.

The site itself was in the center of a volcanic cone which had breached one side. The view to the West was toward the Arctic Ocean ½ mile away. The view to the East was the remainder of the volcanic cone. It was 2000 feet high. The Eskimos on the island described the site as, "a lonely, desolate place."

With the exception of the officer's quarters, all of the rooms were 15 feet long and 12 feet wide and were set up to hold two men and all of their gear. Each room had one window. You could paint your room any color you wanted as long as it was light gray, light green or light tan. The floors were black tile. All of the colors were somewhat depressing according to the first letter I wrote home. One person located some black paint and painted his room black. The commander made him re-paint it.

The only facilities available were a gymnasium where you could play basketball, a weight room and a hobby shop. They were all terribly outdated and pitifully inadequate.

The Inspector General came in on February 19 on a tour. The shakeup came later.

With the exception of the 6980th orderly room, nearly all members of the squadron were assigned to Able, Baker, Charley or Dawg trick. The entire mission of the 6980th was Russian voice and Morse code intercept; there was no radar or electronic mission.

We normally worked 3 shifts from 4:00 PM to midnight and got 24 hours off, worked 3 shifts from midnight to 8:00 AM, got 24 hours off and then worked 3 shifts from 8:00 AM to 4:00 PM and then got 72 hours off and then started the routine again.

The result of this schedule and the short hours of daylight in the winter and the long hours of daylight in the summer really messed up the 24 hour clock your body was attuned to. The end result was a lot of insomnia commonly referred to as "The Big Eye." It wasn't unusual to go a couple of days, or nights without any sleep only to crash at the most inopportune time.

March 02, 1964 the Inspector General shake-up hit and I got a new roommate which was better than the one I had. I still don't know what the visit was all about.

March 5, 1964: snowing an 80 mile an hour wind! All I see around me are unhappy faces! One of my friends from Berlin days got a "Dear John" letter . . . he was devastated and never really got over it.

I got a portable sewing machine from the hobby room and started patching and tailoring clothes and sewing on stripes for guys that got promoted. I charged two bits a set for the stripes and one dollar each for tailoring shirts and pants and fifty cents to a dollar for patching fatigues.

We were able to make one 5 minute phone call on the 10th, 20th, and 30th of every month. You stood in line for a couple of hours to make the call. One method of getting through was to get the MARS boys get a phone patch to a "ham radio operator" close to your home and have him patch you up. Otherwise, you could contact the military base closest to your home and have them make a phone patch to your home. Shortly after I started calling Portland AFB to call off base, they refused saying it was against regulations.

March 25, 1964, my poker winnings for the month were $400.00. I socked it away in a little strong box bolted to my closet floor as the "Anderson Relief Fund."

March 27, 1964 the Alaska Earthquake hits. The story from the site was that a tsunami had hit all of the coast of the Pacific Northwest as far inland as Portland, Oregon, the home of my family. The folks at home heard that there was a tsunami for all of the coast of Alaska. We did anticipate a tsunami at NE Cape as we were very close to sea level. It was 3 days before I could get in touch with anyone to verify that I was alright and that everything was fine at home. It was a very stressful time.

By the end of March, there were pretty normal daylight hours and the ice on the Bering Sea was breaking up. The site was still snow covered.

April 05, 1964, it sure is a slow river that is passing me. It seems like an eternity until it takes me home again.

We had a big "white out" yesterday. The wind blows the snow so hard you can't see more than eight to ten feet. One guy got lost outside and we had to blow the siren on the fire truck and shoot off guns. He finally wandered in unharmed.

April 15, 1964, I turn 26 years old and can feel myself changing. They are starting to inspect the rooms every day now.

April 23, 1964 the AM-FM stereo radio record player kit I ordered from Knight Systems came in today. I started soldering and wiring the whole thing together at 1:00 AM Tuesday morning until 4:00 PM Wednesday afternoon before I could play a record on it. It worked great! It is all finished walnut and polished brass.

27 April, 1964, the Inspector General came in today and we are really in a jam! The morale is so low here that no one gives a damn. The officers are getting tougher and tougher instead of slacking off. I have just pulled into myself.

By the end of April, there was a big problem within the squadron. The USAF Security Service had a program called the Two Tour program where an individual with a good proficiency report had his three year tour curtailed at the end of 18 months, was shipped back to Goodfellow AFB in San Angelo, Texas for six weeks of training and was then promoted to E5, Staff Sergeant and was then assigned to a remote site for the remainder of his four year enlistment. This was great in theory, lousy in practice.

The end result of this was that the 6980th had more brand new E5's at the site than E3's and E4's combined. This resulted in many hard feelings in the enlisted ranks, especially in the 712th AC&W Squadron. We were resented big time by the career people some of whom had spent more than 4 years to make E5.

The Airman seconds and firsts were pulling KP every third day regardless of what shift they worked on. The base commander then decreed that all Staff Sergeants with less than 1 year time in grade would pull KP even though they were Section Chiefs. The only people who met this criteria were the members of the Two T program.

This was contrary to regulations and resulted in a near mutiny. The walls and every available space including the ceiling of the secure area had "TPS" or a stylized finger <<!>> and the initials IGAF scrawled on it. TPS was short for "This Place Sucks" and IGAF did NOT mean "I Go Air Force!"

Rather than attempting to address the problem, the Operations Officer, a captain, threatened anyone who had that written on their equipment or was caught writing it on anything would be subject to a courts-martial.

US Senators and members of the House of Representatives and the Inspector General were contacted. The IG made his second trip to NE Cape in three months. E5s were pulled off KP. Our Operations Officer was so relieved that the whole thing was over that he got thoroughly intoxicated, came into the NCO club, got in a fight with and hit the Tech Sergeant who was the head Air Policeman on the site.

The Tech spent the rest of the night writing up courts martial papers on the captain but they were never served as the Tech suddenly got orders to have his tour curtailed and was sent to an Air Force base twenty miles from his hometown where he finished his 20 years and retired.

We heard later that the captain was RIF'd and left the Air Force before his twenty years were up.

I wrote, "You have to understand that this place is pretty much of a prison for all respects; we have to be here a year without leaving, we never see a woman; men of all types and caliber are thrown together in very close contact with no way to release the tensions which are bound to build up. Any problem at home automatically builds itself up to monstrous proportions."

May 02, 1964, I started to work in the base laundry ironing 50-100 shirts a week for $75.00 a month. The big break-up is going full tilt. The arctic ice floe is breaking up. It sounds like explosions sometimes. The entire building trembles from it. It even makes the needles on my stereo skip lines.

By the middle of May we had no real night and 20 hours of total daylight. The snow was melting but the site was still covered with snow. Then we had a big storm come in, rain, snow and winds up to 120 miles an hour. A bulldozer was hooked up to a Cessna 180 so what was left of it wouldn't blow away. The wind blew the roof off the supply house.

These Guys

The snow had pretty much melted by mid June so the base commander had my group out cleaning rock off the runway at 8:00 AM. We then had to work a full shift from 4:00 PM to midnight.

The next week the work party was ordered out in the rain to wash the windows.

June 22, 1964 got in a game of "Ringo" at the NCO club. I put in my last two bits and rolled 5 fives and won $40.00. Then I got in an all night poker game and lost $15.00. My winnings for the month totaled $80.00.

By late June, the sun was still shining at 11:00 PM. One of the guys in my outfit had gotten sick a couple of months ago. The closest doctor was at Elmendorf AFB in Anchorage, over 2000 miles away. The base medic couldn't figure out what was wrong with him. The operations officer thought that he was malingering so he was made to continue working. This was the same officer who punched the Air policeman after the near revolt a couple of months ago. The person he accused of malingering lost over fifty pounds and was finally too weak to report to work. He was a good sized colored man but he was a deathly gray when they air evacuated him to Elmendorf with tuberculosis and pneumonia. We never heard whether he lived or died. We were all required to take a TB test as a result of that cruel fiasco.

Shortly after that, one of the fellows I worked with started acting paranoid. He would come into my room at odd hours, drink coffee and tell me about how other guys were out to get him. I couldn't convince him otherwise. Finally, one evening, he accused me of drugging the coffee that he was drinking, left my room and went up to officers quarters and locked himself in a spare room and wouldn't come out for anything. They brought food to him, and everything else he needed until he could be air evacuated to the mental facility in Anchorage. I never heard from him again.

Another individual felt that his one year tour would go faster if he slept all of the time. If he wasn't working, or at the chow hall eating, he was in the rack trying to sleep.

By the time the above episodes were over I wrote, "Morale was so low you had to reach up to touch bottom." I was very depressed about the whole situation.

June 27, 1964 another buddy and I went beachcombing and found all sorts of stuff: a Japanese barrel, a fishing float and a bottle with a note in it. The note was from a person on a Russian fishing boat and was dated August 2, 1963. It told the name of the boat, where it was from and where it was going. It said they were having a party in the cabin for another fellow's birthday. The other side of the note said, "May whoever finds this bottle have 25 years of good luck."

In mid July, seven of the men who came to the 6980th with me from Berlin were suddenly shipped to Shemya. There were a lot of fireworks about that and congressmen were written again. No one could understand how the military could have transferred any person to three different sites overseas without any explanation.

By mid July, the snow had melted off the roofs of the buildings but a person could still walk up to the roofs of the buildings on the drifted snow. The temperature got up into the high 50's so one day some of us went sunbathing on the roof.

While we were up there, a Russian 4 Engine Bomber flew over the site. We weren't sure what the hell was going to happen but apparently they were testing our reaction time the same as our airborne platforms did to them.

I wrote on 23 July, "this place is really beginning to get me down again." We went fishing down on the beach more to get away from the site than to do any serious fishing. The candle fish were washing up on the beach to spawn and the sea run Dolly Varden trout up to two feet long were in a feeding frenzy. They would strike on anything that we tied onto our lines, even the pop tops from beer cans.

July 28, a Ph.D. came to the site and gave a lecture on alcoholism that we were all required to attend. I wrote, "really a laugh . . . they lecture us on it but they never attempt to give us any other method of relieving the inevitable tensions that build up here."

August, 1964 the Tonkin Gulf Incident.

August 08, 1964. I bought a three week old eight track tape recorder from a guy for half price and went on a recording spree. I tried to tape every record on the site. I won $0.00 playing poker.

By late August winter had arrived along with very short days, fog, rain and wind gusting up to 40 miles an hour. I had a real case of the blues. I had "The Big Eye" so bad that I went 36 hours without sleep. I finally had to admit that I had a problem and reported to the base medic.

On 27 August, 64, the medic made the following comment in my Chronological Record of Medical Care (Standard Form 600), "Fatigued and can't sleep. Place seems to be bothering him now. RX-Equanil 400 mgm.bid." Equanil didn't work but Jack Daniels did!

By the start of September the weather turned nasty. We had wind, rain and snow mixed. There was a storm that lasted over six hours. The wind was over one hundred miles an hour. It tore the roofs completely off three buildings. Tarpaper, boards ten to twelve feet long, and metal flying all over the place.

September 28 some fool tried to burn the place down last night. He set fire to a wastebasket in the hobby shop.

October 09, 1964 I bought a half share in the base laundry business. My share should bring in about $250.00 or more a month.

On 19 October, the new base commander arrived and everyone is in a panic. There is also another inspection team coming in from the Security Group. Everyone is trying to complete in twenty-four hours what they have been neglecting for three months.

The new base commander is a retread light colonel from the Strategic Air Command and apparently wants to get back there. He declares a Class A Blues inspection for the entire base. Since there were no dry cleaning facilities on the site, everyone had to pull their dress blues out of their duffel bag where they had been stored. The resulting inspection was less than perfect; most of us looked severely wrinkled. As a result of that debacle, we had daily inspections at 0800. For those of us working trick, the results were the same as the Class A inspection. They didn't last very long!

October 22, 1964 was a huge disappointment for me. At that time, there was an Alaskan Air Command regulation that stated that all Non-Commissioned Officer grades have to serve to the end of the month that corresponded to the month that they had arrived.

I received a set of orders changing my date of rotation for separation from the 6980th from 4 February, 1965 to 17 February, 1965! The end result of this was to extend my enlistment beyond the 4 years that I had signed up for originally! I was twenty-six years old and hadn't cried since I was twelve years old, but I did when I got that set of orders.

What was especially frustrating about the above situation was the fact that two days before I got those orders, 3 men that I had trained months after I arrived got a three month curtailment and got to leave three months before I was scheduled to leave.

November 17, 1964 I wrote, "Had a guy get all tanked up here this weekend and pulled a knife on a guy. No harm done but it looks like a courts martial coming up. He has a pretty bad record anyway so they will very likely hang him any way they can. He is confined to quarters now and pretty subdued. A couple of others got caught with booze in their rooms but they skated out with KP for a couple of days."

"I hope that my children are never forced into anything as personally degrading as this year that I have been forced to endure. I guess it is for their sake that I am putting up with the whole mess."

November 22, 1964. Things have really been popping around here lately. I don't really think that he (the new commanding officer) really likes anything or anybody." "It can't stay this bad, I hope!" The weather was so cold that I never got outdoors for nearly six weeks. It had to be pretty bad when the guys on KP couldn't even make the garbage run to the dump. I got in another poker game and came out $160.00 ahead. More for the college fund!

December 1964, bug build up of troops in Viet Nam.

December 9, 1964 got into a poker game and won $80.00.

December 10, 1964, we may have two hours of twilight with the temperature 8 to 10 degrees above zero. The inspection team from Elmendorf, our parent organization, left today. When they arrive, we get to play, The General is coming and we can play the "Alert Game." "When we have that, they wake us up at 10:00 in the morning after you have a midnight to 7:00 AM shift. They have you put on your fat-boy pants and parka complete with hood, gloves and thermal boots. Then we go to the armory and they give us a rifle with no shells for it, and make us stand around the outside of the buildings and play like we are stopping saboteurs and things. This is all accompanied by the din of sirens and officers running around saying, "Did you see anything?"

December 20, 1964, last letter home. On 20 December, my request for an early out to attend college was honored and I got orders to leave "The Rock" on 22 December and report to Elmendorf AFB for out processing. I got to McChord AFB on 24 December and was able to catch a bus for Portland, Oregon and be home on Christmas Eve. I was discharged 30 December, 1964 in time to enroll at Oregon State University to complete my degree requirements.

Thanks to Gary Anderson for sharing his "letters" to the lady who later became his wife, during his stay on St. Lawrence Island, Alaska. These "letters" have enabled us to see what daily life was like on duty in a mighty desolate and cold place.

I asked a few of the guys in this book what SERE is, wanting to know if any of them had experienced it or trained for it or had anything to do with it or what did they know about it, other than the Internet. Here are a few of my replies.

SERE
By Gary Anderson

This is only my conjecture after contacting a few other individuals in the USAFSS about the Air order of Battle (AOB).

To the best of my knowledge, the only linguists that got this training were the airborne guys who went through survival school at Stead AFB.

I personally don't think the USAF wanted us to survive in the event of a Russian attack. On the landing between the 5th and 6th floors at Tempelhof AFB in Berlin, there were about four or five rows of 50 gallon drums full of diesel fuel. Theoretically, they were to power the electric generators in the event of a blackout or power failure. The Officer of the day also had orders to toss thermite grenades into them in the event of a Russian attack. Big deal . . . They only gave us 15 minutes to survive anyway.

It is my understanding that there were thermite grenades in the ops area of NE Cape also. But where in Hell were we going to escape to anyway? Our best bet was to carry jam in our pockets because in the event of a Russian attack, we were all "toast" anyway.

Gary

RE: SERE
By Bill Person

Survival, Evasion, Rescue & Escape.

It's a new term, we had just called it Survival School or "Snake School" in my day. I went to Stead AFB Survival School in 1960, Reno, Nevada. Then it was closed down because when the public learned of it, and how rough it was, it was secretly moved to Fairchild AFB, at Spokane, Washington. It's still there and I had to go back through it in May/June 1967. It was 20 days long with physical conditioning and classroom study for two weeks; then the obstacle course with tripwires and patrolling guards with dogs; a mock prison camp at the end of it. Isolation cells and interrogation treatment; then a prison compound with others, I was the "Covert Leader" in my group. I sort of knew what was coming so I sneaked over close to the POW area and stashed some stuff there. Once in the fenced-in POW compound, I got some of the PJs (Para-rescue) guys to climb out and go get my stash. It was an American flag, some cigarettes, snacks and candy bars; drove the mock guards in black uniforms crazy. We got a debrief on what we did right and wrong, released to recoup one night and then bused to the forest way up north. That part was the trekking through the mountainous forest up near the Canadian border for camping and sort of navigation. Finally 2X2 groups had to run and evade capture for a few more days, to get to specific points each day. I lost 22 pounds and was not fat.

Stead was almost as bad. I also had to go through water survival at Otis AFB on Cape Cod, and at Tyndall AFB, at Panama City, Florida. In class, we studied about actual events of others to help us learn what we should do.

I saw "The Unit" last night and we never had it anywhere close as bad as that but it was not at all fun anyway. I'm sure the training has advanced a lot since my day but stops just short of any real injury. We could ask to see the flight surgeon as a codeword to be taken out of the game.

Nothing can simulate what happens in a POW camp and like in the Hanoi Hilton, everyone breaks at some point. I met and talked to many of them at the River Rats Reunion in Ft. Worth in May 2003. The real heroes are the survivors, the dead didn't learn anything.

Hope this helps.
Fondly,
Bill

RE: SERE
By Bill Person

"Sourtainly you may use my ramblings, as always." (One of the 3 Stooges' remarks.)

They did have a snake school near Clark in the PI. and no one liked it there. I got to see it back in my early days and that was when I had a curiosity about the "headhunters" or "stealthy" guys in my book, "Avatar Dawn."

Some of my fighter pilot buddies were able to avoid the PI snake school but no one ever reported a fun time there.

The classroom covered materials about survival, evasion, escape and rescue in all parts of the world. Some pilots got a course in flying MiG or other foreign aircraft if they got the chance to steal one to escape in. We also had Green Beanies teach us about firing foreign weapons but that was not recommended in North Vietnam if downed there. We also had a monthly letter to use to somehow make into a huge letter so our high-flying planes would see it and send in a SAR (Search and Rescue). I still remember a lot of it but sincerely hope I never have to use it again.

Fondly,
Bill.

SERE
By Vince Wuwert

I spoke one time, with a lady who was a Postal manager, supervisor, she was ex-Army, sort of butchy type appearance, but was always decent with letter carriers. Anyway, she said she had to go through SERE type training for her MOS category and she said they literally tried to beat the "shit out of me," and when she complained, they turned to some other verbal abuse. They never relented, treated her like crap. She finished, bruised, cut up a bit, but "survived" the training and was awarded credit for passing it. No fun, she told us, and it was all real, her gender didn't matter to the "enemy combatants" who detained her and abused her.

Vince

SERE
By Deryl Sadler

Trish, you should be hearing from my USN retired son Spencer soon. He was a SERE instructor for three years at Brunswick, Maine. One would think he might be able to answer your questions from a first-hand standpoint. I forwarded your note on to him along with your e-mail address. He's no stranger to San Diego having pulled about three tours there. If you have specific questions you might just shortcut the relay and fire them at him . . . He's in Renton, WA about twelve miles from me.

Deryl

Trish
by Deryl Sadler

Spencer sent this along to me to forward. He wanted me to look at it first. Having done the USAF version of this course I'm aware of what he's concerned about in certain parts of the course. The 'survival' part of it is pretty straightforward . . . which trees have tasty bark and so on. It's the E&E that gets into touchy areas and leaves different impressions on different people and is the part that people don't chat about. Spencer, being a corpsman, was literally the camp doctor and on his own when they went into the deep woods. Apparently, the Maine deep woods in the dead of winter, is a real fun place. I saw a distinct change in him after he spent three years on that assignment. He had a different perspective and attitude about war and life in general. Really matured him, and he was pretty mature to begin with. That assignment occurred between Gulf Wars One and Two.

Anyway, feel free to contact him directly when you get to something you'd like more info about. He's on broadband but keeps that [other] address as a spam deterrent.

My own experience [Deryl's] was at the USAF school out of Fairchild AFB in Spokane. Their E&E and 'deep woods' training was up along the Canadian border and it was coming on winter as I attended in November of 1975; the school had just condensed their course by several days, and were scrambling to provide the same training in less time . . . and one of the things they had to reduce was each student's personal experience with disagreeable captors. So, as senior officer of this mob, I was sort of the training aid . . . and that was rather disagreeable as well as realistic. At age forty-two, I was considered the 'old man' among all the fresh 2nd Lts. and young Sgts. in the class and people wondered just why in heck I was there - me included. It was a requirement for AWACS duty though, and I led the charge by assigning myself to the first group of us to attend. "It may be that your purpose in life is only to serve as a poor example to others."

What I did find out is that virtually no one seemed to have been a Boy Scout. Boy Scout training is a primer for survival school as I discovered. When we were moving through the woods or spending the nights in the snowy woods, none of these guys (and girls) had done this before. Little things like 'how to stalk a critter, how to be invisible' and 'how to roast stuff in coals wasn't something they'd done before. So I was sort of an additional instructor with my group.

Later the assigned monitor with my group pulled me aside and asked me where I picked up that info as it wasn't in their curriculum and was surprised when I told him "Boy Scouts" . . . but not the Scouts of today . . . the Scouts of the 1940s when we went into the woods with just a pocketknife; even rubbed the two sticks together to make fires. It was something our Scoutmaster felt we had to know.

They taught map-reading and navigation, but I was still ahead of them with my old Scout knowledge. One exercise had us going into the woods at night with our wee compass in groups of two. Been there, done that as a kid all over Texas. We were supposed to go to different points as we found our way to the friendly border. At each point you had to pick up a different compass heading. These points were indicated by a five-foot log mounted vertically in a small clearing. So what did everyone do? They laid the compass on top of it to get a better reading. Some clever instructor had hammered nails in the top of this thing which really screwed over any compass set there. I caught on to this immediately and my partner and I managed to complete the course without trekking over half the state. That was one happy lieutenant, I tell you.

Deryl

Hello,
My name is Spencer Sadler . . . my father, Deryl sent me your request. I suppose because I spent three years as a survival "SERE" instructor. Dad and just about everyone else who may have been listed as "high risk of capture," air crew, or special ops personnel or if there was room in the class, volunteers, have some first hand knowledge of SERE.

I'd be happy to answer what I can about SERE. Understand that there are several dimensions to the training. Some of it is classified and must be respected for what it is. Only the "enemies" of our great nation and our military personnel would ever attempt to document the life and honor-saving principles, techniques and exercises conducted at our SERE schools.

Hollywood has tried repeatedly to get a handle on SERE training and with all their efforts haven't come close to what SERE training really is about. One only has to watch the truly perverse, and totally inaccurate, portrayal of SERE in movies like "G.I. Jane" to see just how little folks are willing to talk about actual SERE training. It is important that the military keep this training from the public and therefore, our enemy's view.

I cannot emphasize enough how important it is to those relying on this invaluable training, to possibly save them one day, that the real experience and training never be made public. Virtually, everything you read or think you know about SERE training is inaccurate. By nature SERE training is a personal experience and no two experiences are entirely the same, by design. Everyone who has ever experienced SERE training has been debriefed and signed a nondisclosure document that is on permanent file, i.e., the training someone took four decades ago is still grounds for prosecution and confinement if divulged. In other words, if you actually know the facts then someone needs to go to jail, for a long time. The actual training itself is dictated by very good and highly intelligent people who continually update, modify and evolve the training to the point that no one can truly say what a student's SERE experience will be until it occurs.

As far as anyone who might try to offer you a "real" insight, I can explain it this way. If you think you have the real story from someone, it will only be half-truths and outright lies. I've spoken to people I helped train and I had no idea what they were talking about. I have been described physically as everything from a superhuman 6'10" Goliath to a half-pint scrawny pencil-necked clerk. I am neither. So, if or, when you read anything "factual" about SERE, I wish you luck. It is a personal experience and only fits the perceptions of the individual experiencing it at that time. Perceptions can be, and often are, wrong, smoke and mirrors, slight of hand, whatever you want to call it.

If you want to talk about SERE, I suggest sticking to the survival training. Most of us really consider ourselves survival instructors anyway.

Best wishes,
Spencer

Trish
by Deryl Sadler

From my personal experience, I'd have to say all that physical mistreatment is BS. We did a certain amount of odds and ends that the Korean and Viet war vets were exposed to as prisoners but nothing that left scars or bruises. Again, this was the AF version. Sleep deprivation, harassment, insults, pushing and shoving. No beating, no electrical games, etc. And, from predecessors who went through the old SAC survival school which was a real bear, none of that bad stuff happened then either. Several in my class were eliminated for physical problems, like catching the flu and pulling muscles, but they came back for a later class to continue the program.

Personally I got injured accidentally during parachute fall training. I'd done this for years and so none of the procedures was a surprise. And I'd been through water survival in Florida including the parasailing and the swamp camp-out amongst the critters. That included a pretty tough parachute program. Anyway I was swimming back and forth on a rope in my harness and some young kid is hanging on to the end. He turns the rope loose and I'm expected to do my landing tuck 'n roll from whatever attitude I strike the ground in. So he turns me loose at the apex of my swing and I dead-drop straight down on the flat of my back. I lay there silently waiting to see if all my parts felt normal as the NCO came rushing up to me. He asked if I was OK. I told him I thought I was well enough to go one on one with the airman out behind the building.

Anyway, they hauled me off to the clinic for X-rays, gave me a sack of pain pills and sent me off on the woodland hike the next morning. I really wasn't up to it but I was damned if I was going to come back and do all of this over again, so I chewed on my pills and merrily tiptoed through the woods, nymph-like. Anyway, it wouldn't have looked good for the leader to fink out just because I dinged my back.

I think Hollywood goes to extremes on some of these things as part of their anti-military bias. I'm tuned to that note and it comes across quite regularly and usually in something like 'how we train sweet kids to be killers and such.'

Sure, we do that but their depiction of it is usually biased. We also train them to be leaders and citizens.

During my employment at Lockheed and Boeing I constantly remarked that we had corporals who had more leadership training than our senior managers did. Lockheed hired me in as a manager but Boeing actually sent me to their three week management school . . . along with two ex-GI buddies. We sat there in amazement as we endured three straight weeks of 'CYA' training. It was all about how the working swine can ruin your day and how to prevent it; you against them, nothing at all on leadership. We were shaking our heads at the end of each day.

I asked Deryl if all of the above was from him and his answer was:

Yup, that was from me. You can use anything I send you with blessings.

Incidentally, when I retired in '77 one of the things you do on your way out the door is to fill out your VA form stating if you have any ailments, injuries, etc., that might qualify you for a disability pension. So, I entered the bit about my back being hurt out at Survival School and that I was X-rayed but sent on my way. And yes, the back had been quirky since then. Anyway, I filled out the forms and two weeks later departed for Saudi Arabia for my two year stint with Lockheed. Some time later I got a note forwarded from the VA saying that my claim for back injury was denied inasmuch as there was no indication of any such injury on my medical records. I didn't fool with it at the time since I was half-way around the world and had other things on my mind, like keeping a sense of humor and avoiding confrontations with a really juvenile customer.

After Spencer retired we were talking about VA disabilities and I mentioned the back injury thing to him and said I was surprised that the survival school clinic apparently hadn't entered anything in my records. He replied that they very likely kept their own records and didn't meld them with my official AF records. He imagined that they destroyed their stuff on an annual basis to prevent lawsuits from whip lashing on them downstream. He was just guessing, he said, but he'd heard of other schools doing that sort of thing. At any rate all trace of my visit to the clinic had vanished.

Deryl

Trish

Hello again,
by Spencer Sadler

First and foremost, Hollyweird is the last place to get any insights into SERE. The have asked, demanded, have tried and will continue to try, everything they can to get an inside look at SERE. Needless to say, today's Hollywood should never be trusted with the truth about SERE. So, Hollywood is left to its own imagination as to what SERE is. Forget "The Unit," I've never seen it but, I'll bet it is way off track.

First, SERE is a school not a proving ground, not a place to test testosterone or determine the "right stuff." Second, it is a military school with all the checks and balances of the military bureaucracy. All of the SERE schools are governed under the umbrella of the JSSA (Joint Services SERE Agency). JSSA is responsible for the training and every aspect of the program. So, JSSA does inspections, audits, verifies the training and the application of every aspect of SERE that both the students and the instructors deal with.

Now, I can't say people don't get hurt. They do, but more likely from twisting an ankle or some other normal accident. The training program is relatively short and at the end of it, members are expected to be able to do their jobs, i.e., pilots have to be able to fly, Marines able to carry a pack and charge a mountain, etc. What you describe in "The Unit" doesn't sound like it would leave people fit for full duty.

By the way, women go through SERE with the men. There isn't any reason to change the program or the training for the females. They are equally capable of experiencing SERE training. I had female instructors who worked for me and I worked for female instructors during my tour. Hollyweird hasn't figured out that SERE is a school and it provides training. The sensitive portions of that training are not to be discussed; if SERE is discussed in public, the bigger and more outlandish the fabrications, the better. It keeps our enemies in the dark and protects our troops.

So, "The Unit" and "G.I. Jane" are way off mark. Stop trying to learn from Hollywood. It'd be better if you just put the characters, in your book, in a school for a few days of warrior bonding. To which they would only speak amongst themselves about it afterward or spin obviously fabricated stories about it when outsiders tried to get them to discuss it. It'd sound almost like real life if you asked me.

Doctors and Lawyers can claim client privileges and keep secrets. Why do people assume the professional secrets of the defense department, especially those designed only to protect our men and women in uniform from our enemies, need to be revealed?

SERE is a school. I really enjoyed teaching people how to fabricate snow shoes and how to trek in snowshoes. Water procurement and food procurement were big ticket items I enjoyed teaching. I taught environmental injuries, treatment and how to prevent them. SERE is more about learning to live than anything else. The first letter is an "S" and it stands for "Survival." That should be the focus for anyone who isn't required to attend the school.

As far as war and POW's: One of my mentors, a man I had the privilege of working with, spent almost five years as a guest in the Hanoi Hilton. He is a very good man. No one can discuss what that experience is like unless they were there. I was never a POW and I have no more license than the man on the moon to assume I know the least bit about being a POW.

I served with the units that kicked in the door to Kuwait during the first Gulf war. I served with the expeditionary unit that kicked in the door to Iraq in the second Gulf war. I served on board one of the amphibious ships involved with Restore Hope in Somalia. In '88 I served with the expeditionary unit that almost assaulted Burma. In September 2001 I served in a brigade on exercise in Egypt. Long and short of it, I found myself too close to the front on five occasions, and officially in the frontal assault twice. So, I suppose I can claim to understand a little about war. Although, I think the wars of my father and his father were far more severe and dramatic. I didn't learn how to fight or act in war from SERE. Boot camp and field training exercises teach that aspect to our troops. War training is normal and continuing training that the armed services provide to all hands who may be assigned such duties.

These Guys

Forgive me if I am too basic here, but I don't know your experience or understanding of the military. I'm happy to answer any specific questions I can. Three things though, I won't confirm/deny any specific Hollyweird depictions of SERE training. I won't discuss any training that might be the least bit sensitive. I do not speak for the Military, government or other service members, past or present, my opinions are only my opinions - I can only speak for myself.

I hope this helps you,

Spencer

Spencer, you have helped me immensely, especially where preserving SERE is concerned. All your points are valid and valued by me, and I hope to others. T.S. [The Editor]. Bless you and thank you for your service.

AN E-MAIL AND A STORY - By Gary Anderson

The e-mail says:
I am attaching an article I wrote for the Berlin Island Association which describes the situation leading up to my assignment to St. Lawrence Island. It is rather caustic humor and reflects the way most of us felt about the entire program. Lt. Sam Skazai is a loose translation of the Russian words meaning, "Myself I said." A1C Buford Bumble is a figment of my imagination.

Keep in touch! Gary

THE 2 T PROGRAM-MY PERSPECTIVE - By Gary Anderson

In September, 1963, things were looking up for me: I had the equivalent of a BA degree but no diploma, I was pretty good at my job as an Analyst, Joe Kinel had stretched the truth considerably and MSgt Cormier had backed him up so I got my third stripe the first time around. I had finished half of my tour and was considering an application for OCS or the possibility of Intermediate Russian at Syracuse University.

In October, it all came undone! It seems someone at USAFSS headquarters read the statistics and realized that Uncle Sam had spent nearly $60,000. in 1960s dollars to train and get a Top Secret Codeword clearance for all of the young airmen in the various intelligence fields, what's more, many of them weren't re-enlisting! Promotions were also in short supply and many of the remote tours in Turkey, Pakistan, Japan and Alaska were short of qualified NCOs. Nobody was volunteering for those sites! Whatta surprise!

The distress filtered down to 2nd Lt. Sam Skazal who had a law degree in Loopholes from the local Home School University and whose father was the head of the draft board in Corncob, Kansas. Second Lt. Sam Skazal has been passed over twice for promotion and his dreams of retirement as a Captain or even a Major were going up in smoke! In desperation, he contacted A1C Buford Bumble, a career man who started his military career as a B17 ball turret repairman and eventually ended up in USAFSS HQS in charge of USAFSS Manual 39-2.

A review of the manual revealed two important facts:

1. An enlisted man could not spend two consecutive overseas tours unless he volunteered for them. You had to have a stateside tour in between overseas tours!
2. There were no criteria for what constituted a length of time for a stateside tour!

According to the deductions of 2nd Lt. Sam Skazal, the solution to all of the USAFSS manning problems was simple. A first term airman 2nd with a good record; no Article 15's or attempts to put in papers on Dirty Marge would receive a "spot" promotion to A1C, have his three year tour curtailed, be given a 6 week stateside tour of duty which included a 30 day delay in route and a two week Mission Improvement Conference at Goodfellow AFB, in San Angelo!

For all of their good work and effort, they would be assigned to a one year tour on a site somewhere in the far reaches of the planet. They would also receive a second "spot" promotion to E5 at the princely sum of $250. a month plus remote duty pay prior to reaching their new duty station!

With the exception of a minor episode involving every air policeman on the base covered under "Damn the Mission, GI the Floors!" and a slight case of overindulgence at the trick picnic, I met the criteria for the 2 Tour Program and on 30 Oct 63 I was relieved from duty at the 6912th and reassigned to the 6980th Scty. Sq. USAFSS, APO 714 Seattle, Wash. (2T Program).

On 26 Nov 1963, I received orders directing me to report to the USAF Air Traffic Coordinating Officer at Rhine Main AFB on 12 Dec 63 for departure to the CONUS and to report to the Comdr., 6944th Sch. SQ Goodfellow AFB 17 Jan 64 for 14 days, TDY for the purpose of attending Mission Improvement Conference and further will report to MATS Passenger Service Counter, McChord AFB, Wash. 4 Feb 64 for transportation to new unit.

Michael Doran, Paul Dorsey and Douglas, "Lightning" Fleming were included on the same sets of orders as were Lawrence Howard, Jerome Setlik, Donald Cretien, Paul Harmon, Carleton Marvel, Phil Blaisdell and Richard Uravitch, all from the 6912th. Jim Blunt and others from our outfit also got their 2T orders.

On 11 Dec 63, I had a last bottle of Becks Bier at The Silver Wings NCO club along with good friends, Phil Adams, Bill LaChance and Ray Yarbrough, pocketed my last 5 Mark bill, collected my Club Silver Wings Zippo lighter, said goodbye for a century and caught the evening train into the zone.

I spent a desultory 2 weeks at home on leave and headed for Nazareth, Texas and spent some time with my Syracuse roommate, who had been assigned to Shemya, Alaska as part of the same program.

Both of us reported to the orderly room at the 6944th Sch Sq and were assigned to a barracks for the start of our 2 weeks TDY. Since my promotion to A1C was effective before the program started, I was a bonafide A1C vs. a "spot" promoted one and therefore, got the dubious honor of being appointed Barracks Chief. Being the first guy to check in may have also had some bearing on it.

There are only two things that I distinctly remember about the Mission Improvement Conference School. The first was a Class A inspection by the 6944th Commander who informed the majority of us that our tailored "Blues" were not regulation and that we were to purchase a new set prior to our departure for our next duty station. Since I had been the tailor who had done the alterations on them while at Syracuse, I had studied the regulation and knew that the 16 inch cuffs on the trousers met the regulation requirements. His orders were ignored.

The last situation occurred when I was marching the group from class to the chow hall for lunch sometime during the second week of our program. We were bobbing along past the orderly room in some semblance of order when the squadron commander burst out of the building, shouted, "Take My Command!" called us to a halt, ordered a left face and proceeded to inform us that the USAFSS had gone to a lot of time and effort to make the 2T Program a success. Since we were the first group to go through the program, he then asked us in very polite terms to "behave." He then gave the command back to me and we went to chow, so much for the Mission Improvement Conference.

On 5 Feb 64 several of us took off in a civilian aircraft for Anchorage, Alaska and our next duty station. During our final approach to Anchorage

International Airport, our aircraft hit severe wind shears, dropped 3 different times for a total of over 1500 feet and finally pulled out 50 feet above the runway, aborted the flight and flew to Eielson AFB in Fairbanks. I got knocked silly by a camera bag, two guys got broken backs, a few banks of seats came loose and quite a few other people had to have some sort of medical attention or a change of underwear. We spent the night at Eielson and caught the same aircraft back to Anchorage the next day.

The next two weeks were spent clearing in to the Alaska Air Command, getting cold weather gear and taking courses in Arctic and Nuclear survival.

On 17 Feb 64 we took off from Anchorage for the flight to St. Lawrence Island, Alaska and the 6980th Security Squadron. The Eskimos on St. Lawrence Island called NE Cape AFS, "A lonely, desolate place." For me, that was the USAFSS equivalent of being sent to Coventry.

In the 10 months and 11 days I was there, the Inspector General visited twice, Staff Sergeants with less than 1 year time in grade pulled latrine duty and KP, the "Baker Trick Bird" reemerged as did a TPS and IGAF campaign which resulted in a near mutiny, an officer struck a Tech Sgt Air Policeman, one poor E5 nearly died from TB and pneumonia because the powers that be thought he was malingering. In addition, we had whiteouts, 120 MPH winds, no mail for weeks on end, 23 hours of darkness during winter and a couple of flyovers by Russian bombers. Someone also tried to burn the place down by setting a fire in the hobby shop and 3 people that I knew had nervous breakdowns and were shipped off in long sleeved white jackets. Today, it would be called Post Traumatic Stress Syndrome.

For those individuals selected for the program who were assigned to a more favorable site, the 2T program was very likely a great opportunity. The Viet Nam war was heating up and I understand the program was still working for some people during that period. I am only aware of one individual during my tour that re-enlisted and stayed in the USAF. Jim Blunt, another good buddy from Syracuse and Berlin completed his education and went back into the OSI as an officer and had a very successful career. I am sure others had similar success stories.

Me, when my re-enlistment conference came up, I was offered a re-up bonus of $800.00 and given a chance to go to Monterey Language School for

Vietnamese. I told them I didn't like to wear a hat, took my discharge and went back to college.

As for 2nd Lt. Sam Skazal, he never made 1st Lt. and ended up having a moderately unsuccessful business in Corncob, Kansas as a combination ambulance service and mobile law office. Rumor has it that he talked to himself a lot.

For his efforts in maintaining USAFSS Manual 39-2, A1C Buford Bumble was made airman of the Week, given a new set of teeth and re-assigned to the 7350th at Tempelhof AFB, Berlin Germany as a cashier at the chow hall.

These Guys

Contained herein is an article from Bruce Ashcroft to me as he knows I was looking for what may have happened to my brother, SSGT Phil Noland, after having returned from a 3 day TDY in London, to the 6901st Zweibrucken, in July 1963. I don't believe this is what my brother had, but I thank Bruce for his devotion in helping me in my research. And I give credit to him for sending this Special News Story from The Times.

From: Ashcroft Bruce Civ AETC/HQ <Bruce .Ashcroft@Randolph .AF.MIL>
To: Pink Flanagan (another of my e-mail addresses)
Date: Wed. 19 Nov 2003

Trish,
I may be way out of line here (but I'm hoping you'll forgive me).
When I read this article, I thought of your brother; sending as a text file. If it doesn't make it through, try Googling "James Alford" AND "Fort Campbell." The Shreveport Times link should get you the whole article.

With best intents and wishes,
Bruce

Robbed:
Rare brain-wasting disease killing area soldier
Gannett News Service
Posted on November 12, 2003

Special to The Times

Spc. Amber Alford sits by her husband, Staff Sgt. James Alford, as he lies in a semi- comatose state from Creutzfeldt-Jakob disease; the degenerative brain disorder assaults the brain similar to how "mad cow disease" affects cattle.

KARNACK, Texas - Under a blue November sky, in the piney woods of this small East Texas town, a soldier lies dying.

Staff Sgt. James Alford, who until last April called Fort Campbell, Ky., home, appears to sleep. Sometimes his eyes blink open, and he smiles. But the monster within remains in control.

His strange, silent ailment is Creutzfeldt-Jakob disease, a rare and fatal brain disorder that causes progressive dementia. It's a human cousin of mad cow disease.

It first robbed Alford of his dignity and the career he craved since boyhood.

Not knowing the monster was consuming his brain and central nervous system, his superiors in the 2nd Battalion of the Army's 5th Special Forces Group berated and demoted him for a pattern of behavior that included losing equipment, going AWOL and failure to carry out commands.

He was knocked down a rank and was about to be stripped of his Special Forces uniform patch, having been shipped home early from Iraq.

Once the diagnosis was made, the Army made amends, and restored his rank and pay (although his pay remains frozen until proper paperwork can be done). Alford's parents and wife wonder why no one questioned how a soldier who had earned a Bronze Star in the 2002 Afghanistan conflict and was praised for his organizational skills could become, 18 months later, the foul-up of the unit. They want answers and apologies.

Today, Alford, who just turned 25, gets liquid nourishment through a feeding tube. A catheter drains his bladder. The Green Beret, a member of the Army's toughest of the tough, is a shadow of his former self.

"We just take it a day at a time. Some days, it's a minute at a time," says Gail Alford, his mother, who worked as a licensed vocational nurse at a nearby hospital in the family's hometown of Karnack, Texas, before her son became ill.

The story began in April, when Gail Alford got a surprise call from one of her son's concerned neighbors: Her son was in the United States, not Iraq. And someone needed to come check on him.

After talking to her son, "I told his dad (John) and Billy (her stepson) that I thought Jamie had had a stroke," she recalled.

John and Gail departed within the hour on a 600-mile drive to Big Rock, Tenn., where the staff sergeant and his wife, Amber, also a soldier at Fort Campbell and deployed to Iraq, rented a house.

They found Alford in bad shape. His right hand trembled. He stuttered and could not string together complete sentences. And he had lost considerable weight, about 30 pounds.

Neighbors who knew the young couple well told the family that Alford had been spotted two days earlier having difficulty unlocking the door.

"He couldn't really talk clearly," said neighbor Stephanie Herndon. "He could say some things but not others. He was very nervous and shaky."

Usually when the staff sergeant would return from a mission, he would tell her it was "no big deal," Herndon said. "When he came back this time, he said it was bad, really bad."

The confused soldier "didn't even know how to use a fork," said another neighbor, Larry Mathis. "We all wondered what in the world had happened."

The Alfords wondered, too, as they began taking him from doctor to doctor. They were told by 5th Special Forces officers that he had been examined by a physician and a psychiatrist while deployed and nothing was found wrong.

However, on April 29, the staff sergeant was admitted to Blanchfield Army Community Hospital following a neurological exam. After a transfer to a Nashville VA hospital, an infectious disease specialist diagnosed encephalopathy, a slow decay of the brain that had begun 12 to 18 months earlier.

While Alford was hospitalized, Spec. Amber Alford arrived from Iraq to find her soldier husband of three and a half years in terrible shape.

"I had gotten a completely messed-up message that my husband had head injuries," she said. "They gave me a number to call at the VA hospital. I thought he was somewhere in Iraq. I wasn't prepared for how I found him." A brain biopsy confirmed doctors' suspicions: The staff sergeant has sporadic CJD, a term that means no one knows, nor likely will ever know, how he contracted the disease.

According to the Centers for Disease Control and Prevention, the average annual death rate of American CJD victims is about one case per 1 million people.

But most cases occur in the elderly. When the patient is younger than 30, the odds of contracting CJD are closer to one in 100 million.

The Alfords speculate that the soldier, who was well-traveled in the Special Forces, could have eaten contaminated beef. He has been to England, where more than 125 humans have gotten the disease by eating beef that had been fed products rendered from infected sheep.

Alford, while he could still speak, offered another scenario. While in the Middle Eastern country of Oman, during 2001, he partook of a sheep's brain at the invitation of locals.

CJD tackles its victims with cruel form, changing their personalities. Forgetfulness is an early symptom, followed by memory loss, wide mood swings, difficulty with speech, lack of coordination and, eventually, coma. Death follows as vital organs fail.

Looking back, the Alfords realize they had seen hints of change.

In August of 2002, Alford became increasingly forgetful, said his wife, who was away at a training school in California during much of the time that the disease began manifesting itself.

In December of the same year, he faced a military hearing for going AWOL. Amber Alford said her husband told her he quit a class he was taking in West Virginia in September 2002 because of headaches and backaches and returned to Fort Campbell. He also lost an Army-issued assault vest and body armor set, valued about $600.

On Dec. 10, 2002, Alford was demoted to sergeant. He dropped from the Army's E-6 pay classification to E-5, a loss of more than $10,000 a year. Eleven days later, he forgot their anniversary.

"Jamie never forgot things like that," Amber said.

When he left for Iraq with his unit earlier this year, the effects of CJD only intensified.

The soldier was ordered in writing to "carry a note pad in order to write instructions down to ensure that they are not forgotten." He failed at least four times to appear for duty. Errands that should have taken 15 minutes took hours. He was charged with stealing a gas mask.

A memorandum dated April 10 from Lt. Col. Christopher E. Conner informed Alford that he was initiating action to revoke the young soldier's Special Forces patch. "Your conduct is inconsistent with the integrity and professionalism required" of a Green Beret, Conner wrote.

A week later, Jamie was flying home, fully disgraced, extremely confused and very ill.

"The real question we want to know the answer to is, why nobody questioned how a soldier went from walking on water to all of a sudden couldn't do anything right?" Gail Alford asked. "How does that happen and no one seems to notice that something is wrong?"

I wrote to Bruce, telling him "thank you immensely! and no, you are not out of line. You are a lot of help and you are a kind person. I cried when I read the part that you sent to me. How awful for that couple. This is only part of the article about Alford - the part that Bruce sent to me. Although there are many things alike, between Alford's disease, and the behaviors of my brother, Phil, they are not the same disease, though both men were treated in the same manner by the Army for Alford, and the USAFSS for my brother, Phil. After many letters and contact with the Pentagon and the White House, my mother managed to get some truths about Phil, and his case was completely reversed and he was given back his rank, rate of pay, and pay due him, and complete medical benefits from the Air Force. The government, our government, knew what had happened to him and refrained from being truthful because of my brother's Top Secret Clearance and work in the USAFSS as a Radio Intercept Analyst. I am still looking for what changed him, completely, after a 3 day TDY to London when he returned to 6901st Zweibrucken, W. Germany, and why his duty MSGT and others didn't perceive that there was something wrong with Phil until October or November of 1963. My brother's papers show him as exemplary in everything he had done until the incident at the 6901st. I have had some men say they remember an incident around that time, but they cannot remember what it was, or won't say. But, I thank them for their information - as little as it is.

THE BLITZ OF WHIP DE COUX
By Wayne Babb

The year was 1970 and San Vito was in its first year of intramural eight-man tackle football. The Able Flight team was coached by Ira Garrett (a tackle football legend in Security Service who had played base level ball and, legend had it, was offered a tryout with the Baltimore Colts) and I was his able assistant. When Ira held tryouts for the team, almost every flight member (almost a hundred guys) turned out. Ira decided we had to "weed out" a few. He lined everyone up and conducted mini-interviews. At the end of each mini-interview, Ira would say, "He stays" or "He goes" and I would make a note on the roster.

One of the last to be interviewed was a young fellow from Yazoo City, Mississippi named Michael David DeCoux (pronounced without the "x"). His friends called him "The Whip". He was skinny as a reed with knobby knees and had on baggy shorts with a faded and tattered "Satsuma Salamander Phys Ed" tee shirt--number 101. Ira went through the interview questions:

"How much do you weigh?"

"140", Whip lied. He didn't weigh 125 soaking wet with rocks in his pockets.

"Did you play in high school?"

"Yup."

"What did you play?"

"Tuba."

"Cut him," Ira said.

I had coached the flag team the previous year and Whip had played for me. I told Ira he didn't look like much, maybe wasn't very big, and, I admitted, was a little on the slow side, but what he lacked in the things that made a great football player he more than made up for in guts, hustle, and raw "want-to". Ira said he could stay.

We only had 22 uniforms, so everybody who made the team didn't get to dress on game day. Whip watched the first two games from the bench in civvies, but by the third game, we had lost so many players to injuries that Ira *reluctantly* allowed Whip to dress out but he didn't start. On the first play from scrimmage, our number one linebacker went down and Ira put Whip in to take his place--a little amazing since Whip was a defensive back.

Able flight lost the game badly that day. I don't remember the exact score, but it was a whole bunch to a little bit. But during that game, Whip DeCoux made the best and worst plays I have ever seen made in a football game--

sandlot, high school, college, or pro. We were working our last mid shift that night and the flight newspaper, "The Mid Rag", was due for publication. I had the editors "hold the presses" while I jotted down Whip's exploits in a poem that was fashioned after the classic "Casey at the Bat". I called it . . .

THE BLITZ OF WHIP DECOUX

A Saga by
T. Wayne Babb

'Twas a bright day in November
And a goodly crowd was there.
Fans had come from far and near,
Football was in the air.

The Animals of Able
And the Browns of Charlie Flight
Were gathered there upon the field
To engage in friendly fight.

The Animals were underdogs
For win they knew not how.
Baker and Dog had beaten them before,
Could Charlie do it now?

NOOOOO! the cry was fierce and loud
From Able's hearty band.
They may have beaten us twice before
But they'll not do it again.

For Able had a secret weapon,
That sneaky so-and-so,
And it's remembered to this very day---
The Blitz of Whip DeCoux.

The game began in earnest,
And it was plain to see,

These Guys

The Animals were undermanned,
The Browns scored wild and free.

Charlie scored left and they scored right
They scored on every hand,
They scored by the pass, they scored by the run,
And then they scored again.

And when the forth quarter rolled around,
It was plain for all to know,
The game was lost, the Animals beat,
Except for Whip DeCoux.

But Charlie had the ball again
'Twas on the twenty-four.
If things went now as they always did,
The Browns were sure to score.

But Whip wouldn't let that happen,
And as the tension grew,
He told his fellow linebacker that,
"These turkeys always go on 'Two'."

"Down!" the quarterback did shout,
And down the line did go.
"Set!" he yelled for all to hear,
He sounded like a pro.

Muscles tensed in readiness
Awaiting the play to start.
The fierceness of the Charlie line
Struck fear in every heart.

"Hut One!" the QB yelled aloud,
As Whip began his move.
He leaped toward the Charlie line,
And hoped to find the groove.

These Guys

He never looked at Whip De Coux,
As through the air he flew.
He kept his eyes on the center's back,
And then he yelled, "Hut Two!"

A blinding blur of green appeared,
Above the scrimmage line,
And as the quarterback took the snap,
The sight flat blew his mind.

For on a downward arc Whip came,
'Twas like a great green bird.
And when the Q.B. stood with the ball,
Whip damn near killed the nerd.

The sound of colliding facemasks
Caused Charlie hearts to crumble.
Q.B. and the ball parted ways,
And Whip recovered the fumble.

A cheer then filled the valley,
It echoed to and fro,
Proclaiming a mighty victory for
The Blitz of Whip DeCoux.

Now Able had the ball again,
But the offense could not stay.
They stunk up the joint with three bad plays,
Then punted the ball away.

Down the field Charlie charged again,
In chunks of ten yards and more.
If things went now as they always did,
The Browns were sure to score.

But Whip remembered the last time,
How they always went on two,
When the Browns broke the huddle again,
He knew just what to do.

These Guys

"Down!" the quarterback did shout,
And down the line did go.
"Set!" the Q.B. yelled aloud,
He sounded like a pro.

"Hut One!" Whip took two steps back,
And waited for his cue.
He charged forward and launched into the air,
As the Q.B. yelled, "Hut Two!"

A blinding blur of green appeared,
Above the scrimmage line,
Could this be a repeat of a fantastic play?
All would know in time.

As Whip came down toward Charlie turf,
The crowd leaned forward to see.
The Q.B. kept his steely glare,
And then he yelled, "Hut Three!"

Flags reined down all over the field,
Like giant yellow raindrops.
Every official yelled, "Off Side!"
As Whip hit the ground with a flop.

Now somewhere people are shouting,
And somewhere folks have fits.
But all is quiet on Able Flight.
Mighty Whip has blown the blitz.

I visited with Whip a few years ago when he came up here on business. He's still skinny as a reed, but now he has a "paunch", his hair is gone, and his face is laced with wrinkles. But the eyes haven't changed. They still twinkle with the kind of mischief that would dream up a "dive-over-the-line-of-scrimmage" blitz. I wish we had had a whole team of Whip DeCoux's that first year of tackle ball at San Vito. We would have gone undefeated.

From August of 1984 through December 1985, I served in the Electronic Security Command Office of the Inspector General. During that time, I traveled to ESC units all over the world with the Inspection Team. Most people we found at those units were highly motivated and were dedicated to their jobs. But some performed at an even higher level. This is the story of one of them.

THE BEST DAMNED 202 EVER
By Wayne Babb

In addition to looking for negative things during an inspection, I.G. Team members also looked for unit members who were performing above and beyond the call of duty. These folk were dubbed "Professional Performers" and were recognized for their outstanding performance during the outbrief when the inspection was over.
Since an inspection only lasted five days, Professional Performers were hard to find. Usually, the unit being inspected would point an inspector at some guy or gal who was doing an outstanding job and hope the inspector would recognize the obvious. That's what happened when I was inspecting Mike Miller's Exploitation Management Shop at the 6924 Security Squadron in Kunia, Hawaii in 1985.
While I was talking to one of Mike's Day Shop analysts, he showed me the activity logs that had been filled out by analysts on the four Flights. Hour after hour on the logs, the information was spotty at best. Then suddenly, the logs showed line after line after line that were filled in completely with good intelligence. "You can tell when Airman Dickson comes on duty," the Day Shop Analyst said, "just by looking at the logs."
 "Looks like a Professional Performer to me," I said. "But I can't give him the award just by looking at the logs. I need to talk to him. What Flight is he on?"
 "He's on Baker Flight," I was told. "They're working Swings."
After the daily I.G. Team meeting that afternoon, I went to the Ops Floor to interview Airman Dickson. I was in a bit of a hurry because other Team members were waiting for me in the rental car headed back to the motel where we were staying.
When I got to the intercept aisle where Airman Dickson worked, he wasn't hard to find. He was a squat little dude wearing unstarched, untailored fatigues. A lock of hair hung over his forehead and one eye, he had a grease pencil behind each ear, a ballpoint pen clinched between his teeth, and carried a clipboard. His lip bulged with a dip of snuff. He zipped from one

intercept position to another like a water bug, issuing instructions to operators and making notes on his clipboard. Other operators yelled questions at him, and he answered on the run with a length of five-level tape streaming behind him as he scurried about his domain.

I tried to get Airman Dickson's attention several times as he swooped by where I was standing. He ignored me. I knew the guys waiting for me in the rental car must be getting impatient, so I finally stepped directly in front of Airman Dickson and asked if I could speak with him for just a moment. He looked me squarely in the eye and said, "Get outta my face, Chief. I've got friggin bombers all over China." And he was off again, leaving the old Chief standing there like an idiot. I made an entry in my inspection notes. "If this ain't a professional performer, I ain't never seen one."

I turned my nomination in to the Inspector General who passed it on to the 6924th Commander. The 24th Commander didn't want to recognize Airman Dickson as a Professional Performer because of "image/appearance issues."

When the I.G. told me about the concerns, I raised the bullshit flag.

"Colonel," I said. "I don't care what this man looks like or what the Commander thinks about him. I say he's a professional performer. That should be enough."

It was.

When the Professional Performers were announced during the outbriefing and Airman Dickson walked across the stage to accept his "Certificate of Achievement," he looked as though he didn't really know why he was there. But I did—Airman Dickson was the 202 I always wanted to be.

THE DAY TESTOSTERONE RULED THE WAVES
By Ted Barker

Trish, the events that I am writing probably are not classified but the events that lead up to this near fatal encounter with the Soviet Navy still may be. I am going to write this in the order I experienced it, which you will shortly understand why I have to do this. The events took place in the Mediterranean Sea in 1976 during the period when the Soviets were flexing their muscle in Lebanon and having the Cubans conquer Angola in Africa. Tensions were high in the world and the USS Independence (CV-62) was reported to be off the coast of Angola with 95 F4 Fighter Bombers, which never happened. We did though, participate in a little exercise called Ocean Safari 75, just 75 NATO ships including the USS Independence, HMS Ark Royal and HMS Hermes and we just sort of sailed up to the Northern part of Norway. We were making a statement to the Soviets. This little adventure will be described in detail in its own sea story. In addition, in 1973 the Independence was in the Med during the Yom Kippur War and the air wing flew combat patrols with live ordnance with the Soviet Naval combatants as their targets . . . SCARY. The Soviets had sortied a large number of additional ships to increase the combat strength of their fleet during the war and kept their surface force at that numerical strength in 1976.

Now for a little background on the key players in this little sea story: the commanding officer of the USS Independence was Captain Serves with air wing CVW7 embarked commanded by one Captain James Flatly, son of Admiral Flatly. The Admiral on board was none other than Admiral Carol, you may have seen him on TV several times, he became one of the first of the talking heads and I never heard him say anything good about the Navy. Now, another little event that happened before the cruise, that if taken alone would not have any cause for concern other than just providing a little of what may happen during the cruise. Captain Flatly was making the rounds of all the Squadrons of CVW-7 and during his brief inspection of HS-5, my first Squadron, he told all hands that he would prefer to be on the Carrier that would have to fight its way back into the Med. Now this was said from the man who landed and took off a C-130 from the flight deck of USS ZIPPO "Forestall" CV-59, which sort of gave all hands a nice warm feeling! During this time period money from the Operational Steaming was, should I say, TIGHT? Being post Vietnam and the politicians were blaming the military for the outcome of the war. Well, Captain Serves liked Palma Majorca, a little lovely, beautiful, and delightful island off the east coast of Spain. I sort of liked it too and so did the crew and air wing. Admiral Carol on the other hand liked France, a dirty nasty place, for whatever reason, who knows. I did not like it and neither did most of the crew and air wing. The people were rude, nasty and cold and that was on a good day! Well the officers who ran strike ops also tracked the daily fuel usage of the Indy and they and the Captain would somehow always have used just enough fuel to prevent but one trip to France.

The stage has been set, the players have learned their lines and it is now SHOW TIME!

The Indy had just completed an at sea period and instead of pulling into port it went to one of its favorite anchorages. The lack of steaming dollars mandated that the ship stop steaming. Since the next scheduled port visit was several days away, to the anchorage we went. The air wing and ship were placed in an alert 30 status due to the uninvited company we had, it was the type of company one would not bring home to dinner. Our company consisted of two Soviet warships and one Soviet oiler. One of the warships was a minesweeper and the other was a destroyer, commonly referred to as a Mod Kashin, a ship with a very nasty punch. For those not familiar with this type of ship it was equipped with twin SAM 1 launchers, one located forward and the other aft. This was a big Surface to Air missile with a surface-to-surface capability. In addition it was equipped with between four and six early Soviet Naval surface-to-surface missiles, the big nasty type that sunk the Israeli destroyer during the 6-day war, with the launchers located in aft part of the ship pointing aft. Well the Mod Kashin was anchored within 1000 yards of our port side and since there was NO WIND the bow of the Indy pointed in one direction and the Soviet Mod Kashin pointed the opposite - it was sort of like a Chinese landing, port side to port. The other Soviet ships were in the vicinity but did not pose a threat.

During this period the weapons officer had his division perform maintenance on the port side Basic-Point-Defensive Missile Battery otherwise called BPDMS. This system was developed to counter anti-ship missiles like the ones carried by the Mod Kashin. It was basically early versions of the Sparrow air-to-air missile modified to be launched from a modified ASROC launcher and it had a limited surface-to-surface capability. Hint, hint at 1000 yards it wasn't a limited capability. At the same time the weapons division was performing maintenance, the Soviets were conducting what looked like a dress white inspection aboard the Mod Kashin.

Now the Admiral and the Captain were in Strike ops having a disagreement on the condition of the flight deck, i.e. was it or wasn't it in a real alert 30 condition. According to persons at the scene this difference of opinions became quite something to hear. With both of the key players in Strike ops during this testosterone vocal disagreement neither had a clue what was going on around them. The Admiral telling the Captain that the deck was not in an alert 30 status and the Captain just as adamant that the Indy would be able to launch the alert 30 aircraft within 30 minutes. With neither one of the men able to think straight due to an overabundance of testosterone rushing to the brain the Captain had the great idea of calling combat and having the ship launch the alert 30, WE WERE STILL AT ANCHOR! I can still hear the 1-MC today, announcing, "Launch the alert 30 initial vectors overhead!" Since I was the closest one at the squadron duty desk I grabbed the helo tower flower book and raced up to pri-fly. What a show I saw, from where I was standing looking down at the flight deck - it looked like something had kicked over an ant hill. There were people running out to the flight deck from both the port and starboard catwalks and the island area racing to their assigned stations. Hands waving, whistles blowing, yellow gear being started and positioned, and just general chaos going on to the untrained eye, like to our good friends the Soviets only 1000 yards off our port side.

In less than 30 minutes the alert helos were airborne along with the E2C commonly called the hummer plus the A-7's, A-6's and the F4's, the A-7's were launched while the Indy was still at anchor, gave the Soviets something to think about.

The dress white inspection being conducted on the Soviet destroyers was cut short and I sort of feel sorry, even pity the poor communications officer of that Soviet ship. He must have been yelled at by the Commanding officer, the XO of the Soviets had that command structure, and the political officer, as to why he missed an important message from fleet HQ. The Americans just wouldn't do something stupid or crazy like what they were seeing. Or would they?

At the same time this was happening, or as soon as the announcement was made to launch the alert 30, the crew doing maintenance on the port side missile launcher very quickly armed all the launch cells and cleared the area. Why they did this was because there was a little Indy instruction that required that if the alert is launched and it isn't stated that this is a drill then the launcher is armed, and the missile director had to be manned. Starting to get the picture, just wait, it gets better, or scarier!

In addition to spinning up the missile guidance systems radars on both sides where showing their might, i.e. FIRE CONTROL RADARS were being turned on and pointing at each other; all over a little too much testosterone! Let me continue: our EW's were reporting nasty type of radar signals coming from our neighbors only 1000 yards to our port and I am sure the Soviet EW's were reporting the same thing about us. Now there are a lot more people having their testosterone levels elevated! Well, neither side blinked or should I say panicked and no missiles were fired. It was close though, according to the guys in combat. Ah, what a lovely thing it would have been, the US Navy sinking a Soviet destroyer with its small missiles. As I said, from 1000 yards it would have been hard not to hit the Soviet ship.

Now for even more fun in the sun, the ROE or rules of engagement for flying over Soviet ships of any kind was you must be at least 1000 feet above them when within 1 mile of a Soviet ship. Well, since this was an alert launch from anchor even after the Indy was making way it still did not have the best winds for the fighters. The Soviets really did not like having the F4's flying no higher than 150 feet from their mast tops in after burner, made for a very loud noise.

The Indy proceeded onward to the next port visit, the Captain extended his tour on the Indy, I think he needed a better fitness report since he really pissed off the Admiral. Captain Serves did make Admiral and Admiral Carol went on to become a talking anti-Navy head.

Not over yet, in the summer of 1976 while the squadron was back in Jacksonville, Florida a message arrived and was required reading by all of the squadron officers. It seemed that the United States and the Soviet Union were going to meet and review and strengthen the incident as sea treaty. The one that stated that neither side would harass, illuminate each other with fire control radars or buzz with their aircraft. We all guessed there must have been an incident at sea, then went to the club and had a cold beer. The cold beer really did not happen, just put it in there, it would have helped.

Subject: Brooks AFB, USAFSS 1950
Date: Mon Jan 19, 2004 17:20
Author: Addis Titus Baxter (t.baxter1@att.net)

After spending three years in the occupation of Japan, Tokyo with the 16th Comm. Sqdn. as a teletypewriter, 1946-1949, crypto operator, I stayed in the inactive reserve and was recalled in Sept 1950 to the USAFSS at Brooks AFB. The SS was just being formed and I was working behind the infamous GREEN DOOR. I only worked there about eleven months and I had an accident and spent eleven months in the hospital in Fort Sam Houston. I was discharged in 1952 and got job as a Dept. of Army civilian and taught crypto, teletype, computer comm., etc. at Fort Gordon, GA for thirty three years and retired. . . .

We thank you for your meritorious service, Titus.

These Guys

A FUNNY STORY ABOUT COURAGE AND POLAR BEARS
By Jack Benjamin

It was late winter ('53) and my "trick" was scheduled for the morning shift. It was such an unusually nice morning I decided that we'd all get some exercise by walking out to the operations building via the plowed road. It was about a half a mile or more, so no one would die of the cold before we got there. I had Bob Carter run the Blue Goose (our insulated 6 wheeler truck) ahead of us, as we needed transportation at 4 p.m. Not everyone was happy about doing the walk, but all 12 of us started out anyway. Now some of the Eskimo's told us that they were looking to shoot a rogue polar bear. A polar bear will attack on seeing you, not like the Alaskan Brown Bear who generally keeps his distance unless provoked.

We all knew of the hunt for the bear by the Eskimos, and since most of us had pistols on our person, no one cared about any kind of danger. As we trekked out to Operations, all the jokes and wise cracking was in full swing. One of my guys, and I don't remember who he was, was walking on top of the plowed snow bank. This snow bank was over eight feet high or more. You couldn't see over it. Your view was straight down the plowed road.

We must have been halfway to Operations when this individual hollered out that he could see something moving our way. We asked what it was, and in the next second or so, he screamed, "it's a polar bear." The next thing I knew I was all alone as everyone was flat out running towards the Operations building. Hell we had enough fire power among us to fend off an army. But there I was by myself at that moment. Well, guess who took off after this brave band of hunters and beat every one of them to the door of Ops. Yes me. I wasn't about to take on a bear all alone.

With all the laughing and joking on the road out to Ops, as soon as one guy took off, they all started running. The funny part of this tale was our base security people had a 30 caliber machine gun mounted on the Operations roof. The guy manning the gun saw all of us running like crazy towards him. He got excited and saw the big threat and proceeded to fire at a lone poor caribou. He could have killed us all. We laughed so hard when we had all the facts, knowing what heroes we weren't. Bob "Stu" Stewart gave me the business for weeks about hunting and what he would have done, etc., etc., etc.
Jack Mastrianni (polar bear hunter).

ST. LAWRENCE ISLAND IN THE SPRING OF 1954
by Jack Benjamin

Background: St. Lawrence Island in the spring of 1954 had incurred a bad fog problem. Every day it seemed the fog got worse with the snow and ice in the Bering Sea. We had had a terrible winter in 1953 and our food supply, along with equipment, was in short supply. So much so, that most of all the c-rations as well as k-rations were being eaten by the troops. The chow hall was offering ham that was packed in cans for the navy in 1947. No bread was to be had as the flour was long gone and so was the corn bread staple. All ketchup bottles were in the possession of airmen who brought them to chow hall when they ate. It helped when eating ham. (The ham had a green tinge to it) We hadn't had a plane in for over a month, so no mail as well. With this background scenario I start my story:

Robert Stewert, Bob to some, but Stu to most of his friends, was a big guy, about six one or two, who always was joking or wise-cracking with a huge smile or impish grin on his face. If he wanted your attention in a formal way it was like hey Mastrianni or hey Belliveau what's with this or that. If not, it was your first name or nick name. With me it was always JB (for John Benjamin) my callsign. Sometime he'd refer to me as Jack, but mostly it was JB. He came from upper Michigan, and in his mind if you weren't an outdoorsman something was definitely wrong with you. Some of us had handguns, mine was a .38 special, Stu's was, well you name it he owned it. He was always on top of the latest weapons being made, for here was truly an outdoorsman's, icon. Could he shoot? You bet. We practiced with barrels on the beach of St. Lawrence to no end when we had some free time. While Stu and I were at Elmendorf Air Force base at Anchorage, he marveled that some of the locals wore side arms in town. There he bought the latest and most powerful handgun in the world, a .357 magnum.

Stu had a love affair with this pistol. He kept it clean and always near by. As our hopes for a supply plane with food and mail kept going by the boards everyday, the fog and weather just wouldn't cooperate in sneaking in a C-47 during daylight hours. Our strip was about 3000 feet if I remember correctly. It was dirt with no lights of course, and it had no parking areas. That meant only one plane could land and take off at a time. I'm pretty sure it was the month of April and day light was getting longer each day. Captain Amerhine (spelling may not be correct) was our unit commander, and a WWII pilot. I know he said he had fifty missions in the big one. He was such a straight, no nonsense guy, you had to like him. He probably was still a Captain because of that.

Well, we finally had a couple of good days forecast, and it lined up with the fact that a C-47 could get in and out with no trouble. I remember our "trick" was off that day. A "trick" was a shift of people who worked three days on the day shift, three days evenings, three days nights and three days off. I was talking to the Captain in our Orderly Room about his course I was taking in navigation, when we got the world a plane was on it's way and it would land somewhere around 10 a.m. For what reason I can't remember, Stu and I were invited to ride out to the strip in a jeep with Capt. Amerhine. We drove out to the strip a little early along with trucks from the motor pool. They were going to unload all the cargo. I remember when the C-47 landed, it wasn't a very smooth one, and he landed long on the strip. Here is where the story starts to get interesting.

The pilot of the plane, and his copilot, were brand new to Alaska. The pilot was a 1st Lieutenant, and his copilot was a 2nd Lieutenant. I don't remember their names and it's just as well. Well, as the unloading of the cargo was going on, we discovered that our new Lieutenant forgot our mail. Over a month with no mail really made this a huge blunder. Capt. Amerhine was so mad he decided to send the plane back to Nome ASAP. Stu offered to fly radio for them, as they came over with no radio operator to start with. He also wanted to help load the mail.

Since it was only late morning they had plenty of time and daylight to get cargo and food off, and then take off for Nome. We would call ahead to have all our mail ready to go when they got there. Stu was wise cracking with me about stupid pilots, or something of that nature before he checked out the weather and the radio equipment.

Well, off they went and the Captain and I rode back to Ops. I hung around at the Orderly Room with the idea that I'd join Capt. Amerhine when the plane arrived at the strip. Now the Lieutenants were not very happy about this whole deal of going back in the first place, and with Stu needling them about being jeeps in Alaska, they were not in a good frame of mind. I remember the call to our Security Officer, Lt. Lee that there was trouble with the plane or the mission as it was returning from Nome to the Island. The Captain, the Lieutenant and me, jumped into the jeep and raced out to the strip. The strip had a small shack that housed a phone, a radio and loud speaker that was part of the radio equipment. I can't tell you why we even had it, but you could talk to aircraft via the radio.

The emergency call came from the Dome. The Dome as we called it housed the radar operations. Shifts of "scope dopes" as we fondly called them, had picked up a bogie on our side of the International Date Line. Yes, it was a MiG 15, and it was flying in formation with our C-47 with the Lieutenants and Stu aboard. Capt. Amerhine was in radio contact with our plane and he put the conversation on the speaker so he could view the situation outside of the shack. The pilot reported that the MiG was flying formation with him and the Russian was inside of his wing. Our pilot was really rattled and Amerhine was trying to calm him down, using his vast experience as a multi-engine pilot on what to do next. What happened next will be just as I remembered it. (Amerhine); "Put down your flaps, the MiG will stall out at 110." (Pilot) "Ok . . . he's still with me." (Amerhine) "Lower your wheels . . . (Pilot) "wheels down . . . he's still there!" "I can't miss at this range, silence . . . (Pilot) who said that? . . . Then there was this blood curdling scream, "Don't shoot, for God's sake, don't shoot," (Copilot). (Stu's voice) I can't miss at this range. . . ."

This e-mail was generously shared with me by Dick Bergman. Thank you Bergie. [The Editor]

THE 136th CSS HQS. AT BROOKS AFB, Aug., 1950-1952

From: "Dick Bergman"
To: "Trish Schiesser"
Sent: Saturday, March 11, 2006 5:27 PM
Subject: Fw: The 136th CSS Hqs at Brooks AFB, Aug., 1950-1952
-----Original Message-----
From: Cecelia njust
To: Bob Morris; Dick Bergman
Sent: Saturday, March 11 2006 6:35 PM
Subject: The 136th CSS Hqs at Brooks AFB, Aug., 1950-Oct. 1952

Hello Bob Morris & Dick Bergman:

Glad to hear from you, Bob. Dick Bergman was an intercept operator who trained at Brooks at some point during the time span in the "Subject Line," above. And Dick, Bob Morris was an Officer who was the Opns. Chief and Commander of the 136th Detachment at Daly City, CA. (just South of San Francisco, CA certainly a "hardship tour.") He can fill you in on some of the details as your address should print-out on the "To Line" above. Bob and I were both stationed at Mather AFB & Randolph AFB at times in our careers. Bob is also a retired Colonel and lives in San Antonio. And Bob, Dick went to and Graduated from at least one University ("G.I. Bill") and became a Registered Psychologist employed in that Profession until he "Retired." He lives in Wisconsin. Dick and I finished our USAFSS assignment at the 136th/36th CSS Detachment in Wiesbaden (which was like Daly City, only colder and the Natives were mostly not "Gay").

I came to Brooks AFB to the 136th Comm. Scty. Sqdn. in the middle of Summer, 1950. I had returned from Tokyo, Japan early that year to an assignment as the NCOIC of a Flight Line Aircraft Radio Maintenance Shop at Westover AFB, Chicopee Falls, Mass. I had volunteered for transfer to the newly established USAF Security Service and was (frankly) a bit dismayed when the Orders came thru four months later! I had been an E-5 (S/Sgt.) before starting Pilot training in 1943 and had accumulated another four years in Grade after (Reenlisting in July) 1946 with no like prospects for advancement in sight (our Wing in Tokyo at Haneda Air Field had promoted only one Staff to Tech in the 37 months I was there). I had a "hip pocket" Reserve Commission as 2nd Lt. that I'd obtained when I was separated from the Army Air Force in 1945.

Some people in the Pentagon decided in 1948, in the first half of the year that followed the Sept. 1947 establishment of the U.S. Air Force, that the USAF would develop its own "Army style" Security Service. Some of the Cadre for the new Air Force Command were transferred as volunteers from Ft. George Meade, Md., the Hqs. of the Army Security Agency. USAFSS then had the same manning tables (T.O. & E) as its Army "Parent." There was an identical Army unit to the 136th. The USAF was allowed to pick up some of the Army's Overseas Company - sized T.O. & E. Organizations and locations (minus the people). The 136th Detachment at Camp Peri (Freudenberg Kaserne), Dotzheim, Germany (on top of a ridge above the Rhine River, near Wiesbaden), is a prime example. It was Det. 3, of the 136th.

The 136th C.S.S. at Brooks AFB was commanded by a Major Barnhart when we arrived on that very hot day in early August 1950. He was soon replaced by a more Senior Major named Carl Krula. Barnhart became the Squadron Exec. Capt. Thomas Hayes was the Operations Officer and soon a newly arrived 1st Lt. Thomas Townley became his Assistant O.I.C. I don't know, for sure, if we had Operational Control of any of the transferable Army Security Detachments at that time. In any event, we soon established our own Training Detachment ("Det. 2,") and a newly recalled Reserve Officer, Capt. Pershing was its Commander. His NCOIC was T/Sgt. Virgil Joselyn, who was, in turn, ably assisted by T/Sgt. Raymond Little. Other Officers and NCOs were detached from the Hqs. of the 136th to Det. 2, as they arrived. We were receiving Radio Operators and Mechanics from Keesler AFB, too.

I already had a Cryptographic Clearance (obtained during my Tokyo assignment). For some reason never explained, Security Service ran another Clearance investigation which kept me unassigned for the first two months at Brooks. I was just one of several Enlisted Men detailed to the Base MARS Station at that time. Then, one day I was ordered to report to M/Sgt. Little at Bldg. 300. After two more months I was "recalled to active duty" as a 2nd Lt. and assigned as the Operations officer of Det. 2. I expected to be reassigned to some other unit because the NCOs I worked for were now working for me! But, that did not happen and it worked o.k. Bob Fenstermaker, who out-ranked me as a 2nd Lt. by a few days, and I, traded back and forth as the Detachment Commander whenever Bob was away at School. And, a couple times newly arrived Captains were sent to the Detachment to gain a little experience before going abroad to one of the other (newer, usually) Detachments.

Military life as a tenant Detachment on a 12th Air Force Base (that's right, USAFSS did not "own" the Base) was sometimes difficult for a very junior Commanding Officer. We found it necessary to do much of the Building maintenance normally done by the Host Command Base Civil Engineer. Our people were some of the very best in the Air Force and they did a lot of work besides our Mission.

One of our own technical problems was the High Frequency Antenna "Sets" furnished to the 136ths Detachments. I was a licensed (Class A) Radio Amateur. And it occurred to me that what our Detachment needed to Monitor the Frequency spectrum between 3000 and 20,000 Kilocycles was a single, omni-directional antenna to feed the 20, or so, Radio Receivers we used to listen to the Strategic Air Command and other Aircraft on our "training circuits." USAF used compact "Discone" antennas on top of our Air Force aircraft control towers to talk with airplanes in the VHF spectrum (100 to 156 Megacycles) why wouldn't it work to up-scale the VHF (18" high and about 14" in diameter) discone design to work with a lower cut-off frequency of 3000 kcs? I did the math and decided to make use of an abandoned light pole as the center support for an "H.F." Discone. We had no money so we built the new antenna from material found in the Base salvage yard. We used a flattened metal garbage can lid screwed-down to the top of the wooden light pole. But, first we screwed a dozen, or so, appropriated lengths of discarded aluminum tubing across the top of the garbage can lid and soldered concentric circles of #20 copper "hook-up" wire to convert the assembly, electrically, to a "disk." Then we used the same gauge (still surplus) hood-up wire to simulate a "cone," with its apex bonded with soldered sheet copper located one tenth of a "wave" below the horizontal "disc." The Cone's numerous wires were spaced equally, in a circle, descending at a sixty degree angle to insulators connected to anchor pegs in the ground. We connected an RG8-U co-ax feed-line (center conductor soldered to the "disk," braid soldered to the copper apex of the cone) 'ran the co-ax in to the Electronic Signal Distribution unit, measured the impedance in and out of the "splitter" to the Radio Receivers and found a perfect 52 Ohms! We turned on the Receivers and found the signals to be 40 decibels higher than those from the Double-Doublet Antenna Farm!!! We were really "in business."

The Hqs USAFSS Engineers heard the news about our "invention," made some measurements of performance and went away muttering that: "it shouldn't work." Twelve years later I happened by a USAFSS Antenna Site at Clark Air Base in the Philippines and there, in plan sight, was "my" H.F. Discone, obviously constructed at no small expense by a Commercial Firm. I stopped by the organization for an address and sent them a picture of our first-in-the-Air-Force (1951) antenna.

Life for our married "troops" was better, financially, in San Antonio than anywhere else I've been stationed. That is, if you didn't mind sharing your home (on or off Base) with a remarkable variety of insects! We did mind, so we bought a brand new "Spartan Royal Mansion" Trailer Home (33' 9" long). The Spartan was an all aluminum mobile home and we lived in and enjoyed it for 10 yrs. (minus a tour in Europe).

I'll look for my 201 file and if I find it (soon) I'll send more info on the 136ths early years.

Manford Carroll Night

Thanks to Dick Bergman for forwarding this part of Night's story. Dick says: "We were never known to the public or the other commands of the AF. We were truly silent warriors. We did our job well." Dick Bergman

These Guys

From: Dick Bergman
To: Clara19126@msn.com
Sent: Friday, December 30, 2005 4:27 PM
Subj: USAFSS - THE GOOD, THE BAD AND THE UGLY

Trish,

I got your address from an E-Mail you sent to the Freedom Through Vigilance Assn. I am a member and get the quarterly newsletter.

Yes, I have several missions you might be interested in and also some funny experiences. I'll put them together in the next couple days and send them to you.

Dick (Bergie)

Trish,
Well here we go. Take what you want and throw away the unremarkable ones.

THE GOOD, THE BAD & THE UGLY

We had a dog (GERMAN SHEPARD) named Di-Da; guess some di-di-boppers named her. She knew every man in the detachment (no women then) and would become very aggressive toward any stranger who came near.

We were advised of an inspection by Wing Officers so we locked Di-Da in a room with lever door knobs forgetting that she knew how to open them.

The staff car arrived with two Majors who entered the operations building and quickly left pursued by a very angry German Shepard. She was corralled and the inspection resumed. I was sleeping because I had worked the previous night but a full bottle of I.W. HARPER was in full sight in my wall locker (they never blinked an eye). A couple of months later wing decided we needed to learn the language so they sent a German woman up to the detachment to teach us. Di-Da got loose and she left in a very great hurry. THE BAD: In August of 1954 a small group of us were ordered to Neubiburg Air Base outside of Munich to participate in the 12th AF maneuvers. Our mission was to covertly monitor phone communications on the base, both incoming and out going. The mission was labeled SECRET and the orders did not define the mission.

One night I monitored an outgoing call from a senior officer to a woman in Munich. He was complaining that he could not get away to see her because of the "Damn Maneuvers."

The next day we were transcribing our recorded calls in a locked room when there was a loud banging on the door. Our mission NCO answered and found a Colonel and two confused MP's. The colonel was shouting that he wanted to know, "Who the hell are you and what are you doing here." He demanded access which our NCO refused and handed him a copy of our orders labeled SECRET. The colonel left in a hurry but I recognized his voice as the man I had monitored on the phone the night before. GUESS HE HAD HIS OWN SECRETS.

AND THE UGLY: Our detachment clerk disappeared one night in 1955. It was later revealed that he had been picked up by special investigators and flown back to the ZI for an arrest. The charge: Murdering German women (Shatzi's) and selling their Ken Karts (ID's) to East German refugees. If he is not dead, he is still in Leavenworth.

That's it for tonight. I'll send more later if you are interested. Let me know.

Bergie

From: Dick Bergman
To: Clara19126@msn.com
Sent: Friday, December 30, 2005 4:27 PM
Subj: USAFSS - EXCITEMENT

It might interest you to know that although the U-2 over flights over the USSR did not occur until July 1956, U-2s were flying over Eastern Europe as of July 1955.

I was a voice monitor with 6931st CSS from Mid 1953 to late 1956 and personally monitored a U-2 flight on UHF in July 1955 from our base at Camp Pieri (Detachment #3) outside of Wiesbaden (Freudenburg Kaserne). We also engaged in Wire tapping during NATO maneuvers in 1954 and 1956 (our own communications) and also collected teletype communications from friendly sources in the European Theater of Operations. So spying on ourselves is not new.

If you want clarification of these activities please feel free to respond.

Trish,

I got your address from an E-Mail you sent to the Freedom Through Vigilance Assn. I am a member and get the quarterly newsletter. *[Actually it was Ray Thompson who sent it in.] (My own, Editor).*
Yes, I have several missions you might be interested in and also some funny experiences. I'll put them together in the next couple days and send them to you.

Dick (Bergie)

Trish,

Here are a couple more:

EXCITEMENT

In late June of 1955 technicians arrived and installed UHF antennas and receivers. Soviet air defense had just switched to VHF.

About a week or two later, at the end of my first day shift (we worked 3-3-3 and 3 off) I was advised to wear my Class B uniform when I reported for duty the next day (we always wore OD'S on SHIFT). On reporting for duty the NCO of operations advised me to take the UHF station as my monitor site.

Shortly after I began to receive voice transmissions from a single aircraft and several high ranking officers entered operations and watched over my shoulder as I typed the record of the transmissions. This went on for several hours, then they left.

I knew it was an important mission but did not get clarification until years later when I inquired of my old Commander as to the nature of the mission and that I suspected it was a U-2 flight.

His reply was as follows: "Hello Dick, You are correct about the special operation in 1955. There were people there from both Sqdn. and the Wing in Frankfurt. Major   . . . was the Sqdn. commander. That was the first operational flight of that airplane over Europe. I was not told the name of the airplane or anything about its mission at that time (no need to know). I found out about what your special operation was about when I went on TDY at Misawa Air Base in Japan in November of 1964, etc.

I have always been proud of my participation in that operation."

SADNESS

Our chief radio repairman was S/Sgt Arthur Mello. He was a nice guy, easy to get along with and always willing to help. He died in September 1958 as a crew member of C-130, #60528 which was shot down by Soviet fighters on the Armenian border. It was an intelligence gathering mission.

He was truly a Silent Warrior Hero.

More to follow in a few days.

From: Dick Bergman In Trier - NATO MANEUVERS
To: Trish Schiesser
Sent: Wednesday, February 01, 2006 4:29 PM

Trish,

Here is one: In April of 1955 we were assigned to covertly monitor phone lines during NATO maneuvers. Our site was in the Black Forest above the city of Trier. There were twelve of us, a British intelligence detachment and a small group of French military personnel. We worked day and night but only two were recording at night because of the low traffic load.

Because of the very cool weather we slept in our mummy bags. One night I awoke to see a French soldier going thru my duffel bag. I tried to silently move the zipper down on my sleeping bag but it was stuck. My only course of action was to roll off the cot and holler HELP as loud as I could.

Pandemonium broke loose with 9 men hopping around in a frenzy trying to get their pants on and looking for the threat at the same time.

Well, he escaped along with a full box of my Tampa Jewels cigars.

More to come,

Bergie

Subj: Re: LITTLE TOY DOG
Date: 10/15/02 3:14:40 AM Pacific Daylight Time

Have a good trip to the Cape (Cape Cod). FYI, we work summers in a campground near the cape, at Foxboro. The campground runs tours to the cape and we get to go from time to time. We also attend some craft fairs when our work schedule allows.

I know about the book: Little Toy Dog, and the details of the RB-47 shootdown as my Air Force duties took us to the area where the shootdown took place. Larry Tart's book, The Price of Vigilance, which I referenced in my last, has a good account of the incident.

Dave Bristol
17 Buccaneer Drive
Leesburg FL 34788

These Guys

01 July 2001/Revised 14 August 2006
Editor, Revetments (to whom we give credit, through the Colonel)
Subject: NO SLEEPING IN THE ASHTRAYS
By Colonel Charles V. Brown, USAFR (Ret.)

The night was ink black and stormy as hell, when Captain Chuck Brown took off from Travis in a wounded C-141. It broke down at: Hickham, Wake, Clark, and finally made a fighter landing at Tan Son Nhut some 52 hours later; very little sleep. The heaters didn't work, so we put Army blankets over our heads - I was wearing 1505s - until we got warm but couldn't breathe. Then out for air and back under. We stank, and we badly needed shaves. Worst of all, the in-flight lunches ran out, and we were hungry zombies when we stepped out into - you guessed it - a driving rainstorm. We were herded into the infamous in-country briefing. We kept falling out of our chairs. The only thing I remembered from that briefing was what the Flight Surgeon said: "All of you have arrived as biological virgins. You will be raped repeatedly. Most of you will acclimate. For those who don't we have a pill." I was on that pill for 367 days in country, along with the anti-malaria pill and the ubiquitous One-A-Day vitamin, which many of us used to track our time. We'd put 365 of them in a big bottle and watch it SLOWLY empty. Of course we also had the connect-the-dots poster of a female. That last dot meant you were homeward bound (in more ways than one). The only other thing I remember from the orientation briefing was that there were NO officer's quarters. "All officers will find their own quarters; we don't even have enough quarters for the enlisted, so you're on your own. You may stay in the transient barracks for 72 hours max, and for God's sake stay on the wooden planking between buildings; there are snakes swimming around in the barracks area." I said my first in country, "shit."

Dropping my duffel bag in the first building I found with an empty bunk, I read the sign posted over the door: "No smoking in bed." Someone had penciled below it: "And no sleeping in the ashtrays." I crashed, slept for 14 hours, got up to pee, actually saw a snake swimming toward me and repelled him with automatic urine fire - the only weapon I had.
Slept another four hours and staggered into the officers club. It reminded me of scenes from Dunkirk during WWII.

I sat down with two Majors, who were bemoaning the fact they'd just lost their roommate to rotation. I had my wallet out and begged them to take me in. "OK, here's the address. Downtown Saigon. Take a dongcart or a peacart." I took a taxi.

"Where you go, GI?"
"En jew yen hue," I said.
"You say same same again, GI." I did.
"Gimmee paper." I gimme him the paper.
"Ha Ha Ha Ha Ha Ha Ha HA HA HA!" he said.
"You go Nguyen Hue (pronounced win way), GI. You velly funny Di Wei (captain)." As the taxi wended its way down Truman Key, at every stop he leaned out the window, pointed to me, and, after a burst of Vietnamese, I heard "En jew yen hue." All the taxi drivers in Saigon laughed at me by sundown. As I paid the driver, a horde of street urchins grabbed my duffel bag and took off, me in hot pursuit. But they were the "baggage handlers" for the hotel (I can't remember its name, sorry). I was in a four-man hooch built on the roof of a seven-story hotel. Boy, did I get in shape, lugging two five-gallon jerry cans full of Army water up seven flights of stairs every few days!

It turned out to be a grand place to watch stuff. Like the night the VC blew up the Shell Oil Refinery. In my basement somewhere are 35 mm color slides, timed exposures, of fireballs, gunships firing red tracers down on the VC - all just two miles away.

Having finished one 12-hour shift and settled down for a long morning nap in my hooch, I was rudely awakened by considerable small arms fire. "Shit," I said. It was about my 3,953rd use of that expression by then.

Well, some South Vietnamese rangers had consumed too many Bam De Baas (does anyone remember how to spell 33 in Veenamee?), got into an argument in a tea house over, what else, a teahouse girl, and fell out on Nguyen Hue to settle it. So I stroll over to the railing, look down, see three bodies in the street while others are doing their best to emulate John Wayne. A stray round ricochets off the railing about two feet from me. I use expression number 3, 954 and drop on my face.

Speaking of teahouses, I'm sure officers weren't supposed to go in them, so please, please don't pass this story on, OK? Deal. Any of you ever hit the London Club? Very last one on the right going down, uh, down - somebody help me here. Lots of Sierra happened in the LC. One night one hell of a fight broke out over one of the girls and an MP battalion arrived. Captain Brown managed to jump through a broken window, narrowly avoiding having to explain to his commanding officer - well, you know.

I was an Intel weenie. My title was Air Force Special Security Officer, 7AF. Among other things my guys ran a communications center to pass Special Intelligence (Signals Intelligence) to 7AF HQ Combat Intelligence. So our Quonsets were behind barbwire and guarded by the Air Police (now called Security Police).

Well, so about 0330 I fired up my pipe for the zillionth time and walked out for a breath of soggy air. I found the guard asleep. Bang! I kicked the door.

"Airman, do you know the penalty for sleeping on guard duty in a combat zone?"
"No, Sir!"
"The firing squad."
"Sir, you are shitting me, right?"
"No, I am not. Don't move, I'll be right back." In 30 seconds I was back with a mug of scalding "combat coffee" from our 24/7 pot in the AFSSO. "Drink this. That's an order."
"Yes sir." He did.
"You awake now, son?" (I could call him son as I had just turned 30.)
"Yes, sir. It won't happen again, sir." We chatted about stuff and watched the parachute flares float down, as usual. Good lad. He asked me why I was wearing such grungie foot gear. I told him I couldn't get any new boots. He asked my size. Next day, as I went through the security guard post, he handed me a brand new pair of jungle boots, my size. "Don't ask sir." I didn't. He was a good lad, and I missed him after he rotated; wrote a letter of favorable communication to his Squadron CO.

Do any of you remember the friendly firefight between two enlisted barracks one night (I want to say early-mid 1966)? They expended six or eight hundred rounds without a single casualty. In those days the AF was the gang who couldn't shoot straight unless flying an aircraft. The two buildings were riddled, however. It was one of those nights God was pulling OD (Officer of the Day).

One night I started a riot in the O' Club. Seems my wife had sent me a pecan pie, which had, miraculously, arrived in pretty good shape. I brought a piece with me to dinner that night, ordered an empty plate (very hard for the waitress to understand), and began eating it. As a group of senior officers were leaving, they saw me eating the pie and sprinted back to their table, demanding from a totally perplexed Vietnamese waitress that they be served some pecan pie, just like the captain was eating. "No habe, no habe precam pie."
"We are NOT leaving till you serve us pie, like the dei wei is eating!" I said the "Sierra" word and slunk out of the club. I learned a lot of hard lessons that year.

I may be the only Air Force officer ever run over while on a motorcycle by a South Vietnamese Admiral in a staff car. He got out and helped me up. It was dark and I was using my entire monthly allotment of the "Sierra" word till I saw two stars on his gold shoulder boards and starched white uniform. Scratched, bruised, my uniform a wreck, my bike fortunately not too banged up. I saluted. He returned it and bowed, so I bowed back. What the hell, the whole world was crazy anyway.

I could go on and on. But maybe these stories have triggered a few memories, maybe a laugh about something. It's good to remember. I salute all of you, and I'm damn proud to be one of your brothers. Welcome home.

YAHOO! Groups: airforcesecurityservice Messages

From: phillconrad@n...
Date Thu Aug 22, 2002 9:47 pm
Subject: RE: {Air Force Security Service} Re: Misdirection to Correction on the 6901st Inflection Section

Question for those who knew The Thurmanator, Thurman Miller: Google makes reference to 6901st.org/obituary(ies).htm, or something like that, and seems to indicate an obit.

Miller passed away a few years ago in a VA hospital in Texas. Miller and I did not see eye to eye. My duty as an NCO was to take care of the troops and his was to screw them. He even had me court martialed but I was found not guilty. He and Halverson were after my a** until I left.

Phil Conrad

Subj: Re: Blessed Christmas (this is trish)
Date: 12/15/02 2:06:20 PM Pacific Standard Time
From: Phil Conrad
To: Idareedblanford@aol.com

Trish:

Watch what u say on the internet. It might be intercepted by the ACLU and a lawsuit could have u in court. We in USAFSS know quite a lot about INTERCEPT. (HA HA) Merry Christmas and a Happy New Year. I pray that the GI's that must go to IRAQ ALL return home.

Phil

IdaReedBlanford@aol.com wrote:

[Unable to display image] Dear Phil, Have missed hearing from you. Sent you a few e-mails and they came back, but had been sending to another e-mail address. Hope this reaches you. I want to thank you for everything this year. You are a wonderful person and your buddies are a hellofabunch of terrific people. See you around, I hope.
Hugs, Trish

This is from Phil Conrad - one of the nicest USAFSS men.

This is a portion of an e-mail I received from ex-USAFSS man, Dale Cox. I am "adding a disclaimer stating that the stories are true and accurate only so far as the story teller can remember what actually happened." This is per Dale's suggestion.

MORALE CAPS
By Dale Cox

This story is now legend since it has been passed down from the guys who were the first to serve at KAS (Karamursel, Turkey) after it started up in 1958.

First, go to the site and check out the cap with our patch on it so you will know the basis for the story that I never experienced first hand but that was passed down to us by the older guys.

In either 1959 or 1960, to boost morale and esprit de corps, a patch was made up that could be worn on a black baseball cap as part of the fatigue uniform. These were called, "morale" caps.

The Soviets, at the time, saw that U.S. surveillance bases were going up around their borders from Europe all the way to the Orient. There was nothing they could do to stop this but they found ways to send messages letting us know they were aware of what we were doing.

A female announcer on Radio Moscow, whom we called "Moscow Molly," once broadcast this message. She said, "You boys at Karamursel Air Station. Black is not a morale color."

This was how close we interacted with the Soviets, and that is why we were proud to have been part of Air Force Security Service. We were actually on the front lines during the Cold War!

Dale

Subj: Re: Oberauerbach 63-65
Date: 9/19/02 3:14:11 AM pacific Daylight Time
From   philcon@localnet.com
To: IdaReedBlanford@aol.com

Trish: I understand your hesitance to not tell what you know. That's okay, Phil. It's yours. So keep it to yourself. I know that 6901st was an analysis center and a think tank, and a lot of goings on, experimental, there. That's why I think the Surgeon General, at that time, was very interested in Phil's case.

Phil: One of our main missions was the collection of data from a listening post west of Moscow. This was consolidated and sent to Meade for further analysis. There were no "experiments" at Zwei. The duty was terrible, we worked shift work 3 mids, 3 swings, 3 days and than a 3 day break.

Trish: I just appreciate that you are being nice and including me in whatever. I wouldn't ask you to give up what you are not able to give up. I understand.

Phil: No I did not know Phil but probably passed him many times in the hallways and was in the snack bar with him many times. We didn't interact with guy's from other shops because of the "need to know." I have asked all the fellow's I still am in contact with and his name does not ring a bell

Trish: Phil showed up on my back steps New Years Eve '65. Something weird was going on. The AF caught up with him and took him to the Vet's home in New Orleans(we were living in New Orleans) and I went to see him - he'd escaped from the vet's hospital for three days or so and hid under a house with a dog for comfort and a hose to drink from. They got him somehow, or he may have just decided to go back to them. I went immediately after they found him and he was in a room with a bed and the door was big, heavy, dark, and had a little slot in it for me to open and talk to him. So I started making noise, 'cause I wanted to see my bros. (brother) and so they let me in. He was reading the funny papers.
"So, why'd you turn your ol bros in," he said, before I could answer, in comes three AP's and a litter and a straitjacket and a shot for Phil. I said, "Is that really necessary!" "Standard procedure, ma'am." They carried him off and I stood there crying, bleeding down my legs (had a real heavy period)

and some gawk came up to me with Phil's belongings in a dirty brown grocery bag. You know what was in there? Just the white pajamas they'd put him in - only they were brown with dirt from hiding under the house. I nearly cracked up, but I didn't. I went home and Bob and I packed up our son and daughter and drove to Key West for Bob's Sub-Sonar School (he was an officer in Naval Reserves.) Phil went all over - they shipped him here and there, as far as I know - someone said he was a double plant and had a lotta knowledge, etc., and that's why USAFSS and Hoover were looking for him. Every time they'd catch him, he'd slip off again - sometimes to return on his own.

Phil: If one of the USAFSS fellows went AWOL or had to visit a shrink the problem was were they going to release classified info. When I had an automobile accident the German police showed up first and were going to take me to the police station. The AP's arrived and said they were going to take me back to the 01st. An argument started and one of the AP's I knew drew his 45 and the German police said OK you take him. If someone got into real trouble he disappeared and was sent back to the US.

Trish: There are two stories about him, Phil, but I hope to try to prove which one is true. Dunno if I'll succeed, but I'll keep tryin',
Love to you,
Trish

Phil: Good luck and if I can do anything that might help I will let you know. Try contacting the fellows that lived in Oberauerbach - they may help.
Phil

Re: Oberauerbach 63-65
Date: 9/19/02 4:25:12 PM Pacific Daylight Time
From: philcon@localnet.com
To: IdaReedBlanford@aol.com

In a message dated 9/19 philcon@localnet.com writes:

Phil: No, that was Army, I knew a Warrant Officer from the Nike site we drank a few Parkies together.

Trish: Would he remember Phil's name?
I've had so many people point me in so many directions.
I talked to someone and they said I may never find out.
At this point, I'm feeling that way too.

Phil: I never kept in contact with the Army guy. It never hurts to keep trying but if the AF (government) is hiding something you will never find out.

To: IdaReedBlanford
From: philcon@localnet.com

Phil: I was told when I first got into the USAFSS that the KGB had a file on everyone in USAFSS.

Trish: Then, I'll bet that's what happened to scare the shit out of him after the three day TDY to London and back to Zwei. Personally, I think you've hit half the nail on the head, my friend.

This is an e-mail I received from Dale Cox - ex- USAFSS man. He calls it, "Karamursel, The rest of the Story." Karamursel, or KAS is in Turkey.

SAILBOAT FOR SALE
By Dale Cox

Trish,
In the summer of 1961 one of the base personnel was rotating out and listed his four man sailboat for sale. Three guys on Able flight, who shall remain nameless in case the statute of limitations has not run out, thought they might buy the boat, but figured they should try it out first.

None of them knew anything about sailing so one dark night they sneaked down to the boat dock and "borrowed" what they thought was the boat for sale and took it out into the bay of Izmit for a little practice. They were doing pretty good until they realized the wind had blown them a few miles away from the base. Try as they may they could not tack into the wind to get back and they kept getting farther away. In desperation they finally pushed the boat into some willows that were growing in the water near the shore, and having no other way to go, started wading along the shore back to the base.

This was no sandy beach. It was marshy, and weeds, thorns and brush grew to the waters edge. By the time they made it back they were covered with punctures, scratches, mud and muck. They only had a few hours to get cleaned up and ready to go to work on day shift. Not having slept the night before, and having to tolerate all their scratches, they spent a miserable day at work. At dinner that night they unanimously decided sailing was no fun and they would not buy the boat.

Oh, yeah. The boat they "borrowed" was not the one for sale. It belonged to the base Fire Marshal. When word got out that his boat was missing everyone on Able Flight was mum.

It took two days to find the boat. They finally spotted the sail sticking up above the willows where it was stuck. Someone suggested the boat had broken loose from its mooring and the wind had blown it into the bay. The guys on Able flight all agreed.

The Fire Marshal didn't buy that story. Why not? "Because," he argued, "the wind cannot hoist a sail."

Now, these three guys just happened to be Russian linguists. If any shenanigans were going on, it seems the Ruskies always had a hand in it. But, the boat was recovered intact. The episode died down, and the three guys: they went on to participate in many other escapades.
Dale

Credit to Ramparts via Fehrs@. . . .

Subj: Interesting Background Info.
Date: 9/29/02 6:41:11 AM Pacific Daylight Time
From: fehrs@. . . .
To: IdaReedBlanford@aol.com

Trish, this will blow you away. I don't know exactly what your brother did, but in the course of researching for my memoirs, I discovered this account that almost parallels your brother's time span (and mine). I bookmarked it, but am not sure why. It's lengthy, but read it top to bottom.
http://www.euronet.nl/`rembert/echelon/nsa-elint.htm

Author's Note: I believe my brother, SSGT Phillip C. Noland, performed the same duties as Perry Fellwock, from all the information I have gathered about him.

Note: The article begins with commentary on information provided by an anonymous former analyst of the National Security Agency followed by the full interview. The analyst was later named as Perry Fellwock, at the time using the pseudonym Winslow Peck.

Ramparts, Vol. 11, No. 2, August, 1972, pp.35-50

U.S. ELECTRONIC ESPIONAGE: A MEMOIR

About thirty miles northeast of CIA headquarters in Langley, Virginia, right off the Baltimore-Washington expressway overlooking the flat Maryland countryside, stands a large three story building known informally as the "cookie factory." It's officially known as Ft. George G. Meade, headquarters of the National Security Agency.
Three fences surround the headquarters. The inner and outer barriers are topped with barbed wire, the middle one is a five-strand electrified wire. Four gatehouses spanning the complex at regular intervals house specially-trained marine guards. Those allowed access all wear iridescent I.D. badges -- green for "top secret crypto," red for "secret crypto." Even the janitors are cleared for secret codeword material. Once inside, you enter the world's longest "corridor" - 980 feet long by 560 feet wide. And all along the corridor are more marine guards, protecting the doors of key NSA offices. At 1,400,000 square

feet, it is larger than CIA headquarters, 1,135,000 square feet. Only the State Department and the Pentagon, and the new headquarter planned for the FBI are more spacious. But the DIRNSA (Director, National Security Agency) can be further distinguished from the headquarters buildings of these three other giant bureaucracies -- it has no windows, another palace of paranoia? No, For DIRNSA is the command center for the largest, most sensitive and far-flung intelligence gathering apparatus in the world's history. Here, and in the nine-story Operations Building Annex, upwards of 15,000 employees work to break the military, diplomatic and commercial codes of every nation in the world, analyze the decrypted messages, and send the results to the rest of the U.S. intelligence community.

Far less widely known than the CIA - whose Director Richard Helms will occasionally grant public interviews, NSA silently provides an estimated 80 percent of all valid U.S. intelligence. So secret, so sensitive is the NSA mission and so highly indoctrinated is its personnel, that the Agency, twenty years after its creation, remains virtually unknown to those employees outside the intelligence community. The few times its men have been involved in international incidents NSA's name has been kept out of the papers.

Nevertheless, the first American killed in Vietnam, near what became the main NSA base at Phu Bai was an NSA operative. And the fact that Phu Bai remains the most heavily guarded of all U.S. bases suggests that an NSA man may well be the last.

The scope of the NSA's global mission has been shrouded in secrecy since the inception of the Agency. Only the haziest outlines have been known, and then only on the basis of surmise. However, Ramparts has recently been about to conduct a series of lengthy interviews with a former NSA analyst willing to talk about his experiences. He worked for the Agency for three and a half years -- in the cold war of Europe and the hot one in Southeast Asia. The story he tells of NSA's structure and history is not the whole story, but it is a significant and often chilling portion of it.

Our informant served as a senior NSA analyst in the Istanbul listening post for over two years. He was a participant in the deadly international fencing match that goes on daily with the Soviet Union, plotting their air and ground forces and penetrating their defenses. He watched the Six Day War unfold and learned of the intentions of the major powers: Israel, the Soviet Union, the United States, France and Egypt, by reading their military and diplomatic radio traffic, all of it fully intercepted, de-coded and translated by NSA on the spot. As an expert on NSA missions directed against the Soviet Union and the so-called "Forward Countries" - Bulgaria, Hungary, Czechoslovakia, East

Germany, Rumania and Yugoslavia - he briefed such visiting dignitaries as Vice President Humphrey. In Indochina he was a senior analyst, military consultant and U.S. Air Force intelligence operations director for North Vietnam, Laos, the northern-most provinces of South Vietnam and China. He is a veteran of over one hundred Airborne Radio Direction Finding missions in Indochina - making him thoroughly familiar with the "enemy" military structure and its order of battle.

With the benefit of the testimony he provides, we can see that the reason for the relative obscurity of NSA of less to do with its importance within the intelligence community than with the limits of its mission and the way it gets its results. Unlike the CIA, whose basic functions are clearly outlined in the 1947 law that created it, NSA, created in 1952, simply gathers intelligence. It does not formulate policy or carry out operations. Most of the people working for NSA are not "agents," but ordinary servicemen attached to one of three semi-autonomous military cryptologic agencies - the Air Force Security Service, the largest; the Naval Security Group; and the Army Security Agency, the oldest. But while it is true that the Agency runs no spies as in the popular myth, its systematic Signal Intelligence intercept mission is clearly prohibited by the Geneva Code. What we are dealing with is a highly bureaucratized, highly technological intelligence mission whose breadth and technological sophistication appear remarkable even in an age of imperial responsibilities and electronic wizardry.

So that not a sparrow or a government falls without NSA's instantaneous knowledge, over two thousand Agency field stations dot the five continents and the seven seas. In Vietnam, NSA's airborne flying platforms carrying out top-secret Radar Detection Finding missions, supply U.S. commanders with their most reliable information on the location of communist radio transmitters, and thus on the location of NLF units themselves. Other methods, the use of sensors and seismic detectors, either don't work or are used merely to supplement NSA's results. But the Agency's *tactical* mission in Indochina, intelligence support for U.S. commanders in the field, however vital to the U.S. war effort, is subsidiary in terms of men, time and material to its main *strategic* mission.

The following interview tells us a great deal about both sides of the NSA mission - everything from how Agency people feel about themselves and the communist "enemy" to the NSA electronic breakthroughs that threaten the Soviet-American balance of terror. We learn for example that NSA knows the call signs for every Soviet airplane, the numbers on the side of each plane, the name of the pilot in command; the precise longitude and latitude of every nuclear submarine; the whereabouts of nearly every Soviet VIP; the location of every Soviet missile base; every army division, battalion and company - its weaponry, commander and deployment. Routinely the NSA monitors all Soviet military, diplomatic and commercial radio traffic, including Soviet Air Defense, Tactical Air and KGB forces. (It was the NSA that found Che Guevara in Bolivia through radio communications intercept and analysis.) NSA cryptologic experts seek to break every Soviet code and do so with remarkable success, Soviet scrambler and computer-generated signals being nearly as vulnerable as ordinary voice and manual Morse radio transmissions. Interception of Soviet radar signals enables NSA to gauge quite precisely the effectiveness of Soviet Air Defense units. Methods have even been devised to "fingerprint" every human voice used in radio transmissions and distinguish them from the voice of every other operator. The Agency's Electronic Intelligence Teams (ELINT) are capable of intercepting any electronic signal transmitted anywhere in the world and, from an analysis of the intercepted signal, identify the transmitter and physically reconstruct it. Finally, after having shown the size and sensitivity of the Agency's big ears, it is almost superfluous to point out that NSA monitors and records *every* trans-Atlantic telephone call.

Somehow, it is understandable, given the size of the stakes in the Cold War, that an agency like NSA would monitor U.S. citizens' trans-Atlantic phone calls. And we are hardly surprised that the U.S. violates the Geneva Code to intercept communist radio transmissions. What is surprising is that the U.S. systematically violates a treaty of its own making, the UKUSA Agreements of 1947. Under this treaty, the U.S., Canada, the United Kingdom and Australia erected a white-Anglo-Saxon protestant nation's communications intelligence dictatorship over the "Free World." The agreement distinguishes between three categories of intelligence, First, Second, and Third Party consumers. The First Party is the U.S. intelligence community. The Second party refers to the other white Anglo-Saxon nations' communications intelligence agencies; i.e. Great Britain's GCHQ, Canada's CBNRC, etc. These agencies exchange information routinely. Non-WASP nations, the so-called Third Party nations, are France, Italy, as well as South Vietnam, Japan, Thailand and the non-WASP allies in SEATO. But the idea of a closed club of gentlemanly white men gets quickly dispelled when we learn that the U.S. even intercepts the radio communications of its Second Party UKUSA "allies." From the U.S. military base at Chicksands, for example, and from the U.S. Embassy in London, NSA operatives busily intercept and transcribe British diplomatic traffic and send it off for further analysis to DIRNSA.

We feel that the information in this interview -- while not of a "sensitive" nature -- is of critical importance to America for the light it casts on the cold war and the anti-communist myths that perpetuate it. Few myths about the aggressive intentions of the Soviet Union and China and about North Vietnam's "invasion of a democratic South Vietnam," can only be sustained by keeping the American people as ignorant as possible about the actual nature of these regimes and the great power relationships that exist in the world. The peace of the world, we are told, revolves shakily on a "balance of terror" between the armed might of the Soviet Union and the United States. So tenuous is this balance that if the U.S. were to let down its guard ever so slightly, if it were, for example, to reduce the ever-escalating billions allocated for "defense," we would immediately face the threat of destruction from the aggressive Soviets, who are relentless in their pursuit of military superiority. Our informant's testimony, based on years of dealing with the hard information about the Soviet military and its highly defensive-oriented deployment, is a powerful and authoritative rebuttal to this mythology.

But perhaps even a more compelling reason requires that this story be told. As we write, the devastating stepped-up bombing of North Vietnam continues. No one can say with certainty what the ultimate consequences of this desperate act are likely to be. Millions of Americans, perhaps a majority, deplore this escalation. But it would be a mistake to ignore the other millions, those who have grown up in fear of an entity known as "world communism." For them Nixon's latest measures have a clear rationale and a plausible purpose. It is precisely this political rationale and this strategic purpose that the testimony of our informant destroys.

We are told by Nixon that South Vietnam has been "invaded" by the North which is trying to impose its will on the people of the South. This latest version of why we continue to fight in Indochina -- the first version stressed the threat of China which allegedly controlled Hanoi, even as Moscow at one time was thought to control Peking -- emphasizes Hanoi's control over the NLF. Our evidence shows that the intelligence community, including NSA, has long determined the NLF and the DRV are autonomous, independent entities. Even in Military Region I, the northern-most province of South Vietnam, and the key region in the "North Vietnamese" offensive, the command center has always been located not in Hanoi but in somewhere in the la Drang valley. This command center, the originating point for all military operations in the region, is politically and militarily under the control of the PRG. Known as Military Region Tri Tin Hue (MRTTH) it integrates both DRV and NLF units under the command. Hanoi has never simply "called the shots," although the DRV and PRG obviously have common reasons for fighting and share common objectives. All of this information NSA has passed on systematically to the political authorities who, equally systematically, have ignored it.

Nixon's military objective -- halting supplies to the South through bombing and mining of North Vietnamese ports -- turns out to be as bogus as his political rationale. Military supplies for the DRV and the NLF are stored along the Ho Chi Minh trail in gigantic underground staging areas known as bam trams. These are capable of storing supplies for as long as twelve months, at normal levels of hostilities, according to NSA estimates. Even at the highly accelerated pace of the recent offensive, it would take several months (assuming 100 percent effectiveness) before our bombing and mining would have any impact on the fighting.

Taken together, the experience of our informant in Europe, in the Middle East, and in Indochina bears witness to the aggressive posture of the United States in the late 1960s. It is hard to see anything defensive about it. Our policy makers are well-informed by the intelligence community of the defensive nature of our antagonists' military operations. The NSA operations here described reflect the drive of a nation to control as much of the world as possible, whose leaders trust no one and are forced to spy on their closest allies in violation of the treaties they initiated themselves; leaders, moreover, for whom all nations are, in the intelligence idiom, "targets," and who maintain the U.S. imperium around the world in large part through threat of actual physical annihilation.

At home, however, the favored weapon employed is ignorance rather than fear. Like NSA headquarters itself, the United States is surrounded by barriers -- barriers of ignorance that keep its citizens prisoners of the cold war. The first obstacle if formed by the myths propagated about communism and about its aggressive designs on America. The second, dependent for its rationale on the first, is the incredible barrier of governmental secrecy that keeps most of the questionable U.S. aggressive activities hidden not from our "enemies," who are the knowledgeable victims, but from the American people themselves. The final barrier is perhaps the highest and is barbed with the sharpest obstacles of all. It is nothing less than our reluctance as American to confront what we are doing to the peoples of the world, ourselves included, by organizations like the National Security Agency.

Q. *Let's begin by getting a sense of the National Security Agency and the scope of its operations.*

A. O.K. At the broadest level, NSA is a part of the United States intelligence community and a member of the USIB, the United States Intelligence Board. It sits on the Board with the CIA, the FBI, the State Department's RCI, and various military intelligence bureaus. Other agencies also have minor intelligence-gathering units, even the Department of the Interior.

All intelligence agencies are tasked with producing a particular product. NSA produces -- that is, collects, analyzes, and disseminates to its consumers -- Signals Intelligence, called SIGINT. It comes from communications or other types of signals intercepted from what we called "targeted entities," and it amounts to about 80 percent of the viable intelligence the U.S. government receives. There is COMSEC, a secondary mission. This is to produce all the communications security equipment, codes and enciphering equipment for the United States and its allies. This function of the NSA involves the monitoring of our own communications to make sure they are secure. But SIGINT is the main responsibility.

As far as NSA's personnel are concerned, they are divided into two groups: those that are totally civilian, and those like me who derived from the military. As far as the collection of data is concerned, the military provides almost all the people. They are recruited through one of the service cryptologic agencies. The three agencies are the U.S. Air Force Security Service (USAFSS), the Army Security Agency (ASA), and the Navy Security Group (NSG). These agencies may control a few intelligence functions that are primarily tactical in nature and directly related to ongoing military operations. But generally, DIRNSA, the Director of the National Security Agency, is completely in control over all NSA's tasks, missions and people.

The NSA, through its sites all over the world, copies -- that is, collects -- intelligence from almost every conceivable source. That means every radio transmission that is of a strategic of tactical nature, or is related to some government, or has some political significance. NSA is powerful, and it has grown since its beginning back in 1947. The only problem it has had has come over the last few years. Originally it had equal power with the CIA on the USIB and the National Security council. But recently the CIA has gained more of a hegemony in intelligence operations, especially since Richard Helms became director of the entire intelligence community.

Q. Does the NSA have agents in the field?
A. Yes, but probably not in the way you mean. It is different from other intelligence agencies in that it's not a consumer of its own intelligence. That is, it doesn't act on the data it gathers. It just passes it on. Generally, there's a

misconception all Americans have about spying. They think it's all cloak and dagger, with hundreds of James Bonds wandering around the world in Aston-Martins, shooting people. It just doesn't happen. It's all either routine or electronic. I got to know a lot of CIA people in my three and a half years with NSA, and it became pretty clear to me that most of them sit around doing mundane stuff. You know, reading magazines, newspapers, technical journals. Like some people say, they do a lot of translating of foreign phone books. Of course I did meet a few who were out in the jungles with guns in their hands too.

But as far as the NSA is concerned, it is completely technological. Like I said, at least 80 percent of all viable intelligence that this country receives and acts on comes from the NSA, and it is all from signals intelligence, strategic and tactical. I saw it from both angles -- first strategic in working against the Soviet Union in Turkey and then tactical flying missions against the VC in Nam. Information gathering by NSA is complete. It covers what foreign governments are doing, planning to do, have done in the past: what armies are moving where and against whom; what air forces are moving where, and what their capabilities are. There really aren't any limits on NSA. Its mission goes all the way from calling in the B-52s in Vietnam to monitoring every aspect of the Soviet space program.

Q. In practical terms, what sort of data are collected by NSA?
A. Before going into that, I should get into the types of signals NSA collects. There are three basic areas. First is what we called ELINT, electronics intelligence. This involves the interception and analysis of any electronics signal. There isn't necessarily any message on that signal. It's just the signal, and it's mainly used by technicians. The only time I ever remember using ELINT was when we were tracing a Russian fighter. Some of them have a particular type of radar system. As I remember, we called this system MANDRAKE. Anyhow, every time this system signaled, a particular type of electronic emission would occur. Our ELINT people would be looking for it, and whenever it came up, it would let them positively identify this type of fighter.

The second type of signal is related to this. It is intelligence from radar, called RADINT. This also involves the technicians. Let me give you an example. There is a particular type of Soviet radar system known in NSA by a codename which we'll call SWAMP. SWAMP is used by the Soviet technical air forces, by their air defense, by the KGB and some civilian forces. It is their way of locating any flying entity while it is in the air. It had a visual read-out display, so that, whenever a radar technician in the Soviet Union wanted to plot something on his map, he could do it by shooting a beam of light on a scope and then send it to whoever wanted to find out information about that airplane. Our RADINT people intercepted SWAMP signals in our European listening posts. From the data they got, NSA analysts were able to go back to the headquarters at Fort Meade and in less than eight weeks completely reconstruct SWAMP. We duplicated it. This meant that we were able to see exactly what the Soviet operators were seeing when they used SWAMP. So, as far as this radar was concerned, the upshot was that they were doing our tracking for us. We knew everything they knew, and we knew what they were able to track over their airspace, and what they weren't.

Q. Does this mean that we can jam their radar?
A. Yes, part of the function of ELINT and RADINT is to develop electronic counter measures. There's a counter measure for every type of Soviet radar.

Q. You said there were three areas. You've gone over ELINT and RADINT. What's the third?
A. This is by far the most important. It's communications intelligence. COMINT. It involves the collection of radio communications of a targeted entity. NSA intercepts them, reproduces them in its equipment and breaks down any code used to encipher the signal. I should say that what I call a "targeted entity" could mean any country -- NSA gathers data on them all -- but in practical terms it's almost synonymous with the Soviet Union.
COMINT is the important function. It's what I was in, and it represents probably 95 percent of relevant SIGINT intelligence. As a matter of fact, the entire intelligence community is also known as the COMINT community.

Q. It would probably be good to backpedal for a moment before we go into your experiences in NSA and get into the way you joined the organization.
A. Well, I'd been in college, was bored, and wanted to do something different. I come from the Midwest, and we still believed those ads about joining the military and seeing the world. I enlisted in the Air Force. Like everybody else, I was shocked by basic training, but after that, when it came time to choose what I'd be doing for the rest of my time, it wasn't too bad. I tried for linguist's training, but there weren't any openings in the schools. I was then approached by three people I later found were a part of the National Security Agency. They interviewed me along with four other guys and asked us if we'd like to do intelligence work. We took a battery of tests, I.Q. and achievement tests,

and had some interviews to determine our political and emotional stability. They really didn't go into our politics very much, I guess because we were all so obviously apathetic. Their main concern was our sex life. They wanted to know if we were homosexual.

At this point, it was 1966; I suppose I had what you would call an analysis of the world situation. But it was primarily based on a belief in maintaining the balance of power. I really didn't see anything wrong with what our government was doing. Also, the few hints about what we might be doing in NSA were pretty exciting: world-wide travel working in the glamorous field of intelligence, being able to wear civilian clothes.

After getting admitted, I was bused to Goodfellow Air Force Base at San Angelo, Texas. Originally, it was a WAC base or something like that, but now it's entirely an intelligence school for NSA. The whole basis of the training was their attempt to make us feel we were the absolute cream of the military. For most GI's, the first days in the military are awful, but as soon as we arrived at the school we were given a pass to go anywhere we wanted, just as long as we were back in school each morning. We could live off base; there was no hierarchical thing inside the classroom.

Q. What sort of things did you focus on in school?
A. At first it was basic stuff. For about two months we just learned primary analysis techniques, intelligence terms, and a rough schematic of the intelligence community. We learned a few rudimentary things about breaking codes and intercepting messages. A lot of people were dropped out of the program at this time because of inadequate school performance, poor attitude, or because of something in their backgrounds didn't prove out. Actually, of fifteen people with me in this class, only four made it through. We had been given access only to information rated "confidential" all the time, but then we got clearance and a Top Secret cryptologic rating.

The first day of the second phase of school began when we walked into the classroom and saw this giant map on the wall. It was marked "Top Secret," and it was of the Soviet Union, for the next three months, we learned about types of communications in operations throughout the world and also in-depth things about the political and administrative makeup of various countries. The soviet Union, of course, was our primary focus. And we learned every one of its military functions: the entire bureaucratic structure, including who's who and where departments and headquarters are located; and a long history of its military and political involvements, especially with countries like China and the East European bloc, which we called "the forward area."

We learned in-depth analysis -- how to perform different types of traffic analysis, cryptic analysis, strategic analysis. A lot of the texts we used were from the Soviet Union, and had been translated by the CIA.

I'm not especially proud of it now, but I should tell you that I graduated at the head of the class. We had a little ceremony inside a local movie theater. I was called up with two guys from other classes and given special achievement certificates. We were given our choice of assignments anywhere in the world. I chose Istanbul. It seemed like the most far-out and exotic place available. After that I left San Angelo and went to Monterey to the Army's language school for a month and a half. I learned a bit of very technical Russian - basically how to recognize the language -- and then to Fort Meade NSA headquarters for a couple of weeks indoctrination about Istanbul, our operation there at Karamursel, and the whole European intelligence community.

Q. When did you get to Istanbul?
A. That was January 1967.
Q. What did you do there?
A. I was assigned to be one of the flight analysts working primarily against the Soviet tactical Air Forces and Soviet long range Air Forces. I had about twenty-five Morse operators who were listening to Morse signals for me, and about five non-Morse and voice operators. It was a pretty boring job for them. A Morse operator, for instance, just sits there in front of a radio receiver with headphones, and a typewriter for copying Morse signals. They would "roll onto" their target, which means that they would go to the frequency that their target was using. The list of likely frequencies and locations and the call signals that would be used -- all this information was made available by the analyst as technical support to the operator. In return the operator would feed the copy to me: I'd perform analysis on it and correlate with other intelligence collected there in Istanbul, and at the NSA installations in the rest of Europe.

Q. Where were the other NSA installations in Europe?
A. The major ones aside from Karamursel are in Berlinhof and Darmstadt, West Germany; Chicksands, England; Brindisi, Italy; and also at Trabesan and Crete. Some of the sea sites have gigantic Feranine antennas. This is a circular antenna array, several football fields in diameter, and it's capable of picking up signals from 360 degrees. They're very sensitive. We can pick up hundreds of signals simultaneously. We pick up voices speaking over short-range radio communications thousands of miles away.

The whole Air Force part of NSA, the USAFSS units, is known as the European Security region. It is headquartered at the I.G. Farben building in Berlin. The Army ASA has units attached to every Army installation in Europe. The Naval NSG has its sites aboard carriers in the 6th Fleet. But mainly it was us.

Q. What does this apparatus actually try to do?
A, Like I said, it copies -- that is, intercepts for decoding and analysis -- communications from every targeted country. As far as the Soviet Union is concerned, we know the whereabouts at any given time of all its aircraft, exclusive of small private planes, and its naval forces, including its missile-firing submarines. The fact is that we're able to break every code they've got, understand every type of communications equipment and enciphering device they've got. We know where their submarines are, what every one of their *VIPs* is doing, and generally their capabilities and the dispositions of all their forces. This information is constantly computer correlated, updated, and the operations go on twenty-four hours a day.

Q. Let's break it down a little. How about starting with the aircraft. How does NSA keep track of the Soviet air forces?
A. First, by copying Soviet Navair, which is their equivalent of the system our military has for keeping track of its own planes. And their Civair, like our civilian airports: we copy all of their air controllers' messages. So we have their planes under control. Then we copy their radar plotting of their own air defense radar, which is concerned with flights that come near their airspace and violate it. By this I mean the U.S. planes that are constantly over flying their territory. Anyhow, all this data would be correlated with our own radar and with the air-to-ground traffic these planes transmitted and our operators picked up. We were able to locate them exactly even if they weren't on our radar through RDF -- radio direction finding. We did this by instantaneously triangulating reception coming through these gigantic antennas I mentioned. As far as Soviet aircraft are concerned, we not only know where they are: we know what their call signs are, what numbers are on the side of every one of their planes, and, most of the time, even which pilots are flying which plane.

Q. You said that we overfly Soviet territory?
A. Routinely as a matter of fact -- over the Black Sea, down to the Baltic. Our Strategic Air Force flies the planes, and we support them. By that I mean that we watch them penetrate the Soviet airspace and then analyze the Soviet

reaction -- how everything from their air defense and tactical air force to how the KGB reacts. It used to be that SAC flew B-52s. As a matter of fact one of them crashed in the Trans-Caucasus area in 1968 and all the Americans on board were lost.

Q. Was it shot down?
A. That was never clear, but I don't believe so. The Soviets know what the missions of the SAC planes are. A lot of times they scramble up in their jets and fly wing-to-wing with our planes. I've seen pictures of that. Their pilots even communicate with ours. We've copies of that.

Q. Do we still use U-2s for reconnaissance?
A. No, and SAC doesn't fly the B-52s anymore either. Now the plane they use is the SR-71. It has unbelievable speed and it can climb high enough to reach the edge of outer space. The first time I came across the SR-71 was when I was reading a report of Chinese reaction to its penetration of their airspace. The report said their air defense tracking had located the SR-71 flying at a fairly constant pattern at a fairly reasonable altitude. They scrambled MIG-21s on it, and when they approached it, the radar pattern indicated that the SR-71 had just accelerated with incredible speed and rose to such a height that the MIG-21s just flew around looking at each other. Their air-to-ground communications indicated that the plane just disappeared in front of their eyes. I might tell you this as a sort of footnote to your mentioning of the U-2. The intelligence community is filled with rumor. When I got to Turkey, I immediately ran into rumors that Gary Powers' plane had been sabotaged, not shot down. Once I asked someone who'd been in Istanbul for quite a while and he told me that it was reported in a unit history that this had happened. The history said it had been three Turks working for the Soviets and that they'd put a bomb on the plane. I didn't read this history myself, however.

Q. You have explained how we are able to monitor Soviet air traffic to the extent indicated, but it's hard to believe that we could know where all their missile submarines are at any given moment.
A. Maybe so, but that's the way it is. There are some basic ways in which we can keep track of them, for example through the interpretation of their sub-to-base signals which they encode and transmit in bursts that last a fraction of a second. First we record it on giant tape drops several feet apart, where it is played back slowly so that we get the signal clearly. Then the signal will be modulated -- that is, broken down so we can understand it. Then the codes are

broken and we get the message, which often turns out to contain information allowing us to tell where they are.

Another way in which we keep track of these subs is much simpler. Often they'll surface someplace and send a weather message.

Q. But don't submarines go for long periods without communicating, maneuvering according to some pre-arranged schedule?

A. Actually, not very often. There are times during a war exercise or communications exercise when they might not transmit for a week or even longer. But we still keep track of them. We've discovered that they're like all Soviet ships in that they travel in patterns. By performing a very complicated, computerized pattern analysis, we are able to know where to look for a particular ship if it doesn't turn up for a while. The idea is that they revert from that pattern only in extreme emergency situation: but during such a situation they'll have to be in communication at least once. We know how many subs they have. And in practical terms, when one of them is not located, NSA units tasked with submarine detection concentrate all their energies on finding it.

Q. How do you know this? Did you ever have responsibility for submarine detection?

A. No. My information comes from two sources. First, the fact that there were analysts sitting right next to me in Karamursel who were tasked on subs. Second, I read what we called TEXTA. TEXTA means "technical extracts of traffic." It is a computer generated digest of intelligence collected from every communications facility in the world -- how they communicate, what they transmit, and who to. It is the Bible of the SIGINT community. It is constantly updated, and one of an analyst's duties is reading it. You've got to understand that even though each analyst had his own area to handle, he also had to be familiar with other problems. Quite often I would get through my operators base-to-base submarine traffic and I'd have to be able to identify it.

Q. The implications of what you're saying are very serious. In effect, it means that based on your knowledge there is no real "balance of terror" in the world. Theoretically, if we know where every Soviet missile installation, military aircraft and missile submarine is at every moment, we are much closer than anyone realized to a first-strike capacity that would cripple their ability to respond.

A. Check.

Q. How many NSA people were there at Istanbul and in the rest of the installations in Europe?

A. About three thousand in our operation. It would be hard to even guess how many in the rest of Europe.

Q. What were the priorities for gathering information on Soviet operations?
A. First of all, NSA is interested in their long-range bombing forces. This includes their rocket forces, but mainly targets on their long-range bombers. This is because the feeling is that, if there is conflict between us and them, the bombers will be used first, as a way of taking a step short of all-out war. Second, and very close to the bombing capabilities, is the location of their missile submarines. Next would be tasking generated against the Soviet scrambler, which is their way of communicating for all of their services and facilities. After this would be their Cosmos program. After those things like tasking their KGB, their air controllers, their shipping, and all the rest of the things tend to be on the same priority.

Q. All this time, the Soviets must be doing intelligence against us too. What is its scope?
A. Actually, they don't get that much. They aren't able to break our advanced computer generated scrambler system, which accounts for most of the information we transmit. They do a lot of work to determine what our radar is like, and they try to find out things by working on some of the lower level codes used by countries like Germany and the Scandinavian countries we deal with. Their SIGINT operation is run by the KGB.
The key to it is that we have a ring of bases around them. They try to make up for the lack of bases by using trawlers for gathering data, but it's not the same. They're on the defensive.

Q. What do you mean by that?
A. That they're on the defensive? Well, one of the things you discover pretty early is that the whole thing of containing the communist menace for expansion is nonsense. The entire Soviet outlook of their military and their intelligence was totally different from ours. They were totally geared up for the defense and to meet some kind of attack. Other than strategic capacities relating to the ultimate nuclear balance, their air capabilities are solidly built around defending themselves from penetration. They've set up the "forward" area -- our term for the so-called bloc countries of eastern Europe -- less as a launching pad into Europe than as a buffer zone. The only Soviet forces there are is air defense forces, security forces. Put it this way: their whole technology is not of an offensive nature, simply, they don't have the kind of potential for a tactical offensive that we do. They have no attack carriers, for instance.

Soviet ships are primarily oriented toward protection of their coasts. Actually they do have carriers of a sort, but they are helicopter anti-submarine carriers. Another thing: they have a lot of fighters, but hardly any fighter-bombers. They do have a large submarine force, but given the fact that they are completely ringed by the U.S., this too is really of a strategic nature.

Everything we did in Turkey was in direct support of some kind of military operation, usually something clandestine like over flights, infiltrations, penetrations. If all we were interested in was what they call an "invulnerable deterrent," we could easily get our intelligence via satellite. We don't need to have these gigantic sites in Europe and Asia for this.

Q. You mentioned a few minutes ago that one of NSA's main targets was the Soviet space program. What sort of material were you interested in?
A. Everything. Obviously, one of the things we wanted to know was how close they were to getting a space station up. We knew everything that went on in their Cosmos program. For instance, before I had gotten to Turkey, one of their rockets had exploded on the launching pad and two of their cosmonauts were killed. One died while I was there too. It was Soyuz, I believe. He developed re-entry problems on his way back from orbit. They couldn't get the chute that slowed his craft down in re-entry to work. They knew what the problem was for about two hours before he died, and were fighting to correct it. It was all in Russian, of course but we taped it and listened to it a couple of times afterward. Kosygin called him personally. They had a video-phone conversation. Kosygin was crying. He told him he was a hero and that he made a great achievement in Russian history and that they were proud and he'd be remembered. The guy's wife got on too. They talked for a while. He told her how to handle their affairs, and what to do with the kids. It was pretty awful. Towards the last few minutes, he began falling apart, saying, "I don't want to die, you've got to do something." Then there was just a scream as he died. I guess he was incinerated. The strange thing was that we were all pretty bummed out by the whole thing. In a lot of ways, having the sort of job we did humanizes the Russians. You study them so much and listen to them for so many hours that pretty soon you come to feel that you know more about them than your own people.

Q. While you were monitoring the Soviet Union what sort of intelligence would have been considered to be very important or serious?
A. In a way you do this almost routinely. That is, there are certain times that the activities of the targeted entity are of such an important nature that a

special type has to be sent out. It is called a CRITIC. This is sent around the world to a communications network called CRITICOM. The people in this network, besides NSA, are those in other intelligence or diplomatic capacities who might come across the intelligence of such importance themselves that the president of the United States would need to be immediately notified. When a CRITIC goes out, one analyst working alone can't do it, there is just too great a volume of material to correlate.

Q. What would be an example of something sent out as a CRITIC?
A. Well, one of the strangest I ever read was sent out by our base at Crete. One of the analysts traced a Soviet bomber that landed in the middle of Lake Baikal. He knew it hadn't crashed from the type of communications he monitored, and he thought they had developed a new generation of bombers able to land on water. It turned out to be a bad mistake because he neglected to remember that about three-fourths of the year this lake is completely frozen over. But actually this sort of thing is rare. Most CRITIC's are based on good reasoning and data. You work around the clock, sometimes for 30 hours at a stretch putting things together. These are the times that the job stops being routine. I guess that's why they have a say about the work in NSA: "Hours of boredom and seconds of terror."

Q. Did you ever issue a CRITIC.
A. Yes, several. During Czechoslovakia, for instance, when it became clear the Soviets were moving their troops up. We also issued a number of CRITIC's during the Mideast war of 1967.

Q. Why?
A. Well, I was part of an analysis team that was predicting the war at least two months before it began. I guess we issued our first CRITIC on this in April. We did it on the basis of two sources. One, we and the Crete station had both been picking up data as early as February that the Israelis had a massive build-up of arms, a massing of men and materiel, war exercises, increased level of Arab territory -- just everything a country does to prepare for war. Two, there were indications that the Soviets were convinced there was going to be a war. We know this from the traffic we had on diplomatic briefings sent down from Moscow to a commanding general of a particular region. And by April they had sent their VTA airborne, their version of Special Forces paratroopers, to

had sent their VTA airborne, their version of Special Forces paratroopers, to Bulgaria. Normally they're based in the Trans-Caucasus, and we knew from their contingency plans that Bulgaria was a launching point for the Middle East; and because some of these forces were being given to cram-courses in Israeli and Arabic languages.

Q. All this leaves the sequence of events that immediately preceded the Six Day War - the various countercharges, the U.N. pullout, the closing of the Straits -- still pretty obscure. Did NSA evidence clear this up?
A. No. Not really. But one of the things that confused us at first was the fact that until the last days before the war the Arabs weren't doing anything to prepare. They weren't being trained to scramble their air force. This is why there was a total chaos when the Israelis struck.

Q. How did the White House react to your reports about all this?
A. Well, in every message we sent out, we always put in our comments at the end -- there's a place for this in the report form -- and they'd say something like "Believe there is some preparation for an expected Israeli attack. Request your comments." They didn't exactly ignore it. They'd send back, "Believe this deserves further analysis," which means something like, "We don't really believe you, but keep sending us information." Actually, we all got special citations when the whole thing was over.

Q. Why didn't they believe you?
A. I suppose because the Israelis were assuring them that they were not going to attack and Johnson was buying it.

Q. You remember about the "Liberty," the communications ship we sent in along the coast which was torpedoed by Israeli gunboats? The official word at the time was that the whole thing was a mistake. Johnson calls it a "heartbreaking episode" in The Vantage Point. *How does this square with your information?*
A. The whole idea of sending the "Liberty" in was that at that point the U.S. simply didn't know what was going on. We sent it in close so that we could find out hard information about what the Israelis' intentions were. What it found out, among other things, was that Dayan's intentions were to push on to Damascus and to Cairo. The Israelis shot at the "Liberty," damaged it pretty badly and killed some of the crew, and told it to stay away. After this it got very tense. It became pretty clear that the White House had gotten caught with its pants down.

Q. What were the Russians doing?
A. The VTA airborne was loaded into planes. They took off from Bulgaria and their intention was clearly to make a troop drop on Israel. At this point it became pretty clear that we were approaching a situation where World War III could get touched off at any time. Johnson got on the hot line and told them we were headed for a conflict if they didn't turn those planes around. They did.

Q. Was it just these airborne units that were on the move?
A. No. There were all kinds of other action too. Some of their naval forces had started to move, and there was increased activity in their long-range bombers.

Q. What about this idea that Dayan had decided to push on to the cities you mentioned. What happened there?
A. He was called back, partly because of U.S. pressure, partly by people in the Israeli political infrastructure. He was somewhat chastened and never given back total control of the Army.

Q. How do you know this?
A. Like I said earlier, NSA monitors every government. This includes Tel Aviv. All the diplomatic signals from the capital to the front and back again were intercepted. Also at this same time we were copying the French, who were very much involved on both sides playing a sort of diplomatic good offices between Cairo and Tel Aviv. As far as Dayan is concerned, the information came from informal notes from analysts at Crete who were closer to the situation than we were. Analysts send these informal notes from one station to another to keep each other informed about what is happening. One of the notes I got from Crete said Dayan had been called back from the field and reprimanded. Obviously, by this time the Israelis were getting heat from the U.S.

Q. What did the Russians do after the situation cooled down a bit?
A. Immediately after the war -- well, not even afterwards, but towards the end -- they began the most massive airlift in the history of the world to Cairo and Damascus; supplies, food, and some medical equipment, but mostly arms and planes. They sent in MIG-21s fully assembled, fueled, and ready to fly in the bellies of their big 101-10s. At landing the doors would open, and the MIGs would roll out, ready to go. Also there was quite a bit of political maneuvering inside the Soviet Union right afterwards. I don't quite remember the details, but it was mainly in the military, not in the Politburo.

Q. We routinely monitor the communications of allies like Israel?
A. Of course.

What other sorts of things do we learn?
A. Practically everything. For instance, we know that the Israelis were preparing nuclear weapons at their development site at Dimona. Once, the U.S. Ambassador to Israel visited there. They had been calling it a textile plant as a cover, and when he went there they presented him with a new suit. It was a charade, you know. They didn't have warheads deployed then, but they were close to it. I'm sure they must have a delivery system in operation by now. It was said that American scientific advisors were helping them in this development. I mean it was said on the intelligence grapevine. I didn't know it for a fact. But this grapevine is usually fairly accurate.

Q. All the material you've been discussing is classified?
A. Almost all of it.

Q. Who classified it?
A. I did. Analysts in NSA did. In the Agency, the lowest classification is CONFIDENTIAL. Anything not otherwise classified is CONFIDENTIAL. But SIGINT data is super-classified, meaning that only those in the SIGINT community have access to it, and then only on a "need-to-know" basis. A lot of the stuff I'd work with was SECRET and TOP SECRET, which is the highest classification of all. But after a while it occurred to me that we classified our stuff only partly because of the enemy. It seemed like they were almost as interested in keeping things from the American public as the Soviets. Hell, I'd give top secret classifications to weather reports we intercepted from Soviet subs. Certainly the Soviets knew that data. I remember when I was in school back at San Angelo one of the instructors gave us a big lecture about classifying material and he said that it was necessary because it would only confuse the American people to be let in on this data. He used those exact words. As a matter of fact, I used those words when I was training the people who worked under me.

Q. How did you relate to our allies in intelligence matters?
A. I'll have to digress a moment to answer that. The SIGINT community was defined by a TOP SECRET treaty signed in 1947. It was called the UKUSA treaty. The National Security Agency signed for the U.S. and became what's called First Party to the Treaty. Great Britain's GCHQ signed for them, the

CBNRC for Canada, and DSD for Australia, New Zealand. They're all called Second parties. In addition, several countries have signed on -- ranging from West Germany to Japan -- over the years as Third parties. Among the First and Second Parties there is supposed to be a general agreement not to restrict data. Of course it doesn't work out this way in practice. The third party countries receive absolutely no material from us, while we get anything they have, although generally it's of pretty low quality. We also worked with so-called neutrals who weren't parties to the UDUSA treaty. They'd sell us everything they could collect over radar on their Russian border.

As it works out, the treaty is a one-way street. We violate it even with our Second party allies by monitoring their communications constantly.

Q. Do they know this?
A. Probably. In part, we're allowed to do it for COMSEC purposes under NATO. COMSEC, that's communications security. There's supposed to be a random checking of security procedures. But I know we also monitor their diplomatic stuff constantly. In England, for instance, our Chicksands installation monitors all their communications, and the NSA unit in our embassy in London monitors the lower-level stuff from Whitehall. Again, technology is the key. These allies can't maintain security even if they want to. They're all working with machines we gave them. There's no chance for them to be on par with us technologically.

There's the illusion of cooperation, though. We used to go to Frankfurt occasionally for briefings. The headquarters of NSA Europe, the European Security region, and several other departments in the SIGINT community are located there, inside the I.G. Farben building. We'd run into people from GCHQ there, and from the other countries. It was all fairly cordial. As a matter of fact, I got to respect the English analysts very highly. They're real professionals in GCHQ, and some are master analysts. They'll stay on the job for twenty-five or thirty years and learn a lot. The CGG is also located in the I.G. Farben building. That's the West German COMINT agency. Most of them are ex-Nazis. We used to harass them by sieg-heil-ing them whenever we saw them.

Once I briefed Hubert Humphrey at the I.G. Farben building. It was in 1967, when he was vice-president. The briefing concerned the Soviet tactical air force and what it was capable of doing. It was all quite routine, he asked a couple of pretty dumb questions that showed he didn't have the foggiest notion of what NSA was and what it did.

Q. But you said that you often sent reports directly to the White House.
A. Yes, I did. But the material that goes there is cleaned of any reference as to where the intelligence comes from. Every morning the President gets a daily intelligence summary compiled by the CIA. This information will probably contain a good deal from the NSA in it, but it won't say where it came from and the means used to collect it. That's how a man like the vice-president could be totally ignorant of the way intelligence is generated.

Q. So far we've been talking about various kinds of sophisticated electronic intelligence gathering. What about tapping of ground communications?
A. I'm not sure on the extent of this, but I know that the NSA mission in the Moscow embassy has done some tapping there. Of course all trans-Atlantic and trans-Pacific telephone calls to or from the U.S. are tapped.
Every conversation, personal, commercial, whatever is automatically intercepted and recorded on tapes. Most of them no one ever listens to, and after being held available for a few weeks, are erased. They'll run a random sort through all the tapes, listening to a certain number to determine if there is anything in them of interest to our government worth holding on to and transcribing. Also, certain telephone conversations are routinely listened to as soon as possible. These will be the ones that are made by the people doing an inordinate amount of calling overseas, or are otherwise tapped for special interest.

What about Africa? Does the NSA have installations there?
A. Yes, one in Ethiopia on the East Coast and in Morocco on the West Coast. These cover northern Africa, parts of the Mediterranean, and parts of the Mideast.

Q. Do they ever gather intelligence on African insurgents?
A. I went to Africa once for a vacation. I understood that there were DSUs, that's direct support units, working against Mozambique, Tanzania, Angola, those countries. These DSUs are in naval units off the coast. They are tasked with two problems: first, they copy the indigenous Portuguese forces; and second, they copy the liberation forces.

Q. Is the information used in any way against the guerillas?
A. I don't know for sure. But I'd be surprised if it wasn't. There is information being gathered. This intelligence is fed back to NSA-Europe, of course. It has

no strategic value to us, so it's passed on to NATO - one of our consumers. Portugal is part of NATO, so it gets the information. I know that U.S. naval units were DF-ing the liberation forces. That's direction finding. The way it worked was that the ship would get a signal, people on board would analyze it to see if it came from the guerillas, say, in Angola. Then they'd correlate with our installation in Ethiopia, which had also intercepted it, and pinpoint the source.

Q. Did you ever have any doubts about what you were doing?
A. Not really, not at this time. It was a good job. I was just 21 years old; I had a lot of operators working under me; I got to travel a lot -- to Frankfurt, for instance, at least twice a month for briefings. I was considered to be a sort of whiz kid, and had been since I'd been in school back in San Angelo. I guess you could say that I had internalized all the stuff about being a member of the elite that they had given us. I was advancing very rapidly, partly because of a runover in personnel that happened to hit at the time I came to Turkey, and partly because I like what I was doing and worked like crazy and always took more than other analysts. But, like I said earlier, I had developed a different attitude toward the Soviet Union. I didn't see them as an enemy or anything like that. Everyone I worked with felt pretty much the same. We were both protagonists in a big game-- that's the view we had. We felt very superior to CIA people we'd occasionally come in contact with. We had a lot of friction with them, and we guarded our information from them very carefully.

Q. Was there a lot of what you'd call esprit de corps *among the NSA people there?*
A. In some ways, yes; in other ways, no. Yes, in the sense that there were a lot who were like me -- eating, drinking, sleeping NSA. The very fact that you have the highest security clearance there makes you think a certain way. You're set off from the rest of humanity. Like one of the rules was -- and this was first set out when we were back at San Angelo -- that we couldn't have drugs like sodium pentothal used on us in medical emergencies, at least not in the way they're used on most people. You know, truth-type drugs. I remember once one of our analysts cracked up his car in Turkey and banged himself up pretty good. He was semi-conscious and in the hospital. They had one doctor and one nurse, both with security clearances, who tended to him. And one of us was always in the room with him to make sure that while he was delirious he didn't talk too loud. Let me say again that all the material you deal with, the code words and all, becomes part of you. I'd find myself dreaming in code.

And to this day when I hear certain TOP SECRET code words something in me snaps.

But in spite of all this, there's a lot of corruption too. Quite a few people in NSA are into illegal activities of one kind or another. It's taken to be one of the fringe benefits of the job. You know, enhancing your pocketbook. Practically everybody is into some kind of smuggling. I didn't see any heroin dealings or anything like that, like I later saw among CIA people when I got to Nam, but most of us, me included, did some kind of smuggling on the side; everything from small-time black marketeering of cigarettes or currency all the way up to transportation of vehicles, refrigerators, that sort of thing. One time in Europe I knew of a couple of people inside NSA who were stationed in Frankfurt and got involved in the white slave trade. Can you believe that? They were transporting women who'd been kidnapped from Europe to Mideast sheikdoms aboard security airplanes. It was perfect for any kind of activity of that kind. There's no customs or anything like that for NSA people. Myself, I was involved in the transportation of money. A lot of us would pool our cash, buy up various restricted currencies on our travels, and then exchange it at a favorable rate. I'd make a couple of thousand dollars each time. It was a lark. My base pay was $600 a month, and looking back I figure I made at least double that by what you'd call manipulating currency. It sounds pretty gross, I know, but the feeling was, "What the hell, nobody's getting hurt." It's hard for me to relate to the whole thing now. Looking back, it's like that was another person doing those things and feeling those feelings.

Q. All this sounds like a pretty good deal -- the job, what you call the fringe benefits, and all that. Why did you go to Vietnam?
A. Well, I'd been in Istanbul for over two years, that's one thing. And second, well, Vietnam was the big thing that was happening. I wasn't for the war, exactly, but I wasn't against it either. A lot of people in Europe were going there, and I wanted to go see what was happening. It doesn't sound like much of a reason now, but that was it.

Q. You volunteered?
A. Right, for Vietnam and for flying. They turned me down for both.

Q. Why?
A. Because of my classification. What I knew was too delicate to have me wandering around in a war zone. If I got captured, I'd know too much, that sort of thing. But I pulled some strings. I'd made what you'd call high-ranking

friends, you know. Finally, I got to go. First I had a long vacation -- went to Paris for a while and that sort of thing. Then I was sent back to the U.S. for schooling.

Q. What sort of schooling?
A. It was in Texas, near Brownsville. I learned a little Vietnamese and a lot about ARDF -- that's airborne radio direction finding. It was totally different from what I'd been doing. It was totally practical. No more strategic stuff, just practical analysis. I had to shift my whole way of thinking around. I was going to be in these big EC-47s -- airborne platforms they were called -- locating the enemy's ground forces.

After this first phase in Texas, I went to a couple of Air Force bases here in California and learned how to jump out of planes, and then up to Washington state to survival school. This was three weeks and no fun at all. It was cold as hell. I guess so we could learn to survive in the jungle. Never did figure that one out. We did things like getting dropped in the mountains in defense teams and learn E&E -- that's the process of escape and evasion. You divide the three-man team up into certain functions -- one guy scrounges for food, the other tries to learn the lay of the land, that sort of thing. We were out for two days with half a parachute and a knife between us. Strangely enough, we did manage to build a snare and catch a rabbit. We cooked it over a fire we built with some matches we'd smuggled. It was awful. We'd also smuggled five candy bars, though, and they were pretty good. Then we got captured by some soldiers wearing black pajamas. They put us in cells and tried to break us. It was a game, but they played it serious even though we didn't. It had its ludicrous moments. They played Joan Baez peacenik songs over the loudspeaker. This was supposed to make us think that the people back home didn't support us anymore and we'd better defect. We dug the music, of course. After this, I shipped out.

Q. How long were you in Vietnam?
A. Thirteen months, from 1968 to 1969.

Q. Where were you stationed?
A. In Pleiku, most of the time.

Q. Is that where the major intelligence work is done?
A. No, there's a unit in Da Nang that does most of the longer-range work, and the major unit is at Phu Bai. It's the most secure base in Vietnam. An old

French base, just below Hue and completely surrounded by a mine field. It's under attack right now. The people based there -- a couple of thousand of them -- will probably be the last ones out of Vietnam. I don't know if you know of this or not, but the first American killed in Vietnam was at Phu Bai. He was in NSA, working on short-range direction finding out of an armored personnel carrier -- you know, one of those vans with an antenna on top. It was in 1954. We were told this to build up our *esprit de corps*.

Q. So what kinds of things did you do there?
A. Like I said, radio direction finding is the big thing, the primary mission. There are several collection techniques used there. Almost all of them are involved with the airborne platforms I mentioned. They are C-47s, "gooney birds," with an E in front of the C-47 because they're involved in electronic warfare. The missions go by different names. Our program was Combat Cougar. We had two or three operators on board and an analyst, which was me. The plane was filled with electronic gear, radios and special DF-ing equipment, about $4 million worth of it, all computerized and very sophisticated. The technology seemed to turn over every five months. As a sideline, I might tell you that an earlier version of this equipment was used in Bolivia, along with infrared detectors, to help track down Che Guevara.

Q. So what would be your specific mission?
A. Combat Cougar planes would take off and fly a particular orbit in a particular part of Indochina. We were primarily tasked for low-level information. That is, we'd be looking for enemy ground units fighting or about to be fighting. This was our A-1 priority. As soon as we located one of these units through our direction finding, we'd fix it. This fix would by triangulated with fixes made by other airborne platforms, a medium-range direction finding outfit on the ground, or even from ships. Then we'd send the fix to the DEUS on the ground -- that's direct support units -- at Phu Bai or Pleiku. They'd run it through their computers and call in B-52s or artillery strikes.

Q. How high did you fly?
A. It was supposed to be 8000 feet, but we couldn't get close enough, so we went down to 3000.

Q. You hear a lot about seismic and acoustic sensors and that sort of thing being used. How did this fit into what you were doing?
A. Not at all. They weren't that effective. A lot of them get damaged when they land; some of them start sending signals and get stuck; others are picked up by the Vietnamese and tampered with. Those that come through intact can't tell civilian from military movements. Whatever data is collected from sensors on the trail and at the DMZ is never acted on until correlated with our data.

Q. How did the NVA and NLF troops communicate their battle orders? They seem to take us by surprise, while from what you said earlier the Soviet Union can't.
A. That's because there are no grand battle orders except in a few cases. Almost everything is decided at a low level in the field. That's why most of our intelligence was directed toward those low-level communications I've been talking about. NSA operations in Vietnam are entirely tactical, supporting military operations. Even the long-range stuff, on North Vietnamese air defense and diplomacy, on shipping in and out of Haiphong - the data collected at Dan Nang, Clark Air Force Base in the Philippines and somewhat in Thailand - is used in a tactical sense only. It's for our bombers going into North Vietnam. They aren't engaged in probing or testing the defenses of a targeted entity like in Europe. It's all geared around the location of enemy forces.

Q. What would be the effect if the U.S. had to vacate ground installations like the ones you've mentioned?
A. Well, we wouldn't have that good intelligence about the capabilities of the North Vietnamese to shoot our planes down. We wouldn't know what their radar was doing or could do, where their ground-to-air missile sites were, when their MIGs were going to scramble. We'd still be able to DF their troops in the field of course. That won't change until our Air Forces, including the airborne platforms I flew on, go out too.

Q. NVA and NLF troops must have some sort of counter-measures to use against operations like the ones you were in. Otherwise they wouldn't be as effective as they are.
A. Basically, you're right, although you shouldn't underestimate the kind of damage done by the strikes we called in as a result of our direction finding. To a certain extent, though, the Vietnamese have developed a way to counteract our techniques. Their headquarters in the North is known as MRTTH -- Military Region Tri Tin Hue. It is located on the other side of the Valley,

somewhere just into Laos. MRTTH has a vast complex of antennas strung all over the jungle. When they're transmitting orders, they play with the switchboard, and the signal goes out over a several-mile area from these different antennas. When you're up in one of these airborne platforms, the effect is like this: you get a signal and fix it. First it will be nine miles in one direction and then, say, twelve miles in another, and fifteen in another. We never found MRTTH. It's one of the high priorities.

Q. But you'd say that the sort of data you collected through DF-ing had some effect?
A. Right, generally; at least in locating field units. It also leads to some large actions. For instance, the first bombing that ever occurred from ARDF data occurred in 1968. There was an area about 19 kilometers southwest of Hue that we'd been flying over. Some of the communications we collected and pattern analysis that was performed on it indicated that there were quite a few NVA or VC units concentrated in a small area, about a mile in diameter. General Abrams personally ordered the largest B-52 raid that had ever taken place in Vietnam at that time. There was one sortie an hour for thirty-six hours, thirty tons dropped by each sortie on the area. Afterwards it was just devastated. I mean it was wasted. It was a long time before they could even send helicopters into that area to evaluate the strike because of the stench of burning flesh. On the perimeter of the area there were Vietnamese that had died just from the concussion. The thing of it was, though, there wasn't any way to tell which of the dead were military and which were civilian. It was pretty notorious. Afterwards it was called Abrams Acres. It was one of the things that began to turn me off to the war.

Q. You said that you're a-1 priority was locating enemy units on the ground. What were the other targets?
A. Mainly supplies. We tried, not too successfully, to pinpoint their supply capabilities. All along the Trail the Vietnamese have these gigantic underground warehouses known as "ban trams," where either men or supplies are housed. The idea is that in case of an offensive like the one that's going on now, they don't have to go north for supplies. They've got them right there in these ban trams, enough to last for a long time at a fairly high level of military activity. They had about 11 ban trams when I was there. We knew where they were within twenty-five or thirty miles, but no closer. I remember the first Dewey Canyon invasion of Laos. I flew support for it. It happened because the 9th Marines went in there to locate a couple of ban trams. Their general was convinced he was going to end the war. It was a real *macho* trip. He got called

back by the White House pretty quick, though, when his command got slaughtered.

Q. What about the idea of an invasion from the north. How does this equate with what you collected?
A. It doesn't. There's no invasion. The entire Vietnamese operation against Saigon and the U.S. is one unified military command throughout Indochina. Really, it's almost one country. They don't recognize borders: that's seen in their whole way of looking at things, their whole way of fighting.

Q. But you made a distinction between VC and NVA forces didn't you?
A. There are forces we'd classify as VC and others as NVA, yes. But it was for identification, like the call signs on Soviet planes. The VC forces tended to merge, break apart, then regroup, often composed differently from what they were before. As far as the NVA is concerned, we'd use the same names they were called back home, like the 20th regiment. Hanoi controls infiltration, some troops and supplies coming down the Trail. But once they get to a certain area, MRTTH takes over. And practically speaking, MRTTH is controlled by the NLF-PRG.

Q. How did you know that?
A. We broke their messages all the time. We knew the political infrastructure.

Q. You mean that your intelligence would have in its official report that this MRTTH base which was on the other side of the Ashau Valley was controlled by the NLF?
A. Of course. Hanoi didn't control that area operationally. MRTTH controls the whole DMZ area; everything above Dan Nang to Vinh. The people in control are in the NLF. MRTTH makes the decisions for its area. Put it this way: it is an autonomous political and military entity.

Q. What you're saying is that in order to gather intelligence and operate militarily, you go on the assumption that there is one enemy? That the NLF is not subordinate to the North Vietnamese Command?
A. Right. That's the way it is. This is one thing I wish we could bring out. Intelligence operates in a totally different way from politics. The intelligence community generally states things like they are. The political community interprets this information, changes it, deletes some facts and adds others. Take the CIA report that bombing in Vietnam never really worked. That was common knowledge over there. Our reports indicated it. Infiltrations always

continued at a steady rate. But of course nobody back at the military command or in Washington ever paid any attention.

Q. What were some of the other high intelligence priorities besides locating ground units, MRTTH and the ban trams?
A. One of the strange ones came from intelligence reports we got from the field and copies from North Vietnam. These reports indicated that the NLF had two Americans fighting for them in the South. We did special tasking on that. We were on the lookout for ground messages containing any reference to these Americans; never found them though.

Q. When you were there in Vietnam did you get an idea of the scope of U.S. operations in Southeast Asia or were you just involved with these airborne platforms exclusively?
A. I was pretty busy. But I took leaves, of course, and I saw a lot of things. One thing that never came out, for example, was that there was a small war in Thailand in 1969. Some of the Meo tribesmen were organized and attacked the Royal Thai troops for control of their own area.

Q. What happened to them?
A. Well, as you know, Thailand is pretty important to us. A stable Thailand, I mean. CAS-Vientiane and CAS-Bangkok were assigned to put down the uprisings.

Q. What does CAS mean?
A. That's the CIA's designation. Three of our NSA planes were taken to Udorn, where the CIA is based in Thailand, and flew direct support for CIA operations against the Meos. We located where they were through direction finding so the CIA planes could go in and bomb them.

Q. You mean CIA advisors in Thai air force planes?
A. No. The CIA's own planes. Not Air America -- those are the commercial-type planes used just for logistics support. I'm talking about CIA military planes. They were unmarked attack bombers.

Q. What other covert CIA operations in the area did you run into?
A. From the reports I saw, I knew there were CIA people in southern China, for instance, operating as advisors and commanders of Nationalist Chinese commando forces. It wasn't anything real big. They'd go in and burn some villages, and generally raise hell. The Chinese always called these "bandit raids."

Q. What would be the objectives of these raids besides harassment?
A. There's some intelligence probing. And quite a bit of it is for control of opium trade over there. Nationalist Chinese regular officers are occasionally called in to lead these maneuvers. For that matter, there are also CIA-run Nationalist Chinese forces that operate in Laos and even in North Vietnam.

Q. Did you ever meet any of these CIA people?
A. Sure. Like I said, I flew support for their little war in Thailand. I remember one of the guys there in Vientiane that we were doing communications for, said he'd been into Southern China a couple of times.

Q. You got disillusioned with the whole Vietnam business?
A. Yes.

Q. Why?
A. Well, practically everybody hated it, everybody except the lifers who were in the military before Vietnam. Even after that wasting of the area called Abram's Acres that I told you about before, everybody else was really sick about it, but these lifers kept talking about all the commies we had killed.
For me, part of it was when we crashed our EC-47. We'd just taken off and were at about 300 feet and it just came down. We crash-landed in a river. We walked out of it, but I decided that there was no easy way to get me into an airplane after that. We got drunk that night, and afterwards I spent two weeks on leave in Bangkok. When I got back to Saigon I got another three days vacation in Na Trang. The whole thing was getting under my skin. I told them that I wasn't going to fly any more. And mainly they left me alone. They figured I'd snap out of it. But finally they asked me what my reasons for refusing to fly were. I told them that it was crazy. I wasn't going to crash anymore. I wasn't going to get shot at anymore, I was afraid. I told the flight operations director that I wasn't going to do it anymore. I didn't care what was done to me. Strangely enough, they let me alone. They decided after a few days to make me Air Force liaison man up at Phu Bai. So I spent the last three months up there correlating data coming in from airborne platforms. Like the one I'd flown in and sending DSU reports to the B-52s. It happened all of a sudden, my feeling that the whole war was rotten. I remember that up at Phu Bai there were a couple of other analysts working with me. We never talked about it, but we all wound up sending the bombers to strange places -- mountain tops, you know, where there weren't any people. We were just biding

our time till we got out. We were ignoring priorities on our reports, that sort of thing.

It's strange. When I first got to Nam, everybody was still high about the war. But by the time I left at the end of 1969, morale had broken down all over the place. Pot had become a very big thing. We were even smoking it on board the EC-47s when we were supposed to be doing direction finding. And we were the cream of the military, remember.

I loved my work at first. It was very exciting -- traveling in Europe, the Middle East, Africa, knowing all the secrets. It was my whole life, which probably explains why I was better than others at my job. But then I went to Nam, and it wasn't a big game we were playing with the Soviets anymore. It was killing people. My last three months in Nam were very traumatic. I couldn't go on, but I wasn't able to quit. Not then. So I faked it. It was all I could do. Now I wish I had quit. If I had stayed in Europe, I might still be in NSA. I might have re-enlisted. In a way, the war destroyed me.

Q. What happened when you mustered out?
A. Well, having the sort of credentials I had, I had my pick of a lot of jobs. Some ex-NSA people get jobs with private corporations. A lot of them run their own SIGINT operations. For instance, oil companies will have SIGINT against Middle East sheikdoms that have pretty primitive intelligence operations. But I didn't want to do this sort of thing. NSA offered me a nice civilian job. The CIA said they'd pay me a $10,000 bonus in two installments if I'd come to work with them -- $5000 on signing up, and $5000 at the end of two years. They said they'd give me a GS-9 rating -- that's about $10,000 a year -- and promote me to GS-11 in a year. But I didn't want any of it.

Q. Why is it you wanted to tell all this?
A. It's hard for me to say. I haven't digested it all; even though I've been out almost two years now, I still feel as though I'm two people -- the one who did all the things I've laid out and another, different person who can't quite understand why. But even being against the war, it's taken a long time for me to want to say these things. I couldn't have done it nine months ago, not even three months ago. Daniel Ellsberg's releasing the Pentagon Papers made me want to talk. It's a burden; in a way I just want to get rid of it. I don't want to get sentimental or corny about it, but I've made some friends who love the Indochinese people. This is my way of loving them too.

[End]

These Guys

Source: Columbia University, Butler Library, Microfilm, No. 3044, Ramparts v. 11. 1-12. July 1972 - June 1973. Call No. Fa612 (2nd of 2 rolls).

Transcription and HTML by JYA/Urban Deadline

Excerpt from *The Puzzle Palace,* James Bamford, Penguin, 1983, (paper), p.334

In August 1972 a twenty-five-year old former staff sergeant in the Air Force Security Service decided to bare his top secret soul to the magazine *Ramparts*. A latent Vietnam War protestor and former traffic analyst at listening posts in Turkey, West Germany and Vietnam, Perry Fellwock wove a tale of much fact and some fancy in a question-and-answer session with the magazine, using the pseudonym Winslow Peck. The Joplin, Missouri, native's claim that NSA was able to break all Soviet code systems ("We're able to break every code they've got"), was most likely an exaggeration, but the majority of the sixteen-page article was, unfortunately for the Agency, quite accurate. Once the magazine hit the stands there was little the red-faced officials of the Puzzle Palace could do except to hold their tongues in embarrassed silence. Prosecution, they must have reasoned, would only serve to confirm all that Fellwock had said.

Additional information on NSA electronic interception:
http://jya.com/echelon-dc.htm
http://jya.com/echelon.htm
http://jya.com/echelon2.htm
http://jya.com/stoa-atpc.htm
http://jya.compp08.htm
http://jya.com/pp09.htm
http://jya.com/pp10.htm

Date: Wed, 15 Apr 1998 00:31:58 +0100
To: ukcrypto@maillist.ox.ac.uk
From: Duncan Campbell, Duncan@mcmail.com.
Subject: The discovery of global sigint networks: the early years, part 2

Ramparts, in 1972, was indeed the starting point. Sadly, many subsequent reporters later confused what "Winslow Peck" [=Perry (not Peter) Fellwock. which *is* his true name] wrote about "keyword" interception of international telephone traffic.

The story from then on:

Early in 1976, Winslow came to London. I interviewed him at length and then carried out my own research on GCHQ. I then published an article in Time Out, June 1976, called the Eavesdroppers which did for GCHQ and the UK what Winslow did for NSA and the US. My co-author was another American journalist, a Time Out staffer called Mark Hosenball.

The Eavesdroppers was the first (and full) description of what GCHQ was and did. There had been no previous article, although World in Action had attempted a program in 1972.

GCHQ's directors were apoplectic. The more so because the combined efforts of the GPO (who tapped my phone from May '76 onwards), the Special Branch and MI5 (who followed MH and me around) revealed that we had actually got the article out *without* breaking the Official Secrets Act. I had done my research from open technical sources, and (!) telephone directories; Peck, as an American wasn't covered by the British law.

But they got even. Hosenball, an American, was declared a threat to national security and deported. Philip Agee, the famous whistleblower from the CIA, was added in to the deportation list.

Seven months later, I *was* arrested in the furor over their deportations together with another Time Out reporter, Crispin Aubrey. We had talked to a former British sigint operator, John Berry. The case became known as "ABC" after our initials. Over the coming two years, I was accused of having too much information and faced two counts of espionage as well as one of breaching section 2 of the Official Secrets Act (a law which was repealed almost ten years ago now). These counts totaled a potential sentence of 30 years imprisonment.

At Court 1 in the Old Bailey in October 1978, this disgraceful prosecution - which marked the high water point of MI5's manic campaigns against "internal subversion" - fell apart. The story has just recently been told in the delightful autobiography of Geoff Robertson QC, who was then my no. 2 lawyer. His book is called "The Justice Game." Maybe its time for me to write my own autobio . . .

Mrs. Thatcher put GCHQ firmly on the world map with the union ban, 5 years later. And now . . .

Philip Agee is married to a ballerina and lives in Germany.
Mark Hosenball is a reporter in Washington.
Perry Fellwock is a lobbyist in Washington.

Crispin Aubrey is an organic farmer in Somerset.
John Berry is a social worker in Somerset.
NSA and GCHQ are still listening.
And I'm signing off for now.

At 13/04/98, John Young wrote:

Peter Sommer noted recently that one of the earliest accounts of NSA global electronic interception was published in a 1972 Ramparts magazine article, which we offer for a bit of history:
http://jya.com/nsa-elint.htm (84K)
James Bamford, Duncan Campbell, Nicky Hager and others have confirmed and extended what was at the time viewed as the fanciful antiwar exaggeration of a young former NSA analyst, named Peter Fellwock, first known by the pseudonym Winslow Peck.
Bamford says in the Puzzle Palace that NSA elected to not prosecute Fellwock in the hope that no one would believe his astonishing claims of NSA, ELINT-ing friends and foes alike. Would anyone know where Peter Fellwock is now? Assuming that the marvelous "Fellwock" is not a NSA-pseudo for "Peck."
These pages brought to you by Floating Point, Rembert Oldenboom, The Netherlands E-mail: rembert@euronet.nl to whom we give credit.

Subj: Re: Zweibrucken 1962-1964-65
Date: 9/25/02 5:13:39 AM Pacific Daylight Time
From   fehrs @ . . .
To: IdaReedBlanford@aol.com

Hi Trish,

My memory is lousy, but I checked some old e-mails and was contacted by a former 6901 A/1c Duren Moffet with whom I worked and he asked if I had known your brother. I told him no, too. I assume he was aware of your search. If not I have his email address. Below are several personnel I do remember from the 6901st.
At 12.28 PM 9/23/2002 -0400 you wrote:

Steve, Thanks so much for your information. The map is great.
I'm pretty familiar with the 6901st site you sent. Haven't had my cup of coffee yet, so I'll get back to you if I have questions.

Steve: I guess what I did is still classified, but I worked or sat behind a desk, side by side with Air Force analysts and Captn. Halverson I can picture, but I don't believe he worked in Ops. He was in charge of the barracks area and all the non-Ops responsibilities. I may be wrong, but that's how I remember it. The other two names do not ring a bell.

On the Ops side or building behind the barbed wire, I worked for USAF Major "stormy" Webber. Later, USN Lt. John Gassner replaced Maj. Webber. Some of the Airmen that I worked with in Ops were: Duren Moffet, A/1C Chuck Baker who married a German girl, A/1C Curtis Coslow, A/2C Addison (don't remember first name), T/Sgt Ramond (sp?) who was married, A/1C Reed (can't remember first name), a friendly, big A/2C first name Chester or "Chet," A/2C Dave Welser (sp?) who had an old Porsche, A2/C Kennedy (sorry can't remember first name). Two other wonderful USAF guys who were roommates in the barracks for a long time were A/2C "Junior" Desist who came from WVA, and S/Sgt Joseph Cooper who was from NC. These two worked in one of the OPS buildings but not with me, i.e., had other classified duties elsewhere in Ops.

These Guys

I received an email last year from a Phil Conrad who served at the 6901; I think he saw my name on one of the websites. He knew Lt. Gassner, USN. I didn't remember Phil Conrad.

I may have mentioned other 6901 personnel in my Memoirs or Letters. I also remember some of the Navy personnel - we all worked in the same area in Ops doing the same duties.

Navy didn't have those MOS numbers like the AF 202xxx etc. and I forget now which was which. The AG rating was for weather observers, but as I complained in the letters, we didn't work in our rate and had to take tests for advancement against people actually doing that job fleetwide. I never revealed exactly what we AGs did, but you might guess it had something to do with codes. *[Look for Steve Fehrs Letters or Memoirs on the Internet - very interesting - The Editor]*

I tried to contact NSA and NSGA re: describing in more detail what I did in the naval Security Group for the memoirs/Letters [on the internet], but got no answers and decided to be safe and say nothing. I must admit I don't remember a whole lot anymore about the job and there would be very little that's exciting. Whatever you can glean from the Letters is all I reveal, but it was mostly boring, mundane paper shuffling and looking for a needle in the haystack at Zwei., although there were anxious moments.
Take care,
Steve Fehr

Steve: We experienced some stressful situations during the height of the Cold War and believed, as my one letter indicated, that the Russians might start a war. If they didn't then our own Gen. Curtis Lemay might. Dr. Strangelove time. We still had alerts in '62 as the Berlin Crisis of '61 lingered, the Russians were still testing nuclear weapons (so were we), the Cuban Missile Crisis almost got out of hand and probings of air space by each side continued. . . .

Hi again,
I meant to tell you in my previous e-mail: Our son was in the US Army for fifteen years (his wife made him get out with only five more to go for retirement! all for the sum of $40,000.) Well, anyway, our son served, I

remember correctly, in: 1st Armored Division; 2nd Armored Div.; 3rd Armored Div; 7th Army.

He had a NRAS - …….. -

a TS/F clearance TSBIG Authenticator

Fulda Gap

E/W German Border.

The main thing I'm trying to say is that he went all the way from wherever he was in Germany (served six years Germany-Field Artilleryman) to Berlin wall, where hundreds of people were tearing it down. Guess who has a nice chunk of the Berlin Wall - yes, ME!

Such a good son. He lives in Kentucky and is an owner-over-the-road trucker.

Trish

Steve was, at this point in time, working on a book interviewing Appalachian Trail hikers. The working title, "Off the AT in Duncannon, PA 2002" 250 page dialogue with hikers containing over 300 photographs. Thousands start this adventure but only several hundred finish, because of the extremes of weather and terrain, swarms of insects, and risk encounters with rattlers, bears and a variety of wild critters. I gave him some advice and some publishing companies who might be interested in his book, which is told in dialogue - an interesting presentation. Wish you well with your book, Steve! and thanks for serving in the USAFSS.

Below are a few "6900th Anecdotes" from J. Fortin, who couldn't manage to make a story from one of them, but said to me, go ahead and use some of them - perhaps they will add to your book. So here goes.

6900th ANECDOTES
By J. Fortin

Official Anecdotes:

*Weekly burn bag detail. (Shredders were not in use yet in 1958-1961). All the offices would bring in their burn bags nightly to be stored in the secured room that I worked in along with T/Sgt. Steve Duncan. Weekly the officer in charge of our office (Capt. Corcoran) and I would take all the burn bags to the incinerator in the basement of the IG Farben building. We would keep a watch on the German national who processed the bags. The funny part of this story is that, I had a .45 that I was supposed to use in case of someone trying to take the bags, etc. I never shot a .45 and it was unloaded!

*Packing electronic parts and making sure that nothing rattled in the packages that were sent via diplomatic pouch to the American embassy in Moscow and I believe the one in Warsaw. The codenames were "Glasshouse" and "Doghouse." Captain Corcoran and I would take these pouches to the National Security Agency office located on the 7th floor of the IG Farben building. The electronic parts were replacement parts for the COMINT operations taken place in the attics of the American embassies mentioned above.

*It was the policy to close the window drapes when working on classified data in the Top Secret Control office. This day the drapes were open and I happened to be looking out the window when two documents floated down. Knowing that CIA, NSA, & ASE were located on floors above us, I went outside to investigate. To my surprise the two documents were stamped "Top Secret." I called a lady I knew in the CIA office and told her what I found. I took the documents to her and she later related that someone at CIA had the window open with a fan going and the documents just flew out without their knowledge!

*The elevators (pater noster as they were called) in the IG Farben building were the old wooden type without doors that just kept going around and around without ever stopping. It was quite tricky to get on and off at your designated floor. It was a standard trick to play on newcomers to take them to the top floor and tell them on the way up, that once we reached the top the elevator would tip upside down in order to begin the downward trip. Of course that was not the case, it would just go across when it reached the top and begin its downward trip. The expression on their faces in anticipation of reaching the top was priceless.

*The following has nothing to do with the 6900th SW, but it is indirectly related to Larry Tart's book, "The Price of Vigilance." A lady mentioned in regards to a CIA document later became my wife (now ex-wife). While we were back in the U.S., Francis Gary Powers was assigned to her office at CIA Hqs. in McLean, VA after his release from Russia (cannot remember which year in the 60's). I had the honor of meeting him at a cocktail party in Alexandria, Virginia.

*Another side note FYI. Prior to USAFSS, I was stationed at Myrtle Beach AFB, SC. My duties there were in the Administrative section of the 354th Fighter Day Wing 9TAC) in the headquarters building. My office was next to the base commander, Colonel "Gabby" Gabreski, the famous WW II fighter pilot ace. He sure was a character and always had that cigar in his mouth. His picture is in the Air & Space museum in D.C.

It is clear to me that I have John Galt's (JG's) permission to use this e-mail he sent to me, enticing me to make comments on USAFSS Lite. When I did go back to commenting I was brought down, again, by the few who commented on the site. I'll never know what I did to "dishonor" them enough to tell me to "take a bottle of pills" and call me "brain dead" among many other things. I suppose, I must have hit a nerve somewhere on that site, and they didn't want me to go any further. Well, I allowed them to affect me and put me into a state of depression that was very deep . . . but as Jim Roper, author of QUOTH THE RAVEN says in his book: NEVERMORE. Here's JG's e-mail to me.

Subj: "Trish"
Date: 1/29/2004 3:45:58 PM Pacific Standard Time
From: John_Galt@muchomail.com
To: IdaReedBlanford@aol.com

Trish -

I'm writing this to you, but I may also write it for everyone else to read on the dumb Yahoo site. Or you should feel free to cut, paste it, and post it if you desire. My entire career in USAFSS I was trick trash. A rack sittin' line dog working rotating shifts: daze, swings, and midz. I worked with a lot of intelligent (?) guys (later on some girls) with a lot of time on their hands, a lot of boredom, and little practical outlet for that pent-up intellect. So here was the plan: Have a little fun anyway you could. And we did. It was pretty childish but it made the time go by. Now, 20, 30, 40 years later, there's a lot of water under the bridge for all of us. Without a doubt, most, if not all of us, have dealt with deaths of loved ones and friends, serious illnesses, family and marital problems, drinking problems, etc. Do I need to mention September 11th? Okay. Been there, done that and here's what I have left and what I have to offer: A sense of humor (yes perverted, juvenile, stupid, but I said I was USAFSS to the core didn't I?) and some dum war stories that prob mean nothing to no one. A small, little, minor, minute, escape from reality. To lighten up the day from the continual bad world news, or the moronic political fighting we are constantly bombarded with. So I will, or may, or may not, write some dum little story, or some scathing dum remark to something I read. And when I write this stuff Trish, I'm NOT a middle aged professional with a wife and 2 sons, I'm a 19 year old rack sitting puke putting a tail on the section analyst and making everyone laugh as we watch the digital clock, set to Greenwich Meantime tick away the minutes of our 8 hour shift. And while you were a squid, I invite you to post some humor, post some war stories, and share a little fun with us dum USAFSS pukes!

Cheers,

JG

THESE GUYS: John Giere and TS e-mail

Subj: Re: Phil Noland/SSGT/Ret/USAFSS/Zwei/
Date: 2/27/02 2:16:52 PM Pacific Standard Time
From: IdaReedBlanford
To: jwgiere@yahoo.com
BCC: TPUGH1@HOUSTON.RR.COM

Hello John,

Your name has been forwarded to me by Jon Horton and Tom Pugh. My name is Trish (Noland) Schiesser. I am the sister of Phil Noland who served at Zweibrucken with you. Would you be willing to tell me what you knew of my brother? I am sorry to say that he passed away in 1986 and is buried at the National Cemetery in Bourne, Cape Cod, Mass., not too far from our mother.
Phil became quite ill (mentally) in June/July 1963 while at Zwei., specifically after he returned from a 3 day TDY to England. He eventually disappeared from 6901st and his wife and two children, Sherry and Billy, on prox. 09 Jan '64.
Phil was found (several times).
It's a long story, but if you will return my e-mail I will tell you what happened.
It would be good to hear from you. I loved my brother a great deal, and I plan to write a book about him, along with some other USAFSS' men's stories, a piece by his daughter and a piece by his son (perhaps).
I look forward to hearing from you. My e-mail address is below.

God bless,
Trish

TRISH (NOLAND) SCHIESSER
LITERARY CONSULTANT/AUTHOR
E-MAIL: IdaReedBlanford@aol.com

Subj: Re: Phil Noland
Date   2/7/02 4:29:06 PM Pacific Standard Time

From: jwgiere@yahoo.com (John Giere)
To: IdaReedBlanford@aol.com

Trish,

Do you have any pics (-.jpg, -gif, etc) of your brother taken when he was at Zwei? I was there between June-62 and March-64. There were probably about 600 AFguys at the 6901st, working in two multi-storied brick buildings said to have once been part of a WWI German cavalry training school.

Dunno if Phil or his wife told you, but the 6901st was what was called a "second echelon" site; i.e., it served as something of an intelligence clearing house for the European and Central Asian areas, or from Bodo, Norway, to Peshawar, Pakistan. Peshawar was the location from which Gary Powers took off on his ill-fated journey over Russia. His U-2 was shot down and he went to the clink for a couple years, later to be exchanged for the Russian spy, Rudolf Ivanovich Abel.

Zwei was not the most pressure-filled place to work; i.e., with some exceptions, the work done there was not "real-time" and usually didn't require real-time reaction. But the guys (and a couple crackerjack lady officers) there were all conscientious and committed to the varied tasks addressed there.

Because security was hammered into all of us, it was pretty typical that a guy sleeping in a top bunk bed had no idea what the guy in the bottom bunk did there. We lived by the acronyms of the sections in which we worked. Some fifty of us worked in an area that might as well have been in the orbit of Pluto, so unrelated was our work to that done by 95% of the others at Zwei. Our section was called OSUP-21, another acronym standing for Operational Support . . . and God knows what the "-21" meant.

Jon Horton and Tom Pugh worked on another floor in another building.

I'm not sure if I knew Phil. I may be trying to wish a working relationship into existence. Pictures would help, as well as the names of others with whom he worked.

These Guys

Although the mission at Zwei was not one that wore people down, there were unusual events that occurred there. Our admin orderly was a SSGT who was married, living on the German economy, and an extremely low-key, well-liked guy. Came to work every day, was always pleasant, did his job, went home. One day he received orders to rotate (relocate) to the U.S. The poor guy simply caved in, had a complete breakdown, and was never again seen by us. Another kid, may be all of 21, broke down when his closest friend became engaged to a German girl. The kid went to the docs at Ramstein and confessed he was gay. So long, kid. An Army 2nd Lt was so depressed when his bar-girl sweetie dumped him, he marched in front of our barracks, put a .45 automatic in his mouth, and pulled the trigger. When our entire section was relocated, in March of 64, to San Antonio, one of our guys pleaded with the brass that returning to the US would be a financial hardship. He was making too much money at the casino tables in Baden Baden.

During the Cuban Missile Crisis, we got the most accurate news by tuning to the BBC on short wave. Despite all the sword rattling between Kennedy and Khrushchev, nothing would stop the 24-hr/day pinochle game that ran for two years in a 24-man barrack room known to all as the "Bay of Pigs." Crazy, fascinating stuff. If you have pics, please fwd to me. I might be able to equate the face to that window in time.

Subj: Re: Phil Noland/Matt Guzzetta/Fred Stassen
Date: 2/8/02 7:53:57 AM Pacific Standard Time
From: jwgiere@yahoo.com (John Giere)
To: IdaReedBlanford@aol.com

Got the pics and have stored them. Matt Guzzetta (last known e-mailmattguzz@pacbell.net) was in my shop, OSUP-21. He was from Vallejo, CA, and was very involved in car design. He bought an MG-TC . . . probably a 1947-49 model, in England, with the intent to ship it back to the US and sell it to pay tuition at the Los Angeles Art Center. The LA Center was, and remains, the premier industrial design breeding ground for the US and Japanese car companies. Matt finished school sometime around 1967-68, about the same time I got my Russian degree. I believe he went to work for a short period for the British motorcycle company, BSA (another acronym: British Sidearms Company). Lost track of him after that, as I went to work for Rockwell Int'l and moved around the US over a 30-year period. Found Matt's name and e-mail on the net a few months ago. Believe he works as an industrial designer for a guitar mfg company in the San Diego area. Haven't contacted Matt in all these years . . . but I will now, and will forward your letter and pics to him. Another name that might have popped up is that of Fred Stassen, a Russian analyst from Zwei. Last e-mail address for Fred was stassen@wwt.net. Fred is a commercial photographer (TV, books), living near Menominee, WI. He finished from the LA Art Center about the same time as Matt Guzzetta. Over the past decade, Fred has been in very dicy health, suffering from cancer. Last I heard from him, he was in remission, although he seemed weak and rather withdrawn. I'll get the info off to Matt today.

Editor's note: I did contact Fred Stassen and spoke with his wife and she said she'd get back to me after talking to Fred. Fred thought he might have known Phil, but wasn't sure. The next time I heard anything about Fred Stassen was that he'd passed away. I received a book he authored, from him, before his passing, and I received a lovely e-mail from his wife after his passing. He is missed by everyone.

Subj: Phil & UK TDY
Date: 2/12/02 12:31:51 PM Pacific Standard Time
From: jwgiere@yahoo.com (John Giere)
To: IdaReedBlanford@aol.com

A previous note received regarding Phil included the name of Matt Guzzetta as one who may have gone to England around the same time that Phil went TDY.

I sent Phil's pictures to Matt and spoke with him Monday about that period. He never went to the UK and did not know Phil. In the summer of 1963, he contracted with a British citizen to purchase a car in England, and have it shipped to Zweibrucken.

These Guys

This communication was to my brother's daughter, to pass on to her brother, Billy, since he cannot remember much about his father, in the beginning of his days.

Subj: (no subject)
Date   10/29/02 2:48:49 PM Pacific Standard Time
From: IdaReedBlanford
To: Phillip Noland's Daughter

Hi, hope this finds you fine.

Did Phil ever mention Menwith Hill? or have you ever heard the name?
I take it from your last e-mail of some time ago that you don't want to be involved in any way with this project, so I haven't been asking any questions, don't want to piss you off.
Here are some things I know: He was a 202, a traffic analyst who analyzed the Morse intercept of 292s to provide information to the Intelligence community on Russian activities in Europe. We know that he was stationed in Turkey and Germany, and that he apparently traveled to England on TDY. We know that 6901st was the European HQ for USAFSS, so can anticipate that Phil may have been involved in a somewhat more thorough and detailed analysis of this radio traffic than was possible at first echelon units.
This is the kind of dull, boring, tedious and extremely vital work most people like him did during the Cold War.
I wondered, by someone's suggestion, if he'd been an airborne backender, and whether he was a linguist. It would have been beneficial for him to have known some basic Russian in his field, so suspect he had some training in that area. But he probably was not fully trained in that area or he would have had orders assigning him to one of the recognized language schools, (Monterey, Syracuse, Indiana U, or Yale.) His papers don't tell everything, so he may well have had Russian training somewhere else, at some point in time.
He could have been involved in airborne intercept activities, but it is unlikely for several reasons. First, the mission of airborne platforms, in his day, is primarily VHF air-to-air, air-to-ground voice, ELINT and exotic comm. signals. Typically the only Morse intercept of interest is to monitor the PVO (Air Defense) radar tracking of their aircraft, so usually there is only a single Morse operator and analyst (preferably, a double threat individual who can

analyze his own traffic.) Second, the only European base at which USAFSS personnel were stationed was Rhine Main AB in Frankfurt, and Phil was never assigned there, that I know of, right now. For those reasons, the guess is that Phil wasn't airborne.

He could have been associated, either at Zwei or in Turkey, analyzing traffic after the mission, but it seems unlikely that he flew the missions. Many of them wished they could fly, but, like Phil, did important stuff on the ground, too.

What Phil did was important. Most of the guys would have liked to do things they didn't get to do - to have been involved in more aspects of the work -- to understand the big picture; for most, that never happened.

Phil was an Analyst; a damned good one, according to his papers. He was the vital interface in some operations. If he didn't fly around with wings on his chest, or intercept exotic radar signals, it doesn't matter. He still performed an important job, and in time, I am told, it will make sense.

There is so much to learn. So far, I've only met via e-mail several guys who actually knew Phil in Turkey-60-61. One sent me a photograph of Flt "C" of which Phil was Supv. Head, and Phil was in it. What a thrill to see him.

Perhaps this will be of some interest to Billy, [his son] that's why I'm writing it.

Bob and I went to Cape Cod and returned Wed. 23 Oct. We visited Phil's grave and my mother's grave at the National Cemetery on Bourne, Cape Cod, MA., went twice. I finally cried at my mother's grave. I understand what she went through a bit more this time, because of my own experiences as a 61 year old woman who has lost a daughter, etc.

I hope this information will be of some help to Billy in forming a picture of his father, since you said, in the beginning, that it would help. If you guys prefer I don't write to you, or don't write to you about any of this, your wish is my command. Just let me know.

I love you,

Trish (Auntie)

These Guys

This is the actual story of the destruction of the bridges that prompted the book and movie, "The Bridges of Toko Ri," written by James A. Michener. The story presents an historical perspective of the dangerous missions flown by Navy pilots and air crewmen during the Korean War. Thanks to Richard Florence and Richard Zeisel for providing this account by LCDR George Everding, USN (Ret) (Former AFCM and current member of the National Chief Petty Officer's Assn.) Every effort has been made to contact Capt. Paul N. Gray to obtain his permission; I owe him the courtesy of printing his story.

THE BRIDGES AT TOKO-RI: The Real Story by CAPT Paul N. Gray, USN, Ret, USNA '41, former CO of VF-54.

Recently, some friends saw the movie "The Bridges at Toko-ri" on late night TV. After seeing it, they said, "You planned and led the raid. Why don't you tell us what really happened?" Here goes. I hope Mr. Michener will forgive the actual version of the raid. His fictionalized account certainly makes more exciting reading.

On 12 December 1951 when the raid took place, Air Group 5 was attached to Essex, the flag ship for Task Force 77.

We were flying daily strikes against the North Koreans and Chinese. God! It was cold. The main job was to interdict the flow of supplies coming south from Russia and China. The rules of engagement imposed by political forces in Washington would not allow us to bomb the bridges across the Yalu River where the supplies could easily have been stopped. We had to wait until they were dispersed and hidden in North Korea and then try to stop them.

The Air Group consisted of two jet fighter squadrons flying Banshees and Grumman Panthers plus two prop attack squadrons flying Corsairs and Skyraiders. To provide a base for the squadrons, Essex was stationed 100 miles off the East Coast of Korea during that bitter winter of 1951 and 1952.

I was CO of VF-54, the Skyraider squadron. VF-54 started with 24 pilots. Seven were killed during the cruise. The reason 30 percent of our pilots were shot down and lost was due to our mission. The targets were usually heavily defended railroad bridges. In addition, we were frequently called in to make low-level runs with rockets and napalm to provide close support for the troops.

Due to the nature of the targets assigned, the attack squadrons seldom flew above 2000 or 3000 feet; and it was a rare flight when a plane did not come back without some damage from AA or ground fire.

The single-engine plane we flew could carry the same bomb load that a B-17 carried in WWII; and after flying the 100 miles from the carrier, we could stay on station for 4 hours and strafe, drop napalm, fire rockets or drop bombs. The Skyraider was the right plane for this war.

On a gray December morning, I was called to the flag bridge. Admiral "Black Jack" Perry, the Carrier Division Commander, told me they had a classified request from UN headquarters to bomb some critical bridges in the central area of the North Korean peninsula. The bridges were a dispersion point for many of the supplies coming down from the North and were vital to the flow of most of the essential supplies. The Admiral asked me to take a look at the targets and see what we could do about taking them out. As I left, the staff intelligence officer handed me the pre-strike photos, the coordinates of the target and said to get on with it. He didn't mention that the bridges were defended by 56 radar-controlled anti-aircraft guns.

That same evening, the Admiral invited the four squadron commanders to his cabin for dinner. James Michener was there. After dinner, the Admiral asked each squadron commander to describe his experiences in flying over North Korea. By this time, all of us were hardened veterans of the war and had some hairy stories to tell about life in the fast lane over North Korea.

When it came my time, I described how we bombed the railways and strafed anything else that moved. I described how we had planned for the next day's strike against some vital railway bridges near a village named Toko-ri (The actual village was named Majonne). That the preparations had been done with extra care because the pre-strike pictures showed the bridges were surrounded by 56 anti-aircraft guns and we knew this strike was not going to be a walk in the park.

All of the pilots scheduled for the raid participated in the planning. A close study of the aerial photos confirmed the 56 guns. Eleven radar sites controlled the guns. They were mainly 37 MM with some five inch heavies. All were positioned to concentrate on the path we would have to fly to hit the bridges. This was a World War II air defense system but still very dangerous.

How were we going to silence those batteries long enough to destroy the bridges? The bridges supported railway tracks about three feet wide. To achieve the needed accuracy, we would have to use glide bombing runs. A glide bombing run is longer and slower than a dive bombing run, and we would be sitting ducks for the AA batteries. We had to get the guns before we bombed the bridges.

There were four strategies discussed to take out the radar sites. One was to fly in on the deck and strafe the guns and radars. This was discarded because the area was too mountainous. The second was to fly in on the deck and fire rockets into the gun sites, discarded because the rockets didn't have enough killing power. The third was to come in at a high altitude and drop conventional bombs on the targets. This is what we would normally do, but it was discarded in favor of an insidious modification. The one we thought would work the best was to come in high and drop bombs fused to explode over the gun and radar sites. To do this, we decided to take 12 planes; 8 Skyraiders and 4 Corsairs. Each plane would carry a 2000 pound bomb with a proximity fuse set to detonate about 50 to 100 feet in the air. We hoped the shrapnel from these huge, ugly bombs going off in mid air would be devastating to the exposed gunners and radar operators.

The flight plan was to fly in at 15,000 feet until over the target area and make a vertical dive bombing run dropping the proximity-fused bombs on the guns and radars. Each pilot had a specific complex to hit. As we approached the target we started to pick up some flak, but it was high and behind us. At the initial point, we separated and rolled into the dive. Now the flak really became heavy. I rolled in first; and after I released my bomb, I pulled out south of the target area and waited for the rest to join up. One of the Corsairs reported that he had been hit on the way down and had to pull out before dropping his bomb. Three other planes suffered minor flak damage but nothing serious.

After the join up, I detached from the group and flew over the area to see if there was anything still firing. Sure enough there was heavy 37 MM fire from one site, I got out of there in a hurry and called in the reserve Skyraider still circling at 15,000 to hit the remaining gun site. His 2000 pound bomb exploded right over the target and suddenly things became very quiet. The shrapnel from those 2000 pound bombs must have been deadly for the crews serving the guns and radars. We never saw another 37 MM burst from any of the 56 guns.

From that moment on, it was just another day at the office. Only sporadic machine gun and small arms fire was encountered. We made repeated glide bombing runs and completely destroyed all the bridges. We even brought gun camera pictures back to prove the bridges were destroyed.

After a final check of the target area, we joined up, inspected our wingmen for damage and headed home. Mr. Michener plus most of the ship's crew watched from Vulture's Row as Dog Fannin, the landing signal officer, brought us back aboard. With all the pilots returning to the ship safe and on time, the Admiral was seen to be dancing with joy on the flag bridge.

From that moment on, the Admiral had a soft spot in his heart for the attack pilots. I think his fatherly regard for us had a bearing on what happened in port after the raid on Toko-ri. The raid on Toko-ri was exciting, but in our minds, it was dwarfed by the incident that occurred at the end of this tour on the line. The operation was officially named OPERATION PINWHEEL. The pilots called it OPERATION PINHEAD.

The third tour had been particularly savage for VF-54. Five of our pilots had been shot down. Three not recovered. I had been shot down for the third time. The mechanics and ordnance men had worked back-breaking hours under medieval conditions to keep the planes flying, and finally we were headed for Yokosuka for ten days of desperately needed R&R.

As we steamed up the coast of Japan, the Air Group Commander, CDR Marsh Beebe, called CDR Trum, CO of the Corsair squadron, and me to his office. He told us that the prop squadrons would participate in an exercise dreamed up by the commanding officer of the ship. It had been named OPERATION PINWHEEL. The Corsairs and Skyraiders were to be tied down on the port side of the flight deck; and upon signal from the bridge, all engines were to be turned up to full power to assist the tugs in pulling the ship along side the dock.

CDR Trum and I both said to Beebe, "You realize that those engines are vital to survival of all the attack pilots. We fly those single engine planes 300 to 400 miles from the ship over freezing water and over very hostile land. Overstressing these engines is not going to make any of us very happy." Marsh knew the danger; but he said, "The captain of the ship, CAPT. Wheelock, wants this done, so do it!"

As soon as the news of this brilliant scheme hit the ready rooms, the operation was quickly named OPERATION PINHEAD and CAPT. Wheelock became known as CAPT. Wheelchock.

These Guys

On the evening before arriving in port, I talked with CDR Trum and told him, "I don't know what you are going to do, but I am telling my pilots that our lives depend on those engines and do not give them more than half power; and if that engine temperature even begins to rise, cut back to idle." That is what they did.

About an hour after the ship had been secured to the dock, the Air Group Commander screamed over the ships intercom for Gray and Trum to report to his office. When we walked in and saw the pale look on Beebe's face, it was apparent that CAPT. Wheelock, in conjunction with the ship's proctologist, had cut a new aperture in poor old Marsh. The ship's CO had gone ballistic when he didn't get the full power from the lashed down Corsairs and Skyraiders, and he informed CDR Beebe that his fitness report would reflect this miserable performance of duty.

The Air Group Commander had flown his share of strikes, and it was a shame that he became the focus of the wrath of CAPT. Wheelock for something he had not done. However, tensions were high, and in the heat of the moment, he informed CDR Trum and me that he was placing both of us and all our pilots in hack until further notice; a very severe sentence after 30 days on the line.

The Carrier Division Commander, Rear Admiral "Black Jack" Perry a personally soft and considerate man, but his official character would strike terror into the heart of the most hardened criminal. He loved to talk to the pilots; and in deference to his drinking days, Admiral Perry would reserve a table in the bar of the Fujia Hotel and would sit there drinking Coca cola while buying drinks for any pilot enjoying R&R in the hotel.

Even though we were not comfortable with this gruff older man, he was a good listener and everyone enjoyed telling the Admiral about his latest escape from death. I realize now he was keeping his finger on the morale of the pilots and how they were standing up to the terror of daily flights over a very hostile land.

The Admiral had been in the hotel about three days; and one night, he said to some of the fighter pilots sitting at his table, "Where are the attack pilots? I have not seen any of them since we arrived." One of them said, "Admiral, I thought you knew. They were all put in hack by the Air Group Commander and restricted to the ship." In a voice that could be heard all over the hotel, the Admiral bellowed to his aide, "Get that idiot Beebe on the phone in 5 minutes;

and I don't care if you have to use the Shore Patrol, the Army Military Police or the Japanese Police to find him. I want him on the telephone NOW!"

The next morning, after three days in hack, the attack pilots had just finished marching lockstep into the wardroom for breakfast, singing the prisoners song when the word came over the loud speaker for Gray and Trum to report to the Air Group Commander's stateroom immediately. When we walked in, there sat Marsh looking like he had had a near death experience. He was obviously in far worse condition than when the ships CO got through with him. It was apparent that he had been worked over by a real pro.

In a trembling voice, his only words were, "The hack is lifted. All of you are free to go ashore. There will not be any note of this in your fitness reports. Now get out of here and leave me alone."

Posters saying, "Thank you Black Jack" went up in the ready rooms. The long delayed liberty was at hand.

When writing about this cruise, I must pay homage to the talent we had in the squadrons. LTJG Tom Hayward was a fighter pilot who went on to become the CNO. LTJG Neil Armstrong, another fighter pilot who became the astronaut who took the first step on the moon. My wingman, Ken Shugart, was an all-American basketball player and later an admiral. Al Masson, another wingman, became the owner of one of New Orleans' most famous French restaurants. All of the squadrons were manned with the best and brightest young men the U.S. could produce. The mechanics and ordnance crews who kept the planes armed and flying deserve as much praise as the pilots for without the effort they expended, working day and night under cold and brutal conditions, no flight would have been flown.

It was a dangerous cruise. I will always consider it an honor to have associated with those young men who served with such bravery and dignity. The officers and men of this air group once again demonstrated what makes America the most outstanding country in the world today. To those whose spirits were taken from them during those grim days and didn't come back, I will always remember you.

PRESIDENT VISITS TROOPS IN COMBAT ZONE
By William C. Grayson

I'm guessing that an overwhelming majority of Vietnam veterans viewed the President's Thanksgiving visit to US troops in Iraq in very positive terms. For some TSN alumni, this recent visit brings back a fading memory that still forces a smile for those who remember a similarly historic presidential trip.

Back in October 1966, a strong rumor rippled through the print and broadcast media that LBJ would visit US troops in-country in Vietnam. The news stories were attributed to anonymous government sources with a caution that any presidential itinerary would naturally be very "close hold" to protect the President's safety.

The mission of my unit, Det. 5 of the 6922nd Security Wing, USAF Security Service, was to intercept and analyze USAF communications throughout Vietnam and to report detected security breaches along with corrective recommendations. Sitting in a special security compound in the shadow of 7th AF headquarters, we were a largely autonomous detachment in the sense that we selected and prioritized our own signals collection targets and issued our security reports directly to 7th AF headquarters elements and tactical units. Having brought with me to Vietnam some experience in producing intelligence from the analysis of foreign VIP travels, I redirected some radio and telephone intercept coverage and asked the listening traffic analysts to look for any indications of a presidential visit, concentrating especially on any attempts to "talk around" the subject in vague or masked terms.

On 25 October 1966, one of Det.5's analysts intercepted a flight plan addressed to the Saigon Air Route Traffic Control Center* for a C-141 flying on 26 October from Clark AB, in the Philippines, to Cam Ranh Bay, on South Vietnam's coast. Transport flight plans to major USAF bases in-country from Clark were unremarkable with many bound for Cam Ranh Bay. The Security Service analyst, however, thought the C-141's tail number looked familiar and researched it in an aircraft card file that served as a database in the days before personal desktop computers. Sure enough, there was recent history of this particular aircraft supporting presidential travel, carrying the President's armored limousine. From this little tidbit, it seemed likely that the rumored visit might occur on the 26th at Cam Ranh Bay. We wrote a "Transmission Security Analysis Report," suggesting that LBJ was possibly going to Cam Ranh Bay on the 26th, and sent it at IMMEDIATE precedence to 7th AF, PACAF, and to various USAFSS units and analysis centers.

Next day, on the 25th, we intercepted a telephone call from the Chief of Staff of the USAF, himself, to the Commander 7th AF, a hundred yards from where we were working. Clearly, our TSAR of the 24th hit the bull's-eye and the Chief of Staff had been briefed. I personally replayed the taped call several times; the Chief of Staff was obviously mightily annoyed. He chewed-out the Commander 7th AF in unkind words and instructed him to find out who had compromised the presidential visit and to hang two of his private anatomical features "from London Bridge."

I knew what the right thing to do was but my autonomy and the great distances that separated me from my Security Service chain of command made me feel somewhat lonely in that moment. I was also keenly aware that I dared not discuss the scenario over a plaintext telephone with my commander in the Philippines or my ops boss in Hawaii. So I conferred with the Air Force Special Security Officer/7th AF, who owned the compound we worked in. The AFSSO, thought I should let the matter lie and not rattle the Chief of Staff's cage. I think he used the word "suicide" in his guidance.

Undeterred, I released a TSAR Follow-Up Report that said the suspected presidential visit to Cam Ranh Bay on the 26th was confirmed and I identified the source. Local predictions of my certain gruesome execution abounded. But there was dead silence from all quarters. No one at any level of authority ever said a word to Det. 5 about it.

Next day, LBJ and General Westmoreland met at Cam Ranh Bay as planned, just as we had reported. As a memento, the troops of Det. 5 gave me a wood-carved turtle with a little plaque that reads: "The turtle only makes progress when his neck is sticking out." That turtle has shared my many offices since 1966.

---

* It wouldn't be till 1967, during a Purple Dragon OPSEC assessment of why B-52 Arc Light bombing missions were generally unsuccessful, that I discovered B-52 flight plans from Guam to South Vietnam were being filed with the Saigon ARTCC in compliance with rules of the International Civil

Aviation Organization (ICAO). As a routine ICAO procedure, Saigon was relaying those B-52 flight plans to its counterpart ARTCC in Hanoi, hours before the B-52s were over their targets. This anecdote serves as the most repeated example for explaining the OPSEC methodology.

EAR ON THE VIETNAM WAR
Securing USAF Tactical Air Communications
By William C. Grayson CSSP, OCP

[Copyright Shefford Press. All rights reserved. Reprinted with permission. The opinions of the author do not necessarily represent the Department of Defense or other government agencies].

Introductory Note: One of the costly lessons learned during the Vietnam War led the Air Force to broadly apply automated security to its tactical communications. Today, cryptography is routinely specified for new USAF communications systems. The old Air Force Security Service was instrumental in leading this advance, a critical force multiplier contributing to astounding air supremacy in the Gulf War, the Balkans and over Afghanistan.

In late 1965, I was an Air Force Captain assigned to the National Security Agency at Fort Meade as a Cryptologic Staff Officer. At the time, I was chief of a special Research Section, responsible for term (as differentiated from immediate) intelligence analysis and reporting of a very high priority foreign target. The work was narrowly specialized and I was the only USAF member assigned in the all-civilian branch to which my section was assigned. When my assignment to Detachment 5, 6922 Security Wing of the old USAF Security Service arrived that fall, my civilian NSA managers sought to have my assignment there extended but I was already completing a 4th year extension and HQ USAF non-concurred. It took two full days to debrief me from all the special security accesses I held.

In July 1966, I reported to Tan Son Nhut AB as commander of a 40-man detachment, working within the special security compound next to the 7th Air Force Headquarters building. Like me, all the troops in the detachment had been drawn from foreign intelligence assignments around the world and brought with them to Tan Son Nhut a wealth of detailed but useless information about various foreign air forces. Useless because Det. 5 was a Counterintelligence unit having among its missions Communications Security (COMSEC) intercept and analysis of USAF and joint forces communications for insecurities. Basically, the "insecurities" we listened for were compromises of classified information which, in a combat environment, could get people killed.

During the Vietnam era, the USAF had no specific technical training program for COMSEC analysts and staffed its COMSEC units with intelligence officers and airmen, who both collected and analyzed the intercepted traffic. My own background, at the time, consisted of eight years of USAF service, including an intensive training course in radio traffic analysis, three years in the UK as a flight commander at RAF Chicksands, and the NSA assignment. Among the detachment's COMSEC staff, the combined knowledge of our own Air Force was sparse. Although the analysts were suddenly assigned to "an English language problem," which should have simplified their task, we struggled with such basics as major USAF command structures and subordinations; aircraft types and variants, USAF tactical weapons, security classification policy, and - most importantly - elementary communications infrastructure and the tactical air command and control process.

Maximizing the complexity of our situation was our lonely uniqueness: we were a detachment of a wing in the Philippines, which itself had no COMSEC mission, and reported operationally to HQ of the Pacific Security Region in Hawaii. Not only were we basically on our own in a combat zone, our "security violation" reporting mission led vast numbers of USAF people to see us as another "enemy." Not as bad an enemy as the VC/North Vietnamese, but bad enough to be denied important information and the support we needed for dealing with Air Force COMSEC issues throughout South Vietnam.

Our "trained-for-the-wrong-war" status put us into many difficult situations - some comical and some highly stressful. I recall a team of analysts - having put their intelligence backgrounds behind them and trying to think in a USAF context - looking for a map location, "Phan Song" not realizing they had intercepted a friendly reference to a heavy radar supplied to the North Vietnamese by the USSR and catalogued as "FAN SONG" by NATO. The only part of my job - and a very small part - that I was immediately comfortable with was collecting information on the enemy SIGINT threat to 7th Air Force and briefing it to all the tactical units I could reach. (During the year I spent in-country, I briefed movie theaters full of troops at every base in South Vietnam at least once; a total audience of over 5000). US and South Vietnamese ground units had captured and turned-in many enemy documents containing USAF radio frequencies, callsigns and key fragments of intercepted voice traffic. News of the reality of this threat confirmed a listening enemy and was the most effective imperative of the detachment's security message.

I will always remember my own most stressful event as a defining moment in my maturation. It occurred less than a month after my arrival in-country, while every aspect of life there was still very much a confusing blur. I took a phone call from the HQ 7th Air Force Command Section, requesting that I come over to see the Chief of Staff, Brigadier General Franklin A. Nichols, right away. The only rationale our Detachment First Sergeant could come up with on such short notice, was that we must have been reported for having "acquired" a refrigerator destined for a neighboring unit. While our detachment analysts didn't know much about the US Air Force, they did know the sound of opportunity knocking and had a refrigerator down off a truck and hidden in one of our tent-billets while the driver was momentarily in the billeting office asking for the intended recipients. So I went over to General Nichols' office ready to plead ignorance and promise immediate cooperation in returning the misdirected refrigerator. But that's not what he wanted to talk about.

The general's aide took me in and I introduced myself. The Chief of Staff cut right to the chase. It seemed that the Operations Plan for 7th AF's newly organized Tactical Ops Control Center (TOCC) had been reviewed at Headquarters of the US Military Assistance Command, Vietnam (MACV) and a reviewer found a lack of meaningful COMSEC detail in Annex K, the Communications Annex. The comments that had come back to 7th AF from MACV suggested that an implementable plan was needed to prevent the compromise of classified target and air strike planning information being communicated among the TOCC, fighter wing operations, airborne Forward Air Controllers and aircrews aloft. General Nichols was hoping I could help. Thinking fast on my feet, I supposed that the detachment's senior NCOs would know what to do and so told the general I could handle it. "Good," he said. "Why don't you sit over there and write it up?" he suggested, gesturing to a table and chair in a corner of his office. He immediately returned his attention to a pile of papers in front of him, signaling clearly that he and I were through talking.

Seated at the corner table, I remember the grip of panic as I tried to think of a way to explain - in terms the general would understand - that all my USAF experience was in other disciplines and that I knew very little of USAF

COMSEC. Fortunately, I quickly recognized that as a path leading to a steep cliff and my mind cleared. Apparently, the general knew even less about the subject than I did and, I told myself, I really did know something I could use. Borrowing from earlier experience with someone else's tactical air force, I decided in real time that 7th Air Force needed to encode radio communications containing pre-strike details, such as target coordinates and time-over-target, with a manual code, if the time of transmission was earlier than an hour before time-over-target. My choice of an hour was completely arbitrary and based on nothing I knew to support it.

I wrote out the whole concept in three paragraphs with a #2 pencil on yellow paper. After reading it through a couple of times, it made sense to me so I walked it over to General Nicholas' desk. He looked up and I handed him the draft, saying something like, "General, here's what I think we need to do." The general looked at the paper, skimmed my very best penmanship in just a few seconds, and thanked me without asking any questions. I was as anxious to be out of his office as he obviously was to get back to whatever he was working on so I saluted and left. Walking back to our secure compound, I realized I had no carbon copy (remember carbon paper?) or photocopy and had no idea where my yellow paper was headed. (Later that day, when I called the general's aide, I was advised the draft had already been typed and would go down to MACV in downtown Saigon in the next courier pouch).

But before I made that phone call, I totally horrified the detachment's senior NCOs by what I had done. However, feeling operationally confident for the first time since setting foot in Vietnam, I called my Ops boss in Hawaii. Having had little more experience with USAF operations than I did, he really didn't understand what I was talking about but suggested authoritatively that I should have first called for back-up. He said I would receive a message ASAP with detailed instructions. My next call was to my principal customer, the COMSEC Officer of the 1964th Communications Group, which provided 7th AF's communications support. The COMSEC Officer, a first lieutenant with about two years' experience in teletype maintenance, also didn't know what I was talking about and seemed unfazed.

Several things clicked into place quickly in the next few days. My expected message from Hawaii arrived, dryly specifying the manual code appropriate for 7th AF's use and advised how it should be acquired. Next I had a very friendly phone call from the MACV COMSEC Officer in Saigon, who spoke to me as though he and I were in the same club. It was he who had rejected the TOCC's original draft. My handwritten draft had been typed, sent downtown, and retyped as three paragraphs of the Operations Plan, Annex K. When I later saw a copy of the signed-off plan, it was my first look at it in its intended context. No one had changed a word of my original draft except for adding the designator of the prescribed manual code.

With a head now two hat sizes bigger than before my encounter with the Chief of Staff, I went to see the TOCC Director and discussed the practical application of the "code" provisions of Annex K. We were in agreement that all pre-strike radio communications that disclosed both target location and time-over-target would be encoded if the transmission was to be made earlier than 60 minutes before bombs on target. We further agreed that there were flying safety implications of tactical aircrews trying to deal with the mechanics of decoding in the cockpit so TOCC controllers would wait till the planned strike was 59 minutes away before making air-to-ground transmissions. Pre-strike transmissions to distant ground controllers at the various deployed fighter wing bases, however, were to be encoded, if they met the early tasking criteria.

Distribution of the codebooks to the field took almost a month and were naturally met with stiff resistance by assigned users. We monitored numerous phone calls between the TOCC and fighter wing operations in which our COMSEC detachment was confirmed as "an enemy." We also heard the TOCC stand its ground, however, and since the pre-strike orders came from Headquarters, the fighter wings had no option but to comply. The brief training period was scary with our intercepted communications revealing significant levels of confusion, error and frustration. On the scheduled code D-Day, however, the secure targeting communications scheme went operational.

It was immediately obvious from our communications intercepts that the TOCC controllers were delaying release of all the pre-strike messages till minus 59 minutes. In the first week, not a single coded message was heard. As the delaying tactic became clearly recognized as sabotage, deep disappointment set in as we had gotten Saigon, Hawaii and Washington excited by the coming proposed great leap in tactical COMSEC. In the second week, however, we had an opportune break: we intercepted a pre-strike message released at minus 70 minutes in un-encoded plain English; somebody in the TOCC had screwed-up. We wrote that one up as a Transmission Security Analysis Report and sent it to a long list of addressees at IMMEDIATE precedence.

I personally walked the TSAR over to the Director of the TOCC and we had an unhappy discussion in which I revealed my disappointment at listening to his controllers circumvent the process. I asked the director if it might not be a good idea to bring the subject up with the Chief of Staff but he didn't think that was at all a good idea and said he'd redirect the controllers, making sure they knew the Security Service was listening. Over the next few days, we monitored a good effort among various controllers. Day by day, the number of encoded messages rose and increases in proficiency were obvious. There was still some confusion and some coding/decoding errors, including a pretty bad one that was blamed (although not confirmed) for a friendly fire incident that I feel guilty about to this day. But between Thanksgiving and Christmas 1966, a captured hand-written document came in from a destroyed enemy position that listed the frequency and call signs of a Da Nang fighter squadron, followed by code groups carefully transcribed by an enemy intercept operator in the phonetic alphabet he had heard. The captured document confirmed that the enemy was still intercepting USAF tactical fighter communications but were prevented by the code form identifying targets and times.

By the early part of 1967, the use of the code was routine. Very likely, controllers newly arrived in-country were told during first-day orientation that using the code was part of the job and so presented less resistance. Nevertheless, we still issued occasional TSARs. The high point of my Vietnam tour came in February, just days before my 30th birthday. A target and bombs on target time were revealed in a plaintext message almost two hours in advance. The TOCC's response to our TSAR noted that the tasked squadron at Phan Rang AB had already rejected the mission because of the compromise. From then forward, the TOCC self-policed itself by either canceling or rescheduling prematurely disclosed strikes.

Detachment 5, 6922nd Security Wing won an Air Force Outstanding Unit Award for 1967.

Ms. Trish Schiesser
THIRD SQUADRON MOBILE-ALASKA-ON ST. LAWRENCE ISLAND.
By Daniel L. Grimsley
CC: Keith Dodd, Dave Bush

Dear Ms. Schiesser:
I understand that you are collecting stories of fellows that were in the US Air Force Security Service. I am enclosing two from men that were in the 3rd Radio Squadron Mobile in Alaska on St. Lawrence Island in the early 1950's. St. Lawrence was a very isolated place and we had a tour of duty of one year. Sometimes we would go three weeks between mail calls and the weather was very harsh so you can imagine why the place left such a deep impression on those who served there.

The first story is by Keith Dodd, 120 Dodd Place, Boaz, AL 35957. As you can tell in his letter, he was one of the first Security Service guys to go to St. Lawrence. He went before the base was built. Later some nice accommodations were built for the troops. At the time of Dodd's crossing to the Island our relations with the Russians were very tense so you can feel the apprehensions the guys on the barge must have felt.

The second story is by one of the fellows, Dave Bush, who was on the Island with me. Dave had a good sense of humor and his write-up conveys the thoughts of many, if not all, of the fellows who served with him. I think it took a little time for all of us to adapt to civilization after being on the Island for a year.

I don't believe either of the two fellows would object to you publishing their tales but by copy of this letter I am giving them the opportunity to give you their thoughts.

I would be interested in learning more about your collection of stories of the USAFSS.

Sincerely,
Daniel L. Grimsley
    Copy: Keith Dodd,
           Dave Bush

DANIEL LAWRENCE GRIMSLEY

Born: 7 July 32
Graduated: Elizabethtown High School (NC) 1950
Joined US AIR FORCE 17 Oct 52
... Flight 1197 Lackland AFB, TX, Oct 52-Jan53
... 3412th Student Sq. Radio, Keesler AFB, MS, Jan 53 - Sep 53
... 3rd Radio Sq. Mobile, Flt B, St. Lawrence Island, AK Dec 53 - Oct 54
... 26 Radio Sq. Mobile (Later 6983 RSM) March AFB, CA, Dec 54-Oct 56
... Discharged Active Duty 16 Oct 56 (4 years inactive duty)
Worked in paper mill Oct 56-Sep 57
NC State College (University) 1957 - 1961
Married Jean Moore Jan 1960
Graduated NC State BS Forest Management May 61
US Forest Service, Holly Springs, MS 1961-1963
US Army Corps of Engineers, Boydton, VA, 1963 - 1969
US Army Corps of Engineers, Wilmington, NC, 1969-1994
Retired 31 Dec 1994
Since retirement: Farm, garden, forestry, and volunteer work.
Two daughters: Laura, Chemical technologist, Wilmington, NC and Amy, Flight attendant, American Airlines, Ft. Lauderdale, FL

28 Feb 2004

Dear Dan (From Keith Dodd)

It was a joy to hear from you and to receive the bits of information related to long-time-ago experiences and memories. I recently had breakfast with Milan Davenport, and he had briefed me on your interest and project of the history of the 3rd RSM. My info is piece-meal - my memory is sometimes fuzzy (Did it really happen this way?) but maybe I can add a piece or two to your bigger picture. I hope so!

I served with the USAF from Feb 1949 to June 1954. During this time the AF was making the transition from the Army Air Corps to the USAF. We were first issued the green uniforms and had Army rank designations until 1951-52 or there abouts. (We "old timers" were allowed to wear the green as long as it was presentable even after the Blue became the official uniform). I was among the first class of enlisted AF to attend the Army Language School at Monterey, Calif. I think there were about fifty that started the Russian Course - all washed out except for about a dozen of us. Some of us who graduated should have washed out, but they had to graduate somebody - and they figured that I had tried. The newly formed Security Service was desperate for linguists and I was one of the early assignees to the Hqrs then stationed at Brooks AFB in San Antonio (moved to Kelly AFB in 1953).

I think it was in July 1950, a class mate from ALS, Vincent V. Dean and I, along with two CW operators whose names I don't remember, were sent to Alaska for 45 days to see if we could hear anything Russian. The Hqs of 3rd RSM was already in place at Elmendorf (consisting of a ring of 8-man Quonset Huts with a makeshift latrine in the middle). As far as I know, there was no intercept activity being conducted at that time. We picked up a couple of Halicrafter receivers and lugged them to several different sites in the Nome - Marks AFB area.(Now, we did fly to Nome and had a support crew to set up our antennaes.) After a month of C-Rations, they sent us back to Brooks AFB. The Colonel at the briefing was not real impressed that the best Russian that we could hear was actually our Voice of America broadcasts. To tell the truth, at that time, we really didn't know what we were looking for.

Back in San Antonio, I was the envy of the barracks. I'd had a 45 day vacation in Alaska - in the summer time. By November, after many briefings on what we were looking for - a larger crew of us were sent to Alaska, PCS, to establish Det B, 3rd RSM at Nome. As you know, the place looked and felt different in Nov. than in August, and somehow the crew felt that I was somehow to blame for the whole idea because I had been there earlier.

Shortly after we got Det B up and running, the Commanding General of the Alaskan Air Command paid us a surprise visit. The guard wouldn't let him in our operations room - and three stars sat and steamed in our latrine while we got his clearance through 3rd RSM Hqs at Anchorage. Later the guard was commended but it was awkward for awhile. The general noted that we did not have a security fence around our operations and gave us like four days to get one up. By then, it's 20 degrees below and covered with snow. The building of the fence is another story, but we did build a fence. We couldn't dig post holes, so we held those 10-12 ft. posts up vertical and poured water around them until they stood by themselves and tacked wire strand after strand. It would have stopped a calf, maybe, until the spring thaw came, and then it fell down by itself.

In the summer of 1951, July, I believe, the powers that be, felt we should try to get a little closer to the transmitters we were trying to copy. Saint Lawrence Island was the most logical place. (We already had a sister detachment at Adak) a crew from Anchorage (or so I supposed) flew into Nome. They had a CW operator but no voice operator, so I got volunteered to go with them. There was no airstrip at NE Cape at that time, so a 60 ft. tugboat, The Kofsebue, was chartered to pull a barge with us and assorted equipment to St. Lawrence. I don't know how long the trip was supposed to take, but it took the better part of five days to get there. We were stuck in a field of floating ice for three days and nights, the fog came in and we weren't the happiest of campers during that time. Fortunately the Bering Sea was at its calmest - the only way we could tell we were moving was by watching the tug's compass. When the fog lifted on the third day we were buzzed by a Russian twin engined plane - later a bush pilot from Nome flying a Grumman Goose came in and radioed instructions on the best way out of the ice pack. (A bit of irony: Our call sign was "Catastrophe One").

I never was real sure of what we accomplished at St. Lawrence. After returning to Nome I was getting to be a "short timer" with plans to be married as soon as I made it back to Alabama. This I did (my wife, Iris, and I celebrated 52 years together last November (2003) and returned to San Antonio where I spent the rest of my AF time with the Hqs USAFSS - first at Brooks then later at Kelly. I taught in what we called a "Pre-language" school screening prospects for the Army Language School at Monterey, Calif.

Let me be more brief for the following years - after getting out of the AF, I went back to college and seminary - the time in Alaska had given me a chance to think about what the Lord wanted me to do with my life, and I became a Baptist minister. After a couple of years in the pastorate, I went back into the Army as a Chaplain.

As a chaplain for the next 16+ years I served in Korea, Vietnam and ten different states. Then retired in 1978 and returned to the family farm where I grew up and where I now live. Since retirement, I have served as pastor of five different churches in this area and participated in numerous mission trips to Montana and points west.

We have three children, five grandchildren, two great grandchildren. I've made a conscious effort to simplify my life, live off the land as much as possible, and rejoice in the good things that the Lord has provided.

I look forward to hearing more about what you've learned about the 3rd RSM

Keith Dodd

Dear Daniel:
I saw your notice in the February issue of The American Legion Magazine and thought I would write and touch base with you about the 3rd Radio Squadron Mobile. I was stationed in the headquarters at Elmendorf from 1953 to 1955. On February 4, 1954 I was among three from the 3rd RSM that boarded a flight headed to Fairbanks and then on to St. Lawrence Island. WE NEVER MADE IT! We crashed that day in the mountains between Anchorage and Fairbanks north and east of Talkeetna. There were 16 on the C-47; ten were killed and six of us survived.

We probably know some of the same people just the same. I had a lot of friends that went to St. Lawrence Island after a short time at Anchorage. After the crash the three of us that survived had the option to stay at Anchorage and we did.

We have been having reunions of the survivors and family members of those who perished since 1996. This year (2003) it will be at Evansville, Indiana. I'm enclosing a clipping from our first one at Dayton.

I know this doesn't quite fit what you asked for in your notice but I thought you might enjoy hearing from someone who tried to go to St. Lawrence Island and didn't make it.

I hope you hear from a bunch of the guys!

Sincerely, Ed Olson

ARTICLE OF REUNION - thanks to Ed Olson submitting an article from PEOPLE.

AFTER THE FALL

Forty two years later, survivors of a mysterious air disaster met to look back on the trauma. In a nightmare that recurred for years, Pratt found himself flying on an airplane, when suddenly the plane fell to pieces and he began falling endlessly into a cold, black void. The nightmare may well have endured because it was based on a real-life incident, itself more terrifying than any dream.

On Feb. 5, 1954, Pratt was a young airman aboard an Air Force transport plane that suddenly, and mysteriously, broke up in midair over Alaska. Seven passengers and three crewmen fell to their deaths, but Pratt and five others--all wearing parachutes--were somehow thrown clear of the splintered, plummeting fuselage. They survived not just the disaster in the air but the bone-chilling days that followed in the wilderness.

Over the years, Pratt, 63, now a retired elementary school teacher in Scotia, N.Y., wondered about the other survivors but lost hope of seeing them again. "I guess with all the time that's passed, [finding them] seemed a pretty daunting task," he says. But when the 42nd anniversary of the disaster came around in February, Pratt says, "I woke up thinking about it and decided to give it a shot." He was prompted by a Christmas gift from his son Greg, 25 - a CD-ROM containing 85 million U.S. phone listings, every phone book in the nation.

The next day, in his Ellenton, Fla., home, Eli LaDuke picked up the phone, and a voice he didn't recognize asked, "Mr. LaDuke, do you recall where you were on Feb. 5, 1954?" LaDuke, 62, a retired electronics engineer, thought for a second before saying the words Pratt had waited so long to hear: "In Alaska, near Mount McKinley." It wasn't long before Pratt had contacted all five of his fellow survivors.

Their doomed journey had begun as they stepped onto a C-47 on that winter day in 1954 for what was to have been a routine 260-mile flight from Anchorage to Fairbanks. There was only one hint that the day might go awry: "This was a real scroungy-looking plane," recalls Huey Montgomery, 63, now a retired logger and strip miner in Evansville, Ind. An hour after takeoff, the flight got rough; the plane went into a dive and then leveled off. Suddenly "there was a loud bang and the engines stopped," Pratt recalls. The fuselage tore apart, and before the plane plunged into a mountain, the six men were sucked out into the frigid sky. "I opened my eyes, and I was about 10,000 feet up," recalls Ed Fox, 65, of Palm Bay, Fla., who retired from the Air Force after 20 years.

Saved by their parachutes--none of the six had ever used one before--each man landed alone. "It was the loneliest time in my whole life," says Ed Olson, 62, a city-development manager in Elkader, Iowa. Eventually, Pratt, Olson and Fox met up and huddled for warmth through the night in the remnants of a parachute, rotating places to give each a turn in the middle. Two bush pilots spotted them the next day and returned with food, coffee and a doctor to attend to their wounds, including frostbite, cuts and bruises. When the weather cleared the following day, the trio were flown out.

Fifteen miles away, up the mountain near the crash site, LaDuke, Montgomery and Bobby Sallis formed a second group. For them, the wreckage became a makeshift camp. Before an Air Force helicopter rescued them, they had no food and endured three days of howling winds and temperatures of 35 degrees below zero. "I was afraid to fall asleep for fear of freezing," says Allis, 64, a retired Huntsville, Ala., government contracts negotiator.

The six were briefly hospitalized in Anchorage and within two weeks had returned to duty. "Today, they bring in a whole planeload of psychologists after a thing like that," says Fox. "But back then, you fall off your horse, you get back on." They never got together again--that is, until recently, when the reunion Pratt orchestrated took place in Fairborn, Ohio, near Wright Patterson Air Force Base.

Not surprisingly, they discovered that the experience had left deep scars. Most suffered a chronic fear of flying (only one of the six, LaDuke, had flown to the reunion). Some, like Pratt, suffered nightmares, and all were troubled by the mystery of why the flight ended in disaster. They did not know that the Air Force had prepared an accident report. Says Pratt: "We never really discussed the crash while we were out there or in the hospital. That was part of the problem." Some of the mystery was solved when Keith Betscher, 44 son of the C-47's pilot, Earl, read aloud a 1954 letter to his family from one of his dad's fellow officers. Step by step the writer related how ice built up, the right engine stalled, the plane went into a steep dive, and G-forces literally pulled the aircraft apart. "That letter explained a lot," says Montgomery.

Now that they've reunited, the men have already made plans for the future: a memorial plaque at Wright Patterson and a newsletter to keep in touch.

Nothing, however, is likely to erase their memories. "It never leaves you," says Sallis of the crash. "Every time you hear about a plane crash anywhere, you're reminded. And you wonder: Why did I survive and others didn't? That's always the question."

Dave Bush's recollections of St. Lawrence Island tour (1953-1954)

Following graduation of the Radio Intercept Operator Course at Keesler AFB on June 4, 1953, three friends and I bought a 1948 or 49 model car and drove home. The last guy was from PA and wrote later that the car died a final death as he drove into his driveway. Anyway the cost of buying the heap was cheaper than buying airline or train tickets home, so we came out ahead.
Sometime around the middle of July 1953, I remember flying into Anchorage just after a volcanic eruption and seeing black snow. We spent about a month at Green Lake and then were transferred to Nome. We were in partial status awaiting assignment and transportation to St. Lawrence Island.
While in Nome, we met the grand dame of Nome, one Jennie Wylie. Who owned a fur/gold training post and a hotel, which had a good restaurant. Jennie, who was in her late 60s at the time, more or less adopted me and a couple of friends. She had a Chinese chef who could do magic with wild game. I'll never forget the great Caribou steaks we ate there.
One of the guys was a commercial artist who did some pastel drawings of Eskimo scenes around Nome. Jennie was so impressed with his art that she offered to bring his wife to Nome and set them up in business. She implied that since she had no children that if they decided to stay on in Nome that she would consider them as heirs. Jennie's husband had passed on 10 or 15 years previously and I think she was lonely for a family. The guy's wife told him in no uncertain terms that she was not going to move to Nome, Alaska and that was the end of that story.
After a couple of weeks in Nome, we caught a C-47 to St. Lawrence. As I climbed off the plane, a fellow met me there and introduced himself. Turns out he was a RDF operator and he told me that it was a great job - working by himself outside the main operations building, answerable only to himself. He, having taken a great liking to me, decided that perhaps I might be his replacement if I was so inclined. Being an independent type, I opined that it might just be the job I was looking for. It took me four months in isolation

to find another "sucker" to take that job. I was nearly stir crazy by that time and learned first hand what cabin fever meant.

The RDF job did have its incentives. I was allowed to drive the half-track to work, discovered an Arctic fox and tamed it with C-Rats bacon. Unfortunately, I had a habit of throwing tracks on the half-track/sno-cat and an Eskimo trapper trapped the fox.

Dan Grimsley swears I was the guilty party behind a "mayday" episode after I got out of stir and on B Shift operations. According to him, someone (allegedly me) cut into the voice operator's intercom and simulated a Mayday call. Of course all hell broke lose, and one of those smart-A voice types pointed the finger. I just can't imagine that I would be guilty of doing something like that.

I do recall some things that happened. One of my favorite recollections was the Sunday morning I was in the dayroom, sitting in the barber's chair when an airman walked in and asked for a haircut. I threw the sheet on him and gave him a haircut that was something to behold - charged him $.50 and sent him on his way. I doubt if he ever found out that I wasn't the regular barber.

I also remember the hard days and nights we spent on Mona Lisa - the sea borne barge re-supply operation. We worked our tails off for a week either 12 on or 12 off at Operations of the same unloading barges and stacking boxes. Seemed to me that it was a lot of work to then have to spend the rest of the year eating powdered eggs, powdered milk, and powdered everything . . . We learned quickly where the term "green eggs and ham" came from.

I also remember the time that the alarm clock went off and I staggered out of bed, went to the mess hall, had breakfast and drove out to operations in the Arctic darkness and relieved the operator on my position. He left immediately and returns to the base and 30 minutes later I realized that it was only 2 a.m. He had arranged to have my alarm changed - after I was asleep. If I remember, I caught him a few days later in the hall, sprayed him with water and threw him out the emergency exit in minus 30- degree weather. I can still hear the sound of his clothes freezing in those extreme temperatures. I also remember the day I grabbed the handle of the snow-cat with my ungloved hand and had to be thawed off.

Probably the most memorable event at St. Lawrence was the week of the major Arctic Storm. The weather was so bad that the crew at operations was unable to be relieved and after 2 or 3 days they were running out of supplies and heating oil. A relief party was organized and of course being the pioneer that I am, I was one of the first to volunteer. Six of us loaded the sno-cat with supplies and, tying a long rope on the front of the cat, we took turns searching out the next telephone pole in the long line leading to operations. When we would find a pole, we would signal the rest of the guys in the cat and the cat would follow the rope to the pole. The next guy would get out and repeat the process.

All went well until we came to the last pole. If you remember, the power lines went below the cyclone fence around operations. As luck would have it, I was the next guy in line. I went to the end of the rope, but no fence. Having made that trip a hundred times, I knew the fence was within reach of the rope. My next move was a major error in judgment. I laid the rope down and took two or three steps forward to find the fence. Alas, it was not to be found - and neither was the rope when I turned around and took three steps back to where I had left it.

The wind and snow was blowing so hard nothing could be seen. Not the sno-cat, not the fence, not the rope - nothing. What to do? I made a decision - I just knew the fence could be found, so I turned and walked toward the operations building. I don't know how far I walked, but just as I was about to panic, I walked into the side of the white operations building - at the second story level. Snowdrifts had piled up to the point they covered the fence - that was why I couldn't find it. I banged on the window and was immediately pulled inside where I had to explain that there was a sno-cat out there with five guys in it who had no idea where I was or where they were. The Operations Officer formed a human chain and we anchored to the front door and swept an arc around the front of the building. We were fortunate that we found the sno-cat - as it was moving away from the building headed toward the Arctic Sea. Another 10 feet and we would have missed it.

Needless to say, after everyone was inside safe and sound I received a thorough dressing down by the Operations Officer for letting go of the rope. I've often wondered what might have happened to that crew had we not found them in time. It was a lesson learned about individual responsibility and judgment.

I also remember some other lesser incidents - the boxing matches at the end of the barracks wing lounge - just enough to let off some pent-up energy during the long winter.

Some individuals couldn't handle the isolation and went bananas - one quietly and one violently (the cook with the meat cleaver that was lured into the covered walkway and tackled).

I still have the photos I took on the seal hunt with the Eskimos in skin boats. They were real hunters, seldom wasting a shot.

I also recall my introduction to classical music. My roommate (whose name I have unsuccessfully tried to recall over the years) was a classic pianist who spent hours practicing in the day room and who had a great collection of classical records. I went to sleep every night listening to Ravel, Bach, Beethoven and other great music. I still do.

One last item, you may recall the USO show that came to St. Lawrence in the spring/summer of 1954. Of course they had some females in the show, and to me one red-head in particular was a queen . I was totally infatuated with her. I followed her to the snack bar, the chow hall, was almost touching her on stage and shot tons of film - I was smitten.

Lucky me, when I caught the flight out of Alaska to Seatac - who was on the plane, and who had a seat beside this beauty. Yep, me! We talked and talked. I really thought I some kind of Lothario. The rest of the story, as Paul Harvey says, was that a month later after I had been home on leave and around civilians for a while, I had the rolls of film that I had shot developed. What a shock. That raving beauty was a major dog. She was at least 55 years old, in bad need of a dye job, and not all that pretty to look at. Do you suppose it was the year-long isolation and absence of women on the island that affected my sense of perception?

There's probably more that I will recall about that year when I get together with some other St. Lawrence veterans. Looking forward to hearing from any of the 3rd Radio Mobile gang.

Dave Bush

dave.bush@verizon.net

FREEDOM THROUGH VIGILANCE ASSOCIATION

August 30, 2002

Daniel L. Grimsley
Sir,
Thank you for your interest in the association.
The enclosed brochure describes our association. We publish four newsletters yearly. We also publish a membership directory that is periodically updated and very handy for finding old friends. Our membership has been close to 2000 over the last several years. We hold our general membership meeting in San Antonio the last weekend of September each year. Along with the meeting we have a golf tournament, picnic, hall of honor induction ceremony, and a dinner/dance. We have both ex-USAFSS/ESC/AFIC/AIA and active duty personnel attending the festivities. If you decide to join, please fill in the card and return it along with a check for the amount of $15.00 for a one-year membership, or the appropriate amount for a lifetime membership. Upon receipt of your payment we will send you a membership card and the most current membership directory. If you have Internet access, our homepage address is listed below.
Again, thanks for your interest.
Sincerely,

Bob Baert
Membership

Homepage: http://www.ftva.org
E-Mail: info@ftva.og
NOTE: "You may want to contact this organization for more stories."

"Remain in Touch"

Daniel L. Grimsley
1258 Liberty Landing Road
Winnabow, NC 28479
(910)371-2017

December 18, 2004

Dear Mr. Grimsley:

It was a pleasure to speak with you on the telephone several days ago. As I said, I received your lovely letter and Keith Dodd's, Dave Bush's, and Ed Olson's writings.

I will use all of what you sent to me, including your letter, as I said, for a book that I am researching for, entitled THESE GUYS. It will contain USAFSS stories written by those people who served in that part of the military and some other stories.

I find your information a treasure, since my own brother, SSGT Phillip C. Noland, AF12392047 spent many years in the USAF and USAFSS. He is deceased and buried at the National Cemetery in Bourne, Cape Cod, MA. He was 55 in 1986 when he was hit by a New York City Taxi and after three weeks, he died of a blood clot (he'd broken his leg).

Phillip did serve at Kisarazu, Japan, during the Korean War and so he did earn the Korean Service Ribbon. Ultimately, he became a Radio Intercept Analyst and his last assignment was in 1962-64 at 6901st Zweibrucken, W. Germany, holding a temporary TSGT. Phillip was one of the men who suffered and eventually went crazy, after returning from a TDY in London, from Zweibrucken. He was a gentle, fine man. Intelligent. Did a good job getting me off to school when I was a youngster. ha ha

If you have any further questions - anything - please contact me and I will be happy to answer them. If you can get someone to allow you to use a computer, there are many fine websites which you would enjoy. If you do get the chance, just let me know, and I'll send the website addresses to you.

God bless you for sending these wonderful stories. They are a goldmine, as far as I'm concerned. I am very proud of all of you who served.

I have moved since you mailed your letter. My new address:

Trish Schiesser, Author, Literary Consultant
One Harbor Court, #19D
Portsmouth, VA 23704

I wish you and yours a healthy and happy holiday and hope to hear from you again. Meanwhile, know that these books take a long time - I am working on three books right now, but they all get published sooner or later. I have two

of my first books to send to you and will send them to you at the address on your letter as soon as the holiday rush slows down.
Again, Thank you, Daniel
With Respect,

Trish Schiesser . . . I have, once again, been moved by the DoN, for which my husband works . . . and we are living in Portsmouth, VA.
My husband is the Principle Port Engineer of the USNS GRASP.
My new address is:
Trish Schiesser, Author, Literary Consultant
One Harbor Court, #19D
Portsmouth, VA 23704

NOTES RE: PHIL NOLAND FROM BOB GUEST - 6933rd KARAMURSEL, TURKEY FOR PERIOD OF 1960-61.

Bob Guest - I served with a SSGT Phil Noland in Turkey in 1960. If it's the same Noland, I can tell you he was a very nice guy with a good sense of humor and seemed to enjoy life. I'm sorry to hear that he has passed away. God bless him. Bob Guest 1/20/01.

Bob Guest through e-mail to and from: Pete Johnson: Here's a note Bob Guest sent about Phil Noland. The cc on this e-mail is Trish Schiesser, Phil's sister:

Pete, the SSGT Noland I knew is definitely her brother. He was assigned as our Section Head (203xx) after Dodi (CAPT Aspell) had to transfer out the existing Section Head after busting him. The former Section Head (I can't remember his name) was a master at several languages, (Russian, Rumanian, Polish, Czech, etc.) but was very antisocial and an alcoholic. He could not accept women in authority and got abusive with Capt. Aspell several times when he was drunk. She finally busted him, but he did it again and she had no recourse, but to remove him. That's when we got Phil. The fact that he spoke Russian, was being cross-trained, and lived on Long Island clinches the ID. I cried real tears tonight because I was so saddened that he had such problems at the end of his life. He was a really nice guy.
Please forward this to his sister.

Bob Guest

From one of the two TUSLOG Det. 3 Airman Performance Reports . . . a partial quote from the APF:
FACTS AND SPECIFIC ACHIEVEMENTS: Sgt. Noland replaced a man who was considered to be one of the best in his field . . . Since Sgt. Noland is in a cross-training status, . . ."

From Bob Guest to Trish Schiesser: 2/1/02
Trish,
I know that Phil sang in Russian. One of his favorite songs was "Pod Moscovniye Vechera" (Under Moscow Evenings). A musician by the name of Kenny Ball came out with a jazzed up instrumental version in the 70's, but the version that Phil and I knew was done as a love song I had learned at Syracuse University, and Phil was delighted to discover that I remembered all of the lyric. I had sung in our High School, a capella choir and several other choirs and could harmonize at the drop of a hat. We used to sing it together from time to time.
By the way, I'd love to get a copy of that book when it is completed.
Bob Guest.

Dear Trish, 2/12/02 from Bob Guest
I had no idea about Phil's problems, nor the fact that he had anything but an Honorable Discharge. No wonder you have been going bonkers! I can't imagine Phil as a "spy" because he didn't look or act Russian even though he was fluent in the language. My guess is he would have been a double agent plant. That might also help explain why he finally went off the deep end. Both sides came into some pretty nasty business and I can imagine how Phil might have become disillusioned when faced with the realities of how dirty things can become. He was a nice guy and was somewhat altruistic. The realities of what both sides were willing to do to gain the advantage might have just been too much for him.
Thank you for filling me in and I am so sorry that he had to go through that. I really liked him and he was a sweet gentle man. Bob Guest

2/14/02 Trish, Happy Valentine's Day! I'm not sure what they mean. I speak Russian, German and some Turkish, but never was very good at Military or Federal Govt. acronyms. I know that HQ means Headquarters and 1401st would be the organizational designation.
ABWG probably means Air Base Wing, but I'm not sure.
SO sounds like special operations.
G-15 sounds like a rank or another organizational designator
6901SCG sounds like Special Communications Group
I'm sorry I'm not much help on this, but if you send your inquiry to the KAS group address, I'm sure somebody can tell you for certain.
Bob

Trish 5/21/02 from Bob Guest

Trish, I have been in touch with a couple of Senator's Offices and have gotten a positive response from one of them. They have sent me a form to fill out and I will check the details with you before I send it in. By the way, the first thing I was asked was my authority to inquire, and I told them I had been given a Power of Attorney by you and they asked me to send them a copy.
Bob

Editor's Note: Nothing further was done on this case. Bob Guest said that the Senator's Office lost Phil's file, which I had given him in power of attorney to investigate Phil's background in the USAFSS.

CONGRESSIONAL RECORD article 57 of 64
By HON. RALPH M. HALL

IN RECOGNITION OF CAPTAIN D.L. "PAPPY" HICKS -- HON. RALPH M. HALL (Extensions of Remarks - June 16, 1999)

[Page: E1294]

HON. RALPH M. HALL
OF TEXAS
IN THE HOUSE OF REPRESENTATIVES
WEDNESDAY, JUNE 16, 1999

Mr. HALL of Texas. Mr. Speaker, I rise today to honor and pay tribute to a true American hero, Captain D.L. "Pappy" Hicks. In a recent trip to Washington, Pappy was honored by Congress for his dedication and service in the Secret Army, which operated in Laos during the Korean and Vietnam Wars.

Pappy was a deep, covert operator in clandestine operations in South Asia from 1959 until 1982. Many of these operations have remained concealed over the years as a result of their top secret nature. American citizens and U.S. troops, alike, were unaware that any fighting was occurring in Laos during the Vietnam War, hence the operations have often been called the "Secret War." The Secret Army was comprised of Hmong and other Laotian Mountain people in cooperation with the Royal Laotian Army and American advisors such as the CIA, U.S. Army Special Forces, and U.S. Army covert operators. Yet, as a result of the covert nature of their service, the men who gave their lives serving in the Secret Army in Laos are not recognized on the Vietnam War Memorial. Their mission was to find potential enemies of the United States operating within the Laotian borders with the North Vietnamese. Reportedly, these men saved thousands of American lives through their efforts; thus, their recent Washington tribute was an emotional one for Pappy.

At the ceremony, Pappy was given a pa'ndua, a ritualistic cloth used to tell the history of the Hmong people, by General Vang Pao, his Laos commanding officer. In his speech, Pappy struggled to fight back tears as he recollected his time in Laos and the injuries he sustained while operating in that area. As he spoke to his fellow soldiers, Pappy remarked, "Every so often, years after the fact, when we become old men, we who worked in the dark are let out in the light for a moment of glory. For me, this is the day."

Captain Hicks, from the Fourth District of Texas, currently resides in Troup, Texas, with his lovely wife of forty-five years, Marjorie Ann Tupa. Mr. Speaker, as we adjourn today, let us do so in honor of this true American hero--Captain D.L. "Pappy" Hicks.

[NOTE: *This is a Congressional Record article from the Texas House of Representatives in honor of "Pappy" Hicks' heroic service in the "Secret War" in Laos during the Vietnam War.*]

RUSTIC YANKEE - OV-10 GIB
By Rog Hamann

In 1997 my wife and I had just returned from a vacation trip to Rochester, NY, home of an old Air Force buddy of mine. As I walked up to the entrance of my home, I saw a note taped to the door, a note from another Air Force bud I hadn't heard from in 25 years.

"Hi Rog. Was in the neighborhood and thought we'd stop in to see you. Sorry we missed you. I have some information about a Rustic reunion. Call me at . . ." The note was from Joe G., with whom I'd been stationed at Ubon RTAFB, Ubon, Thailand back in 1971-72. Joe had gotten my address from Ralph D. as all three of us had served at Ubon together.

Twenty-five years ago . . . it had all been put in the back of my mind . . . not intentionally, mind you. Or was it? How could I forget something that was so opposite of my character, something I had never envisioned doing when I first enlisted in the Air Force? Something that now is on my mind daily.

No. 27, that was my number, no, not my lucky number . . . 27 was my draft lottery number for the Selective Service in 1970. I was attending art school in Portland, Maine, a non-accredited school at the time. Having full independency at this time of my life was something I was truly enjoying . . . maybe a little too much. Though I seldom missed classes, it became clear to me that this was not going to work out. I had to go to a school where my courses would be accountable for something once I graduated. Simple solution - transfer! And where better than to the college my girlfriend was attending, just a twenty-minute drive away. Well, as luck would have it, (my kind of luck anyway), I was told I'd have to start from day one, that the courses I'd taken so far didn't mean much at this school. Number 27, start all over . . . 27, start all over. I never really cared for school, be it grammar school, high school . . . or art school. The Vietnam War was still going on although it had begun to subside some as far as fatalities were concerned. The television news carried daily updates of Americans being killed, questioning whether we should be there at all. Was the "domino affect" of Communism really something we as Americans should be worried about? It wasn't anything I lost sleep over. This whole Vietnam thing was going on a long, long way from home and I knew no one serving there. Fighting, be it in a war or otherwise, was not something I was familiar with, even boyhood fist cuffs. Never was I in a situation where I had to fight my way out. Now, a decision had to be made. Join the Army or Marines and there was a good chance they'd eventually send me to Vietnam. The Navy option did not entice me at all since being on water and remaining afloat had proven to be a sinking feeling as my swimming instructor at Boy Scout camp could attest to; and the Coast Guard, much the same feeling. So the choice was obvious, I'll enlist in the Air Force and see the world! How dangerous could it be serving in the Air Force? I certainly wasn't going to be flying as Officers Candidate School was never in my plans - remember my dislike for school?

I was sworn into Uncle Sam's Air Force on June 24, 1970, and proceeded directly to San Antonio, Texas for basic military training at Lackland, AFB. This was my first time in an airplane and my first time away from home for any length of time.

After six weeks of training in the hot Texas sun, I was anxious to head back home to Maine on leave before reporting to my new assignment at Wurtsmith AFB in Oscoda, Michigan. There were only four airmen from my training flight who received DDAs, Direct Duty Assignment, no technical school training before assignment to a new duty station. I was one of those four. Again, I had not tested too highly on any of the aptitude tests given while in BMT, my highest score being in the administration career field, lowest being in mechanical. And so, I was assigned to a supply squadron as a POL specialist, Petroleum-Oils-Lubricants, in other words, a gas jock. My job involved driving a truck filled with 5000 gallons of jet fuel or AV-GAS (for prop driven planes) and refueling whatever aircraft needed fuel on the base, from B-52 bombers, KC-135 tankers, F-106 fighters to T-33 trainers, T-39 and the C-47 gooney birds. If the B-52's or KC-135's needed a full load, we'd bring out a hose cart to the flight line near the specific bird that needed fuel, attach the cart to a hydrant coupling on the flight line that ran back to fuel pump houses all along the flight line and then attach another hose coupling to the bomber/tanker itself and begin the long process of refueling, at all times holding on to a cabled switch box that controlled the fuel pumping hose cart, ready to shut it off should an emergency occur. It was mandatory that we have that control switch in our hands at all times, no matter how cold it was out there on the flight line, and believe me, it could get wicked cold up there in Michigan on the shores of Lake Huron. I witnessed a B-52 actually being moved around on an icy flight line by the winds coming off that great lake.

My tour at Wurtsmith wasn't too bad as it reminded me of my home state of Maine. The area and the weather were pretty much like that back home. The only downfall was that there really wasn't too much to do there outside the base for a single guy as the base itself was somewhat remote. Girls from the Detroit USO club would come up to the base once a month and that meant that once a month the Airmen's Club was the scene of a feeding frenzy . . . maybe a dozen girls and one hundred lonely GI's! Fortunately, my barracks was right across the street from the movie theater and bowling alley. My mouth still waters at the thought of those juicy, loaded cheeseburgers we'd get to eat after catching a movie for fifty cents.

But all this working and not much playing became rather boring after awhile and I decided it was time for a change. Some of the POL guys I worked with had returned from bases in Vietnam and Thailand and all seemed to have made it without too much difficulty, so why not me? I put in a volunteer statement for either Vietnam or Thailand. How dangerous could it be refueling aircrafts at an Air Force base in Thailand, away from where the real action was? After all, it's not like I was going to be in that airplane flying missions amidst enemy bullets and risking my life to save someone else's life on the ground below me. I was nothing more than a gas jock? Let's go for it!

Sometime in early summer of 1971, while on my way to the barracks from the chow hall, our bay orderly clerk saw me and told me I had orders to go to Vietnam . . . oh, and they were special orders. Special orders, I thought, I wonder what that's all about? I quickly made my way to the First Sgt.'s office and inquired about the message given me moments earlier. I was told that I indeed had special orders to report to Phan Rang AB in South Vietnam . . . but not as a POL specialist. No, I was told these orders had something to do with the fact that I spoke French. Now I remembered taking an optional language test back at Lackland but had never given any more thought about it since . . . until now!

They told me in personnel that before reporting to Phan Rang, I'd have to go through altitude chamber testing at Wright-Patterson AFB in Ohio, survival school training at Fairchild AFB in Washington and jungle survival school at Clark AB in the Philippines. That look of confusion on my face must have been fairly evident because without even my asking they told me that was all they could tell me. That, and the fact that I WOULD be flying!

What had I gotten myself into? Flying? Now that sounded great, but in Vietnam? And what about speaking French? Where did that fit into the picture? Well, I figured since I HAD volunteered, I had no choice but to follow through with this, whatever THIS was; granted, I had not volunteered to fly in Vietnam but to go over there as a POL troop, refueling airplanes. You know the old saying, "Nothing ventured, nothing gained," so I decided to venture out, not exactly knowing where this road would lead me to career wise, other than somewhere in Vietnam.

It was on my last leg of training at Clark AB that I first got an inkling as to what I was being prepped for. Mention was made, (by who I do not recall), of enlisted guys being sent to Nam to fly in the backseat of a two-man reconnaissance plane called an OV-10, to be used as airborne interpreters. Wow, this was becoming more "warlike" by the minute, and I wasn't a "warlike type" of guy!

It wasn't until I arrived at Phan Rang AB in mid-October that I was finally told my official job description, that's IF they decided to keep me there. Seems that with all the time I'd had to take in preparation for this assignment, by the time I arrived at Phan Rang the powers that be had decided they probably no longer needed any more enlisted interpreters. The question now was whether to send me back to the states, along with other guys who had also reported for this same assignment, or keep me in Southeast Asia and allow me to fulfill my duties as a POL specialist, seeing as that's what I had originally put in my voluntary statement for.

Capt. M, the OIC (Officer in charge) of the enlisted backseaters program stated he would interview us all, there were about 8-9 of us, and that he'd then decide who would stay on as an interpreter with this, the 19th Tactical Air Support Squadron, and who might be assigned to another unit. After a few weeks of anxious waiting and trying to become acclimated to the sultry weather that is Vietnam, word came down that I had been chosen to continue with the program. The squadron, however, playing its part in the Vietnamization process, was now moving from Bien Hoa AB, SVN to Ubon RTAFB in Thailand. Bien Hoa had been the home base of the OV-10 squadron known as the Rustics, a group of men known as FACS, Forward Air Controllers. I soon learned that I would be joining them as their newest backseater, acting as an interpreter between the pilot and the ground commanders. Didn't these ground commanders speak English, I asked? Well, some did . . . but most spoke only Cambodian and French. Wait a minute, I thought, Cambodian and French? Turns out I wasn't going to be flying in Vietnam after all, but Cambodia. And the ground commanders referred to were Cambodian Army ground commanders and their radio operators (RO). Finally, I now knew what, where and how I was going to perform my new duties as an airborne interpreter. The question of why, still needed an answer and that would come soon.

On November 10, 1971, I saw my first OV-10 and after being strapped into the back seat with all the necessary safety harness, parachute, helmet, gloves, revolver and with my duffel bag thrown in the cargo bay, I was off on my first OV-10 plane ride to Ubon, Thailand, approximately a two hour ride, and new home of the now 21st TASS, the Rustics. With the constant change over of aircraft and personnel due to Vietnamization, the Rustics would soon become part of the 23rd TASS with its home base being at Nakhom Phanom RTAFB in Northern Thailand.

I remember little of that first time in the OV-10 save the fact that flying in that small bird was quite a contrast to what I'd experienced on the planes I'd flown in until then, not a whole lot of maneuvering space to say the least! But I was forever grateful that Maj. A. had managed to get me to my new duty station unscathed and unfired upon, at least as far as I knew.

The OV-10 taxied off the runway and Maj. A. brought her basically to the front door of the Rustics Ops. Building. It was there that I met my new commander, Lt. Col. C. and my new NCOIC (Non-commissioned officer in charge), Tsgt. Joe G. Joe was from Maine as well, as was another backseater, Ralph D. Imagine my surprise and a rather "feel good moment" knowing I was in the company of fellow "Maineiacs."

We all came from different parts of the great state of Maine, Joe from the southern end, Ralph from the north and I from central Maine, but the bond was there, that special uniqueness that had landed us all in the same place far from home . . . our French-Canadian background. Mine came from both of my parents who were born in Canada and had moved to Maine to work in the mills in Lewiston, a city with a heavy population of French-Canadians. To their credit, my parents insisted that all of us kids retain our ability to speak French as we'd been brought up to do. When my siblings and I were in our teenage years, Mom went so far as to put up signs in the dining room to remind us to "Parlez Francais" (Speak French) as she could see we no longer used our French much once we were attending high school. Now, some three years later I was going to get the chance to do some serious "Parlez Francais."

After a few days of briefings on map reading, use of the code wheel, proper usage of radios in the OV-10, proper military terms used in reconnaissance work and of course, familiarity with the OV-10 itself, my name was added to the Rustic flying schedule. I had chosen the call sign of Yankee since the interpreters had a choice of choosing a letter from the phonetic alphabet for their call sign. I figured since I was from Maine, Yankee was a good moniker for me. The Rustic pilots had numbers for their call sign and so on.
Nov. 13th, 1971, I, now officially known as Rustic Yankee, set out on my first Cambodian adventure with Rustic 18, Lt. C. We took off from Ubon on an early afternoon and set our sights for Rumlong, which had been the scene for approximately two weeks of many confrontations between Cambodian Army soldiers and the NVA. When we arrived on scene, we were told that the enemy had finally overtaken the area and that we were to destroy any weapons that now lay abandoned by the fleeing troops and civilians who had fought in vain to protect their town. I found it so ironical that my very first mission as a Rustic would have us destroying friendly weapons instead of the enemy's but this was done in order that the NVA would not have access to an extra supply cache of weapons.

We put in four sets of air (air strikes) on that particular mission and although my French speaking abilities were not needed, I had all I could endure just trying to keep my meal down as we constantly pulled G's going up and down with our dives, marking the target area for the fighters. Looking through a set of binoculars while making marking passes also proved worthless as I was getting nauseous just trying to keep sense of where the target was in relation to what I was seeing through the binoculars, dealing with the G forces and a pilot who was obviously delighted to have a rookie in his backseat. I didn't use the barf bags that day however, or on any other mission for that matter. We returned to Ubon almost five hours later and upon landing, I felt like I was on top of the world, with a sense of pride I'd never experienced before in my life. In a matter of one month, I'd gone from driving a fuel truck in Northern Michigan to flying my first combat mission in the backseat of a two-man recon plane in Cambodia, from oil stained fatigues to a sweaty, thoroughly drenched flight suit, from delivering JP-4 jet fuel in an F-106 fighter jet to directing A-37 fighter jets on an enemy target in South East Asia. Now THIS is what being in the Air Force was really all about and although I initially never saw myself as being part of THAT Air Force, I certainly was mighty proud to be a part of it now!

As time and the missions themselves began to fly by, I became more accustomed to each pilot and his manner of flying a mission. Some preferred flying solo and the thought of having someone in their backseat seemed to cramp their style. In such cases, it was best to keep notes and let the pilot do most of the talking to the fighters as well as to the ground commanders. Others enjoyed having an extra set of eyes and ears in the plane with them, better to see and hear more of what was going on in our AO (Area of Operation). With a UHF, VHF, HF and two FM radios aboard the OV-10, having a backseater gave the pilot the opportunity to share the work load, a critical component when we were involved in a TIC (Troops in Contact) situation where we could be talking simultaneously to the Cambodian ground commander, his radio operator, a set of fighters engaged in bombing runs on the target area, another set of fighters in a holding pattern awaiting their turn to hit the target, another Rustic FAC leaving/arriving at the target and BlueChip, 7th Air Force Headquarters. Yes, communications at times such as this were vital and all had to be absolutely sure we were all talking on the same page. An erroneous placement of a bomb could be devastating and it was our job as the FAC to make sure this never occurred.

The daily missions into Cambodia developed into a strong bond between our Cambodian allies and us Rustics. It got to the point where the distinct sound of one's voice was all that was needed for some of the ground commanders or their RO's to identify which Rustic pilot or GIB (Guy in back) they were talking to. We could often times hear the relief in their voices just knowing a Rustic was flying over their area, providing a sense of security, if for only an hour or so or until another Rustic FAC arrived on station.

As we arrived over a certain town such as Kampong Thom, the first voice we most often heard was that of Sam, a captain in the Cambodian Army. Sam proved to be one of the most endearing characters I would ever meet via the airwaves. Although his entire life dealt with the ravages of war in his homeland, and maybe because of this, it was not uncommon for many a Rustic to become involved in a dialogue with Sam about life after this war was over or even what it was like at the end of another day in the field of battle. Sam would ask whether we had a honey back home waiting for our return from SEA, our favorite foods (his seemed to be spaghetti), even whether we had any "ankle biters." I'd never heard that term before. When I questioned him about that, he laughed so profusely I was caught somewhat embarrassingly. He asked if I was married and I replied that I was too young to be married yet. Sam laughed some more and told me an ankle biter was another name for a small child, specifically, a crawling toddler . . . an ankle biter! Strange, even though I was a naïve and very young 21 year old, I found myself flying over a war torn country talking to a Cambodian Army officer about children.

Children was not something I'd given any thought to at this point in my life but it proved to be a subject that would, years later, come back to fruition in the form of three ankle biters of my own; and, 18 years after the birth of our youngest child, the children of Cambodia would come back to me in a dream, no, a nightmare, that would forever leave a question in the back of my mind regarding my personal accomplishments as a Rustic GIB. Was I ever responsible for the dropping of an inadvertent bomb resulting in the death of an innocent child/children on the ground below me? It's a question that will probably never be answered, until maybe my day of reckoning.

It wasn't until Christmas morning, 1971, my 32nd mission, that I actually saw people on the ground, people, in the target area. Rustic 06 and I had the first mission this day, Christmas Day, and an 0500 take off. Shortly after we "crossed the fence," the Thailand/Cambodia border, I began my ritual of trying to rise up our Cambodian allies on the FM radio. Soon, I heard the familiar voice of Sam in Kampong Thom. There was no more friendlier voice to hear over those airwaves than that of Sam, always cheerful, thankful and most of all, sincere. He loved talking about "Wine, Women and Song," but not necessarily in that order! On the dawn of this particular day however, Sam's voice came across the wavelengths with a serious tone and impending doom. His troops and the villagers of KP Thom had been the recipients of heavy mortar fire throughout the previous evening, resulting in many being mortally wounded. Sam passed the map coordinates to me by way of a code we used and changed on a daily basis. He stated that at these coordinates we would find two hooches located on the Northwest corner of a bend in the river and that his scouts reported this is where the VC/NVA were launching their mortars the previous night. We flew to the area described by Sam and did a visual recon of the sight. As my pilot circled above that bend in the river, high enough so as not to attract any attention, I looked for any signs of activity through my binoculars. There was none; no people, no guns, nothing, save for the two hooches.

The soldiers in KP Thom were outgunned and under supplied. Sam asked that we put an immediate air strike on said location. Sam, as well as the Rustics, knew that approvals for an a/s did NOT come that quickly. Nevertheless, R-06 pleaded Sam's request to Bluechip/7th AF (Saigon) and in a matter of ten minutes or so (maybe Bluechip was in a giving mood, being Christmas and all), we were notified that a set of A-37s would soon be headed out to our AO. The fighters checked in about 15 minutes later, Hawk/Rap flight (CRS as to what call sign they were using) and R-06 proceeded with his briefing, describing the target, elevation, weather, enemy and friendly locations, best possible bailout areas and so on. While this was going on, I kept in touch with Sam, notifying him that we were about ready to put in an a/s for him and to make sure there were no friendlies in the target area. This flight was carrying MK-82s, 500-pound bombs. Lead went in on his first pass and dropped his first bomb shy of the hooches. The results however, were, shall we say, a wake up call. Suddenly, amongst all the dust and debris, about fifty or so black pajama clad humans came running out of those two hooches, heading into and under the coverage of the nearby jungle canopy. Before any of them got very far, Two was in with his first pass and this one found its mark! R-06 called for the fighters to hold high while we went down to VR the area for BDA (Battle Damage Assessment). As soon as the dust settled we slowly circled our way down to see the after effects of two MD-82S; total annihilation. That's the only way I can describe it, nothing but bits and pieces of black, blood and bodies. Neither 06 nor I said anything to each other for a few minutes. But then, in an uncharacteristic moment, I keyed my mike and said, "Merry F***in' Christmas." My pilot simply responded with a double click of his mike. Anyone who knows me would say I never could have said that . . . but I did. And to this day, every Christmas, I think of that mission . . . and those words . . . and that scene below me.

Up until then, the targets I had been involved with were usually that of suspected ammo dumps, VC training areas or mortar/gun pits, always under the cover of triple canopy jungle. But this one target, these two hooches sitting quietly by the riverbank, seemingly unoccupied on a Christmas morning . . . this one was an eye opener. This time I saw humans, obviously fighting for their own cause, much like myself . . . but for different reasons. We got the best of them that day . . . but there would be other days, with different results. Sam was ecstatic with the results of the a/s and thanked us endlessly for our support. His people would be able to rest now, if only for a day or two before the whole process would begin again in earnest.

One may find it difficult to believe but I now barely remember most of the 169 missions I was involved in during my ten months of flying as a Rustic GIB. It seems unbelievable to me anyway that these missions don't come back to me as if they'd only happened yesterday; is it because they basically became "just another day on the job?" Or has my subconscious completely blocked out this chapter of my life, for reasons I may not want to search out. Surely, there were missions that proved to be rather mundane, with hour upon hour of flying into deserted areas of Cambodia or the occasional foray into Laos, looking for enemy activity and that ever present possibility of spotting a truck convoy loaded with ammo and fuel. This rarely happened during daylight hours, which is when we flew our missions.

I do remember meandering into the Laotian skies one day while listening to music from Australia on one of our radios. My pilot motioned to me that he'd spotted something of interest below. I turned from one side of the aircraft over to the opposite side to check things out for myself. Below us was a peasant farmer, or maybe a VC soldier, or maybe an NVA informer or a Khmer Rouge combatant sitting on his dilapidated oxcart being pulled by a water buffalo; the cart was loaded with something in the back, covered by some type of tarp. My pilot asked me what I thought the guy below us must have been hauling. My personal opinion was that this was just some poor farmer minding his own business, going about his daily chores. This wasn't what he wanted to hear. He began to lay out this elaborate theory as to what he thought was going on below us. Obviously enemy, as this was not a recognized friendly area. Obviously a cart loaded with weapons, probably AK-47s. I could sense an impending self-expenditure coming. The thought no sooner crossed my mind than the pilot stated he was going in for a dive run. On this particular day, we just happened to be carrying a rocket pod of flechettes. These were rockets filled with basically small pieces of metal fragments, small darts, if you will. I almost didn't want to look as he fired away our first flechette rocket then quickly pulled on the stick to bring us back safely away from this menacing target. Our suspect was no longer a threat to deliver his supply of guns and ammo to awaiting enemy forces. My pilot said something to the effect that there was now one less bad guy to worry about. Obviously, fortunately, most of the pilots I flew with were a lot more reserved about hitting such a target and carried the responsibility of bringing death and destruction below with great personal morals, based on their own beliefs and the ROE's (Rules of Engagement) that governed their actions. Missions such as the one I described above were rare . . . maybe that's why I remember it.

The majority of the Rustic missions went smoothly and all my fellow GIBs and pilots who flew the trusty OV-10 were sincerely dedicated to the mission at hand. We were always anxious to get out to our AO in order to help our Cambodian allies in any way possible. The possibility of being shot at was a constant therefore there was also a good chance one could be shot down as well. We were often told by the ground commanders as an air strike was being conducted that we and the fighter jets were taking ground fire but that never seemed to bother anyone, maybe due to that all too familiar scenario, "in the heat of the battle." As stated before, we flew day missions therefore tracers coming at us were rarely visible unless one happened to be flying the dawn of dusk mission of the day. The familiar "They shooting at you sir" warning from Sam or any radio operator was always taken seriously but never impeded the Rustic FAC or the fighters he was controlling from defending our allies below. During my ten month tour as a Rustic, no one was ever shot down in our AO but three of our fellow Rustics were shot down and killed prior to my tour and after I returned to the U.S. The names of Garrett Eddy, Michael Vrablick and Joseph Gambino are inscribed on the Vietnam Veterans Memorial in Washington, D.C. Though all Rustics did indeed give some, these three gave their all.

There were many special or eventful things that happened during my tour at Ubon that are now but a hazy snapshot in my mind, a vague memory of joys and fears, highlights and rock bottom tragedies. Writing this piece has helped bring some of those memories to the surface. The "highs" include meeting Sam and his commander, Col. Oum when they visited the Rustics at Ubon in May, 1972; flying with and fighting for some of the greatest people I have ever known in my life; being privileged to have been a Rustic GIB and sharing our unique role in that secret war in Cambodia; having been given the opportunity to fly combat missions when I thought pumping gas into USAF aircrafts was about the closest I'd ever get to seeing war "up close and personal."

That little note left on my door by Joe G. in the summer of 1997 was the igniter of memories of events long forgotten, the start of a life now filled with reminders of a chapter in my life I'd put away for 25 years. But now, 34 years after I last flew a FAC mission in Cambodia, I think about those times on a daily basis.

My wife recently told me that she felt I was evaluating my entire life's worth based on what I did during that tour as a Rustic GIB those many years ago. I think she may be correct. Even with all the riches I've gained as a father of three wonderful children and grandfather to currently two beautiful grandkids, I feel my latest personal accomplishments can't compare to what I got to do as a young 21 year old, enlisted two-striper in the back seat of that OV--10, flying the skies of Cambodia in 1972.

As a side note . . . In October of 2002, on the occasion of the Rustics 3rd reunion in San Antonio, TX, about six of the Rustic GIBs were presented with the award of the Distinguished Flying Cross, awards some 30 years overdue. Being the youngest and the only one not to have made the Air Force a career, I was the last to receive my DFC with 2 OLCs. As a gesture of thanks and most importantly, as my own personal way of showing respect for the Cambodian people and the soldiers who fought for their convictions, I presented one of my DFCs to Col. Oum, the Cambodian Army commander with whom the Rustics worked with on a daily basis from 1970-73 and who now resides in Austin, TX.

FW: RE: EMAILING: S&W 38'
From Pappy Hicks through Bill Person

Now that time has passed and some of us are old and don't give a damn, I'm in my seventies, I got my goods in Nha Trang at 5th SF where a man who worked for the CIA had all the goodies. Not only did I get suppressed (a device that masked out the sound and the telltale flame when fired) weapons, but I got money to pay the people working for me. I'd put it in a duffle bag, throw it in the back of my jeep and drive off, not signing for anything. In the good old days we got Louie de Ore. then it got down to sheets of gold, plus dong and 20 dollar bills. If I haven't told it before, I would cut a small square, roll it up and place a batch in a cigarette pack. I didn't smoke, so it was handy in my pocket. I'm an honest man and did not bring back one Louie or one damned sheet of gold. It wasn't mine, so I don't have any of it. I know men that did, but there are asses in every crowd.

I always say suppressed weapons, not silenced. One night, December 1966 when it's raining like hell, we went into a safe house and my little guy popped off a round from his grease gun. I had told him not to fire that damned thing when it was wet; he did, made a damned good shot, but it sounded like a small cannon went off. We grabbed NVA info bags and took off like scalded assed apes. We only had to shoot one guy on the way out. The rest stayed hid in their hootches, except for the two men who went down on our way in.

Next time I've got to tell you a real combat story about apes. Goddamn, I can feel the adrenalin just writing about it.

Pappy

I feel that this story was too good to pass up. It was his first crash landing. [The Editor]

I WAS A SERGEANT PILOT...
By Bob Hazlett

I was a Sergeant pilot during World War II. Due to a situation that occurred when I was first drafted, I arrived in the Pacific without a crew. When I was first drafted into the Army, one of my best friends was Jewish. We arrived at the induction center together. While we were filling out our paperwork one of the questions was "Religious Preference." I started to put down "Protestant" and Len nudged me with his elbow and said "Put down Jewish." I said to him that he knew that I wasn't Jewish. He replied "Yeah but you will get twice as many holidays." So I erased "Protestant" and put down "Jewish."

So when I arrived at the overseas replacement station with my B-24 crew I was told that I couldn't go to Europe because I was Jewish. My crew shipped out to Europe and I ended up as a single pilot with no crew in the 819th Bombardment Group in the Gilbert Islands. We were then stationed on Abemama in the Gilberts. I was assigned to the 819th Bombardment Squadron.

It was decided that since I had no crew that I would be a "stand-in" pilot for anyone that could not make an assigned mission. I sat in on several mission briefings before I finally had to replace a pilot that had come down with malaria. This was my first mission and I was flying with an unknown crew. I was somewhat apprehensive and I suppose the crew felt the same way.

Our mission was to bomb the Japanese held island of Truk. Truk was well guarded by both Japanese fighters and ground anti-aircraft guns. Our formation was attacked by fighters on the way into the target but the formation managed to hold them off. The fighters broke off as we approached the target and we began to take ground fire. The flack became heavy as we neared the target. We took a couple of minor hits and then as we were on our bomb run we took a forty millimeter round into the fuselage. We had an augmented crew as this B-24 had radar and therefore we had a radar operator. The round into the fuselage killed the radar operator and the navigator and the engineer both took some flack in their legs and the copilot took a hit in his left arm. I did not receive a scratch. I had blood splattered all over my right side. Our radio operator, that sat right across from the radar operator was saved because he had decided to watch from the waist gun positions on the aircraft.

We took quite a pounding as we came off the target. Our B-24 took some minor damage from the flack and we took many hits from the fighters. None of the crew members were hit coming off the target and I managed to keep up with the formation even though our B-24 had taken quite a lot of damage. Our squadron lost four aircraft out of twelve.

When we got back to Abemama we were one of the first in the traffic pattern for landing as we had wounded aboard. When I called for gear down the main landing gear extended but not the nose wheel. So we had to break out of traffic and attempt to do an emergency extension of the nose gear. The emergency procedure was for the engineer to lay on his back aft of the nose gear, which was covered with a canvas cover, and put his feet against the gear and shove it forward and it would drop out and fall into position. However in our case the nose gear strut had been shot off and the gear just kept going when it dropped out of the aircraft.

Since I was going to have to make a crash landing we had to remain clear of the runway until the rest of the aircraft landed. On landings the normal procedure was for all the crew except the pilot, copilot, engineer and radio operator to stand in the bomb bay just aft of the flight deck due to the B-24 being a little tail heavy on the ground. In this case I had all the crew except the copilot and I go to the rear of the bomb bay and as I touched down on the runway they were to walk, one at a time to the rear of the fuselage. Thus I managed to stop the aircraft on the runway on the main wheels and the tail skid. We stayed in this position until the ground crew had a dolly in position under the nose. The crew in the rear then started walking, one at a time, forward to the bomb bay. The B-24 slowly came nose down until the nose rested on the dolly.

At this time the crew was taken off the airplane and it was towed off the runway. It had over two hundred fifty holes in it and it was never repaired. It became a supply source for needed parts for other damaged B-24's.

This was my first crash landing.

MY SECOND (AND ONLY OTHER) CRASH LANDING
By Bob Hazlett

I need to lead into this and give some background. In 1958 I was assigned as Training Officer in the Deputy Commander for Plans Office (DCOP) in the 4751st Air Defense Missile Wing at Hurlburt Field in Florida. Hurlburt Field is Auxiliary Field Number 9 of Eglin AFB. I was also the Chief of the Standardization Board for the T-33 jet trainer and the C-47 military transport planes.

In around 1949 to 1960 the DCOP was in an accident with a T-33 jet trainer. I was appointed as Accident Investigating Officer for the accident. I did everything I could do to exonerate the Colonel I worked for. He came out of the accident smelling like a rose. The accident was declared a mechanical failure. I won't say that my findings were instrumental in this decision but they contributed greatly.

Now to continue the story: I usually requested a T-33 for cross country training at least once every month. I always put in a request for a T-33 to go to Nellis AFB at Las Vegas, Nevada. I had been doing this for over a year when I thought the Wing Commander might be a little hesitant to grant me T-33 to fly to Las Vegas every month. So one month I decided to change my request. I asked for a T-33 to go to Phoenix. This meant I could land at Luke AFB and refuel and hop over to Las Vegas. I put the request in on Monday of the week and on Wednesday the Wing Commander called me and said that he had my request for a T-33 to fly to Phoenix. I confirmed the request. He replied, "God Damn it! If you want to go to Las Vegas put down Las Vegas." So I never worried about the situation after that.

On one of my week ends to Las Vegas, I took a friend of mine that I will call John. We spent Friday night and Saturday night in Las Vegas and had a great time. We were returning to Hurlburt Field on Sunday evening. On these trips we always took turns in the front seat. The front seat pilot made the landing. In this case it was John's turn to be in the front seat and make the landing at Hurlburt. Technically, however, as a Standardization Board Pilot I was always in command of the aircraft.

Repairs were being made on the runway at Hurlburt and only approximately six thousand feet of the south end of the runway was usable.

Also the overrun at the south end of the runway had been torn up for re-paving and there was a sixteen inch lip on the end of the runway. We were not notified of the lip on the end of the runway. When we arrived at Hurlburt on this Sunday evening there were thunderstorms all around the area. We made a normal approach for landing and everything was normal until we encountered a down draft just off the southern end of the runway. The left wing dipped about fifteen or so degrees, which was enough for the left main landing gear to impact the lip of the runway. The airplane bounced and set down on the runway again at about the one thousand feet marker. As the airplane slowed the left main gear collapsed and set the airplane down on the right main gear, the nose gear and the left tip fuel tank. We skidded up the runway for some distance and then slid off the left side of the runway into the dirt.

There was a small fire started at the left wing tip tank. We could not get the canopy to eject so we were trapped in the cockpit. I had a pocket knife in my flying suit so I opened the blade of it and tried to jab it through the canopy. The canopy was made of plexi-glass and was close to a half an inch thick. On the first jab the blade broke off the knife. I managed to punch a small hole through the canopy with the stub of the blade and the knife handle itself. I then slid down in the rear seat and kicked the top out of the canopy. We were both out of the airplane when the fire department arrived and put out the fire. I tried to demonstrate what I had done several times after this and was never able to slide down in the rear seat and kick the canopy.

To continue the story: The Colonel that I worked for was the President of the Accident Investigating Board. The same Colonel that I had helped when he had the accident. His board found that the accident was Pilot Error for not landing at Eglin AFB where they had ten thousand feet of runway. So I had to meet, along with the President of the Accident Investigating Board, with the Commanding General of the Air Defense Command.

General Robert E. Lee (not the Civil War General) was the commander of the Air Defense command at that time. There were two other pilots that had accidents that met the General before me. The general ordered Flight Evaluation Boards for both of them. This meant that they had a good chance of being grounded. I figured that I had really had it when I was called in with Colonel R. We both saluted General Lee and were seated. General Lee said that he had read the report and that he had one question for Colonel R. He said "Colonel R, if you had been flying that T-33 on that night, where would you have landed?" Colonel R said that he probably would have chosen his home base at Hurlburt Field. General Lee replied "You're damn right, and so would have I, so don't blame Captain Hazlett." So my accident report just disappeared. It was never entered on my records.

However the man that I pulled strings to get him out of a mess tried to hang me. Poetic Justice.

These Guys

Although Bob Hazlett, USAF Lt. Col. (Ret.) was never a member of the USAFSS I put down these stories and information about him as I feel his contributions were relative to the Cold War era, and beyond. His comments:

Trish, Yes I applied for selection as an astronaut and met all the requirements and passed all the tests but I was about six months past the maximum age for selection at that time. I was about the same age as John Glenn. The Navy gave Glenn a waiver on his age but the Air Force decided against giving any waivers so I was dropped. I checked out in jet fighters in the same group as Gordon Cooper and was quite well acquainted with Gus Grissom. I was never assigned to the USAFSS but I did do some work for the old Air Technical Intelligence Division at Wright Pat. I helped analyze the capabilities of the Russian Bison Bomber when it first appeared. I also was a Top Secret Currier for about a year in the 50's. I also went through Russian language school in the mid 60's in preparation to being assigned to Moscow as an Air Technical Liaison Officer (licensed spy). But instead I ended up going to Southeast Asia. I had a Top Secret Crypto clearance and a Top Secret Special Intelligence Clearance and was cleared for ridiculous! For some time in the 50's and 60's I was not allowed to fly on a commercial airliner flying into Florida.

The squadron that I was assigned to in WWII was on the island of Edimama. I spent a 30 day R&R in Sydney after I was shot down. I also made a trip into Karachi when it was still in India. We were also stationed in the Phillippines and Java. I was also stationed in Panama during WWII and spent some time on the Galapagos Islands. I was stationed at Nakom Panom in northeast Thailand. When the Gulf War I occurred I was working in Saudi Arabia. So as you can see I spent a lot of time in the Pacific; Japan, Okinawa, Taiwan, Hong Kong, Philippines, and Hawaii. I also worked with a squadron on Johnson Island.

I went through Russian language school at Ft. Carson, Colorado. I was stationed at Ent AFB. I was Chief of Space Defense in the Deputy Commander for Plans in the Air Defense Command. I was not allowed to fly commercial into Florida because of the commercial airliners that had been hijacked into Cuba.

I flew three C-47 gun ships from Florida to Viet Nam. When I flew the first one into Saigon I wanted to stay overnight and see the city. The Col. in charge insisted that I be on the next airplane for the states because of my clearances. He didn't think I should have been allowed to fly into Viet Nam. When I was assigned to Southeast Asia at Nakom Panom I was debriefed in the states and told that I should forget everything I knew and my clearances were removed. When I returned to the states I was told that it was ok for me to remember and my clearances were reinstated. Makes sense doesn't it?

In the 50's I was one of these guys that had a briefcase hand cuffed to his wrist and had to carry a 45 in a shoulder holster. Stood out like a sore thumb. There were always three of us sent to the same destination on different routes. We never knew which one of us had the top secret info and which of us just had a satchel full of blank paper. I rode the centrifuge at Wright Pat. They had me up to ten g's for about four to five seconds!

KOREAN STORY NUMBER ONE
By Bob Hazlett

Let me give you a little more of my background. I learned to fly by hanging around the airport. I soloed my first time in 1934 when I was fourteen years of age. I started flying with an airline in Central America when I was nineteen years old. I flew as a production test pilot after the war started in 1941. Although I wanted to be a fighter pilot I ended up flying B-24's during World War II.

I checked out in the F-80 fighter in 1950 and was immediately assigned overseas for combat in the Korean War. I arrived at Itazuki Air Base, in Japan, and was assigned to the 35th Fighter Bomber Squadron. The 35th was the Black Panthers and was part of the 8th Fighter Bomber Wing.

The F-80 was a work horse and was the first operational jet fighter in the U.S. Air Force. It did not have long range capability in its original configuration. To give us long range the Air Force devised three hundred gallon under slung tip tanks. This approximately doubled the fuel capacity of the aircraft but made it a little over two thousand pounds overweight for takeoff when loaded with ammunition and bombs, rockets or napalm.

Itazuki had five thousand feet of runway with a thousand feet overrun on each end. The normal way that takeoffs were made was for an element of two airplanes to taxi to the end of the overrun on the runup end of the runway. Each ran their engines up to 100% for take off and at the signal from the lead airplane you released your brakes. No attempt was made to stay in formation for takeoff. Maximum flap down speed was 165 miles per hour. Usually you rolled until your wheels hit the dirt at the far end of the runway and then gently pulled back on the control stick and hoped it would fly. We always said that if you didn't pull back the stick, you lifted.

Anyway, the story I want to tell you happened on one of my combat missions somewhere around the 10th to the 15th mission I flew. We were assigned to bomb and strafe a town in North Korea. There were troops and supplies in the town. My flight leader was Mack Maclim. I was flying the number three position which was the element leader. The weather was not good, it was very hazy, with visibility of about three to five miles. Since weather forecasting was not very good we had no idea of what was coming in later. We made our takeoff at around 0500 hours. It didn't get daylight until we were well up into Korea.

Mack managed to locate our target, and for some reason that I can no longer remember after 56 years, we decided to strafe the town before dropping our 250 pound bombs. We lined up in trail and each picked a target. I was lined up on a house with a thatched roof. I was just about to open up with the F-80's six 50 caliber machine guns when I saw a larger building a little to the right of my first target. Before I could correct my course the thatched roof opened up and quad 12.5 millimeter guns came out. Their first burst shot my right tip tank off. However I was lined up on the gun position and I pulled the trigger and that was the end of the quad 12.5's.
The worst part of this was that I still had about 100 gallons of fuel in each tip tank and since they were pressure fed from the engine compressor I could not use the fuel in the other tank and it was nothing but a drag and made the aircraft out of balance. We strafed the town and dropped our bombs. I dropped my left tip tank and hoped I could start a good fire with it. We took quite a lot of fire from the ground. I was not hit again but my wing man took several hits and lost his tip tanks and lost his radio so he was not able to communicate with me from then on.

Mack formed the formation and we started to climb out. We had only gone a few miles south until we encountered dense cloud formations. We normally climbed to about twenty-five thousand feet on the way home to conserve fuel. My airplane was a real dog and I could not keep up with the formation, so my wing man and I were on our own. Mack kept climbing until he was on top of the clouds. He said he leveled at forty thousand feet. I finally managed to break out on top with my wing man but I was very short of fuel. I had no idea of my wing man's condition. I called Pusan at the southern tip of Korea and they advised me that the clouds were solid from the ground up to forty thousand feet. I called Itazuki and they advised me that they had a three hundred feet ceiling and three to five miles visibility. I called a B-26 base about 50 to 60 miles north of Itazuki and they informed me that their weather was worse than Itazuki.

I decided to make a try for Itazuki. We had an in route let down for Itazuki so I started the letdown. I had Itazuki radio tuned in for heading but I had no idea how far I was from the station as our aircraft did not have distance measuring capability at that time. We broke out of the clouds at a little under 300 feet over the bay near Brady field. Brady field had C-46's, their runway was not long enough for F-80's. I had about 20 miles to go right over the city of Fukuoka. I crossed the city at a little above roof top level with my fuel gauge bouncing on zero. We had to go to the opposite end of the runway at Itazuki as they had a tail wind of over 20 miles per hour if I landed straight in.

I made a close down wind leg to keep the runway in sight and made a short base leg and final approach. I didn't put my gear down till the last minute. I still had engine power on the final approach but when I shoved the throttle up to turn off the runway there was no power. The engine had run out of fuel and flamed out on the landing roll. My wing man's airplane flamed out on the final approach and he hit in the dirt about a thousand feet short of the overrun. His airplane bounced and he touched down next on the overrun. We both had to be towed into the line.

I decided that I would never purposely run myself that short on fuel again if I could avoid it in any way. I do not remember my wing man's name but we were both lucky to be alive.

KOREAN STORY NUMBER TWO
by Bob Hazlett

Shortly after flying my fifteenth mission in combat I was put in charge of the checkout school to check newly assigned pilots and to introduce them to the tactics we used in combat. I had four F-80's assigned to me every day for this purpose. Each day the new pilots were assigned missions to strafe and napalm the small Japanese island of Shimea.

We did not use tanks of napalm on the island. Rather we used napalm tanks filled with water. That way we were not fire bombing the island. Dropping napalm required a special technique. Since the tanks were not stabilized in any way they had the tendency to roll over end to end. The technique used in dropping the tanks for the greatest advantage was to come in to the target as low as possible and drop the tanks. Thus the napalm spread out over the greatest area.

To those of you who do not know what napalm is I will explain. Napalm is jellied gasoline. It was carried in bomb shaped tanks that held approximately one hundred sixty-five gallons in each. The tanks had a fuse or igniter that actuated on contact. Normally each F-80 carried two tanks of napalm in combat. Napalm has now been discontinued by our armed forces. It is considered inhumane to kill with fire - as though the person being killed preferred one method over another!

There were, many times, fishermen around the island of Shimea so they had to be chased away before any live rounds of ammunition were expended. I was leading a flight of four F-80's to Shimea one morning and there was a Japanese fisherman near the approach end of the island. I flew in low over him and rocked my wings to warn him to leave. He merely waved back at me. I made two or three passes over him with the same results. Finally, I came in low over him and fired the six fifty caliber machine guns well over his head. He took off with his boat rowing like an outboard motor. He was nearly jet propelled!

One day there was a large convoy of tanks and vehicles spotted in North Korea. Every available airplane in the 8th Fighter Bomber Wing was scrambled to attack the convoy. This included my four training aircraft loaded with eight napalm tanks full of water. I could only imagine what some

North Korean thought when he was doused with ice cold water! I think this was one of the most comical events that happened during my combat tour in Korea.

KOREAN STORY NUMBER THREE
by Bob Hazlett

In June of 1951 the 8th Fighter Bomber Wing moved from Itazuke Air Base in Japan to Kimpo Air Base in Korea. Kimpo is just south of Seoul. It is now Kimpo International Airport. I remained at Itazuke for about two weeks and kept the checkout school running. It was decided after this to close the school completely so I moved to Kimpo at the end of June. Kimpo was very primitive, we lived in sixteen man tents with canvas cots. In fact everything on the base was in tents. The base had been shelled and bombed by the North Koreans and there was nothing around except rubble.

The runway was just five thousand feet long and had several craters in it. The craters had been hastily repaired by the Army Engineers and some of the repairs had sunk several inches below the rest of the runway. We could not take off in formation any longer and had to take off individually. The reason for this was that you started your takeoff on the right side of the runway to avoid a sunken spot and then about half way along the runway you switched to the left side to avoid another sunken spot.

We were being harassed every night by a North Korean biplane that was so slow that the night fighters had trouble intercepting it. They would come over around nine o'clock or later and drop mortar shells on us. It was really more of a nuisance than a danger as they were not very accurate.

The media people called it "Bed-check Charlie," however, we in the military were not so polite, and we called him "Piss-call Pete." When he would approach the siren would blow and we were supposed to get into fox holes that had been prepared outside of the tents. The first night I was there the siren blew and I had an end cot next to the entrance to the tent. I jumped up, exited the tent and dived into the fox hole and landed on top of the guy that followed me out of the tent. How he managed to get by me I will never know. Anyway, after a few nights of doing this I decided it was worthless and just decided to stay in my cot.

Since we were not going such a distance on our missions the large tip tanks were removed and the old one hundred sixty-five gallon tanks were reinstalled. This meant to the brass that we could carry a heavier load. For instance, instead of two, two hundred fifty pound bombs we could carry two five hundred pound bombs. Or instead of only two, two hundred fifty pound bombs we could add eight 5.5 inch HVAR rockets. Anyway with only five thousand feet of runway we were having difficulty getting airborne with the loads we were carrying. Several pilots jettisoned their load to get airborne. I rolled several feet on the dirt on the end of the runway several times before becoming airborne.

There was a small village at the north end of the runway. One pilot could not get airborne and went right through the village. There were many people in the village killed, many of them children. He ejected but since we did not have zero level ejection seats it only sent him about ninety feet in the air, and he was traveling about one hundred-fifty miles per hour or more forward speed, there was not much left of him. I was the investigating officer for the accident and I couldn't look at a piece of meat for some time.

We had a special mission where we were each carrying two one thousand pound bombs. We had to use JTO (Jet Assisted Takeoff) for takeoff. These are two rockets attached to the fuselage of the aircraft. We were to start our takeoff to the north and when we reached ninety miles per hour we were to fire our JTO. I was about the ninth aircraft to take off and as I approached ninety miles per hour I ran into a cloud of smoke where the visibility was near zero. I was just about to fire my JTO when two bombs bounced over my wings. The pilot ahead of me had jettisoned his bombs and they bounced and tumbled right over my wings without hitting me. These are just a few of the things that happened because of the lousy condition of the runway at Kimpo. We actually lost more pilots to the runway than we lost to enemy fire.

One of the flights that we made out of Kimpo was to hit an antiaircraft battery in North Korea. Mack Macklin was again leading the flight and I was flying as his wing man. A man named Lorch was element lead and his wing man was Willie. When we arrived at our target area there was only one approach we could make to hit the antiaircraft guns. We had to fly down between two mountains and try to come in low enough to drop our napalms. It was a difficult situation and we were not able to get low enough to be effective. Each time when we came out from between the mountains the gun positions were really nailing us. Willie called and said "they're shooting at me," Mac replied, "what the hell do you think they're doing to us, throwing rocks?"

I seemed to be getting hit by flack on every pass. Mack called and said to shove the power up to 90% but my throttle was already against the stop and I was barely keeping up with Mack. I had several holes in my wings that I could see and my engine did not seem to be performing the way it should. I finally called and said I had to head south. Mack called, asked if I needed help and I told him no that I thought I could make it. I climbed to about twenty thousand feet and headed straight for Kimpo. This route took me right over Inchon harbor which was restricted airspace. As I approached Inchon the Navy called and told me I was approaching restricted airspace and they would have to shoot at me if I continued on this course. I called them and said to go ahead and fire as I didn't think they were as good as the guys up north. So I flew over Inchon harbor and no shots were fired.

I set the aircraft down at Kimpo. It had over two hundred holes in it. One shot went right through the compressor wheel of my engine which caused the engine not to perform well and gave me a lot of vibration. I also had a piece of flack in my survival dingy about an inch below my butt. I had a few shots of scotch to calm my nerves. I had a little trouble keeping the first one in the glass because I was shaking so much.

COLD WAR STORY NUMBER ONE
by Bob Hazlett

After receiving my first master's degree from the Air Force Institute of Technology at Wright/Patterson Air Force Base located at Dayton, Ohio, I was transferred to the 29th Fighter Interceptor Squadron at Great Falls, Montana. The 29th was located on Malmstrom Air Force Base. The squadron was flying F-94C aircraft. These aircraft were sort of a souped up version of the T-33 trainer (a two seat F-80). The F-94C had a more powerful jet engine equipped with an afterburner. It also had a swept back tail and the winds had more dihedral than the T-33. The rear seat was occupied by a radar operator. The radar was located in the nose of the F-94C. The aircrafts armament consisted of forty- eight two point five inch rockets. Twenty-four of the rockets were in the nose of the airplane and twenty-four rockets were carried in two pods in the wings. It had a top speed of mach point eight two. If you exceeded this speed the aircraft had a very definite nose tuck. From straight and level you could lose five thousand feet in just a matter of a few seconds.

The F-94C was a very stable airplane and handled very nicely in weather. This was good since we were an all weather squadron. The big disadvantages of the F-94C were its speed restriction and it had a limited range. The maximum time you could stay airborne was in the vicinity of two hours. This time was decreased if you had to use the afterburner for any period of time except for takeoff.

I had to make a series of training flights before I was qualified to stand alert for the squadron. I no longer remember the number of flights required. I had read somewhere that you could take the F-94C supersonic straight down. I decided that I would try it. I was going up for my third training flight and my newly assigned radar operator asked if he could ride along. I told him that it was ok with me but that I intended to take the airplane supersonic on the flight. He just laughed and got his equipment and we did our checks and climbed into the airplane. I made the takeoff and climbed out to the north to an altitude of about forty-five thousand feet. There I rolled the airplane over and headed straight down with full power on. The airplane went through several gyrations called a Dutch roll. It was very loud and we had a lot of vibrations but we went supersonic at about thirty-eight thousand feet and the aircraft became very smooth and was very stable.

Around twenty-nine thousand feet the denser air slowed the airplane and we went back sonic. We went through all the vibration and gyrations again and I pulled out of the dive at about fifteen thousand feet, about ten thousand feet above ground level in Montana. The rest of the flight was uneventful and I landed back at Malmstrom AFB after about an hour and a half flight. I taxied the airplane onto the fuel pit and sat in the cockpit and filled out the paperwork. My radar operator got out of the airplane and went in the hangar. When I walked in I was told that the Squadron Commander wanted to see me right away. I went to his office and reported. He asked me what I had done on my flight and I said nothing unusual. He said that my radar operator came in his office and said that he would never fly with that crazy sob again. I told the Command what I had done and he liked the idea. Within a month or so just about every pilot in the squadron had taken the F-94C to supersonic speed.

I had been in the squadron about five or six months and was on "alert" when this episode happened. Perhaps I should explain. We had four flights in the squadron and each flight was on alert status for twenty-four hours. When you were on alert you stayed in the alert facility for twelve hours. If the scramble bell rang you had to be airborne within five minutes or you had to write a letter to the Division Commanding General explaining why you exceeded five minutes.

In this instance I went on alert at 1900 hours (7:00 PM). The weather was very bad, we had heavy snow and gusting winds. The ceiling was zero and the visibility was near zero. In this condition the senior man on alert took the number one position. I was the senior man. This meant that if the scramble rang I was the pilot that had to be airborne within five minutes.

About 2100 hours the scramble bell rang. In this case me and my radar operator manned the airplane and started the engine while the number two pilot called and asked if the scramble was mandatory. In every case prior to this, in bad weather, the scramble was not mandatory and the number two pilot would run out and give the cut signal. This is what I expected to happen but in this case he ran out and gave me the go signal.

I gave the aircraft the power and we headed from the alert hangar directly to the runway. I made the takeoff in zero-zero conditions in well under the five minutes. I climbed out under the direction of the ground controller that was guiding me with his radar. I broke out on top of the clouds at about twenty thousand feet. It was a moonlit night and visibility was very good. The ground controller brought us into position where my radar operator could lock onto your intercept target. We locked on at about twelve miles. When I had a visual on the target it was a four engine airplane and the markings on the tail looked like Russian from my point of view. When I got closer I realized the markings were the letters DC-7 interlaced so that it looked somewhat like a Russian letter.

I had a hard time catching the airliner as he seemed to be attempting to outrun me. I had to use afterburner to catch him and I had the F-94C setting right on mach point eight two. When I finally caught up with the DC-7 the pilot cut the power and I went shooting by him like a freight train passing a bum. I had to make a large circle to the right and pull back up beside the airliner. It was United Airlines flight from Anchorage to Seattle. He was about seven hundred miles off course.

I was quite disgusted and I pulled in tight in formation. I was actually inside his wing tip. The ground controller asked me if I could read his aircraft number and I told the controller that I could tell him what color the copilot's eyes were if he wanted to know. There was a head in every window. I thought that the pilot might report me for pulling in so close but nothing ever happened.

After the intercept, because I had had to use the burner so much I was running low on fuel; the ground controller steered me back to Great Falls. The Division Commanding General came up on the radio and asked me whether I wanted to make a Ground Controlled Approach (GCA) at Malmstrom or Instrument Landing System (ILS) approach at Great Falls International Air Port. I had had some unsatisfactory GCA approaches at Malmstrom so I chose to make an ILS approach at Great Falls International. With the ILS the ground stations send signals to the airplane and an instrument, with cross hairs, on the instrument panel guides you to the runway. The General told me I had one chance to make the landing and if I failed to land I was to pull up to about ten thousand feet and eject. Neither I nor my radar operator wanted to eject in this weather so we decided that we would make it on this approach.

The ground radar guided me into the ILS approach and I kept the needles centered on the way down. My radar operator kept telling me how far we were from the runway. He told me when we crossed the highway that runs beside the airport and when we crossed the end of the runway. I still had the ILS needles centered and when we crossed the end of the runway I pulled the power off and pulled the nose up slightly. We touched down smoothly and I could see runway lights go by on each side so I knew we were on the runway. I got the F-94C stopped and called the tower. I said I could not see to taxi and that they would have to send a tug to tow me to the apron. The tower said he could not see me and had no idea where we were but he would send a tug to tow us to the line. Even though it was cold and snowing and blowing, we climbed out of the airplane to get on the ground. It was good to be there.

COLD WAR STORY NUMBER TWO
by Bob Hazlett

In November 1956 a request came into the 29th Air Defense Division for an F-94 pilot to go on exchange duty with the Navy. It specified that the person chosen had to have at least four hundred hours in the F-94 and be a regular officer. There were only two of us in the 29th squadron that had these qualifications. One was a Captain Bill Cunningham and then I. Bill already had orders for another assignment and was not interested so that left only me.

I heard about this assignment when our squadron commander came into the ready room and told me about it. He said he sure would like for me to get the assignment but that I was on a directed duty assignment and couldn't go. I went to the Personnel Office and asked them about the assignment and they said that there was nothing to prevent me from going. They said that my directed duty assignment would not interfere. They said that the only thing I needed was the squadron commanders ok. I told them that he said he would like for me to get the assignment. They called him and he told them that under no circumstances was I to be put in for the assignment. I asked what I would need to get the assignment and they said that I would now have to have a letter from my commander recommending me for the assignment.

I was at a loss as what to do. I went back to the squadron and went to the commander's office. He greeted me by saying he sure would like for me to get the assignment to the Navy. I said, "Would you please put that in writing sir." He had backed himself into a box and finally agreed to write a letter recommending me for the assignment. So my name and qualifications were submitted and the Navy accepted me.

I received my orders on the 20th of December and was authorized thirty days delay in route to Miramar Naval Air Base near San Diego. The only catch was that I was to report no later than 7 January 1957. I cleared the base at Malmstrom and my wife, son and I headed west to Seattle on the 22nd of December. We were the last car to get over the pass west of Missoula because of heavy snow. We arrived in San Francisco on Christmas Eve and spent the night in a very nice motel. The people treated us just great. We spent Christmas day in San Francisco and had a wonderful time. We left San

Francisco on the 26th and arrived in San Diego on the 28th. We stayed in a motel for about a week while we looked for a place to rent. We finally got settled in a house before I reported to the Navy on the 7th of January. The only problem was that we did not have any furniture. Our furniture got caught in the snow storm and we were not sure just when it would arrive.

I reported to Navy Air Group 5 at Miramar Naval Air Station on the 7th of January. I was given the choice of any squadron that I wanted in the air group. I chose VF-141 the Iron Angels. The squadron skipper was Commander Klahn. This was the first squadron to become operational with the Douglas F4D Skyray. I immediately had to start training as the group was to go on cruise to the Pacific in July. The navy pilots had to have at least two hundred fifty hours in the F4D to make the cruise but it was decided that because of my flying experience that I could deploy with a minimum of fifty hours.

The Squadron Executive Officer insisted on making a courtesy call before our furniture arrived so we entertained the Exec and his wife on the floor. Not the greatest way to entertain, but the only way we had since he absolutely insisted.

I became the Training Officer for the squadron. The training was intense both for me and for the other members of the squadron. The F4D, known to its pilots as the Ford, was a high performance aircraft. It held the worlds climb record of fifty thousand feet in four minutes and was capable of maintaining supersonic speed in level flight. It was the Navy's newest interceptor aircraft. It was a single place airplane, the pilot operated the radar and flew the airplane. It had Westinghouse radar and would easily lock onto a target at thirty-five miles. It was a very enjoyable airplane to fly. It was very stable, very maneuverable and handled very well. The only big problem was the radar. Sun proof radar monitors had not yet been invented and without shading the monitor it was impossible to read it. Someone in the squadron came up with a rubber shade that we called "elephant ears" to shade the scope. It was said, however, that the pilots needed two heads and three hands to do a good job on an intercept.

The Navy did not have any training guide for this kind of training and did not have any written directions on how to make an attack on an enemy aircraft with rockets. I wrote the first training guide and the manual on how to make an intercept on an enemy aircraft with rockets. Thus an Air Force officer wrote the Navy's first instructions on this type of interception.

The first time I had ever seen a naval aircraft carrier was after I arrived in San Diego. I had never seen anything but pictures of a carrier prior to that. I was flying around San Diego at about thirty thousand feet when I noticed a carrier in Mission Bay. It looked terribly small so I dropped down to ten thousand feet. It still looked like a postage stamp. I called North Island control tower and asked for permission to make a low pass by the carrier. They granted me permission and I flew by the starboard side of the carrier at about one hundred feet above the bay. The carrier still looked like a postage stamp. I kept thinking that I was going to have to land on that postage stamp!!!

The squadron started the carrier qualifications in about April of 1957. Six arrested landings were required to qualify. Some of our officers that were ahead of me in training did their qualifications on the Lexington. I started my qualifying on the Bonne Homme Richard; the USS BHR -- the Underway Saturday and Sunday Big Hunk of Rust. This was the carrier we would deploy to on to the Pacific. It was a World War II carrier that had been modified with a canted deck. It was CVA-31.

The day I was to start my qualification flights the VAH-2 (Heavy Attack squadron 2) were practicing approaches to the carrier. VAH-2 flew the Douglas A3D twin engine bombers. It was a fairly large aircraft and had never landed on a carrier before. The squadron commander was finally given the ok to make a "touch and go" landing. He came in a little too low and hit just in front of the main gear on the round down on the aft end of the deck. His airplane split in two and the rear dropped into the water behind the carrier and the forward part came up the deck skidding on the engine nacelles and dropped into the water and exploded. I was watching this from the crow's nest. I kept thinking I'm next. I didn't think I could fly after watching that. However flying was called off for the day.

The next day I received my briefing and was told that I would make two "touch and go" landings and then I would be told to put my tail hook down and make an arrested landing. I was instructed that if everything was ok I would give a thumbs-up and taxi onto the catapult and would make a second flight and landing. I had been warned about the catapult that accelerated you from zero to one hundred eighty knots in one hundred eighty feet. I taxied my airplane onto the catapult and did my run-up. I saluted the catapult officer and I was off. It really didn't seem to be all that bad.

I climbed into the traffic pattern and received permission for my first touch and go landing. We used a system of lights on the carrier to steer the aircraft in for a landing. You set up a rate of descent with the lights and flew the aircraft into the deck. I made one touch and go and was climbing back into the pattern when the Landing Signal Officer (LSO) called and told me to put my hook down. I replied that I had made only one touch and go. He replied by saying, "I know how many touch and goes you have made, put your damn hook down."

This shook me up so much that I took a wave off on my first attempt to land. I was not in position to make the landing. So I climbed into the pattern again and made my second approach. I really watched it close and set it down on the deck as I had been taught. No one had warned me about the arrested landing. What a shock. I came out of the arresting gear and taxied up the deck. I gave them a thumbs-down and they wanted to know what was wrong with the airplane. I told them nothing was wrong with the airplane but the pilot was not in condition to make another landing.

I completed my six carrier qualification landings in May and my skipper made a trip to Washington and had me designated a Naval Aviator. Thus I am one of the few pilots ever that were qualified to wear the silver wings of the Air Force and the god wings of the Navy.

We deployed to the Pacific in July of 1957. My room mate, Lt. (JG) Joe Muca, and I attempted to take a refrigerator on board. We were refused permission and were told that Captain Brush, the carrier skipper, did not allow refrigerators. We took the refrigerator to the paint shop on North Island and had it painted Navy gray and had U.S. Navy stenciled on the front. We then returned to the carrier and they helped us load it and take it to our state room. We carried enough beer aboard, in boxes with a few clothes on top, to fill the refrigerator. Thus Joe and I had a cold beer before evening mess each evening.

After deployment we went first to Hawaii where we were tested and passed as being combat ready. Top Guns did not exist then but if they had our squadron would all have been Top Guns. I might point out that it is said that the three most enjoyable things in life are a good bowel movement, a good urination and an orgasm. Navy pilots say that all three can occur on a night carrier landing. I whole heartedly agree. On one of the exercises I came in for a landing which seemed to be quite normal. However, my left main gear landed directly on one of the arresting cables. It split the wheel in two and I came up the deck skidding on the left wheel break rotor. I was completely unaware of what had happened until my airplane started to turn to the left and I saw a tire and parts of the wheel going up the deck in front of me. The arresting gear brought me to a halt and several deck hands rushed to my airplane and lifted the left wing on their backs so that a dolly could be put under the left main strut. In only a few seconds my airplane was taken up the deck out of the way for aircraft to land. The landing aircraft had forty seconds spacing between them. Only one aircraft missed its landing position behind me.

From Hawaii we went to Japan and then we started a patrol of the Pacific. We were harassed by Russian subs and Russian bombers flying over the fleet. We were in the Pacific with the nearest land being about a thousand miles away. We were in the mid-Pacific directly west of Hawaii and southeast of Japan. We were in rough weather with the aircraft carrier pitching up and down about a hundred feet. I was called to the squadron ready room and told that there was an unknown target circling the fleet at about fifty thousand feet. I was to launch and make a maximum performance climb to make an intercept and identify the object.

The launch was uneventful and I made a maximum performance climb to fifty thousand feet. I was told that the object had started to climb rapidly from fifty thousand feet and had disappeared off radar at a speed of over mach 2 headed toward China. My distance measuring equipment (DME) indicated that I was about one hundred-fifty miles from the carrier. So I started my let-down and headed for the carrier.

When I arrived at the carrier and started my landing approach I was unable to keep the control light known as the meat ball centered in any way. It was going off the top and off the bottom. I could not control the airplane to keep it centered because the ship was pitching up and down about a hundred feet. I asked for permission to have the LSO bring me in with paddles but my request was denied. I then asked for an LSO that we knew as "Red Dog" to come to the landing platform and bring me in. I was asked how much fuel I had aboard and I lied and doubled the amount I really had. I came around in the traffic pattern and started my final approach. Red Dog talked me in, I paid no attention to the meat ball. At the last second he gave me a wave off because the aft end of the carrier started up. Captain Brush came up on the radio and asked me how much fuel I had remaining. I again lied and told him that I had a little over twelve hundred pounds. This is approximately two hundred gallons which was not enough to make another attempt after this one. Actually I had only about six hundred pounds which is about one hundred gallons. This was barely enough to complete the landing pattern.

Captain Brush told me that if I did not land on this attempt that I was to pull up to at least five thousand feet or as high as I could get and eject. So I entered the pattern again and this time Red Dog talked me in till I passed over the round down. When I say he talked me in it consisted of him saying you're too high or too low. We made no use of the landing system what so ever. When I passed over the round down Red Dog said "land it." I jammed the stick forward and slammed the F4D onto the deck. It wasn't a good landing but I was down. I shook for the next two or three hours. I tried some coffee in the ward room but even holding the cup with both hands I was unable to keep the coffee from sloshing out.

We never did figure out what had been circling the fleet but whatever it was it climbed out at a very steep angle at speeds of over mach 2. As you are aware this falls into the category of an UFO. This was not my first encounter with UFO's and was not my last encounter with these mysteries. Of course these are other stories. I do not know what I would have done if I had been able to make an intercept on the unknown target. We were completely unaware of any Russian aircraft that had the capability to perform as this unknown.

COLD WAR STORY NUMBER THREE
by Bob Hazlett

My closest encounter with a UFO occurred while I was assigned to the 29th Fighter Interceptor Squadron stationed at Malmstrom Air Force Base near Great Falls, Montana. The insignia of the 29th was a fighting cock. The squadron always had a fighting cock as a mascot and the newest Second Lieutenant assigned to the squadron was always designated as the "Keeper of the Cock" and had to take care of the mascot. The 29th was a typical Air Defense Fighter Interceptor squadron that was assigned to intercept any unidentified aircraft entering the United States. We were guarding the northern border and operated in the area from Spokane, Washington to approximately Minot, North Dakota. There were approximately sixty pilots and sixty radar operators assigned for flying and approximately two hundred enlisted personnel assigned for maintenance and support. The pilots and radar operators were divided into four flights. The flights rotated on alert so that each flight was on alert status every four days. This was three hundred sixty five days a year.

When a flight was on alert status the pilots and radar operators assigned for duty that day had to stay in the ready room for a twelve hour shift. On each shift there were two pilots and two radar officers. We normally rotated into the number one position; that is the crew that had to take a scramble if the bell rang. We had two F-94C aircraft assigned for alert each day. When you went on alert you each inspected your assigned aircraft and set your parachutes in your seats ready to go. You normally placed your helmet on the edge of the cockpit and plugged the oxygen hose into the seat connection so that it was ready to be donned as you got into the cockpit. Starting units were plugged into the aircraft and were set so that the ground crew only had to start them and turn on the power to start the jet engine. The flight crew members that were not actively on alert had to remain at home near a telephone and had to be ready to fly with a half hours notice. After a flight's alert day they received a day off and then had two days of training and then back onto alert on the fourth day.

I was going on "alert" one evening in August or September of 1956 and as I finished my check of my assigned F-94C and set up my equipment I received a telephone call from the local radar station. It was seven o'clock in the evening (1900 hours for you military types) and I would be on duty until seven o'clock in the morning (0700 hours). We had several radar stations around the area. The call was from the local radar site on the base at Malmstrom. The call was from the Ground Controlled Intercept (GCI) officer. The GCI officer is the person that commanded the scramble and the one that activated the scramble bell in the ready room; he informed me that the ground observer's corps at Kalispell, Montana had sighted a UFO hovering over the city. The ground observer's corps was organized during World War II to scan the sky and pick up any flying objects and report them to a central agency. They were made up of volunteers and the corps was in existence. They claimed that it appeared to be about five thousand feet above the ground. It had windows with bright lights and was just hovering in place over the city. My first comment was "what brand are they drinking?" Anyway I was told that as soon as I was ready they would give me a scramble but they would lose contact with me before I got to Kalispell, which is in western Montana, as I would be out of range and there were no other radar stations in that area. I told them that I was ready anytime so the scramble bell rang in a few minutes. The reason that the radar station lost contact with me was because we used ultra high frequency radios (UHF) that were "line of site transmission" which meant that the maximum range was about two hundred miles at thirty thousand feet or above.

I ran out to my airplane and climbed into the cockpit. The procedure was that as soon as I hit the seat my right arm went through my parachute harness and hit the start switch which was on the right console. My left arm went through the other side of the harness and grabbed the throttle on the left console. While the jet engine was spooling up I donned my helmet and fastened my oxygen mask across my face. My radar officer was climbing into the rear seat at the same time. He had his own procedures. In this case my radar operator was a Lieutenant Storz (I am not sure of the spelling). As the jet engine started I signaled the wheel chocks to be pulled and shoved the throttle up to taxi. The radar officer read the check list to me as we taxied out. I performed the checks and fastened my shoulder harness and seat belt while we were on the way to the runway. I still did not have my parachute harness fastened and on some hot scrambles I never did get my harness fastened before we landed.

I had clearance onto the runway and immediately shoved full power and cut in the after burner. We were airborne in less than four minutes after the scramble bell rang. If we exceeded five minutes I would have had to write a letter to the division commander and explain why I didn't make it in less than five minutes. The radar station guided me as far as he could toward Kalispell. In this case I had time to fasten my parachute harness on the way to the target area. I arrived over Kalispell at about fifteen thousand feet indicated. The aircraft altimeter indicates feet above sea level and not feet above the ground. There was cloud cover over Kalispell but I could see a faint glow in the clouds over the city. This is common as you can normally see the clouds lit up over cities if the clouds are not too thick. I had no one to talk to for guidance and the clouds looked fairly thick. Kalispell is located in a valley at an elevation close to five thousand feet so I was about ten thousand feet above the valley floor. The mountains on either side of Kalispell go up to an elevation of eight thousand feet or more.

I circled around and tried to find a hole in the clouds but the cloud cover seemed to be quite solid. Since there was no published let down for any airport around Kalispell, I had no safe way to let down through the clouds. Some of these clouds, no doubt, sat right on top of the mountains and I didn't want to take a chance of making a letdown into the mountains. I stayed and circled around as long as I could but the F-94C had a limited range and I was fast approaching the time when I would have to leave to get back to Great Falls. I finally shoved the power up and headed home without seeing anything but the tops of clouds over Kalispell. I climbed to about twenty-five thousand feet to go home because the jet engine is far more efficient at high altitude. On the way to my home base I passed my wing man who had been scrambled to take a look also. I told him what I had found and he said he didn't know just what more he could accomplish but that he would take a look. I am sorry I no longer can remember my wing man's name. I can see his face but I just can't place a name.

When I got back to Malmstrom I taxied my aircraft onto the fuel pit and filled out the forms. The F-94C had single point refueling and could receive fuel for all tanks from one connection. When I got to the ready room the radar station was already on the telephone. They told me that the ground observer's corps could hear my airplane when I was overhead and that the object that they were watching seemed to follow me. They again said that the object was round and seemed to be about one hundred fifty feet in diameter and had windows with lights around the edges. They asked if I could devise a letdown for Kalispell. I told them that I would try and that I would let them know as soon as I had something. I got the charts out and looked at the area. I made up a let down procedure for Kalispell using the Missoula radio range. This was the old type of radio range that had four legs for approach to a station. One of the legs extended right over Kalispell.

I called the radar station and relayed the information and told them that the aircraft was ready and they could scramble me at any time. The scramble bell rang and we were off again. I passed my wing man on the way. He was on the way home with the same results that I had. I lost contact with the radar station again as I was letting down toward Kalispell. I started the letdown that I had devised. I went into the clouds at about thirteen thousand feet indicated (above sea level), about eight thousand feet above the valley floor. I broke out of the clouds at about eight thousand feet indicated (about four thousand feet above the valley floor).

I could see the lights of Kalispell off to my right, I was heading southeast. About this time we picked up a terrific squeal in our head phones. I could not talk to my radar officer. There was no way to turn off this squeal without turning all my radios off. I was too busy at this time to mess with the radios as my airplane started losing airspeed. I kept shoving the throttle forward but I was still losing airspeed. Due to the night time situation, and being near the base of the clouds, I immediately went onto instruments so that I could be completely aware of my airplane's attitude. I was straight and level and losing airspeed. I reached full power and then went onto afterburner. With full power and afterburner the J-48 engine in the F-94 produced approximately ten thousand pounds of thrust. I could hold about one hundred eighty knots and climb very slightly. The F-94C stalled at around one hundred fifty knots without flaps extended. It stalled at around one hundred thirty knots with flaps extended. A knot is a nautical mile per hour. A nautical mile is approximately 1.15 times longer than a mile. All aircraft instruments indicate in knots and nautical miles. An aircraft stall is when the wings stall. When this occurs the wings lose their lift and the aircraft noses down. A stall at this altitude in the F-94 would have been fatal as it takes about five thousand feet to recover with the F-94. I could never make a recovery before hitting the ground.

The terrific squeal continued and I decided to climb the airplane as much as I could. With the afterburner going I should have had a climb rate of about eight to ten thousand feet a minute at this altitude. I was able to climb at two hundred feet a minute or less. Around twelve thousand feet indicated, about seven thousand feet above the valley floor, the squeal stopped and it felt like something let loose of the airplane. The airplane just shot forward and I was up to three hundred knots and climbing at over six thousand feet a minute in just a few seconds. My radar operator told me that as soon as we picked up the squeal that his radar scope lit up like a large electric light bulb. He said it was so bright that he was blinded and could not see a thing outside the airplane. I wanted to go back down through the clouds and take another look but I was very near to minimum fuel to make it back to Great Falls. So I started a climb out to about twenty-five thousand feet and headed home. On the way I passed my wing man again. I briefed him on what had happened to me and continued on my way home.

I landed at Malmstrom and taxied onto the fuel pit and filled out the forms. When I entered the ready room the radar station was on the telephone for me again. He relayed the information from the ground observer's corps. They said that they saw me break out of the clouds and that I headed straight for the object that they were watching. They said it looked like I was going to hit it but that I went just over it or under it. I, of course, saw nothing as I had my eyes inside the cockpit watching the instruments. The GCI controller said that he wanted me to make a third trip to Kalispell and I told him that I was ready.

As soon as I hung up the telephone it rang again and it was the Commanding General of the 29th Air Defense Division. He told me that, when I broke out of the clouds on my let- down into Kalispell, if the radar operator could lock onto the object that my orders were to salvo all of my forty-eight rockets into the target.

I passed my wing man on the way to Kalispell and he said as soon as he broke through the clouds he picked up the squeal on the headphones. He immediately gave the airplane full power with afterburner and climbed out. By the time I made my second letdown into Kalispell it was day light. I cruised up and down the valley and looked everywhere I could but found nothing. I was sort of disappointed. I finally had to climb out and head home. I had spent more than twelve hours chasing something I never saw. I landed back at Malmstrom and taxied the F-94 onto the fuel pit. I was tired and somewhat disgusted.

When I got into the ready room the radar station was on the telephone again. It was the GCI officer and he told me that the ground observer's corps said that as soon as I broke out of the clouds on my last pass the object, which appeared black or gray in the morning light, took off to the west and was out of sight in seconds.

My radar officer and I had to go through a debriefing by our Intelligence Officer and after we finished we were informed that we had to remain in the ready room as some interrogating officers were on their way from Wright-Patterson AFB at Dayton, Ohio. They were from the office that keeps records on UFO occurrences. They were due to land in a few minutes. When they arrived they asked us to tell them everything that happened. We went over what had happened on each flight. They also interviewed my wing man and his radar operator. They asked me if I felt heat in the cockpit and I informed them that I could not say for sure that I felt heat but that I had about six inches of sweat sloshing around in the cockpit while the airplane was losing airspeed. They told me that what we had experienced was very similar to what every other pilot had reported except that the others all said they felt heat.

Anyway this is the story of my close encounter with a UFO. I was not told that I could not talk about this and was not sworn to secrecy. I have heard others say that they were sworn to secrecy but this did not happen to me. I wish I could say that I saw the object but I did not. Was there something there? You can bet there was. However there is no way I could say just what it was. There are at least three other crew members that can verify this story and there may still be some members of the ground observer's corps that could verify the story.

This is an e-mail to Trish Schiesser from Pappy Hicks in which he includes his letter to the Tyler Courier-Times-Telegraph, Tyler, Texas. He says: I thought I'd send this along. I'm getting kind of ticked off at Murtha, and other people, who are called our leaders. Plus our idiotic fringe fellow citizens. These people are kicking our Congressman because of his comment on Murtha.

LETTERS
By Pappy Hicks

As a young teenager, I ran up and down hills, across rice paddies, killing people I didn't even know in Korea 1951-52. I was US Army, infantry, a "grunt." It was our people who were wounded by bullets, knocked down by artillery and mortars, and torn by shrapnel. You haven't been in combat until you have had bullets pop past your ears or shrapnel whiz past your head.

Between wars I got a US Army commission, infantry. Since I was a combat veteran with a Combat Infantry Badge, I was asked to go into deep covert special operations in 1959. I went on operations early on to Laos, South Viet Nam, Congo, Central America and other spots, always shooting and fighting my lifetime enemy, communists. Many people in the Special Forces and CIA know me. Besides the VFW here in Troup, TX, I belong to the Special Forces Association Chapter 15 in San Antonio. Before I got shot out of the saddle, so to speak, I made my last operation to Laos in March, 1968. I know war and I know combat.

It ticks this old soldier off to hear these "generals" here at home and other parts of the US defending House Rep. Murtha. "You can't condemn him. He is a war hero from the Viet Nam War!" We combat sergeants and officers, I've been both, don't feel that a man with a Purple Heart is a hero. He just happened to be standing in the wrong place at the wrong time. I've fought among heroes, knew many and most of us say a hero has had his flag folded and is no longer with us. And it doesn't mean you know much just because you are a veteran. Look at John Kerry. Less than four months in Viet Nam and he is an expert on all things military?

Now I hear people bad mouth our House of Representative Gohmert for attacking this phony named Murtha. Murtha, a guy who is calling for all kinds of things we should do and condemning our soldiers at the time they are in combat fighting and getting killed. My GOD! That's a soldier's job, to fight and die. We have kept our country free, and yes, Korea stopped the spread of communism. We tried to top it off in Southeast Asia but Americans who had rather condemn their own country and soldiers more than the enemy brought us home and would not let us finish the job from the beginning. If you think we could not have won, that shows your ability as a general.

But, stay off Gohmert's back. I don't know the man, but I know he is doing a great job for our district.

D.L. Pappy Hicks, US Army, Retired, Troup, TX 75789

This poem is by Jon Horton, a wonderful and talented writer, today. His site is: www.sunlightpublishing.com. Please feel free to go to his site and see the great writings he has to offer. This particular poem was written by "Johnny" Horton, Cheyenne, Wyoming, while he was stationed in the USAFSS at the 6901st SCG, Zweibrucken in the fall of 1963. This poem was originally brought to my attention by John Oberg (USAFSS) and I was given permission to use it by Jon Horton.

THE RETURN OF THE TEUTON HORDES
or
ROME OR BUST!

MY HEAD A'SWIMMING, THE TRAIN A'JIGGLING,
THE WIND A'GURGLING AND THE WOMEN A'GIGGLING

THE MOON LOPES BY ON THE BACK OF THE NIGHT.
THE REVELERS LAUGH IN THE BOWELS OF THE TRAIN
LEAVING GERMANY AND ITS ETERNAL RAIN
TO THE CLACK-SLAM! OF THE WHEELS AND THEIR SMALL SPARKS OF LIGHT.

"PASS THE JUICE!" COMES THE SMALL, SMALL VOICE OF A CHILD.
'TIS LITTLE JOHNNY H.; HAIR TOUSLED - EYES WILD
WITH THE SPARKLING BLOOD OF THE GRAPE.
ONE GLANCE WILL ATTEST - MURRAY'S BENT OUT OF SHAPE.

OUR SPARSELY LIT SERPENT SCREAMS AT TUNNELS AND LAKES
AS SWITZERLAND RACES BY CLOAKED IN DARK.
RED AND GOLD TREES WAIT FOR WINTER'S SNOWFLAKES
AS THE WINDOWS AFFORD GLIMPSES OF THE STARS' ICE COLD SPARK.

THE EYES OF OUR IRON HORSE WINK OUT ONE BY ONE
WHILE ABOVE ALPS WAIT FOR THE CARESS OF THE SUN.
BUT LO AND BEHOLD!! FAR BELOW ON THE TRAIN
ONE HEARS THE CROAKING OF AN OFF-TUNE REFRAIN:
"SHE WAS ONLY THE DEAN OF MEN'S DAUGHTER . . ."
ISSUES OUT FROM ONE CAR.
THE TEMPO IS BROKEN: "WHAT THE HELLSH THE NEXSHT BAR?!"

MEMORIES OF THE PO AND THE TIBER, THE APPENINE HILLS,
MULTITUDINOUS TUNNELS WITH THEIR DANK SMELLS AND
CHILLS ARE BURNED IN THE BRAIN BESIDE CASTLES AND RUINS
AS MYSTERIOUS AS THE MOURNFUL NIGHT CRY OF LOONS.

A BEND IN THE TRACK BRINGS THE FIRST GLIMPSE INTO SIGHT --
THE ETERNAL CITY, HOME OF DEAD ROMAN MIGHT,
AND HOME FOR A WEEK FOR THE RUBBERY-LEGGED CREW
NOW ABANDONING THE TRAIN FOR THE ROMANS TO VIEW.
AND VIEW THEM THEY DID WITH THEIR MOUTHS ALL AGAPE;
RED EYES AND RED NOSES -- THE SIGN OF THE GRAPE.

ROME IS A CITY OF FACADES AND WALLS,
ASHAMED OF HER POVERTY YET PROUD OF HER HALLS.

IF ROME IS A WOMAN AS ANCIENTS CLAIMED
I SEE HER AS A BEAUTY DEGRADED AND SHAMED.
HER FACE IS ANCIENT YET WONDROUS TO BEHOLD
WITH THE DARK POOLS OF HER EYES FILLED WITH TALES BEST
UNTOLD. IF HER FACE IS A BEAUTY THEN WHAT FOR A TORSO?
COUNT THE GIRLS ON THE CORNERS OF THE VIA DEL CORSO.

BUT ON ONE CORNER OF THIS CITY THE SCENE IS A RIOT
OF LUGGAGE, CHIANTI AND SCREAMS OF "I'LL BUY IT!!"
THE VENDORS OF ROSARIES AND BEESWAX CANDLES
AND RAZOR SHARP SWITCHBLADES WITH VATICAN HANDLES
HAVE SPOTTED THE YANKS POURING OUT OF THE BUSES. YOU
NAME IT, THEY'VE GOT IT, FROM PIZZA TO TRUSSES.

THE FIRST EVENING IN "ROMA" IS A JIGSAW OF IMPRESSIONS;
FOUNTAINS LIT BY THE MOON, ST. PETERS' DOME, THE TOMB OF
EMMANUEL, ECUMENICAL SESSIONS.
BELLA ROMA TE AMO, I LOVE YOU MY ROME!

THE HALLS OF THE PENSION ARE A CACOPHONY
OF SUITCASES SLAMMING (THE WINE STILL FLOWS FREE).
BUT ONLY THE HARD REMAIN ON THEIR FEET
WITH GENE ON A LEDGE NINE STORIES O'ER THE STREET.
WITH HEARTBEATS SLAMMING AWAY IN EACH CHEST,

THE FACES CONTORTED, EACH ONE PLEADS HIS BEST.
"COME BACK THROUGH THE WINDOW!!" HIS ARM THEY TUG,
FOR THE SLIGHTEST MISTAKE AND HE MIGHT DROP THE JUG.

THUS ENDETH THE FIRST FULL DAY OF THE TRIP.
"SIX DAYS TO GO!!" IS HEARD FROM ONE LIP.
AS FATHER MCCONNEL KNEELS AT HIS DEVOTIONS
THE PAGEANT OF THE TRAIN RIDES THROUGH HIS EMOTIONS.
ONE THOUGHT SITS IN HIS MIND AS THORNY AS CACTUS: "IT'S NOT SATAN WE'RE FIGHTING BUT THE ROMAN GOD BACCHUS!"

THE NEXT DAY DAWNED WITH UNACCUSTOMED LIGHT.
TO THE SOUL ACCLIMATED TO THE COLD GERMAN MORN
THE SUNLIGHT WAS WARM; WHAT A JOY TO BE BORN!
THEN 'TWAS TIME FOR THE RITUAL OF THE RAZOR'S BITE.
BUT THE RITUAL WAS CHANGED THIS PARTICULAR TIME
FOR IT WAS SHAVING OF TONGUE THAT WAS CALLED FOR --
SUBLIME! NOW A RAZOR IN AN UNSTEADY PAW
MUST BE RECKONED WITH CAREFULLY WHILE SCRAPING YOUR JAW BUT WHILE SHAVING THE HAIR FROM A FUZZ-COVERED TONGUE THE CEREMONY DEEPENS AND QUIET PRAYERS ARE SUNG. FOR THE SLIP OF ONE FINGER AND YOU MAY REST ASSURED DURING YOUR BRIEF FLIGHT THROUGH LIFE YOUR PROFANITY'S CURED.

THE BALANCE OF THE WEEKDAYS WERE SPENT TOURING THE TOWN FOR THE CITY IS RIFE WITH SITES OF RENOWN.
A FULL LIST OF PLACES WOULD FILL A SMALL BOOK
BUT FOUR DAYS ARE SUFFICIENT FOR A GOOD HEALTHY LOOK.
THE LIST READS IN PART AS FROM HISTORY TOMES:
CHURCHES ST. MARY MAJOR AND ST. PETER IN CHAINS, TREVI FOUNTAIN, COLOSSEUM, ROMAN FORUM, CATACOMBS. ST. PETER'S BASILICA (ALONE WORTH THE TRIP) ALONE COULD THE SISTINE CHAPEL OUTSTRIP.
VARIOUS MONUMENTS SET ON ROME'S SEVEN HILLS
ARE A TRIBUTE TO ITALIAN SCULPTING SKILLS.
BUT THE FEVER FOR WORKING IN MARBLE IS DEAD,
THE MEDIUM IS NOW STUCCO APARTMENTS INSTEAD.
THE MULTI-HUED PASTEL MONSTERS HAVE CREPT
TO WALLS THAT ONCE WHISPERED TO THE SENTRY'S STEP.

PERHAPS ROME SHOULD PUT SENTRIES BACK ON HER WALLS
AND, AS IN ANCIENT TIMES, HARK TO THEIR CALLS.
BUT 'TIS NOT LIKELY THEY'D CALL OUT OF HORDES
OF TEUTONS AND HUNS WITH THEIR INFIDEL SWORDS
AND BANNERS OF SKULLS A 'DRAPED WITH HORSEHAIR
BUT IN SPRING RAISE THE HUE: "THE TOURISTS ARE HERE!!"

THE EVENINGS AND NITES FLEW BY MUCH TOO FAST
BUT 'TWAS A MIRACLE OUR MONEY DID LAST.
FOR TO SEE ROME AS YOU SHOULD YOU NEED GROUPS OF
GOLD AND 'TIS FOLLY TO GO WITH A LIMP MONEY BELT.
LIMP WASN'T THE WORD FOR OUR MONEY RESOURCES
OUR IDEA OF A FEAST WAS TWO PIZZAS (IN COURSES).

I DON'T WANT TO BORE YOU WITH TALES OF OUR TRIP
ON THE "ZUG" BACK TO ZWEI SO I'LL BUTTON MY LIP.
JUST ALLOW ME TO SAY (OBJECTIVE I'LL BE) THAT NEXT YEAR
THEY'LL HAVE TO RETURN WITHOUT ME.
'CAUSE I'LL BE IN THE STATES (O BEAUTIFUL THOUGHT)
HOLDING FORTH IN A PUB AND SIPPING GROG FROM MY TOT.
AND MANY AN HOUR WILL BE SPENT REMINISCING
AS OUTSIDE, THROUGH THE SNOW, THE AUTOS GO SWISHING.
YES, MANY AN EVENING WITH FRIENDS GATHERED ROUND
WILL BE PASSED OH SO COZILY WITH ONLY THE SOUND OF
TALES OF EUROPE BREAKING UP THE ENNUI OF THE LONG
WESTERN WINTER THAT OFFERS NO GLEE. THEY'LL SWEAR
THAT I'M STRETCHING IT, (I WON'T CARE IF THEY SMIRK) I'LL
REST ON MY LAURELS AND FORGET ABOUT WORK. 'CAUSE IT'LL
BE: "FIND ME A SEAT AND STAND ME A DRINK AND A TALE TO
YOU I'LL TELL OF MY GERMAN HOME, A TRIP TO ROME AND THE
REASON THOSE WOP WALLS FELL!!"

IT WAS LOTS OF FUN, FOLKS, IT'S BEEN A BALL
SO REMEMBER THE MEMORIES AND TALES TALL
WE HARVESTED OUR FUN AND RETURNED TO THE RAIN
BUT IN 40-ODD YEARS IT'LL OFFSET THE PAIN
OF THE OLD AGE AND WHEELCHAIRS THAT WILL BE OUR DUE
BUT WITH MEMORIES LIKE THESE IT WON'T BE QUITE SO BLUE.

And now, I give you a recent work by Jon Horton, most likely around 1991. It's about his father, dying. Jon is a published author and his works are admirable, but this piece about his father dying has hit me right in my heart. [The Editor]

EPITAPH
By Jon R. Horton

On November 17, 1991, a message came from the office in Sana'a that there was a family emergency and to phone my sister in California. That was impossible inasmuch as the nearest phone was about six hours away by 4-wheel drive vehicle. I asked them to phone Stormy and get the details. The next morning they radioed and said that Dad was in the hospital, unable to speak, and the doctors had given him four to six weeks to live. I knew immediately that it wouldn't be that long.

I took a walk after they gave me the news, just climbed over the bandit berm surrounding the camp site and headed out into the strange country.

The camp was on top of the high central plateau, near the heads of two gorges, waadis in Arabic. I wandered about a mile to the southeast and found myself on a ledge of limestone which looked out over a valley. Below there was a village, probably two miles away from the high rim rock where I was standing.

The ledge came to a point. A few hundred feet below me was a narrow waadi, running roughly north-south, with high vertical walls. Its boulder-strewn bottom was green with brush and small trees so there must have been spring water running underground.

I don't remember actually thinking about what I was going to do but it suddenly seemed fitting that I build a cairn. They are not uncommon in Yemen, though the significance of the ones I saw in the countryside were a mystery to us, the farangi - foreigners. Perhaps they memorialized someone as well. Spontaneously, I began to build a monument to my father.

I picked a flat place near the edge, where one can look out over the country but also down into the narrow, rocky waadi, which is an isolated and starkly beautiful place. I put up a half-dozen courses of large rocks, narrowing the structure as I went, until it was about four feet tall. Then I sat down and scratched onto a piece of flat grey limestone:

+ + +

JACK HORTON
1915-1991

I broke down as I scratched the epitaph. As I placed it in the hollow in the heart of the monument I cried aloud, my voice coming out in wails for I knew in those moments that I would never see him again.

I cried more as I searched for rocks to finish but the tears finally stopped and I went on about the last several courses of the work till I found a large flat cap rock and put it in place. Then I found another, small rock which was flat on two sides. On one facet I scratched three small crosses then set the rock on its bottom facet, facing it toward the east and the rising sun.

When I search my feelings for my father he is somehow mostly associated with our lives in Nevada. Yemen is very much like Nevada. So in this impossibly remote place, so far from where he lay at the moment, I did all I could do. It was very little but, then, so are the rest of our works here on this earth. But it was something. I did it out of love, respect and sorrow, the three emotions I associate most with the man.

I pray for clouds of angels to care for him and have no doubt that my prayers are answered. I hope that after he left us one of those angels took him to see what was made in his memory. It was a work of the hands, something he respected for he was a man molded by work.

I think that he will like the site, I am convinced that it was a gift from God to us in our sorrow.

It is as distant and as alone as he was in much of his short time among us. But it is also very near a green and hidden place in that strange, sun blasted land. The searing sun will find it every morning when the weather is clear, which is most of the time, to bathe with light the memorial and its trinity of small crosses.

And when cometh the rainy season, the season of the resurrection of the desert's life, I promise you that there is a place at the monument's foot, in the hidden waadi, where he can hear the greatest gift in that land -- the sound of precious water falling in abundance; a gift from God for all his thirsty people.

A VERY MOVING STORY
By George Huffman through MMCKAY

From: IdaReedBlanford@aol.com
To: MMCKAY@satx.rr.com
Sent: Wednesday, September 10, 20003 1:57 PM
Subject: Re Karamursel 1960-61

Hi MCKay: I was wondering if George L. Huffman remembers my brother, SSGT Phillip C. Noland from "C" Flt. I have a photo with George's signature on it. At that time period, Phil was brought in to replace "the best man in the business" as Supv. Head under Captn. Dodi Aspell.
If George remembers anything at all about Phil, would you kindly ask him to respond to me at: Idareedblanford@aol.com
The photo I have was contributed to me by Jack Wood, who was also at kas.

Thank you and God bless,

Trish (Noland) Schiesser
e-mail: Idareedblanford@aol.com

Subj: Re: Re Karamursel 1960-61
Date: 9/11/03 8:15:51 AM Pacific Daylight Time
From: mmckay@satx.rr.com
To: IdaReedBlanford@aol.com

This is George Huffman and yes, I remember Phillip very well. We worked together for almost the full two years I was at KAS. We both worked for Dodi Aspel, who I understand has passed on. We always had a great time at work, it was a great group of people and everyone seemed to get along very well.

If there is any other information you would like me to respond to, please feel free to contact me at any time.

Different e-mail:

Oh, this is very nice and kind of you to take the time to answer me.
Do you recall that Phil had a sense of humor? He did, I know. Also, did you ever hear him sing a Russian song? He sang it with another fellow who worked with you. I know what Phil's job was, but if possible, would you be willing to write a little bit about what he looked like on a typical day at work? and what he wore and if he was fluent in Russian, as we (family) knew him to be? Also, he spoke other languages - do you know which ones?
Tell me if I'm being a pest. I don't want to be a bother to you and I appreciate hearing about Phil.
I will try to attach a photo of him and his wife and two children at that time. And also hope you can open the photo I'm attaching, of "C" Flt.

In a message dated 10/14 2003 2:27 PM In a message dated 10/14/03 mmckay@satx.rr.com writes:
Subject: Re: A VERY MOVING STORY . . .

I don't know the name of the person that Phil replaced. Phil arrived at KAS before me and left before I did so I don't know the persons name. We lived on base and as I recall Phil lived in Yalova so we didn't really see each other except at work. I was an analyst and was the TE Controller on Charlie flight. I was a TSgt at that time.

E-mail: 10/15/03 5:59:21 AM Pacific Daylight Time
From: mmckay@satx.rr.com
To: IdaReedBlanford@aol.com

I am having problems with my computer in that I am unable to open attachments, so I can't view the picture. I never heard him sing and I don't know what languages he spoke. We all wore fatigues to work so we all looked pretty much the same. You must remember that this all happened 40 years ago and although we worked on the same flight, for a short period of time, we never really worked "together." I wish I could tell you more but I just don't know any more.

E-mail from IdaReedBlanford
To: mmckay@sats.rr.com

I thank you, very much, for what you have told me. You are a big help and it's good to know that you knew my brother.
If there's anything I can ever do for you, please let me know.
Thank you for your graciousness.
Take care, and be well,
Trish.

THESE GUYS - Don Levesque and T.S.

From: IdaReedBlanford@aol.com
Date: Tuesday, November 04, 2003 19:30:17
To: Dr.Levesque@adelphia.net
Subject: Hello, Don, this is Trish

Been doing some researching today, don't know why, it gets more and more frustrating . . . I saw some interesting stuff on your site the other day, which is coming along beautifully, I might add.
What do you know, I came upon that same stuff, flower, etc., today, AFTER locating Oberauerbach - the NIKE defense missile training center back there in old days - wasn't that about 6 miles or km from Zwei?
My brother happened to live in Oberauerbach, or so my niece told me awhile back.
Something else, I always wondered why he told me, sometime around 1957-59 that he was going to "Cheyenne." I know what was in Cheyenne - didn't know then, but know now.
I also know that he was at Goodbuddy in '59 studying Analyst stuff. . . .
I also know that he came home to Hollis, NY (Queens) in middle Nov. 59 to stand Godfather (& I stood Godmother) to our mom's newborn, Downs' Syndrome baby (our half sister) Ellen. We stood together, with pastor, in the hospital in Manhattan - Phil on one side of the isolette and I on the other side - we wore masks in case of giving little Ellen an infection. It didn't help though, she died when she was seven months old.
I remember, distinctly, Phil getting into his 1957 Black Beauty (his Ford Fairlane car) and waving goodbye to me - and as he cranked up the car and started to pull away, he said, "See ya kid. I'm off to Cheyenne." Never heard anything before that nor after that.
I know he was a SPOOK in 6901st though.

Question: What did SPOOKS do at 6901st? I know some stuff, but not all. How are you? Are you feeling good today? Do you have snow? Do you know how proud I am of you because of your past service and for what you continually do to keep the 6901st alive? Well, I'm pretty damned proud.

Hugs to all,

Trish

These Guys

Subj: Re: Hello, Don, this is trish
Date: 11/15/03 7:45:56 AM Pacific Standard Time
From: dr.levesque@adelphia.net
To: IdaReedBlanford@aol.com

Hi Trish, "Cheyenne Wyo." during the 50's was mostly schools for communication "teletype oprs" Linemen communications repair and install. We used to call them "Pole Jackers." During the late 60's it became an ICBM Silo base.

We were the spooks of the Cold War because we in many fields of our operation spied on the Evil Empire (USSR). Intercepting communication and evaluating their combat status. Like the Japanese "Blue Code" broken by our 2nd world war intelligence spooks which gave us the edge and victory at Midway. Combined with U-2 flights. During my tour, at times the stress was heavy. I remember several times, during the Hungarian Revolution, working 36 to 40 hours without sleep. During this time many of us experienced stressful moments.

In September of 1958 we lost one of our intel C-10 shot down in Turkey by a Russian Jet. I believe you can find a picture of that plane in flames in one of our USAFSS sites. Those intel flights were similar to the Navy plane that had to land in China some months ago. I am feeling much better this week, they changed my medication last week.

God Bless
Don
Say hello to Robert and your cat.

Editor's note: I have a dog.
Also, through the FOIA I recently received a communication that my brother, Phil, went to school in Cheyenne at the Frances Warren AFB as a student for one month learning: Supervisory duties. [The Editor]

Thanks to retired Captain Joe Jamison for sending this interesting report. The book is available through Amazon.com entitled: "MISTY." Credit is given to MJami!@aol.com

MISTY REPORT
By Joe Jamison

"Misty: First Person Stories of the F-100 Fast FACs in the Vietnam War" By Don Shepperd, USAF. Major General Don Shepperd (Paperback- Dec. 2000)

BAT CAT (EC-121R) MISSION
By Jim Roth

From: MJami1@aol.com
Date: Mon, 20 Oct 2003 21:21:16 EDT
Subject: Fwd: Misty report

Subject: Misty report

During the recent Misty Forward Air Controller reunion at the Air Force Academy we put on a leadership seminar for the cadet wing. We were given six minutes to tell of our war experiences. It was a moving evening. Here are my six minute remarks:

So, you want war stories, six minutes to describe the experiences of a lifetime: I'll try.

The old men you see in front of you are not terribly impressive, but we WERE. We flew in the Vietnam War when we were in our 20s, 30s, 40s and 50s. We are now in our late 50s, 60s, 70s and 80s, like rejects from a recruiting fair. None of us ever wanted to be this old; until just recently.

I went to Vietnam fresh from a fighter tour in Europe where I flew F-100s at Hahn Airbase West Germany. I sat alert on a one-way target deep into a Soviet block country. I had a 1.1 megaton nuclear weapon tucked under my wing and would have blown the world up to save it. I doubt that I having a nuclear weapon scared the Soviets, but it would sure have concerned the folks from Wheat Ridge, Colorado where I grew up just north of here.

These Guys

I left the US in October 1967 with a stop through the Philippines for Jungle Survival School. Our Escape and Evasion exercise was conducted during a typhoon with torrential rains. My buddy and I shared a six square foot piece of high ground with every rat in the Philippines, just me and him and 400 rats.

I reported Bien Hoa Air Base northeast of Saigon and came under rocket attack my first night. Welcome to war, Capt. Shepperd. I flew about 10 missions, half of them checkout, and came down with dengue fever, a mosquito-borne virus. If you ever get dengue, I recommend you just go ahead and die, it will be easier on everyone involved.

In December I volunteered for Misty. Some of my old friends, classmates and squadron mates were up there, Jim Mack, Chuck Turner, Jim Fiorelli, Glenn Jones, Charlie Neel, and Gary Tompkins. I heard it was an exciting mission. IT WAS.

I reported in just before Christmas and stopped into the squadron where Bob Craner and Guy Gruters were just stepping to the airplane for a mission up north.

I had known Guy (a great football player) at the Academy, shook his hand and said, I'll talk to you when you get back. Little did I know that it would be almost six years later-welcome to Misty, Capt. Shepperd. I then learned it was the second time Guy had been shot down while in Misty - what have I got myself into?

My first checkout ride was with Jere Wallace. The weather was bad, but Jere tried to provoke some gunners to shoot at us through holes in the clouds. So I, the green bean, could see some gunfire on my first ride. My next ride was with Jonesy Jones.

The weather was good so he took me low level through AAA University, first provoking 50 cal. (the Kid on the Karst), then 37 mm, then 57 mm sites to shoot at us so I could learn to ID the sites - see the color of tracers and flak bursts - and feel the concussion, BAM, BAM, BAM of the AAA rounds as they came close to the airplane. [After the mission] I told Jonesy, honest, I'll believe you if you just brief me about these things. I don't need a demo.

Next ride was with Charlie Neel where he showed me where he and Guy Gruters had been 'hit' and then gone down in the water just off the beach. He was grinding his teeth, saying he would sure like to find those bastards that shot him and attack them. I was secretly hoping he wouldn't

By the time I had finished five rides and was 'checked out' I was pretty much convinced that I had joined a bunch of 'madmen.' I considered desertion, heart transplant and a sex change, but alas, a sex change would probably have made me more desirable. I was convinced there was no way I was going to make it out of there alive. So all fear vanished as I became one of those 'courageous Mistys' as I calmly awaited my own sure death.

Many missions later, many successful attacks on target, seeing AAA, missiles, rescues, and losses of comrades - seeing this group of guys hang it all out every day, throwing caution to the winds when a comrade's life was in danger. I was 'selected' for the Great Risinger Raid about which you have just heard. I was selected because I was one of three guys in the vicinity when Ed Risinger went mad, stole three airplanes and we rode off into the weather to attack a SAM site under the clouds with napalm, high drags and CBUs; a terrible idea.

As a young captain I was caught up in the excitement. We launched but en route as I looked out at my wings with high drag 500# bombs and CBUs, both requiring multiple passes at low level . . . it struck me that this was a really dumb idea. But, it was too late. I was already a henchman in the crime. I was a pretty good kid and felt if anything happened I was destined for heaven, but it all changed that day.

As we proceeded inbound, I was 'Tailend Charlie' with bullets whizzing past my canopy. To maintain my courage I repeated my mantra, "That goddamned Ed Risinger; that goddamned Ed Risinger; that god . . ." I repeated that for almost 100 miles, so now I'm destined to hell, courtesy of Ed Risinger.

That story and all the others are in the book "MISTY," a 602 page book; a labor of love. I could write a book about writing this book. I put it together, but it was the idea of Ed Risinger. Why is everything hard in my life tied to Ed Risinger? I cannot over-emphasize the difficulty of getting stories out of a group of 155 elderly, cantankerous, renegade fighter pilots, dealing with sensitive issues, copyrights, editing. In the final analysis about 50% of those still alive sent between 1 and 7 stories which you will find in the book.

As I shopped the book around to the usual suspects, the publishers. They all told me the same thing. "We love it." "We'll buy it BUT you must give us editorial control and the book will have to be cut by two thirds to make it commercially viable AND several of the authors will have to be eliminated because their stories are somewhat repetitive, or quite frankly, not very good."

I could not do that.

So, we self-published the book through 1stBooks Library. The book is not for the general public . . . but for us . . . our families and for history; to let people like you know what we went through, what war is really like in our words and who we were. The book will never go out of print. It will be there for our great, great grandchildren and theirs.

My greatest satisfaction has come from the children of some of our dead comrades who have told me, "I feel like I finally know something about my Dad." With that all of the work of our authors and those who assisted in editing and assembling this and those who flew with us to make the stories possible, has been worth it. I hope you buy it. You will learn something.

Finally, I have a piece of advice for you. Yes, we were a special group of guys, but the women you see with us were even more special. They waited, they feared, they suffered, they waited for the blue car with bad news, they buried us and accepted the flag. Here is the advice: "When you marry, MARRY WELL. Marry someone of character and strength. Like these women. You will be well served.

Let me close by reading the Postscript from the "MISTY" book:

One day an old, gray, bent and stooped former Misty will hold his great grandson in his lap. The young child will be fondling a dusty set of military medals. He will look into the eyes of his great grandfather and ask, "Were you a war hero?"

The old man's eyes will mist. His mind will flood with memories. He will see tracers passing close to his canopy and feel the shock waves of AAA rounds beating against the fuselage. He will see black flak exploding in the air and hear the depressing sounds of parachute beepers. His heart rate will increase as he gets low on fuel and warning lights flash on his instrument panel. He will feel the sharp thump of rounds impacting his aircraft and smell acrid smoke in the cockpit. He will look in the rear view mirror and see flames. He will hear the voices of men on fire and in danger. He will once again encounter the depressed feeling of landing, after losing a comrade . . . or failing in a rescue attempt. He will wipe his eyes, clear the lump in his throat and whisper quietly and truthfully, "No, Son. But I flew with men who were."

Thank you and welcome to our great Air Force.

These Guys

BAT CAT (EC-121R) Mission

Jim Roth

We were flying the Blue Orbit. Just south of the DMZ and east of Laos. Two acoustic sensors started going off, one louder than the other. Didn't know what the sound was. We would visualize what we thought the sound was and see if it matched.

I tried trucks and airplanes (the most common sounds) no luck. After several hours I contacted TFA and asked them to put it on the sonic analyzer. No luck. After several hours I had them try again. No luck. After 4 more hours I finally made a match.

It was a small generator Charlie was using for a tunnel complex. I had the Marines at the Rockpile give me four for effect on the loudest sensor - no effect. After several more attempts at that location I had them fire at a location between the two sensors.

No more generator. That messed up Charlie's card game for that night.

VINCE'S LETTER FROM CONGRESS
By Marcy Kaptur, U. S. Representative

This is a letter to Vince Wuwert from Marcy Kaptur from the Congress of the United States, House of Representatives, Washington, DC 20515-3509 dated 3/17/2000.

Dear Mr. Wuwert:

It is with great pleasure that I write to you and your fellow veterans of the 6950th Security Group and its forerunner the 10th Radio Group Mobiles at Chicksands, Bedforshire, United Kingdom. I am pleased that the men and women of these units are holding a reunion and it is my wish that it will be the best reunion ever as you renew old acquaintances and friendships.

I especially wish to thank Mr. William Grayson for his efforts in making this reunion a success. Without Mr. Grayson's work, this reunion would not be possible and I am confident that all involved appreciate his tireless leadership in making this gathering possible.

Please extend my deepest appreciation to Brigadier General Chris Holtom, Commandant at Chicksands, for his willingness to open his post and facilities to the American veterans. Acts of kindness and hospitality such as this do more to cement relations than the best effort put forth by London or Washington.

I have been told that the British Wireless Service veterans of WWII will be joining you for the reunion. The veterans of WWII have a special place in my heart. President Clinton, in an address at Normandy said, "When these men were young, they saved the world." This is true! As free people we must never forget how our freedom was preserved by these gallant veterans of WWII. Please extend my heartiest appreciation for their sacrifices and my best wishes for a wonderful reunion and may we always remember the sacrifices of the men and women who served our nations in the Second World War.

The Cold War was a period in world history when my generation could not imagine the end of communism in Europe. To think of the Iron Curtain crumbling was a dream. The reality is that the walls did come down and the barbed wire was rolled away and the freedom we have known in the West was extended across Europe and into the former Soviet Union. The Cold Warriors who served in numerous posts throughout the world must be given the credit for this astonishing victory.

These courageous men and women accomplished nothing less than a miracle as they broke the back of communism and freed millions from isolation and oppression. I salute the veterans who served the free world by standing shoulder to shoulder in defense of our great nations. It is my hope that this reunion will be a joyous and momentous occasion for the Cold Warriors who stood between communism and freedom in the dark days when the Soviet Union appeared to be invincible.

The United Kingdom and the United States of America have been close allies and friends for many decades. May all of you renew old friendships and make many new ones and may this reunion instill a deeper sense of patriotism in all of you.

On behalf of the people of the 9th Congressional District and all of the citizens of the United States of America, please accept my deepest appreciation for your service. I wish each of you the very best!

Sincerely,

MARCY KAPTUR
U.S. Representative

MK:dff

SAFB
By Gus Kilthau

Subj: Re: Phillip C. Noland, SAFB Nov. 1951-52
Date: 11/7/02 9:13:37 PM Pacific Standard Time
To: IdaReedBlanford
Hi Ms. Trish . . .

Thanks for the note about Phillip and the photograph.
We are in the process of changing the Web site over to some new hosting and software, so I cannot tell you when (and even if) the data and the photo can make it to the pages . . . However, I would suggest you get onto the "Guest Book" of the current Web site and repeat the typed information you provided in your note. Most members look at that Guest Book first thing when they get onto the site and will see your information there. Be sure to include your E-mail address for possible replies.

Best regards,
Gus Kilthau

IdaReedBlanford@aol.com wrote:

Phillip C. Noland, AF12392047, did his boot at SAFB.
He is deceased 1986, buried full military honors: National Cemetery, Bourne, Cape Cod, MA.
He ultimately became 20270, last duty at 6901st Zweibrucken, before that TUSLOG Det. 3, Karamursel, Supv. Head for Captn. Dodi Aspell, "C" Flight.
Would anyone remember him?
How do I discover exactly where he went from SAFB?
I attach his photo, taken at SAFB right after a bout with pneumonia up there, as many of those fellows had.
I am Trish (Noland) Schiesser and I am Phil's younger sister.
I am researching and writing a book. Any info. would be helpful.
Please pass the word?
My e-mail: Clara19126@msn.com
Thank you, and please add the downloaded photo of Phil to your site.

Respectfully,

Trish (Noland) Schiesser
Literary Consultant, Author

This was a note, like many others, that I sent to many sites, and people over the past five years, to try to obtain information about my brother, Phillip C. Noland.

The real history of Zweibrucken as taken from a pamphlet prepared by the Special Services Libraries, US Army Area Command which was distributed around 1966. (For all other addressees, this is a courtesy copy of a very interesting place). I received this from anonymous http://www.6901st.org/histzwei.htm. The 6901st made its home here for a time, during the Cold War.

ZWEIBRUCKEN - A SHORT HISTORY
Credit is also given to David King

A horse, a rose, and two bridges -- the symbols and essence of Zweibrucken. The very name Zweibrucken is derived from the fact that there are two (zwei) bridges (bracken) in the town. The horse represents one of the oldest and most venerable occupations of the city, horse-breeding.

Horses bred and raised in Zweibrucken since 1744 are known throughout Europe and the world. Many winners of races throughout Europe can be traced to stud farms here. The beauty of roses grown here is legend and are to be seen in the "Rosengarten," a special park which offers roses and a variety of other flowers every spring and summer.

Zweibrucken is located in the western sector of Germany not far from the Saar, which because of its great concentration of industry, was extremely important during World War II. Crumbling and damaged bunkers which surround the city form part of the famous Siegfried Line.

In April 1957, Zweibrucken celebrated its 600th anniversary as a city. The foundations of the city were laid when the Merovingians, the Counts of Saarbrucken, established a custom-house at Zweibrucken to control the resources of this area and nearby Hornback in the mid 1350's. The independent line of the Dukes of Zweibrucken arose following the sale of the city to the Count Electors Palatine.

During the Thirty Years War, Zweibrucken was held and defended by the Swedish fighting under King Gustav Adolph. Three Swedish kings were descended from the Zweibrucken Dukai line, Charles X, Charles XI, and Charles XII. Under Karl XII the Duchy became a Swedish province. Friendly ties with Sweden continued for many years after the end of Swedish government and recently were renewed when the Swedish legation in Germany informed the city authorities (in 1966) of the country's intention to include Zweibrucken in the list of places to be visited by the Swedish International Tourist Organization.

Zweibrucken was the cradle of the last royal family of Bavaria, the house of Wittelsbach, whose ancestral castle is still standing. The architecture of the heart of the city reflected the Swedish Renaissance under the influence of the architect Sundahl, and mingled with the baroque to give Zweibrucken a distinctive character. Of all the building in the Palatinate, Karlsberg Castle built by Duke Karl August was the most impressive. Set in a park which contained specimens of exotic plants and animals, it looked like a fairy castle and rivaled in splendor those of Ludwig II of Bavaria.

Like Ludwig, the Duke was a solitary person and resented any attempt to approach the castle, so spacious rooms and inviting hallways remained empty.

The beautiful building was so completely destroyed by the French in 1794 that scarcely a trace remains today. During the American Revolutionary War, the Zweibrucken Regiment, "Royal Deux-Ponts," under the command of Wilhelm von Zweibrucken-Forbach, stormed and captured Yorktown, Virginia. Von Zweibrucken-Forbach was the first man to enter the bulwark.

The regiment lost twenty-nine men in this attack but the assault resulted in the surrender of 8,000 British troops under the command of Lord Cornwallis.

Wilhelm von Zweibrucken, wounded in battle, was made a Colonel and decorated with the High Order of St. Louis while his brother, Christian (the regimental commander), was awarded the rank of General.

Three diaries kept by officers of the regiment are still in existence giving proof to the events during the campaign of 1780-1782.

Of all the wars, the most destructive to the city was World War II. On the evening of March 14, 1945, Baroque Zweibrucken was completely destroyed.

The castle which was reduced to rubble was restored in 1964. The Alexander Church with the Wittelsbach Royal crypt was also destroyed and has been rebuilt according to the old plans.

This was completed in 1958. Located on the Main Street only a block from the city hall stands the oldest Gasthaus in Zweibrucken, the Zum Hirsch, dating back to 1600. This is one of the most picturesque places in the city and attracts a large number of people with its good food and quiet atmosphere.

For centuries Zweibrucken, as well as its vicinity, has been the residence of many royalties. A short distance outside the city stands the Fasanerie Gasthaus, surrounded by large old trees.

Refreshing to visit in summer, history states that the building once was used by Stanislaus Leszcynski, one of Poland's kings during the 18th century after he had dethroned King August, the Strong.

Horse racing attracts many to the area and another type of racing, gass tract, or motorcycle racing is also important. The award for the winner of this race is fittingly, a silver rose. Located near the Rosengarten, the Festhalle attracts a number of patrons of plays, operas, dramas, and concerts during the year. The modern city of Zweibrucken of concrete, steel and glass is a worthy successor to the honored ancient home of kings. In the little town of Hornbach, only twelve kilometers away, stands the old Riechenau monastery.

During the many wars of the area, farm houses were built up around the monastery to shield and to hide it. Only a few years ago the grave of St. Primin, who founded this, his tenth, and last monastery in 743, was discovered and a chapel erected over the site.

The borders of Saarland, Germany and France once met at Hornbach forming the "Three Country Corner."

Zweibrucken is within easy traveling distance from many of the great cities of Europe, only 227 miles from Paris, 55 miles from Metz, 85 miles from Frankfurt, 47 miles from Strasbourg, and 205 miles from Munich.

Credit is also given to: Respectfully submitted by David King, inhabitant 1963-1966.

These Guys

THANKS FOR THE INVITE TO WRITE SOMETHING FOR YOUR BOOK
By Paul Laffitte *(Editor's note: This is usually the type of kindness shown to me by Paul and many others like him during my research. This, from Paul's e-mail to me).*

The only thing I did most of my early life was the Military. Graduated from High School, took a short tour of France and then enlisted in the Air Force (Feb 48). Graduated from Radio School and was assigned to the Air Force Security Service. Departed NY on a Hospital Ship to Bremerhaven, Germany and went to a Repo Depo (Replacement Depot) and was misrouted to the Berlin Airlift as they needed Airborne Radio Operators badly.

When the Airlift was over in August '49 we were returned to the AFSS and sent to our original assignment to the 2nd Radio Squadron Mobile, in Darmstadt Germany (just South of Frankfurt).

The 2nd RSM really started out as the 3rd RSM in England during the war and landed shortly after "D" day and was later changed to 2nd RSM (AAF/Army Air Force). In Feb. 49 those 2nd RSM AAF guys were transferred from the Army Security Service to Darmstadt and then the real Air Force personnel arrived and the outfit became part of the AFSS.

We were living and working on the Ernst Ludwig Kaserne in Darmstadt and worked in the attic of our four story barracks. It was a great time to be in Germany and it was a fine outfit and we contributed to the monitoring of the Russian Air Force radio traffic, both voice and C/W (Morse Code).

We expanded rapidly and when Phil *(the editor's brother)* arrived overseas, the AFSS was all over Europe, Africa and out to Pakistan and beyond. Everything we did was classified at least Top Secret and above and was finally released a few years ago.

Some books have been published listing some of the things we did. Don't know if this is stuff you *(Trish)* want but there it is.

I also served with the Security Service out in the Philippines and on the island of Okinawa. Returned to Germany 1955-57 and married a German National and lost my security clearance and *need to know*.

Spent until 1975 with the Air Force Communications Service and had other tours at out of the way places around the globe.

This is a little bit about my service. Use or discard what you want or don't want.

Don't forget that if you get more on Phil's orders and you want to know what it means, let me know and I will try to get you an answer.

Take Care,

Paul

I want to thank Dave Lally, a former member of the USAFSS, for his note about the Cuban Missile Crisis. I had been talking on Bravenet Web Services and this was an answer to what I had been saying about the crisis.

Re: Cuban Missile Crisis new info.
By Dave Lally

Great subject Trish. I was at Kelly when the crisis started. My roommate and I, Ted Dawson a 203 started getting Navy and CIA reports tracking ships. For the sake of our own curiosity we got maps and started charting the Soviet freighters Sverlovsk and Poltava, both known to be carrying missiles on deck. We did this a couple of times a day and drew a lot of interest, to the point we had to give daily briefings. Right after Kennedy made his blockade announcement, we charted through the night. U Turns were made in the mid-Atlantic, it was awesome to see.

ON THE INDY: 19 August 1961
By Tim Lally

When I was on the Indy, during one of our Med cruises I was an EM/2. I'd just relieved a watch stander from the #4 generator control room so he could go to chow. I don't think I was there more than five minutes when I noticed that my generator was losing speed. As I was trying to bring it back to 60 cycles the 1/MC sounded a fire alarm for #4 engine room, which was just below the room I was in. Within seconds the circuit breakers, some of which were huge, started tripping with smoke, flames and sparks. A curious person, I naturally wanted to know what the hell was going on.

I went to the access door, which is normally very warm to the touch and cracked it open. I was greeted by copious amounts of thick black smoke.

I think my first though was, "Oh Shit!"

The ship's chief engineer and electrical officer called me and asked for a status report, and to let them know when I'd evacuate the compartment - I never did - I told them what I'd found, asked for an OBA as the smoke that got in was nasty and the deck was so hot the rubber mats and paint were blistering and smoking. My feet got so hot because of the deck I had to climb up onto the control panel!

We fought that fire for most of the day, were dead in the water, had destroyers alongside, and if memory serves, I think all non-firefighters mustered on the hangar deck in preparation for leaving. We went to flight quarters - the aircraft were going to go too!

After the fire, #4 engine room was virtually unusable, all the electrical systems were destroyed and we didn't have enough parts on board to make repairs. We got stuff from every ship in our battle group and got #4 engine room and generator back online within a few days of working around the clock.

An unsecured cap on one of the two-lube oil filters that served the #4 generator caused the fire. When the MM changed filters (done every watch) the unsecured cap came off and 400 gallons of hot oil was pumped out, hit the turbine that powers the generator and burst into flames.

Giving credit where it's due, the MM was not responsible for the loose cap, and was severely burned trying to re-secure the cap and put out the fire.

We were very lucky in that there were no fatalities, and other than the MM, only minor injuries. He received the Navy Commendation Medal some time later for his actions, and somewhere in my archives I have an award for one, for not leaving the switchboard room during the fire, but I never received the medal as I was transferred to a reserve DE in Whitestone, New York.

I don't think we made the Discovery Channel.

This was written by Lally during his service aboard the Carrier Independence during the Cold War era.

These Guys

This is for the "navy" guys who "miss" being aboard ship during the cold war. Thanks, guys, for your service, and I hope this gives you a chuckle and a remembrance or two. It was sent to me by Tim Lally, but he says the author is unknown, so I give credit to the unknown author for such a good laugh.

SEA DUTY - as sent to me by Tim Lally

Miss Sea duty?
If you're longing for sea duty, here are 22 simple steps to simulating life in the Navy.

1. Sleep on the shelf in your closet. Replace the closet door with a curtain. Six hours after you go to sleep, have your wife whip open the curtain, shine a flashlight in your eyes and mumble, "Sorry, wrong rack."

2. Renovate your bathroom. Build a wall across the middle of your bathtub and move the shower head down to chest level. When you take showers, make sure you shut off the water while soaping.

3. Every time there's a thunderstorm, go sit in a wobbly rocking chair and rock as hard as you can until you're nauseous.

4. Put lube oil in your humidifier instead of water and set it to "High."

5. Don't watch TV except movies in the middle of the night. Also, have your family vote on which movie, then show a different one.

6. (Optional for ex-engineering types) Leave lawnmower running in your living room six hours a day for proper noise level.

7. Have the paperboy give you a haircut.

8. Once a week blow compressed air up through your chimney, making sure the wind carries the soot across and onto your neighbor's house. Laugh at him when he curses you.

9. Buy a trash compactor and only use it once a week. Store up garbage in the other side of your bathtub.

10. Wake up every night at midnight and have a peanut butter and jelly sandwich on stale bread, if anything. (Optional: Canned ravioli or cold soup).

11. Make up your family menu a week ahead of time without looking in your food cabinets or refrigerator.

12. Set your alarm clock to go off at random times during the night. When it goes off, jump out of bed and get dressed as fast as you can, then run out into your yard and break out the garden hose.

13. Once a month take every major appliance completely apart and then put them back together.

14. Use 18 scoops of coffee per pot and allow it to sit for 5 or 6 hours before drinking.

15. Invite at least 85 people you don't really like to come and visit for a couple of months, and call them Marines.

16. Have a fluorescent lamp installed on the bottom of your coffee table and lie under it to read books.

17. Raise the thresholds and lower the top sills on your front and back doors so that you either trip over the threshold or hit your head on the sill every time you pass through one of them.

18. Lock-wire the lug nuts on your car.

19. When making cakes, prop up one side of the pan while it is cooking. Spread icing really thick on one side to level off the top.

20. Every so often, throw your cat into the swimming pool, shout "Man overboard, ship recovery!"

21. Run into the kitchen and sweep all the pots/pans/dishes off of the counter onto the floor, then yell at your wife for not having the place "stowed for sea."

22. Put on the headphones from your stereo (don't plug them in). Go and stand in front of your stove. Say (to nobody in particular) "Stove manned and ready." Stand there for 3 or 4 hours. Say (once again to nobody in particular) "Stove secured." Roll up the headphone cord and put them away.

23. Wake up at 0-Dark-30, line up in the driveway in a light drizzle, and have your mother-in-law criticize your clothes and read you the newspaper.

This is what Tim Lally, ex-navy, during the cold war, who served aboard the carrier Independence, did after he exited the navy. I thought it a good article for THESE GUYS, because he served when the cold war was still going on, and we get to see what he did when he got out. He is also a former boyfriend from my High School days!

"206" - By Tim Lally

The telephone rang at about 0900 on a typical Tuesday morning in February. By typical I mean cold, wet, foggy, and of course rainy. I'm surprised it isn't snowing too! I answered, "Lake Union Air Service." The voice on the other end was heavily accented, and I recognized it as belonging to David Chang of "International Shipping" as he said only, "Port Angeles." I replied "OK when do we leave" and was informed he would be ready in 15 minutes.

Just as I was completing the pre-flight check of our aircraft, a Cessna 206 float plane, David Chang arrived, we climbed aboard and were airborne from Lake Union in the heart of Seattle within 5 minutes. Nice not to have ATC delays like every major airport in the country. Since this was a typical February day the ceiling over the lake was about 400 feet, and that usually meant 40 feet out over Puget Sound.

Port Angeles is located about 65 miles NW of Seattle, and on a clear day the trip would only take 30 minutes or so. Today however with a 40 foot ceiling and visibility at 1/4 mile I will stay over water the entire trip and reduce speed by about 35 knots which will at least double our travel time. As we flew away from Seattle and finally lost site of land behind us I still could not see the west side of Puget Sound. I hate it when that happens. For some reason my palms always sweat when I fly in this garbage. Finally the shore line. Damn. The trees on the beach are higher than we are. So much for cutting across the point. Following the shoreline we will fly north across Oak Bay toward Port Townsend then turn West toward Port Angeles. That is as long as "Mr. Murphy" is not with us today. He is!

The bridge at the north end of the bay is visible, but the mega volt power lines above it are not. Being the prudent person that I am I made an immediate 180 degree turn, had to stand the bloody plane on a wing tip. I hate it when that happens. Now we must go around Port Townsend and the two islands to the south of it.

With Port Townsend behind us I can hug the shore line and not fly over any houses. This section of shore is actually cliffs and very steep hills with not much beach, and the houses are actually built quite close to the edge. Well, will you look at that, there was a woman standing in her kitchen drinking a cup of something and she waved at us. Yes we were that close as we flew by.

The weather seems to be improving a bit, looks almost clear further West in the Straits of Juan de Fuca. "Murphy" must have bailed out when I made that turn back there. I can see Port Angeles, I'd better wake up Dave. He didn't tell me the name of the ship we are meeting.

WOMEN AND WHISKEY AND WAR - Sent to me by Tim Lally *(done by Robert A. Hall of the Scottish American Military Society)*.

They are trying to gentle the gender,
To civilize Western man.
They think that your thoughts are too dirty,
Not to mention your heart and your hands!

They bid us to banish our weapons,
For bravery is "macho" they say.
We must learn that weeping's not weakness,
And put it on public display.

They know not of weeping that's private,
They know not how our hearts can break.
They think that a soldier's not human,
The arrogance of the mistake!

Let us charge our glasses for drinking,
A dram to our friends in the Corps,
A toast to a life worth the living,
To women and whisky and war!

Not women to serve as our playmates,
But partners to stand at our side,
Our equals under the heavens,
And first in our hearts and our pride.

Not whisky to burn out the senses,
But a dram of fine Highland malt,
To share with our friends over stories,
And to ease the pain of our faults.

Not war as a game for the sadist,
But honor for men who would fight,
Refuse acquiescence to slavery,
And lay down their lives for the Right!

These Guys

They are trying to gentle the gender,
But there are wolves in the world,
And who will answer the summons,
When a Fuhrer's next flag is unfurled?

They are trying to gentle the gender,
But when the old wolf's at the door,
They will beg for men who are living,
For women and whisky and war!

A Nation Calls to USAFSS LITE: Ed Leonard remembers his time with USAF Security Service from 1959-1965. Ed, or, "Mr. Ed" as I called him when in contact with him, is a gentle and helpful human being. His site, USAFSS LITE, when he was in command of it, was a good site; one where members could air their memories or thoughts on politics or whatever came to their minds. Since he has left the site for someone else to "mind" it, well, it has changed. Below, you will still find how Ed begins USAFSS. Many of his stories have not been removed, and are of great interest and should you have a mind to, please visit the site, especially, Transcriptions, where there are many good stories; and The Attic, where there are many good poems.

USAFSS - The Lighter Side:
Many Web Pages have been devoted to USAFSS alumni and the vital role they played in winning the cold war. Some focus on specific units, some honor those lost in the line of duty, and there are others like "Freedom Through Vigilance Association (FTVA)" which salutes in its Hall of Honor the career officers and NCOs who hold the organization together.

But, the USAFSS I best remember was made up primarily of young first and second term airmen who manned (and later women) the intercept positions and analysis desks day after day. They were young men (and women) deadly serious in their professionalism and devotion to excellence when it came to their jobs, but irrepressible and irreverent in their dealings with nearly everything else, including their approach to the military establishment.

Perhaps their flippant attitudes were defense mechanisms to help them retain their sanity in a high-pressure environment, or maybe they were just immature. No matter - as an amateur cartoonist, I found them refreshing, and their memory is forever etched in my mind.

This site is devoted to those young airmen I worked beside for 85% of my short military career - the grunt airmen who recorded the action, interpreted its importance, and relayed the vital warnings to others in a prompt manner. They were our real first line of defense, and they should be remembered as they would prefer - with a smile.

The last time I went to find the USAFSS Lite site I clicked on it and immediately got a virus. Maybe it's just reserved for me, but I'd check it out before you attempt to click onto it. [The Editor]

This is a short story written by Ed Leonard who served in the USAFSS.

DON'T ASK WHY
By Ed Leonard

So, you ask me, "What made you decide to join the Air Force and become a Russian linguist engaged in intelligence collection against the Soviet Union?" and you expect a simple patriotic answer. As we were prone to say in my day in the military, "Never happen, G.I."

I wish I could give some simplistic answer pointing to my overdeveloped sense of patriotism, or my highly focused hatred of the Soviet system and fervor to defeat the Communist infidels, or even to fall back on some mercenary master-plan to become a millionaire and retire before age twenty-six. I guess I could tell you that, but it would be blatant B.S. and you'd probably know it.

What I did and why I did it is more complex, and far less organized than that. The first part of the question, about joining the Air Force is pretty simple. I joined the Air Force because that was preferable to being drafted into the Army. Back in those days we had a draft, and young men who didn't join the Navy, Air Force or Marines got drafted into the Army.

Well, yeah. If I was drafted into the Army I could get out in two years instead of four, but I'd get out with the skills of an infantry grunt (not that they lack skill). Imagine getting home from your time in the service and you apply for a job.

"And what skills do you have?"

"I can shoot people."

"We don't do much of that here at Slickfix Industries. Is there anything else you can do?"

"I can blow people up with hand grenades."

"I see. Anything else?"

"I can stick 'em with a bayonet, too."

"Well, we'll keep your name on file. Thank you."

I opted for an opportunity to do something that might help me get a job when I got out. Well, at least I thought that was what I was doing.

Besides, I grew up in an era that fostered and reinforced the belief that military service was the right thing to do. I was born in 1940, immediately preceding America's entry into World War II. During my formative years I was bombarded by patriotic hoopla and worship of our heroic fighting men, standing tall in the cause of freedom on foreign shores. My own father wore the uniform of the U.S. Navy and sailed the pacific in that war, and my grandfather had served in the Army in an earlier war. Even my friend, Bugs Bunny who spoke to me from the pages of my little cardboard covered comic book was kicking the crap out of Tojo and Adolph Hitler in every episode.

I grew up worshipping John Wayne, who won the war on the screen. I played soldier, sailor and marine -- whatever the Saturday matinees dictated. As a teenager, I was a Civil Air Patrol Cadet, and made my mark in that organization as Cadet of the Month on several occasions, and a recipient of a CAP Certificate of proficiency just a little over a year after signing up in the three-year cadet program. You might say I was predestined to join some branch of service, and my interest in airplanes nudged me in the direction of the Air Force.

But, the leap from airman to linguist is a big one. I really didn't seek out the job; it sort of found me. I took French in high school and flunked it miserably. In retrospect, I have to admit that I failed the course because of lack of interest and insecurity when it came to speaking before a group of my peers in an unaccustomed tongue. At the time, however, I was in full agreement with my teacher, Miss Margaret Leatherbury, who advised me, ". . . you will never be a great linguist."

If I had my "druthers" I would have joined the Air Force as a pilot because my dream from childhood was to soar with the eagles. I suppose every kid has such dreams. But, in 1958 contact lenses were unheard of and the military required perfect vision to gain access to an airplane cockpit. With severe myopia, flying airplanes was not an option.

Another childhood interest was amateur radio, so I decided to shoot for an electronics school. After all, I reasoned, I liked the subject and it showed pretty good promise as a civilian vocation when I re-entered the civilian world. I was showing troubling signs of mature thinking by this time.

The Air Force seemed sorely in need of people with this aptitude and practically dragged me off to basic training the day I took the test. That's one thing about the vintage advertising, "Uncle Sam Wants You!" sign that was quite literal. If Uncle truly wanted you, he would move mountains to take you right damned now. As it was, I had planned to go off to basic with a high school friend who was enlisting in a less critical mechanics quota, but I nearly had to beat the recruiters off with a stick to wait until his enlistment date.

So, I was a hot commodity as an electronics candidate, right. Fame is fleeting in the Air Force of the United States. At Lackland Air Force base, the great Air Force feedlot where new airmen are fattened, sorted and screened into the careers the military machine has selected for them, I took another battery of tests. This battery included a "Radio Operator" test and a "Language Aptitude" test. Radio operator was no problem after all, I was interested in amateur radio at the time and the test only required me to recognize and distinguish a handful of similar sounding Morse code combinations. I scored high on that test and was most likely a target of renewed interest as a candidate in another critical field.

But, to my surprise, flying in the face of Miss Leatherbury's respected opinion, I also scored well on the Air Force Language aptitude test, displaying an ability to memorize vocabulary, apply grammar rules, and discern meanings of strings of vocabulary words in a little known or made up language. While my success on the test might have made Miss Leatherbury a little red-faced, it didn't put the lie to her assignment. While I did show sufficient aptitude to gain entry into the Russian language program at the Army Language School in Monterey California, my score was too low for selection to the Yale University Chinese program.

By this time the Air Force had completely forgotten their interest in sending me to electronics schools. They had shelved the idea of having me chase dits through the ether as a "radio operator." Now, I was a truly hot commodity in the Air Force, a prospective linguist. Well, hell yes, I was honored. I thought they were crazier than a March Hare, but if I somehow survived, I could always go back and look Margaret Leatherbury right in the eye and say, "You were wrong."

The fact is, I not only survived, but once past the initial shock of contorting my mouth and tongue into what I considered totally inhuman configurations for a couple of months, embarrassing myself in public daily and being threatened with expulsion if I didn't redouble my efforts, I fell into a groove and discovered that I really could learn a language. I could actually excel in that field, and I did.

I also found that, thanks to my upbringing in wartime and immediate postwar America, in a semi-military environment, I was reasonably adept at playing the military game without surrendering all intellect to the point of total submission. This seems to make me an ideal candidate for a position in the intelligence community since I can function relatively independently without running amuck and doing anything too unreasonable.

In the field, I knew I had found my niche. When I reached Berlin and found myself sitting at a radio monitoring Soviet air activity every day, I could put myself in the cockpit with that pilot and nearly anticipate his moves. I never knew whether what I was doing was vitally important to the future of America or the world. But, I always knew that what I did was the best I could do, as accurate as I could make it, and if it were the missing link in a puzzle, it would fit properly. Every day I could tackle my assignment with pride.

And, I knew that others surrounded me with similar pride in their work. Many of them drank too much, got overly exuberant and did things that ran them afoul of the law, but on the job they were the most professional bunch with which I ever worked. Probably, I would have spent my life in pursuit of that profession if I hadn't met a woman born outside the United States. Her place of birth made the Air Force question my integrity, thanks to the Cold War myopia of the time, and I let the service of my country into the outside world.

But, I was never sorry for the eight years I served, or for marrying my wife and leaving it all behind me. I was never ashamed of being a "spy" as some people would call my former work. I was a soldier serving my country, gathering vital information to defend against potential enemies. Perhaps I was able to assist my country and contribute to preventing an armed confrontation somewhere. I'll never know.

I'll always know that as a group, we gave our all every time we took our places on the line. Our war was never one of brief, but violent confrontation. It was, instead, a long tedious and tense confrontation, always alert and poised to react, never able to blink. We served, but we served in silence. Nobody will ever know our contribution. Few will even know our losses. However, we can take pride in what we've done.

Subj: Re: Call for submissions for Cold War era short stories/Trish (Noland) Schiesser
Date: 3/12/02 2:52:41 PM Pacific Standard Time
From: Idareedblanford
To: eleonard.geo@yahoo.com

In a message dated 3/12/02 2:31:24 PM Pacific Standard Time, eleonard.geo@yahoo.com writes:

Trish,

Will be glad to provide you anything within my poor powers of composition that you'd like. You already know about all the trash I have posted on USAFSS Lite and you are welcome to use any of it as long as it is something within my knowledge and recall (and isn't one of them dratted classified thingies.). If you want something in particular, let me know and I'll give it a shot.

Ed

Hi Ed! Thanks so much for replying. I would like YOU to be the one who chooses the two short story submissions.
BTW . . . YOUR WORK IS FAR FROM BEING TRASH!!!! YA GOT THAT!!!!!
You are a beautiful and creative writer. I love everything you've written. You're the one who first got me started with this research, you know. I trust in your judgment. Let me say this, if I don't like what you choose, you get to go back and choose something else. And, it's all as I said in my call for submissions, nothing classified, etc. Also, if you need more time that's okay, just let me know how much. I should have asked: How are you? Hope you're having fun!!!!

Trish

A Hotmail Message to me, under the name of Pink Flanagan, from Ed Leonard

Subject: Re: Language
Date: Fri, 23 Aug 2002 01:29:44 -0500

Hi Trish,

Good to hear that things are leveling out some for you. Got lots of items to try to answer since I last wrote to you. To answer a question you had about JWG and Ray are doing, both seem to be OK, although guys often don't share a lot with one another about how they are doing.

You asked about HALO and at this point I don't have a clue, but it sure sounds like it could be a codename of some sort. Might be interesting to pursue.

In answer to your question about records of those attending classes at Monterey in 1957, I can tell you right off that nothing is available from DLI (Monterey). The subject has come up numerous times on the DLIWC group bulletin board and people currently on staff out there say that no history of class rosters is maintained at the school. Most people who have had any luck at all locating names of people there have done so through copies of orders or old graduation programs that packrats like me save. The problem is that such documents don't cover the whole school or the whole year, just individual classes. If Phil attended a class there, he should have had orders in his file assigning him there, then reassigning him elsewhere when he finished. At least, that is the normal method of moving military people around.

I did receive the package the other day and the book is Japanese. I can figure out enough to tell you that it is Japanese language - reading it is something else again.☺ Thank you for thinking to send it.

I will be leaving for Japan on September 3, but will probably head up to Kansas City a couple of days early to visit my brother before I leave. Will be flying out of KC to Chicago, then to Tokyo.

These Guys

I hope everything went well with picking up Andrea's ashes. I think there are generally mixed emotions involved there - at least, there were for me. On one hand, you know logically that those ashes are her remains and not her spirit, yet you don't want to admit that she is gone. I had to tell myself that Toshiko was not in the ashes, but in my heart, and there she lives forever, as Andrea will with you.

Take care, take time to heal, and come back strong.
You still have much to do.

Pink Flanagan had written:

Dear Ed,
Tomorrow, Bob and I definitely go to pick up our bit of Andrea's Ashes . . .sounds like title of book. . . . I am hoping that - I don't know what I'm hoping - wondering how I'll feel. Knowing Bob and I we'll make some jokes, while sorrowful.
Ed, how would I obtain information, on the internet, about Monterey (Language School) specifically the roster for 1957. Phil said he was going to Cheyenne, WY in 1957 and off he went in his '57 Black Beauty. He was at Wright Pat., before that (it could have been after, but I think it was before). I'm not doing any type of anything that's going to "hurt" me at this point. Here's the scoop, I don't want to go looking all over the darned Internet for this and that about each phase or whatever about Monterey. So, it would be helpful if you could (or are able to say) ask someone how I would find that year's roster, possibly 58, but think it was '57.
I hope you received your package. When do you go?
(Thinking of you, buttercup).
Trish

By this time I have figured out what HALO means: High Altitude Low Opening - Free fall from 30,000 feet to about 3,000 feet before popping the chute. This is done by Jumper's, SEALs, Airborne, Rangers, etc. [the editor]

A priceless "gem" buried in your "Attic" brings forth memories of how my brother SSGT Phil Noland, USAFSS lived the "rest" of his life till he was killed by a NY taxi cab as he stepped off the curb one cold and bitter night in Feb. 1986. He was 55 years old and had served his country a long time, in Excellence, like you, in the USAFSS. Only, he survived on his USAF pension from his Honorable Discharge in 1965 . . . the USAF kept him in till 1968 . . . I don't know why. Thank you, "Mr. Ed," for this beautiful and heartfelt poem.

WELFARE CASE by Ed Leonard
(1968)

He's just a pitiful welfare case,
his home is the Three-Point Bar.
He's a no-good and a drifter,
dreams riding a falling star.

His family just ignores him;
real friends he has not one.
With only his bottle for comfort
he thinks of battles he almost won.

Who cares if he sleeps in a flop house
or the gutter outside the bar,
If he takes his soup at the mission
or he dines on caviar?

When his check comes in, he's wanted,
and the drinks flow fast and free.
Then again he's suddenly lonesome
when he can't pay friendship's fee.

Now, with winter's snows a'flying,
with his dole in a post office box
A man lies still in a railroad yard,
cheek cold against the rocks.

These Guys

He's gone and there are no mourners.
He has vanished without a trace.
A spade shuts the book on a wasted life,
just a pitiful welfare case.

Subj: Re: Mr. Ed
Date: 1/13/03 8:03:43 PM Pacific Standard Time
From: eleonard.geo.Yahoo.com
To: Idareedblanford

Hi Trish,

Good to hear from you about your trip and that you are able to enjoy it all. Unfortunately, the visual didn't make the transition to my server (got lost enroute), but I'll just use my vivid imagination to enjoy the beauty of it anyway.

Have been meaning to write you a note about the orders gobbledygook from Phil's separation orders, but somehow never got the job done until now. Reading special orders is an acquired skill, so don't feel bad if you missed a few less than intuitive abbreviations.

Re Fr AD translates to "Released from Active Duty"

ENLISTED IN OR TRANSFERRED TO A RESERVE COMPONENT: YES: COMPONENT AND BRANCH OR CLASS: AFRES: indicates that he was transferred to the Air Force Reserve. This was the normal transition of a first term discharge in those days because your total military obligation was 6 years. If you served 4 years active, you were held in inactive reserve status subject to recall for two additional years.

COGNIZANT DISTRICT OR AREA COMMAND: HQ CONAC (NARS) AIR RES REC CEN, DENVER 5, COLO. His inactive reserve assignment was to Headquarters Continental Air Command (Can't remember what NARS stood for) with records held at the Air Reserve Records Center in Denver.

As far as his flying over Korea, that is certainly a possibility. Another would be if he was on TDY (Temporary Duty to the Korean end of one of his unit's operations for a period long enough to make him eligible for the award). His records would still reflect assignment to Japan, but a secondary TDY order would have shown a temporary duty there.

All of this probably just muddies the waters and I don't mean to do that. Just trying to cover all the possibilities.

Enjoy yourself and, you and Bob support each other as you go through this time. *[Editor's Note: death of our daughter, Andrea]*

Had a good encampment. Got to see the B-2 "Stealth" bomber up close and personal. Maybe you can't see it, but it has a firm feel when you touch it. We also got some hands on experience with some veteran A-10s and some new Apache helicopters.
Highlight of the encampment was the formal "Dining in" on the last night of encampment. I think the kids all had a good time.
Take care. Ed L

THE REAL WORLD
By Ed Leonard

I sat in the kitchen, holding my steaming coffee mug between my hands as I watched the thin figure across the table from me. I tried to concentrate on what she said so that I could formulate a careful response. The frail woman opposite me, with intense brown eyes, reddish hair, and crooked little smile, was my stepmother. The day was Thanksgiving 1961. The occasion was a visit with my family following my return home after two years service with 6912th Radio Squadron Mobile, United States Air Force Security Service in Berlin Germany.

"I was just wondering, Edward," she said, sort of twisting her head to her right side as she spoke and caressing the back of her neck with her thin, wrinkled hand, "what you think of the world situation?" The use of my full first name was a signal of her mental state. Nobody at home ever addressed me so formally under normal circumstances.

The wheels in my head spun, seeking an appropriate answer. First, there were so many things happening in the world that it would be hard to pick the appropriate response. Mom was like that. Although the question she posed was a broad, non-specific one, the issue in her own mind was more defined in her own unique parameters.

Nothing in her world was what it seemed in ours. My stepmother lived in the demented world of a schizophrenic and her perception of the world situation often differed from the real world experienced by other family members.

"I don't know," I answered carefully, hoping for a little more definition in what she was seeking. "The world is so complicated today."

"I know," she responded, reaching across the oilcloth covering the kitchen table and touching the back of my hand lightly. "I was so worried about you there in Germany."

"It wasn't bad," I responded, feeling pretty hypocritical in view of the fearful last day I had spent in the city, wondering whether I would get home before the guns of war could take us all out. "I wasn't in any danger. I just have an office job."

Now I was really going out on a limb of falsehood, going against everything I had ever been taught about honesty. And, I wasn't just lying to some stranger. No, I was telling falsehoods to a family member, and not even to one in full possession of her senses. I felt ashamed, and yet I had sworn to secrecy about my work and there were no exceptions.

"I knew you would be all right," she confided in a sage whisper. She patted the back of my hand again and winked. "I got your messages on the radio."

I looked slightly to my left in Dad's direction and he lowered his eyes slightly to signal his embarrassment that she was about to go off into a fantasy.

"At first," she explained, "I couldn't understand them. But, then I realized that they were in code, and I knew that you were okay."

I took a sip of hot coffee while I tried to fight back the panic that followed her references to radio and code. Of course, I knew that this was my stepmother, my poor mentally diminished stepmother, not a diabolical Soviet agent. Still, I had never mentioned coded messages, or even suggested that I spent my days hovering over a radio. But, then she was just schizophrenic, not stupid. I shrugged off the implications.

After all, the entire family knew that I had studied Russian at the Army Language School, and the Air Force didn't send me to Russia, they sent me to Germany. So, how would I be associated with Russian? Radio was a good guess. Then, oh, yeah, my mailing address was a "Radio Squadron Mobile," wasn't it? It would take a much more serious disorder than schizophrenia to let you miss that connection.

Damned good job of analysis, I thought as I gently lowered my cup back to the oilcloth. Maybe she's the sane one and all the brass is crazy for trying to disguise the obvious.

"There's nothing to worry about, Mom," I said with a confident tone that was only half sincere. I knew that I was probably right, at least in most cases. But I also knew that there were occasions when danger was only a breath away, not just for my comrades, and me but also for everybody.

I yearned to tell them just how dangerous everything really was, and how scary the world outside could be. I wanted to reassure them that there were people working at jobs like mine, around the clock, every day to keep them safe. But, I was sworn to silence, and these same family members sitting around the kitchen table had taught me to keep my word.

It would have felt so much better to be able to share my pride in the work I did, and how it contributed to protecting them from harm; to tell them of the wonderful people I worked with who daily brought a phenomenal reserve of intellect, talent and dedication to the workplace to provide intelligence for our nation. But, my lip was zipped.

Mom looked through me with those soft brown eyes and Dad moved his head almost imperceptibly from side to side. My younger brother, eight years my junior, sat silently in the adjoining living room, watching a cartoon show on the television with an intensity as overwhelming as the concentration of my fellow operators listening to their target radio frequencies back in Berlin.

That was the first time I had stopped to consider the impact of my secretive work on the folks back home. Perhaps it represented our impact on the real world. It made sense to the mentally impaired, was a source of embarrassment to others, and was of no consequence to the rest. Still, Mom seemed concerned about what was happening in my world, and that worried me.

It was time for me to go back to school to sharpen my skills to improve my performance.

"It'll be okay, Mom," I said, making a promise that meant nothing.

"Robbie, you take care of yourself," I yelled into the living room at the young innocent whose brain was being sucked into the television set.

"Come on, Dad. Drink up. I got a bus to catch."

MY WAR WAS PSYWAR
By Ed Leonard

It's not every day that a man gets such a direct call to arms, yet probably no one remembers the day as I do. I had served a fairly uneventful two years of my life as an airman in Berlin Germany during the height of the Cold War, between October 1959 and October 1961. it was 25 October, my last day in the divided city, more than one hundred miles inside Soviet East Germany.

There had been exciting times, especially in the intelligence collection business, my assigned specialty with the Air Force. There had been occasions when I had been ringside at what appeared to be a major offensive by Soviet long-range bombers en route to the West, but that had downgraded to an exercise in long-range navigation for the Russian aircrews. And there had been an assortment of Soviet intercepts of civilian and military aircraft in the assigned air corridors to and from the city, but they had all ended in the Soviet fighters escorting the aircraft into Tempelhof Air Base peacefully.

Without a doubt, the most ominous event in my two years in the city had been the surprise move to seal off West Berlin with the concrete and barbed wire barrier, the Berlin Wall in August 1961, followed by a threatened curtailment on ground transportation in and out of the city and further restriction of air travel. These events, coupled with the creation of an East German propaganda radio station beamed to the American military community in Berlin created a very real siege mentality for those of us who stood ready to defend the Island City in the event of hostility.

But today that would all end. I had experienced my last wake-up in the divided city. I had eaten my last breakfast and my last lunch in the Tempelhof Air Base chow hall. My bags were all packed, my orders translated into Russian to travel by Military Duty Train from Berlin to Frankfurt, and I had cleared the final stop in my checkout itinerary; turning in my bedding at unit supply. All that remained was my wait until time to go to the bahnhof to catch the train in the evening.

Back in my room for the last time, I took off my fatigue shirt and tossed it on top of my B-4 bag, later to be stuffed into the side pocket, where it would stay until I reached my destination back in Kansas City where I hoped to reunite with my young wife who had disappeared from my life some six months earlier when I started getting my letters returned marked, "Moved, No Forward - Addressee Unknown." But, that was all behind me now. I was confident that I could locate her and we could put it all back together. My two-year separation was over and I was heading home.

I sat on the edge of the bare mattress on my old bunk. Actually, bunk is a misnomer. The term bunk conjures images of a three foot wide steel frame with metal link webbing and a thin, lumpy mattress, capable of being stacked. The ones we had in Berlin were twin size beds with wood head and footboards and real innerspring mattresses. I guess they could have been stacked. The drilled holes in the center of the corner posts and the reduced size of the post ends at least suggested fitting some sort of adapter onto them to facilitate stacking.

I dug a novel out of my AWOL bag, leaned back against my B-4 bag and began to read.

Suddenly the door burst open, and a short A2c wearing glasses poked his head in the door shouting, "Get your fatigues and field gear and report to Ops on he double!"

I sat up on the bunk, startled by the sudden intrusion, then recognizing the airman as one of the jeep linguists from operations, I laughed and responded, "Too late buddy, I've turned my field gear in. I'm outta here on the evening train."

The guy looked a little surprised at my response. I could see the color draining from his face and he remained deadly serious.

"I'm not kidding," he said, "this is for real." Then he disappeared and I could hear other doors opening and closing as he worked his way down the hall checking for occupancy.

I sat there for a couple of minutes trying to understand what I had just seen. Finally I concluded that the airman had, indeed, been serious. Something was going on, and whatever the something was, it required an unprecedented muster of personnel in the operations area with field gear -- not a good sign any time, but an absolute slap in the face on the day you're scheduled to leave. I stood and slipped my fatigue shirt back on, grabbed my cap and stepped out into the hallway. There was no further sign of activity in the hall, but most of the Security Service residents of this short third floor wing were day workers who were already on duty.

I turned left and made my way toward the squadron supply room in the main hall of the third floor near the shaft where the continuous movement of the two person lift carried personnel up and down the six floor structure. As I rounded the corner into the main hall I discovered that a long queue was already forming outside the supply room as off-base personnel who were allowed to stow their field gear in the supply room lined up to check out their gear.

My quick spot evaluation of the situation was that if this was the real thing as the airman at my door had stated, then I damned sure wasn't going to be taken out standing in line to check out a steel pot and shelter half. I passed them by and went straight to the elevator, stepping onto the first available down bound car and jumping off as the car neared the first floor level, not waiting for any easy step off position. I pushed through the heavy doors onto the sidewalk under the portico.

As I emerged from the building, three jeeps belonging to the First Battle Group (Reinforced), 18th Infantry Regiment, careened around the corner, descending the ramp from Eagle Square, under the portico and out into the open street leading to the Main Gate. As they streamed through the enclosed area at the door, the soldiers hanging on the machine gun mounts in the rear of the vehicles swung back and forth in response to the quick turns. I remember thinking to myself that while it was certainly a macho sight, they'd probably be a lot better off to just sit down on the back seat until they got where they were going.

But, the sight of these theoretically battle ready soldiers, temporarily quartered at Tempelhof since they were sent in to reinforce the Berlin Command troops in August after the wall was built, hot on their way to some pre-selected defense position in response to a still unknown emergency, added extra haste to my step as I pointed myself toward our Operations building.

Actually, the Tempelhof building is a series of six story buildings set in a semi-circle and connected by covered hangar spaces between the buildings. Each of the main buildings which housed military administrative function, enlisted and officers billets, supply areas, chow halls, service clubs and other support functions was constructed of heavy stone, capable of withstanding anything less than the direct hit of a nuclear weapon, and it was all built before anybody even started tapping on an atom, let alone cracking any. That's the German way - they always did build hell for strong. Security Service Operations were located on the sixth floor of the building at the far end of the semi-circle.

As I neared my destination, I saw little sign of activity outside the entrance. Everything appeared normal enough. Civilian vehicles whizzed by on the street outside the fence carrying on the normal commercial routine of the city. I saw nothing inside the chain link fence marking the Air Base to indicate that any increased security was in effect. I guess I had expected to see squads of Air Police patrolling the perimeter, or at least a few German guards with their dogs.

I entered the building and opted to climb the broad concrete stairs rather than waiting for the often malfunctioning elevator. As I reached the landing intermediary to the second and third floors, I saw my first indication that the situation might actually be as serious as the airman at my door had painted it. Soldiers from the ASA unit on the fourth floor were busy setting up a machine gun to command a field of fire covering the whole stairwell.

"Very good," I thought as I passed them. "It'll probably surprise the hell out of the first wave of enemy coming up those stairs after they encounter no resistance on the first or second floors. But, the second wave will probably be a bit more cautious and send a grenade up first." The thought of grenade shrapnel rattling around in the stone cavern of that stairwell sent a chill through me as I continued up the stairs.

I reached the AP guard house at the fifth floor landing and explained to the guard on duty that I had already been debriefed to ship out and no longer had an entry badge, but that I needed to get to the armory to draw a weapon if this alert was for real. The guard frowned, unsure of what he should do in this situation, but eventually handed me a carbine and two clips of ammunition that he had in the guard shack.

I took the weapon and asked, "What do I do?"

The guard thought for a moment, then improvised, "Go back down to the front entrance and take up a position there."

I knew he had just pulled that off the top of his head, so I didn't ask for any further instructions about what to do. I figured I'd just make my plan as I went along if things got out of hand. Back down the stairs I went, past the machine gun and the soldiers, heading in the opposite direction of the airmen straggling up the stairs toward the operations area and the armory. I reached the first floor entry.

"Now what?" I asked myself. It didn't make much sense to stand here and challenge my former co-workers that I knew damned well belonged upstairs or, for that matter, even to challenge the soldiers that I may or may not recognize as belonging to the ASA unit. First of all, if this was the real thing, the Russians weren't going to send in one or two spies dressed as soldiers or airmen. They'd more likely send a flipping battalion dressed like Russian soldiers and armed to the teeth.

My mind raced. If they did send a battalion, or even a platoon, what the hell chance did I have with my .30 cal. Carbine and two clips of ammo? The answer was obvious. Not much, dummy! I cursed my phenomenally bad luck, that I could spend two years here and have the world end on the day

I was due to go home. "Damn," I thought, "what a sorry commentary on my worthless life."

I surveyed my dimly lit post in the stair well. At least that would be to my advantage, I reasoned. Anybody entering the building from the bright outside would have more trouble seeing me than I had seeing them silhouetted in the doorway frame. I began to resign myself to the concept that if it became real we were probably dead men. At least I could take a few out with me, and maybe gain a few minutes for the guys upstairs to destroy documents and equipment.

Suddenly a thought struck me that brought a smile to my lips. Throughout my stay the rumor had circulated that in the event of any threatened hostility the Security Service Air Cops had orders to shoot the operations personnel to prevent their capture and interrogation. If that was the plan, and there had always been serious doubt, then the guy on the gate sure screwed up when he handed me a carbine and two clips of live ammunition; so much for that bit of folklore.

I began to imagine what might happen if Russian or East German soldiers stormed the building. It wouldn't be easy to gain entry. The walls were too thick and strong to be easily breached and the narrow doorway would force single file entry making them extremely vulnerable. Probably, they would first toss in a grenade, then rush a chance to even fire a shot at the bastards.

I sat there in the gloom for a few minutes contemplating how to best extend my life for a few more useless minutes. Then it struck me . . . the staircase. Those stairs were reinforced concrete, and underneath them, with that concrete between the door, and me I would be protected from the direct blast of a grenade, and to some extent from the ricocheting shrapnel, if I squeezed as tightly as possible into the angle formed by the stairs meeting the floor. "Ok, then. That's it," I told myself. "That's the plan. If the damned thing happens and they toss in a grenade, I dive into the area under the stairwell and hope for the best."

Well, so much for my goal of taking out a couple of Russians before they got me. I just lost my advantage of picking them off as they came through the door. Hiding under the stairway you can't even see the door. On the other hand, maybe they wouldn't see me either. If, somehow, they missed me there, could I get clear of the building? Then what? Where would I go? How could I get out?

I decided that in the event I could clear the operations compound and the base, I'd need to find some German clothes. I could somehow, in the confusion of the Soviet takeover, clear the city; I could best travel East and South, away from the area they would expect straggling allied forces to move until I was well clear of the city. If I encountered Russians and could not avoid them, I would be best off to speak German, while meeting Germans would be occasion to speak Russian. I reasoned that speaking what my interrogators would view as a foreign language would better conceal my accent, buying me time to try to find a way out, and I acknowledged that whatever happened, if I wasn't shot on sight, I'd probably be treated as a spy, no matter how I was captured.

The afternoon passed slowly, with fantasy scenario after scenario spinning through my otherwise unoccupied mind. Occasionally someone from operations would hurry up or down the stairway, and as they passed my position I would call to them, asking for some kind of update on what was happening.

Eventually, it became clear that a showdown was taking place at Checkpoint Charlie, a principal border crossing between East and West Berlin, manned on the West side by American Military Police and on the East side by East German VoPos or VolksPolizei (People's Police). The result was that American and Russian tanks were now faced off against one another across the checkpoint in a giant game of chicken with world peace at stake.

Was there any promise that the situation would resolve? Nobody knew. Had the duty train departure been delayed or canceled? Nobody knew. Was there any word about reinforcements from the Zone coming in? Nobody knew.

Finally, two hours before the Berlin-Frankfurt Duty Train was due to depart, Lieutenant Nikula descended the stairway and I flagged him down, explaining my need to know whether I was still leaving the city on the train, or whether we were in a state of emergency that precluded my departure. He told me he'd check and let me know, and then disappeared back up the stairs. A few minutes later he was back and I was on my way to pick up my luggage and catch the bus to the bahnhof and Train 349.

My war was over without a shot being fired. I guess it was what you'd call a psywar. It was all in my head, but during those long hours of waiting, not knowing what might happen next, the war was real. And, I'll tell you for sure, I wasn't ready to die for God or country or anything else. I was mad, and I wanted to get even with whoever was messing with my life, but I was resigned that if I must die in the process, by God some sonuvabitch was gonna join me. I sure as hell wasn't going to die alone.

But, my private war, fought solely within the confines of my mind in the solitude of a dimly lit stairwell was over now. I had won the battle in my mind, and whatever the Russian threat was, it had stabilized to the extent that I could leave the city.

Today the incident doesn't even rate an entry in most histories of the divided city. Even the web site devoted to the Berlin U.S. Military Veterans dismisses the incident with two short lines, "On 25 October came the famous standoff at Checkpoint Charlie between the M48A1s of F Company, 40th Armor and the Red Army. The Soviets backed down."

One of the few photos of the incident I have seen shows six U.S. tanks plus armored personnel carriers arrayed at the checkpoint, but does not show the opposing force. A soldier who was on the scene that day describes it as a laughable situation.

"I had the occasion to be in the M-59 APC behind the tanks on that day at Checkpoint Charlie. I was able to watch the 'State Department' types that panicked and ran for the doorway of the German Gasthaus on the right before you get to the actual Check Point Charlie. They were running when one lone DDR BTR152* turned onto Friedrichstrasse and drove in the direction of Check Point Charlie. The entire incident started because the VOPOs were hassling the sedans that were going over to provide access. The Military wanted to send in the armor and infantry to escort, but the state department opted to send in a MP escort. We were working close with the tanks from the 40th Armor who were close enough to the wall to lay the ninety tube on the wall. . . . According to the "Spooks" we would have had little or no resistance had we sent the "Heavies" over that day in October."

So, in retrospect maybe the crisis loomed far larger in my imagination than in life. But, I had experienced a highly personal bit of the Cold War that day, and felt ready to tackle whatever awaited me back in the United States. Now I was catching that damned train and I was going home.

This is Ed Leonard's (former USAFSS) story of his life and his wife's death. He had married her during the Cold War.

MEMORIES
By Ed Leonard

It was all I could do to contain my tears as I looked down at my wife's expressionless face, framed in a fine halo of black hair against the white pillow of her hospital bed. Her eyes were open and aimed in my direction, but I was unsure whether she recognized me sitting next to her bed or not. I felt that she probably knew that I was holding her hand though.

I knew that time was very short now, and I think she did too. I knew because the doctor had met with me earlier, explaining that there was nothing more they could do to prolong her life and that all they could do was try to ease her passing by dosing her with morphine to ease her pain. Reluctantly, slowly and painfully, I had accepted the reality that I was about to lose my partner of the past thirty-five years. Her knowledge probably came from within her, from the feeling that she was losing her grasp on the will to fight back.

Pick's disease, the neurological ailment that had robbed her of her ability to walk independently, feed and dress herself, talk or function productively in any way, was now stealing her ability to respond at all. It is a cruel disease, eating up the brain cells that allow us to function normally, distorting our realities into nightmare episodes, yet leaving enough intact to allow us to track our own inability to respond. I knew my dear Toshiko had fought her disease every step of the way, eventually losing each succeeding skirmish, and with each loss becoming more depressed at her inability to overcome the illness.

I squeezed her hand lightly and spoke softly. "Darling-chan," I began, using the private Pidgin English we spoke to one another. The term was a double endearment - the English *darling,* coupled to the Japanese diminutive *chan,* deriving from the honorific *san,* but used only in speaking to children and close loved ones. "Darling-chan, I have been asking you to hang on and fight back because I want you with me."

My eyes were burning and I paused to bite my lip. "But, I know how hard it is for you," I continued, "and I won't ask you to hang on for me anymore. You do what you want to do. Don't worry about me. I'll understand."

I swallowed hard and willed myself to stand by my word on that issue. Having released her from any obligation to suffer on my behalf, I wanted more than anything to help her recall some of the good times, to somehow take her mind off of her present suffering.

"Do you remember when I asked you to marry me?" I asked, and directed us back into a time warp to Christmas 1964 when I had given her two Christmas gifts.

The first gift was a small box, maybe ten inches long and four by four in the other directions. I had asked her in advance what she wanted for a gift, and she had jokingly responded that she wanted a red sports car. It was an obviously frivolous request for several reasons. First, my income was far too limited to allow such extravagance; second, she didn't drive, so such a gift would be of little use to her. Obviously, whatever was in the box was not the response to her request - or was it?

There was a puzzled look on her face and certain urgency in her fingers as she hastily stripped the wrapper off the box to reveal a carefully assembled model of a red Honda sports car with working headlights. The gift carried many messages. While she had asked for a seemingly impossible gift, I had done my best to meet her request, and in a special effort, had provided a "Honda" car, and Honda was my wife's family name.

Her face melted into a warm smile and she hugged me in thanks for her gift. But, that was not all. I produced another gift-wrapped parcel. This one was about seven inches by nine inches and a mere quarter inch thick in bright wrapping paper and a neat bow.

Toshiko stripped the paper off quickly to find a slender book, titled: *So You Want to be a U.S. Citizen?* She looked first at the book, then at me, and it was obvious that she didn't understand the significance of the book.

"I hope you can find a use for it," I explained. "You see, I want to ask you to go with me to America, as my wife.

"Do you remember that, darling-chan?" I asked again. There seemed to be a sparkle in her eye, but maybe it was my imagination.

"Remember how hard it was to get the permission to get married?" I asked her, continuing my reminiscence. I went through a recitation of the obstacles thrown up by the military hierarchy to prevent marriages to foreigners in the Far East. I strung out the shared memories of the documentation and translation requirements, the exhaustive medical testing, and the reams of seemingly useless paperwork stretching out over a six month period, then the announcement that all of the assembled documentation had mysteriously disappeared just short of the Base

Commander's stamp of approval. I recalled the personnel clerk's contention that we would just have to start over, a totally unworkable solution since my tour of duty ended in less than a month, and my own suggestion to the clerk, that he rig a bomb in a box addressed to the Base Commander, triggered to explode when the box was opened, then search through the rubble wherever it detonated until they found our papers.

I smiled at the memory of the somewhat frightened look in the personnel clerk's face as he tried to decide whether my remark was a threat or simply frustration. But, Toshiko's face remained still and I was unsure whether she too remembered.

"Then, they relented and decided we didn't really need all those papers after all. Remember that? And we went to Sapporo, to the American Consulate to be married?

"Remember how seasick you got riding the ferry across the strait to Hokkaido. You started getting sick before we even left the dock. But, we got there.

"And then, how devastated we were when there was no wedding ceremony, no exchange of wedding vows. Instead, we only witnessed a flourish of bureaucratic name signing, rubber-stamping and seal-applying, first in Sapporo City Hall, then in the Consul's office. The ceremony consisted of the Consul shaking my hand and saying, 'Congratulations,' but it has worked for us, hasn't it?

"Then you had to go down to Tokyo to get your visa. Remember when you rode the train down there for that and I had to wait in Misawa? Boy, I was scared then. I was scared you wouldn't come back. In Tokyo you were so much closer to your family's home than to me, and I was afraid that you'd go home and decide that you were afraid to come to America with me - that you wouldn't come back. I didn't sleep much that night.

"The next day, I kept reassuring *Punk,* your dog, that you'd be back, but I think I was trying to convince myself, I went to the door every time a car slowed down outside the house, expecting your cab, until you got back late the next night."

I kept talking most of the night, remembering those days and the highlights of the years that followed. I slept occasionally; resting my head on a pillow over her bed rail, then awoke and continued talking. I don't know how much she heard, or whether she understood. But, she stayed with me through the night and into the next morning, and from time to time it seemed as though she squeezed my hand slightly in response to what I said.

At noon the next day my brother arrived. The Doctor had dropped in to check on her condition, and she suggested that my brother and I go down and get some lunch since Toshiko appeared to be resting comfortably at the time.

I left the room and headed down the hall toward the cafeteria, but before I could sit down to eat a nurse came to summon us back. When I reached her room my Toshiko was gone.

Perhaps the timing of her passing was coincidental. Maybe my imagination chooses to focus on fragmentary evidence to conjure a distorted reality to match my own needs. But, in my mind my lovely Toshiko made one last effort to protect me by holding on until I left the room, then dying alone to save seeing her go. It was a re-enactment of her mother's passing, when mother sent young daughter Toshiko into the kitchen to fetch her an apple so she could pass on in solitude. It was a last stoic show of immense courage in the face of the unknown.

Toshiko was a Buddist, as are most Japanese, and since her passing my Western friends, all products of Judeo-Christian cultures, have counseled me to forsake her belief lest I burn in Hell for my blasphemy. Of course, the implication is that Toshiko, whose only transgression was to call her maker by a different name, and imagine his form in less personal and more spiritual terms, is doomed to an eternity of torture, and I should forsake her and save myself from such a fate.

On reflection, Toshiko's religion does not advocate inflicting harm on her fellow man for such minor variances in belief, nor does it portray an afterlife of suffering to those who refuse to kill and maim others in God's name. Maybe a God who would punish so gentle and kind a person for her failure to embrace such beliefs is not worthy of my obedience either. I will stand by my wife through eternity. I love her. If we must suffer after death for being honest, kind and gentle, even as we did in life, then we will do it together. That is the depth of our enduring love.

Subj: VETERAN'S DAY NOVEMBER 2002
Date: 11/11/02 6:22:50 AM Pacific Standard Time
From Don Levesque (drlevesque@adelphia.net
To: IdaReedBlanford@aol.com
CC: RJJones@amvets.org, tpugh@houston.rr.com, Jewens@ . . . com, IdaReedBlanford@aol.com,HikerPaul1@aol.com,edwatts@mindspring.com
File: Untitled-1.gif (63178 bytes) DL Time (763408 bps): 1 minute

Hi, everyone, herewith a big thanks for serving faithfully our country, all of us in the 01st made a difference in protecting the freedom that many in our country today seemly don't care. Let's all of us support our men and women who have taken the torch and are carrying on.

Don

An e-mail from Don Levesque, "Pastor Don," speaking to me of the 6901st and other things ... like my brother, Phil, ex-USAFSS.[The Editor]

THE 6901ST ZWEIBRUCKEN
By Don Levesque

Glad to hear you are doing better. About Phil, I wish I could get any information, it's been so long ago, and I can't even find more than three guys I worked with. Yes the government stinks about getting information. All my records were burnt supposedly. They even said the 6901st was not USAFSS in their records. Hmmmm, wonder where I spent three years, I must have been AWOL! We had a lot of people crack up under the stress of the work we did. I had one guy stealing rain coats, he must have had over 60 of them in his locker; they took him away. Also several guys lost their clearance and ended up from what I understood in a mental hospital. They would not let anyone who cracked up loose because of the information they had. I remember when I got discharged I had to sign a paper saying that I could not go abroad for something like ten years, unless I worked for the government.

I had applied to work for NSA (none such agency we used to call it.) The National Security Agency wanted to hire me, because I had a Top Secret Cat #4, the highest clearance one can get. It took three security background checks from the FBI to get it. So, I was worth much. But, they wanted to send me back overseas to some Embassy in Turkey for another three years, and I wanted to get married and that would not have worked out.

By the grace of God I took the right road. Remember, we are living in a 4th dimension of time, and eternity lies on the distant shore. Then, all things will be revealed and we will know what happened to Phil, and many other things. Was Phil still in the AF when passed away? I know he is one of us Sampson AFB Vets, I took my basic there, and I belong to the Sampson AFB Association. I just bought a nice jacket from them with the inscription in the back, "Sampson AFB Veteran."

Well, I have to sign off for now, wishing you and blessing you with the best of health and wisdom.

Jesus loves you ...
PD

FERRET MISSIONS
By Don Levesque

Subj: Thanks
Date: 12/20/02
From: dr.levesque@adelphia.net
To: IdaReedBlanford@aol.com

Just got your books this afternoon, planning to sit down over the holidays and enjoy them, especially "Ida's Ride."
I see you're an old salt also huh! I had a boat till a few years ago and I really miss it. The coast of Maine is really rich with scenery. I was the chaplain for the local power squadron. Again, have a great Christmas and New Year.
Don

Subj: More on the 6901st
Date: 4/13/03

Ida, those ferret missions were very dangerous, a C-130 like the one the navy plane that was forced down in China last year. Loaded with intel. equipment. We had two of those shot down in the 50s. Those Missions flew next to the borders sometime over the borders, collecting radar, telecommunications, etc. They were very dangerous missions. I have a book I gave to my son on it, and I will try to get it and send it to you. It speaks about those missions from the time I served to during the Nam war.
Don

DON LEVESQUE SOUNDS OFF
By Don Levesque

Subj: SO GS-15/6901/SCG/1963
Date: 4/13/03 2:08:17 PM Pacific Daylight Time
From   dr.levesque@adelphia.net
To: IdaReedBlanford@aol.com

Dear Trish, Phil was serving during the Vietnam War, and those of us who served Jan 1955 to Jan 1962, never got one single medal, and we were tagged "PEACE TIME VETS:" which makes me very angry to even think about this, we were not even able to join the American Legion, barred from States benefits for us.

A few years back they gave us a stinking piece of paper thanking us for serving during the Cold War, which included all those from 1945 to 1990. Yet, even today we are still classified under this d... title. We could not even go to any VA hospitals till 4 years ago. Here, in Maine we could not be buried in Vets cemeteries till a few years ago, but we are still barred from other benefits. We all served, wore the same uniform, took the same oath, some of my friends were shot down on the Turkish border in 1958, lost eleven brave men. Those were the ferret missions you mentioned besides other ops in Berlin, where we lost other men. They stopped awarding the "NATIONAL DEFENSE MEDAL" in Dec of 1954, and once re-instated it during the Nam war, stopped it again and I understand they just re-instated it. I wonder who we defended? I have been fighting with others to change this awful status. It's an insult . . . to all of us, I served 4 years and 2 years reserve. We are trying to get the Govt. to award a "COLD WAR MEDAL" and yet the Defense Dept. is bucking us. Take a look at these sites. I belong to a new Service Org called "COLD WAR VETERANS." The sites are at:
http://members.aol.com/dggoodrow/coldwarvets.html
http://www.coldwarveterans.com/press_release.htm
The American Legion looks down on us, they haven't fought Congress to change this, and boy you should see my face, It's RED HOT. . . . For forty some years I had to fight to get examined by a VA doctor and get a disability rating, I finally got rated 100% last year for the injury that occurred while serving my country. I think of the two airmen who died on each side of me often and they are worthy to be our heroes like today's brave young men. The SCG/1963 they were special ops, during the Vietnam War by the 6901st. We had different classifications because we did things that never happened

and they were never recorded on our records. Even our USAFSS patch was forbidden to wear on our uniforms. A few years back I tried to get the History of the 6901st so we could have it on our site, and they could not find it in their records to be a USAFSS unit. So, I guess we never existed. I'm sorry but I had to lift off some steam about this. . . .
God Bless
Don

This e-mail is in answer to my e-mail to Don Levesque about whether dogs were used at the 6901st, Zweibrucken, W. Germany while he was there.

GERMAN SHEPHERD DOGS
By Don Levesque

Subj: Re: (no subject)
Date: 8/26/2004
From: dr.levesque@adelphia.net
To: Idareedblanford@aol.com

Good morning, I never saw dog's used during my tour in Germany. But, some units used German Shepherd Dogs for perimeter security. Some bases had nukes stored in bunkers. At Zweibrucken we only had the double fence. We worked on the top floor, with a big vault steel door with a code we had to punch to enter. Also entering the building was a check desk where you had to present yourself to get your badge with your picture on it. In Landsberg in the 6905th, we were working in an underground facility which had been the German Army Security Service communications center during the war. Landsberg was the best of all my duty stations during my tour in Germany. Landsberg also was the place where Adolph Hitler's imprisonment had been. A Roman road built by the Romans went right through this old town. The Appian Way I believe is the name for the road if I am correct.
I arrived in Landsberg on the 19th of May 1956, on my 18th birthday. In 1957 I can't remember which month it was the 6905th was disbanded and most of the guys were sent to the 6901st in Zweibrucken. So the 01st opened shop somewhere in 1957; located on a muddy hill above a town that sits between two hills. It was far short of what we had been accustomed to at Landsberg with private rooms for two persons, and now living in what we called bays, with forty persons. Landsberg was lush green. We could see the Alps from our windows, and here there was a pond of muck and mud. It was also a missile base for the Army. Later on in 1958 a company of German Army moved in on the base. It was also called Tureen Kaserne. One night a friend got drunk and wanted to go join the French Foreign Legion at the French base in town. They would have taken him; they took everyone that wanted to enlist, criminals, etc. We talked him out of it, lucky for him. I was a cryptographer; I held the highest clearance in the country, a TOP SECRET Category #4, which means I had 3 security clearances to do the work I did. The 6901st was the biggest communications, and intelligence center in

Europe. We worked around the clock, rotating in 3 shifts. All intelligence from all Europe and our sites in Turkey, Pakistan, was relayed to the 01st. It was digested, evaluated, and sent to the States through NSA, and USAFSS in San Antonio communications centers. Well, so much for now. I pray you do have a good day.
God Bless.
PD

PD stands for Pastor Don. Don Levesque is a pastor.

AT FRANCIS WARREN AFB
By Don Levesque

At FE Warren AFB, I arrived there in the fall of '55 after Sampson AFB to be a Communications specialist. I wanted to be an aerial photographer, since I had been working for the local newspaper while in High School, attending teletypes from the Associated Press. My job was to retrieve the news coming off the teletypes and photo facsimile (the early fax machine that sent pictures by telephone from the National News like Associated Press. Therefore they automatically classified me for this type of work. I had to learn to type on a teletype with speed up to 35 words per minute, read teletype tape, and learn the full realm of a military communications center. This place was worse than basic training, the barracks went back to horse cavalry, a leftover from the Indian wars, matter of fact, Custer had been stationed there. Cheyenne sits between mountains and the wind always blows there. I thought Maine was cold till I got there, that winter was terrible, snow drifting in from the windows. The furnaces were outside, therefore during the night we had extra duty to shovel coal from one barracks to the other all night in sometime blizzard conditions, the coal bins were next to the furnaces, each barracks, had there own furnace, by the time you got finished from one end of the barracks maybe ten, if I can remember, you had to start again till 7 in the morning. Then go dress up and clean for breakfast and school started promptly at 9. Now this extra duty was every three days, and it does take much of your sleep time. So, I used to doze during the class many times, maybe more than anyone I suppose, and I was caught sleeping several times.

Now, came the final tests, and the instructor told me that if I did not pass, I would be busted and probably go into the stockade. Fortunately, that weekend I was free, and I studied all weekend. Come Monday morning I was ready for the tests, the instructor thought I was going to fail, I can almost see him looking at me during the test, with a grin. I finished first, and his eyes almost went through the papers, he could not believe his own eyes. I had a perfect score of 100%.

He responded to me by saying, "I know you didn't cheat because you finished first." Also, he mentioned, "Well the school is taking the first twenty with the highest scores for Cryptographic school." And he then added with a smirk, "You're not leaving here soon, because you will have to be standby, till your Top Secret Crypto Clearance is cleared, that means full time coal shoveler."

I debated at that time if I had made a good choice of getting a high score on my test. This was in January and it's cold there. After all I did not join the AF to be a coal shoveler specialist. I was what they called "casual duty," awaiting my orders for the Month of January and most of February.

Then one day, as I mentioned, I got out of what I considered hell. I was transferred to Scott AFB Ill. to Cryptographic school, and this was like heaven, no extra duty after school, no KP, and treated like a human being. I graduated there also with honors, and was chosen to be assigned with the United States Security Service, awaiting another clearance, but this time I spent the time awaiting my clearance on leave at home.

From there I was assigned to Landsberg AB in Germany in the Bavarian Alps, former SS Communication base. This was even better than Scott AFB. I arrived there on my 18th birthday on the 19th of May 1956. In February of 1957 the New German Army took over the base, and the 6905th was deactivated and we were moved to the 6901st in Zweibrucken. It was a US Army Missile Base with the old Persian IRBM. So, we were guest of the Army with their terrible Army chow. It was another traumatic change from Landsberg with all the great food we enjoyed there.

Before we moved from Landsberg to Zweibrucken the then famous "Moscow Mollie" a replica to Tokyo Rose, said one evening, "You little spies from Landsberg, you're going to be moved to Zweibrucken." No one in my squadron knew about this, and to this day I wonder how she ever found out.

FOR YOUR EYES ONLY . . . hahaha love PD
By Don Levesque

From: Don Levesque
Date: 6/23/05 22:35:01
To: wladyboss@cox.net
Subject: FW: God loves you

Edna, are you sure your dad was in charge of the mess hall for a fact? I remember in 1957 during the Hungarian Revolution that was crushed by the former Evil Empire (USSR), that we were on high alert, and we had a meeting in the mess hall of all places. And told that by the base Commander, if anyone asked what we did, or what our job description was, our response was to be "we all worked in the mess hall," officers and enlisted. I still don't know the date your dad served in the 6901st, our unit was a Top Secret intelligence communication unit. You mentioned the Russian person; he possibly was one of our Russian spies. Turkey was also another intelligence gathering site. It probably was at Ankara Turkey, or one of our sites there. You also mentioned he spent some time at Langley which is CIA Hq. So, like all of us we could not tell even our family what we did or what our job was - classified even till after the end of the Cold War. In Sept.1958 we lost eleven of our men from the 6910th who were shot down on the Turkish border on one of our regular intelligence missions. The relatives weren't told the truth about what happened till 1998 and their bodies were only brought and buried at Arlington that year; prior to that the story was that the plane had crashed in the Mediterranean Sea. Their names are now inscribed on a stone in front of the NSA building. I served in the 6905th in Landsberg, Germany with the United States Security Service from 1956 to 1957, then I was transferred to the USAFSS 6901st in Zweibrucken, spent some time in Turkey. One day two airmen were killed instantly next to me and by the grace of God I survived, but I received a serious head and back injury. I was discharged afterward in 1963. I went to Bible College, earned a doctorate later and ministered to a local church till 2002 due to my former injury and a newcomer "Parkinson." I am now a totally disabled veteran. I am the Maine Chaplain Commander for the United States Corps of Chaplains - a strictly volunteer organization. We are not part of the US military, because we are all ex-military, we have military ranks. Our mission is to help and support military personnel and families. On 9/11 it was found that there was a lack of trained chaplain professionals to deal with that awful disaster. The

USCOC was then organized in all 50 states, to deal with any emergency which would demand our expertise. Just last year our Maine Guards were all in Iraq and there was no chaplain here in Maine. We were called and asked to assist to notify the next of kin with a military officer.

I love your trust in the Lord, I assume you know Jesus personally, I will also pray for your son.

That must have been some experience going to West Berlin, no wonder all heck broke loose, hahah - the things we did when we were young.

I will continue to write to your son, and I told him I would be sending one of our Spiritual deployment packages which has a Bible and some other goodies.

God Bless You,

HIS

Chaplain (BG) Donald R. Levesque
United States Corps of Chaplains
Commander Maine Brigade, 1st Division

Trish,
Some more interesting stuff for your book.
Love, PD

From: Edna Whittemore
Date: 6/24/05 09:57:30
To: Don Levesque
Subject: Let's Back Track

Hi Chaplain,

My Dad was stationed at the 6901st in Zweibrucken Germany from 1961-1964. Prior to that, we were stationed in Clovis, New Mexico (AF Base closed). You know what, come to think of it, every base we were stationed at closed, even Victoria Texas when I was in second grade! The only one that did not close was Langley. We always came back here to Langley, always! Daddy started out at Langley.

All of us kids have often wondered if he really was a "Mess Sgt." because he sure didn't act like one! Nobody else's Daddy went TDY like ours. We would come home from school, especially in Germany, and find he was gone again. Captain Bush always checked on us to make sure everything was okay and always told us to call him if we needed anything. Hell, I spent most of my time at his house anyway because his daughter and I were such good friends and have been for a number of years now.

The Russian wasn't the only "strange" individual trekking in and out, there was Regina, who all of a sudden disappeared too. There was Frau Weiss, whom we rented from, but the relationship was a strange one with her too. Then my Dad decided one day that my sister Barbara and I had to make friends with these two German girls across town. Well, we had our own friends we wanted to be with, so our first encounter was at their house and I was the only one fluent in English and German both, so I told one of the girls if she didn't shave under her arms the hair would grow all the way to her wrist. Needless to say, among the other things of this nature I felt necessary to tell these two young krauts, we were never invited back! Were we ever so glad. Of course, I denied everything they accused me of!

Barbara (sister) and I went to school in K-Town and my two younger sisters went to school in Zweibrucken (all on Post schools). I decided in 9th grade that I wanted to participate in the student exchange program whereas I went to a German school and a German kid took my place at my school. I wanted this badly because I knew that German kids only went to school until Noon each day, and boy did I want a schedule like that. I begged my Dad, and finally he signed me up. NOBODY TOLD ME THEY WENT TO SCHOOL ON SATURDAY AND DID NOT GET A SUMMER BREAK! I begged to get out of it, but my Daddy *made* me complete the assignment. So when I went back to school in the fall, I had no summer break! It was one of the most treasured experiences in my life. I learned so much, and they were so far ahead of American Schools.

While we were in Germany, we vacationed to Austria, Switzerland and Luxembourg. We also saw France and Italy while we were there. If Gregg gets the station in Germany, I will certainly visit. He is so interested in what his Grandpa did while in the Air Force. Gregg is so much like his Grandfather, it's not even funny! I caught him punishing my granddaughter once. He had her scrubbing the kitchen floor with a tooth brush . . . yes, Granny, intervened! I told him my granddaughter was not one of his troops and she wasn't going to be treated like one, and that ended that right there!

I am also disabled, degenerative joint and disc disease (excelled) and lupus of my connective tissue. I used to go 200 mph and God just slowed me down one day in 1998, what for, I don't know yet, but there is a reason for everything on this earth. I was the only female Maintenance Engineer in the State of Virginia at the Hampton Roads Bridge-Tunnels. I supervised 67 men and 5 women. I was responsible for the maintenance of the Hampton Roads Bridge-Tunnels, I-564 Tunnel under the Naval Air Station, and the Coleman Bridge, plus 10 miles of the new I-664 tunnel approach. I spent 28 years there, and loved every minute of it. My Dad was big on education, and I am glad. I was a rather odd one being a female engineer in a "good 'ol boys" environment, but I can give as good as I get! They tagged me as the "Dragon Lady," I really didn't care as long as they did their jobs to my satisfaction, because the buck stopped with me, not them!

Well, enough this time, take care, stay well, and God Bless.

Just,
Edna Whittemore

From: Don Levesque
Date: 06/24/05 11:38:39
To Edna Whittemore
Subject: Re: Let's Back Track

Good morning Edna, I believe he was a spook administrator, never a mess sergeant. There are so many things I could say, but I don't know what is declassified and what is not. They have had much declassification since the Cold War ended. We had so many classified ops during that time. Regular enlisted personnel aren't that close to ranking officers. Some of us had false rank, an A1c could be a LT. or Captain. Those TDY missions occurred frequently. We needed to get people in and out of the East Berlin, and other locations. Greg can be proud of his warrior grandpa. Sorry to hear about your disability. You sound like a friend of mine that I write often, her name is Trish, and she got in touch with me concerning her brother and wanted to know what happened to him and other information. She is an author of many books and she is presently writing a book about the guys who served in the 01st and other USAFSS outfits. I will tell her about you and what I know about your dad. You could share your time over there. This is all great stuff. You were a part of this great outfit and contributed to the Cold War victory.

God Bless - have to go to the VA hospital this p.m. - regular stuff appointment.

PD

Interesting, that now I live in the Norfolk area, like Edna Whittemore and all her experiences as the only female Maintenance Engineer in the State of VA at the Hampton Roads Bridge Tunnels. Hooray for Edna!!!! [The Editor] I live in Portsmouth, not far from where Edna worked! I also suffer from degenerative joint and disc disease. But, I keep on going and going and going - maybe not too much in the way of walking, but writing books on my computer and researching for my books, takes up my time and I not only learn more each day, but I love it.

From: IdaReedBlanford@aol.com
Date: Friday, December 13, 2002 01:35:20 AM
To: dr.levesque @ . . .
Subject: Re: Hi

Well, perhaps: Can you tell me if SO GS-15 6901SCG/1963 (which was under decorations on Phil's DD214) means Special Operations at a GS-15 level for 6901 SCG is an award for Phil doing some kind of Special Ops (how do I find out WHAT special ops) from the 6901 SCG? Any ideas? I'm not asking you to break any of your code of silence, 1963 is when Phil cam back from a TDY to London and he cracked up when he came back from that. The rest is history.
God Bless,
Trish

Subj: Re: Hi
Date: 12/13/02 2:04:09 PM Pacific Standard Time
From: dr.levesque@adelphia.net
To: IdaReedBlanford@aol.com

Trish, I left the 6901st in March of 1959. The SO GS-15 is a civil service grade at a security level. I don't believe it was any decoration. We never got citations during my tenure. The National Security Agency "NSA: OR WHAT WE CALLED IT "THE NONE SUCH AGENCY" may have given special citation after I left, I don't know.
We had many men end up with mental breakdown during my tour there. Long hours and much stress. We did have many ops, but still to this day I believe they remain classified.
Have a great day.

It turned out that information from the FOIA said the SO GS-15/6901st SCG/1963 were two Good Conduct Medals with two bronze loops from the 6901st

From: IdaReedBlanford@aol.com
Date: Friday, December 13, 2002, 06:10:11 PM
To: dr.levesque@adelphia.net
Subject: Re: Hi

God bless you, Don, that's what I thought it meant.

Many, many things are becoming de-classified, but I don't know them all, so better to stay safe and sound rather than sorry.

Thank you and I appreciate your time. If you ever need anything . . . all you have to do is let me know.

Do you have my two books that I wrote? I'll send them to you in Maine-not sure if I have your address or not, but will use the one on your site.

I am missing my Andrea, who died of cancer July 19 of this year. Christmas music and all makes me feel dead. Could use a bit of prayer.

Trish

Subj: Re: Hi
Date: 12/13/02 6:15:48 PM Pacific Standard Time
From: dr.levesque@adelphia.net
To: IdaReedBlanford@aol.com

I understand it must be hard to have lost Andrea, and especially during this time of the year. The loss of our loved ones makes us sharply aware of our own mortality and ultimate death. But the Scriptures proclaim the even greater reality of life beyond death, so our hope in God reaches beyond death. Jesus once told a young lady who had lost her brother: "I am the resurrection and the life, he that believes in me shall never die." Then he popped the question to her, "Do you believe this?" (John 11:25) Yes we do miss our departed ones, but to know that they will suffer no more, and have just graduated to a better place, where they await our departure from this place of sorrows and hurts, once again we will meet with them, and be together forever. Trish, I will be praying for you, especially during this season. How old was Andrea? Yes, it would be an honor to read your books. My address is Donald Levesque, 19 Smith St., Lewiston, ME 04240. Snowing here this evening, cold, brrrrrr. I wonder if I told you that I am retired now, due to my condition. It has brought some depression, hard after having to step down from my ministry after all those years. The VA has finally granted me a 100% disability. I don't plan to be retired from ministering to people. Don

ONE NATION, UNDER GOD
By Senator John McCain (as told by Donny Mayer)

In light of the recent appeals court ruling in California, with respect to the Pledge of allegiance, the following recollection from Senator John McCain is very appropriate.

The Pledge of Allegiance - Senator John McCain

From a speech made by Capt. John S. McCain, USN, (Ret) who represents Arizona in the U.S. Senate:

As you may know, I spent five and one half years as a prisoner of war during the Vietnam War. In the early years of our imprisonment, the NVA kept us in solitary confinement or two or three to a cell. In 1971 the NVA moved us from these conditions of isolation into a large room with as many as 30 to 40 men to a room. This was, as you can imagine, a wonderful change and was a direct result of the efforts of millions of Americans on behalf of a few hundred POWs 10,000 miles from home.

One of the men who moved into my room was a young man named Mike Christian. Mike came from a small town near Selma, Alabama. He didn't wear a pair of shoes until he was 13 years old. At 17, he enlisted in the US Navy. He later earned a commission by going to Officer Training School. Then he became a Naval Flight Officer and was shot down and captured in 1967. Mike had a keen and deep appreciation of the opportunities this country and our military provide for people who want to work and want to succeed.

As part of the change in treatment, the Vietnamese allowed some prisoners to receive packages from home. In some of these packages were handkerchiefs, scarves and other items of clothing. Mike got himself a bamboo needle. Over a period of a couple of months, he created an American flag and sewed it on the inside of his shirt. Every afternoon, before we had a bowl of soup, we would hang Mike's shirt on the wall of the cell and say the Pledge of Allegiance. I know the Pledge of Allegiance may not seem the most important part of our day now, but I can assure you that in that stark cell it was indeed the most important and meaningful event.

One day the Vietnamese searched our cell, as they did periodically, and discovered Mike's shirt with the flag sewn inside, and removed it. That evening they returned, opened the door of the cell, and for the benefit of all of us, beat Mike Christian severely for the next couple of hours. Then, they opened the door of the cell and threw him in. We cleaned him up as well as we could.

The cell in which we lived had a concrete slab in the middle on which we slept. Four naked light bulbs hung in each corner of the room. As I said, we tried to clean up Mike as well as we could. After the excitement died down, I looked in the corner of the room, and sitting there beneath that dim light bulb with a piece of red cloth, another shirt and his bamboo needle, was my friend, Mike Christian. He was sitting there with his eyes almost shut from the beating he had received, making another American flag.

He was not making the flag because it made Mike Christian feel better. He was making that flag because he knew how important it was to us to be able to Pledge our allegiance to our flag and country.

So, the next time you say the Pledge of Allegiance, you must never forget the sacrifice and courage that thousands of Americans have made to build our nation and promote freedom around the world. You must remember our duty, our honor, and our country.

"I pledge allegiance to the flag of the United States of America and to the republic for which it stands, one nation under God, indivisible, with liberty and justice for all."

PASS THIS ON . . . and on . . . and on!

And I am passing it along . . . [The Editor]

AN EARLIER TIME
By Dr. Al Leinweber (52-53)

Ed. Note: A cover letter: Barbara and I had the good fortune to meet Al and Betty Leinweber at the 2001 BIA Reunion in Berlin, Germany. We got to know each other while scurrying between U-Bahn trains as we worked our way across that great city to the various BIA events.
Because Al served in Berlin before many of us, I asked him to write something about those years that could be edited for use in a BIA Newsletter later this year. The result was so fascinating to me that I asked Al to let me share it in it's entirety with those of you at the reunion. It is presented here just as Al drafted it.
Thanks, Al, and our best wishes to Betty.

BerlinerPhil 9/9/02

It was a time of transition for Flughafen Tempelhof 50 years ago. Eisenhower was just then forming NATO. The Korean War was going full blast. Joe Stalin was still alive, and had only recently desisted from his attempted strangulation of Berlin. The Air Force was only about three years old, and lots of us were still in OD uniforms, and had to polish gold-colored brass.

The recently-departed Red Army had tried to burn everything above ground in the great arc of an operations building at Tempelhof (largest building in Europe?) which we all came to know so well. They flooded the subterranean floors where Luftwaffe fighters were kept. I never could find out how many levels were below ground. Stone and steel don't burn very well, so quite a lot of building was left - about 3/4 of a mile of it.

Detachment "D" of the 2nd Radio Squadron Mobile occupied one long room "Am vierten Obergeschoss," with a glass-lensed peephole in the door, so that one could be eyeballed from within before he entered. Thirty years later, someone knowledgeable told me the peephole was still there. Also, the 3-man elevator boxes were still said to be continuously running, carrying voice and CW operators to their workplace.

Inside were numbers of Collins 51J and Hammerlund receivers, along with "Bendix Washer" Radar sets. A pair of powerful binoculars was kept over by the one window, south-facing. There was a direction-finding facility out between the runways, made to look like another GCA shack. Communications with the site was via Deutsche Post land-lines between teletype machines. Communications were encoded securely by NSA codebooks which were changed periodically. A weak spot was having those code books out in that shack, with East Germany scarcely a mile away. The shack area was surrounded by multi-lingual signs, warning that access to the area was "Streng Verboten," "Zapreschchenno," and "Interdit." I came within a whisker of having to ice a German Shepherd Lad, who was probably illiterate and couldn't read the signs, in any language. Trouble was, he was wearing a ground-length sheepskin cape, and I couldn't see his hands, nor the Uzi he might have had.

Shift changes at the shack were made by a jeep coming and going, always awaiting an all-clear visual signal from the control tower, before crossing the tarmac. Shifts were four days, then four night shifts, then four graveyard shifts, with a day off in between.

Det "D" comprised about a dozen of us, voice and CW operators, covering all shifts. T/Sgt Darrel Hanson and 2/Lt Kenneth Piersall were our authority figures. The guys were a multi-talented bunch. One had been a ghost writer in New York City, another had been a superintendent of schools, and another was an electrical engineer. The latter was probably the most valuable man on Tempelhof: he could fix any of our electronics, though he was there as a voice operator. All of us were in our early 20's.

In the late 40's, there were 3-year enlistments. One of our guys, Dallas Clark, was approaching the end of his enlistment, and was actually enroute to the port at Bremerhaven, for his voyage back to the land of the big PX, when he was involuntarily extended for another year due to the NATO build-up, and he was turned around and sent back to us. I've always admired the good grace he exhibited, ever a cheerful and responsible member of the outfit.

On my arrival, in January 1952, I was shown a smoke-blackened room, about 50' x 50', where I was to be billeted. It was just a few steps from the operations room, but that was the only attractive thing about it. I set up my folding metal GI cot in one corner, drew bedding from supply, and I was then in residence, with all my worldly possessions in my footlocker and barracks bag. Later, some other guys moved in with me, and painters finally came and brightened up the place.

Berlin had been destroyed over its wide areas, as no other comparable place had ever been done in. The Kaiser Wilhelm II Gedaechtniskirche on the Kurfuerstendamm was blasted as it now stands, only it had not yet been stabilized for safety, and entering it was dangerous. The huge, cast-metal statues in the Tiergarten were still full of Red Army bullet-holes. I remember a massive bison having a spear plunged into his side by a huge Nordic huntsman. There were a lot of extra "eyes" in and around his helmet. All this, but the U-Bahn could still whisk you from Neukoelln to Spandau in less than an hour, through 370-odd square miles of debris. We were told not to ride the U-Bahn across intervening portions of East Berlin, even though we didn't get off. Vopo's were everywhere in the East. Even if they had no arrest power over us, it was crucial that we were not interrogated. The monument depicting the three air corridors had already been erected on Platz der Luftbruecke. An eagle facing it across the quadrangle had already had the Swastika blasted from his claws.

A wonderful bright spot happened during that time. Harry Truman's last term was drawing to a close, and he wanted to do something to draw Germany back into the family of nations. He hit upon a cultural exchange program, Harry was always accused of operating "government by crony," and this time was no different. There resided in Independence at that time one Blevins Davis. He had been a high school literature teacher, but he had a football romance with a very rich elderly widow. By that I mean he married her, then waited around for her to kick off, which she eventually did, making him a very rich fellow indeed. He became a patron of the arts. Harry knew all this, so we called on him to act as impresario for our end of the cultural exchange, and what he did was sheer genius. He assembled a cast that was never to be forgotten to do Gerschwin's "Porgy and Bess." Porgy was William Warfield, who had just sung "Ol' Man River" in the current movie "Showboat" better than anybody ever had, before or since. Bess was Leontine Price, then about 21 and unknown, but had a long career as a diva at the Met, famous for interpreting Verdi. Cab Calloway was Sportin' Life, already well-established as a "Scat" singer. Berlin was one of their first performances in what became a triumphant world tour, and I was there to see it. The Berliners had trouble with the dialogue, but when Leontine's voice soared up into the high registers doing "Summertime," the whole place went wild. Cab did "'Taint Necessarily So" as no one else could. It was a glorious time.

Now a little about the beginning of it all - Brooks AFB was Security Service HQ, with a wire-enclosed compound where we mounted guard all too often. The big outfit there was a giant "casual" squadron, with about 2000 of us going to schools or waiting for shipment elsewhere. Naturally, everything was overseas except for the schools. I lived in a 200-man barracks with holes in the roof, where Eddie Rickenbacker had lived when he was a cadet in 1916. In this setting, we went through 2 weeks of English Grammar instruction, then two weeks of Russian Language, during which we mastered the Cyrillic alphabet and got a good start on Russian grammar and, of course, some vocabulary. Then came the Army Language School at the Presidio of Monterey, CA. There was a year-long Russian course, but we were in a 6 month course which had its genesis when Russian voices were heard flying air cover for North Korean troops. It was an all-Air Force program, designed to quickly get us into the Aleutian Islands, small islands in the sea of Japan, and assorted places in Europe, all surrounding the Soviet land mass. I was in R6-3 (Russian, 6 months, 3rd group to start). R6-1 was still there and in session at that time. Twenty-three languages were being taught, but half the resources and students were there for Russian language study. Our day was split up into times for vocabulary study, speech patterns, conversation, dictation, and some other things, with a different instructor every hour. There was a language lab, the first I'd seen. Tape recorders hadn't come along for personal use just yet, but there were wire recorders. R6-3 was divided into sections A, B, C & D. The group in D section were just hanging on, maybe including some guys from the deep south who couldn't quite get their tongue wrapped around Russian vowel sounds. The guys in section A contrived to look bored, while they fondled their Phi Beta Kappa keys. Every two weeks, there was a large oral and written exam and a reshuffling of the sections, with now and then someone being sent off, presumably to learn another trade.

If there are those of you who have never ridden a troopship, you have my congratulations. I and 2500 poor lost souls were sailing on the stormiest North Atlantic in history during Christmas of 1951. There were 50-foot waves, and the normal 8 days from NY to Bremerhaven took us 11 days. We were locked below for most of the voyage, to avoid scattering bodies into the ocean. Capt. Kurt Carlsen, a Danish skipper of the Flying Enterprise, a Merchant Ship, made big news when he was snatched off his bridge just as she foundered and went down. We were near enough for visual contact somewhere off Lands End when this was happening.
A shipboard troop bunk is a piece of canvas laced to a pipe bent into a "U" shape, and hinged so it can be turned upward to allow daily swabbing of the deck. These hinged bunks were stacked five high, with very little space between, so the top guy almost had to get into his bunk last, and be the first to arise. The guy on the bottom had maybe three inches between his derriere and the deck. One night when the ship was heeling over and pitching more than that for which it was designed, the bulkhead door up above flew open and the sea gushed in. Shoes and barracks bags began floating around, and

some colorful language was heard. The guys on the lower bunks were in great danger, but everyone (200 of us in that compartment) responded immediately, and no tragedy occurred.

Nowadays, whenever someone suggests a sea cruise, it falls on my deaf ears. When I was recalled and sent back to Europe then years later, someone was grousing because our C-118 had to remain overnight in Labrador. I made an impassioned plea to the person to count his blessings.

Heard in a compartment on a troop train going across Germany about midnight our first night there:

"Damn, I never seen so many furriners in my whole life."

"This train is going in circles. That's the third time we've gone through this town of Ausgang."

"Can you speak German?" "I dunno. Mebbe. Ain't ever tried to before."

In 1961, when the Berlin Wall went up, the jet age was upon us with full force. Fighter-plane reflex time was needed against the East, which brought into being a string of hitherto unused bases well back of the Rhine, mostly in Eastern France. I had recently qualified in dentistry, and had recently settled into a small-town practice in Missouri. Almost overnight, I found myself Chief of Dental Services at Etain AB, very near the Argonne (Sergeant York) battlefield area of WWI. In a few months, I got some leave time and, burning with curiosity, made my way to Berlin and Tempelhof. There, I was greeted by (my jaw dropped) a Major. I realized that I no longer had a proper clearance and "need to know," but I explained my curiosity to him, and he was most cordial, without telling me anything. He said I'd be surprised at some of the new technology.

The doctor draft (to age 52) was in full effect in those days, but I had signed on as a reserve officer, USAF, DC: thus my quick call-up. After years of grinding poverty, I was trying to make a buck wherever I could. The Korean GI Bill had paid only a small fraction of my tab. Student Loans? They were for later coddled generations.

During my career, most of which was in military service, fame and fortune have eluded me. Quite the antithesis of fame, I worked in a "silent service" in divided Berlin as a Russian language operative, within months after leaving Westminster. That was when Josef Stalin was still alive and probably livid with rage when his attempt at strangulation of Berlin was frustrated by the enlightened actions of President Harry Truman and Generals Hap Arnold and Lucius Clay.

Very likely Stalin had issued a blanket "shoot-down" order to his 24th Air Army across East Germany, the only exception being the air corridors, covered by the 4-power agreement.

The three air corridors were 10,000 feet up and ten miles wide. They radiated out of Berlin at 237, 270 and 310 degrees respectively.

One memorable day I was on a work shift, in multiple locations around Tempelhof Air Base with two or three other linguists operating receivers, radar sets, recording devices, and direction-finding equipment, all of us with earphones on and engrossed in an exercise involving a controller in the 24th Air Army directing maneuvers of Yak fighter-planes beneath one of the corridors. Incredibly, an Air France pilot picked that moment, near the fighters, to do some sloppy navigation and stray out of the corridor. We heard the controller give the "shoot-down" order and the Yak fighters' assent. Via some circuitous but almost instantaneous communication (we were there in secrecy) the Air France pilot had his ears blistered, but was in time to find some cloud cover and get back into the corridor; not, however, before having a burst of machine-gun fire rip through his cabin. Thankfully, none of the 60 odd passengers were injured or killed. In a few seconds, there would have been no survivors.

As the airliner limped into Tempelhof, I stepped outside my "office" momentarily to watch it land. Then, and often later, I've reflected on the fact that none of those 60 passengers would ever know who saved their lives.

That kind of communications intelligence was then in its infancy. There were perhaps a dozen of us there, covering all shifts around the clock, doing some rather intricate things in a rather skillful manner, considering that we had no predecessors to instruct us in those days.

A huge part of my own contribution could be chalked up to the fact that Westminster had an iron-clad requirement that, in order to graduate, one must pass an exam involving a foreign language.

I was born in a Missouri farmhouse and learned my "three R's" in one-room country schools. Left to my own options for course selection, I never would have equipped myself to be instrumental in preserving 60 lives that day.

ROSEMARY
By Dr. Al Leinweber

My arena was in a large common room inside an unremarkable dwelling in Saigon. In that room were dozens of toddlers to about age 12, all orphans. Babies were in an adjoining, quieter room. The place was the creation of a modern-day saint, an Australian lady named Rosemary. She was ably assisted by an East German nurse. They had a cadre of young girls, both Caucasian (mostly Australian) and Vietnamese. Rosemary had an uncanny intelligence network, which told her of impending battles, and fights just concluded. Before the smoke had cleared, she was in those villages, looking for orphaned children. Also the Viet Cong did a lot of selective assassination of officials in supposedly "pacified" villages, leaving their children to perish. Instead, Rosemary showed up in a short time.

Living and working in a different culture can be tricky. Rosemary knew the ropes, and the correct strings to pull. A thing to be guarded against was causing someone to "lose face;" particularly important in maintaining good relationships with co-workers, and especially with elders and superiors. Even an Oriental government or regime will "lose face" if its orphans are shipped out wholesale to other countries to be adopted. Rosemary knew this, but found she could get the children out singly, or by twos, as long as she kept a very low profile. No publicity, no neon signs, and nothing to make her house different from the ones around it. I found out about Rosemary and her operation from a Catholic chaplain, with whom I often broke bread in a mess hall. He thought some of the children might be experiencing dental ailments, and at least should be examined.

My job, for which I was in Viet Nam, was to be the advisor to the Chief of the Republic of Viet Nam Military Dental Corps. Typically, I was at the Chief's side, and we were out visiting his clinics all over South Viet Nam, whether in hospitals or line fighting units. Through me, the Chief could get equipment and supplies, education and specialty training for his doctors, laboratory technicians, etc. There were times when he was dealing with personnel and cultural matters and there would be less distraction if I wasn't present. We developed a close friendship and synchronization, so there were times, never predictable, when I would go to check on Rosemary's children. Dozens of kids were always there.

I had no one working for me, but I was always in and out of American military clinics in the area, and knew all the guys. They were (young assistants & technicians) itching to get out of the four walls where they worked 7 days per week. Their bosses almost always gave permission for them to go with me; I had a jeep every day from the Vietnamese motor pool. They'd prepare sterilized materials and instruments for every eventuality. We'd pile into the jeep and off we'd go. From the moment we'd enter the big common room, the kids, always starved for adult attention and affection, would be clinging to our legs with little faces upturned, wanting to ride on our shoulders, etc. Of course, we really ate that up. Every time I'd see the young guys after that, the question was "When can we go again?"

I learned things from those fellows, i.e., a ladder-back straight chair, strapped firmly in a tilted position to a ceiling supporting column, with cushions for the head and under the knees, makes a useable dental treatment chair.

We couldn't communicate verbally with our little patients, and at first they had little reason to trust us. Imagine feeling the numbing effect of local anesthesia for the first time if you're three years old. Fortunately, I had unknowingly assembled a troupe of ham actors and pantomime specialists. They simulated grotesque rubber faces, crossed eyes, stood on their head, etc. Instead of cries of anguish, there were peals of laughter. Some of the most heart-warming episodes of a lifetime were spent in that common room.

During one break in the action I noticed a pretty young matron, Australian I learned - one of Rosemary's adoptive parents who had come for her daughter, and with whom she was cooing and communicating. I went over and sat nearby and said hello and admired her little girl, about two or three years old. We chatted a little, very pleasantly, then I had to go back to work across the room. On the way, I talked to one of Rosemary's helpers, and commented on the beautiful mother-daughter bonding I had witnessed. The young lady was strangely evasive, and I later found out that the baby girl had a medical problem which would limit her life to only two more years or so. As I inquired later, the young mother adopted her, took her home, and cared for her, knowing about the short life of her beloved little one, another saint in that room, and maybe lots of them.

After my tour of duty in Viet Nam was over, I wrote to my Congressman about Rosemary and her work. That was the first and only time I ever wrote to a Congressman and that was the only subject I ever discussed with him. It was a story that needed telling, I thought.

A letter from Chau N. Lam, D.M.D., former Chief of the Republic of Vietnam Armed Forces Dental Corps, follows:

Chau N. Lam, D.M.D.
F.A.D.I., F.P.F.A., F.A.C.D., F.I.C.D.
7008 Lake Run Drive
Birmingham, AL 35242-7501

September 29, 2003

TO WHOM IT MAY CONCERN:

It is with great pleasure that I write this letter in strong support of Dr. Alfred Leinweber whom I have known since 1971. I was the Chief of the Republic of Vietnam Armed Forces Dental Corps in Saigon, South-Vietnam, and he was my Advisor. At that time and for approximately a year, Dr. Leinweber and I were reasonably close, we worked together almost daily.

He maintained contact with the Senior Dental Officers of the U.S. Army, U.S. Air Force and U.S. Navy to set up some short Residency Training in Maxillofacial Surgery, Prosthetic Replacement and Periodontal Specialty in Cong-Hoa General Hospital in Saigon. He made sure that we had adequate dental supplies and equipment for the various Republic of Vietnam combat units, to maintain oral health of the fighting forces where they were located. He was responsible for reporting on the status of the above activities to his U.S. Military Superiors, Chief of Professional Services and the Command Surgeon, Military Assistance Command, Vietnam. He sent quarterly reports of all these activities to the Assistant Surgeon General for Dental Services, USAF in Washington, D.C.

I have no reservation to write this letter of recommendation for Dr. Alfred Leinweber for I know his integrity is beyond question. Dr. Leinweber demonstrated great enthusiasm, energy and intelligence in his capacity of Dental Advisor during his tour in Vietnam. Since then, he is in New Mexico and I am here in Birmingham, Alabama as a Dentist at the Jefferson County, Department of Health and for 31 years, have stayed in touch by letter and by phone. Dr. Leinweber and I were military colleagues, then, and good friends now.

Sincerely,

Chau N. Lam, D.M.D.
Former Chief of the Republic of Vietnam
Armed Forces Dental Corps.

Dr. Leinweber's note: Unfortunately for us, and for the world, Dr. Chau Ngoc Lam died about a year after writing this item. ADL.

These Guys 335

This is a story sent to me via e-mail by Irv LeVine, its subject, someone whom Irv knew who had owned and flown his own p-51's. It brought tears to my eyes, said Irv, and it did to mine, also. Thanks, Irv. T.S.

P-51: sent to me via Irv Levine.

I don't know who wrote the piece but he's a Canadian and a damned good wordsmith.

It was noon on a Sunday as I recall, the day a Mustang P-51 was to take to the air. They said it had flown in during the night from some U.S. airport, the pilot had been tired.

I marveled at the size of the plane dwarfing the Pipers and Canucks tied down by her, it was much larger than in the movies. She glistened in the sun like a bulwark of security from days gone by. The pilot arrived by cab paid the driver then stepped into the flight lounge. He was an older man, his wavy hair was grey and tossed . . . looked like it might have been combed, say around the turn of the century. His bomber jacket was checked, creased, and worn, it smelled old and genuine. Old Glory was prominently sewn to its shoulders. He projected a quiet air of proficiency and pride devoid of arrogance. He filed a quick flight plan to Montreal (Expo-67, Air Show) then walked across the tarmac.

After taking several minutes to perform his walk-around check the pilot returned to the flight lounge to ask if anyone would be available to stand by with fire extinguishers while he "flashed the old bird up . . . just to be safe." Though only 12 at the time I was allowed to stand by with an extinguisher after brief instruction on its use - - "If you see a fire point then pull this lever!" I later became a firefighter, but that's another story.

The air around the exhaust manifolds shimmered like a mirror from fuel fumes as the huge prop started to rotate. One manifold, then another, and yet another barked -- I stepped back with the others. In moments the Packard-built Merlin engine came to life with a thunderous roar, blue flames knifed from her manifolds. I looked at the others' faces, there was no concern. I lowered the bell of my extinguisher. One of the guys signaled to walk back to the lounge, we did. Several minutes later we could hear the pilot doing his pre-flight run-up. He'd taxied to the end of runway 19, out of sight. All went quiet for several seconds, we raced from the lounge to the second story deck to see if we could catch a glimpse of the P-51 as she started down the runway, we could not. There we stood, eyes fixed to a spot half way down 19. Then a roar ripped across the field, much louder than before, like a furious hell spawn set loose -- something mighty this way was coming.

"Listen to that thing!" said the controller. In seconds the Mustang burst into our line of sight. Its tail was already off and it was moving faster than anything I'd ever seen by that point on 19. Two thirds the way down 19 the Mustang was airborne with her gear going up. The prop tips were supersonic: we clasped our ears as the Mustang climbed hellish fast into the circuit to be eaten up by the dog-day haze.

We stood for a few moments in stunned silence trying to digest what we'd just seen. The radio controller rushed by me to the radio. "Kingston radio calling Mustang?" He looked back to us as he waited for an acknowledgment. The radio crackled, "Kingston radio, go ahead." "Roger Mustang. Kingston radio would like to advise the circuit is clear for a low level pass." I stood in shock because the controller had, more or less, just asked the pilot to return for an impromptu air show!

The controller looked at us. "What?" He asked. "I can't let that guy go without asking . . . I couldn't forgive myself!" The radio crackled once again, "Kingston radio, do I have permission for a low level pass, east to west, across the field?" "Roger Mustang, the circuit is clear for an east to west pass." "Roger, Kingston radio, we're coming out of 3000 feet, stand by." We rushed back onto the second-story deck, eyes fixed toward the eastern haze.

The sound was subtle at first, a high-itched whine, a muffled screech, a distant scream. Moments later the P-51 burst through the haze . . . her airframe straining against positive Gs and gravity, wing tips spilling contrails of condensed air, prop-tips again supersonic as the burnished bird blasted across the eastern margin of the field shredding and tearing the air.

At about 400 mph and 150 yards from where we stood she passed with an old American pilot saluting . . . imagine . . . a salute. I felt like laughing, I felt like crying, she glistened, she screamed, the building shook, my heart pounded . . . then the old pilot pulled her up . . . and rolled, and rolled, and rolled out of sight into the broken clouds and indelibly into my memory.

I've never wanted to be an American more than on that day. It was a time when many nations in the world looked to America as their big brother, a steady and even-handed beacon of security who navigated difficult political water with grace and style; not unlike the pilot who'd just flown into my memory. He was proud, not arrogant, humble, not a braggart, old and honest projecting an aura of America at its best. That America will return one day, I know it will.

Until that time, I'll just send off a story; call it a reciprocal salute, to the old American pilot who wove a memory for a young Canadian that's stayed a lifetime.

This was sent to me by Bill Person, a Viet Nam Vet.
Sent: Thursday, January 13, 2005 7:47 AM
Subject: FW: ANOTHER REMEMBRANCE BROUGHT TO MIND . . . THANKS TOBY. . . .

From Irv LeVine, my F-105 pilot buddy,

Toby et al you can add a very thankful Marine, name of Mike Bradbury to [that list]. Mike was at Khe San when the big NVA push was on to take it. Took a bullet through the helmet, it circumscribed his head and came out a few cm's from where it went in. It knocked him out and the blood poured down his face and neck and he was "added" to the pile of dead that were to be evacuated if and when such time came. He "groaned" and they realized he wasn't ready to go. He has told me many times of the hope and relief they all felt when they saw the smoke of the F-4s as they roared in for the kill against the attacking NVA. He feels he owes his life to "luck and f-4 fighter jocks who swept in so low he could see the pilots clearly as they went over the hill he was on." Khe San, of course, didn't become another Dien Ben Phu because of the gutty guys in the air, both Arc Light and TACAIR, the airborne sensor monitoring and the determined, Marine Fighting Spirit on the ground.

Semper Fi,

Irv

TA-RA-BOOM-DEE-AAAAA - by Irv Levine

KORAT ROYAL THAI AIR FORCE BASE, THAILAND, 1967! TA-RA-BOOM-DEE-AAAAA WHO WILL GET STUFFED TODAY . . ." The semi-musical notes came from the mouth and throat of the Wing Flight Safety Officer Major 'Billy' Givens. It was 3 a.m., and as always, too damned early that Thailand morning. We had eaten a light breakfast, used the urinal and were trucking down the flight line for the early morning "go." Most everyone else in the truck was half asleep - but not Billy. Billy was one of those non-descript guys you see . . . but don't, really. He was fun, usually laughing or with a big smile on his face, with something nice to say about the day, the weather and life, in general. The "Ta-Ra . . ." etc., however, was the bile raising in Billy's throat as he thought forward to yet another early morning flight when he again, with fifteen other men, would ride the Thunder of his F-105 Thunderchief into yet another battle in the skies over North Vietnam. Sixty percent losses! - Twice as high as any other outfit over there. The THUDS (105's) were a major part of the air war back then. Billy let his nervous frustrations out through his little song. It tended to relax the rest of us more than it did Billy - and maybe he meant it that way. We lost Billy. Not to SAMS, or Flak or MiGs over the target area but to a tiny mistake that mushroomed into a very large crash. As the Wing Life Support Officer it was my job to inspect what was left of Billy and his Life Support Equipment to see if any of it had failed. None of it did. Billy had simply lost control of his aircraft when he asked it to do more than it was capable of. But you don't forget a guy like Billy Givens. It's been almost 40 years since that bleak day I had to say good-bye to him but he remains a bright spot in my life for the fun, warmth and enthusiasm he gave to the guys around him. I still find myself humming and thinking, "TA-RA-BOOM-DEE-AAAAA," but in a positive sense . . . not a negative one. Billy had that effect on a lot of us who out lasted him in life. He's out lasted himself and it's something we all should strive for as we too pass through this hallway-of-life.

This story was written by Irv Levine, another F-105 Thunderchief pilot, in memory of Billy Givens. Irv flew many, many missions over North Vietnam.

These Guys

From: Irv LeVine
To: Trish Schiesser
Sent: Sunday, March 05, 2006 4:46 PM
Subject: RE: AN OBJECTIVE LOOK AT THE WAR WE'RE IN . . .

OPPS! Hi! I've been going over OLD EMAILS and rereading them more closely. I recently sent you a "true story" from the Vietnam Era but find you WEREN'T asking for such. You were interested in COLD WAR stories. Sorry about that! Here's one . . . AND a picture of me in my SHIT HOT HAT, in front of my aircraft, "THE LIQUIDATOR."
Perhaps this little tale doesn't fit the mold you had in mind for telling about the COLD WAR . . . but I tried . . . ☺ IRV

[EDITOR'S NOTE]: The Cold War was from 1945 to Aug. 21, 1991, so any of the stories THESE GUYS send fit just fine. T.S.

The Cold War got "hot" at times but most of such was kept from the general public. The fighting forces were kept on constant ALERT and the hours of "waiting" seemed worse than combat. There were many, many, many "practice flights" to keep us "sharp" and "ready." The amount of tension on the men and aircraft wasn't humor but when they arrived those "moments" helped to lower the tension to manageable levels. We weren't allowed to say ANYTHING on our radios that wasn't germane to the mission . . . especially cuss words.

A night mission to Alaska and back from Little Rock AFB; Little Rock AFB at the time was a SAC base. The Strategic Air Command often entered into exercises as the BAD GUYS and this night was no different. A line of 15 B-47, Stratojets were to fly nose to tail separation of 1 mile and were "stacked up" 500 feet above each other in a long stair step line. We were to fly to a point in Alaska above our northern most radar lines and then turn south towards the United States. The Air Defense Forces would try to pick us up as quickly as possible on radar and launch fighter aircraft to intercept and shoot us down before we could penetrate the North American Area Defense Intercept Zone. (ADIZ) It got pretty hairy doing all the things required on the mission: air to air refueling, navigation, shooting the stars with manually operated sextants, managing fuel loads, setting up bombing equipment, etc.

The exercise would eventually end and the ground plotters would start "second guessing" at how many bombers made it through, how effective the fighter defenses actually were while the bombers flew home. We kept our 1 mile separation and landed one after another. As one aircraft was slowing to turn off the runway another was touching down a mile behind it on the opposite end of the runway. Jaded voices came over the radios. "ROBIN 72 TURNING OFF THE ACTIVE." "Uh, ROBIN 73 IS TOUCHING DOWN." On and on . . . one after another.

Suddenly an anxious voice came over the radio that didn't identify itself but said, "BULL SHIT! WE'LL NEVER MAKE IT!"

The tower control officer couldn't tell if it was the aircraft about to turn off the runway that was maybe going too fast to make the turn and might run off the end of the runway and crash. Or it was the aircraft about to make the runway thereby knocking out approach lights, getting a set of flat tires, etc. Another accident in the making.

Whatever his "guess" the tower control officer wasn't brooking any breaches of radio etiquette. His voice cracked like a whip over the airwaves, 'AIRCRAFT TURNING OFF THE END OF THE RUNWAY . . . WAS THAT YOUR "LAST TRANSMISSION." That copilot, equally sharp snapped lazily, but clear as a bell, answered, "NEGATIVE ON THE BULL SHIT."

NOT ANOTHER SOUND WAS HEARD over those radios as more and more aircraft touched down or turned off the active at the far end.

But, you can bet that the tension dissolved to "0" as heads were thrown back against head rests and explosive laughter penetrated the quiet air of the dimly lit cockpits of every aircraft on that frequency. The tower officer knew when to quit and he did. I'm betting that he was smiling, too.

These Guys

These stories, sent to me via e-mail, are from Patrick Mower and another crewmember of an RC-130 during the Cold War. And, also Patrick Mower says," Just make sure my uncle gets his credit . . . he is in the big day room in the sky and deserves everything he should get!" So, Pat, here is credit to your uncle as you wish, and to all of you aboard the RC-130's. Well done.

SHORT TERM SEPARATIONS
By Patrick Mower and a crewmember of the RC-130

Ya know, when I say that I earned (and some laugh), 11 air medals during "peace time" (remember, to the WWII vets, the cold war wasn't). Some people just stare. I liked your answer - "free" Air Medals.

I never had an Air Medal presented until my last one. I was on my way out, working at the recruiting station close to Omaha, the HQs for the Nebraska recruiters. Crash McFall (one of the Combat Sent Pilots I knew) was the commander. He asked me how I wanted to do it. He suggested that he present it to me at a little ceremony right there in the office. I had them present me with my Uncle Charlie's only WWII Air Medal. He was a Ball Turret gunner on B-24's, and made every single Ploesti Mission. All were happy, even my now departed uncle, when I informed him of my doing this.

I don't think we were crass; young, yes, and probably too dumb to realize that we were not far from the Almighty. But, that is what youth is for.

If they said, you need to strap on a flight suit and go out again . . . my bags are packed.

Pat

Re: SHORT TERM SEPARATIONS
By RS-130 Crewmember

Well said, Pat. There is nothing quite like 6" of jet fuel sloshing around in the cockpit and down the aisle while everything is still powered up off the coast of some country that didn't want us off their coast. There are many other stories, many of which you are familiar with . . . You are right about not being scared at moments like that, when the jet was self destructing, we were too damn busy trying to stay alive to be scared. Same as when a missile is in the air. . . .

Give me another one of those "free" Air Medals,

Signed,
RC-130 Crewmember

From: Patrick E. Mower

The flyers among us will tell you about flying. For the most part it was safe. I just said, "The most part." Remember, we were aboard "government" aircraft built by the lowest bidder with union contract labor for the lowest cost! And remember, we were NOT flying in the "Friendly Skies" either. I saw enough "bogies" along side us to know we were not flying "safe," even though the statement - "Safety of Flight is of paramount importance" was the key in every briefing I attended.

The art and science of what we did, on the ground or in the air (Na bastes I Na zaemlya) (VIZ for you Russian Linguists), made what we did dangerous not because of being constantly fired upon, though some were fired upon and weren't hurt, but just because we never knew what would happen. I came back from more than a few missions and had to clean out my shorts and kissed the ground because the old RC got us back, but nobody knew why or how.

I can truly say that I was never "scared" to fly, or while performing the mission. A few times, some of the incidents that occurred happened coming home, or even "in area" when we had fuel leaks, or a crash landing or two (or my mid air on AWACS in Saudi Arabia with a TANKER), made me realize that life is fragile. I still lived life to the fullest then - and now.

Pat Mower

Permission from Global Spy Magazine-2001 Edition

NSA ABANDONS WONDROUS STUFF

January 07, 2001

Surprises: Astronomers who took over an abandoned spy base find remarkable, expensive and often incomprehensible stuff at every turn.

TRANSYLVANIA COUNTY, N.C. - Along the long, twisting road through the Pisgah National Forest, the first sign that something is out of the ordinary is a line of giant transformers. Then, around the bend, a barbed-wire fence, guard shack and surveillance cameras protect what looks like nothing more than another hill of trees and dense shrubbery.
It is anything but.
This is the entrance to one of the National Security Agency's former spy stations, a place shrouded in secrets and denials, the source of local lore that seems right out of "X-Files."
What is inside that giant geodesic dome that looks like a golf ball? Where do the tunnels snaking beneath the 202-acre site lead? Why are the rugs welded to the floors of the windowless buildings?
Few people have been beyond these gates, deep inside the Appalachian Mountains, 50 miles southwest of Asheville.
The NSA abandoned the site to the U.S. Forest Service five years ago, leaving behind a deserted mini city in the middle of nowhere. Now, some of the secrets are being revealed.
Last year, with the base boarded up and close to demolition, the property was transferred to a group of astronomers in exchange for a piece of land in western North Carolina. Over the past year, they have begun piecing together the site's past.
"There are things on this site you will never see anywhere else," said site manager Jim Powers. "I've never had someone come here that wasn't blown away."
The astronomers, who formed the Pisgah Astronomical Research Institute, were attracted by two 85-foot satellite dishes on the site - some of the largest in the country - which could be repositioned to catch deep-space radio signals and allow them to study the life and death of stars.
When the group arrived in January 1999, they expected a basic, albeit large, government facility, but as the weeks passed they realized little about the site was what it appeared.

As they began to install their computers, they found hundreds of miles of top-of-the-line cabling running under every floor. They discovered that the self-contained water and sewer treatment plant could handle tens of thousands of gallons of water at a time and the generator could produce 235 kilowatts of energy - powerful enough to light up a small city.

In a basement room of one of the larger buildings, they found the entrance to a 1,200-foot tunnel system that connects two of the site's main buildings. Every inch of floor in more than four buildings was covered with two-by-two-foot squares of bleak brown carpet. When the astronomers tried to replace it, they discovered it was welded with tiny metal fibers to the floor. The result, they eventually realized, is that the rugs prevent the buildings from conducting static electricity.

Even the regular lighting looks different, covered by sleek metal grids that prevent the light bulbs from giving off static interference. The few windows are bulletproof.

But what fascinated the astronomers was the still-operable security system that, among other things, sounds an alarm in the main building any time the front perimeter is crossed. The group can watch on monitors as cars approach from miles away.

Inside the site, the agency had taken further measures. One area is in a small, sunken river ravine surrounded by barbed wire and an additional guard post. Steps, with reflective metal paneling, to shield the identity of those walking beneath, lead down a small hill, and wind their way to two small buildings with conference rooms inside - both of which once emanated, "white noise," to prevent electronic eavesdropping.

What Powers and several others in the group find remarkable, though, is not just the expansive network of buildings and security, but the extraordinary cost of all the items they have found - items the agency discarded.

He said the extensive fiber optic cabling that runs for miles under the floors and through the tunnel system is the most expensive on the market.

When a state regulator came out to issue a permit for a massive underground storage tank with a double lining, the astronomers said he told them he wished he had a camera. He wanted to take a picture to show his co-workers because he had never seen a system so sophisticated.

And the agency didn't just install one water tank; it installed two. In a basement room, beneath a system that pressurizes wells, is another system just like it.

"You see this kind of thing everywhere here," Powers said. "They never have just one of something."

Even most of the heavy bolt locks - which every door has - are covered by black boxes locked with padlocks.

Despite the site's stark appearance, there are some human - and humorous - vestiges. A bright happy face is painted on the smallest of the four satellite dishes on the site, something one former employee said was done so that they could "smile back at the Russians."

Inside the tunnels, too, are chalk drawings of animals and warriors, resembling those found in caves thousands of years ago.

Aside from the rustling of deer and the wild turkeys that run rampant across the hundreds of vacant parking spaces, everything about the place is now eerily quiet.

Paperwork in the guard shack is held in place by a stapler though no one has been inside the small building in years. Security cameras still work and alarms all still sound, though no one is listening.

When the agency withdrew in 1995, some of the 300 workers, especially those who grew up locally and got hired on as groundskeepers and mechanics, returned to the nearby towns, though many say they are still forbidden to talk about their work.

Most of the others - the security officers, military personnel and cryptologists - left the area for their next Department of Defense post.

The site dates back to the early 1960s, when a scaled-down version was carved out to support the space program. It was operated at first by the National Aeronautics and Space Administration, and scientists used the early satellite dishes to track the flights into outer space and kept the door open for school groups and visitors who wanted to learn more about space missions.

But suddenly in 1981, the NSA took over from NASA. Local hikers and hunters who stumbled onto some of the agency's acreage would be suddenly surrounded by armed guards who appeared as if from nowhere to escort them out of the woods. Vans with darkened windows shuttled past the local coffee shops, fueling rumors.

The agency's presence was hard on the local employees as well.

Don Powell began working on the site in 1967 as a car mechanic and spent the next three decades learning the mechanics of every inch of the satellite dishes for the Defense Department. He also learned to avoid questions about his work and to lie to his neighbors.

For 15 years people would approach him and the few other local workers, asking what was out there, what they did and, of course, what is that golf ball?

"The kids would always ask, what's in [that] giant dome?"

He would tell them it was "filled with chocolate pudding," he said. "I couldn't even tell my wife. I couldn't tell anyone."

The 1995 closure appears to have caught the agency by surprise. It had recently cleared several more areas and laid the foundations for additional smaller satellite dishes that were never built. One newly built satellite dish, which one insider says was never turned on, was dismantled and shipped to England.

The Forest Service tried unsuccessfully to engineer a land trade for three years, hampered by a site that posed many problems for the few interested parties - from the remote location to the expense of removing satellite dishes embedded 80 feet into the ground.

The agency was about to return with a bulldozer when the astronomers group, headed by benefactor J. Donald Cline, a scientist and former computer executive, offered to buy and trade 375 acres along the French Broad River in North Carolina for the spy station.

What made the site, shielded from interference in a natural bowl-shaped terrain, so perfect for the NSA made the site perfect for the astronomers as well. They plan to use the satellite dishes to read the characteristics of elements given off by dying stars.

"This area is free of light pollution," Powers said, as he stood in the middle of a vast, empty parking lot. "It's also clean in terms of electromagnetic interference like cell phone towers or things that create electromagnetic noise.

"And we can be sure there won't be any in the future because the Forest Service owns everything around here. . . . It's easy to see why they liked this place."

Recently, in one of a dozen large empty rooms in one of four mostly empty office buildings where the group decided to set up shop, four scientists stood around a portable panel of monitors and computers, watching the results of a test appear on a screen.

"It's stardust," said the site's technical director, astronomer Charles Osborne. "This stuff is just floating around out there. It's the building blocks of life."

In order to use the satellite dishes, they had to spend months trying to slow them down. Both of the 85-foot dishes swing on two axis, an extravagance the astronomers suspect allowed the agency to swing the face around swiftly to catch up with satellites orbiting Earth. The astronomers need the dishes to move no faster than the speed of Earth itself.

But there is much on the site that the astronomers don't know what to do with, such as the paper-shredding building up on one hill, the large helicopter pad on top of another, and down in a valley of well-manicured grass, that giant golf ball, similar to those seen at NSA headquarters at Fort Meade.

Close up from the outside, the ball is a circle of triangles, no two identical, that feel like Gore-Tex to the touch. When one triangle at the bottom is pushed, several triangles around it gyrate, letting off a low grumbling sound of bending metal echoing through the ball.

Inside, past a small door less than 4 feet tall, the ball glows white, lighted by the sunlight outside reflecting and bouncing inside from one triangle to another.

In its center is a 40-foot satellite dish, cleaner and smoother than any of the others. It looks new, though it has been there for years. There are unusual numbered patterns on the dish's white panels, laid out like a cheat sheet to a jigsaw puzzle. The astronomers believe that the triangles vary in size as a clever way to minimize the effect of interference that comes from patterns. Enclosing the dish under such a surface, they speculate, would protect it from the weather, and prevent anyone else from seeing it or reading the direction it is pointed.

For the astronomers, though, this curious dish is somewhat irrelevant. They need dishes with large faces, like the two bigger ones, to read the radio signals of stars millions of light-years from Earth.

From far above on the perfectly level, perfectly painted helicopter pad with a view of miles of mountains and green trees, Powers laughed at the differences between the previous owners and the astronomers, a group short on staff and scraping for funding. He studied the golf ball.

"You'll go a long way before you find anything like that around anywhere else," he said. ". . . but nothing about this place is what it seems."

Subj: Update: Havana conference on Cuban missile crisis reveals dangers unknown at the time.
Date 10/11/02 2:04:26 PM Pacific Daylight Time
From: mevans@GWU.EDU
To: NSARCHIVE@HERMES.GWU.EDU
Sent to me: IdaReedBlanford who was on the NSARCHIVE list.
National Security Archive Update, October 11, 2002, 5:00 PM EST

For more information contact:
Thomas S. Blanton or
Peter Kornbluh 011 537 880 1845

Havana conference on Cuban missile crisis reveals dangers unknown at the time;
New documents show US located only 33 of 42 missiles, zero warheads during crisis;
US Navy dropped grenades on nuclear-armed Soviet sub at height of crisis;
Cubans thought malaria more dangerous on Oct. 24, but expected invasion by 27th.

http://www.nsarchive.org.nsa/cuba_mis_cri/press3.htm

Havana, Cuba, 11 October 2002, 5 p.m. - During the second session of the historic 40th anniversary conference on the Cuban missile crisis, participants including Cuban president Fidel Castro and former US secretary of defense Robert McNamara discussed newly declassified documents showing that events were spinning out of control at the height of the crisis, with the danger of an accidental or deliberate nuclear exchange even greater than policymakers believed at the time. US intelligence never located the nuclear warheads for the Soviet missiles in Cuba during the crisis, and only 33 of what photography later showed was a total of 42 medium-range ballistic missiles.

On the most dangerous day of the crisis, Saturday, 28 October 1962, notes from the Joint Chiefs detail a crescendo of alarming news, ranging from a U-2 spy plane straying into Soviet airspace (1341 hrs.), a U-2 missing and then determined shot down over Cuba (1403), the Joint Chief's recommendations (1600) to the President for the air strike and invasion plan starting no later than Monday, low-level reconnaissance pilots reporting anti-aircraft fire from the ground in Cuba (1800), the President commenting to his top advisers that "time is running out" (1830), and a briefing on the latest photography showing "the missiles are on the launchers" in Cuba (1940). Within five minutes of this briefing, the President's brother was meeting with Soviet ambassador Dobrynin to tell him "time of the essence and we shouldn't miss the chance," reiterating the President's pledge not to invade Cuba and assuring Dobrynin the US missiles would come out of Turkey in 4-5 months as long as nothing was said publicly about it.

In the middle of this sequence of escalating tensions, according to new documents released today, the US navy was dropping a series of "signaling depth charges" (equivalent to hand grenades) on a Soviet submarine at the quarantine line. Navy deck logs show the depth charges at 1659 and 1729 military time. At the conference table in Havana were the US Navy watch officer, Captain John Peterson, who ordered the depth charges as part of standard operating procedure for signaling submarines, and the Soviet signals intelligence office, Vadim Orlov, on the receiving and inside submarine B-59, where the depth charges felt like "sledgehammers on a metal barrel." Unbeknownst to the Navy, the submarine carried a nuclear-tipped torpedo with orders that allowed its use if the submarine was "hulled" (hole in the hull from depth charges or surface fire).

Further evidence of the escalating danger came from a series of military documents declassified by the Cuban government. In an October 24th meeting with his commanders, Fidel Castro remarked that they needed to resume fumigation flights because the danger from lack of fumigation (i.e., malaria) was at that point even greater than the danger of invasion. By October 27, however, commander in chief Castro had ordered his anti-aircraft gunners to fire on US reconnaissance planes and fully expected an all-out US air strike and invasion within 24 to 72 hours.

The conference is meeting at the Palacio de Convenciones in Havana, Cuba. Most participants are housed in the Hotel Palco next door. Phone: 011-53-7-337235. Fax: 011-53-7-337236. The conference room itself is closed to the press but the organizers are holding daily press briefings each afternoon summarizing the discussion and releasing key documents addressed that day.

The National Security Archive co-organized with Cuban institutions the highly successful 40th anniversary Bay of Pigs conference last year in

Havana; this year, the Archive is also working with Brown University's Watson Institute. Peter Kornbluh directs the Archive's Cuba project.

For today's press release and a selection of reconnaissance and other photographs from the crisis, follow this link:

http://www.nsarchive.org/nsa/cuba_mis_cri/press3.htm

To check for daily press updates, 10-13 October 2002, use the following link, or simply wait until you received the next e-mail update:
http://www.nsarchive.org/nsa/cuba_mis_cri/index.htm

THE NATIONAL SECURITY ARCHIVE is an independent non-governmental research institute and library located at The George Washington University in Washington, D.C. The Archive collects and publishes declassified documents acquired through the Freedom of Information Act (FOIA). A tax-exempt public charity, the Archive receives no U.S. government funding; its budget is supported by publication royalties and donations from foundations and individuals.

This information was received by the Editor who was registered with this archive at the time.

Of interest re: the Cuban Missile Crises

THE CUBAN MISSILE CRISES, 1962: A POLITICAL PERSPECTIVE AFTER 40 YEARS news release 12 OCTOBER 2002 1:00 p.m. EST Cuban missile crisis not over in 13 days; Soviet tac nukes in Cuba until Nov. 20;

THE NATIONAL SECURITY ARCHIVE - The George Washington University
Havana, Cuba, 12 October 2002, 1 p.m. - During the third session of the historic 40th anniversary conference on the Cuban missile crisis, participants including Cuban president Fidel Castro and former US secretary of defense Robert McNamara discussed newly declassified documents showing that the crisis did not end after the famous "13 days," but continued at a high level until late November, in large part because of Cuban rejection of Soviet concessions. The documents show that the Soviet nuclear-armed tactical weapons in Cuba stayed there after the missiles were withdrawn, and may even have been intended for Cuban custody.

Documents released today included, verbatim, Soviet records of the contentious meetings between top Soviet leader Anastas Mikoyan and top Cuban leaders including Fidel Castro and Che Guevara during Mikoyan's trip to Cuba in early November; Soviet orders first preparing the tactical weapons for training the Cubans and then, on November 20, ordering their withdrawal; and a prophetic summary of the crisis written by the British ambassador to Cuba, who predicted that the crisis could ultimately rebound to the benefit of the Castro regime and the long-term survival of communism in Cuba.

The conference is meeting at the Palacio de Convenciones in Havana, Cuba. Most participants are housed at the Hotel Palco next door. Phone.... Fax.... The conference room itself is closed to the press but the organizers are holding daily press briefings each afternoon summarizing the discussion and releasing key documents addressed that day.

The National Security Archive co-organized with Cuban institutions the highly successful 40th anniversary Bay of Pigs conference last year in Havana; this year, the Archive is also working with Brown University's Watson Institute. Peter Kornbluh directs the Archive's Cuba project.

GHOSTMAN'S FIRST E-MAIL TO ME
By Herb Neeland

From: Ghostman <HerbLesRN@cox.net>
To: Clara19126@msn.com
Sent: Saturday, November 19, 2005 1:53 PM
Subj: Responding to your mail, "bill person"

Hey Trish, sorry you had to apologize for accidentally getting into a group of "Crotchety" old retired USAF, and Army men." I am the 'Ghostman'. I'm also the youngest. I'm 53. When I saw the mail, regarding your faux paux, I thought, "here we go again." I saw some mail that said, "Who the Hell is this Trish?" I knew what happened right away. I knew that someone had replied all, and they stepped on a bunch of Senior Citizen's toes. Sheeesh, what a bunch of ole gripes. Huh? Ha! ha! ha! ha! ha!

No apology necessary for this old trooper. I was a medic, late in the war. I was there, "73-74." Yeah, I'm a member of the "Secret War." When I used to say that, I would cover my ears. I would sit like I had a board up my back. Ha! ha! ha! No more. The veil is off. I'm part of a group that took care of "Hmongs." A brave bunch of mountain folk up in the Laotian Mountains. They were under the command of General Vang Pao.

I was at a hospital in "Udorn Thailand." I worked the hospital there. When I first arrived, I thought someone had told me it was an R&R center. "Wrong!" Well, some squadrons on the base partied, we took care of casualties. Many. No one, even on the base, knew what was going on, and they were completely oblivious to the human waste coming through our ER.

When I found similar type X GI's that had the same experience, only earlier, I was thrilled. When I first got home, I told my best friend when he asked what I did, I said, "I took care of war casualties." This was well after the March 28, 1973, treaty.
HE was a Lib, and a non believer. He said, "Herbie, your freaking delusional." Well, I wanted, and now I have, the proof. Thank God, I found these crotchety old men. Ha! ha! hah!

And for you young lady, you'd better watch what your doing, ah! ha! ha! ha! ha! I'm just kidding. Take care, good luck with your books. And may your

daughter be sitting at the Right hand of our Lord . . . God bless you Trish, "The Ghostman" . . .
Herb Neeland

"Ghostman"
90250
"Don't mean nuthin"

From: Ghostman <HerbLesRN@cox.net>
To: Trish Schiesser
Sent: Thursday, December 22, 2005 10:50 AM
Subj: "The Young Pilot"

This is a true story written and sent to me [The Editor] by Herb Neeland, better known as "Ghostman."

THE YOUNG PILOT
By Herb Neeland

I woke with a start. "F*****g alarm, damn, I'm gonna be late." I had been at the Airmen's club till closing trying to block out the day before. Or, should I say, The Day's before. I was one of the new Medic's but I felt like I had been there a life time. I was at Wilford Hall Med. Ct. The Jewel of the USAF Hospitals. I had only been "permanent party" for three months, but already I felt three times my age.

The new medics had come from "Sheppard AFB" with three weeks and three days under their belts, with training that you would give a "nurse's aide" in a nursing home. I would have nearly a year and a half of OJT, before I would be trusted out on the floor by myself, or so they said.

During the last four days, I had been "Specializing" a patient. "Specializing" meant that a medic would have one patient, by himself, and maybe one medic with even less training than myself. So, when you were thrown into a situation, you were literally thrown into a situation. Of course there was an RN you could call on, but hell, she had nearly thirty other patients to take care of; medications, treatments that she would have to do, along with some brand new medics. So, calling on her kinda made you feel guilty.

I had pushed myself out of bed, head thumping from all the "Lone Star beer" I had drunk the night before. I had only drunk small amounts before coming into this man's Air Force, so I wasn't used to the sheer volume it took to drown out a daily memory. Besides, one could not drown out this memory I had been faced with the last four days.

I showered quickly, kicked the side of my roommate's bunk, and yelled, "Mikey, get your ass up, we're late." Mike was a South East Ohio boy, like me, and was raised, "never to be late." He cussed me for not getting him up sooner. He threw on his Medic whites and went to the head to brush his teeth, and comb the small amount of hair we were trying to grow out. No one wanted to look "New."

These Guys

Since we had only been at "Big Willy," our pet name for Wilford Hall, for such a short time, we did not have a car as yet. So, it was "beat feet" over to the hospital, which was a good half mile from where the Medic's barracks were located; didn't seem fair. Hell, "no car, tough shit."

We took our usual route to the hospital, through the WAF Basic training facilities, then across the busy highway, then up the nearly quarter mile sidewalk to the front of the hospital. We were walking so quickly, that it was hard to salute the night crew of assorted officer's that were coming out the door. There were very young RN's that loved the salutes. Made them feel good, after a tough night at Big Willy. They would report you in a heartbeat if a salute was not given. I mean, after all, they were officers. Then there were the young intern's that were paying off their loans, by giving Uncle Sam four years of their lives. They were so dog tired, that if you saluted them, you might get a half hearted, incorrect salute, or maybe none at all. Those always made me and Mikey laugh.

When we entered the hospital, we had to make sure we were spit and polished. Checking each other for wrinkles, rubbing spit on our combat boots to take off scuff marks, and making sure your belt line was even with your zipper. It was hard enough just to make it to the elevator, to ride up to ole, "T-2," the Neurosurgery Ward . . ."

Upon arriving, Mikey looked at me and said, "Hey, Herbie, do you still have the Pilot?" I said, "Hell yea, and man, he doesn't look so good." Mikey, who had been there as long as I, turned to me and said, "Maybe this is the day?" I said, "Not on my shift asshole, no sir." We made it to the long report. This was a report on each and every patient, other than the "ICU," but did include, the young pilot. I found myself shaking when they got to the Pilot's room. They saved him till last, 'cause he had the most to report on. The report went like this:

In room 101, we have a twenty-five year old Caucasian male, Captain, with multiple and various traumas. I was sitting there thinking, "Good God, to say the least." The night nurse went on. "Patient was on a routine training mission, when the student co-pilot, accidentally put the Trainer over, and it landed upside down." Again, my pen started to shake. "Patient slid down the runway on face shield, then face, and upper torso." I could feel myself getting a little queasy. "Arms were traumatically amputated, along with some of both shoulder's, face is unrecognizable, and he has two tubes that were surgically placed for breathing, and for ice lavaging, to control the bleeding in his stomach, and upper intestines." I was listening every day, trying to pick out the physiological reasoning for all these tubes. The ice lavaging was finally sinking in.

The report went on. There was the Foley cath, which was measured every fifteen minutes for output. The constant IV's that the Nurse handled when she had time, otherwise, I would take down the empty ones, and put up the new one's that were clearly marked. The Stryker Frame that he layed upon, was not turned, otherwise, he would have been turned every fifteen minutes. He was too fragile to turn, so pneumonia was going to set in, just as sure as I was sitting there listening.

My main job, when the nurse came to me, was the "ice lavaging." What we would do, was put a fifty cc syringe in the tube coming out of a surgical hole, where a nose used to be. The breathing apparatus, or the respirator, was in a hole that used to be a mouth. There were no eyes. There were no ears. Only a "melon" like object, that resembled a head. I would take my syringe, fill it with "Iced Saline," or part sterile water and salt. It was in cases, stacked up in the room.

When I first would enter the room, I would make sure the supplies were freshly stacked, and that I did not have to want for anything, that morning. I did not look inside the boxes. I "assumed," that the boxes were full of bottled "Sterile Water, and half Saline." I said my good mornings to the young Pilot's mother and father. The father was in his dress Blue's. He had a "full Eagle" on his shoulders, and many decorations on his chest. He was definitely an "Airman's Airman." His command wings in place, and his nameplate. He was a VIP, as the NCOIC of the unit told us. Or Very Important Person.

After my introduction's, I would glove up. Check the Urine. It had gone down slightly from the day before, and even less output on the night shift. I briefly looked at the young pilot's head, which was featureless as I said, and could feel a small twinge of nausea, repulsion, but yet a deep, deep, sadness for this poor young man. I did all the quick check's of the IV's, and started to get my pan, to start the non-stop Saline washes that I was about to perform, all eight hours.

In this room, you were told, "No lunch," and that was just the breaks. This young man could not be left for a moment, let alone thirty minutes. He was "Constant care," or he would die. We did not have a "Respiratory Therapist," so we had to make sure the respirator was giving its constant, "Wish, whoosh, wish, whoosh." We would have to give him four breathing treatments that day, and every day, just to keep the pneumonia from setting in. We knew this was not going to help, because he could not be turned onto his belly. If he could, then it would move around the secretions, and he could be suctioned out, with a long tube, through his trach tube in his neck. The thing was, he was so fragile, with the bleeding from his stomach, we were not comfortable with him coughing through his trach; so, another serious problem.

I got my pan, filled it with ice from the cooler provided, added my Water and Saline, and started lavaging. Over and over, watching the return from his stomach contents, just to see if the bleeding was becoming less, or the color was less red, and more of a pink color. Behind me, up on the wall, was the TV. They kept it on 24/7. Just in case the patient could hear, he might be comforted.

Well, the TV was turned up to about medium listening, and I could hear a television program. It was the "New Zoo Review," a kid's program that my little sister would watch, before I left for the service. There was a guy and a girl, some people dressed as a female Hippo, an Owl, and I think a giraffe or something like that. They kept singing over and over this insipid song.

When my help came in to check on me, a brand new WAF, she walked over to me. She said, "Airman Neeland, is there anything I can get for you?" I said, "Yes, Patty, would you please go and get me some fresh boxes of Sterile water and Saline, I noticed the night crew didn't replace any they used, and I'm getting real short." She said, "Oh God, I have to go clear to Central Supply for that." I said, "Airman, please, go and get me the water."

This WAF was very immature, and all she had to do was get me what I needed. She swung her arms and left. She didn't even look at the patient. She said before, "This makes me sick." Christ, it made us all uneasy, but this was our job, and we had to do it. We had to bring this kid back. Besides, his father was the Superintendent of the Air Force Academy. I didn't know that just because the more rank you had, maybe heightened your chances of survival. Well, I would learn that it didn't; no, God could take you at anytime on this floor, any time, and I was getting ready, unbeknownst to me, that this was going to be the day.

As I was lavaging, and that damn, stupid program was playing behind me, Airman Patty walked in with a dolly of my Water. She looked up and said, "Oh, Airman Neeland, I used to watch that when I was. . . . At that time, it was like someone had hit oil, only instead of oil, it was fresh, and very red blood that hit me right in the face. The patient had hemorrhaged so hard, it bent him at the stomach. The second hemorrhage was even worse; it hit the TV, where those Goddamn creatures were telling me how "to be nice, and to mind my fucking parents."

I yelled for Airman Patty to go get the Nurse, and the Doctor and anyone else she could find. I started to yell again, and she was just standing there in shock, covered in blood, dripping from her short blond hair. I didn't know he was hemorrhaging that bad, I was just trying to control the uncontrollable situation. I screamed again, "Patty, Patty, Goddamn it Patty, get the Nurse." She awakened from her hypnotic state, and ran screaming out of the room, right by the parents, which sent them into a panic. I was trying to get more iced saline down his tube, but the flow of blood was just too much. The Nurse ran in with two pints of blood, and hung them quickly on the pole. She opened the clamp up all the way, and the blood was just pouring into a subclavien vein on his chest. The more that went in, the more blood came out.

I continued to push the water in; I didn't know what else to do. They hadn't gone over what to do, when something like this would happen. Again, "Whoosh, the blood hit me in the face, the wall, and that fucking TV that kept blaring, "It's the New Zoo Review, Coming Right at You." NO, I thought, "The fucking blood is coming right at me." They kept singing, these damned creatures; and the blood kept hitting me in the face. There was an array of people coming in and out. Why didn't anyone stay? It was like everyone was trying to help the parents, and not the patient, or me. I thought, "For Christ sake, this kid is bleeding to death."

Well, everyone knew that this was the last roundup for this young Pilot. The main thing was to comfort the patient's family. Not the patient, because, every last stitch that was put in surgically, to hold his stomach together, had come loose. I didn't know that. I started yelling, "Help, someone give me a fucking hand in here, please, he is bleeding to death." Not a soul came. I kept hearing, "It's the New Zoo Review, Coming right at YOU." I heard myself say, "Someone turn off that Goddamn TV, I can't hear myself think." I was still trying to push the iced saline down the tube.

Suddenly, there was no noise; only the "Whish, whoosh," of the respirator, and two hands placed on my shoulder. It was the Nurse and the NCOIC, or the "Non Commissioned Officer in Charge," my immediate boss. I heard them say, "Airman Neeland, it's ok, come on, come on Airman, let's get out of here." I kept saying, "Get me some more saline, I gotta stop this bleeding." I heard someone say, "It's all over Airman Neeland, he's gone." I thought, "in the three months I have been here, I had seen death, but not on my patient, not mine." I was forced from the table I was working on. Another whoosh of blood came out and hit everyone in the room, his final liquid that kept his heart beating, and his organs functioning was leaving him. It was slower now; just trickling down the tube.

I looked up at the TV. It wasn't off, but someone had turned it down. I could see the blood running down the creatures that were singing to me. Those fucking Hippos and Owls, and those two cutesy people in their slacks and shirts, were being covered in blood; this kid's blood. Why weren't they screaming, too? Why weren't they trying to help, like shutting the fuck up, or just turning themselves off? Had they no fucking respect?

I was led out to the Nursing station and a blanket was put around me. I was covered in blood. My face could feel it hardening, cracking, like after you had a bloody nose or a cut on your forehead. The WAF was in her hypnotic position at one of the report tables. Sobbing, sobbing, crying, and crying for her mother. I was just watching her. I was led to a shower room, one of the Doctor's shower rooms that were on the unit. I was given a fresh pair of scrubs that only the surgeons wore, and told to clean up. I did. I couldn't wait to get this kid's blood off of me.

After I came out, I was asked if I wanted to go back to the barracks for a little while. I told them, "No, I wanna go get drunk." There was some small amount of giggling, but that stopped quickly, when I said, "I am not kidding, just get me the fuck out of here." I was told to take the rest of the day off. I rolled up my Medic whites in another blanket, and walked off the floor. I saw other Airmen I knew from Tech School, but didn't want to stop and chat. I just wanted to get back to the barracks, find someone that was off that day, and go get drunk.

As I sat at the Airman's club later, Mikey found me and said, "Hey Herb, you OK?" I said, "Fuck, no man, I want the fuck out of here." He sighed, sat down, and said, "yea, me too, but I don't think we gotta choice." He said, "Hey, Airman Patty is on T-4." I said, "The Psych Unit?" He said, "Yea, she went full tilt goose bozo, man." I said, "She never came out of it?" Mikey said, "Fuck no man, she is gone." I said, "I wonder what will happen to her?" He said, "Some cush job, where she doesn't get her fucking panties in a wad." I said, "Hell Mikey, that was some fucked up shit today." He said, "Yea, I know, but guess what the good news is?" I said, "What, good news?" He said, "You and I are going to the Unit." I said, The NICU?" He said, "Yea, man, ain't that great?" I said, "Oh, yea Mikey, that's fucking wonderful, we can see this kind of shit every day." He said, "Naw man, we will be in the Veggie room for at least six weeks, we will have it made."

I thought, "I have heard of the Veggie room. Didn't I just come from one? Wasn't this kid a vegetable?" I finished my beer and walked out with Mikey.

I could feel the hot burning tears coming to my eyes. I didn't want anymore to do with this shit. But, I did. I had three years to go. Three years of DEATH. Would I make it? Damn, what a fucked up thought.
We walked back to the barracks in silence. I was quietly crying to myself. I kept thinking, "I can't do this anymore, I just can't," but I did, and it drove me fucking crazy. . . .

Herb Neeland, aka Ghostman, actually went through the story above. He said to me, "Thanks for reading it Trish . . . I hope you liked this story, it's not that I like it. It's just one of those that I dream about every so often. . . . Love, Herbie" Well, Herbie, it is I who thanks you for sending me this poignant and true story and thanks for letting this editor know what you went through as a Medic, while serving your country and serving the servicemen, well, and beyond the call of duty. T.S.

THE MEDIC - By Herbie (Ghostman) Neeland

OK, Trish, I had just finished my "tech school" at Sheppard AFB, in Witchita, TX. I was now to learn by "on the job training" for the next year, at Big Willy.

Anyway, I walked onto the unit, scared to death. I was the "FNG," "Fu***ng" New Guy." So, I knew there was something going to be put on me, big time - I just didn't know what. Everyone in tech school said it would happen my first week as a "Permanent Party."

I was introduced to the "NCOIC" or my top Sarge, then, the CO of the unit, a male nurse by the name of "Major Biangardi." He was an "As*****," from the word go. NO sense of humor, straight down the line, and you'd better have your stuff together. Then, there were the guys who would show me around, Staff Sarge Erbe, and one other butt hole I can't remember.

Sarge Erbe was told to take me around, and get me used to the daily duties I would be expected to carry out. This being a "Neuro Ward" there was ton's of work to be done. I was waiting, and waiting for the first sign of a "Trick." Well, it didn't take long, or so I thought it was a "TRICK." I was escorted into a regular room. I was not in the NICU, until weeks later. I was introduced to a Tech Sergeant, lying on a "Stryker Frame." He had "Vinkie tongs" in his head, and he was flat on his back at the time. He was to be turned at that time, then, the bath was to be given, but first, the first thing these two Sergeants did was to turn the patient. It was tedious, I could tell. I could also tell, very dangerous for the patient, but these guys were experienced, and the turn was second nature to them. When they had him face down, they undid the top part of the bed, took off the pillows he was laying on when he was on his back, and then rubbed him down with lotion to prevent any pressure sores.

Sergeant Erbe took me aside and told me. "OK, he had a suppository last night, and his feces has to be removed digitally." He lost me at "Feces." I had never heard, "Shit, poop, crap, whatever" called feces. I said, "I don't understand Sarge."
He said, and looked over at his buddy, "You have to put on a glove, and put your finger in his ass, and dig out his shit." I laughed and said, "Awww, here it comes, the ole LEFT HANDED MONKEY WRENCH deal, huh?" They both looked at each other and laughed. I said, "Yea, I got both you guys, huh?" Again, they laughed.

After they had laughed a little, they said, "No Airman, this is for real deal, you will put on your rubber gloves, and dig the feces from his rectum." I said, "Yea, right, and what are you guys gonna do?" I was still trying to make light out of this strange request. But, deep down inside, I had this knot, growing in my stomach, and I was thinking, "What if this is true?" Well, it didn't take them long to use their rank. "Listen Airman, we all gotta do this, and if you think it's that funny, you can talk to Tech Sergeant Kolterman, and he will tell you just how real this is." I stopped smiling.

I said, "Is this some kind of cruel joke, Sergeant Erbe, cause if you think I'm gonna do something like this, your crazy. I signed up, and learned to do vital signs, and blood pressures, and give baths, I didn't sign up to do this." Well, he got red in the face, and very pissed off. "Airman Neeland, you will do what you are told, and you will do it now, if you want I will demonstrate." I said, "Well I guess you'd better do that, cause I'm not doing it . . ." He said, "Do you know what insubordination is?" I said, "Yes, Sergeant, I know what it means." He said, "Well, if you don't follow my lead, I will report you." I had nothing to say after that.

He inserted his finger deep inside the ole guy laying on the Stryker. He made a twisting move with his hand and out came a soft, but large piece of stool. He wiped on the "Chux" that was laying beside him, and said, "There, like that." Without saying a word, I ripped off my gloves, between gags, and walked off to the utility room. I banged in the door. Then Sgt. Erbe, and Tech Sergeant Kolterman came in, Kolterman said, "What's the matter Sgt. Neeland, are you OK?" I was just about in tears. I said, "Do you know what they want me to do?" Like this was gonna make any difference. He said, "Well, Sgt. Erbe told me you refuse to dig out an impaction, is that true?" I said, "Damn right Sarge, I have never done anything remotely like that, and the only ass I have been near, has been my own." Well, they both laughed, but it wasn't as sarcastic as before. Sgt. Kolterman said, "Well, it's just the first day jitters, so just get back in there, and do what you have to do." I said, "Don't you guys get it? I am not going back in there and do anything of the sort." Well, the day started to go downhill further now.

Tech Sergeant Kolterman said, "Come on now, Airman Neeland, let's go in there for a talk. I walked behind him. Kolterman leaned over to the patient and whispered to him, "you don't feel a thing do you, Sarge?" The Sarge had been listening to all of this going on, (bless his heart) and said, "Hey young'n, I don't feel anything, go ahead and get that damn stuff out of me." I felt kinda sorry for the guy at first, then I told the two Sarge's standing there, "Sergeant Kolterman, Sergeant Erbe, I don't think you are understanding what I am saying here." They looked puzzled for God's sake. I said, "I don't want to insert my finger into this man's rectum and dig out anything, do you understand me?"

Well, out the door we went again. We went back into the utility room. Sergeant Kolterman, trying to be professional said, "Sgt. Neeland, this is part of our job, and these people need help. There is no other way to get this out, unless we do an enema, and this is not called for at this time, because the ole Sarge there just needs a good "start," and he will start moving on his own." It's called, Peristalisis. The involuntary movement of the muscles of the stomach." I just stood there, I couldn't believe what I had gotten myself into. I just couldn't. I wanted to go home. I wanted my Mom, Hell, I wanted anyone to tell me, I didn't have to do such a disgusting thing. But, I was alone, and I was going to do one of the most disgusting things in my life.

Well, I put on my gloves. I was thinking, "Jesus H. Christ, Herb, run, get out of here, don't do this, but common sense took over and I started to do it," I put my finger in, and twisted, I could feel the hard impacted stool, and that if someone had done their job the day before, I would not have to be doing this.

Anyway, the procedure was done, by me. The day was over in nearly "A Year." Or it felt like a year. I went back to my barracks, laid my head down on my pillow and cried like a baby. I thought, "Could I get back to the Appalachians, and hide out, go AWOL, and then have my father find me?" No, I couldn't do that. Neeland's didn't quit. That was beat into me at an early age.

So, the days, weeks, months went by. One day I was on the floor, supervising some young troops that had just come on as permanent party. It was their first day. Sgt. Erbe said, "I will take them for their orientation." I said, "Sgt. Erbe," I'm still one stripe below you but I wouldn't mind taking you outside, and just beating the shit out of you." He said, "What, what are you talking about?" I said, "I will give them the orientation. I will see to their needs, and I will dig out the first impaction for them." Well, Sgt. a*****e Erbe just kinda stomped off into his "Lifer Land," and I took the young troops around and showed them some of the jobs they would have to do. I told them, "Guys, there are gonna be some jobs that your not even gonna believe that you have to do around here." One of the young troops said, "Like what, Sgt. Neeland?" I said, "Follow me, and I will show you, this is just for you to observe today, so don't let it get to you, ok, or at least try." That was it. A nineteen year old, who was a master of "Shit removal," telling an eighteen year old, how he was gonna be "Digitally removing a fecal impaction."

Love and Prayers buddy, Herbie.

THE BOYS IN THE MIST
By Herb (Ghostman) Neeland

I guess it was a dream,
only things like this can happen in dreams.
Or can they?

A lady sitting at an easel,
pallet in hand, a smile so wide,
it was almost a
laugh.
The arm going
this way and that,
brush strokes, painting, hair blowing as feathers.
Occasionally a feather would blow off her lovely head.

A boy standing with a rifle;
watching.
The Rifle would drop,
and in his hand the feather would land.
He would look at it,
with a smile and a tear.
He would walk off into a mist.

This kept happening.
Rifles dropped, feathers caught,
then the walk to the mist.

How long would this last?
How long would her arm last?

She had to be exhausted.
But the strokes only got stronger.
The smile wider. Floating now.
Watching right from her soft shoulder.
What was she painting? Well,
they were words.
They poured from the pen like colors I have never seen.
Reds, blues, yellows; colors I can't describe.

These Guys

A feather flew from her head. I tried
to grab it. I tried. I
ran, I floated, just out of reach.

I heard a voice. It was the Lady.
She said, "Why do you run? These are not your feathers.
They belong to those boys, there, in the mist.
The boys, can you see them?"
I said, "Yes."
"You see, they have no rifles; they choose something else now."

I wanted a feather so desperately.
She said, "You have much to do.
I have your feather. You just can't have it yet."

She turned; without losing a stroke, the letters flowed.
Again, colors I have never seen before.
I looked again in back of me.
There was another boy. He dropped his Rifle, and reached so
carefully and easily for his feather.
He took it gently in his hand. He walked to the mist to
join the others.
I wanted so much to have my feather. I wanted to go with those boys.

I turned to the lady.
She was walking. She was so far now. Walking, almost floating.
Her feathers were just hair now. Golden.
She turned and looked at me. She smiled.
She cried out in a voice, nearly like a song.
"Wait now for your time, your feather will come.
Go now and live, and love.
Make paintings of your own if you wish."

I could barely hear her now; she was so
far. I thought I heard her say, "Live boy live."
Then the softest
laughter; she was gone,
but she was everywhere; I could feel her.
The boys had long since gone

into the mist.
I thought there must be one of those beautiful feathers here somewhere.

Then, I heard her voice again . . .
"In time boy, in time."

All I could think of was,
"Thank you lady with the
colors, the laughter, the feathers . . . 'The Dream.' "

Herb Neeland was a Vietnam Medic and is now an RN and TLCB Member. He tried to save them all. "To Chrissy: This was a story, a poem or maybe just a small gift for you on Memorial Day. Your big brother, Herbie ." xxoo.

BRAVE THAI SOLDIER
By Herbie Neeland

It was late 1974. By now I was probably psychologically immune to all of life's "Kicks in the teeth." Well this night was little or no different from the rest. Buddha, my partner, and I, just sittin' back, feet propped up on the desk. Then, the RED PHONE. Couple of casualties comin' down from the North. Word had it that a couple of Thai Army had walked into a Claymore Mine that the VC or Pathet Lao had turned around during the night. Well we knew what to expect. Blown completely apart, or some severe traumatic amputations.

When the jeep got there, I could hear the soldier's scream before even reaching the loading dock, Hell, at least he was alive. The other one was DOA. We got to the jeep, and there was blood flying in all directions. The soldier had lost both his legs from the thighs down. The guys who kept him alive from Laos to here, I thought, should have gotten a medal. We just grabbed arms and stumps, and got him to the gurney inside the ER. The Doc was waiting, and he was putting in the IV lines. I grabbed some sterile towels, and literally jumped on to the left thigh. The femur bone was jutting out, and I got a nice puncture right in the middle of my abdomen. I held him with my body on top of him. I was screaming for some thread and clamps, so I could start tying off bleeders. By this time the entire crew was blood soaked. We had a nurse pumpin' blood to him, IVs were giving him much needed volume, due to severe blood loss. He finally passed out from shock. I remember sewing, tying, clamping at anything that oozed. We had an ET tube down, he had two chest tubes. The entire surgery crew was called in, and we slipped slided down the hall takin' this mangled boy to the OR.

Well me and Buddha's job was done. We hadn't noticed, but three and a half hours had passed. We were blood-soaked and exhausted. At a time like this, the damnedest things are funny. Buddy looked up at me, smiling, and said, "Well, wonder who's gonna clean this mess up?" We laughed and did what we were supposed to do. I went out on the back dock, and thought that I better get a "Box" ready. I thought for sure that this boy would be in the morgue before morning.

The morning crew came in, and immediately told us to get the Hell out. We were still covered with blood, and God knows what else. I made a detour, and went down on the ward. I saw, much to my surprise, a half conscious soldier laying on the bed. He was groaning a little, and I could see it was him. I thought, "Well, I'll be a son of a bitch? He made it." I walked out the back of the hospital, turned onto the sidewalk, over the Klong and into the barracks. Right before I got undressed and gave my soiled uniform to one of the house girls, I just looked at the Heavens and said, "Well, thank you God." Or maybe I said, "Thank you Buddha." I don't really remember. 'Cause over there, I think you had two guys on your side. I can see that boy's face in my dreams to this day. Maybe selfishly I'm thinking he is thanking us too.

BABYSAN
By Herbie Neeland

During the Monsoon, it is hard for all of us to see a hand in front of our faces. Well this so happened to be one of the Staff Car Driver's problems one morning in Udorn, at the RTAFB. I was on duty, getting' ready to get off after a very busy 14 hrs. The Red phone rang, and whoever was on the other end, said that they were bringing in a babysan that was hit by a Staff Car. A "babysan?" Heck, I had seen every wound known to man, I thought. Panic hit me like a hammer. I have done everything there is to do . . . two and a half years on Neuro ICU, now ending my tour over here, and I don't know anything about babysans.

Well, in he came by SP jeep. They handed him to me. He was thrashing, vomiting, bleeding all over the place. I carried him to an open gurney, and literally had to hold all four extremities down. A fellow medic came to my aid. I knew by his Neuro signs, and it was mach, mach, my dee. The other medic looked at me and said, "Now what?" "Well, let's get an airway, get some 02 to him and hold him down. Dr. Simpson was just coming into the room. Well, I won't repeat what he said. I gave him the stats . . . Thrashing, pupils fixed and dilated, pulse was like a rabbit's and B/P was just barely audible. He told me to get an IV line, using a butterfly needle. God was with me, and I got it on the first try. He said, "Pump some Dilantin in him, and try to get hold of those seizures." I asked, "Uh, you know the dose on a baby?" "No, airman, I don't, but give it in small doses." He was busily trying to get an NG tube down. Heck, we didn't even have that size. But, hey, we were a "Can Do," kinda place.

Well, the CO was notified and came to the ER. He asked a very interesting question, "What in the Hell is a baby doin' here?" Well, I thought what I wanted to say, but bit my tongue. I informed this Col. Andrews, that we needed transportation to Bangkok, or we were going to have to put this child in a bag. Well he fumbled about, pacing, and said, "I will call someone to take this child to a big hospital." God, he was brilliant. Well, we held this baby and worked the best we could for SIX hours. We all knew, who were standing there, that this child, if he made it, would be a vegetable in the end. After all that time, someone from the flight line came over, and the three of us worked on this baby all the way to the flight line, where he was boarded on an aircraft to Bangkok. We never knew the outcome.

It continued to rain that day, and the three of us shouted obscenities, cried, and got a ride back to the 432nd Hospital. I don't know about the rest of my crew, but I didn't sleep. I went back at 1630, and started all over again. My thoughts were selfishly, not of the babysan. I had maybe 10 days and a wakeup . . . "How did I get all this blood on me? Damn! God, please let it be an easy night."

DATE OF SEPARATION
By Herbie Neeland

Wow! The Water Festival! How can a holiday such as the Thais', get carried away, so out of proportion that the American GI can make it his own? That's our nature I guess. Well, I was in the ER. My partner that night, Ed Burdine - called him Buddah. Hah! He was as big as Buddah anyway. We had a maelstrom of Water Festival casualties that day. Severe eye infections, yeah, from Klong water, broken toes, from way too many drunk GI's, droppin' Fire Extinguishers on their toes, lacerations from broken glass, guys with busted noses, hands, you name it, because of the fights that were the result of, "I got you first!" Terrible day. We could only think what the night would bring from the North. What sort of God awful wounds would we see tonight? Seems that Mine wounds were the last two nights, and you know, comes in threes.

Well, during this nightmare of a Water Festival, a Senior NCO, came walking in, green in the gills, holding his stomach. "Hey Sarge, what can I do ya for?" He just looked me in the eye, and said,"Got any Paragoric?" "Sure sir, just have a seat on the gurney, I keep this for the really sick ones." He sat up on the gurney, and started giving me a history of the previous day and night. He said, lots of nausea, diarrhea, just felt like crap. Well, I sure had heard that a million times. I told him I would go and get his records, and be with him in a second. I turned to go, just rounded the corner, and I heard a big thud. I looked around, and Sarge was on the floor. Experience told me from the look, that this was not a viral thing.

He immediately went pale, and on to blue. I quickly grabbed a bottle of 02, put a mask on him, screamed for Buddah, and started checking for pulses. None, no breathing. Oh, God, he's had a Heart Attack. Buddah grabbed the phone right away and called the Doc, who was trying to catch up on some needed sleep. I heard his footsteps come flying up the hall. Well, we performed CPR, while Buddah was getting the Heart drugs. I could hear the dismay in the background, of drunk, hurting GI's, with their little problems, regarding their injuries from the day's partying. I am a big guy, and I can be loud when I want. I said, "All you guys get out NOW." Most knew me, so out they went to the dock outside.

We worked on that guy for 3 hours, we gave him every drug. We had a nurse come up and draw blood for the, oh, so important tests. Well, Sarge didn't make it. When working on a patient like this, I usually had to be bodily pulled off. This time was no different. Sarge had passed. I threw stuff around me in disgust. I wept, along with the nurse and Doc. I helped put him back on the gurney, and did the never ending cleaning of the patient. Packing the orifices for his ride to the Philippines.

His Squadron Commander was called. When he showed up, he was as shaken as I have ever seen a man. "My God Doctor," he said. "His DOS is tomorrow!" I came to find out, this Senior MSGT, had extended for a couple of months, and his second DOS was in the AM. He died on his last day. There would be no "Wakeup." I cursed my usual curses, took him out to the morgue, prayed for him, and went back up to the dock amongst the crying, laughing, drunk GI's . . . "Hey Sarge, give me something for this cut" . . . "Hey Sarge, what kinda dope ya got?"

What an absolutely shitty day. . . .

Another woman writes for THESE GUYS, your book, your stories, but I couldn't help including this woman's war story.

DO YOU REMEMBER ME . . .
By Renate Nishio

Do you remember me, "he does not hear you, he does not know you are here," the Doctor said, but I did see a tear ever so slowly rolling down his cheek; how can that be, if he is not aware. I said, *he does hear me,* and the doctor repeated, he cannot feel or hear anything, the stroke caused massive damage to his brain, so he can't hear or notice you. I had placed my hand under his and I was staring at his index finger where a thin layer of skin was not enough to cover a little piece of bullet, a residual from the war where he was in the air force; now it appeared innocently as a light blue spot, not more. My father could never move that finger, it was slightly bent, now I was staring at it and I could swear, it was moving, I felt a twitch. The doctor had left the room, and I did not want him to hear me, so I whispered into my father's ear to press my hand if he could hear me. There we go, I felt it again, and that one tear kept slowly rolling down his pale motionless face and I could swear I detected another one in his right eye, trying to break through. That gave me the courage to now speak up and say loudly what I had to say. "I love you father, what a life we had, there is nothing to forgive and nothing to forget; everything made me into what I am, and I am glad about who I am; I am part of you, and *that* is what I want you to know I am proud of." And as I expected, I clearly felt another squeeze. I was so relieved, that I found a minute to go within myself and recall. I did not remember too much about us, me and my father, only, that he was always gone to work to rebuild what had been lost in the war, and he therefore never had enough time to notice my requests for attention. I often thought when I felt lonely, how much he had to miss me. One day, I was about five, when I climbed my favorite tree all the way to the tip, swaying in the wind, dreaming of sailing to America. I heard my father's voice calling from below. He was leaning out of the window and yelling, 'you come down here, right now.' I did, and I got some spanking for my daring adventure; but then I knew that he really cared about me. I did make my dream come true. I lived in America, and when I got the phone call, I came to be here by his bedside, just in time. Father, dear father, I wish we could talk now, just about a few things that I never got to mention or to hear from you. But don't you worry, I always knew that you loved me, that made me very self confident . . . and independent . . . and positive. I just feel so sorry now that time has left me so little to remember about you. But I will never forget that at every Christmas, when I was little, I would cry for you when Santa entered the room, only to find out over and over again, that when the white beard came off and the bushy brows moved away from those blue eyes, it was you who brought those wonderful presents; I know now how difficult it must have been to make my wish come true in those times after the war. One of my other favored memories is mothers story, about when you were released from Russian prison years after war end; you had walked like so many others all the way back to Germany; when you got to our home town, you saw us walking on our street and gently tapped mother's shoulder, as you were saying *'do you remember me?'*

We did, and we always will! For now, your eyes have not opened again, but I am still listening.

Love and Light forever,

Your daughter Renate

The "attachment" that John Oberg refers to is listed in this book as THE RETURN OF THE TEUTON HORDES by Jon Horton. I hope you will enjoy reading Jon's writing as much as I have. [The Editor]

AN E-MAIL FROM JOHN OBERG

Subj: Hey ditto!
Date: 10/20/03 8:42.49 PM Pacific Daylight Time
From: Jcoberg@shaw.ca
To: jonhorton1@earthlink.net
CC: Idareedblanford@aol.com
File: THE RETURN OF THE TEUTON HORDES.doc

Jon,

Yes, what a surprise! I'll fill you in on various details later, but now I just want to establish two-way contact.
And, to add to that I am going to try to send an attachment that just may knock you off your chair!
Stand by!

So, have the 40 odd years offset the pain?
This year would be the 40th year! Prost mit Parkbrau . . . or ???????.
. . . can't find access to Cyrillic script so: za vashe zdorovyeh!

Surfing the net on topics related to 6901st, I came across Trish Schiesser in Chula Vista, and she - bless her heart - is the one who has been instrumental in my making contact with you. I'll cc her in this e-mail just to let her know that contact has been made.

Tell me what goes through your mind when you read your own words contained in the attachment.
Cheers for now!

Elaboration to follow.
Semper Fi!
John Oberg

These Guys

Jon Horton wrote:

John,

What the heck are you doing in Canada? I have a good friend in Nova Scotia and I'm trying to figure out a way to get up there to visit.

I was in the book store the other day and Steve said, "I have a note for you from John Oberg." I just about dropped my teeth.

Let me know where you are and what you are doing.

I hear from some of the others from Zwei, Fred Stassen (via his wife), John Giere, and others. Many more are on the web site <www.bat69.com>

Drop a line.

Horton

The person, Fred Stassen, mentioned in Jon Horton's e-mail is now deceased. The Return of the Teuton Hordes is a poem that Jon Horton wrote, which is included in this book, while at Zweibrucken at the 6901st.

This e-mail from John Oberg is one of helping me discover what happened to my brother, Phil Noland, after a 3 day TDY to London, when he came back to the 6901st Zweibrucken a changed and broken man.

Subj: and mega dittoes to you! could be a bonanza here for you
Date: 10/23/03 12:02:57AM Pacific Daylight Time
From: Jcoberg@shaw.ca
To: IdaReedBlanford@aol.com
File: PILGRIMAGELIST . . .

Trish:
That IS a possibility. Funny how certain topics and names come to the surface. I seem to remember a Sgt. Lincoln Stockwell. I have had his face in my mind for some time, but only tonight did his name "surface" so I can pass it on to you. Sgt. Stockwell would now be in his mid - to late - 70's, if he is still alive. But, as to how to find out his whereabouts, I am stumped for the moment. Through Jon Horton, you (as it now appears) should be able to get in touch with Fred Stassen's wife. I don't know what the "status" of Fred is these days, but perhaps Mrs. Stassen could be a useful contact. Funny how little bits of info can be useful. Good Luck. I assume you have Jon Horton's current email address, but just in case, here it is again. . . . I just found my original copy of the special orders (which I have typed faithfully in the attachment - minus my name because you already know who I am and where I live).

My hunch is that from #1 of the orders, anyone may have known of your brother. But the odds are that those listed at the rank of Airman First Class (AFC) or higher are much more likely to have known him or heard of him simply because people at this rank and higher were simply stationed longer at the 6901.

I used to know what the first 4 digits of an airman's service number referred to: for example "1972" was the Pacific Northwest - specifically Seattle/Everett area. I am sure that "1139" included the Connecticut area,(as that is where Roger Cyr was from) up to the Worcester, MA area (where another buddy was from); SSGT Bernard (Bernie) Bolduck was originally a French Canadian (or had family ties in that direction, but considered somewhere in Massachusetts to be his home when I knew him); "1970" was the Portland, Ore area; "1761" was the Southern Illinois/St. Louis, Mo area;

"1672" was the Kenosha, WI area; and "1478" was the Erie/Union City, PA area; and "1374" was the Pittsburgh, PA area.

And in #3 of these orders, A1C Robert G. Kiefer, may well have been taking/delivering his vehicle purchased somewhere in Germany to the docks in Bremerhaven prior to his going home. If that is the case, there is a chance he had been around for a long enough period to have perhaps, met/known your brother.

And, finally, 1st Lt William A Miller, as the Chief of Administration Services at 6901SCG in April 13, 1964, could have been in a very good position to have known/met your brother.

On another set of 6940 AIR BASE GROUP (USAFSS) [Goodfellow AFB, in San Angelo, TX orders dated 13 May 1963, I see the name of one A1C Gene K. Winn (AF12312571) who was to be reenlisting in the Reg AF on 27 May 1963 for a period of five years. If that is true, he too may have known/heard about your brother.

WOW! When I began this about two hours ago, I had no idea that this email would evolve into this lengthy document. I just thought, as the well-trained researcher you are, you might appreciate some of these names and serial numbers.

I do have a clear image of Fred Stassen being a sergeant, possibly a Staff Sgt, who was a person of quiet and high integrity. Very polite and utterly dedicated.

IdaReedBlanford@aol.com wrote:
>*Would Fred Stassen have known my brother?*

Fred Stassen thinks he knew my brother. But Fred died shortly after I contacted him.

John Oberg helps in searching for my brother, Phil Noland.. One can appreciate the bits and pieces of information I would glean from each ex-USAFSS person to another during the past three years or so.

In a message dated 11/27/2003 9:58:53 PM Pacific Standard Time, jcoberg@shaw.ca writes:

Trish:

This might come as some good news on Thanksgiving.
And it just occurs to me that you said your new computer arrangements do not include access to attachments.
You can try the attachment here, but just in case that does not work, I will copy (cut & paste) verbatim Jon's message to me.

On 11/25/03 9:22 PM, John Oberg at jcoberg@shaw.ca wrote:

Jon: I still have not answered your second question, but I will get to it. Meanwhile, I have kept Trish in the loop as to what you said about her brother Phil and Matt Guzzetta. But here is her reply to me:

So, my question for Jon Horton is: If he thought "Noland went to England with Matt Guzzetta then, did Jon know Noland? Tom Pugh never said he'd known Noland."

Jon, with your permission I will pass on your e-mail address to Trish, but I have not done that yet. Do you have any idea how Trish might locate Matt Guzzetta? Do you remember Phil Noland?
Is it okay that I pass on your e-mail address to her?

John, I was at a party in the NCO quarters and there was a guy there with Mat Guzzetta. I had never met him before but the two of them had just returned from England, driving an MG-TC Matt had bought. When I heard the name Noland I flashed on that guy. Never saw him after that. I hesitate to mention the incident because it's all foggy after 40+ years.
Sure, pass the address.
Jon

Jon might know something about your getting in contact with Fred Stassen or Fred's wife.

Does the info above help . . . ?
John

JOHN OBERG'S RIDE IN A C 124
By John Oberg

This e-mail begins with present day, but leads up to the Cold War experience. John Oberg tells.

Subj: Re: Check out the AOL Photo of the Day!
Date: 8/5/2005 6:04:38 PM Pacific Daylight Time
From: Jcoberg@shaw.ca
To: IdaReed@aol.com
cc: franzhome@hotmail.com

IdaReed@aol.com wrote:

In a message dated 8/5/2005 12:33:26 PM Pacific Daylight Time, jcoberg@shaw.ca writes:

Quite an effort by the USAF and US Navy to help out the Russian bathyscape off the Kamchatka Peninsula. I hope they make it there in time.

Cheers!
John

Your story gave me goosebumps. You should have been in the Navy or Coast Guard with all your shipping savvy. I'm certainly glad to see that you are hail and hearty today, after having gone through such unsettling winds and seas.

Yes, quite an effort by the USAF and US Navy to help out the Russian's. Bob had called me from his office on Pt. Loma (opposite where the C-5 was loading our two bathyscapes) and asked if I could see them from the condo - I couldn't - but he was willing to come home and get me to go see them in action - I declined due to the bronchitis that still has a hold of me. However, in three weeks, I am to get a personal tour aboard the Ronald Reagan aircraft carrier, so that should make up for missing today's events in person. It has always been my desire to catch a ride on a C-5 or C-5A, however, all I've managed are all the ships in the navy, except submarine, and a hop on a

helicopter, which was fun. I should also like to catapult off a carrier in a jet, however, I don't see that happening. You can see I have a lot of Ida in me, even today, I just saw the ship that carries our bathyscapes go up the bay, most likely to 32nd Street Naval Station, where they dock. I've seen them, fully loaded, while moored.
Well, that's about it for the day. Got my adrenalin running too, John. Sweet talk - this naval stuff.

Trish

I envy you having the chance to tour the Reagan! Back in my days in the Air Force, I hitch-hiked a lot on various military aircraft.

One story: I flew from Frankfurt to Naples, then to Wheelus AFB (in Libya; before Gaddafi's time); then to Kenitra, Morocco; then to Gibraltar, before arriving at Rota, Spain where my brother was an armaments specialist of some kind on a P2V Neptune bomber. I sure surprised him! It was like dropping in out of the blue, dressed in my air force uniform, walking up to the orderly at his unit's front desk. "Are you," he asked, having glanced at my name tag. "Yes, I am. Is he here?" I replied.
"Hey Oby!" there's somebody to see you here!" the orderly shouted toward the back room.
My brother came out from the other room and his mouth just dropped. "Where the hell did you come from?"
That night his skipper and crew invited me to come with them to a beach party, and the skipper then gave my brother a week off so that my brother and I could have some great times together. And we did!
Where's this leading? You said you wanted to fly in a C5. Well, my trip back to Germany involved hitching a flight from Rota to Torrejon AFB, outside of Madrid. I thought I was going to have to wait for a long time for some aircraft - any aircraft - going north toward Paris, London or Frankfurt. Well, after a mere 20 minutes or so, I was summoned to a departure desk and offered a ride on a NOPE - not a C5.
I was offered a ride on a C124, the old Globemaster with the clam-shell doors at the front of the fuselage. I went in and found a canvas-strap 'bench' sort of sitting area on one side and looked at two jet engines and a couple of trucks being sent back to . . . Frankfurt! Wow, I was lucky! I was the only passenger in the cargo area.

We taxied toward the end of a runway and then began the slow, ever so slow, take-off. I swear I could probably have reached out and touched the chain link fence at the end of the runway! Anyway, we slowly gained altitude as we got on a northerly course that would ultimately take us over the Pyrenees and southeast of Paris before heading off to the northeast to arrive in Frankfurt.

As we gained altitude, the temperature in the cargo area steadily dropped! Pretty soon, I looked around for some entry to the crew's quarters. I found a metal ladder giving access from the cargo deck up probably 20 or 30 feet to a regular door - regular just like a door in a house! I opened it and found warmth! And I found hundreds of dials and gauges and sundry items apparently needed to fly the beast. I even found a food-dispensing machine (minus a device to take coins; you would simply select what you wanted and then would bang the machine with your fist to get what you wanted!). The navigator and the engineer waved greetings to me and welcomed me to the rest area behind/aft of where they were working. After 30 minutes or so, the pilot came back and introduced himself. We chatted and inquired about what each other did as Air Force members.

And then the pilot invited me to go to the front and sit in HIS SEAT! Would I like to do that, he asked. Well, I was off like a scalded rabbit!

I walked by the work area of the navigator on one side and we chatted a bit. I stopped by where the engineer worked, fascinated by all the dials and levers so he could synchronize the engines and fuel characteristics. And then I walked further to sit in the pilot's seat, at the front on the port side!

The wind noise coming over the front of the fuselage was immense. I waved at the co-pilot, but we couldn't hear each other over the wind and engine noise. As a result, the co-pilot just waved me into the pilot's seat and motioned for me to put on headsets so he and I (and the crew) could talk to each other over the intercom inside the aircraft.

Can you imagine what this experience was like for me who, although wearing an Air Force uniform and in the USAFSS and having gone through Indiana University for Russian language training, had never actually (to that point) ever flown in an Air Force aircraft?

Gads! I looked out the pilot's port side window and looked way back at the wing. I saw huge exhaust pipes coming out of the engines, each pipe belching out maybe 8 to 10 feet of blue flames! I joked to the co-pilot that it looked like we were on fire, but he assured me that what I was seeing was normal.

The co-pilot then asked me if I would like to steer/to actually 'fly' this C-124. Well, not being the shy type, I quickly said, "Yes, I'd like to!"
After about 10 minutes with MOI at the stick, flying off into the starry sky, watching the portside wing 'fall' away when I would steer to the left, being utterly thankful the co-pilot was there to catch any stupid action I might come up with that might jeopardize all on board, ... after about 10 minutes, the co-pilot tapped me on my right shoulder and, shouting, told me to flip one particular switch in front of me so that we could actually hear each other without having to shout.
After doing as I had been instructed, I resumed 'flying' this C-124 for about 5 more minutes when, all of a sudden, the navigator came on the intercom and asked the co-pilot, "Hey, which switch did Oberg hit?"
I pointed at the one I thought the co-pilot had told me to turn on, but then in a moaning tone exuding all sorts of disbelief, he asked the navigator, "Ok, Jack. Where are we? Oby just turned off the auto-pilot!"
And I thought I had already been flying this beast! Well, the co-pilot then said, "Well, you got us off course. Now you can get us back on course!"
So, now I think the auto-pilot really was off. The first 'flying' exercise was apparently to see if I would survive being in the pilot's seat in the first place! Now, I would have to steer without the aid of the auto pilot. Now, when the wind dropped out of sight on my left, I knew I had caused that to happen. This time, though, it simply stayed down until I brought it back to something resembling level flight.

We were at 9,000 feet doing 220 knots, and I actually moved that beast left and right, took it 5 or 10 degrees off course and then took it back to the original course. Wow! What an experience! I was excited and still am over 40 years later! I was just a Russian linguist, etc., and here I was moving this whale of a plane through the sky.
But, you know what? To this day, I think that air crew was pulling my leg. Sometimes, I think that I probably didn't even get them off course. They probably just said that to thrill the you-know-what out of me! (And they almost succeeded!)

For you? Beware of the C5 pilot handing the controls over to you! They might be simply having some fun at your expense! But you too give the impression of walking on the wild side (when a reasonably safe opportunity arises!), so go to it with gusto! May I suggest this, though: Instead of 'steering' left or right, put the C5 into a very, very steep dive, and let the rest of the crew clean out their pants!

Since I am sending a copy of this to my sister, I'll provide some links to two photos:

1) A C5 like you want to fly.
http://community.webshots.com/photo/24918828/24919317mQMzTATrqM#

AND

2) A C124 like the one I flew:
 http://www.connect.net/titurner/124.jpg

Finally, I note that you have written, "I should also like to catapult off a carrier in a jet, however, I don't see that happening." Trish, just be careful (if this ever happens) that you get catapulted WHILE SITTING IN AN AIRCRAFT WITH A CERTIFIED PILOT LEADING THE WAY!" Getting catapulted in your street shoes would be an experience that no other human has ever gone through (or at least I hope so!)!! ☺

Cheers!
John

And, here we have another fun-filled story from John Oberg, ex-USAFSS. I salute you, John.

This is a partial e-mail from an ex-USAFSS guy during the Cold War giving me permission to print what he has written. He writes in the first graph of my husband's job on a USNS ship being overhauled in Todd-Pacific Shipyard in Seattle, WA. A little levity never hurt anyone, eh?

JOHN OBERG AND THE CAPTAIN
By John Oberg

From: John Oberg
To: Trish Schiesser
Sent: Wed. November 09, 2005 1:50 PM
Subject: Home again.

JCO replies: Nov 9, 1:45 PST

What a pissy (oops!) I mean what a pity: the Captain's toilet broke? (Editor's Note: Bob Schiesser's Captain's toilet broke, on his ship after an overhaul at Todd Pacific Shipyard, Seattle, WA and he had to ride the ship all the way home with a broken toilet.) John's answer to this is:
Maybe that is why some people think the Captain is full of s***!

Some captains I have known have been really great people (my most memorable is a fellow) in the RAF at Gatow Airfield in the Berlin area back in the Cold War days. Technically in all aspects of our work, he was truly outstanding: very well trained, very knowledgeable about goings on, 'on top' of absolutely everything. Personally, he was a true gentleman. Academically, a humanities AND an engineering background from Cambridge and . . . somewhere else, (can't remember where in the UK). Squadron Leader Jamieson, was his name.

One of the most objectionable captains I knew was right there at Zwei: Thom. He thought he knew everything and tried and tried and tried to prove to everybody that he knew everything. Fortunately, most of us knew that he didn't know squat! He was always in the way, and I remember so well when we were monitoring an air defense exercise underway in the Ukraine/Polish forward area and he got so close behind me that I accidentally stepped on him and almost lost my balance. The colonel in charge saw this and ordered, "Captain! Back off and don't interfere with what Oberg is doing!" All I could do was give an appreciative glance at the colonel, and then I went back to work. Besides, I am quite sure that the captain I am referring to was gay, or at least he certainly impressed many of us as being that way! A few months later, I understand, he was transferred to somewhere in Korea. Bad assignment. Nobody wants to go to Korea!

Later,
John

ZOOMIES/TESTS
By Bill Person

From: Bill Person
Sent: Wednesday, January 12, 2005 9:24 pm
To: A listing of people
Subj: Re: Zoomies/tests

Okay guys,

The Army had ASA, the Navy had NSG and the AF had USAFSS. All working for NSA.
Enlisted men with high test scores went to electronics schools, manual Morse school, Intelligence Analysis school, and language training at a university. Like now, the enemy does not wear a placard saying, "I'M ENEMY, SHOOT ME!"
When "Rolling Thunder" started on March 1965, we knew nothing about the air defenses of North Vietnam or potential targets to bomb. I was Queen Bee Delta Project Officer and it was my job to oversee the intercept of enemy radios and how they reacted when we sent drone and fighters over them to photograph their facilities.
Someone wrote that without intelligence, military leaders tend to appear more brilliant or more stupid than they truly are. It does little good to do any shooting if you don't have a target, or know where to find one. And it does little good to find those targets if we can't kill them. I applaud the smart guys who read good books and help determine which targets need shooting, and I truly applaud the shooters who get the job done, comic book readers especially. I also know I would not be happy flying combat with a major who reads comic books. I have raised hell with pilots who put the bird on auto pilot and opened a book to read. I want every pair of eyes watching out for danger while my ass is up in the wild blue yonder. So, no one needs defending or running down, if anyone let down on his job, we all hurt. Semper Fi, do or die, HOORAH! catch you later in the sky, GI.
Regards,
Bill Person

RE: EJECTION AND OTHER THINGS IMPORTANT
By Bill Person

Yup, Ray,

The F-16 and all high performance fighters have the glide path of a hurled brick. Back in August 1960 when I soloed the T-33 down in Laredo, Texas, the bird ahead of me had his ailerons working together, not opposed as they are supposed to and as the bird started a roll to the left, he punched out close to a 90 degree bank. He didn't have his zero anchor lanyard hooked so his chute didn't get fully deployed. I had a good seat to watch it all. He died enroute to the hospital. The plane ahead of me broke right so I had to fly over his smoke. Taught me a lesson to use my rudder to turn out of the roll and gain some altitude in case I needed to punch. At low level, you don't have time to react and pull the string after ejecting so you keep your zero anchor lanyard hooked to pop your chute immediately for you. I never had to do it but I did crash land once though. That was a rough bucking ride getting the T-28 to settle dead stick on not-so-soft elephant grass. I did hit the emergency air jam to force the two canopies full back and open before slam down just like the old Navy jocks did. These newer fighters don't have slide back canopies so they have to punch out and have the Plexiglas blown away in the process since the newer jets don't "ditch" and stay on the top of the water worth a damn. Raise your canopy at 100+KIS and you have a speed brake with the bird being pitched up about 60 degrees nose up. You can't negotiate the water in that attitude, it'll flip, tumble forward and take you straight to the bottom and if you punch out then, you'll be like a launched torpedo at a few fathoms down. Hard on the body, they tell me.

Beef is still up there and I like tamer cows. A neighbor put a Guar from Ceylon on his Charolais to get Guarolais. They're kin to the kwai we saw in SEA and American insects didn't like the taste of them but that was not enough to make it work here. They were kind of white, long legged and had a sort of a topknot on their horn area. They could jump an 8 foot fence with ease so he couldn't keep them. They had to dart them to bring back to a holding pen. Guess they all got a free trip to McDonalds. They just got one mean assed Watsui bull that they plan on breeding. This sucker has horns that are at least 5' from tip to tip. We buy alfalfa hay by the ton out of Oklahoma at 600 + bales at a time and they put it all in the hayloft of our barn. It goes for about $5.00 a bale by the truck load and we don't have to feed cubes like our neighbors. We really don't make any money off them we get our money from oil & gas and get to pay less property tax for agricultural land use. The dairy and horse folks here feed alfalfa too.

On the subject of punch out's they had a program on the Military Channel about modern carrier planes. There was footage of several punch outs and the de-briefs afterwards. The worst one was an Intruder that just left the ramp and lost power. It rolled right before they punched out and both guys went into the ocean sideways just as their chutes deployed. I couldn't believe they survived. They said they didn't believe they survived. In the debrief, their CO told them they should have punched out sooner, but the pilot said he was too low and busy trying to fly the plane at the time. Lesson learned. Another was an F-14 that was to do a fly by the carrier and let the "nugget" go supersonic. As soon as he hit the after burners the left engine just exploded. Fortunately he had plenty of altitude when he punched out. All of these pilots said it was an experience they never wanted to repeat. They also came out of the ejections an inch shorter. EJECTION SEATS USE A 20 MM SHELL TO PROPEL IT OUT. I'LL BET IT IS A KICK IN THE ASS GETTING CLEAR OF THE SICK BIRD. I RODE THE EJECTION TRAINER A FEW TIMES AND IT USED AN UNDER CHARGED SHELL THAT STILL GAVE YOU A HELLUVA BOOT IN THE BUTT. GLAD I NEVER HAD TO DO A SILK DESCENT OVER HOSTILE SEA. I KNOW HOW THE GOMERS LOVE TO USE YOU FOR TARGET PRACTICE.

Regards,
Bill Person

From Ray:

In the program that I watched a pilot said their ejection seats in the F-14 had 2 rockets to launch the seat. The RIO went out first and the pilot went out a split second later so he didn't get burned by the Rio's rockets; it's split second and automatic, once they pull the handle. The two that punched out in a right roll had their chutes deploy just in time to drag them into the ass first position before hitting the ocean. The chutes saved them despite the fact that they hadn't fully opened.

My comments about helio crews riding them down, wasn't bragging. It's the only option. You have a chance unless you lose that tail rotor. Without it you auger in and break up bad. Both times that we got hit and went down the tail rotor was still intact so we went straight in sans flare, once into some trees and one pancake. Bent skids, broken tail boom and a brief religious experience. Once the area was pacified, the Hooks would come in and haul them back to the bone yard for parts. They always gave us another one.

I'm waiting to see the first calves that come out of that Watsui/Corinth mix. Could be some strange critters.

Ray 774

From: Bill Person
Sent: Wednesday, March 01, 2006

Well, Ray, I suppose you could technically call it a rocket on ejection seats. The jets of my day used a 20mm shell with a bigger charge and no projectile. The shell case is like a rocket body but it requires solid recoil to toss the ejection seat, pilot still strapped in, up the rails and into the air, free and clear of the cockpit. The ones with a red top headrest would burst though the Plexiglas canopy even if it failed to blow first, protecting the pilot, somewhat. The fire from the shell would continue to burn with the oversized charge so it looked like a rocket spewing fire as it was driving the ejection seat up and away from the plane. Rockets might not have the initial recoil that a 20mm shell does but it would quickly build up thrust and propel the seat upwards. The key here was to boot the pilot up clear of the cockpit so quickly that he didn't get slammed back against the plane or the rear fin, especially at 600mph+. The wind blast at that speed would be devastating. That's why the helmet had a drop visor and the oxygen mask to protect the face from wind sheer. Also, we had a tiny O2 bottle with a green bulb handle to pull and it had a separate hose to the O2 mask to give the ejectee good air to breath while descending from high altitudes. Passing through ten thousand feet we had a check to disconnect the zero anchor lanyard so the chute didn't open immediately, giving you a chance to free fall until you manually pulled the D ring. You didn't want to deploy your chute up high and give the enemy more time to gather and use you as a target while descending and be there when you reached the ground. The "unofficial" manual said to try not to eject over the area you just bombed, it tended to piss off folks on the ground, especially the ones with guns; lots of stuff to think about at such a time when you had a sick or shot up bird. That's why we have procedure trainers to practice all kinds of emergencies so the pilot knew what to do in each instance.

Don't know much about choppers except they had that big overhead fan to keep you cool while the ground raced up to impact you. And it was difficult to jump out when the whirling rotors were coming down on top of you and preventing the chute from filling up with air for a desired unobstructed descent. If it had been up to me, I would make it a law that our enemies can only use blanks cause, hell, even our own planes can kill you without any help and we soldiers don't need to be hurt, on purpose or otherwise, right?

Regards,
Bill Person

Bill Person, ex-USAFSS, kept me apprised of some of his background, from time to time, and the history of the moment. This is one of those times. [The Editor]

TURKEY STUFF
By Bill Person & Others

Trish, here a synopsis of what I sent to Jim in case you didn't get it.
Fondly,
Bill

When I got to the 685th ACT Squadron at Las Cruces, NM, I got to meet some of the people at White Sands Missile Test Range just over the Oregon Mountain Range. Mr. Johnson kept me up with the fact that early in 1960, the Atlas was launched to be tested against the Nike-Ajax or the Nike-Zeus (??). The Atlas had a special avoidance system if it encountered a reactive threat before discharging its multiple warhead payload. The Atlas was launched and the defending missiles, Nike, was fired to intercept it; probably both from Vandenberg AFB to be over the Pacific. The guidance system of the Atlas did not perform as programmed so modification work was ordered. The Thor missile removal from Turkey was put on hold as a back-up system and a nightmare of trial and error modifications ensued. The Intelligence Community and especially the Air Force Security Service was extremely active on Russia southern border. We had intercept sites on the northern coast of the Black Sea at Trabson, Samsun and Karamursel, and we had the big missile monitoring site at Diabakir, plus the intercept site at Ankara. We also flew U-2s out of Incirlik. We had a system called Trackmaster that monitored both the Soviet ICBM launch facility at Kapustin Yar and the ESV launch site at Baikonur near the town of Tyura Tam. The Peshawar, Pakistan site (Fieldpiece) monitored the launch facility activities and reported it on a manual Morse radio net in connection with the island intercept site at Shemya, Alaska on the Aleutian Chain (Newcomer). This was in line with the impact area of Kyluchi on the Kamchatka peninsula. At Wakkanai, the 6986th RSG was under the path of both type of space tracks. I was there from September 1963 to May 1965.

Back to the Cuban Missile Crisis of November 1962; the Turks knew that by having Thors IRBMs pointing north towards Moscow posed a highly visible threat to the Russians and this served as a potent dissuader for any aggression towards them. They saw Soviet photo recce planes fly along the Black Sea taking pictures of the Thors and this delighted the Turks. They had a really big stick. I had gone through pilot training with two Turks, Aden Austin and Chelating who later became the top general for the Turkish Air Force. They both told me that the Thors were a self-confidence factor for the Turks and also a threat for Russia to keep away.

It is well to remember a period that America saw the poor performance of our early day missile efforts. TV depicted a number of missiles blowing up on the launch pad. It was said, federal employees were like our missiles, they won't work and you can't fire them. When the Atlas missile guidance and also the evasive system proved to be unreliable, the order to remove the Thors from Turkey was stopped. It is true that they were obsolete but they would still do a lot of damage to Russia if they were launched. At the time, November 1962, the Turks relied upon those Thors as a bulwark against Soviet aggression. In America, we were still practicing reactions to a nuclear attack from Russia in the Cold War. I went to Chemical, Biological and Radiological CBR school for ADC. And too, the Soviet people were not completely aware of the new threat of our Atlas ICBMs; they certainly were of the Thors in Turkey. The Soviets didn't tell their people stuff like we did in America.

Jim Stampher wrote:
I knew two people assigned to the Thor missiles in Turkey. The decision had been reached early in 1960 to remove the missiles as soon as the multi-warhead Atlas became operational, the Atlas missile shooting from 8,000 miles away (later in scattered underground silos along with the Minuteman) was in fact more accurate than the Thor shooting from Turkey. The site at Cheyenne became operational in early 1960, I helped off load the first 6 Atlas missiles at Cheyenne. Two more delivered as I was clearing the base to leave for Alaska in May of 1960. I was at Las Cruces by then. Later, I toured the Cheyenne complex in 1965.

Bill wrote:
That's what JFK told the public so he would not appear to be the woosie. He started crating them before the SS-4s were removed from Cuba. We had to pay the Turks millions for reducing their threat hold over the Russians. Khrushchev wanted to reduce this threat, or show a force of power to his Kremlin goonies.
He reduced his Warsaw Pact in a real threat to their position against NATO. We had Thor medium range missiles there and elsewhere to mount an over-

kill threat including Swift Strike/Roll Back, F-105s in 6 bases, B-52s armed and airborne, B-58s poised, not forgetting the subs in place and the ICBMs here at home.
Russia knew they were overmatched and when Reagan started the SDI, they had to collapse, unable to keep up.

Jim Stampher wrote:
The missiles were coming out of Turkey anyway. They were a stop gap solution waiting for the ICBMs to become operational. Some of the guidance systems in Turkey were already crated to be shipped back to the CONUS.

Bill Person wrote:
Yep, old Uncle Waltie was sitting at the bar for newsy folks in the Caravel Hotel in Saigon, sipping his martini when he heard shots ring out closer than he felt comfortable with and went on TV saying, "The war is lost!" like Chicken Little in the story by the same name, when an acorn fell and hit him on the head, he proclaimed, "The sky is falling, the sky is falling!" He was wrong of course but the other chickens believed him since he was the "Dean of Journalists, and the most trusted man in the news business." So I call him "Chicken Little" Cronkite. If Uncle Ho had still been alive, he probably would have awarded him the NVA's Red Star Hero medal for doing more to win that war for them than Gen. Giap had during the Tet '68 offensive. When Dan Rather touted a fake document about Bush's AWOL as real, I dubbed him, "Little Chickenshit." As I say, "the odor of liquor was strong on his breath and the truth was not in him!" The North Vietnamese knew the difference but apparently few people got it right back here in the good old US of A. Still don't. Trained/schooled at the Walter Cranched/Dan Rather school of Journalism, all newsy folks still say we lost that war. Then here comes Tom Broke-all to proclaim WWII vets as "the Greatest Generation." Guess he wanted to distance himself from us "Baby-killer" Nam vets and the "Lost the peace" vets of Korea. And, "WHAT COLD WAR generation?" I watched the History Channel version on the Cuban Missile Crisis and shouted at the TV. Nikita Khrushchev pulled 30 medium range SS-4 missiles from the Warsaw Pact in Poland and East Germany, severely weakening that part of his defenses and shipped them in crates to Cuba in October 1962. Our Intel guys knew it but no one ever reported that

part of it. Nikita wanted to give JFK a dose of missile-itis since he and the Kremlin felt the threat of our missiles in Turkey.

The Rooskies never trusted Fidel to have nuke-tipped SS-4's so they never sent the warheads.

We knew where the SS-4's were and could have easily wiped them out with mini nuke-tipped cruise missiles in an instant. What scared our defense generals were the location of their sub-launched nuke-tipped missiles off our coasts. Anyway, JFK agreed to remove our "out-dated" missiles from Turkey if the Soviets took back their SS-4's. We knew that the Warsaw Pact Russian generals were clamoring to get back their missiles, feeling naked by the threat of superior NATO forces. We had to pay off the complaining Turkey leaders for stripping the missiles from there and put more of our subs in the area to take up the slack of an "over-kill" capability, which we certainly had over them all along.

And that's all I know about Walter Cronk-case.

Regards,

Bill Person

WEAPONS
By Bill Person and Irv Levine

Ray, I change the subject so I will know which incoming ones refer to me. Periwinkle struck a tickle chord with me. Anyway, back when I was a brown bar, I got tapped to drive down to Biggs AFB at El Paso to get the payroll. And on the days the CO wanted a cash payday, another young 2nd Lt. would go along as an extra armed guard. We wore .45 cal (semi) automatics in those days and my buddy was from Long Island, NY and not used to weapons. He was an electrical engineer and a radar type but we all had to fire the weapon to be qualified to carry it. Anyway, he made a comment the first time that the payroll was only money and if anyone tried to rob us, he wouldn't bother to even draw his weapon, they could just come and take it. I laughed at him and told him that if anyone tried to rob us of the cash, they would see that we wore pistols and would probably think that us being military, they'd have to kill us to get the money. He looked kind of funny when I added that our only chance of survival was to kill them first, so he'd better get used to the idea. I'm sure he didn't like that answer but he admitted I was probably right. In all my times to serve as an escort to classified materials while in Japan, and on TDY, I always had to wear the big .45 cal. Colt. That was a mean weapon to fire and I worked my tail off with it because when I had four years in and was to wear the two-tone blue longevity ribbon, I swore I was not just going to wear one ribbon so I managed to earn the Small Arms Expert Award to go with it. Then we changed to the .38. We also had to fire the .30 cal carbine but only as a familiarization, not as a weapon we ever carried like the airmen did. Then came the M-16 and another round of familiarization firing for a weapon we'd probably never use.

More later,
Regards
Bill Person

P.S. I sent the part about me carrying the tracers to ward off the sharks if I ever got shot down in the Gulf of Tonkin to my Thud pilot buddy, Irv, and here is his reply.

MORE Shark story:
You too, huh? I didn't see ME having a WAR with six bullets in my Combat Master Piece, so I gave it back to them and carried a 9mm with 80 extra rounds . . .hollow points. I never thought of sharks, but I damned sure

thought of SNAKES. Sheesh! "Dingy" Dengler (now deceased) said he "buried" his .38 because he couldn't see himself starting a war with six bullets. Then he thought better of it and went back to get it . . . but couldn't remember where the f*** he'd buried it. Guess all that jungle looks alike. He also claimed to be "chicken" to "punch out" so he "dead sticked" it down and landed in a swamp without so much as a scratch. (Note: the F-105 will not fly straight and level below 200 mph. At a nose-high touchdown, it breaks in half and explodes.) He (Dingy Dengler) lied about so many things I give no credence to most anything he said. BUT, he was rescued at the last moment, made LIFE Magazine and was forever listened to by and of the rabid young folks that he could draw around him. I've had people write to me and ask about him. They DIDN'T like my answers, 'cause they were looking for a real life HERO. Deiter (notice my appellation for him above) Dengler was most certainly a LEGEND IN HIS OWN MIND. (Note: we sure grew a bumper crop of those legends in SEA.) Ya know, they also LOCKED UP the ammo for the marines and army troops IN COMBAT AREAS. How unstable were those f***ers? When attacked they had to run down to their armory and be "issued" bullets. Sigh! I read a book by a former Navy SEAL, and he said they did the same thing to them in Beirut. They had to show their guns were "empty" when they went out the gate. The SEALs carried LOADED WEAPONS at ALL TIMES. He said they'd OPEN THE BOLT and show the guard at the gate the empty chamber and they'd pass them through. As soon as they got out of ear shot they "locked and loaded" and were ready for business.

You were certainly "prepared" for survival. But, see, BECAUSE YOU WERE nothing ever happened. If you had a finger nail file, been roaring drunk the night before (1 hour between bottle and throttle, so to speak) and not a drop of water, food or medicines . . . you'd surely have been hit, shot down, ditched or parachuted and suffered for your folly.

I had a friend in B-47's that had flown F-86's in Korea. He was hit and forced to bail out, but he made it to the Gulf of Tonkin, and they told him a Navy Destroyer was on the way to pick him up. His ejection was good and he was floating in his life preserver vest when he looked down and saw "something" coming up from deep in the waters below him. First thing he thought was SHARK! As it approached him, getting larger and larger, he was terrified and finally in desperation "KICKED" at it in a weak attempt to "drive it away" or at the very least maybe "discourage it." He made contact and the thing "exploded" into an even LARGER looking mass and he realized it was the Sea Marker Dye that had been leaking out of its package, which he had forgotten about completely. And when he "kicked it" it burst the package even more. A great POST SCRIPT to this was THEY DIDN'T HAVE ANY PROBLEMS FINDING HIM WHEN THEY GOT WITHIN EYE SIGHT OF HIS POSITION. Ha!

Have to run to Las Vegas for a week, starting in about an hour. Take care and we'll be "back up" and "on the net" in a week. Back the 27th of Feb. Save all the GOOD STUFF for me then.

Irv

These Guys

Here is an answer from Bill Person, to my question, "How does the Starburst happen? Are those missiles? Also, who took the photos and from where - a tanker or something?" Damned beautiful! (I had been sent a photo of a C-130 with starbursts shooting out of it and it looked like the fourth of July!) [The Editor]

PLANES
By Bill Person

These are flares. Pods are placed in certain places on the plane in recesses and then replaced when fired. Our shoulder-fired Stinger and the Soviet-built SAM-7 Strella have an internal heat-seeking detection and guidance system. They try to fly up your exhaust ports. Jets are even better. Fighter pilots try to aim for the sun and then reduce power, hoping the heat-seeker will lock-on to the sun and then pass by and use up its fuel, die and fall away. The bigger SAM-2 Guidelines have a 50-foot proximity fuse that detonates when it senses an object as close as that. The pattern you see is just like a fireworks display, electrically timed to form a shape for the heat-seeker to lock-on to which is brighter and hotter than the plane. You may have seen Russian transport planes in older films as they fired starbursts one at a time in all different directions to dissuade heat-seekers being fired at them. If you are on the ground ready to fire one, and you see those, your rocket will not likely down the intended target. The pictures are made from a chase plane to photograph and monitor the results for adjustments. Air Force One has them as do a lot of special planes. Certain Airlines want them but they are expensive. Yes, it is a beautiful pattern and at almost 10 miles a minute, the burning flares make a hotter and more attractive target for the rocket. The SAM-2 was radar controlled by a man on the ground. As you ran away from it, the faster telephone pole sized missile's path was corrected to intercept you. So the way we defeated it was to detect it on our ARN-249/250 dash-mounted detector and that told you where it was coming from (you were dead meat in anything but a fighter) turn and fly directly at it. You could see the white double-winged rocket coming and it was then a game of chicken. The ground controller was not likely to be able to make corrections with a closing rate of over 2500 mph. At the last minute, you dived under it and let the thing zoom past you. The last minute tuck. SAM-2s can't make a 180 degree turn at 1000-1800 mph.

Of course if your judgment is bad and you got within 50 feet, the damn thing exploded and got you. No one looked forward to ejecting at 600 mph or faster. Sometimes the explosion broke the plane into pieces and you in the cockpit got spun around like in a washing machine and the g-forces kept you from raising the handles to eject from the tumbling wreckage. A lot of pilots were badly injured with broken limbs from high-speed bailouts. When I was at Eglin AFB, Florida, my office was next door to the paramedic school. They used goats for training. They broke one or more of their legs and let the trainees learn how to splint a broken bone, "direct hands-on." They knew that rescuing a downed pilot in Vietnam would make them have to deal with such injuries. They didn't want a new PJ to deal with his first broken bone on a downed pilot in SEA. Some people found out about the mistreatment of goats and the school was moved (slightly). We had a Mexican family who got the injured goats and barbecued them; excellent cabrito. Most US pilots never complained of the system.

Regards,
Bill

A TRIP TO NEVERLAND
By Bill Person

Subj: Re: How old I are 2
Date: 6/20/03 2:00:15 PM Pacific Daylight Time
From: fcentaur35@hotmail.com
To: IdaReedBlanford@aol.com

RE: now I know why you write so many sex scenes in your books. [The Editor]

Well, that and some of it happened as a part of the pertinent part of the story e.g., watching the ships come in at the port of Wakkanai at night. Perhaps I wrote in too many descriptive scenes as an after thought. You'd have to read the part in my Queen Bee Delta when my pregnant girl friend was killed in a plane explosion. So, you can't determine what an elephant really is by feeling its trunk.

I went through 18 sex partners and refused 10 in my 4 books. Actually there were a few more and I can recite their real names as well as the names I used in the books.

In April 1965, I flew up to Lulang Prabang, Laos with the "civilians" and was not supposed to have been there. The hardest thing I ever wrote was about those 3 days and I wrote that as a short story.

I was part of the cover-up when a British MI5 agent who had followed 4 French-made atom bombs to Sihounikville, Cambodia only to have the Mossad steal them right off the ship while the "sellers" were being assassinated in Thakhet, Laos. These bombs were to have been used against us in South Vietnam when we started the air war up north. I have always believed that by Israel having those two years later, during the 5 Day War, kept the other 13 Arab nations out of that war.

The DeHavilland Otter, DHC-3, was very forgiving for the likes of me.
It's spacious and roomy, but very slow, and painted dull gray so it won't show.
British letters painted on the side, their pilot sick, so I gave the ride.
I flew it north to the Me Kong shore, at NKP, we stopped, 'twas unsafe to venture more.
The 600 horses drew us along, the load was too heavy, a safety wrong.
But in this clumsy, hulking crate, I made the trip, tho' a scary fate.

The air was heavy to thusly fly, I heard the blame thing shudder and give a sigh.
A wounded Sandy (A1) had the lead, I touched down next, my sweat did bead.
Out in the brush, in smelly tents, the Tommy listened to VC radio sends.
Was told of evils done in spite, for loot taken, it was not right.
Dressed in sarongs, we crossed the stream, the ferry boat was a nightmare's dream.
In Thakhet, (Laos) we saw the horrid deed, of men driven by sinful greed.
But the revenge was taken, quick and sweet, the culprits then chanced their Maker meet.
A circle of tribesmen formed round to glare, at the springing of their deadly snare.
Screams of pain and moans rang out, as five mens legs were sawed off and strewn about.
Rough-hewn planks on the raised up dock, were coated crimson red with human stock.
I witnessed these evil men who died, and held my gag, no tears were cried.
Their fiendish deeds were not condoned, and the natives' act, had now atoned.
When asked, I joined and did my part, but alas, it sickened me to heart.
I flew back home in a saddened mind, to have seen such gore on my humankind;
War does exact an awesome price, but I checked my shock and ate my rice.
There was no time to rest nor stew, the air war was a go for each combat crew.
Hanoi was short of MiGs and SAMs and triple A. Twas ripe a time for us to play.
LBJ and his pal Mac, delayed destruction, lest our taxes pay for new construction.
America paid in lives and mental pain, for misdeeds in that land of monsoon rain.
Many speak of misplaced shame, but D.C. leaders must forever bear the blame.
Then, later, I perchance to take, the ruptured Otter up to Bailiwick (Burma)
That's on the Dana Range's steep side, above the Salween (River), down low, but not so wide.
I touched down hard on a muddy road, and let them take off my explosive load.

Midst thunderclaps and drenching rain, my skill tested lest we there remain.
I flew in natives, and British moles, but left there quickly as Burmese filled the tail with bullet holes.
I sat out two nights of fear that made me gag, while the locals played games of deadly tag.
Red Flag Commies were thinned all out, by Burmese and natives who led the rout.
In morning's light, the sights were strange, as I made the hop back over the mountain range.
Bandages and salves, they awful stank, on wounded Bees (natives), and vomit rank.
To Bangkok, I flew us, all safe and sound, no more to traverse over hostile ground.
Three short months in Spring of '65, but the nightmares would stay while I'm alive.
When I am asked of this to speak, my tears do flow and my knees grow weak.
Yet, back I went to Korat in '67-'68, to once again tempt my test with fate.
More deaths were taken by the score, and the Air Force gave out medals galore.
Somehow, this too, I did endure, would I go back? No, I'm too old and had the cure.

SHORT ROUND
By Bill Person

An e-mail of interest copied to me by Bill Person, Captain, Vietnam Dated 7/11/03

Hi Trish,
I sent this to a distant relative I've never met. Thought you'd enjoy reading it:

Hi Barbara,

I took the scenic drive once I got into Virginia and wound up at the court house. I took pictures of the John Smith plantation monument and the house where John Rolfe and Pocahantas lived. I even went into the clerk's office and made copies of John Person Jno's will. Then I crossed over on the ferry to Jamestown. No, actually I didn't spend any time in Williamsburg except to drive around and look it over; so many fine old houses. I was more interested in seeing the location of where our ancestors were.
According to the documents, John Person came over in 1648 and only had one son, Jno Person. And he was granted property on the Blackwater River in Surrey County. I wished I could have stayed longer to check records and look around but I did not allow myself that time. In fact I had not really planned to do all that I did. Then I had to cut short my time in Charleston at the reunion because I had promised some people to give some input at the museum at Ft. Walton Beach, Fl. The beaches from Panama City to Pensacola were swamped with people and then there were lots of heavy thunderstorms.
The KH San Vets have decided Charleston was not the right kind of place to hold a reunion. Many of them took a bus back to Parris Island where it had all started for them before Vietnam.
There were so many with missing limbs. One little guy called "Short Round" was there and he is missing both hands with stumps about half way to his elbows. He can surprise you with what he can do with that. One Marine jokingly commented that he could no longer do the manual of arms with a rifle. He snapped back that he could too. Another Marine pulled off his leg, nearly up to his hip, and handed it to Short Round so he could use it as a rifle and do the manual of arms with it. I knew Short Round from Dallas last year and happened to walk up just as he finished doing all the maneuvers with his buddy's artificial leg. Seeing him holding it like that, I walked up in the middle of a bunch of Marines and said, "Damn it Short Round, I told you, arms, you

need arms, not legs!" Everyone got a big laugh out of that. Short Round laughed the loudest. That incident will be told and retold for several reunions. I have to wonder what the Marine Drill instructors thought when these guys climbed off the buses. They were supposed to be treated like new raw recruits as a joke. I can only imagine that the toughest DI must have lost it when he saw them as very few escaped major wounds in that 77 day siege. It must have been hell listening to the VC dig tunnels under them with the intent of placing an explosive charge to blow them up and not being able to do anything about it. Then the VC lobbed mortar rounds and rockets into the base at all hours. I flew on three different orbits, 20,000 feet for 8 hours above, and got to talk to Henry on the radio several times. He reported that their boots were rotting away and that they couldn't get anything from supply. I told him to make a list for me. He did and I took it to our supply at Korat, Thailand. I knew that we had two big Air Force Wings there and that we had all come over with all the things we needed but supply would have ordered things anyway just in case; Henry had a list of: boots, watches, flight jackets, socks, tee-shirts, underwear, toilet articles and a bunch of stuff. I got some of our guys and went to the Base Exchange and we bought beer, cokes, shaky-puddin', cans of spray cheese and all sorts of crackers, cookies and snacks. We loaded them in some big cardboard boxes and flew to Da Nang and I marked them for 1st Lt Hank Norman, Khe Sanh. We put them on a C-130 going there and I told the pilot that it was classified stuff. Hank's buddies thought he knew Santa Claus personally. A few days later, a mortar round hit him in the chest and killed him. He was hot and had undone his flak vest. His boss, Ken Pipes held him until he died. That was March 30, 1968 and I e-mailed Ken frequently. Hank's widow, my ex-wife's sister, requested I escort his body back and I did since Henry and I were close. He graduated North Texas in pre-dental but could not get accepted in dental school before he was to be called up. So he joined the Marines and trained as a 2nd Lt at Quantico. I was the SSO up at Newburgh, NY and got to come down to visit him a time or so.

They say the reunion next year will be in Dallas again, only in September, then maybe Las Vegas.

I drove south from Williamsburg and went thru a tunnel to get back to I-95 passing a lot of Navy stuff.

Yes, I wish I had planned it better and left sooner, I would have enjoyed meeting you all.

Regards,
Bill Person

The Editor's answer to Bill Person's e-mail about blonds, is made by me, tongue in cheek.

BLONDES
By Bill Person

From: "Bill Person"
To: Pinkflanagan@hotmail.com (Editor's different e-mail)
Date: Sun. 31 Aug 2003 09:08:48 -0500

Concentration occurs when a certain amount of energy is generated to excite a host of electrons in brain cells to jump from the orbit of one brain cell to another. And if likened to a jet engine, 75 percent of the energy generated is expended in the form of exhaust gases to drive the turban which in turn drives the compressor intake turban so only 25 percent is available to be applied to propel the craft. On that premise, if 75 percent of the energy is needed to make the minuscule electrons bounce from one orbit to others and thus carry a thought, then if a blond dreams, will it deprive her of her much needed beauty sleep? And will only 25 percent of that available energy be enough for her to even have a dream. And like the tree falling in a forest when no one is there to hear, if a mere 25 percent of energy is all that is available, will that blonde even remember it if she does dream?
Don't even think about it.
Fondly,
Bill Person

The Editor's answer to Bill, because I'm a blond and must defend all blonds, or at least certain blonds, or at least THIS blond.

BAH HA HA HA HA AH HA HA HAH. I didn't think about it. But the blond knows about the tree in the forest, no matter the % of energy. (I sure wish I'd saved some stuff on this site, but I didn't - se la vie). Instinctively, blonds drive better than any other hair color, male or female. Blonds have the innate ability to feel the gears, plus great acuity in sounds, especially if they have e.s.p. passed on through the mother. Dreaming does not affect a blond, and particularly does not rob her of her beauty sleep, however, we cannot assume this for all blonds, as no sociological study of any consequence, if any has been made atall, and without that, who in hell can compare blonds to jet engines - who would want to except some rascal Captain outta nowhere, not supposed to be there, and has some wild ass adventures being there - why outrunning whoever that pilot outran must have seemed like nada, after chasing blonds during his beauty sleep - one eye awake for the next asshole jungle devil ready to pounce upon his heaving chest which has calmed in order not to betray his whereabouts. As are pilots, so are certain blonds, crafty devils. Actually, if one studies the brain cells of any colored haired male or female, chances are that the crafty, intelligent ones are borderline bi-polarites, which comes from the voodoo nigras from way back in the south and we do not speak of Brooklyn, heah. A male can teach a blond, but she will outdo him, eventually, perhaps not in quantity, but in quality, not only in his field, but in any field she chooses to undertake. It is in the dreams that we solve our problems, particularly if one wakens and writes them down immediately - then the day starts fresh. However, if a pain in ass male is still at home, asking, how she is before she gets her eyes open, well, this keeps her from her concentration and she may have the urge to kill before that first cuppa java, or before. Take the jet engines and deal with percentages, but nevah with a woman, especially a blond who lights all types and colors of candles and can convince the most assuming engineer that he will suffer strange problems brought upon by her voodoo, if she feels the need. Belief- that is the thing, plus, for God sakes, gentlemen (women) check your engines! Unlike engines, brain cells can bring forth great information and entertainment for certain masses. Blonds don't care to bother with the minuscule, unless it is greatly needed.

Do or do not - there is no try. So take off the turban, and fart - therefore 75% of exhaust is now reduced to 25% and there's no problem.

Firmi once told me - oh, well, it's getting late - time to hit the sack.

This is SNOWBIRD WHQ2514 over and out.

Fondly,

Trish, the blond

AVATAR DAWN
By Bill Person

From: Bill Person
Sent: Saturday, December 20, 2003 7:19 AM
To: pinkflanagan@hotmail.com
Subject: Re: I may be way out of line . . .

Hey Trish,
I found it.
I answered him and told him what was taking place back then, it's in my book, "Avatar Dawn."

John Balabouhin (wrote)
G'Day Chaps,
Firstly & foremost, yes I did enjoy your website, very informative. I am in a process of researching an incident which occurred in Borneo approximately in 1964. I was on HMAS Vendetta as a stoker PO. We used to pick up British commandos from various locations Singapore and mid ocean from RN submarines, brought the commandos as close to shore as possible & dropped them off at various locations. As well, we recovered quite a number of them from shore. My question to you is, have you had any reports from your members of any recollection of human head incidences. I was picking up some of your chaps in the presence of another Petty Officer when I discovered a human head in a bag, this caused an unpleasant situation between myself & the person (British Commando) who had the human head, his remark to me was that it was going to be a present for his son (sounded ridiculous to me at the time), I threw the human head overboard which infuriated him further. Just recently during my research I was told that the British Government issued a bounty for any sympathizers who were anti-coalition forces, any truth in that?

I would like to mention a short story which also occurred a year previous to the above, HMAS Vendetta was steaming through Sunda Strait, just on dusk when an object was located on radar, the Skipper sent word to me that he required full power. I was the Stoker PO on duty in number 1 boiler room, incidentally the second boiler was shut down (that's another story). Full power is not obtainable on one boiler, by this time I got word that a surface vessel was ahead which turned out to be a whisky class Russian submarine, they were training Indonesian crews. Bear in mind that only a short time ago we had the world on its toes in fear of having a nuclear war with Russia over the Cuban missiles in 1962. Premier Nikita Khrushchev took his shoe off in the United Nations assembly and hammered the desk top to be heard without interruptions from others. Having described the general atmosphere which existed at the time, I will now focus back to the submarine issue. Normally if there is one submarine, then more likely one can assume that another one is within close proximity. Shits were trumps, by this time I had another PO flashing up the second boiler, all sorts of possibilities were imminent. I have located sufficient information regarding the Russian Submarine 512 sighted at 1830 Wednesday 24th July, 1963, from our naval archives.

As a coincidence, some twenty years earlier in approximately the same location HMAS Perth & USS Houston were sunk by the Japanese fleet. This year marks the 60th anniversary of the event. More information is available if you require it.

Please try to help me out with the head issue, I know it's a long shot, but one can never tell, research brings out the information.

All the best & Regards,

John Balabouhin

At the time I was there, '48-'49 at RAF Butterworth, the bounty was issued, usually to the Malayan police. Usually the sympathizer was caught in the jungle and it made sense to just carry the head rather than drag a body for ten miles or so. I think I was nearly in the bag once - I had been working late and rode a bicycle back to camp from the airstrip about 2 am. About a dozen armed men jumped out at me - recognized me and let me go after saying "we usually shoot first and see who we've got afterward."

SHITHOT PILOT
By Bill Person

From: Bill Person
Sent: Sunday, January 18, 2004 4:44 AM
To: pinkflanagan@hotmail.com
Subj: FW: F-14 Tomcat Ride (from jimharber@juno.com, Thursday, Jan. 15, 2004 8:41 PM)

FUN is where you find it, I guess. It looks like a lot more fun than it truly is unless you are a young shithot pilot.

I remember we were never to exceed a wings level 9 G pull out in high performance aircraft or a rolling pull out to exceed 6.5 Gs.
The wings were not stressed for that, uneven wing loading you see and they come off. The reason you sweat is that your heart has to pump harder to get blood to your head, and elsewhere, at "G-created" greater distances. G suits, when activated by air pressure when sensing G loading, acted like a giant squeeze to prevent your blood from settling down past your waist. You still have to grunt to take it above 6 Gs. They say you experience 18 Gs on ejection but you have to clear a plane doing 600+ that's about to explode. AH, but I regress. Hey, note Alcatraz off the port bow of the carrier under the Golden Gate, entering San Francisco Bay. And the Tomcat jock-scraping paint off the side of a carrier as he makes a low flyby.

Unfortunately, the photos taken of the above are not available.

Pending your approval, I, Bill Person, have decided to make the dedication: *(to the first of his books to me, says the Editor of THESE GUYS):*

To Trish Schiesser

My good comrade in letters.
Ida Reed Blanford,
My kindred spirit in adventure
And Pinknees,
For all the other reasons.
Because I love you dearly.
Enjoy this, my very first copy.

With great affection.
Bill Person.

I'd say that is a pretty darned nice dedication on the pages of his first book, and what a book!!!! "Critic Makers." I learned a lot reading that book and I suggest you "guys" go to Bill via E-mail and buy all four of his books on his life and the times during the Cold War.

THAILAND, BURMA
As sent by Bill Person with, Ray, Ghost Rider 774 and Pappy Hicks

Hi Trish,
This makes for an interesting read in the light of my books about that area. The tsunami probably wiped out a bunch of pirates in the Malacca Strait between Sumatra and Malaysia. But the mess in Thailand, Burma and the upper part of Malaysia still exists. I describe some of it in my books. I wrote Ray about the states and hill tribes I knew about in Burma.
Fondly,
Bill

Pappy,
Thailand was, to say the least, open to anything. Immigration forgot about you for the right amount of baht; same, the police. We got into quite a bit of side business, but had been warned off dealing arms. We did not have the right connections for that and it was one of the few things the Thai's were touchy about. Carrying an unlicensed 32' Browning auto, in my western boots, when just traveling or partying was never a problem. Say traveling the road from BKK to Sattahip for sun and fun wasn't all that safe. Our regular pooying wouldn't go with us because of the bandits that preyed on the roads. Girls sold into brothels along the way and people robbed/murdered along the way also. That 32' wasn't much fire power, but we never got bothered fortunately. I also heard they had pirates out in the Gulf of Thailand that took off everything, from Yachts to small freighters. Thailand was the wild, wild east for sure.
The infamous Red Dragon Bar was a hiring hall, Intel center, a place to make connections with the civilian contractors and a general hang out for the unsanctioned. Read NVMS types. Luckily I hooked up with a running partner that had taken his discharge in Thailand after RVN. He'd been there for four years when I hooked up with him and knew the customs, language and the drill for how you approach Thai authorities.
Aside from just plain hating the Chinese, the Chinese were also cutting into the Thai's black economy. They were competition and there wasn't much investigation done if one turned up dead. Shit I'm getting hungry for some Khow Phat right now. I'd love to go back there, just to visit, but I know I'd end up in some kind of shit in no time. It's a personality flaw.
All that I remember about the king was how much his people loved him. Coup of the week or not, he remained.

From what I've been hearing lately, is that Hanoi is exerting more pressure on Laos than before and appear to be almost running the country, got a take on that.

I don't now if I still have the legs, but it's about time we get around to "liberating" Burma. That's one government that could stand a good ass kicking. Screw that Myanmar crap, it is still Burma to me, like Saigon is still Saigon.

What's your take on the Free Burma Rangers? Are they just an aid group or do they have an operational side to them?

Ray   Ghost Rider 774

Ray,

I enjoyed the story.

Most people who have never been to Thailand, and some that have, do not understand what can be done in the country. And, yes, the Chinese are hated by the Thais. I don't blame them. I hate them also.

But in Thailand, after a period of time, I learned who and where I could go for info and even the people where I could buy enough equipment to set up my own army. Being who and how I worked, I had many military officials I could go to. Of course, all of those old guys are my age, retired to mountains of Laos when I was in country.

Well, hell, that was a long time ago. I still wake up thinking about the sounds and smells of the country I'm in. Usually the sound will bring back a memory faster than anything.

Sometime when I'm feeling better, I'll tell you about the plans we had in the 1990s to protect the King of Thailand if the Viets or Chinese came calling.

Pappy

Evening Pappy,

The crew I was in was a lot less sophisticated and had no connections that I knew of to any US control. What I don't know would fill volumes. Don't ask questions and don't get caught, applied. Ex Nam combat vets looking for that adrenaline they couldn't get back in the States and more money than I've ever seen. Unsanctioned as hell, but the Thai military was awfully indifferent to us. A necessary evil to keep the trade flowing and something they could not be seen getting directly involved in. Would you get paid or terminated? Keep alert, you have no friends. Secured some remote airstrips, took out small time competition and got deep into side business. Some vets I met back in the states told me who to see in BKK about work. Two weeks later and I was there. I met some active duty Spec-5's that guided to our game and after a week of "acclimatizing" in BKK, we headed North. I'd rather crash and burn in a helicopter than drive on Thai highways. Three months later and I return to BKK to stand down and party. A guy I had buddied up with was into dealing with the Chinese gangs in BKK; passports, counterfeit $20.00's and black market gold. The Thai Police did not appreciate this and although well paid off, we came back to the World Hotel one day to see two Land Rovers full of Thai Police parked in front of us. No pay-offs this time. Stop screwing with their economy and take out this Chinese hump they didn't care for or most likely go to prison for a damned long time. The Thai's really hated the Chinese gangs there. So, me and my partner find ourselves walking in from two directions of a street in the Chinese District looking for this hump at night. Not a good situation or place to be in. What happened next was weird, this one Thai cop pulls up in, I swear, a big old Plymouth that almost took up the width of the street. I'm carrying a Belgian made Browning 32' auto in my western boot and this little cop is trying to get me into the damned car. Then he hears a gunshot down the street and starts to take off in that direction, when I make my exit. Any cop made to work in the Chinese District alone must not have been in favor, but it's still bad to shoot one of them.

Another thing we'd been told was to stay out of BKK unless we were flying out of the country. The Thai's had told the FBI Liaison that they could not approach or question us, but the Feds must have taken rolls of photo's of us. My first trip over and I found my bank account frozen. The bank told me to go see immigration. Immigration told me to show up with a plane ticket out of the country within the next 24 hours and they'd unfreeze my account. I complied. The second trip over and Thai immigration kept my passport hostage and well . . . I had to go to the Chinese District for another one. This time I understood the rules better. Stay out of the cities and away from any military installation. No sweat. When we weren't doing our day job, we switched our side business to smuggling which the authorities found acceptable. Supposedly some of this illegal revenue financed the secret war. We were no secret that's for sure. I got some carnal knowledge of USAID and Heroin Airlines, but to this day have no idea who paid us. My best guess was those making the most profit, were the Thai's. All I knew was the guy running us was a Nam vet and didn't ask questions.

Ray   Ghost Rider774

These Guys

Morning gentlemen,

Thank God winter will end soon; can't live with it like I used to.

RVN is Republic of Vietnam. Those who ran covert in special operations played the "Game." Over time we learned of each other, and there were only a few. All operations are very compartmentalized. The only persons who knew my mission, or even who I was, was my Control, always a general officer, and my One-on-one. Our rules were simple. Don't get caught. We ran the Game because we could not get vital info out of the CIA or MI. You would think that their intelligence was theirs and theirs alone. We used contingency money, I worked and still had my "Day Job," and it was hell at the time. I would go on a TDY and the old man would ask me where I was going. He reminded me that he wrote my report card. HA! One asshole kept pushing me, so I told him the truth. "It's on a need to know basis, sir, and you don't need to know." Went over like a broken tie rope on a bull ride or a parachute that lost its canopy.

The Game was a hell of a run, if you survived. Disease and being slapped around in fights with the enemy usually took its toll. I was lucky and survived the Game. I was always ready to go on any operation, no matter where it was. Control and One-on-one was having a meeting and Control commented that I went, I did my job and I always returned. He asked if I would even run an ops to Antarctica. I told him that I did not wish to capture, interrogate nor kill a damned penguin. He and One-on-one had a good laugh. I thought it was a pretty smart answer. They knew how much I hated cold weather. It got cold in the mountains of Laos, but not ice and snow.

I was wounded in the left side of my neck and left shoulder in Vietnam near the Cambodian border in February 1961. The CIA operative and the Aussie MI man brought me back to Ban Me Thuot. They couldn't keep me there. All they could find leaving was an old DC-3 heading for Bangkok. They put me on board with my little hand bag and off I went, neck in a bandage. Only trouble was, I would have a hell of a time getting out of Thailand. I had no papers; my blue and red passports were left behind and held by Control, so. . . .

Anyway, I was taken to the Seven Day Adventist Hospital in Bangkok. They did not like soldiers, but they liked the money the USG gave them for taking care of our men back then. They did a good job on me, in fact. I was sitting on a gurney when a man walked in, handed me a bottle of Jack Daniel's in a bag. I knew I was in good hands. Then he told me my code name. I told him that I didn't have any papers to get out of Thailand. He told me that was

his mission. I later learned that he was Jack Shirley, CIA and worked that area, all the way over to Laos. He worked with an old friend, Vang Pao. In fact he was back from Laos to the US Embassy, Bangkok on business when he got the call to pick me up and take me to the airport. I had no idea who had brought me to the hospital. I flew back to Bragg, nursing that bottle of Jack until it was empty. My Control picked me up at Pope and drove me over to the Womach Hospital on Bragg that night. The doctor told us that whoever worked on me did a good job. He wrote me up as having a growth removed from my neck and shoulder. Unlike Kerry, I didn't get a Purple Heart. Why? Simple; I wasn't even there. I don't think he could have played the Game. I would have gone, found him and killed the sonofabitch.
Enough of my crap.
Hang tuff,
Pappy

Pappy,
One thing you wrote here stands out. I never heard the word in RVN, when I was active duty, but heard the phrase "the game" for the first time in Thailand, as a civilian. Hell of a game. Few rules, but don't break them.
Ray   Ghost Rider 774

These Guys

To: Person Bill; Sadler Deryl; Ray Hoagland
Sent: Thursday, February 10, 2002 6:51 AM
Subject: Cambodia

Bill, Ray and Deryl,
A lot of things have been surfacing the past few years about Cambodia, mainly because of the Montagnards.
A friend said he found this article that was written a few years ago. The MAJ Carl Bernard is COL Carl Bernard, US (RET), who now lives in Virginia just out of DC. A great soldier, we have been friends for a number of years. The UK Pappy is yours truly.
The last time I was in Southeast Asia was when I went with General Vang Pao in 1987. Five days after I returned, our youngest son, Ty, 18 years old, had a wreck, and wound up with a closed head injury and was in a coma for two and a half months. It took about three years of much therapy to get him back on his feet and operating some. Of course, Little Margie shut me down of going back to Central America where I worked with the Nicaraguan Indians against the communist Sandinista, or from going over seas anywhere for any reason. She said after 40 years it was time for me to stop. It was the first time she has ever questioned me about my running in the "game." The article is on site: http://www.worldnetdaily.com/news/article.asp?ARTICLE_ID=19063.
The reporter is a guy LoBaido, who spends most of his time in Southeast Asia. After I got back from Southeast Asia with Vang Pao, LoBaido collared Carl and I in Washington, DC and said he had heard about his and my involvement with Vang Pao in the old days in Laos and of my last trip with VP. This article he wrote wrong in many ways, what article isn't screwed up, the US was giving aid to pro-Western Cambodians, not Pol Pot, and I did try to find three plane loads of equipment that had disappeared in Thailand. Well, well, is that really a possibility? But he had some of this pegged right. That SAS man was telling about my story of the frag vest given to the Cambodians and their attack from Thailand against the Vietnamese inside Cambodia.
Hang tuff,
Pappy (A lot of back slapping crap.)

SENSORS GO TO WAR
By Bill Person

From: Bill Person
To: Clara19126@msn.com
Sent: Friday, October 14, 2005 2:45 PM
Subject: RE: BATCATS: Sensors go to war

Hi Trish,
Here's the updated version.
Fondly,
Bill

Just read your story about the above on USAFSS Lite. It's quite a good one. I am considering using it in THESE GUYS.
Fondly, sending from Seattle, Lake Union - Trish

BATCATS: SENSORS GO TO WAR
(By Bill Person)

The Air Force had purchased 30 converted Navy Willie Victors to use in a McNamara Priority One Project called a lot of names. Many are not listed here and rightfully so. In early 1967, nine college professors were invited to a Pentagon funded Think Tank. Their objective was to devise a plan to "Impede the flow of men and materials down the Ho Chi Minh Trail." America, regardless of Robert Strange McNamara's insistence to President Johnson, was not winning the minds and hearts of the Vietnamese people in the south. The other part of that was to destroy the will of the people in North Vietnam to support a war in the south.
The supreme Perfumed Prince, General William C. Westmorland was not "being all you can be" Army's idea in the Vietnam War. Operation Rolling Thunder, originally intended to last only a few weeks, was still in progress. The Rules of Engagement that prohibited actually inflicting injury to North Vietnam, served to stir the people against us, not dishearten them as Secretary of Defense RSM claimed. It was an inconvenience rather than being outright destructive. Each time the president called for a 'cease fire,' North Vietnam used that time to succor and strengthen their defensive positions.

The nine professors did propose a cheap method, a relative term for merely a billion tax dollars, of 'impeding' Hanoi's waging a war against South Vietnam. Their recommendation was to use surplus Navy C-121 Super Constellations as an airborne platform to detect movement with sensors that were seeded along the trail in the Laotian panhandle. This was dubbed "College None" for the Think Tank authors. Their recommendations included the use of modifying radio receivers, ARR-52s, with submarine sonobuoys also modified as sensors, all in house available items. This was renamed "Practice None" and ordered into R & D. Apparently the Pentagon knew that because LBJ was not going to employ their plan to bomb ninety-four strategic targets within three weeks of the real Rolling Thunder, McNamara convinced LBJ not to focus on an outright total devastation type bombing of North Vietnam, but rather hit more inoffensive obscure targets with the intent of demonstrating our capability. It failed of course and the Pentagon did not bother to use "halt" because that was not a possibility, 'impede' was. By June 1967, the Defense Communications Planning Group, DCPG, an offshoot of Navy at Washington, took charge and initiated testing and developing now dubbed "Muscle Shoals" and "Dune Moon." Forty-one crews were amassed, processed and training commenced along with testing. A huge Air Defense type blockhouse was constructed at Nakhon Phanom along with four massive rotating frame-work type dish antennas on derrick mounts. The 553rd Reconnaissance Wing with its two Squadrons, the 553rd and 554th deployed to Korat (Nakhon Ratchasima) Royal Thai Air Base, Thailand before the end of the year. A crew consisted of nineteen members, an aircraft commander, a co-pilot, two navigators, an electronics warfare officer, EWO, two flight engineers, a radio operator, a Combat Information Control Officer, eight Combat Information Monitors and two electronics technicians. A plexiglass plotting board was positioned across the aisle from the CHICO's position in the back.

As the CAMS called in "hits" on their radios, indicating activity down on the ground, this movement was plotted on the board. The CHICO had an encrypted radio, an ARC-109 with a KY-8 paddle set scrambler to communicate with other BATCATS aircraft and Task Force Alpha at Nakhon Phanom. The CHICO panel also had other UHF, VHF and HF radio capabilities. The plane employed, in addition to the CAMS, who were considered as merely backup, an "X" band transmitter to relay all the sensor beeps on the NKP. At TA's blockhouse (Task Force Alpha or as we called it, "Task Farce Awful"), giant computers processed the signals and plotted them on a printer. Once a truck convoy was determined, as programmed by the computer, a report was generated. TFA was staffed by civilians, highly over paid, tax-deferred who sent off a "Spotlight Report." TFA members had gone to 7th AF and most of the bases, 7/13th AF at Udorn to sell the importance of these reports. The Airborne Communications and Combat Control ship, ABCCC maintained two orbits in the Laos panhandle around the clock. "Cricket" day and "Allycat" night flew "Barrel Roll" and "Hillsboro" day and "Moonbeam" night in the south part. Forward Air Controllers, FACs were assigned a sector and when they had targets, ABCCC sent them fighters to strike them.

The computer at NKP, Nahon Phanom (Naked Phanny) was programmed to detect movement of trucks going past a string of four sensors placed along a road on the Ho Chi Minh Trail. TFA erroneously thought truck convoys formed up at Hanoi and drove down close to Saigon much like back in the states. In fact, it was a shuttle/relay type of supply system designed to dodge our ever-watchful eyes of FACs and bomb-laden jets. Sold on the importance of "Spotlights," ABCCCs sent FACs to check on these high priority targets. But, as it turned out, the trucks never responded as TFA's computers thought. When the FAC got to the predicted location indicated in the "Spotlight," nothing was there. The trucks had pulled-up and stopped or else turned off the road in a covered area, but did not get to the place predicted by TFA. After a while, ABCCCs and FACs stopped responding to the urgent "Spotlight" messages. Again, TFA would make the rounds selling the importance of their highly prized "Spotlights." I knew about this and back during the middle of January 1968, I punched in the illuminated on/off button to listen in on one of our Accubuoy (acoustic/sonic) sensors. I heard the unmistakable squeaking buttons sounds of a tracked vehicle moving down the road. Curious, I began to punch buttons to hear several more of these tracked vehicles. I consulted the detailed map of the area to see that a lot of bomb craters were blown in that section of Route 9 of the trail. These vehicles were going around them and proceeding on down the trail. This old Texas boy knew the sounds of a bulldozer from growing up in the oil patch and also in ranch and farm country. The powerful diesel engine is set at a high rev. while the gears are changed to move back and forth while working the blade to do the dirt moving work. This was not the case here and I heard more and more of the tracked vehicles move down the trail in a widely spread spacing. I kept notes and when I got back to Korat, I insisted our Operations Center fire off a message reporting tanks moving down the trail towards South Vietnam. I will never forget the enthusiasm I generated at the newly constructed 553rd RCW Ops Center when we sent out that message and waited for an answer. In fact, I had served in the additional duty special project as Wing Beautification Officer. I had driven one of our pick-up trucks into Korat and instructed some airmen with me to dig up banana plants and a bunch of other flora to plant around the new headquarters buildings. I suppose that I was thought of as something special by ranking members of my fellow Batcats. When the message came in from PACAF and 7th AF at Ton Son Nhut, it stated that Air Force estimates did not assess NVA with possessing tanks. It went on to suggest what I had heard might have been bulldozers doing repair work on bomb craters on the trail. I fumed and exclaimed that this Texas boy sure as hell knew what a bulldozer sounded like, and these were damn sure tanks. I had served as Queen Bee Delta Project Officer from March to May 1965 and oversaw the monitoring of communications of North Vietnam at the start of Rolling Thunder.

I knew that the enemy had no air defense capabilities when we started bombing low grade and ineffective targets, contrary to JCS recommendations. As our target selection was raised, so were Hanoi's capabilities to defend against us. I had served as the SNO to Eastern CONAD/NORAD Region at Stewart AFB, New York, and had seen the CIA report and briefed the general on how the Soviets were paying 100,000 Chinese Coolies with shovels to fill in bomb craters along the Ho Chi Minh Trail. Obviously the bulldozers and other support personnel could not keep up with the inflicted damage to keep the re-supply route open. So, in the mindset of AF intelligence, it was logical that the sounds I heard were a bulldozer, not a tank.

A little more than a week later, on February 7, 1968, the Special Forces camp at Lang Vei reported tanks. David "Bulldog" Smith was the commander there at the time. As a matter of fact, it was at 0035 hours, Sergeant Nikolas Fragos the Tactical Observations Center tower reported, "They've got tanks!" He went on to say, "I don't know how many, but they have tanks out there!" Captain Frank C. Willoughby asked, "Where the hell are they?" "We have two tanks in our wire!" Fragos shouted. An unknown station then added, "We've got five tanks in line right at our wire!" Then the same voice said, "We've got tanks inside our wire - I said inside our wire!"

When our headquarters did acknowledge this fact, they said that these were 11 Soviet-built PT-76 amphibious type armored vehicles, not tanks. Whatever they were, they sure as hell kicked the shit out of our Army Special Forces at Lang Vei and then moved against the Marines at KH San. That was the start of the infamous Tet Offensive and the 77 day siege of KH San. My brother-in-law, Marine 1st Lt Marion Henry (Hank) Norman was killed there on March 29th. Hank was the FO to B Company, lst Division, 26th Marines. An FO or Forward Observer is a trained artillery director that is the liaison between his unit and the big guns. Because of the technicality, headquarters never admitted to my correct assessment about tanks, not bulldozers. I did read about the PT-76 not being a tank, but an amphibious armored tracked vehicle. I seriously doubt the Special Forces at Lang Vei appreciated that distinction.

At some time later, while flying up near the DMZ, I was watching the lights go on and off on the CHICO panel display and checking the activity on the plotting board, against the area map, I noticed that a truck with a rather loud exhaust, and running in low gear at high rev would go past some of the sensors but never get to the fourth one in a string of four. Then, a bit later, it went back north again. This was just south of the Ben Hai River on our Blue Orbit, which was up near the DMZ and above the Rock Pile and Con Thien, all just south of the river.

I began to observe a repeating event of the truck and I just employed my old Security Service creative thinking process. It occurred to me that this was where the NVA brought supplies and ammo down the coast on Route 1 to the DMZ, then west to a point where their sampans ferried the stuff across the Ben Hai River. I managed to imagine that there were storage parks on both sides of the river. Running south a short way, the road had a spur back to the west and I imagined that there under a grove of trees, was another, a third ammo dump.

I got the timing down for the repeating trips of the truck and then called ABCCC. This time, I wasn't going to leave such an important discovery up to some weenie up the chain of command. I knew damned well TFA would want their computer to make the call about its 'target worthiness' and nothing would ever be done. The TAC Air fighters were fussing to find them targets before they ran out of fuel and had to drop their bombs in a safe area to then be detonated by ground ordnance techs. They wanted 'counters' for their bombs with real BDA (bomb damage assessment). The ABCCC answered and I asked him if he could go secure voice with me on a discrete freq. He said he could and we made contact via scrambler on a different frequency from TFA. I didn't want them to hear me. I told Moonbeam about my suspicions and that I had heard the jet jocks screaming for targets, not wanting to drop their ordnance on a harmless disposal area. They were running low on fuel and wanted the mission to count for something. The EC-130 ABCCC controller probably was surprised to hear from another aluminum cloud like me, up there crowding the 'friendly skies of SEA' but he was so desperate for good target info he'd probably have talked to anyone. I gave Moonbeam the coordinates and he sent Covey in to check it out. I had timed it so the truck would be back at the river taking on another load. Covey, A FAC, spotted what he thought might be something under some trees.

He marked it with a Mighty Mite smoke rocket and two Ubon-based F4Cs were cleared in hot. Luckily, they were spread and Two barely veered off because Lead's bombs set the entire grove off in a tremendous series of explosions. I could hear him on the other clear tactical frequency.

"My God, watch it, Two! Looks like the whole world blew up!" Lead shouted. Two broke it off and barely missed the billowing fireball. Moonbeam got a BDA, bomb damage assessment of an estimated 270 secondary explosions from that ammo dump. ABCCC relayed, as I heard also, a call for another target like that one. I gave him the location I was sure was the place where the truck might be loading up again. I checked myself in telling Moonbeam that I could hear the explosions on several acoustic sensors on the ground but I was afraid he might relay that and compromise our mission. It was frustrating to be the cause of what must have been a brilliant fireworks display down there and not see it. I was in the darkened back end of a Super Connie boring holes in the sky and back where it made no difference if it was daylight or dark outside. This time, Covey marked it and F4C Two, the wingman delivered his load. (Two Hundred Seventy was a number they used when it happened too quickly and was too many to count).

"BOOM!" another estimated 270 secondaries, and probably a truck to boot. From the illumination of the explosions, the FAC could see activity across the river. A bunch of the tiny square green lights on the CHICO panel lit up also. The area across the river was called Tally Ho, Route Pack One. When Covey swooped over to mark it with another Mighty Mite white phosphorus smoke rocket, he accidentally hit and ignited that ammo supply dump himself. The next two F-4Cs from Ubon had already been cleared down to their perch for a strike but when their target erupted in fire and explosions, they were cleared in to make road cuts along the access road east of there where Route 1 joined that position. They hoped to bag a supply-laden truck but nothing spectacular was detected by Covey as he orbited nearby to check it out; just some nice bombs exploding on the jungle road that evening.

Needless to say, Moonbeam and a bunch of jet jocks got all highly enthused about the Batcats from Korat. However, like all good wars, fun is the first casualty. TA also learned of this inter-unit unauthorized communication cooperation and all future such direct contact with ABCCCs was prohibited. I tried it directly with FACs and jet jocks too, but that too, was banned. So, it was back to ignoring Spotlight reports, gaining a term for a Lamar Cranston, or the Shadow Reports. If anybody was going to take any bows, it had to be Task Farce Awful, OOPS, Task Force Alpha.

I did get a chance to officially pose the question, "Since the TA complex was just across the Me Kong from Thakhet, Laos, a known VC rife town, and in range for a mortar barrage, who would serve as back-up to TA? TA proudly announced a planned solution. They were simply going to build another complex down south of there on the Me Kong, maybe near Ubon. That never happened, thankfully.

They say, never stand too close behind a high-ranking civilian, (military officer either). You might get beat to death when he pats himself on the back. I had the distinctive honor of learning that lesson anew when I returned to the states in September 1968. I had been directed to personally brief President Johnson when I got to the Ft. Meade area.

I called the number I was given back at Korat and was directed to a rather plain Army office to wait. When LBJ arrived, he wanted to know how the sensor program was working and I told him, great, if you let the Air Force handle it and send the Task Force Alpha civilian jokers home. I tried to explain that their approach was not geared for tactical combat, but they wanted us to try to make it work anyway. I told him that it was just pissing off the jet jocks and wasting a lot of ordnance busting trees back in the "Enemy Friendly War," as the pilots were calling it. Up until then, I thought it was LBJ's advisors who were 'ruining' the war but my disappointment came when I discovered that it was the big Texan himself as well as "Number-cruncher" McNamara.   I don't think LBJ liked my answer and I suspect he had friends in "high pay, show places." He never understood the war he had inherited from FDR and each ensuing president before him. Franklin promised Stalin that this U.S. would not go to war with Russia over any country west of Japan as a condition to entering the war against Japan. We didn't, but the Soviets killed a lot more Americans than anyone will ever admit, war or not. That was America's price for saving lives by letting Russia capture and occupy Berlin, East Germany, Poland, Czechoslovakia, Romania, Albania, Yugoslavia and Hungary, and for entering the war against Japan on the day we dropped the second atomic bomb. The Russians held us to our promises but they reneged on some of theirs. Guess they were better at détente than we were.

\# \# \#

These Guys

This is a rough draft of a piece of a book entitled:
BATCATS: SENSORS GO TO WAR #2
By Bill Person

Otis Air Force Base is located on the wind-swept lowlands of Cape Cod amid scraggly, short pines that look like a poorly tended nursery for a forest-to-be. A victim of the Cold War's cut back, the "Mole Hole," as it was called, had been a ready room for Strategic Air Commands KC-135 tankers, but now it was to be the Operations building for the newly formed 553rd Reconnaissance Wing. I was the SNO at Stewart and got classified messages in to brief Major General Gordon H. Austin about the progress. He was the CO to Eastern NORAD/CONAD Region and 26th Air Division at Newburgh, NY. We flew over in his T-39 Saberliner to check on things and I asked to join the 553rd over his hesitations.

College Nine was the codename for the nine college professors in the think tank who came up with the project. Practice Nine-codename for the antifiltration project using sensors and it was implemented by the White House in National Security Action Memorandum No. 358 on January 13, 1967. The Subject: "Assignment of the Highest National Priority to the Mk 84, Mod 1 2000 lb Bomb and to Project PRACTICE NINE. (This was first used for the MANHATTAN PROJECT, the development of the atom bomb.) It was changed to Illinois City on June 14, 1967. Then again to DYE MARKER on July 14, 1967. MUSCLE SHOALS was the new codename on September 3, 1967. Then once in place in SEA in December 1967, as a part of Task Force Alpha, a mostly civilian outfit at Nakhon Phanom, it finally named IGLOO WHITE in June 1968.

John's Pond was where we had water survival. We had to wear life preservers and swim out to a big doughnut life boat. I got a leg cramp but could not do anything about it so I limped around for a couple of days with a sore, strained right calf muscle.

ESD/MITRE (Electronic Systems Development/Massachusetts Institute of Technology for Research in Electronics) was involved in sensor development. Vitro Services handled the field installation of sensors at Eglin AFB, Florida. Defense Communications Planning Group, DCPG moved into the Navy bldg at DC. I later got them to let us use their fund account for our TDY expenses for Ignition Switch. Ignition Switch was the codename for the testing phase of newer sensors and equipment.

Rooftop trainer played tapes that simulated sensor activations to train CAMS on their 8 ARR-52s at their consoles. It had been called Music Box down in Florida when it was used for test purposes at Eglin.

Button bomblets washed ashore at Ft. Walton beach and the press reported that it was a fireworks prank. These little button bomblets were seeded along trails to make sure the acoustic sensors were activated. They did not necessarily activate seismic sensors but made the walkers go where the sensors worked. We also had iron half moon shaped mines that were placed along side the trails. These were called Dragonteeth and would blow off a truck tire or a foot if stepped on.

These Guys

Apparently there is a photo involved in these e-mails, but I never got them, so know that what is written here is being referred to as a S&W 38' Special.

AS SENT TO ME BY BILL PERSON
FW: RE: E-MAILING: S&W 38' SPECIAL

More commo from my grunt buddies,
Fond Regards, BILL
By Pappy Hicks and Ray Hoagland

From Pappy:
Damn if that pistol doesn't look like a S&W 1917 .45 cambered for a .38 special. I've got to get my "Small Arms of the World" book back from my son. By the way, if you want to kill somebody far, far away, get a 1918A2 BAR. Now, that will do the job. Had one in Korea and didn't know a damned thing about it. Squad Leader said, "Here it is, Cowboy, now shoot that sonofabitch." I learned to take that thing apart in the middle of the night, ChiCom bugles blowing and whistles sounding over and bullets cracking over my head. I didn't know until then that you had to put the buffers in a certain way down the stock of the rifle to get it to fire properly. I was more worried about the Platoon Sergeant who crawled over to my hole, cussing and ready to kick my ass than I was the ChiCom. But I got it straightened out. Next, the Platoon Sergeant told me that since I would stand and fight in my hole, he made me Assistant Squad Leader of the 1919A4 Caliber .30 Machine gun Squad. I learned to shoot far, far away with the thing too. The Company Commander kept getting pissed off because I could use those tracers to hit the ChiCom commo trenches across from us. It pissed them off, which I wanted to do after killing some of them. I was in that squad until I rotated back to the States. We didn't call it "the World" back then. Just to the States.
Pappy

E-MAIL FROM RAY HOAGLAND TO PAPPY
I don't remember if it was a 38' special or not, but despite having some barrel it was an inaccurate piece of aging crap. I have no doubt they could have been made in 1917. They did look good on us in the photos, but didn't impress the VC I'm sure. With the M-60's I had an understanding with our armorer. I am one crazy mutherfucker and you will repair, machine and trick

out this weapon for me. He got my drift. I think the higher cyclic that we got out of it from being "tricked out" may have something to do with me missing my left eye, but that was also due to a worn barrel I was cowboying to, (set to fire faster.)
One thing in common Pappy and that's using the tracers to target instead of the sights. Try hitting something with the sights from a moving helo and you'll just end up with eye strain. On target by the second tracer or you needed to find another job.

I once saw 2 ARVN's carrying a BAR near Pleiku. I guess it took both of them to hump that thing, but would have only taken one VC to pack it. I had nothing but bad experiences with ARVN up to having to throw them off the bird on hot CA's. The Yards fought and have my respect, but the ARVN was as bad as the enemy.

I would really love to try a BAR. I think they're in the .30 .06, 7.62 range of calibers but have never fired one. How does it fire hand held? - recoil, ride and accuracy. I would like to see a larger clip on them, but have no doubt they were a fine weapon.

Korea and Nam were two very different wars. In Korea you had the ChiComs trying to come down your throat and in Nam we had to go out and find the bastards. Fortunately, we had some sharp LRRP's that found them, then we made the house call. In 68'-69' the VC were eating it bad from us. A shitload of assault help companies - Infantry, Arty and those fun-loving Greenies. I can only imagine what those mass charges from the ChiComs were like. We only had sappers and probes. The VC in the AO knew our Snakes (Cobra's) and Charlie model gun ships were on hot start and would be on them in under 10 minutes, so they didn't get too bold around Camp Holloway. Mostly rockets and mortar attacks and not too accurate ones either. Camps Carrol and Holloway were up near the DMZ and attacked in February 1965 when LBJ decided to start Rolling Thunder.)

The caption on the picture sent with e-mail: This is the S&W 38' flight revolver setting on the deck of my bird. Col. Bill Fraker may care to comment on how we got issued this paper weight instead of the 45'.
Ray - Ghost Rider 774

From Pappy to Ray

When it comes to the 1919A Machine gun and the M-60 there are things I like about both. One thing for damned sure, I like the .30.06 caliber over the 7.62mm. It shoots further and it hits harder. I don't know why in the hell the US went to the NATO round. Let 'em all borrow ammo from us and leave us to hell alone. Reckon some colonel wanted to make general or some general wanted recognition he couldn't get as a leader. But the 60 was an improvement for the gunner. I do like the idea of a quick twist to get that barrel off. It is one hell of a job when in a firefight to pull the barrel from a 1919 at night. You had to take a cartridge and turn the driving spring rod to release the tension. You lifted up on the pistol grip to lift off the back plate. This allowed you to take out the guts of the gun and get to barrel extension. It was as hot as the barrel. Most of us "stole" extra barrel extensions so we could have a barrel attached with head space. All we had to do was, clip that sucker to the lock frame spacer, put the rest of the guts together, and start firing again. Damn! It got kinda scary at the time, especially when you had to kick the shit out of the man in your hole to get him to do his part.

The BAR! I had a couple of Montagnards in my teams who loved that weapon. Of course they took off the bipod and flash from the barrel. It still weighed over 16 pounds. But hell, if a guy can't carry a BAR, he don't need to be in the infantry. Maybe even in the god damned army. None of my men full fired any automatic weapon. That was a no, no. Aim at a target and then shoot the sonofabitch. It was fired full out when used for covering fire.

I had one man who was a wizard with the old M3A1 "Greasegun." It was a great weapon at short range and especially when in a VC or NVA safe house; unsafe, that house. He had a suppressor and would walk up to a bed and pop off one round shots. Now I didn't do shit like that. I am an honorable army officer and don't kill the enemy in his sleep.

Old fashioned, I like most of the old weapons. They were made to kill people, not scare them. A scared man will come back to kill you.
Pappy

From Ray to Pappy

We never did the spray and pray bullshit, but coming in the first flight of a CA, when none of our people were on the ground yet, we did spray to keep their heads down coming in. Once closing on the LZ we would use direct fire and target the movers. We were always doing the in and out and stayed on the trigger until we were out of the fire and had some air under our ass. Same if we were picking up a team under fire. If they were heading towards my door that 60' was all the close air support they had. I'm sure it was a lot different working one on the ground. At the time mine went up in my face we had no new barrels in the whole damned company and no spares either. Someone in supply needed fragging. There was supposed to be protective gloves for us to change barrels with, but I never saw one. We wore flight gloves and would cut up a piece of canvas for changing a hot barrel. Even the release lever would burn through a flight glove.

They still had the .30.06 1919A4, BAR and grease guns when I was in Nam in 68'-69', but they were few and mostly given to ARVN or just left over from WWII. I remember my second CO mounting a 50' Browning in a Slick and going out hunting along the rivers one night; a Slick with a bank of lights out front, him behind and looking to get some. I know nothing about the 50' and apparently neither did he. Reportedly he would only get off one shot, double cock it and get off only one shot again. Read abort. I heard something about having to time the barrel on a 50' or at least put in the proper way. What can I say, we were aviation, not 11 Bravo. I think every assault helo outfit tried a 50' at one time. First, your ass was sticking out one door and the barrel out the other so you couldn't really see anything unless the AC had it on one hell of a bank. Second it would shake the bird like mad and send hot brass at everybody aboard.

I saw what, I, believe to have been an SAR team in Thailand that had MAC-10's or the like with suppressors, but in Nam only the SF's had them.

I'm with you. Shit can the 9 mm for the .45, .30.06 instead of the 7.62 and my personal desire is to sell the M-16 to our enemy's. The US can design a better weapon or at least buy German steel. I wasn't that surprised that they went to the 9mm because of the NATO shit, but buying Italian designed weapons? I have nothing against Italians, but they are not known for winning wars. I wonder how that deal got through the DoD; probably a lowest bidder thing. Now what is this thing about a "buffer" in a BAR. I have no doubt you were an honorable Army officer and am sure you would have wakened the hump up first before doing his ass. Sure.
Ray Ghost Rider 774

These Guys

From Pappy to Ray
A buffer tube ran from the bolt link down the stock of a BAR. Inside the buffer tube was a spring, also other springs called buffer springs, a lot of other crap, and a buffer head. I'm sure I don't have all of it, but all of this gave some recoil resistance to the pounding of the .30.06 we were firing. I've forgotten a lot about the BAR. I did show my Montagnards and ARVN how to use it.

I'm well known to have carried and left many Gurkha knives in the Central Highlands. Like my weapons, I want something to take a head off or split his belly open so things will fall to the ground before he does. Use a Gurkha kukri or a big Bowie. I prefer the kukri.
Pappy

From Ray to Pappy
First let me qualify this for my first CO, Bill Fraker. It was Major Morrison that followed him in command of the 189th AHC that flew gunner that night with the 50' Browning. Bill saw Morrison as a bit of a loose cannon from the gate and he did have some off moments (like with the 50'), but he was a real cowboy and we liked that about him. Anyway Pappy, that's what we heard when they got back. Something about the barrel not being timed and Morrison being much more pilot than gunner. Fuck, a gunner would have asked the armorer how to operate it! Doctors think they are pilots and pilots think they are gunners. You get my drift.
Ray Ghost Rider 774

Ray to Pappy
I've always assumed that BAR had a kick to it. In the Slick's we had the 60's mounted on a post because sometimes we had to get out on the skid and pull people in, etc. On a post, restricted you in a way, but mostly gave you a solid platform to shoot from; hence more accuracy.

We had an M-16 that we carried under our seats if we went down, as the aerial version of the mounted M-60' wasn't worth a damned hand held on the ground. With it came the M-16 bayonet. You know, the one you couldn't sharpen regardless of what you did! We all had issue switch blades like the Airborne guys carried I guess. These were for cutting ropes on guys that got hung up on trees on rappel, to cutting of the safety straps on our pilots after a crash. No fighting knife, but sharper than that bayonet.

As you know they sold all kinds of switch blades in Thailand, mostly to the R&R types and tourists. Mine was custom made with a teak handle. I must admit that I never killed any enemy with it, but did take out a Thai taxi driver that tried to set us up back in BKK. I've seen a lot of the fighting knives used by Spec-Ops types in books. You guys could get anything (and usually did), but I just like that big old Ka-bar. I'm sure having the technique to use it is better than having just pure meanness, but whatever it takes to be the one that walks away is all I need.

The Central Highlands; my first AO; it's not only the place where I became a man, but the place I feel my life started in. Staging at Duc Co, waiting for the load and go.
Ray Ghost Rider 774

These Guys

This is an e-mail from Bill Person, who served in the USAFSS during the cold war, who forwards a great story.

I DROVE A TRUCK - By Richard Jarrett

A good 'un!
It says - author unknown but there's a name at the bottom.
Bill Person

This is a funny story I received from my ex-CO. Jose could probably appreciate it. It may start out serious, but goes south real quick.
I think that the following is pretty humorous. Have a great Veteran's Day (Nov. 12, 2004) and stay healthy.

"I Drove a Truck . . . You got a problem with that?"
-author unknown

Recently I have been force feeding myself the book: "Stolen Valor," by B.G. Burkett and Glenna Whitley. I recommend it - with some reservations.

Mr. Burkett did a thorough ten year investigation of phonies and "wannabe" veterans who have surfaced since the end of the Vietnam War. Or, to be more precise, since it is now "ok," even "in," to say that you served in Vietnam. He has exposed phony Veterans in politics, show business, and everyday life. People who have the so called "Secret Discharges," or who cannot produce a DD-214, because everything they did was all very 'hush, hush.' These guys have medals that they can't verify, because they were awarded them for "Black Ops," or "SOG Activities." Of course all of these phonies were SEALs, or Special Forces. Back before most people knew about the SEALs, most people lying about their Navy experiences would tell you that they were in Riverboats, or Swift Boats. I have, for years, said that only about 800 SEALs served in Vietnam . . . and I have met ALL 2000 of them.
Now to the meat of the subject; Mr. Burkett repeats, several times in his book, that most Veterans who lie about their Vietnam experiences were probably "truck drivers," or "cooks" or "clerks." Now, if I was a cook, or a clerk, or a First Sergeant, or a lieutenant, I may tend to stretch what I did in Vietnam. But, dammit . . . I WAS a truck driver!

Why does he keep throwing us truck drivers in with that undesirable element who lie about what they did in Vietnam? I drove my truck through the jungle, paddies, sand flats and villages. Over the Hi Van Pass and into Arizona Territory. One eye on the road the other on the tree line. Talking on the radio, shooting my M-16 through the raised windshield, swinging a machete out the window and changing gears with my feet, all while opening a can of Ham and Lima beans and drinking a warm Ballentine beer. Then I'd get back to the rear, stand Guard duty all night and start it all over the next day. On top of all this, as near as I can figure, I was the only truck driver in Vietnam in '68 and '69.

So, you can imagine the burden I had to carry. I thought that I saw other truck drivers while I was there, but I must have been mistaken. You think with all this, people would be "exaggerating" what they did in Vietnam by saying stuff like: "I drove a truck for the Special Forces, or the SEALs." Or, "My favorite truck got blown up on a SOG, LRRP mission. I loved that truck man. I'll never forget the day they towed her down to salvage. I stayed drunk for a week."

Or, how about: "I had a top secret driver's license."

Whatever you did in Vietnam, the fact that you went should be enough to instill self pride, just as much as having served elsewhere would. I mean after all . . . "We couldn't all be truck drivers!!"

Richard S. Jarrett
4242 N. Capistrano Drive
Apt 146
Dallas, Texas 75287

These Guys

Received this bit of juicy material from Captain Bill Person, USAFSS (Ret.) Subject: FW: TLC-Mission: FROM COL. JIM BUTLER

Hey Jim, Thought you'd like this. Bet Toby Hughes knows him, living so close by. Regards, Bill Person.

COL. RALPH PARR: A fighter pilot's fighter pilot.
A veteran of three wars with 641 combat missions, an Air Force Cross and 10 DFC's.

By Bob Hieronymus Wingspread staff writer
In the book, "Army Flier", Gen. Ira Eaker wrote:

ARMY FLIER
By Gen. Ira Eaker

"The fighter pilot is a throw-back to the knights of King Arthur; his safety, his success, and his survival, lie in his own keen eyes, steady arm, and stout heart." This is the story of one fighter pilot who embodies that description.

"I was 5 years old when my dad, who was a Navy pilot in Manila, strapped me on his lap in an observation plane. When we were airborne he told me to grab hold of the stick and I 'flew' that plane for a few minutes. I was hooked. All I wanted to do from then on was, fly."

Col. Ralph Parr told the story with a chuckle, the way he's told it a thousand times. At 81 years of age, he has lots of stories to tell and he enjoys the retelling. His eyes sparkle as he talks about flying his favorite airplanes; the P-38, F-86 and F-4, although he has flown many others along the way. Among his many assignments, Colonel Parr was commander of the 12th Tactical Fighter Wing in Vietnam, before the wing relocated here in 1972. His military flying stories begin in 1942 when he finished high school and signed up for aviation cadet training. He pinned on his second lieutenants bars and wings in February 1944 at the age of 19 and landed a slot in a P-38 squadron. He didn't get into a combat unit until the last two months of the war in the Pacific. The Japanese Air Force was pretty well done in by then, he said, but he did fly over both Hiroshima and Nagasaki while they were still smoking from the atomic bombs.

He recalled one mission in his P-38 when a leak in the carburetor of one engine was siphoning gas out into the slipstream. He was losing fuel fast but he had to keep up with his flight or wing - it alone across hundreds of miles of open ocean and possibly ditch the aircraft at sea. He tried some unusual engine manifold pressure and throttle adjustments Charles Lindbergh had described in a conversation with him a couple months before and managed to keep up with his flight. As he approached his home base, the tower told him to go around again because some transport aircraft were in the pattern. "I told the tower to clear them out of the way," he said. "I'm coming straight in!" He rolled onto the parking ramp with only five gallons left in his fuel tanks. Afterward he shared his fuel tanks with his squadron and the technique became a standard operating procedure.

He flew P-47 Thunderbolt fighters after the war with a Reserve outfit while attending American University in Washington, but requested an active duty position again shortly before the Korean War broke out. He flew the F-80, the new jet that was just coming into the inventory then. In November 1950, he was working on the ground as a forward air controller with the Marines when the Chinese army smashed through the American lines. He and five other FAC's raced back from the front in their Jeeps but he was close enough to watch as the Chinese captured two of his fellow FAC's and executed them on the spot. Two years later, he returned to Korea flying the F-86 Sabrejet. On June 30, 1953 he was in a flight of four F-86's near the Yalu River looking for enemy MiGs. The flight was at 41,000 feet when Captain Parr caught a glimpse of something shiny, moving fast, far below. His flight commander told him to go check it out. Pointing the nose down, he went to investigate. Pulling out of the dive with the G-meter pegged at over nine G's, he found himself at 300 feet on the tails of two MiG 15's. He noticed two more MiGs close by and then another four, and then another eight not far away. He had a whole squadron of 16 MiGs to himself. "Oh well, I'd best splash their leader and the others will scatter," he said, relishing the story once more. "I threw out the boards (speed brakes) to bleed off some speed and rolled inverted to lose some more but I still was overtaking him. I found myself upside down, right above him. My canopy was within a few feet of his canopy." His hands turned and twisted to "fly" the aircraft again, as he told the story. "We looked at each other for a second, then he tried to speed up to get away. I rolled in behind him-couldn't have been more than 10 feet away when I hit the trigger of my six .50 caliber guns. I chased him all around from 100 to 500 feet above the terrain. Pulling so many G's made my gun sight circuit blow a fuse, so I had to guess at my aiming. I could see my bullets hit him every time I pulled the trigger and finally the fifth time he lit up. The flames almost scorched my canopy, we were so close. Then I jumped his wingman and sent him down, too. I was working on my third MiG when my flight commander called for help. He had ingested debris from a MiG he had scattered so I went up to cover my commander and stayed with him until he had a restart and we went home." Captain Parr's gun camera photos confirmed two kills that day and a third probable. That episode earned him a Distinguished Flying Cross. He shot down nine MiG 15's and one Il-2 transport aircraft in 30 missions during the last seven weeks of the war, earning double ace status, the transport aircraft event caused something of an international stir because some Russian officials were on board. It was later determined the transport was the last enemy aircraft to be shot down before the armistice took effect, Colonel Parr said.

In 1967, Colonel Parr was assigned to the 12th TFW at Cam Ranh Air Base in South Vietnam as deputy for operations. He flew 226 combat missions during his 12-month tour. One of those missions stands out from the rest. On May 16, 1968, he was escorting C-130's that were trying to deliver supplies to the Khe Sanh Marine base. A forward air controller called for immediate help because a major North Vietnamese force was about to overrun the base. "The FAC directed us to two NVA mortars that were no more than a hundred meters from the Marine's defensive positions. I couldn't identify them so I asked the FAC to mark the targets," he said. "He rolled his O-2 in and tossed a smoke grenade out the window. I laid a napalm can right on the smoke and finished off one mortar crew and the FAC told me where to find the second mortar. Another pass and another napalm can took care of that one. Then the whole hillside lit up as six 14.5 mm, four-barreled anti-aircraft guns opened up on me," he said with the tension still showing in his voice. "They were evidently trying to stay hidden until the C-130's arrived to re-supply the Marines." He made six passes into the teeth of the AAA using his 20 mm Gattling gun, even though the Marines on the ground radioed him to clear out for his own safety. Because of the terrain, every pass had to be made on the same heading, meaning the enemy knew exactly where he would be. "I saw the bullets coming at us," the Colonel said, "but I knew the Marines desperately needed the ammo on those C-130's. The hillside looked like it was covered with ants as the NVA soldiers lay down on their backs to fire their rifles at us. Some of them were even firing down at us because we were so low in the valley. That F-4 could take a lot of punishment." The maintenance people later counted 27 holes in his airplane, one large enough for the Colonel to put his head and shoulders into. After making two napalm and six strafing passes, Colonel Parr stayed on the scene to show his wingman where to lay his 500-pound iron bombs effectively. The official after-action report stated there were five AAA guns and two mortars destroyed and 86 enemy troops killed by air. The C-130's were then able to off load the needed supplies. For his part in the action, Colonel Parr received the Air Force Cross, the second highest decoration, one step away from the Medal of Honor.

Two years after that tour of duty, Colonel Parr was back with the 12th TFW, this time as wing commander, and flew another 201 combat missions. He retired after 34 years of active duty with an unmatched record of one Distinguished Service Cross - the only person to win both awards - 10 Distinguished Flying Crosses and 41 Air Medals. He holds some 60 U.S. and foreign decorations, more than any other Air Force officer.

Except for a two-year tour as head of the officer assignments section at the Air force Personnel Center here, his duties were all in cockpit related assignments where he accumulated more than 8,000 flying hours. He lives now in New Braunfels, Texas, with his wife Margaret and is a regular visitor to the base. When asked how it felt to get so close to his enemy, he smiled and said, "You can't shoot 'em down if you don't mix it up with 'em."

These Guys

This is an e-mail sent by Bill Person to all his buddies and me [The Editor.]

A SCARY TIME
By Bill Person

I was assigned to the 685th ACT Sqd. at Las Cruces, NM. and had been picked to be sent on a highly secret mission. I drove to Biggs in El Paso where I was flown in a T-33 to Homestead. There, a helicopter flew me to Key West. Once inside, I saw airmen technicians listening to radio signals emanating from Cuba. I saw the big bold dull colored markings TOP SECRET DAUNT and asked what it meant. They said I wasn't cleared to codeword, SI material and made me sign an inadvertent exposure oath but since I was there as liaison officer, it was too late to get a cleared replacement, so I had to be it anyway. The hurriedly positioned intercept site crew monitored Cuban and Russian communications from ships, planes and the ground. Detailed reports were sent to "Big Brother" at Strike command in case things got hairy.
Actually, we had confirmation, not readily made available to anyone outside the Intelligence Community and the Presidential Executive level - the Kremlin was not on a war status. As it turned out, Khrushchev only wanted to place missiles in Cuba that he had secretly "robbed" from the Warsaw Pact area to pose a similar threat to JFK that we had in Turkey against Moscow. We knew from photos where the SS-4s were and could have easily have knocked them out if and when it became necessary. The Soviet submarine "Polaris type" missiles posed a much more serious threat to us. In the end, it was JFK who blinked and agreed to remove our "out-dated" missiles from Turkey. This weakened that part of NATO and we had to pay the Turks a lot of cash to quiet them as we promised to keep more U.S. subs in the area to make up for the diminished protection of the removed missiles. A Junior High School in Arlington did a project on Cuba, both the Bay of Pigs and the Missile Crisis. I provided them with some info. I am scheduled to go talk to two classes on November 10. I am also going to the Book Fair in Austin the 30th for a book signing for my four books. So, the Cuban Missile Crisis was a much hyped story to tout JFK as a hero but Khrushchev proved him to be a zero. He won that round and the SS-4s were returned a few weeks later to their Warsaw Pact positions while our Turkey-based missiles were brought back to the U.S. well out of range of their intended targets. End of story . . .
Regards, Bill Person

An e-mail from Bill Person, ex-USAFSS, about Intelligence.

THE CIA AND OTHER INTELLIGENCE STUFF
By Bill Person

A lack of capability on the part of Mainline China made sense when considering the unprofessional manner that Maoist Chinese Communists did things. First, Mao Tse Tung had purged all those who might pose a threat to his particular brand of Communism. He banished or had all the competently educated technicians killed off which seriously handicapped his ability to develop his own military hardware. Then, Mao directed a schism with Russia, claiming that Soviet Premier Nikita Khrushchev had allowed the élan of the Marxist principles to flag. This foolish effort only served to cut off China's primary source of military arms.

There was a report about how the People's Republic of China Air Force once tried to build a copy of the Soviet Air-to-Air unguided rockets. These were the ones that came equipped on the MiG-21s they originally got from Russia. When the Soviet military aid stopped, the Chinese began building their own Air-to-Air unguided rockets with make-shift proximity fuses. But, when they tried installing them on their older MiG-19s, the results were disastrous. The MiG-19 had a small, inefficient electric generator that drew so much power from the jet engine that it frequently caused a flameout. To further complicate the matter, some of the rockets exploded while others did not release from their mounts under the wings when they were fired. Each time a Chinese-built rocket was fired, the MiG carrying it was destroyed instead of the intended target. In one's mind's eye, you can visualize a MiG fighter firing one or two of the big unguided rockets. The spew of flames that belch from the tailpipe as it stubbornly clings tightly underneath the wing. The thrust of one rocket propellant would send the plane in an uncontrollable spin while two would act as a sort of afterburner to rapidly accelerate the plane. Then, once the proximity fuse activated, the fighter would erupt into a fireball and do a meteor imitation crashing to earth. In the rare instance when the rocket did launch, the MiG-19 had a flameout and crashed anyway.

There were some things to learn from AAI radars, but they were less complicated than ground based surveillance radar systems. The invention of some transistors, the traveling wave tube and a better tuner gave fighter/interceptors a big edge on unsophisticated intruders. The Soviets had not fully shared their airborne radar detection system with the Chinese. This is likely because much of it had actually been stolen from the West through spies.

The U.S. Intelligence Community had the equipment and certainly the know how to analyze radar emissions as to its operating parameters, frequencies, constant or shifting, type of modulation, power strength, scan rate, pulse rate, pulse shape, polarization, sharp spike or soft pulse and a myriad of things not generally available to outsiders, only to the esoteric of Allied ELINT.

The Chinese had another problem in their hi-tech technology when testing large surface-to-surface missiles. All their multi-staged rockets exploded with the start of the second stage and their missile threat capability was a joke. So, the Chinese quickly put that project on hold.

Another such incredible story of Chinese incompetence involved a massive Chinese effort to make engine blocks and other parts for truck engines. They set up a host of tiny helter-skelter, almost comical foundries all over the rural countryside. The inept steel-makers burned charcoal with a primitive billows system to melt the iron. A lot of the paper and cloth billows burned up from the sheer heat before the iron had melted sufficiently. In the fiery furnaces that did work, the molten iron was haphazardly poured into earthen molds in countless numbers. High grade know how and quality control was non existent. When completed each of the engines exploded when the inferior, untempered metal castings disintegrated as soon as the engines were started. There was a joke about more Chinese were killed by terrified, stampeding iron makers than from the explosions of the engines. Their Great Leap Forward suffered a severe setback.

During the Vietnam War, Chinese advisors were actually purchasing agents to buy badly needed parts for China's military weapon systems. As any military leader knows, without sufficient spare parts, planes, trucks, tanks and just about everything else, is junk. The Hanoi officials gladly pocketed profits as middlemen when ordering spare parts from Moscow. And too, Moscow was only too glad to have a paying customer, for a change, even the hostile Chinese. The Soviets made certain that China did not become too well equipped so they posed a threat to them. They were shooting at one another across the Amur River in border disputes anyway. This meant that each part was highly overpriced because Russia controlled the price at their factories, a layered structure of middlemen were there with sticky palms and finally, the poor farmers who had originally earned the spendable currency to supply Hong Kong were cheated out of their pay. Beijing intercepted this payment to further its military needs. Thus China was less than friendly to all Western faces.

On January 13, 2000, at page 7 of San Antonio Express-News "Repressed-News" as I call it, two items caught my attention. "Senator seeks clearer Colombia goals." Sen. Pat Leahy, D-VT is asking where the 1.6 billion is going. This smacks of early day Vietnam, training the unmotivated and disinterested to fight a seriously more determined threat. Hence the quip: "Hey, want to buy an M-16? It once belonged to a young South Vietnamese draftee. It's never been fired and has only been dropped once." And, the big money goes in right here, then it goes round and round and it's supposed to come out here. OOPS "Heck, the drug cartels have more of our cash than we do . . . whose kidding whom?"

Then, just below, is "Pentagon warns of China links in Panama." "Surprise, surprise, Gomer Pyle, even Goober knew that, fer shore." Now just why the heck would the Commie Chinks want to glom onto a piece of real estate down at the canal? They leased the huge shipyard in San Diego and they own some other businesses in America. Perhaps we should analyze it from the oil situation. Most of the crude oil is processed on the Gulf of Mexico in Texas and Louisiana. Crude oil from Alaska is loaded onto super tankers that can not pass through the canal. They must off-load their oil onto smaller tankers for the trip to the Gulf. Environmentalists prevented any attempt to lay a pipeline from the Pacific coast to Texas. Oh well, most of the North Slope oil goes to Japan anyway, but since China is there, perhaps they could start buying this oil off the super tankers at the same reduced price as the Japanese pay for it. Then, too, a bit of sabotage to shut down the canal would stop the sale of oil from Pacific sources. Anyway, most of U.S. crude arrives from the Arabs and they have a bone to pick with us over Israel, much as the Chinese do over Taiwan. It is an interesting potential threat that does not seem to bother Clinton and the other Democrats. They've been bought off.

I used to work for Brantley Helicopter Inc. in Vernon, Texas. I learned about a guy named Mike Hynes who had a contract with the army to build drone helicopters as targets for the Soviet-built Hind D. Mike had gone broke trying to develop the radio-controlled Brantley model of the larger five-place helicopter. I approached Mike at his plant at the airport at Frederick, Oklahoma and offered to assist him in solving his problems. However, by that time it was too late and the Hynes Helicopter Company was in bankruptcy. The problem was that the unshielded radio controlled mechanisms were responding to extraneous signals and resulting in a disastrous crash. I later got involved with a Japanese man named James T. Kimura who acquired the company through the bankruptcy court in Oklahoma City. I tried to convince this naturalized citizen whose Japanese name was Toru Kimura, to salvage the army contract. I knew that the control problem could have been corrected easily, but a portion of the pre-acceptance tests had been done with another company's remote control system. Vega's system had been done with another company's remote control system. Vega's system cost six million per and Hynes was opting to sell his Brantley 305 remote controlled drones for $185,000 each. As I got more involved, I learned from Mr. N.O. Brantley, the original creator, and another man that there were other serious problems with the larger model of the helicopter. Someone had to cheat to pass the static run test for FAA. The load bearings had cratered during the 100 hour run test and while the inspector was "entertained" elsewhere, the load bearings and three new rotor blades were attached so it appeared to be on the same test. A Korean named Ching Kook Chaing, C.K. for short, was the translator for Mr. Kimura and once the company had been moved across Red River to Vernon, Texas, the new plan was to build the smaller B2B model helicopter. Red China desperately wanted to buy them for use and later, production in Beijing. Kimura did not want to pay for the liability insurance to sell in America.

There had been several attempts to quash production of the B2B because it was better than most of its competitors. I tried to let Kimura to let me modify the two-place version to a new production method and use the larger engine, but he wanted it to remain as it was. I explained that the old method of construction was labor intensive and too costly. I had obtained data on an injection molding system to greatly reduce the production costs and greatly increase the rate of manufacturing them. Also, I wanted the larger 200 horsepower Lycoming engine so it could carry two 200 pound men. The Lycoming IVO-360 developed only 180 horsepower and would barely carry two 170 pound men.

The U.S. Army finally came for the three remaining drones to take them to White Sands Missile Test Range in New Mexico where they were to be targets for some other highly destructive ordnance. That ended a highly profitable enterprise.

Next, I proposed we use a small plane to test my remote control system and autopilot. We did buy a Cessna 150 but that was to be used for Mr. Kimura to take flying lessons. I tried to explain that it was too risky and expensive to use a B2B as a test bed. A Cessna 150 was much cheaper to fly and maintain, and it was a lot cheaper to buy than a B2B Brantley. I would fine tune my electronics gear before we put them in the helicopter. The dullard C.K. Chaing had another agenda, not mine.

I had made friends with Olvis Jones and Harold Jenkins who were the only qualified mechanics and pilots for the Brantley. Neither of them really wanted to go to Japan or China to work. Tragically, Mr. Norris Brantley died before he could help me convince Kimura what needed to be done. Then, whatever Kimura's plans were, they died with him before anything was established and once again the bank had to foreclose on a superior helicopter.

Red China was the next successful purchaser of BHI, Brantley Helicopter International. I later went back to see the plant and watched as twenty imported Chinese used long poles as levers and a stack of wood blocks to set a big press down in place. It was like stepping back a century to before the internal combustion engine. When I had worked there, I used a forklift and my two helpers. By my calculations, the project would have taken an hour at about $35.00, but they took over two hours with twenty men. Of course at Red Chinese pay scale, that was probably ten cents and hour so the method was still cheaper at maybe five bucks or less.

C.K. Chaing had gone back to Los Angeles to work at a 7-11 convenience store where he was infinitely more qualified. Mrs. Kimura went back to Japan with her family where she needed to be and the helicopter plant was in new incompetent hands for yet another time. A local glib-talking fellow took over C.K. Chaing's position to also direct the new owner's direction in a similarly wrong path.

I had made friends with the bank president and quietly advised him to get the FAA issued Type Certificates so that neither the Japanese nor the ChiComman could not sneak it off to Asia and leave the bank with an empty sack. Since no one was going to take my advice to make the Brantley fly, I took my leave in a fusillade of cusswords.

I made contact with the CIA through Ft. Sam and an agent out of Dallas came to see me at the Bowie Airport. I explained to this young fellow how I could arrange for CIA agents to be trained as the only qualified pilots and maintenance techs for the Brantley. It would involve a small investment in the company to be harnessed up with the chinks, but that would place spooks inside their company and country. I told him that this would buy out the bank's note and provide a CIA-owned company the control to dictate certain undercover men within the management of the company.

Beijing desperately wanted a helicopter to be used for flying tourists to the Great Wall and on sightseeing trips around the country. Spendable foreign currency was high on China's wish list, and that would come from selling food supplies to Hong Kong and a budding tourist trade.

I explained to the CIA Agent that they could have a reason to fly around China and sneak pictures and whatever they wanted with complete cover. They even had reason to communicate back here for parts, and pass information. I still have the fella's card. He told me that CIA could not get involved in local situations. That was the FBI's area. I told him that I had the contacts and could put his guys onto the only men who knew all about the helicopter and since it involved a covert setup to insert agents in China, I didn't see why it was exclusively FBI's bailiwick. He said it would have to be a joint operation and that would likely kill it. That was about 1992 and they could have had the best possible cover to plant agents in Red China since that time. I had asked that once I passed along my part, I wanted no part in it, but I had invented a remote control to be used on the helicopter for training and also a cheap autopilot system. The only three pilots and mechanics that I knew of didn't want to go to China so their guys could be trained by the best and no one except me would know that they were CIA. I even explained that by placing TV cameras on the helicopters and a small airplane I had proposed for training, they could photograph anything they wanted to around Peking. It would be sold to them as a training aid effort. Do you realize that by sending back small parts for repair and having a direct line of communications back to the States was something that the CIA I used to know would kill for. Hell, they could send back microdots in the greasy parts and no one would be the wiser. Good old (CIA) pilots could have made fast friends with ChiCom military pilots and gleaned a wealth of intelligence.

Now, it would seem that the last major bastion of hard-core Communism is capitalizing on a long denied practice of capitalism. They made a sizable contribution to Bill Clinton's campaign for which they wound up with priceless information on super hi-tech nuclear weapons and missile technology. North Korea has recently demonstrated their capability of a much improved medium range ballistic missile threat.

China has detonated "devices" to prove they have made super great advancements in nuclear weapons. Clinton has managed to thwart efforts to investigate just exactly what the Chinese really got for their contributions to him. Even more recently, a news item reported that Mr. Steven Liu, a Chinese citizen who worked for a U.S. military contractor was fined $4,000.00 and placed on probation for one year for gaining unauthorized access to a $148 million computer at Wright-Patterson AFB, Ohio. Since it is not certain what all Liu managed to steal, mostly passwords for access to other systems, it has been termed a misdemeanor, not a felony.

I suppose when our new, all-volunteer military is faced with super hi-tech weaponry, they'll be too weak from all the anthrax and other vaccines that a "pork barreled" congress imposed to be able to withstand a grossly under-rated enemy like China, North Korea, Iraq, Iran or just about any country who wishes to confront us.

When I read these three articles, it brought back a lot of memories of things that once really pissed me off. After more thought, I recalled how the Ravens and the rescue guys were the ones that came up with Alpha Mike Fox. Down in Eglin, or closer still, nearby Hurlburt Field the Air Force trained rescue pilots, and T-28 pilots for highly specialized jobs. We trained Cubans to go to the Congo to fight the commies there. That was because their darker faces blended in better in darkest Africa, while the pale faces went to Laos. All "civilians" you understand. Only "game wardens" and "forest rangers" crossed the staging area from Udorn, Thailand, over the Me Kong River into Laos. Once in Vientiane did they get their USAID ID cards, and were photographed at a distance from the Embassies of the North Vietnamese, China and the Soviet Union, if the opportunity availed itself. Having the close contact with Cuban trainees back in Florida got the whole thing started. Pedro was the call sign of Air America's H-34 Choctaw helicopters operating in Laos. Air America flights and Ravens were involved in the secret war up there. Also deep cover CIA case officers who led groups of Hmong natives against the Pathet Lao and the NVA. All during the war, Hanoi denied ever violating the neutrality of the DMZ, the lying MIKE FOXES. Anyway, it was the exposure to the Spanish influence from the training at Hurlburt that carried the terms to Laos. Then, anything that catches on, is magnified through use by others. Sierra Hotel, for shit hot and AMF for the other. My BATCATS group initiated the Lamar Cranston for the Shadow theme. This was for the secrecy involved in Igloo White. Milton Caniff came up to our dining in before we deployed to Korat and he had drawn our logo patch, the BATCATS with the term, "CAVETE CATTAM" meaning beware of the cat. Also, Batman was popular on TV about that time. I recall the notices posted on the office at the Texas Courts where we stayed in Ft. Walton Beach reading: "Bat bus will depart bat cave at 0600 for the bat plane." The term for "NO NOTICE NAP" was coined then too because of the long hours we put in and when we dozed off during brief idle times. I had been through the initial testing parts in June 1967 so I slipped in the opportunity to do some training of other newcomers while down in Florida. Defense Communications Planning Group, DCPG, the civilian boss wanted us blue suiters to use only our best people to participate in the testing of the system, but I managed to bring along a goodly number of men to train as we did. I never admitted to it though.

Anyhow, that's how the term AMF was originated. A lot of terms just got started when some glib-tongued pilot said it and it was immediately adapted. Terms like going Christmas tree. That's when a pilot made a low pass over the target at night with all his lights turned on. It was intended to draw ground fire and those above watching could see where to strike to suppress the flak positions. Once you heard the term, you knew very well what it meant. Winchester meant out of ammo, bingo meant out of fuel and RTB was return to base. Clean the wings meant bombs are dropped. Gomer was enemy and I stop here as a flood of terms come screaming back to me from the past.

Most of the war-horses of my era have given way to a bunch of FNGs (f__king new guys) who wouldn't know a good deal from a Peter Paul's Almond Joy candy bar.

THE END

This piece, was written and sent to me, [The Editor], by Bill Person, ex-USAFSS.

NOT ALLOWED TO KEEP NOTES
By Bill Person

I was not allowed to keep notes back during the Cold War or Vietnam, classified, you see. I was able to write about my stuff by looking up and setting down major events and recalling what I was doing then, that was my skeleton. I didn't need to make one for my story, I already knew that. It still took a while to get it all said.

I think everyone in the intelligence business, USAFSS, ASA and NSG, NSA too, all bought and read Ian Fleming and Matt Helm books back then. We also watched what else was happening around the world as we read our classified reports and made comparisons. You must know that we lost a lot of good people back then in the Cold War and our government will never admit to it. I got the impression that some of the guys you talked with may have thought better on it and decided to clam up about Phil. It ain't over until it's over. When you read all four of my books you'll understand better. What I wrote to you was indeed cryptic, multi-meaning. Guys like me with active imaginations had to work extra hard to keep on the subject matter that was critical although driven by cerebral sparks to distract me. Then too, I have been told, by men and women, that they were curious about amorous encounters that were always left out; especially with foreign women. I know that ranking people in positions of importance with families to protect; never included the intimate things the way I do. I'm divorced (twice) and no longer give a crap about protecting anyone. I have had men ask me why GI's marry foreign girls and I sought to explain it in my books. Deep abiding love is wonderful but with foreign women there was total pleasure and no sense of guilt that you get with an American woman.

I knew a friend who wrote me to meet him at Travis when he got back from Nam. He was an Army major and I knew his lovely wife. He wrote me that he was so horny that a needed a few days with other wild women before he could face his wife. I could tell that he had a lot of emotional anger and frustration stored up and thought he would be a different husband than his wife knew. I thought about it as a bachelor and decided he was wrong and would probably regret doing what he planned. I called his wife and asked her to fly out from the east coast to meet me. I told her what her husband had asked me to do and that he had not touched any females over in Nam. Our plan was simple, we told him that the Army had notified her of his arrival date and she contacted me to come out to meet him. I had a nice apartment in Carmichael, CA, near Sacramento and arranged for them to have their reunion there. When he arrived, I told him that he had to spend at least a night or two with his wife since she knew of his return and had come out to meet him, but then, if he still needed to, we could make an excuse of him being debriefed about his classified knowledge and then slip off and have his much "needed" orgy. A few days after they had been at my apartment, they thanked me and flew back home to be with the kids. She knew every detail of her husband's plan but he didn't know she knew and she left me a very thankful note for my role as cupid. She even admitted that she had even felt the same way in the manner of a wild catch-up reunion.

So, I have come to believe that people want to know more, not less.

Fond regards,
Bill

Subj: A Very Unique Status Board
Date: 4/13/5:02:26 PM Pacific Daylight Time
From: Bill Person
To: Trish Schiesser

Howdy Trish,

I don't remember Phil, but a lot of intel types suffered from what was called "syndrome of the labyrinth," meaning toiling away in a dungeon-like environment with no expectation of ever receiving any praise because of the secrecy of the work. Being sworn to secrecy and living it took a serious toll on a lot of our people.
Yes, Sampson was a boot camp like Lackland and despite what the other services allege, USAF is tough. So, I'm not surprised he caught pneumonia while he was there. There are other "schools" all over the country for languages and special intelligence vocations.
 I don't remember Kisarazu/Kisarasu, but there is a Misawa, Japan and he would have served in Korea, probably Osan-ni to earn the Korean Service Medal. If he was TDY to London in June '63, he likely spent time in White Hall with liaison duty with MI6, and I don't doubt he was a "changed man" afterwards. Some say once you've killed, the seeds of your own destruction are forever embedded inside you.
When I came back from Wakkanai, Japan, I was assigned at Newburgh, 60 miles up the Hudson from the City. I was the Special Security Officer and gave high level intelligence briefings to the general and his staff at Eastern NORAD/CONAD Region. I used to drive down to the City to check out the girls and bars on the east 60s.

The SO G-15/6901SCG/1963 in his DD214 means "Special Order number 15, for the 6901 Security Group and dated 1963. It should say something then about AFCM for Air Force Commendation Medal or some other medal in abbreviated form. The next letters tell what it is. Thanks for the kind words on my HONORED VETERANS.
Intro and chapters coming separate.
Fondly,
Bill Person

These Guys 451

This is a story of Bill Person's flight in his T-28 during the Secret War in Laos back in 1965 (plus another incident with which he begins his story). He crash landed, hit by bullets from the Laotians who carried fully automatic AK-47s in the Plaine de Jars. This story in part, puts Bill in a position with MI5. But don't tell anyone I said this. ☺ *[The Editor]*

THE WAR UP TOO CLOSE AND PERSONAL: MY STORY
By Bill Person

I didn't really sleep that night, March 7, 1965, because of the sounds and being in a sure enough combat zone. There were distant, sort of muffled reports of rifle fire all during the night as the army was tending to its business of parting bodies to rot from souls to who knows where Buddhist's go. I made kind of a compromise with my tired body and drifted off into a sort of sleepless doze, a relaxed twilight.

An Army Ranger nudged me awake and signaled for me to keep silent and follow him out to just inside the sandbagged entrance. I followed and kept low with my two strapped on pistols making my way to join the other defenders.

A few others had gathered there and were peering down the side of the mountain. It was not time to start getting light and my eyes had yet to focus on anything in the direction they were looking. They had their weapons trained down to some brush a short distance down the hillside. Then, after a few moments, I too, saw a slight movement there. I wanted to ask but saw the grave expression on the Ranger's face to keep quiet and decided to look like I was joining them by taking out one of my .38 caliber pistols to appear to arm myself. I opened the cylinder a couple of times to make sure it was loaded with live rounds and then closed it again. Of course it was loaded, but I couldn't think of anything else to do to keep from appearing terrified.

My heart raced as the silent, shadowy figures emerged from the brush and suddenly began to fire as they rushed the entrance to the vital intelligence complex. The Rangers began to return fire and when the dually .30 caliber machine-guns opened up I also began to fire my pistol in the direction of the approaching enemy figures. When the six rounds were fired, I took out the other pistol, and still holding the pistol I had rounds in the other pistol. I fired at the place where I saw the figures of Victor Charlie's coming up towards the entrance, my location. It was an exhilarating several moments and then it was over with an echoing of gunfire ringing in my ears. Only then did I realize that I had heard the enemy bullets whizzing around me all that time and now stood there with an empty pistol in each hand. One at a time, I opened the cylinder to discard the expended brass rounds. My ears continued ringing for several minutes after I watched the expended brass fall to the ground.

"Want some more ammo?" an AP Sergeant asked when he saw me eject the expended shell casings from the two cylinders.

"Sure, thanks," I said accepting enough shells to reload.

It was a strange feeling to have actually fired live rounds at an enemy and wonder if I had even hit anyone let alone killed anybody. It's an entirely different experience when you shoot and hear bullets whizzing all around you. I wondered if that meant I was now a real combat veteran. It was not exactly the kind of thing you asked a ground - pounder Ranger if you didn't want to invite him to laugh at you. I listened to the others talk and tried to understand what they were saying but too many things buzzed around in my head to really focus on what was being said just then.

Several of the Rangers went down and examined the enemy dead before bringing them back to be loaded onto a truck to be taken down to the main base for a more thorough body search. Unsure of the safety of being down where the dead gooks were being loaded onto a truck, I elected to watch from a position of cover there next to the machine gun mount. Anyway, I should never be able to tell if any of the enemy had been killed by one of the .38 slugs with all the .223, .30 caliber and 9mm rounds that had been fired. Those with multiple bloody wounds would not be a pleasant sight to witness anyway, I decided.

The morning came and went before I knew it and on one end of the flight line, countless numbers of Marines were forming. The Marines had just made a beach type landing over on China Beach.

It was too early to meet my plane but another C-130 taxied in to park in front of Base Ops. This was a cargo plane from CCK, Taiwan, and another unit. It had flown in from Clark Air Base and as soon as it had lowered the big ramp door in the back, three almost new blue Air Force Chevrolet pick-up trucks were driven out and parked on the edge of the flight line.

"Is there a Captain Person here?" a Lieutenant Colonel in a flightsuit came over to the trucks, asking.

"Right here, Colonel," I answered him.

"Sign here, Captain. These are from General Gordon Blake at Fort Meade. His outfit picked up the tab. They're all ready and gassed up for you," the Colonel said handing over a multiple addressee receipt.

"Thanks for the prompt delivery," I said, signing it.

"Well, at least they'll get some service here rather than be washed and pampered to death back in the Philippines like they were in a dealer's show room display," the Lieutenant Colonel grinned.

"Oh, they'll be used alright," a voice answered, it was the Base Commander.

The Colonel had just driven up in his car with the orange and white checkered flag mounted on the back bumper. He was obviously glad to see some form of support in response to the mounting tasks levied on his hectic tour of duty there. Once the visiting C-130 Lieutenant Colonel had his paperwork completed, he gave the start up signal to the big cargo bird cranked up and taxied out. A few of the officer's close by were invited into Base Operations for coffee while the new vehicles were assigned to impatient unit leaders. I stayed there and watched the activity until it was time for my plane to arrive.

My spirits rose to see my EC-130 with tail number 31532 taxi-up to take me back to Bangkok. The canvass bag containing a couple of dozen 7.5 inch reels of intercepted enemy traffic was handed off to a sergeant as I climbed aboard to enter the plane.

"Welcome aboard, Bill" Captain Greg Somers shouted over his left seat, did you get to fire my pistol?"

"No, it's still a virgin," I teased noting his disappointed frown.

I decided to wait and tell him back in Bangkok so he wouldn't pester me all the way back. As the plane turned to taxi away from the ramp, I could see the faces looking up at the cabin, smiling and waving at my departure. I had only been there 24 hours but they had to stay for a tour and I both envied them and felt a strange kind of guilt, but I was grateful to be leaving there.

The flight back was uneventful though a relief to get back to relative safety and away from Da Nang and the war area.
I would be a civilian again before I would learn that the intelligence complex commander had put in a request for all the defenders from the VC assault be awarded the Bronze Star with a "V" clasp. Luckily someone remembered me

from the pick-up trucks delivery incident that day and vouched for me so I got the medal also.

Apparently word does get around because some time later I had two visitors waiting for me in the Park Hotel lobby. Both wore civies so I did not know if they were military or civilian but from their respectful manner towards me, I would guess they were NCOs. They used first names only and invited me to come join them for a late breakfast at the USO Villa Club a few blocks on out on Sukemwit Road. It was about half way to the Crown Hotel where the backend linguist flight crew stayed.

The Thais were still learning to cook for Americans and the omelets were made with white pizza cheese, provolone, Swiss or something. Certainly not American or cheddar cheese as you would expect in an omelet. Anyway, I had coffee and made small talk with them until they decided to tell me the reason for inviting me there.

I would later learn the significance of a casual comment Ben gave to another man in the Villa Club. He gave a deep, throatily greeting in a mocked Mexican accent, "Hey-ay-ay, PEEDro!" I laughed openly at the mispronunciation "Paid-ro." This had been started at Hurlburt AFB, Florida where these men had trained along with Cubans. The darker faces, Cuban mercenaries were sent to the Congo while the lighter face gringos were assigned to Laos.

The man called Bin joked about a rogue captain who seemed to be able to get things done had been mentioned to them and he looked at me when he said it. The gist of the meeting was that San Francisco or some place in California was preventing some badly needed stuff from the secretive folks up at Luang Prabang, Laos. I did know that secret war activities were handled separately so as not to arouse suspicion and bring uninvited news people to that 'by invitation only war'. A local outlaw strike by some freight handlers had refused to load this much needed supply order. In all fairness, the freight was disguised like it was not military but merely stuff for some foreign civilian company in Thailand.

As it happened, these 'spooks' got word on me and came to ask a huge favor. I assumed that they were CIA, Air America or something, though only the name "company" was used. The two men I met at the USO, Villa Club there on Sukemwit Road were obviously prior military from their demeanor. They seemed to know that since I was in the intelligence community that I was to be trusted not to tell about our meeting and their request to get their supplies there from stateside. I knew that one of the EC-130s was back in Greenville, Texas at E Systems getting modified for The Queen Bee Delta Project and would be about ready to be flown to Yokota before coming on to Bangkok. I wrote down the information and when I went out to recover the recon bird, I stopped off at the Security Service Detachment to send off a message. I addressed it to the 6940th at San Angelo for them to call Greenville and have the flight crew pick up the stranded supplies while passing through California.

A few days later, the newly modified Ec-130BII arrived at Bangkok with the 'secret civilian supplies' on board. I contacted the two men through the Villa Club and they arranged to get the stuff on up to Laos. As a favor, I asked to tag along and see their strange world that I had been reading top secret codeword reports about since 1963 while I was in Wakkanai, Japan.

We flew up across the wide, muddy Me Kong River into the land of 'a million elephants' and 'the land of the mountains of the moon' in a C-447 that had no markings on it, just a number in small black numerals. I remember seeing the mighty Me Kong River there close by as we landed at the base. There were lots of T-28s parked close together and off in the distance, I saw rows and rows of MK-81 250 pound bombs, rockets and crates of .50 caliber ammo.

The liquor flowed freely that evening and in a drunken frame of mind, I bravely asked to fly one of those planes as a return favor for helping them get their supplies to them. A man I had met and never knew his name nodded and said, "we'll see in the morning."

I was drinking coffee the next morning when a man approached me and asked if I wanted to go up on a checkout ride with him in a "Tango," a T-28. A little hung over but in elated spirits at the offer, I eagerly agreed. The T-28A I had flown back in pilot training had a smaller 800 horsepower engine but this one had a Pratt and Whitney R-1820 1425 horsepower engine with a three bladed prop. I was given a hurried cockpit check and then we were airborne. My check pilot had me make some passes over a big wooden framed square target before letting me arm the red covered toggle switches and actually fire the two .50 caliber machine guns mounted midpoint under the wings. He cautioned me on keeping the ball centered with rudder pedals when I fired. The little black ball was in the turn and bank indicator on the console. It was like holding a pistol straight instead of letting it be held crooked in your hand, else the bullets would go askew. I watched the red dirt kick up past the target when the .50

caliber slugs slammed through the cloth center just as I pulled up from my run. My check pilot said I did okay and I snapped the red covers back down to safe the guns and we flew back to enter the traffic pattern for landing.

I was invited to attend a briefing for an air strike over in the northern part of the Plain of Jars. It was a place east of the Nam Khan River, a tributary that flowed west to empty into the Me Kong. I was to take a photographer with me in the back seat and let him photograph the aerial assault. It seems that a large force of Pathet Lao was attempting an end run around the neutralists to cut off their slow retreat into their mountain stronghold well north of Vientiane, the capital on the Me Kong.

The CIA's secret base at Long Tieng, known as Alternate 20 was General Van Pao's headquarters and his Meo command did not trust the Neutralist forces. General Kong Le and his Neutralists were forbidden to enter Vientiane of Long Tieng.

I made my take-off last and followed along the formation gaggle of T-28s. Noting the easterly heading, I made a mental note of the direction back to the base. The country was mostly flat as we winged our way to the target. 'Lead', or the flight leader, called for the attack and I bored in to be in position to his left, following the plane in an attacking dive. The photographer snapped away to record visual evidence of what we were doing as I kept making sort of right-handed landing patterns to mirror the routes of the attacking 'Tangos'.

Finally, 'Lead' called a halt and instructed the strike force to RTB, return to base, and hit targets of opportunity on the return leg. I stayed with two T-28s that claimed they were 'winchester' or out of ammo.

What happened next was close to indescribable.

As I stood surveying the wreckage of the crashed North American-built T-28D Trojan that late morning of April 16, 1965, a lot of thoughts raced through my mind. All of them make a good case for me to not be there, but wistful thinking does not give way for reality. The dull gray colored plane lay partially crumpled up like an empty beer can. The Trojan had been designed to be a trainer, but now, numbered with a big black "O" on the high tail for obsolete and given a coat of drab gray paint, it had been armed for combat. This one had become an official war bird in that secret war in Laos. Now, there was countless bullet holes in it, the most damaging ones were, of course, in front on the underside of the cowling. The deadliest of the bullet holes were not visible because the gear was up so that part was resting on the ground. The irreparable engine gave off angry hisses and a dull grayish smoke like an angry beast not yet dead. The heavy radial engine had bent the mounting frame so it was tilted down slightly to buckle the skin in front of the cockpit. The bottom lip of the cowling had become a scoop to plow up a strip of grassy turf that braked the skidding plane to a more sudden stop.

Once the plane had come to a stop from its rodeo-style wheels-up landing on the rough terrain, like all pilots, I had sweated out the threat of sitting in a resulting fireball, charred crisp, never to move again. Luckily, if that was a proper term for the occasion, swirls of white smoke escaping the ruptured skin immediately in front of the cockpit, the earth-bound plane had no sign of threatening flames that I could see. The two .50 caliber mini-gun pods had been jammed backwards to peek through the flaps of the trailing edge of the wings. The black rubber fuel cells were ruptured and fuel was draining on the ground underneath on both sides.

The battle-damaged plane lay in a small, narrow, sloping grassy area below a ridge that I had managed to clear before the plane quit flying altogether. I could see the heavy line of foliage ahead, but could not see the Nam Khan River there somewhere west of my position. I knew that the muddy tributary where I had seen and angered a large force of Pathet Lao, was not far behind me. My fear was that they had seen that their concentrated ground fire had brought down the enemy plane and were now scrambling to collect their prize, "Yankee Air Pirate" me.

It was a hot, muggy morning in the spring of 1965, despite the surprising chilly, almost cold nights up there in the land of the mountains of the moon. Perhaps in a bit of shock, I stood there as if the world was now in slow motion and my mind was on super fast speed.

Plaine de Jarres was named by the occupying French of an earlier time. This northern central part was so named because of all the hollowed out massive boulders made to appear to be giant jars. No one knows for certain what these vessels were ever used for, but one thing for sure, they are far and away too heavy to be moved from this desolate and mystical location where they must have been resting for centuries. It was a cinch no one was going to move them now. The mystery of Laos is further enhanced by some other odd phenomena there in the land of a million elephants. The national emblem is an Erawan which is a three headed elephant with a white parasol on top; something to do with royal authority according to Lao history. Asian neighbors call it the land of the mountains of the moon because one had to cross the mighty Me Kong River to get to a land that seemed to rise up with many gigantic tooth-like protrusions. These strange obstacles are the white lime karsts that look like a rough designed multi-storied office building that never got finished, or perhaps they were like the abandoned ancient pyramids of Egypt. It was eerie the way these peaks stood out from the jungle floor with vines and other strange types of vegetation climbing up their white, almost alabaster steep walls that seemed to loftily reach for the heavens. The thin wispy clouds that collected to certain of the karsts looked like spider webs spun by mystical giant spiders.

I could still make out the tooth-like hills in the distance and up on a rise, some distance beyond a row of trees perhaps a hundred or more vengeful enemy communist Pathet Lao soldiers were shouting and firing their weapons as they ran towards the plane they had managed to shoot down. This swarming host that appeared to engulf the hilltop was the enemy coming to avenge their anger with a highly visible enthusiasm. They were clad in black pajama-like material, some in flat lampshade-like straw hats and others in the ever popular funny pith helmet. Perhaps the 'jungle' style helmet was a sign of authority. Authority or not, they all were brandishing AK-47s as if to make the downed Yankee Air Pirate rabbit for their hunt.

For certain they had seen their bullets slam home on the fast-moving, low-flying T-28 that had spotted their sizeable force. Caught off guard, they could only glare angrily up at the initial pass of the dull gray plane. Then, the T-28 circled and dived on them spraying two .50 caliber machine-guns at them. They answered with full automatic AK-47s in withering fire. I had seen the glowing tracers stream up at me in arcs from them and knew that there were five metal slugs or more in between each of those fiery projectiles. They were not all missing their intended target, my ride home.

Throaty cheers must have risen from them on seeing the tell tale smoke and the silenced roar of the engine. They had vanquished the annoying hornet and gave spirited pursuit to where the trail of smoke would lead them to their disabled quarry.

I had elected to stay down low and use the speed to buy distance from the enemy on the ground. I was at tree-top level when the engine made a last revolting squeal and went silent.

These Guys

I saw that the airspeed read 300, or there about and pushed the stick forward to barely clear the trees. At that speed, the plane buffeted as it slowed and my eyes strained to pick a place to set it down where there would not be any obstacles to cause too sudden a stop. Just before I let it settle onto the tall blade type elephant grass, I pushed the canopy handle back and pressed the button to use pneumatic air to blow back the two part canopy and lock them open. I certainly didn't want to have to try to open the canopy after I was on the ground. I pulled my lap belt and shoulder harness as tight as I could and mumbled a prayer for a touchdown that didn't incapacitate me.

The initial touchdown was like in slow motion, but then the bird entered into a wild bucking tantrum. That was a helpless feeling waiting for the plane to stop gyrating. As soon as the plane stopped moving, I released the latch on my lap belt and bolted up out of the cockpit. It seemed a lot longer to me as I watched the guy in the back seat fumbling with his stuff, still strapped in. I leaped back up on the left wing to plead with the civilian photographer passenger to expedite getting out of the plane. The disoriented man had not un-strapped from the back seat and acted like he intended to take all of his cameras with him as if we had landed back at our base. I looked up at that forbiddingly beautiful landscape that I knew held death and worse, capture and torture at the hands of these inimically alien Asians. An enemy that my own country denied even having any combatants in so there would be no admission that I was ever there. I certainly had no permission from anyone in authority and if killed or captured, no one would even admit to my predicament or being there. In fact, my country would cook up a flat lie about my disappearance and demise, never admitting I had bought the farm in Laos.
How could this be happening to me? My mind went back to how it had started and then fast forwarded to the present again. It was an exercise in futility, I knew, but it was a part of confronting this un-welcomed situation by recalling how I came to be there. I had been safe down in Bangkok as Queen Bee Delta Project Officer getting Rolling Thunder kicked off. I had used my influence to be there and after a reasonably safe observation and photographic part of the strike mission and while en route back to the base, the man in the back seat and I spotted a large force crossing a stream. It was a good guess that this was a flanking effort by a large enemy force to encircle the Neutralist forces and cut them off from the capital of Vientiane. At the request of the photographer, I dropped down to make a low, flat pass and get pictures. Caught flat-footed, the enemy looked up at the lone plane and some even waved. The man had asked for an action shot and eager to be a real combat pilot, I pulled up to make a circling pass to fire the two .50 caliber machine-guns at them. As I was

pulling off, they fired back and managed to hit the oil cooler to cause an immediate engine failure. Too low to bail out, I used this high speed to soar over the treetops in search for a clearing to put down the crippled bird. I opted to gain distance from the enemy rather than height to bail out within sight of the enemy. A dead T-28 doesn't coast far in spite of the high rate of speed and both of us were going down in a place a lot closer to an enemy than we wanted. The three-bladed propeller froze in a loading pitch that became a sort of air brake to slow the airspeed much quicker than expected. I reached down to set the fuel lever to "OFF" then drew the lap belt and shoulder harness as tight as I could before locking the harness reel lever in anticipation of a rough crash-landing. I moved the canopy control knob back and pressed the button to use the emergency pneumatic system to slam the two part canopy back and locked open because I did not want to be trapped in a burning plane on the ground. The wind whistled in as an annoying diversion but I forced my concentration to set the plane down as softly as possible. The approach glide looked good and flat right down to touchdown and then it became a wildly bucking beast that was intent on punishing the occupants for the shoot down mishap.

Once on the ground, our only hope was to hail the returning T-28s for covering fire while an Air America helicopter was dispatched to bring both of us home. I slapped at the lap belt locking lever, freeing me of the restraints and I bolted upright to scramble out onto the left wing the instant the plane came to rest.

Pistol in hand, I shouted that I intended to shoot holes in the wings to spill out more of the avgas and then set the plane afire. I warned my dawdling passenger that he only had mere seconds to escape the fire and likely resulting explosion. Finally, the passenger emerged from the back seat. He made his way over to hop off the wing and start waddling off towards the west, away from the advancing enemy, cameras bobbing on their straps. I fired my .38 pistol three or four times into the fuel cells in the left wing to expose more fuel. I determined more shots might start a fire before I was ready. After retreating to a safe distance, I fired the miniature flashlight-sized flare gun to set it ablaze; pausing only moments to see that the plane would indeed make a massive fire with a billowing column of black smoke before I too started to run for my life. There was no explosion, only a roaring fire that fed black smoke high into the air.

A last look at the converging black-clad commies, and aware of the bullets raining all about us, I turned and ran after the passenger. Just ahead of me, I heard the man yell out as I began to close on the heavily laden guy with all the cameras dangling from his shoulders. His right leg crumpled under him and he fell headlong into the weeds. When I reached him, I saw that he had been shot in the butt and the bullet had jerked his right leg bone right out of his hip socket. Blood was gushing out from the ruptured vessels and there was little hope of stopping the flow that high up on his torso.

Panic struck, in severe pain, he yelled and cursed as he pulled at my flightsuit more for solace than any real help. I had nothing to give him for pain and could only stare blankly down at him. Not knowing what else to do, I removed my webbed pistol belt and removed the canteen attached to it so it could be used as a sort of tourniquet around him there. I pulled off my kidskin gloves and jammed them into the wounds to try to stop the blood loss. A Band-Aid would have been about as useful, but it was all I could think of to do at the moment, except to try to keep from looking like I thought the poor wounded man was going to die, which in truth, I did.

I had forgotten the man's name because I had been slightly hung over that morning when I flew a quick checkout ride and fought to keep a clear head. Then again at the briefing on the mission before we took-off from that secret base at Luang Prabang, Laos.

I decided to try to hide the wounded man in a ditch with small shrubs for cover and attempt to draw the line of rapidly closing enemy away from him. The pained, pitiful look on his face would always be etched in my mind's eye, never to fade with the passing of time, but I could do nothing more for him. His name, like some other things may have buzzed about in my head like angry bees but for the life of me I could not recognize any of the blurry objects.

I had not reloaded so there were two or three live rounds in the pistol that I had fired into the wing and placed this one in the man's hand. I then took out the other pistol that was loaded before take-off and in my shoulder holster. Earlier, the man had refused to wear one on this photographic mission which was to cover the bombing raid against the Pathet Lao and suspected North Vietnamese forces operating in the north central Plaine de Jarres. It was totally out of character when the man asked me to make a firing pass on the enemy while he took pictures.

I forced a less than reassuring last look on my face, pulled myself loose from the man's grasp and left him there. I began to run towards the southwest away from his cover, avoiding the nearing of the Commie Laotian horde. As I ran, I could hear their shouts much plainer now and the incessant barks of their gun fire hurt my eardrums. I took out the compact rescue radio and holding it close to my mouth, yelled the mayday call for help, identifying myself as a downed pilot in the midst of many hostiles. The radio crackled and I managed to call in two of the T-28s returning from the bombing raid. The blazing T-28 with the rising column of black smoke made a great reference marker for the pilots to spot the large numbers of Pathet Lao troops. The purr of short bursts could be heard as the twin mini-guns quickly exhausted their pitiful supply of .50 caliber ammunition of the two planes.

Then came the sound of the pilot's voice in the tiny earphone to say, "Good luck; out of fuel and ammo. Have to leave you now."

The short sprayings of bullets had served only as a minor annoyance to the host of enemy there below. They paused only long enough to fire back at the angry wasps buzzing above them and to try to down yet another Yankee Air Pirate. I felt like a sacrificial lamb, trembling at what were inevitably my last few moments on earth.

I openly sobbed and I could feel my body shake in response to what I perceived as my hopeless doom. Tears were streaming down my face when suddenly, the radio crackled again and an American voice spoke to me. At first I did not catch the words of the reassuring voice that informed me that he was Navy. I was shaking too much to really catch the call sign. There were four A4D Skyhawks up there on the perch. As luck would have it, these particular Navy pilots were in a holding pattern waiting their turn at some already burning enemy trucks on the Ho Chi Minh Trail. They were over a hundred miles and more back to the east when they heard the call and responded. Flying well out of their range, they brought their five hundred pound bombs and a generous supply of 20mm cannon fire to help save the life of a downed pilot.

Shouts of joy and cheers to the Navy jocks reverberated around inside my chest cavity but with all the bomb-bursts, likely never came out of my throat. Later, I learned that the Navy A-4s were from the USS Coral Sea which had landed at Tahkli to spend the night and refuel on the Air Force's tab. Navy pilots never got to buy a drink at an Air Force base over there because they usually had just helped save an Air Force pilot's life. And too, Air Force pilots knew that Navy pilots did not get to drink on a carrier, legally, but, more to the point, Navy and Marine pilots rarely carried money on combat missions, especially not MPC, the type of Military Pay Certificates in use in Vietnam.

As soon as the Navy jets spent their ordnance, four Republic-built F-105 Thunderchief fighter/bombers from Tahkli jointed the party and put six 750 pound bombs each on the enemy, greatly reducing them in numbers and resolve, and sharing lots of the deep, rasping whir of more 20mm. I was starting to regain some lost spirit by then and enjoy the aerial display when the Sandys made an appearance. These were propeller driven Grumman A-1E Skyraiders with lots of time-over-target and lots of .50 caliber ammo to dissuade the enemy from going after downed American pilots. Even from that distance, I could make out the mayhem and carnage of body parts of the enemy being blown off and flung into the air like so many rag dolls. It was surreal like being entrapped in my mind's eye but not fully registering as to what I was seeing. Years would pass and that vision would flash back without ever accepting it as people being killed like that. I was so engrossed in watching the expertise of those beautiful dull gray painted Sandys that I scarcely saw the helicopter touch down almost on top of me. It was an Air America contract rescue chopper, a Choctaw H-34, call sign "Pedro."

I shouted and pointed towards the badly wounded photographer and he lifted off immediately in response; scant minutes later another helicopter touched down to rescue me. This one was also a Sikorsky-built H-34 medium sized Air Force chopper that was in use before the arrival of the big "Jolly Green Giant" HH-3s, and even bigger HH-53s.

I was flown down south to Udorn, Thailand, making a quick refueling stop at the mountainous secret base at Long Tieng. A drunken party ensued at the Sand Box, a name given to the club by the Skyraider A-1E drivers. There, the helicopter pilot officially presented me with one of the first "Jolly Green Giant" footprint patches which became a tradition with the rescued pilots after that. A company Tech Rep, a North American technical representative who was over there to see to the needs of so many of their aircraft presented me with a silver lapel pin in the shape of a T-28. The men were so busy spreading cheer and getting us all drunk and what with everyone involved in congratulating each other on saving a life that I didn't have time to think about the grim alternative. The chances of me not coming through such an ordeal alive were frightening and even worse, the possibility of being a corpse, rotting away and forgotten by everyone except for legions of those awful, big, ugly, hungry, rats and also the hosts of crawling insects hungry for human flesh.

The North Vietnamese had eagerly brought their communist war for "independence" to share with their heretofore ignored neighbors there in the land of the mountains of the moon. Their real purpose in involving the sleepy little backward jungle and mountainous country of Laos was to secure a major portion of their vital Ho Chi Minh Trail. It served as a major lifeline artery in routing men and materials into South Vietnam, thus, avoiding crossing the Demilitarized Zone. The commies were petitioning the U.N. to call for the United States to end their 'illegal aggression' in Southeast Asia and knew that violations on the DMZ by North Vietnam were more easily proved there, but not so in the Laotian panhandle. The North Vietnamese and Pathet Lao forces pushed westward into the Plaine de Jarres to protect its western flank and insure that the Ho Chi Minh Trail stayed open.

While at the bar, pilots liked to tell a mock story about a poor peon civilian pressed into Uncle Ho's resupply service. The story went that this poor chap had spent arduous months braving the perilous Ho Chi Minh Trail through the Laotian panhandle, dodging Yankee Air Pirates who rained fire from the air, poisonous snakes and damnable stinging insects from the ground, drenching rain during monsoon, sickness and disease everywhere. Then, when he finally delivered the two heavy rockets he had carried on his back all that distance, 600 miles or more, the VC quickly placed them in launching tubes and sent them off along with several other rockets in a blinding instant. Turning to the tired old man he shouted, "quick, go get me some more rockets."

One favorite ploy was to have a Laotian employ an elephant and owner from Thailand to cross the Me Kong to do some heavy work in Laos. Once there, the elephant and the Thai owner were pressed into Ho Chi Minh's service and forced to haul supplies down into South Vietnam. Many elephant's and their owners were killed by allied warplanes. This did not endear either the Americans or the communists to the families suffering such a loss. BDA, or bomb damage assessment reports often included trucks, bicycles, an occasional elephant and, as a joke but too true, 10,000 deaf monkeys.

France had joined Russia and the European bloc countries in the United Nations advocating neutrality for Laos. Laos had a King who, along with his Premier, was in charge of his Royalist forces. The Neutralist forces had been linked to the Chinese doctrine form of communism and they were shunned by the Royalists. The Russian brand of communist leaders in North Vietnam mistrusted the neutralists so they created the Pathet Lao directly under their dominance and heavily recruited from the neutralists. Then, the remaining neutralist forces were forced to either join the Pathet Lao or fight. The option to join the Royalists was never an option and the Royalists hoped to avoid the conflict altogether which was a hopeless position. The Royal forces stayed in the river city of Vientiane and in nearby Thailand away from the fighting.

The United States had officially brought all its military advisors out of Laos on October 7, 1962. These Special Forces advisors were called White Star and numbered 666. The North Vietnamese claimed that they had removed all their forces but their army and its dominate control over the Pathet Lao Communist forces stayed to fight for control of Laos. U.N. inspectors were not permitted to enter North Vietnam or northern Laos to verify claims made by Hanoi. To counter this, America sent in 'volunteers' much like General Chennault's men in China prior to the U.S. entry into the war after December 7, 1941. Few members of the press were permitted up in the mountains of the moon country, only a handful of photographers were allowed there to make a record of the unreported conflict for historical purposes. This was a "by invitation only" kind of war and the only way anyone got to go up there was through participation and vowed secrecy.

In combat you don't sleep much, at least not on purpose. You may pass out from too much to drink or be so tired you doze off a bit unexpectedly, but horrible thoughts force themselves into your mind and linger there when you lie down to try to sleep. If by chance you do drift off to sleep, the nightmares come to haunt you and you bolt from that troubled sleep in a gripping fear and a pounding heartbeat that makes cold sweat flow to completely drench you.

I did think about the four Navy pilots and hoped they were down in Tahkli having a much deserved bash just like this one because they could not drink onboard their carrier. I tried to visualize them as they had taken off, or actually had been launched off the deck of a big ship. A moment so intense as to make you dry-mouth scared when you are tossed off the ship in a slingshot manner; then to be staring out at that vast, potentially dangerous and cruel sea. Just thinking about it was enough to give me cold feet, sweaty palms and uneven breathing. The A4D would have borderline flying speed as it was skimped back on precious fuel and laden with 20mm ammo and heavy with five hundred pound bombs. My mind refused to accept ever doing such a thing in the first place. Hell, it took a lot of moxie just to get one of those big scary, heavy fighter/bombers off the ground anyway, especially one with all that ordnance hanging under it. Add to that the fact that you were going to take that deadly cargo to a place where the people were going to shoot holes in your airplane but, other than that, a pilot is still just a pilot.

I was feeling no pain from sucking down all that golden liquid from the glass and the whiskey no longer burned going down. The thoughts ceased to race through my mind about my near capture. Back in survival school, we had been shown some captured films about how appallingly downed American pilots were treated. The enemy liberated your flight boots along with all detachable personal belongings, identification, dog tags and the like. Airmen were discouraged from carrying personal items on combat missions because such things would be used against them during interrogation and torture. According to the school's information, they tied a man's elbows behind his back, usually with a bamboo stick about one inch in diameter and about three feet long to leave the arms and hands free and while you were ambulatory, you were completely defenseless. This also served to provide your captures with a handle to wrest you to cover should a plane fly overhead. Also, they put a rope around your neck to drag you along if you lagged behind or, heaven forbid, you fell down. It was better to lose the skin from the bottom of your feet than be dragged to your death by the noose around your neck.

A very descriptive account had been offered about how a hanged or strangled man's eyes bulged out to have an awesome stare, the face turned white and the mouth gaped open with the tongue lolled out. All aircrew members had all been motivated well enough back in training, but it was another matter when such a situation came so near to being an eventuality. The liquor was a good temporary despoiler of fear and the shock that follows close calls like I had just experienced.

One fact came through my dulled mind as an afterthought and that was because of certain questions I had been asked. I had inadvertently been bait for a much larger enemy force up there than had previously been observed for that area. From the sheer numbers in that force, that must have been a desperate effort to move in behind the neutralists and cut off their retreat towards Long Tieng and Vientiane. This would have greatly lessened the effort in fighting on the Plain of Jars and permitted the enemy to concentrate more on protecting their lifeline to the south, the infamous Ho Chi Minh Trail. Because this force that seemed dedicated on getting me instead got bombed into oblivion, the balance of that part of the secret war was back to square one.

Obviously General Giap decided more men were needed to keep his supply line open in the Laotian panhandle rather than the lesser threat in the secret little war on the PDJ.

A man in a gray flight suit approached and informed me that they had found and brought the other guy back. The man was a contract Air America rescue helicopter pilot and his face was fixed in a seriously concerned mask. The man that had been left behind had used the revolver to shoot himself under his left ear. He said the poor guy was still bleeding from his hip wound, but would have likely made it if not for his suicide. Another man added that if he had been captured, he would have bled to death within hours so he must have opted to go out this way.

These Air America guys truly did a great job over there, they were mostly ex-military and in the same type of business General Chennault of the famed Flying Tigers began before America got into the war after Pearl Harbor. It's doubtful the Japanese would toast him, but they'd sure as hell respect him. The pilot who had brought back the dead cameraman told me about a mission he had flown a few days before. It was up at the site of a major bloody battle up near the Plaine de Jarres. He described how the place was completely covered with slain bodies, almost as if they had been purposely stacked that way. It must have been an eerie feeling as they shut down the helicopter and the three crewmembers got out to walk among the silent dead numbering almost a hundred, counting the natives, CIA, Rangers and enemy. They were mostly Homng native troops. He said the rats were thick, scurrying over the bodies and the crows and vultures made caws of protest at them, the unwanted late arrivals. As they walked among the helter-skelter strewn dead, the pilot froze when he felt a hand grab and hold onto his boot. He leaned down to move a dead Laotian to uncover the owner of the gripping hand. It belonged to a wounded American advisor who had pulled the body of a dead man on top of him and lain there unmoving for hours. He explained some time later that he recognized the American made combat boot and grabbed at it because his throat was too dry to call out for help. Any pilot or member of a rescue team over there knew that the very first thing anyone wanted was water. Fear parches the throat in unimaginable proportions, especially in combat. As soon as the pilot saw the face of a live American in the heap of bodies, he immediately, without being asked, reached down to take out his canteen to give the wounded soldier a much needed drink of water.

The story touched my heart and I felt lucky that this experience had not been any more harrowing and drawn out than it was. America was only getting started over there and I knew that once the war effort really got underway, the stories would be as countless as the falling leaves on a cold, crispy autumn day.

I didn't sleep in a bunk that night as I, like some others got stewed and passed out outside the sand box. The rank smell of vomit was strong all around me and I felt totally unwell. I looked around to see that several men had barfed during the night including myself.

A Major in full flight gear, pistol, knife, radio, survival vest, canteen, everything, brought me some hot black coffee in a paper cup and he held out some white tablets. "What?" I remember asking, trying to focus my blurry eyes on the offer. "They're APCs. Here, down a bunch of them. Maybe some of the painkiller will get into your bloodstream to help before you have to throw up again," the Major smiled down at me and when he saw that I was unable to speak, added, "We always have breakfast for guests whenever you're able to eat. Oh, a C-45's leaving for Bangkok in an hour or so in case you're ready to go by then."

"Thanks Major, " I managed to say in a hoarse, raspy voice after downing the white pills that the Air Force used as aspirin and a few more sips of scalding black coffee.

"No problem, the extra service is included in our bill," he grinned.

"Well, I feel guilty trying to drink up all your whiskey last night," I told him.

"Nothing like good old Kentucky bond to make you feel lousy in the morning," he said giving a laugh, leaving.

I removed my dirty flightsuit and shook it before taking a cold shower in a primitive, canvass walled facility. The shower had a gravity feed for the ambient temperature water which helped clear the cobwebs from my head. The smell of food made me nauseous so I went to the flight line to check on transportation back to Bangkok. Sure enough, a silvery little twin engine C-45 was parked on the ramp. Someone there in the twin engine C-45 was parked on the ramp. Someone there in the operations building had a hotplate and a pot of coffee, which was also freely offered and accepted. About an hour later, two men came and began pre-flighting the plane.

"You're going to Bangkok I understand," I asked the one I assumed to be the Aircraft Commander.

"Yeah, straight run down, we've got a medevac to take to the hospital there," the pilot answered biting an unlighted cigar stub as he spoke.

"Who do I see to get on the manifest," I asked.

"Me, here's the list," he handed me a clipboard with the flight cargo/manifest form on it.

"Thanks," I told him writing my last name with a different first and simply the 91st unit rather than the 6091st as information on it to be included on the flight hoping no one would bother tracing it back to me.

The temperature climbed even faster than the morning sun and the cargo part of the little plane was rapidly becoming an oven. Finally, the air crew, pilot and co-pilot as some call them, boarded and squeezed into the tiny cabin to begin the cockpit part of the check list. I sat on the end of a bench like seat, which was rather like a small, uncomfortable army cot. It was attached to the left inside wall of the plane and hung from two web straps. Two other enlisted men sat down next to me, sharing the cot as it were and another sat on a pull down jump seat attached to the forward bulkhead, facing backwards.

After awhile, three men in protective type white hospital operating gear, round white caps and masks over their faces came on board bearing a stretcher. The metal framed canvass litter was lifted and straps slipped over the ends of the bearer handles to suspend it there on the right side of the plane directly in front of the passengers. We could see the black man who was wrapped in a blanket so only his head was uncovered. He was firmly strapped onto the stretcher and his eyes were closed, evidently unconscious. He was sweating profusely.

"What's the matter with him," one of the other passengers asked.

"We don't know. That's why we're sending him down to the hospital at Bangkok," replied a masked medic just prior to closing the door, locking the astonished passengers inside the crumpled space with a man who could quite possibly infect and kill us all before we ever got to Bangkok.

Someone up front closed the round, flimsy door to the flight deck. As the engines began to crank into a loud roar, the passengers in the back began to breathe through their handkerchiefs or other pieces of cloth. That was seemingly the longest ride we would ever experience. My stomach was still all a-churn and my head was throbbing in pain from the booze from the two nights before so I had no way of knowing if I was catching something that might kill me or not.

The enlisted men had been noticeably busy filling sick sacks most of the way down and that had really fouled up the air back there. Then too, the landing at Don Muang Airport was a bit bumpy to momentarily distract the sick passengers from their concentration. I was very grateful when I could finally open the door and step shakily down onto the scorching tarmac, breathing deeply for the first time in a long while.

Outside, I saw three medics who had their faces covered with masks, also wearing the white protective gowns. I gave a hand/thumb signal towards the plane to them lest they mistake my shaky body for the really sick man inside. My flight suit was partially wet from sweat and it had some white streaks from the salt that had dried out of me in other places. My legs felt weak and rubbery as I managed to make my way past the curious eyes of those medics who were watching to see if maybe I needed to go with them also.

"You gonna be alright Captain?" someone asked.

"Yep, just a little woozy from the flight," I managed to reply, waving my hand over my shoulder.

I got a taxi outside the operations building and began shaking as the hot blast of air blew over me from the open window. The taxi driver helped me out of the little Japanese made car and I went into the Bath and Massage Parlor which was just around the corner from the hotel. I asked for and got two Thai girls to give me a bath and a very thorough massage. The cold beer helped also. It was a marvelous healing experience to my nerve-wracked body. I had to put my stinking flight suit back on as it was all that I had, but I had the girls throw my underwear and socks away. It was just dark by the time I reached my hotel room and I took a hefty pull from the bottle of Crown Royal. I was totally exhausted and lay across the bed feeling my head begin to spin a bit at first, likely when the stiff belt of whiskey reached my blood stream. I drifted off to sleep knowing a severe headache was going to wake me later, but I had the little gold and green Zactrin tablets close at hand for that. It was still dark when I was awakened by the charging, throbbing pain in my head so I took some pills and went back to sleep again when the pain subsided.

At five in the morning, the phone woke me to inform me that it was time to go down to have breakfast with the flight crew.

"Good morning Captain, you look like you just escaped from a body bag. Are you okay," Major Evans asked.

"Yeah, you look like you're a few quarts low, buddy. Here, better have some coffee, "Captain Conroy offered pouring coffee into the white china cup.

I looked down into the blackness there in contrast with the bone white cup to see the steam rise and finally, feeling the pain-killer medication start to ease the pain and then sipping the tongue-numbing hot coffee before I answered.

"A bit too much celebrating the last two nights, I'm afraid. I'll be alright as soon as I get something in my stomach," I announced.

"Maybe like a stomach pump to extract the booze," Major Evans teased.

There was no way I could tell them what had happened. It was all highly classified and no one would ever be permitted to confirm or deny those events that should never have happened anyway. So, I only nodded agreement amid the laughter and sipped my coffee, thinking how great it was to just be there.

The End

These Guys

A story told to me by Bill Person, ex-Cold War Warrior, ex-Vietnam Era. This story (or Affidavit-Declaration) is by Stephen Crittenden.

AIR CIA
By Stephen Crittenden as told to Bill Person

This is just one of 11 such Airlines operated by "Uncle Sam," many more have been created as some disband or disappear. (What's in a name?).

AFFIDAVIT-DECLARATION

I, Stephen Crittenden, do hereby declare:

I make this declaration-affidavit with the intention that the information will be used to bring to an end the wrongful activities that I witnessed by high-level government employees in control of the Central Intelligence Agency, the Department of Justice, and other government entities. I operated a covert CIA proprietary airline from 1986 to 1988, and in this key position I discovered the wrongful acts described in this document.
I joined the Army at 17, and was in the Army Special Forces program. I did three nine month tours of duty in Vietnam, from 1969 to 1973; I then went with Air America from January 1974 to December 1975. During this time I was checked out as pilot in the C-123 and C-130 aircraft. In 1976, the Central Intelligence Agency formed a proprietary airline for which I was made the titular head. The Agency provided me with five C-123 military aircraft and $20 million in start up capital. My name was placed on the CIA proprietary airline operation, and it was called Crittenden Air Transport. It was based in Bangkok. I was 24 years of age, and did not have the financial resources or expertise to have formed and operated the airline until a later date. The CIA provided management personnel and did most of the scheduling from CIA headquarters at McLean, Virginia. I was provided a mentor to organize and operate the airline. This CIA assistance and operation permitted me to fly many of the flights. This CIA operation continued from 1976 to December 31, 1988. I had no mortgage payments to make, and engine replacements and aircraft upgrading were provided by the CIA.
Initially, Crittenden Air Transport aircraft flew to seven different countries flying arms, including Thailand, China, El Salvador, Nigeria, South Africa, Saudi Arabia, and the USSR. Payment to Crittenden Air Transport for the flights were initially received from the CIA's Shamrock Corporation through

the Bank of Bangkok. Payments were based upon full loads and at five dollars per pound of permissible cargo weight.

The first flight of Crittenden Air Transport, in 1976, under orders of the CIA, was from Bangkok to Beijing. This flight was arranged, authorized, and directed by the CIA. The cargo was unloaded at Bangkok, where another CIA proprietary airline, Southern Air Transport, picked it up for shipment to Los Angeles. At that time, Crittenden was flying short range twin engine military C 123s, and Southern Air Transport was flying long range four engine C 130s. Crittenden Air Transport received a $100,000 check from the Shamrock Corporation for that flight.

In 1978, two years after the formation of Crittenden Air Transport, the CIA provided me at no charge, seven military C 123s, and one Boeing 707, which came from Evergreen International Airlines operation at Pinal Airport near Marana, a small town north of Tucson, Arizona. Again, no money was paid for the aircraft, and no money was owed on them. Eventually, Crittenden Air Transport had over fifteen aircraft that were provided by the Central Intelligence Agency.

With these additional and longer range aircraft, the CIA ordered Crittenden Air Transport to fly into additional countries, including the United States, Mexico, France, Germany, Great Britain, Egypt, Italy, Columbia, Bolivia, and Panama. Payments for each flight increased, and the checks were made out by Shamrock Corporation with accounts at the BCCI bank in Grand Cayman, Valley Bank in Phoenix, Arizona, Barclays Bank in Miami, and Gulf Bank in the Bahamas.

Common destinations included Sydney, Australia; Manila; Philippines; Singapore; Miami, Florida, San Salvador, El Salvador; Guatemala City, Guatemala, Managua, Nicaragua; San Jose, Costa Rica, Panama City, Panama, Mena, Arkansas.

A typical flight from Manila or Bangkok to the United States would make the first stop at Honolulu for fuel, and go non-stop to locations in the south eastern part of the United States. Special codes were used in air traffic control procedures to advise customs to ignore the aircraft and not make any customs inspection.

After receiving the long range C-130 Aircraft, Crittenden Air Transport handled much of the Pacific Rim cargo for the CIA which was formerly handled by Southern Air Transport. SAT then confined its operations mostly to Central and South America, until it returned to the Pacific Rim.

The CIA's Shamrock Corporation, which paid for most of the flights conducted from 1976 to 1988, paid Crittenden Air Transport approximately

$571,350,000 from 1976 to 1988, with checks written on various bank accounts, including the bank of Credit and Commerce International (BCCI), Valley Bank in Phoenix, and Barclay Bank in Miami.

I flew several flights for the CIA into Moscow during the Cold War period, including one flight in the summer of 1976, when a load of M-16 rifles were off loaded. The load had been brought to Crittenden Air Transport at Manila by Southern Air Transport. A load of Russian AK-47s were then loaded on the C-130 and flown to San Salvador in El Salvador. At San Salvador the unloading of the arms was coordinated by John Forsyth, who worked for James Pennington, the CIA's liaison to Anastasio Somoza, who headed the Nicaraguan government.

I received my instructions from the CIA for the various missions by phone, or by instructions on floppy disks. The floppy disks would be delivered by courier, and in one case the courier was G. Gordon Liddy, former CIA operative.

In some cases I called my CIA handler at CIA headquarters in McLean, Virginia, Ross Lipscomb, and upon reaching the CIA operator would give them my access code, responding, "Access code 4613." The operator would then transfer the call to my CIA contact.

Among the CIA proprietary airlines with whom I had contact was Ports of Call Airline, based in Denver, Colorado. Crittenden Air Transport C-130s hauled four loads during 1983 and 1984 to Guatemala City, where the loads were transferred to Ports of Call Convair 990 jets. Each C-130 carried approximately 20,000 pounds of cargo, that were distributed into two Convair 990s. Ports of Call aircraft operated in close liaison with Evergreen International.

By 1988, I recognized that some of the CIA operations were inflicting harm upon the national interests of the United States, causing me on December 31, 1988, to shut down the Crittenden Air Transport operation. Aircraft were abandoned in various locations, including three C-123x and vice C-130s at Caracas, Venezuela; and seven C-130s at the airport outside Bangkok, Thailand. My CIA handlers were angry at this shut down, and based upon what I knew about past CIA conduct, I knew that some form of retaliation would follow. Also, the knowledge that I possessed of corrupt activities by the CIA against the United States caused me to be a serious danger to those in control of the CIA and related government entities.

As expected, a year later, in 1991, Justice Department prosecutors charged me with a wire fraud offense, for a matter that occurred in 1986 while I was still working for the CIA, and which involved covert CIA operation. This is the scenario of what happened in 1986. One of my contacts at CIA headquarters in McLean, Virginia, Ross Lipscomb, wired $100,000 to Valley Bank, instructing the bank to place the money in escrow, to be released upon the possible purchase of a Boeing 707 aircraft in which a subsidiary of Crittenden Air Transport, C and C Brokerage of Phoenix, Arizona, acted as aircraft broker. After I inspected the Boeing 707 at the CIA proprietary, Evergreen's Marana facility, I determined that it was an earlier model and not what Lipscomb wanted. I met Lipscomb in Long Beach, California, and advised him of this fact. Lipscomb then notified Valley Bank that the deal was off, and Valley Bank then returned the $100,000 deposit money to Lipscomb. Prior to this return of the escrow money, Valley Bank had placed the $100,000 escrow deposit by error into the C and C Brokerage account, increasing the previous balance of approximately $30,000 to $130,000. While this extra money was in C and C's account, the financial officer, Rick Challis, wrote checks that used up $87,000 of that $100,000 deposit. One check for $50,000 was to one of his friends, who had no relationship to C and C Brokerage. Challis had no authority to make that payment.

I had a practice of signing checks in blank because I was often out of the area on CIA business. Challis would then write checks relating to the business, placing the required second signature on the checks. I learned of these unauthorized payments when Valley Bank management asked Challis and me to sign a promissory note to cover the overdrawn funds.

Even though Challis had written the unauthorized checks, he was never charged by Justice Department prosecutors. Only I was charged, even though I was not involved in the writing of the checks that resulted in the overdrawn condition, and was unaware of the wrongful acts perpetrated by Challis. After the charges were filed against me, my CIA handler, Lipscomb, urged me to plead nolo contedere after the charges were filed, assuring me that I would be shortly released. I considered such a plea to be a not guilty plea. Court appointed attorney Titterington did not provide any defense, urging me to sign a plea agreement that was handed to me several minutes before the hearing started. U.S. District Judge Roger G. Strand then sentenced me to five years in prison and five years probation after release, which was far beyond the sentencing guidelines that went into effect after the 1986 date. Shortly after my 1995 release, I was arrested and charged with parole violation for failure to keep the probation officer aware of my home address.

It is my strong belief that the charges against me were an attempt to silence and to discredit me, in the event that I disclosed the serious corruption within the Central Intelligence Agency. The charges against me were a sham, based upon:

*The person writing the checks, Rich Challis, was never charged, even though he committed the act of writing checks that exceeded the bank balance prior to the accidental deposit of funds into the C and C Brokerage account.

*I was not aware of these checks as they were written, and had never authorized the writing of these checks.

*The person wiring the $100,000 escrow funds to Valley Bank, Ross Lipscomb, a CIA employee at CIA headquarters, never lost any money.

*Valley Bank requested, and received, a promissory note for the amount of money that was placed into the C and C account in error, and was dissipated by the check writing of Ricck Challis. Any financial loss would have been a result of the bank's error; was compensated by a promissory note, and due to the acts of someone other than myself.

*My CIA contacts at McLean, Virginia, urged me not to raise a defense (which I complied with), and assured me that I would spend only a short time in prison.

*I didn't realize the legal aspects of the charge, or the nolo contendere plea, and was not advised properly of the errors or dangers of my pleading.

*During the court hearing in 1991, FBI agent Gill Hirschy testified that he had contacted the CIA and that they had told him that they had no connection to me. Either he lied, or the CIA lied to him.

*On July 5, 1995, a CIA contact in McLean, Virginia contacted me by phone, ordering me to stop talking to Rodney F. Stich (who was seeking to expose government misconduct) and offered me a CIA position in Belize, starting up an airline. The CIA indicated that FBI agent Hirschy had contacted them and disclosed that I was exposing CIA activities. Reference to the FBI agent indicated that the FBI knew I was a CIA asset, and had not only failed to disclose this to the court, but testified under oath at the 1991 hearing and sentencing that I had no connection with the CIA.

I have disclosed considerable information about my activities to former federal investigator "Rodney Stich" in the hopes that he can make known the corrupt activities occurring within the Central Intelligence Agency. Mr. Stich has sought to expose high level government corruption that he had uncovered through various means, and by publication of books intended to inform the public of this corruption and its cover-up.

If needed to establish my prior CIA association, I can provide the names and the phone numbers of CIA contacts at McLean, Virginia, and at other locations.

I have offered to provide information on high-level drug traffickers to DEA agents, and to the U.S. attorney and to the FBI, in exchange for halting the prosecution of me associated with the charges filed in 1991. To this day they have refused to receive this information. It is my belief that this refusal is due to the fact that any exposure of these high-level drug traffickers would reveal the role played by the CIA in a pattern of drug trafficking into the United States.

I declare under penalty of perjury that these statements are true and correct, to the best of my knowledge and belief, and known to me as a result of my long association with the Central Intelligence Agency. I understand that this declaration-affidavit may be presented into court proceedings.

Aug. 14, 1995 Stephen L. Crittenden

MORE BOOKS & STUFF-*This is what Bill Person wrote for one of his four books, this one being "The Queen Bee Delta Project."*
By Bill Person

This is what I wrote as a description for:
THE QUEEN BEE DELTA PROJECT

The top secret story behind the Vietnam War and why we were not supposed to win: Moscow set the time bomb and President Kennedy inherited it from Truman and Eisenhower, but it didn't explode until Johnson's term in office. Stalin and Krushchev had gotten a commitment from three U.S. Presidents that America would not go to war with Russia over any territory west of Japan, namely Korea and Southeast Asia. Kennedy's demonstrated lack of resolve in Cuba in 1961 and 1962 sealed America's fate in Vietnam. Secretary of Defense Robert S. McNamara and his civilian planners defied the military plan of the Joint Chiefs of Staff and with the staged Gulf of Tonkin incident and then the bloody attacks on Camp Halloway and Camp Carroll, the war was precipitated. Ignoring the viable plans recommended by the Joint Chiefs of Staff, hitting 94 selective targets in North Vietnam within three weeks that would strategically cripple Hanoi's ability to wage war, McNamara and other civilian leaders convinced President Johnson to demonstrate U.S. airpower without destroying important facilities that we may later have to rebuild. Anti-war activists managed to get the word to Hanoi that our resolve was not all that decisive in winning a war against them. This was made obvious in the fact that our government permitted merchant ships from communist and democratic registry to deliver materials essential to waging a war in the south to the port of Haiphong unmolested.

The Queen Bee Delta Project was tasked with determining enemy air defense capabilities which was a prelude to initiate the bombing of North Vietnam. It was intended to induce Hanoi leaders to the negotiating table in Paris. The humiliating defeat at Dien Bien Phu in 1954 convinced the French to abandon their colony of Indochina. Ho Chi Minh had recruited and tested the mettle of his Communist Party inner core fighting the Japanese. This taught him that bullets were more positive than ballots when trying to take over all of Southeast Asia, his long stated objective. Ho Chi Minh, studied Communism in England, France and Russia for thirty years. He helped found the Communist Party in France before returning to Vietnam in 1941. He organized a resistance to the Japanese, forming the Communist Party there.

"Uncle Ho," as he was known, was no stranger to hard core Communism and an avowed enemy of any form of democratic free choice. The war did not end with the defeat of Japan for "Uncle Ho's," followers, and while the Allies concentrated on peace, his Viet Minh sought to take over all of Southeast Asia by bloody revolution. Ho Chi Minh was the main player in the "Domino Theory."

The project officer for this pending air war over North Vietnam, and Air Force Captain happened to learn of an incredible scheme by the two French-Canadians to steal items of value from Laotian war victims. They had the "blessing" of someone in the CIA and with total sanction from certain U.S. Congressmen who authorize a bogus agency to receive the life savings of desperate Laotian businessmen and then have them killed to keep their money. A British MI5 agent arranged for the assassination of these two French-Canadians in this money stealing project. Then, in another separate activity that involved these same men, Israeli spies steal four French made atomic bombs from them that were intended for the enemy in Hanoi. Captain Perry eagerly participated in the cover-up after he discovers that his girl friend had been killed by a bomb on board a plane intended to eliminate the last of the Laotian depositors. He learns that revenge is not as sweet as he had believed and that compromise is a means of survival.

AND while I'm at it, here's one of my short stories that got published in some other Vet publications.

INTELLIGENCE MATTERS

I have given some thought to the overall and complex intelligence effort back during the Vietnam War. There seemed to be no really good place to begin.

I was assigned to Eastern NORAD/CONAD Region at Stewart AFB, New York as the Special Security Officer, SSO and the inheritor of a real mess. It had little to do with security but was instead an SI (Special Intelligence or codeword material) intelligence complex.

When I arrived at Stewart AFB, New York in June 1965, a Major Dubrow was most anxious for me to relieve him. He had been there for a few years and had been completely ignored by the senior officers on his billet. That means personnel cleared to see Top Secret codeword material. The Director of Intelligence, an Army Lt. Col. had tried to get him to become one of the "consumer" intelligence types in his outer office but he had become sort of a recluse inside his vault-like compound. He continued to receive materials and keep the facility open with two sergeants in the communications field. He also had a Japanese wife which is a "no no" for holding a SI clearance. No foreign wives of most nations allowed. The exception was Canada, U.K., Australia and New Zealand where background checks could be conducted to determine if they were subversives.

In 1965, the Air Force Security Service relinquished its control of the Special Security Offices to Defense Intelligence Agency. This was a system to present highly classified Special Intelligence information to the commanders and their staffs of the other commands, i.e. SAC, TAC, ADC, etc. I was greeted with a pale green covered book by the Department of Defense, DOD Directive 5200.17 which was the new authority and operating procedures for a Special Security Office.

Once I assumed the office complex, I went to see Major. Gen. Gordon H. Austin and told him I was his new SSO. I informed him that Defense Intelligence Agency had just assumed control of this facility and that I planned to conduct weekly briefings in the SSO briefing room at 1000 each Friday. My briefings would consist of world events that, in my opinion, he and his staff needed to know. In the event of a war, the first indications would come from this source and if he did not make use of it, he would not know how to use such information if we ever do have a war. I told him that if he and those cleared on his staff chose not to attend, I planned to go to Washington where DIA was located in the Pentagon annex and close the facility because it served no purpose being there if it was not used. From that day on, no one missed a meeting and most of them came in for special background information. My two NCOs operated the secure communications equipment and with the courier bringing material in weekly, I believe my briefings were the equal of any SSO anywhere. Because I was the one preparing and presenting them, I know what was presented to the commander and his cleared staff.

My experience in the intelligence field gave me a sound background to be able to talk with ease about almost every subject since I had studied the materials since October 1962.

In early 1964, while I was at Wakkanai AS, Japan, my intercept technicians intercepted a special signal and after we determined its significance, and I reported it, I was criticized for meddling in what was "not my area of responsibility." Later, a thick, illustrated report was disseminated to the upper levels of certain commands to confirm what I had reported as fact.

In mid February 1965, the White House military planners had already approved the commencement of bombing north of the 1954 U.N. truce line. The bombing was intended as an inducement to encourage the communist leaders in Hanoi to abandon their pursuit of the war in the south. The project codename was "Queen Bee Delta" and it was to use a specially equipped Lockheed transport aircraft with four prop-jet engines and was dubbed the EC-130BII. A crew of ten highly skilled intelligence professionals operated electronics equipment installed in a secure metal container in the cargo compartment. This cocoon-like container was outfitted with an array of super sophisticated communications equipment that could intercept and record signals from North Vietnamese radios to determine the enemy's air defense capabilities. By listening in on the North Vietnamese radio transmissions, the U.S. intelligence community could determine if the enemy could detect our planes flying close to and indeed over North Vietnam's air space. Small drones and U-2 spy planes were photographing every square inch of the country in broad daylight while the EC-130BII monitored their reactions. If there had been any serious capabilities to shoot down a drone, the big plane with the "ears" would soon detect it and report it. Gathering information about a country, its air defense capabilities, passive radars and hostile guns, the most likely targets to bomb and a host of other information is called intelligence. This tasking of the Queen Bee plane was deemed essential because no non-communist military observer had been up north of the 17th Parallel since the fall of Dien Bien Phu in 1954. This cease fire line established by the U.N. was designated as the DMZ, the Demilitarized Zone.

U.S. fighter/bombers were going to cut the supply lines of men and materials to the south, and also deliver an ever increasing punishment on the north. This approach was intended to crater their rods, knock out their bridges and destroy their supplies in a like manner of a giant hand squeezing the neck of a snake. It either stopped wiggling or was crushed to death. To a non-military press, the plan by the Secretary of Defense sounded convincing. Often called "king of the number crunchers" and a man who knew the cost of everything and the value of nothing, McNamara made it look viable on paper and maps. He was a most convincing speaker and could vocally destroy anyone who was not absolutely precise with his facts. President Johnson liked this characteristic in McNamara and relied upon his judgment. The Secretary of Defense was determined to gather his facts slowly as he began to wage an air war even more slowly. McNamara was absolutely certain that if he proceeded ever-so-slowly in his bombing objectives, the risk to American airmen would be lessened. But the scarce amount of wherewithal for North Vietnam to be able to wage a war in the South was in concentrated areas around their port at Haiphong and at Hanoi, not scattered all along routes to South Vietnam as McNamara reasoned. Merchant ships registered to Canada, France and other nations friendly to America, as well as the Soviet Union lay at anchor off the coast. These ships were providing the very life blood to Hanoi to resist our initial bombings that did little real damage. The U.S. State Department did not want to risk offending anyone by bombing close to their ships there at Haiphong. The fighter pilots would laughingly call this the world's first enemy-friendly war.

The targeted areas that were approved by the White House were divided into seven parts. These were called Route Packs or packages for short. Actually, these parcels were targeted sections north of the DMZ and they were numbered Rout Package One or RP-1 through RP-6. The lowest numbered Route Pack was RP-1 and it was located at and immediately north of the DMZ. It later became known as the infamous "Tallyho" for fighter pilots who logged missions there. RP-6 was a zone stretching from Haiphong up to Hanoi. The ensuing numbered Route Packs were parcels of territory in between and the intention was to encourage the enemy to come to the negotiating tables through a show of force without directly conducting an all-out frontal assault, total destructive type warfare. It was in fact a new approach to warfare by slowly inflicting the least amount of injury as a means of demonstrating rather than actual punishing. No U.S. General worth his salt bought this approach while those who did were put in command.

While I was Queen Bee Delta Project Officer, my back-end intercept crew began to monitor Navy's Task Force 77 transmitting launch activities over hand-held radios. I knew that the Russians had ELINT/SIGINT/COMINT fishing trawlers operating nearby and that they would be intercepting vital intelligence about our strike force composition, ordnance and intended targets. I directed my 10-man intercept crew of linguists to record these transmissions and I sent seventeen reels of tapes to the Director of Intelligence to confirm my identification of a major breach of security. CNO and other members of the Pentagon sent a scathing message back, through channels, to say that the only means of getting such information was Queen Bee Delta and that was not my tasked mission. I went on to state that I was neglecting my primary mission by wasting time recording these "friendly transmissions." It also stated that Navy's Task Force 77 was not violating any security transmissions. I responded that the tapes had been recorded while en route to Da Nang from Bangkok to pick up fighter escort prior to taking position at Yankee Station. I was directed not to do this anymore by the Pentagon. Gen. Blake, DIRNSA sent me an "Eyes Only" message to keep doing it and to send him the tapes via courier and not to tell anyone. Actually, Blake, the Director of National Security was the boss over me and the Queen Bee Delta project and as such, should have been the one to make that call, not the Pentagon.

As the war progressed and I was seeing MiGs practicing an intercept technique that I had seen Soviet IAPVO pilots perform back while at Wakkanai, I sent a special message suggesting top cover for fighter/bomber strike forces for both Air Force and Navy. I was told to let command decisions be made at the appropriate level and keep to my assigned mission which was intercept and report, leaving the planning to Washington. After we lost four f-105s to a single MiG that command said the North Vietnamese didn't have the capability to do and the Navy lost four F4s to Chinese MiGs, that changed. This took place on April 3 and 5 of 1965. In a little more than a month, North Vietnam had gone from a near defenseless condition to a level that started to seriously challenge America's air power. I was concerned aircraft commanders and Navy ship captains were not cleared to know what the mission of those vessels were which I considered vital in the decisions for their own safety. By vessels, I include submarines and other ships that the Navy used to listen in on foreign communications.

I doubt any of the aircraft commanders or their flight crews knew exactly what was taking place in their planes as they flew EC-118s, EC-47s, EC-130s, EC-135s. Perhaps the SAC crews knew a little more in their RB-47s and RB-57s but I know that neither captains, Cmdr. Lloyd Bucher of the Pueblo nor Cmdr. William L. McGonagle of the Liberty knew the extent of their missions.

The intelligence community had a myriad of collection efforts all over SEA and this was fed back to Wheeler AFB, Hawaii in what must have been a river of intelligence. We knew that the world press published everything they could find out about the day-to-day activities of the war and this served as a very good intelligence source to Hanoi. Perhaps because of this, special intelligence and the information picked up by CIA was sent directly through their channels and denied to combat commanders at all levels. PAC Security Region had reams of vital intelligence at Wheeler that could have been shared with the intelligence Directorate at Hickham but this did not happen. The information went straight to NSA and the White House. President Johnson and Robert S. McNamara were the ones to review this intelligence and make the major combat decisions.

In January 1968, while flying as a Batcat on an EC-121R over the Laotian panhandle, I detected tanks moving down the Ho Chi Minh Trail on Route 9. I sent a message from Korat to report this, by-passing Task Force Alpha at Nakhon Panom. The same intelligence office at Hickham that Larry Clum worked replied that Air Force intelligence estimates claimed that the Vietnamese had no such tanks. On February 8th, 11 Soviet-built amphibious PT-76 tanks and 400 NVA troops with supporting artillery attacked the Army Special Forces camp at Lang Vei overrunning it. The term, "tanks in the wire!" was used routing U.S. forces from their base on Route 9.

The Siege began with Tet '68 with the Rangers at Lan Vei reporting tanks in the wire, overrunning them. Later, it was reported that these were not tanks, merely amphibious PT-76s. I doubt the Rangers could truly appreciate the significant difference when this assault woke them with boring through the protective barbed wire.

I believe that President Johnson and Defense Secretary McNamara did not want the Commanders in the area to have such intelligence for fear that it might leak out to the press. This in turn might, as the Intelligence Community always reasoned, would deny us that intercept source in the future. Like the press always knew, to reveal a source denies that and other such sources in the future, so you don't make them public. There was supposedly enough other source intelligence back then: photo-reconnaissance, trail watchers and direct reports from the forward areas.

I can only imagine what the commanders from Hickham, Tan Son Nhut, and Udorn must have thought when they examined the intelligence information they did see and then to have directions from Washington to assign a specific target where they may not have any information at their levels. During World War II, Churchill severely limited his ULTRA and MAGIC to but a few top people. In the Pentagon, an Army General threw a codeword document into his trash basket. He was removed from the access list. Churchill would have shot him.

We have all seen a tiny part of that war and it is doubtful that all of the real story will ever be told. I was privileged to see more than most and I write about some of it but I still have a lot of questions to ask if I could ever know who might be able to answer them. I do not accept the term "we lost that war" but rather we were not allowed to win it and then ordered out. The Queen Bee Delta intercepted tapes that we recorded and dropped off at Da Nang for transcription to be read in Washington, told us peons that we could have destroyed North Vietnam's ability to fight a war in South Vietnam if we had bombed the 92 targets recommended by the JCS in March and April 1965 before the enemy had a chance to prepare for a protracted war. I personally gave a briefing to LBJ in September 1968 to tell him about the sensor war. Until that time, I thought he was the good guy and he was being advised badly. I met the real enemy that day but it took me a while to realize it; 58,000 Americans did not need to die over there if we had had a good military leader. Good generals do not make good presidents and good presidents do not make good generals. I stand corrected, we did have George Washington, didn't we but they broke the mold after him.

I recall briefing President Johnson that September day in 1968, about the sensor war. He came to meet me in an office at Fort Meade, Maryland, sat me in a chair and took one facing me. He grabbed hold of the armrests of my chair and pulled me up close to face him and started asking questions. He really did not seem interested in what I had to say but kept asking questions that seemed to have no bearing on what we were doing over there. I got the impression he was not interested in being effective, only in us doing what we were directed to do regardless of the result.

THE END

This story appears here courtesy of Bill Person who served in the USAFSS.

TURTLENECK

We've written lately about the great lengths the White House has to go to in order to maintain secrecy surrounding President Bush's unscheduled visits to Iraq - an item that brought "a smile" to the face of one William C. Grayson, who practically compromised a similar surprise presidential visit 40 years ago.

Mr. Grayson forwards to Inside the Beltway an anecdote he's written - "security-reviewed and approved for publication" by both the National Security Agency and U.S. Air Force (USAF) headquarters-that goes back to 1966, when a rumor rippled through U.S. ranks that President Johnson would be making a surprise visit to troops in Vietnam. "One of the missions of my unit, Detachment 5 (Det 5) of the 6922nd Security Wing, USAF Security Service, was to intercept and analyze USAF communications throughout Vietnam and to report detected security breaches along with corrective recommendations," Mr. Grayson recalls. (NOTE: Trish this was TRANSEC for Transmission Security.) Sure enough, on Oct. 25, a flight plan was intercepted addressed to the Saigon Air Route Traffic Control Center for a C-141 transport flying from the Philippines to Cam Ranh Bay in South Vietnam. The plane's tail appeared "familiar" to the security analyst, and upon checking records he confirmed the same C-141 once carried the president's armored limousine while on other official travel.

"From this little tidbit, it seemed likely that the rumored visit might occur on the 26th at Cam Ranh Bay." We wrote a secret 'Transmission Security Analysis Report' [TSAR], suggesting that LBJ was possibly going to Cam Ranh Bay," says Mr. Grayson, who sent the report with "immediate precedence" to Air Force contacts in Vietnam and the United States. At which time, the security analyst almost lost his neck.

Next day, on the 25th, we intercepted a telephone call from the chief of staff of the USAF himself in the Pentagon to the commander 7th Air Force, a hundred yards from where we were working. Clearly, our TSAR of the 24th had hit the bull's-eye and the chief of staff had been briefed. "I personally replayed the taped call several times; the chief of staff was obviously mightily annoyed," says Mr. Grayson. "He chewed out the commander 7th Air Force in unkind words and instructed him to find out who had compromised the presidential visit and to hang two of his private anatomical features 'from London Bridge'. I knew what the right thing to do was but ... the Air Force Special Security Officer, SSO who owned the compound we worked in, thought I should let the matter lie and not rattle the chief of staff's cage. I think he used the word 'suicide' in his guidance; local predictions of my certain gruesome execution abounded.

"But there was dead silence from all quarters. No one at any level of authority ever said a word to Det 5 about it. Next day, LBJ and General [William] Westmoreland met at Cam Ranh Bay as planned, just as we had reported. As a memento of the moment, the troops of Det 5 gave me a wood-carved turtle with a little plaque that reads: 'The turtle only makes progress when his neck is sticking out.'

"That turtle has shared my many offices since 1966."

To be assured by Bill Person that it was Grayson who got the turtle, as I had thought Bill had gotten it, when first reading this story, Bill wrote in an e-mail, to me: "Hi Trish, I didn't get the turtle, Grayson did. I stuck my neck out and felt it get tromped on a few times, hard. Once I got a small wood carved statue of a spy with a pointy hat and cape holding a crooked edged dagger behind his back but someone stole it. I have looked everywhere for one but never found another."

Fondly,
Bill

Here's hoping you do find another statue like the one that was stolen from you, Captain. [The Editor]

I asked Bill Person, Capt.(Ret.)USAFSS, to write a poem for this book. He did so and I gave it the title. Thank you Bill, and all of my cold war "buddies" for your interest in making this book come to fruition. God bless you all, and God bless America. Here's to you, and all those who didn't make it.

REFLECTIONS OF HONOR
By Bill Person

Let's take a silent moment
To reflect on what's been done
That made our country what it is
With so very much for everyone.

There's no way to tell the whole of it
Or even barely just begin
Behind the terrible battles
In wars we had to win.

So much was passionately given
Their deeds might not be told
Of our vanquishing belligerent foes
In the hot wars and the Cold.

Now evil words are uttered
Casting wrong on what was right
By those who seek now surrender
From heroes who went to fight.

View the gauntlet cast in dare
A challenge to cleanse the air
In battle now of verbiage
To bestow honor bold and fair.

These Guys

FROM BILL PERSON'S BOOK: QUEEN BEE DELTA
By Bill Person

From: Bill Person
To: Trish Schiesser
Sent: Friday, February 03, 2006 3:22 PM
Subject: Re: .45 ACP

This is from an excerpt of Bill Person's book Queen Bee Delta towards the end of Chapter 10.

P.S. Pappy wrote:
The Army pilots were given the .38 revolver as were other military pilots. My brother, army chopper driver, wanted a carbine to be beside him in that bird. Don't blame him.

Bill Person answers:
I agree Pappy, the .45 kicks ass!
When I got to Las Cruces, NM in 1960, we had .45s and .30 cal. M1(3) carbines.
I had to qualify on both since I was pay officer. We had a problem with the local cops back then and one day, the Highway Patrolman came to my office there 15 miles west of the town and said he was tired of having airmen hide out from him on the base. I had the additional duty of Security and Law Enforcement, over the handful of Air Cops. I called in the Sgt. in charge and gave him instructions that any airman being chased by the police were not to be permitted entry, and held for the cop.
After that we never had any more problems. The patrolman, Dave, stopped by on his patrol and would have coffee with me. Then, sometimes we'd go to our range, nearby and fire our weapons. He had a .45 cal magnum. Never saw another one. Anyway, I got to do a lot of firing of the old .45 back then. As I was coming up on my 4th year of service and was to receive a longevity ribbon, I decided I didn't want to wear just one lousy, meaningless blue and white ribbon so I really went to work practicing up to be able to earn a Small Arms Marksmanship Ribbon. It was an ugly green and white one but it was better having two. I also scored high with the carbine.
Back in college, we carried the M-1 Garand in the AFROTC Sabres Drill Team and a couple of them still had firing pins. We got some ammo and came here to Post Oak and fired them. I loved that rifle, it was awesome.

Then, before I went to SEA in March 1965 from Japan, I had to qualify with the .38 cal. Combat Masterpiece and the M-16. I didn't like the M-16 but the pistol was kind of okay. On the night of March 7, 1965, I was at the entrance of the highly classified complex on Monkey Mountain at Da Nang, waiting for a message to come back from DIRNSA, Gen. Blake. That was the night before the Marines landed at China Beach and the Rangers were out scouring the countryside for VC. Couldn't let the Marines get sniped at on their amphib landing. Hell, two Jarheads did get hurt when their legs were caught between two barges. No shots fired in anger though.

Anyway, that night, a Green Beanie nudged me awake from my bedroll and shushed me, pointing to the hillside below. I had two .38s with me, one on a pistol belt and one in a shoulder holster, one was on loan from the pilot of my EC-130. I stood blinking into the dark and suddenly all hell broke loose with shooting from some VC being rousted and trying to rush the compound and us firing back down into them. I squeezed off my 6 rounds in first one then the other pistol, sort of shell shocked at all the loud reports of weapons around me. When the shooting stopped, some Green Beanies went down and checked on the VC dead. They were loaded up on a truck and taken on down to the air base the next morning.

Later, after I was separated from the AF, I got word that I had been awarded the Bronze Star for my "defending role" of the "complex." The CO put everyone who fired a weapon, in for it. I also got two other ribbons for that time as Queen Bee Delta Project Officer, the Presidential Unit Citation and the Outstanding AF Unit Award. I had to send in my orders and itinerary to get the awards belatedly.

Hey I saw a .50 cal pistol and it looks like a big dude.

I'm still recovering and feeling improvement each day. Radiation sure takes a while to get over.

Regards,
Bill Person

Bill Person was recovering from cancer at the time, hence the "radiation" message. He's still with us, doing just fine, I am pleased and proud to say. [The Editor]

These Guys

These songs, sung by some guys Bill Person knew and sang with, are from their days at old Korat, sent to me via e-mail October 20, 2005. With courtesy to Irv Levine and Dick Jonas, who wrote these songs. I thank you all for allowing me to put these into THESE GUYS, because the songs tell the stories as they were way back then.

RED RIVER VALLEY
(Song of Teak Flight at Takhli)

From this valley they say you are leaving
I will miss your bright eyes and sweet smile
For they say you are taking the sunshine
That has brightened this place for awhile.

Come and sit by my side if you love me
Do not hasten to bid me adieu
And I'll tell you about the Red River Valley
And why it always makes me feel blue.

Way up yonder they say they've been going,
Where the Red flows by Hanoi to the sea,
And we call it the Red River Valley,
Where the flak is as bad as it can be.

To this valley he said we were flying,
But he never saw the pay that he earned,
Many jocks have flown into that valley
And a number have never returned.

So I listened as he briefed on the mission
That night at the bar Teak Flight did sing
About going to the Red River Valley
And how I was to fly on his wing.

Oh the flak was so thick in the valley,
That the MiGs and the missiles we don't need
We'd fly high and down sun in the valley
And I'll guard well the ass of Teak Lead.

Now if things turn to shit in the valley
And the briefing he gave I did not heed
They'll be waiting at the Hanoi Hilton
Where it's fish heads and rice for Teak Lead.
              (NOTE: TEAK ONE or the leader, LEAD)

Now the roar of the jets on the runway,
Is a sound that the MiGs may well heed,
As we climb and head towards the valley,
Keeping close on the tail of Teak Lead.

We refueled on the way to the valley
Back in the States it had always been fun
But with thunder and lightning all around us
"Twas the last A-A-R for Teak One.
              (air-to-air refueling)

The boss weasel warned of Fan Songs past the target
              (Boss weasel leads the fighters to attack)
Tall white poles would rise to meet us in the sky
When we pulled up off of our bomb run
              (Fan songs=SAM radar.)
The SAMs were fused to hit us where we fly
              (surface-to-air missiles).

Our MiG chaser jets were up high to guard the strike force
While twenty-ones took off from Yep and Ph.C. Yen
But gomer planes would be in place to jump our slow ones
And their cannon bursts would surely do them in.
              (F-4s on Cap. fighter protection)

The triple A rained up thick from the gunners
The orange flashes changed to black the sky
I followed Lead on down from the IP
              (IP-initial point or start of bomb run)
Dared not look up to see else I might die

These Guys

Well Lead bore down through the flak toward the target
With his bombs and his rockets he drew a bead,
But he never pulled out of his bomb run
"Twas fatal for another Teak Lead.

So come and sit by my side at the briefing
We'll say a prayer as we tickle the beads
For we're going to the Red River Valley
And my call sign today is Teak Lead.

THUNDERTHUD
(Irv Levine, Korat-1968)

I'd like to tell the story about the Thunderthud,
The bad you heard about it, is just a bunch of crud.
It took a lot of us up north and brought us back again
And the man who speaks against it will hear our mighty hymn.
HIM, HIM, F**K HIM!

Oh hallelujah, hallelujah, throw a nickle on the grass,
Save a fighter pilot's ass. Hallelujah, hallelujah. Throw a
nickel on the grass and you'll be saved.

Oh, it's heavy as heavy and you'll curse it like a cob,
It ain't no dinky sports car, it's built to do the job.
While the (F4s) other cry for Jollies to come and pick them up,
It's the One-Oh-Five that brought you to a cool one in the club.

So hallelujah, hallelujah, throw a nickel on the grass,
Save a fighter pilot's ass. Hallelujah, hallelujah.
Throw a nickel on the grass and you'll be saved.

Oh the F4 jocks are brazen, they're balls are made of brass,
They're shit hot and they'll tell you they're in a special class,
But let the bastards take one, to head them for the trees,
Then it's Mayday, Mayday, Mayday, won't you save me please.

Oh hallelujah, hallelujah, throw a nickel on the grass,
Save a fighter pilot's ass. Hallelujah, hallelujah, Throw a
nickel on the grass and you'll be saved.

So don't you growl and grumble like a dog without a bone,
It's the one bird in the whole damn war that's built to bring you home,
While the others stayed below the Red, you risked your ass and blood
so don't forget what took you there, the good old Thunderthud.

So hallelujah, hallelujah, throw a nickel on the grass,
Save a fighter pilot's ass. Hallelujah, hallelujah.
Throw a nickel on the grass and you'll be saved.

At last you did your hundred and now you're headed home,
Remember you were king up there while on that thunder throne,
With your hand upon its throttle, you're in a separate class,
You're a fighter-bomber pilot, let the other kiss your ass.

So hallelujah, hallelujah, throw a nickel on the grass,
Save a fighter pilot's ass. Hallelujah, hallelujah.
Throw a nickel on the grass and you'll be saved.

THE RED RIVER RATS FIGHTER PILOTS' BATTLE HYMN
(Dick Jonas , 1969)

The Red River Rats meet again,
Telling tales, remembering when,
Battles joined in the skies,
Shed our blood, gave our lives,
The Red River Rats meet again.

War is never a beautiful thing,
But we fought for the right on the wing,
Dropping bombs, dodging flak,
Fighting MiGs, we'll be back,
Shouts the Rats' battle cry, let it ring!

These Guys

Look around, there's a few empty chairs,
Honored comrades should be sitting there,
Some are dead where they fell,
Some fought on in a cell,
Charge your glass, raise it high, drink to them.

I'll tell you a tale that'll curl your hair.
I'll tell you the truth 'cause I was there,
About what happened in Ho Chi Minh's back yard.
Gyrine, sailor and Air Force type,
Black smoke pouring from a hot tailpipe,
Flying and fighting and living a life that's hard.

Black smoke, flak smoke, red SAM fire,
Pressing your luck right down to the wire,
Then pickle 'em off and boot that mother for home.
But the battle's not over 'til you're parked and chocked,
So if you fly and fight, keep your guns unlocked,
And don't try to fly and fight when you're all alone.

What's that telltale wisp I see?
It's a contrail pulled by a Fishbed C
And the cards are stacked and it looks like time to deal.
Lead's got bandits at twelve o'clock high,
So let's bend 'em around and scramble for sky,
And arm your guns, this ain't no game, it's real.

We flew the valley and the railroad lines,
From Dien Bien Phu to the Cam Pho mines,
And the price was high and measured in rich red blood,
When the deeds are told in the halls of fame,
And the warriors gather, you'll hear these names:
Skyhawk, Crusader, Intruder, Phantom, Thud.
The Red River Rats meet again,
Telling tales, remembering when,
Battles joined in the skies,
Shed our blood, gave our lives.

DOWNTOWN
(Irv Levine, 1968)

Well if the briefer speaks drawly
and your skin gets all crawly
you can bet you'll go,　　　　DOWNTOWN.
There's fear in your heart
and you're too scared to fart
Because you know you'll go.　　DOWNTOWN.
You'll bomb a nit noy bridge in the heart of the city,
and get your ass shot off, oh it's really quite a pity.
Who logged this frag?
The SAMs are much brighter there
You hair turns much whiter there, 'cause you are
Downtown, please don't send me there
Downtown, my pants always get peed there
Downtown, they're always waiting for me.

Now when I feel panic and I run to the clinic
And not have to go,　　　　　DOWNTOWN.
Get sick in a hurry and not have to worry
'Bout having to go　　　　　　DOWNTOWN.
I tell the doc about my aches and how I feel so shitty,
He gives me lots of APCs and very little pity,
What should I do?
Should I take in stride or try to save up my hide but go
Downtown, where they will shoot me up,
Downtown, I'll throw my breakfast up
Downtown, they're always waiting at me.

Now, there is a solution and it won't take much goosing
to get me to go,　　　　　　　DOWNTOWN.
Just load one right on me any old atom bomb me
and I'll take it Ho.　　　　　　DOWNTOWN.
Watch the shitheads run as I disintegrate their city,
Oh where did they all go? My that fireball's sure pretty,
Tough break there Ho
Well your town is much thinner now, I'll go eat my dinner now
and not have to go again,

DOWNTOWN, "cause it don't thrill me none."
DOWNTOWN, where they will kill me some,
DOWNTOWN, they're always waiting for me
DOWNTOWN, Hanoi, DOWNTOWN.

THUD RIDGE
(Irv Levine, 1968)

Oh there are some hills in North Vietnam,
They call "old Thud Ridge" and they point on down
Towards the heart of town, past Hia Gia bridge.
For those who fly up yonder, through a hail of SAMs and flak,
Or a MiG on your tail, can really be hell
For some won't be coming back.

I can't recall his name now, and I can't show you the place
Where a friend was shot down near the heart of town
While tears ran down my face.
Woe to the kids and widow
Who bear their grief alone,
For their man who flew up yonder,
He won't be coming home.

I don't know that it's worth it,
That we hold a sacred trust,
There are those at home burn draft cards and groan
But they don't speak for us.

Now there are some hills in North Vietnam,
They call "old Thud Ridge" and they point on down
Towards the heart of town, past Hia Gia bridge.
Yes there are some hills in North Vietnam,
They call "old Thud Ridge" and they'll be there
'till the trumpets' blare to call the lost pilots home.

From Yahoo.com Mail

OKAY GUYS! LET'S HEAR YOUR STORIES!
By Red

My story involves two of my roommates when I was stationed in the 6914th RSM at Sembach. We had worked a mid shift and after about three to four hours of sleep, I woke up to go to the latrine. When I got back in bed, I tried to go back to sleep when all of a sudden my roommates began talking to each other. The odd thing was they were both still asleep and they began to talk shop. They both were intercept operators and at the time we were working in H-1 vans at Grunstadt. These vans had five positions and the only intercom was with the ID desk, so most conversations were yelled back and forth between vans. Anyway, one of the guys had evidently found the other guy's target and started yelling to him what the guy was doing. "He's sending V's, now his call sign," and on and on. . . . They finally got so loud they woke up my other roommate. We laid there and listened to the other two roommates for a good hour as they conversed back and forth.

They did report themselves to the Flight Commander and nothing ever happened about it.

I am sure someone has a good story out there we can all appreciate, so let's hear them.

Red

(*Red was talking to the members of an Air Force Security Group of some kind, on the Internet*).

These Guys

SOME INTERESTING CRYPTOLOGIC HISTORY FROM THE PAST.
Contributed by William Reed with W. Craig Reed, with their kind permission.

I have read volumes about the Cuban Missile Crisis, but nothing about the Cuban SUBMARINE Crisis, and for good reason.
That story has never been told.
It is buried in the vaults of the National Security Agency.
I know.
I was there, and intimately involved.

I have waited almost forty years to tell this story. It is long overdue. I believe that the general public has a right to know and understand what really transpired between President Kennedy and Soviet Premier Khrushchev: Why Kennedy made the decisions that he did during that conflict, and why Khrushchev backed down. It had a lot more to do with submarines and potential long-range missiles located in Cuba.

Never before revealed to the American public, the Soviet submarine force played a key, if not the major role in the Cuban Missile Crisis.

Thanks to a National Security Agency Top Secret Codeword project termed BORESIGHT, every Soviet submarine at sea, not only those advancing into Cuban waters, but around the globe, was located and targeted by our own Polaris missiles. Confronted with this sobering reality, Khrushchev had no choice but to back down or face World War III. This was the secret ace in Kennedy's hand with which he bluffed the Soviet Premier. It was a hell of a strategic poker game, and should not be buried in the graveyard of secret history.

The Cuban Submarine Crisis started long before 1962:

In 1956, after Nikita Khrushchev emerged as the new ruler of the Kremlin, he exercised his newly found power by appointing Sergei Gorshkov, seasoned naval veteran at the relatively young age of 45, as Commander in Chief of the Soviet Navy. Gorshkov, had earned his sea legs early in life, attaining the rank of rear admiral at the age of 31. Khrushchev compelled Gorshkov to begin dismantling larger surface warships by stating that, "these large warships are only useful for hauling around admirals." In the years that followed many of the once proud gray veterans of the Soviet Navy were dismantled and sold as scrap.

Gorshkov pointed his new navy towards the development of missile armed small craft and submarines to counter U.S. Naval forces then being augmented, especially submarines. That was to be the first line of defense and offense program for the Soviet Navy.

The nuclear-submarine program was put in full swing, but diesel powered units were also updated, especially the deadly Foxtrot class, which could stay submerged for ten hours or more, operating on batteries, during which time she was considered to be virtually undetectable.

November, 1960, Karamursel, Turkey
"We've lost them!"
"Commander, I kid you not. Been over two weeks now, and not one peep. We've lost them!"
"Reed, you can't just lose a Russian submarine, especially not a few dozen Russkie subs; they're out there all right, and they're transmitting."
"Of course they are, I just can't find them. They have to be in the high frequency range, somewhere between 3,000 to 30,000 kilocycles, but I've covered every frequency used for the past thirty years by Russian subs, surface craft, and maybe even life rafts, and not even a smell of a transmission."

Commander Petersen scratched his head, along with the rest of us. I should qualify that. The Commander never scratched his head exactly like the rest of us. He was inclined to baldness, had a skin disease which was to him, I'm sure, a constant irritant, and when he scratched his head, numerous obscene flakes emerged from his scalp, and he then carefully removed them from under his fingernails with a small pocket knife blade and ate them. It was hard to concentrate on any conversation when the Commander was eating his dandruff.

As head of Operations he was our immediate boss, but nobody took him seriously. He had long since been promoted beyond his level of competence, and wouldn't have dreamed of making a decision without first consulting the senior chiefs. Petersen was later transferred to NSA and kicked upstairs into a policy-making billet where he could do little harm. No good field man paid the slightest attention to official policy. The rules of the game in the field were formulated around experience and balls - enough to follow gut level instincts. We all understood the risk and reward factor of such a course of action: guess right and you were a hero; guess wrong and you were crucified. Blindly follow the directives of a Petersen, and you were forgotten.

These Guys

At least in this one instance, Commander Petersen was correct. We all agreed that the Soviet subs had to be communicating with their Fleet HQ in some manner. Gorshkov didn't trust his sub commanders any more than had his predecessors. Historically they had always been required to check in at least once daily, and if they were in foreign waters that could expand to four times a day. There were a lot of Russian subs out there, and that translated into one hell of a bunch of signals bouncing off the ionosphere, day and night, and now, nothing.

The Naval Security Group, and the National Security Agency were very concerned or one might even say, angry.

"Where are they?" "We don't know." "Well find them!"

I had been stationed in Turkey for about one year, on a three-year tour of duty. We maintained a number of military stations throughout that country, and one of these was Karamursel, an Air Force base without aircraft (Air Force Intelligence), located some hundred miles southeast of Istanbul. The primary function at Karamursel was to monitor, by means of massive antenna fields, any electronic emission from Turkey's Big Bear neighbor to the north and east, as well as any transmissions from Soviet fleet units, surface or subsurface.

Special attention was focused on major Soviet missile sites, such as the massive one at Tyruatam. By monitoring their transmissions we were able to determine beforehand (by utilizing a number of complex analytical processes) when a missile was to be launched, what type it was, and its probable destination. By maintaining such monitoring stations around the world, we could detect and analyze the special types of transmission associated with specific types of missiles: short-range, medium-range or long-range. If an unusual amount of long-range missiles were detected in the preparation stage, then we had time to take defensive measures. If it came down to hardball, we would also have time to launch a preemptive strike; we hoped.

Karamursel was important, and the details of its operation very, very Top Secret. A small corner of the station housed a Naval Security Group (NSG) detachment. I was the Chief-in-Charge of the NSG intercept operations section.

As far as my real boss, Captain Frank V. Mason, was concerned, I was the guy responsible for losing the Russian subs. I was also the guy responsible for finding them again.

Captain Mason (then, Commander Mason) had also been my commanding officer some years earlier at the Naval Communications

Station, Guam, and Marianas Islands. My son was born there, and Mason and I together celebrated his birth. We were old friends, so we could talk man to man in a manner unusual between enlisted and commissioned ranks. It was Mason who arranged for my transfer to Skaggs Island Communications Station outside Napa, California, following Guam, for specialized training, and then to Turkey, to coincide with his takeover there. He had recommended me for a commission; I was his boy. I was letting him down. He wanted to know why.

I said,

"Captain, I don't know why. I agree with you that they are transmitting, but if they are it has to be a "burst" signal.

"A burst signal's nothing new, by the way. The Germans used it towards the end of WWII. They recorded standard Morse code signals, then compressed them and sent them out in bursts of a few seconds or less. We lost the German subs then, and we've lost the Russians' subs now. Given time and enough technological expertise one might expect to eventually DF(direction find) a signal of some sixty seconds, although highly unlikely, but if Ivan is using a burst of under a second, which I suspect he is, we will never DF it, and even if we did find it, we can't break it. You know as well as I do that they don't send position reports in any code breakable. It will probably turn out to be a one-time-pad sort of thing, and if we don't have the key we sure as hell can't break the code, and get a DF on a signal of one second or less? Forget it! I am doing all I can, Captain. If he is there I'll find him, but that isn't going to do us a hell of a lot of good, because you will never locate him. Unless, of course, you can't tell me how we direction find from a recording!" The captain and I got a good laugh from that one. Dreamland.

It was Christmas, 1960, when I finally found the lost Soviet submarines. It happened by accident. I had been hearing a "scratchy" sound for some time on various monitored circuits, but had passed it over as some kind of an anomaly, a spurious emission, whatever. It was sort of like a burst of static, but not quite. Then, one day, I made a sonograph-enlarged picture of another signal that happened to have one of these scratchy sounds almost on top of it.

Years earlier at Skaggs Island what we did primarily was to record and analyze Soviet radio transmissions. Everything was signal coded, naturally, so the trick was to break the signal codes in order to "read" the Soviet military or diplomatic or whatever type of correspondence. In the process we used what was called a sonograph machine, which utilized a large drum around which a photographic type of paper was hand wound by the operator for each signal to be analyzed. On playback of a recorded signal, the structure or positive-negative bauds of the signal was imprinted and enlarged for inspection by the analyst. That work required 20/20 vision and the patience of Job. Once we broke a signal code, which entailed figuring out from the baud formations their equivalent letters in the Russian Cyrillic alphabet, we sent this information to the National Security Agency. NSA engineers were then able to construct machines that could read out these messages just as did the Soviet machines. When NSA began to read Soviet traffic in volume, they passed on relevant excerpts to military or political end users. Good information could not be obtained over long periods of time. Like us, the Soviets changed signal codes frequently. Then it was back to the drawing board to start all over again, vital, boring work.

It was the sonograph machine that enabled me to locate and analyze the "scratchy" signal. I spread it out and took a closer look. I'll be damned! It had bauds! They were tiny bauds; the most compressed signal that I had ever encountered. Bauds! It was a man-made signal, and it obviously was not one of ours. Gotcha! It was a burst signal, and it had to be a Russian sub. It just had to be!

We fired the recording directly to NSA and they were ecstatic! All was forgiven. NSA put their best analysts on it and instructed us to concentrate on obtaining as many recordings of this new signal as possible. Suddenly we (and other NSG intercept stations began to find them all over the spectrum. Scratchy signals were music to our ears, now that we knew what to listen for. As we obtained better recordings, I measured them carefully and deduced that the signal had a "trigger" heading, probably meant to activate a Soviet recording device. The trigger was a series of bauds at 345 cycles per second, followed by a series of bauds at 142 cps. Next came the obvious text of the message. NSA confirmed our suspicions shortly. The subs were back! They had, of course, been there all the time.

Captain Mason received a Letter of Commendation from the NSA (he was bucking for flag rank), and I received a Letter of Appreciation from Captain Mason (I was bucking for a commission). We were buddies again.

We had found the Soviet burst signal. Now his question was, "What can we do about it?" Even before NSA put their best code experts and computers to work trying to break the text, I knew that it was unbreakable.

If we could read the text of a position report, we would obviously know the exact location of the submarine. The Soviets would never use a repeating or rotating code on such a transmission. There is an old saying in the code business: "Whatever man can make, man can break." That was true in most cases, but if you used a one-time-pad or a random scrambler device, the code was breakable only if you were in physical possession of the "key," fat chance. Our only hope, I realized, was to devise a means to locate the transmitters by direction finders. With existing technology, that was impossible. A new concept was required.

The reason a spy tried to get on and off the air as quickly as possible was because he knew, as we all know, that it takes time to get a bearing on any transmission. One direction finder will give you only the direction from which the signal is emanating. It does not tell you how far away the transmitter is. Three direction finders zeroing in on the signal will give you a triangulation, and the approximate location of the transmitter. A number of direction finders will give you a multiangulation and a much closer location of the transmitter. That's what we needed. But the typical burst signal was on the air for less than a second. That was okay for the operator at a Soviet receiving station, since his triggering device would automatically turn on his recorder. Once recorded, the operator had all the time in the world to feed the signal into a decoding machine that contained the key to translate the coded bauds into Cyrillic alphabet and thence to Russian plain language. We could (and did) build a triggering device to record the signal, but that left us with nothing more than an unbreakable code.

Since direction finders didn't have time to get a live bearing, our only hope was to devise a means whereby we could obtain a bearing "after the fact" from a recorded signal. That had never been done before. I didn't believe that it could be done, but I was wrong.

NSA engineers did exactly that during a crash program on a par (almost) with the Oak Ridge development of the atomic bomb during WWII. Within months after intercepting the first Soviet burst signal, we had stations set up and operating to detect, record and direction find Soviet submarines. At first this was limited to areas of primary strategic importance, but soon expanded to cover every body of water in the world.

In common with most great discoveries, the concept was, in retrospect, basically simple: it consisted of constructing huge circular antenna fields in areas around the world which would be well able to receive transmissions from critical bodies of water in which Soviet submarines normally operated. These antennae were connected to large banks of receivers, tuned to narrow bandwidths, which overlapped and covered the entire spectrum that the submarines might conceivably use. When a receiver encountered a trigger on a burst signal, a wide (two inch) sixty-inch-per-second recorder switched on immediately and recorded the signal, along with a marker, indicating the time to the millisecond that the signal was intercepted. Since the antenna field was circular, and divided into segments every few feet, it was also possible to determine, tangentially, the general direction from which provided a triangulation, or multiangulation, indicating the general direction from which the signal had managed, one was able to determine after the fact, the approximate location of the submarine.

Later, when we had obtained ample space at our site locations to construct separate antenna fields for both intercept stations and direction-finding stations, we were afforded the luxury of comparing notes between the two to obtain even more precise evaluations of direction. Ample space on site was a prime consideration since, besides the large antenna fields, the space required for the reception and recording equipment covered an area as large as a full sized New York apartment, and had to be fully air conditioned, since the receivers in those days still used vacuum tubes, and generated considerable heat. Land area sufficient for construction of a base, with housing and other facilities for the operational personnel, had to be taken into account. Large power plants and ancillary units had to be installed.

The project was immense in scope, and was classified Top Secret: CODEWORD. That codeword, which designated the entire program, was BORESIGHT.

What I am saying here is so outdated that it is no longer classified, or shouldn't be. HF (high frequency) systems such as this are obsolete because of VHF (very high frequency) and UHS (ultra high frequency) satellite communications technology. The U.S. Navy, for example now uses the SSIXS (submarine satellite information exchange system) for communications between its submarines and shore stations.

Other nations have their own versions of this sophisticated and extremely secure communications system. So what I have been saying is ancient history. Interesting and, I'm sure, never before revealed, but history nonetheless. The BORESIGHT system which I have just described is now as outdated as the Model-T Ford. It was, however, extremely critical as a factor in solving the Cuban Missile Crisis.

But, back in 1961 we were in the experimental stage regarding BORESIGHT, and we had to train operators at outlying stations what to look for, and how to analyze the signals when they received them. You couldn't mail them a tape, and of course you couldn't describe anything by telephone or radio. The tapes containing examples of burst signals had to be hand carried. That meant by armed courier, with the tape in a briefcase attached to his arm by lock and chain. In other words that meant me, and others like me, who knew the signal first hand and could train operators in the field. During the next few years I circled the globe many times helping to install BORESIGHT stations.

In early 1962 I was notified that I had been selected for a commission in the United States Navy. All those years of correspondence courses, night school, and hard work at my profession had finally paid off. I was directed to report to the LDO School, Newport, Rhode Island, in August 1962, for "fork and knife" training, where they would teach me how to act like an officer and a gentleman. But I actually received my commission and ensign's bars in Turkey on July 1. Following LDO School, I was assigned to the NSA for duty.

National Security Agency, Fort Meade, Maryland: 1962-1965

Upon reporting in at NSA I was assigned a minor desk in Section A22, the Soviet Submarine or, effectively now, the BORESIGHT section. As the only man in the section with any actual BORESIGHT field operational experience, I encountered a great deal of confusion and misunderstanding about what the equipment could and couldn't do. We brought in other field-experienced personnel, and eventually worked into a competent BORESIGHT Control headquarters.

In September 1962, our U-2 over-flights finally confirmed what had been suspected: the Soviets were installing missiles in Cuba. As far as I know, that's all the American public ever heard about. I'm not sure that this has ever been officially acknowledged, but I can assure you that there was a Cuban Submarine Crisis going on simultaneously. We had received evidence of Soviet submarine-pen construction in Cienfuegos, Cuba. How much of this came from air surveillance and how much from onsite penetration would be pure speculation on my part, but we were advised by reliable sources that it was so. Soviet submarines with potential long-range-missile-launching capabilities (boomers) stationed that close to U.S. shores, with the resultant increased ability to range up and down our coasts, posed a much greater threat than medium-range fixed missiles in Cuba. That danger had to be eliminated at all costs. We were told to maximize efforts to locate the position of every Soviet submarine possible. We did so, and started to get hit after hit on BORESIGHT.

In late October we obtained BORESIGHT fixes, and later visual sightings, of four Soviet Foxtrot-class attack boats converging on Cuba. We suspected more were on the way. That's when my boss, Commander McPherson, who was Chief of Section A22 (Soviet Submarine Section) at the NSA, was called to the White House. The president and his inner circle had previously been briefed on BORESIGHT of course, but in light of these new developments they wanted an up-to-date confirmation of just how good it was, and a technical explanation of precisely how it worked. Should the U.S. decide to blockade Cuba, a Wolf Pack of near-silent Foxtrot submarines carrying nuclear-tipped torpedoes could spell disaster . . . unless we could find them.

Commander McPherson was a sharp, competent, naval officer, but he only knew BORESIGHT second hand, mostly from me. In fact, he and I together had worked up his presentation. Operationally he was on solid ground, but he was a bit intimidated by some of the technical aspects.

"I'm sure I've got it, but I don't want to get hit with a surprise technical question and have to tell the president that I'll get back to him on that later. You'd best come along Reed, just in case."

A lowly ensign in the U.S. Navy invited to the White House? Unheard of. What the hell, I thought; before I was an ensign I was an old grizzled Navy Chief. Nobody screws around with a Navy Chief . . . right? Sounds tough, but to tell the truth, I was as nervous as a seaman recruit on the first day of boot camp.

The briefing was actually held in the "little" White House, or annex, off to the right side of the White House proper. I was disappointed that it was not to be held in the Oval Office, but when I saw the size of the crowd attending I realized why it was not. The Oval Office is in fact a small office in size.

Commander McPherson gave a very good presentation, but as the briefing progressed and the questions became more technical and precise, I was called upon frequently to amplify. I had brought along charts and graphs, which I had previously prepared for use in a BORESIGHT manual, which I was in the process of writing. Most of the questions came from the panel of technical experts from various agencies of the Defense Department. But there were also occasional queries from a group of quiet "gray" men in the outer gallery. I didn't know who most of them were, and did not especially care. We were here to brief the president. If he wanted someone else present that was his decision to make. I later discovered who the gray men were after reading a book by Robert Kennedy (written in 1967 and published in 1969) titled: Thirteen Days. Robert Kennedy was present at the briefing as well as the other members of President Kennedy's Advisory Committee (ExComm), which in Robert Kennedy's own words included:

". . . Secretary of State Dean Rusk: Secretary of Defense Robert McNamara; Director of the Central Intelligence Agency John McCone; Secretary of the Treasury Douglas Dillon; President Kennedy's advisor on national security affairs, McGeorge Bundy; Presidential Counsel Ted Sorenson; Under Secretary of State, George Ball; Deputy Under Secretary of State, U. Alexis Johnson; General Maxwell Taylor, Chairman of the Joint Chiefs of Staff; Edward Martin, Assistant Secretary of State for Latin America; Llewellyn Thompson as the advisor on Russian affairs; Roswell Gilpatrick, Deputy Secretary of Defense; and, intermittently at various times: Lyndon B. Johnson, Adlai Stevenson, Ambassador to the United Nations; Ken O'Donnell, Director of the United States Information Agency. This was the group that met, talked, argued, and fought together during that critical period of time. From this group came the recommendations from which President Kennedy was ultimately to select his course of action. The general feeling . . . was that some form of action was required . . . I passed a note to the President: 'I now know how Tojo felt when he was planning Pearl Harbor.'"

President Kennedy asked very few questions. He appeared to me to be tired. Secretary of Defense Robert McNamara, a man whom I had always admired and respected, seemed to be pretty much in charge, at least at the beginning of the briefing, but as we began to cover the more detailed technical aspects of BORESIGHT, he looked like he was falling asleep; head down, almost on his chest. We had put in a hell of a lot of work on this thing, and I was annoyed that SECDEF didn't seem all that interested. I learned that my fears were totally misplaced. When the presentation concluded McNamara's head came up. The first question (or rather first review) came from him. He said, "Now let me see if I understand this," and proceeded with the most precise and comprehensive explanation of BORESIGHT that I have ever heard. He had memorized just about everything that we had presented in a two-hour briefing. He had the ability to make even bauds and bits and radio-wave-propagation theory sound interesting. Robert McNamara was (and probably still is) one scary guy.

As we were leaving the conference room Commander McPherson said to me in an aside, "Now what do you suppose that was all about?" I knew what he meant: SECDEF engineers must surely have known how BORESIGHT worked. They shouldn't have to be told that again. In hindsight, I think what they really wanted to know, and what the president had to be assured of, was: What did a BORESIGHT position report translate to in terms of precise target location? Was it 100 yards, or 500 yards, or five miles? A big difference to one of our ASW weapons. If this came down to a shooting war, could we take out one or two of the subs moving in Cuban waters, or all of them, if needed, with one concentrated strike?

The point that we made to them, over and over was that we had a very limited number of BORESIGHT stations installed and operating. We would be lucky to get a simple triangulation fix. That would put them in the right ballpark, but it would not guarantee (without luck) the precise base pad. Once in the ballpark, it was up to their ASW forces to find the base runner. Given more locations, which would provide us with multiangulation fixes, maybe six or seven DF line bearings converging on the target, we could tell them WHO was on first and WHAT was on second.

The Cuban Missile Crisis:

My son, William Craig Reed, spent six years aboard nuclear submarines (late 70's and early 80's) as a fire control technician, espionage photographer, and SEAL-trained navy diver and was involved in the most devastating collision between a U.S. and Soviet submarine during the Cold War. Together, we compiled a precise day-to-day account of U.S. Naval operations during the Cuban Missile Crises, including the vital role that BORESIGHT played in bringing that operation to a successful conclusion. In the details of those day-to-day operations of the U.S. Naval ASW forces, we point out time and again how the ships of our fleet were directed to the precise locations of various Soviet submarines. They had made the mistake of raising their antennae and sending off position reports by the burst signals that they were convinced were undetectable, and BORESIGHT nailed them.

There was no militant exchange involving Soviet submarines, because by this time Khrushchev was having second thoughts. His Fleet Commander, Admiral Gorshkov, continued to assure him that the Foxtrots, operating on battery power, were invisible; they could not be detected by the Americans! But Khrushchev was receiving reports hourly from his submarine commanders contradicting this assurance. His "invisible" Foxtrots were being prosecuted around the clock by U.S. ASW forces to the point that they were often forced to surface under threat of depth-charge attack. Khrushchev began to realize that he could no longer back up his threat to "sink the American naval vessels," should they try to affect a quarantine of

Cuba. On the contrary, his Foxtrots were in imminent danger of being sunk! The deciding factor in this exchange was, of course, BORESIGHT.

Admiral Anderson later commented in his unpublished memoirs:

"... We concentrated our whole area antisubmarine coverage to the point that every Soviet submarine in the western Atlantic was made to surface at least once, or several times in some instances. I had excellent cooperation from Admiral Dennison in that regard, and I did follow very intensely our successes in that respect. One incident occurred. We knew where one of these particular submarines was located. We had that information from the most highly classified intelligence that the Navy had at that time, BORESIGHT. We were very anxious to preserve that intelligence, and very few people knew about this type of intelligence. We had a destroyer (USS Charles P. Cecil, DDR 835) sitting on top of this submarine (Foxtrot pendant number 911). One evening, McNamara, Gilpatrick, and an entourage of his press people came down to flag plot and, in the course of their interrogations, they asked why that destroyer was out of line. I sort of tried to pass it off because not only were there some of McNamara's people there who were not cleared for this information, but some of my own watch officers were not cleared for it in the general area of flag plot. After some discussion, I said to McNamara - he kept pressing me - 'come inside' and I took him into a little inner sanctuary where only people who had clearance for that particular type of classified information were permitted, and I explained the whole thing to him and to his satisfaction as well."

At 10:30 AM on October 27, 1962, Secretary of State Dean Rusk turned to McNamara and spoke words that would make history, "We're eyeball to eyeball and I think the other fellow just blinked." All Soviet ships headed toward the quarantine line had stopped or turned toward the Soviet Union. The Essex received her next orders: do not fire; allow the Soviet ships every opportunity to turn around!

What made the other fellow blink? Volumes have been written trying to answer that question. Alexsandr Fursenko and Timothy Naftali suggest in their book: "One Hell of a Gamble," that it was because of a Russian immigrant from the Balkans named Johnny Prokov, a bartender at the Tap Room in the National Press Club, Washington, D.C.

They contend that Prokov passed to Anatoly Gorski, A KGB officer, information that he had overheard during a conversation at the bar between two celebrated American journalists, Robert Donovan and Warren Rogers, both correspondents of the New York Herald Tribune. "Apparently Donovan was supposed to fly south that very night 'to cover the operation to capture Cuba, which is expected to start the next day . . .'" The story was that the KGB passed that information immediately to Moscow, and Khrushchev had it on his desk within hours. He was finally convinced that Kennedy was serious about going to war over Cuba, and that was why he backed down. Khrushchev backed down because of a conversation overheard at a bar? That smacks of a pretty desperate bid to find an answer.

To this day, I contend that Khrushchev almost surely received and understood a message from Kennedy in words to the effect that:

"We can find your boats, you can't sink our blockading ships with your Foxtrots, and you won't be able to hide your submarines in Cuba.

"We know about the submarine base that you are building in Cienfuegos, but it will do you no good, because we will make sure that no Soviet missile-capable submarine ever gets near Cuba again!"

Khrushchev knew as well as Kennedy that if we had their submarines pinpointed, the ball game was over. The land-based medium-range missiles sited in Cuba could damage a considerable segment of the United States, but the use thereof would result in massive retaliation against both Cuba and the Soviet Union. He stood to lose all of his Foxtrot subs now converging on Cuba, and he would lose his submarine pens in Cuba from which he had planned to service nuclear powered boomers in the future off the shores of the U.S.

Khrushchev fully expected to lose the fixed missile sites in Cuba during the first missile exchange, but he had counted on the long-range missiles aboard his boomers to tip the balance, since those submarines (like the Foxtrot under battery power) were heretofore considered to be undetectable. Suddenly, it appeared that none of his submarines, not only in Cuban waters, but also perhaps around the world, were undetectable! He was playing a losing hand. It was poker that Kennedy was playing, but it was good poker:

I can visualize the scene: Khrushchev bet Cuba. Kennedy said, "Call and raise. We're going all the way on this one Nikita," and pushed the world into the pot. It was the highest stake poker game ever played. Khrushchev threw his cards on the table and said, "fold!" His ace-in-the-hole had been exposed.

Khrushchev discovered to his regret that he was now dealing with a new Kennedy, not at all the Kennedy of the Paris fiasco. This was a man who had assuredly grown into his presidency, and a president who was obviously backed by a United States Congress ready and willing to risk WWIII. The Soviet Politburo, on the other hand, was not, and prominent members thereof were pressuring Khrushchev to ease off. This was a reckless game that he was playing! They did not wish to risk all-out war at this time. Khrushchev was left with no other choice but to turn his ships around, or face WWIII, and probably a bullet.

And WWIII it would have been had there been one small miscalculation by either side. After that hair-raising confrontation and a short cooling-off period of rational exchange, Khrushchev agreed to pull out all offensive-capable weapons systems from Cuba in exchange for assurance that the U.S. would not launch or back an invasion, and would also remove missile sites in Turkey which were targeted on the Soviet Union. The Cuban Missile (and Submarine) Crisis was over. I'm sure Kennedy didn't trade off any BORESIGHT secrets to the Soviets, because we used the equipment to good effect for some years to follow, but I can't doubt that he told them the exact number and the exact location of their submarines in Cuban waters, and probably elsewhere. How we knew must have driven Ivan crazy! There is no doubt in my mind that Kennedy did it right. We owe him.

There is also no doubt in my mind that two technological breakthroughs, one called RADAR (developed by English scientists for combat operations just prior to the German aerial assault against Britain in September, 1940), and one called BORESIGHT, were highly instrumental in achieving victory in two of the most decisive world conflicts of this century: the Battle of Britain, and the Cuban Missile (submarine) Crisis, respectively. And one should never forget the tenacity and the courage of the British Bulldog and the Irish Wolf hound behind them.

Following the Cuban Missile Crisis, BORESIGHT quickly became the hottest program at the National Security Agency. We had the full backing of SECDEF McNamara. He insisted upon a crash program. We were to install BORESIGHT in every corner of the Globe! He pressed our allies for the use of choice locations in which to install the large antenna fields required, and in which also a secure environment obtained. Security was paramount.

The remainder of 1962 and all of 1963 was a period of system refinements and expansion. Major installations included: Adak, Alaska; Kamiseya, Japan; Guam; Pearl Harbor; Port Lyautey, North Africa; Edzell, Scotland; Cheltenham, England; Recife, Brazil; Winter Harbor, Maine. These were backed up by a number of secondaries, constantly expanding.

By 1964 BORESIGHT had been designated the number two U.S. military priority, second only to the development of U.S. Polaris ballistic-missile nuclear submarines. It remained so closely guarded a secret for the next twenty years or so, that nobody ever questioned publicly what effect this program might have had in the crucial final-day talks between President Kennedy and Soviet Premier Khrushchev. How could they have? If there had been so much as a rumor of BORESIGHT, the NSA, the CIA, and even the President of the United States would have sworn under oath that no such program had ever existed. And nobody ever asked questions about the Cuban Submarine Crisis either, since that also never existed. Right?

But, there are still a few of us around who know better, including the former Secretary of Defense, Robert McNamara. He knows the story about BORESIGHT and the Cuban Submarine Crisis as well as I do; ask him.

A more comprehensive account of the part that BORESIGHT played in the Cuban Missile Crisis is offered in the new book by W. Craig Reed and William Reed, titled: Crazy Ivan, and now available from Barnes and Noble.com and Amazon.com

WILLIAM REED, a retired mustang (up from the ranks) Naval Intelligence officer worked for eleven years during his career for the Naval Security Group and the National Security Agency, primarily as a cryptanalyst and Turkish linguist. From 1962 to 1965 he also worked internationally for the NSA as a trouble shooter, lecturer and briefer to Department of Defense and NATO Intelligence agencies. At the onset of the Cuban Missile Crisis, Reed briefed President John F. Kennedy regarding the Soviet submarine threat and the NSA proposed solution thereof. Following his naval retirement in 1967, Mr. Reed earned a master's degree in history from the University of San Diego and, while working on his doctorate in Spanish Borderlands history, was the co-founder and president of Frontier Heritage Press, Inc. of San Diego. He wrote biographies of two famous South Western artists: "Olaf Wiehorst," (foreword by Senator Barry Goldwater), Northland Press, Flagstaff, Arizona, 1969 (which won the Wrangler Award that year from the National Cowboy Hall of Fame, Oklahoma City), and "DeGrazia: The Irreverent Angel," Frontier Heritage Press, 1971. San Diego.

Since his permanent retirement in Puerto Vallarta, Jalisco, Mexico in 1972, Mr. Reed has written eight other books which include: "The Art of Living in Mexico," Wilkie Publishing Co., 1974, Los Angeles; "An Open Book," John Huston (ghost writer), Alfred A. Knopf, 1980, New York; "Crazy Ivan," (with son. W. Craig Reed: the inside story of father-son Top Secret programs targeting Soviet Submarines), Writers Club Press 2001, Lincoln, NE; "Tarzan: My Father", (with Johnny Weissmuller, Jr. and W. Craig Reed), "Sentenced to Life," (Thematic condensation of his two-volume Memoirs), and Mike Oliver's condensation "Acapulco", (with Mike Oliver's short personalized history of Acapulco as seen through the eyes of publisher-journalist Oliver for the past fifty-seven years), Writers Club Press 2001, Lincoln, NE.

In 1999 Reed started Reed Writing, Inc., with his son, W. Craig Reed, a company specializing in biography, military history, and memoirs. Research and writing assistance offered to new authors. Web Site: www.reedwriting.com

W. CRAIG REED

W. Craig Reed served six years in the U.S. Navy as a Fire Control Technician First Class, SEAL-Trained Navy Diver and Special Operations Photographer, deployed on nuclear fast attack submarines. Mr. Reed was the recipient of Navy Expeditionary medals in relation to the completion of several Top Secret operations. During his tour of naval duty he received Marksmanship and Sharp Shooter rifles and small arms medals and the Navy Good Conduct Medal. Mr. Reed earned a degree in marketing after receiving an Honorable Discharge in 1981. He has published several articles in leading high-technology publications and has received numerous industry awards for advertising and marketing programs. He currently provides communications, sales and marketing expertise for high-technology companies. Web site: www.reedwriting.com.

Credit given to: Troika Magazine.com.

William Reed and W. Craig Reed are authors of the book "Crazy Ivan." The book is available at Barnes & Noble and at Amazon.com.

Subj: Re: Bye-Bye
Date: 5/23/02 4:21:53 PM Pacific Daylight Time
From: IdaReedBlanford
To: e14660@yahoo.com

In a message dated 5/23/02 4:15:09 PM Pacific Daylight Time, e14660@yahoo.com writes:

I have a lot of things to do between now and next Tuesday, but wanted to contact you before I go in for surgery. I won't be adding my input to you until later on this summer. Between the course I have coming up, and health problems. I don't want to commit to anything more until things improve. My prayers are also with you and your family.
Take care.
Ray

My dear Ray,

You are in my prayers, daily, and I know you will be just fine.
I will wait for your contribution to my book as long as I have to and will be looking forward to receiving same.
Meanwhile, if there is anything I can do for you, please just ask.
If you can, will you let me know how your surgery goes?
I will drop you an e-mail from time to time just to say hi and I won't expect an answer, so don't you worry about that. Get Well & Stay Well.

With respect and admiration,

Trish
Trish (Noland) Schiesser
Literary Consultant/Author
E-Mail: IdaReedBlanford@aol.com

p.s. Ray, I don't know your last name. It can't possibly be sendai onuma, which is in the Details of aol.
Will you tell me what hospital you'll be in? I want to send you something. Also, if you want to give me an address, I can send to you at your home, or if not, you can tell Ed Leonard and I'll send it through him.

Whatever you wish.
Good luck, will be thinking of you,
Trish

Answer from Ray: 5/24/02

Trish,

My last name is Rose.

Although I appreciate the offer, no need to send anything. This all came as a complete surprise two days ago, but my doctors are the best in the country at Johns Hopkins. There are currently four options: catherization, stents, open heart or the cemetery. It's not often a person has 3 out of 4 choices. We don't know what will be needed, but my stay will be a minimum of 2 days.

When I was with the intelligence community, I met some first class people. Since leaving the intelligence community, I've continued to meet some first class people in law enforcement, who have offered every conceivable method of getting me up to the hospital. I appreciate the sincerity of people I have met along the way. In the past 35 years I've met the crews of SR-71s and U-2s, been on a Russian ship (Zelenogorsk), met FBI agents and chased foreigners through the streets of Washington, D.C., been asked to "supervise" a U.S. missile exercise in Europe, was the only U.S. analyst to work at my specialty on the Iranian Rescue, had a B-52 put out on a runway for my inspection, inspected a Minuteman silo, worked on the INF & START treaties, have a signed personal signature of J. Edgar Hoover when I was accepted into the FBI, personalized picture of a medal of honor winner, picture of me with my Congressman, picture of me with the Baltimore Police Commissioner, and an award from The White House. That's only part of my collection. But unlike most others inside the community, I never asked for one of them! It was their way of saying "thank you." I've had a "different type" of career than most people once I left Security Service. And this will be what I am writing about; the uniqueness of my career. I will provide details and the outline of this as we go along this summer, a little at a time.

Oh, your brother was at Karamusel, Turkey. There are two sites that have pictures from the sixties. I'll pass them to you separately, since I can't cut and paste easily on this site.

Take care.
Ray

The words above, by a man named Ray "Rose" were written to me in May of 2002. I have not been able to contact him - even on the USAFSS Lite site. These words were written to me when I was in the "good graces" of USAFSS Lite as a personal e-mail. Every effort has been made to contact Ray, but no answer has been forthcoming. I credit Ray "Rose" with the words he has sent to me and congratulate him on excellent service in the USAFSS and other factions of our government of the United States of America. Well Done, Ray. And may you be well.

These Guys

Here is some information written and replied to, back and forth, among the members of Bravenet Web Services, New USAFSS Club, of which I was invited to become a member by Ed Leonard, Webmaster. For awhile, I was accepted, then apparently, I hit some nerves and no matter what I said, I was put down, way down, at times, but I feel their comments are remarkable and shed some light on some of those who were different while serving in the USAFSS during the Cold War ... these are their memories and comments of the USAFSS during the Cold War, today.

USAFSS Lite
By Ray Rose

Date: 06:43:02 PM
Name: KHC
Subj: Re: Re: Privacy, Cookie Zappers, Corsicana Conspiracy

Everyone knows about pop-up zappers/suppressors/whatever. Many folks here employ them and they work pretty well to get rid of ads, which fall into the nuisance category. Cookies are another matter because they can be, depending on the intent of the techie coder, insidious. Of themselves, they produce neither Spam nor spam. But they can trigger actions which produce both.

At the far end of the spectrum are the black-hearted trolls from Corsicana, waiting to check all the cookies returned with customer names from ISP/e-mail providers. If you start receiving e-mails for fruit cakes, know ye that De Lawd hath judged ye wanting.

Replying to:
As some folks may not be familiar with 'cookies,' they are the little software agents which can, among other things, report how many times a PC user visits a given site, what subject(s) the PC user is interested in, buying habits, etc. They can also be used to trigger pop-ups from any number of sources. Both individual and more generalized demographic data can be developed. If during the past year you have received rather undecipherable love letters from your bank, credit card companies, etc., saying they will never sell personal data they have about you on file, but just might 'share' that information with other reliable businesses, don't believe any of it. Even in the late 1960's computerized name lists sold to anyone interested for five cents a name. Cookie data can be sliced and diced into reporting date many

times more sophisticated than that of 3 decades ago. If you like all sides to play fair, and don't really want to open your kimono to the entire world, a cookie zapper like Cookie Pal (and many others openly available) may help you to retain at least a modicum of privacy. Good example: while posting this msg., Cookie Pal has zapped 19 cookies from Bravenet.

'S late. Paterno righteously laid it on the Neb Hucksters. Approaching an unexpected death, Johnny U finally got his teeth straightened. Hope his high-tops go to Canton.

Replying to:
FYI
For the past month have been evaluating COOKIE PAL 1.7c from http://www.kburra.com/ Will cost $15 after eval but it looks worth it. You can kill cookies with a high-order wild card, as in*crudclick.com,* or *pics.crudclick.com.* Or you can nail absolute IP addresses, or simply wild-card the low-order, as in 123.456*
If you frequent Yahoo and Bravenet, you can selectively suppress some of their cookies without killing your own session.

Also use a pop-up killer, about the third or fourth tried over the past several months. POW from analogx.com is free and seems to work very well. Have killed 700 pop-ups since mid-June

8/22/02 05:58:54 PM
Name: Ray
E-Mail e14660@yahoo.com
Subject: TUSLOG site

Thought I'd pass on this site to everyone. Interesting from the point that it doesn't bombard the viewer with pop-ups all the time, shares numerous pictures of Sinop from about 1956 through the 1970s, and also discusses good, pleasant times. I know it's not an Air Force site, but the Army SIGINT sites did almost as good a job as the Air Force sites. And the Army guys didn't look as perdy as we did in the Air Force blue. Plus Air Force guys were much better looking than the Army guys. And if the Army guys would have played their cards right, they could have joined the Air Force and gone to Peshawar with a golf course and swimming pool. And, hey, I'm not even gonna mention that we were the top 10%. It took 30 years for me to

understand that meant we did 90% of the officer's work for 10% of their money!
G'Night
Ray
http://www.pics.com/~bsimons/sinop/sinop.htm

Replying to:
8/22/02 7:21:56 PM
Name: Ed L
Subject: Re: Re: TUSLOG Site

Sorry Ray, Ed sez G'night.

Replying to:
Anonymous
I'm not even sure I understood all of that. "Specially the part about the AF guys looking better than the Army guys - That would seem to be a by-product of a tour in Peshawar (at least, in some cases). Nevertheless, try to stay on friendly terms with Ahrmee. They's gots th' guns. Hooah! G'night,
Ray

BRAVENET HANSSEN AFFAIR
By Ray Rose

11/16/02 - http://pub33.bravenet.com

You bring up a good point. In all of these documentaries, they are describing people that used their clearances and accesses to sell information, for personal gain. I just can't get interested in Hanssen stories or Pelton stories, or Ames stories, etc. However, maybe we can get a movie made of someone being dropped in a C47 up in the Anadyr or Norilsk areas in around 1960 getting some pictures of the pork plant, which eventually gave way to the Starbuck coffee factory. We could get the Commie-sar band to play the theme song, and probably get a bit part for Sugar (Putin). We could end the movie by having a scene in the Montana Himalayas in January, howling snowstorms, 40 below zero with a lone voice crying out, "I think the duct tape is frozen to my leg. Can I come in the house now?" The Commie-sar band could play a Dr. Zhivago type song and as the French said in World War II, "Let's surrender," er, I mean, "voila." Hell, this is a better idea than having movies of cowards on for a whole hour! We could probably get a New Yorker to play the part of the guy from Montana. We know what it's like to get to 40 below zero. I look in my freezer every night and see how cold my frozen chicken is. THAT'S COLD!!!!!!!

Ray

Replying to:
Personally, I did not want to waste my time. Seems today the television people have discovered the "spook" business and want to make as much hay out of it as possible. Everyone has become an "intelligence" expert.
Examples: the TV program on the CIA, leaks from the congressional intelligence oversight committee (not sure of the official title), Hanson movie, etc.

Replying to:

I've said this many times before, but depending on your background, and the time in USAFSS, will determine "how weird" we all are. Outside of NSA, we couldn't tell department stores our telephone numbers, but also not the telephone numbers at the Agency. When we did provide the 688 exchange, everyone knew it was NSA, but we had to say "Department of Defense." Because of my job inside the Agency, there were things we couldn't even discuss INSIDE the agency.

I was "familiar" with Hanssen back in 1981-82, and all of his co-workers. I actually traveled with them throughout D.C. in their cars "doing stuff." Great bunch of guys at the time, but "weird," because everything was hush hush and secretive. Because FBI is so weird, they are incestuous; similar to NSA. Many things were presented in the movie, so I turned it off. For instance, Hanssen's debriefing, wound up on the Internet - All of it. Also, one of his bosses that was also in Dorpus Dei, is retired and runs bus rides down in D.C. for $40 a pop, along with the KGB agent he used to follow. They bring you to all the drop zones throughout D.C. But here's the kicker. This ex-boss of Hanssen's, still working with the retired KGB agent, is still working on contract to teach FCI agents how to "work their profession" at a facility in Virginia. That part won't be in the movie. Just here between the few of us that read this site. Okay, and each persons service provider and the guys at the servers, but that's all ok, and their families and friends, not any newspapers. I guess the Today Show would be okay, and Playboy but that's it.

Eventually, there will be many things come out about the people of FBI that will criticize the organization, but I'll tell you the middle echelon of FCI is a great bunch of guys, hard working and extremely competent to do their job. Hanssen was a misfit that was in with his bosses, and a PERSONAL friend of Louis Freeh; hence the promotion system kept promoting him. He had access to NSA stuff that was normally restricted to FBI/FCI. The movie concentrated on the individual and not the system, which may show a good movie to some people, but I turned it off after 15 minutes. The movie did not provide the truth.

G'Night

Ray

Replying to:
Last Sunday or Monday, I watched that CBS 2-hour special about our friend Robert Hanssen. Was there only one installment on the thing, or was it followed up later in the week? I guess Wm. Hurt did a good acting job. At least he made our friend come across as a very strange individual. His old man, too. And his wife.

EW

This story (of his father) was sent to me by Deryl Sadler, a vet of the cold war in the USAFSS.

DO YOU BELIEVE THIS?
by Deryl Sadler

Dad would be proud to have his advice immortalized. His name is Lloyd Spencer Sadler, by the way. Born in '07 in Coryell City, Texas, entered USN in '25, four years later when enlistment was up he enlisted in the USCG where he spent the rest of the time until retirement in '55. Coryell City is anything but a city, then or now, and is right next to Crawford, Texas.

Comes WW2 he was an E-7 Quartermaster and he received a call from an ex CO who was now at CG Commandant's staff telling him he was an Ensign, to which he said, 'no thank you, sir.' To which the guy replied that he was refusing to obey a direct order which was brig time in war, or worse. Dad decided he'd really like to be an Ensign. So his career was roughly half enlisted, half officer. He always sneered at my brother and I for becoming officers through ROTC ... 'can't be a proper officer without enlisted time, etc. etc.'

His war effort culminated in hauling barges of war supplies across the Pacific behind a sea-going tug of about 100' length at six knots. He said you could see the screw turning. The two barges were behind him on a mile of cable to compensate for wave action. They were sort of being herded westward rather than towed. He did this twice. Dad said the ship went six knots with or without the barges behind it ... so it was 3 months over, 3 months back.

The problem at the other end was getting rid of the stuff. Where he was supposed to leave it was never where they needed it by the time he got there and what with radio silence they never knew this. So he'd refuel, reprovision and off they'd go again to some other island ... at six knots.

On the last voyage he chugged into Leyte just as the battle of Leyte Gulf was commencing and here he is with two barges strung out and one .30 cal machine gun on board.

The first voyage, I think it was, he pulls into the final harbor and is greeted with, "What the hell are we supposed to do with this stuff?" To which he replied, "Not my problem." The conversation went downhill further: "How in hell are we going to unload it? We have no cranes or dock equipment?" Dad showed - told them to sink the barges, then they could float the crates to shore. He really enjoyed a warm greeting after three months at sea by some smartass.

JUST LIKE THE 40 FOOTER USCG BOAT THEY "ROLL OVER" IN OREGON

My father was CO of the USCG crowd at Astoria, Oregon for three years or so, back in the early '50s. That was before the fancy boats they have now. He scraped the bottom off on a sand bar doing a rescue and had to attend a board hearing on the event and figured he was to be hung . . . the admiral chairing the board said, "Well, this is your first one, hey? Let me tell you about my first time. . . ." and it went great from there on. The mouth of the Columbia is the pits for uncharted sand bars and rogue waves. Dad retired from USCG with thirty back in May, 1955. He's still kicking at 99 ½. Said he intended to soak the government three-fold for every day he had to float around and he's doing it. He retired in May and I came in the USAF in Nov. of '55. During that interval I asked him what advice he'd pass on to me based on his vast experience.

He left me with the following:

"Don't be first, don't be last, don't volunteer and you're going to screw up on all three of those."
"Don't loan money to anyone, especially relatives."
"Advice is worth what you pay for it, which is usually nothing."

So, armed with this sum of his thirty years of experience, I went off to do battle for the next twenty-two. And he was right on all three of those, which I passed on to my sons for what it was worth.

Dad always liked to keep things simple.

An e-mail sent to me by Deryl Sadler, a warrior of the cold war, re: some info. about 20270's, my brother's rate, another proud warrior of the cold war.

YARNS by Deryl Sadler

You asked about GI experiences; 68-12 is one that dang near got us killed in more ways than one. But it resulted in many saved lives. This odd little project became the beginning of the Nellis AFB "Aggressor Squadron" and the "Red Flag" exercises. In late '69 and the early '70s many pilots of the AF, USN and USMC were rotated TDY through this training prior to going to SEA. In a Congressional hearing they testified that this training not only saved their lives but cost the enemy some of theirs.

Regarding your brother, are you dealing with the USAF Records people or some other agency? I've had some luck getting records from them, and from the AF Safety people about aircraft accidents.

I'm most familiar with 20270 folk. [This would be my brother's number, Editor's note]. The five years I spent in Germany I dealt very closely with them and had the same clearance. When the godless commies took a poop we knew how many sheets of toilet paper they used. We used to jerk the commies' chain via the Intel people and really rattle them and we'd set up a sort of 'sting' for our Intel guys to enjoy. Those were the days!

As for him sort of dropping out, that happened more than once I think. My little group of five officers in a very odd job all had this same clearance and worked 24/7 shifts. No one could fill-in for us if one got sick . . . we just had to double up and keep covering the duty. Of the five, four came down with various nervous ailments from polyps to shingles to just plain worrying themselves into a dither and becoming useless. The shrinks were quite concerned and were going to shorten our three year tour to eighteen months since they thought our effectiveness was being tested beyond limits. I stayed in the job for five years and loved it. Got three eastern-bloc commie counter parts fired, I was told. That might or might not be fact but it was good for morale. But your brother was indeed sitting on the edge with what he had to deal with over there.

This is an answer to a question I asked some of "These Guys" about ECI COURSE INTELLIGENCE FUNDAMENTALS. I discovered it on a performance report of my brothers by reading the type that was under the top typing, (overtyping I guess you'd call it), by using a mirror and a magnifying glass. The answer comes from ex-USAFSS Lt. Col. Sadler. This wasn't the only thing I discovered with my trusty mirror and magnifying glass, but that will come in a later book. [The Editor]

ECI COURSE INTELLIGENCE FUNDAMENTALS
By Deryl Sadler

Yup, I took most of these ECI courses. . . . "Extension Course Institute," out of Maxwell AFB, which was what one did to get 'things' on one's record so that it'd be there when forwarded to a promotion board. The idea was to be working on something all the time so's your boss would have something nice to put in the efficiency report. Think I did well over 100 of them. I have such titles as "Tank tactics" "Portable Flamethrower" all the Special Forces courses, Army Command and General Staff College, USAF Command and Staff College, the Infantry Basic and Career courses, the Civil Affairs Basic and Career courses, a bunch of USMC courses and on and on. The 'career courses' were one-year courses and mandatory for army guys. I was desperate to fill all the available space on my record . . . and did. The USAF ECI courses were basically geared to a career title . . . intelligence, cook, you name it. Strangely enough a bunch of these were actually useful. If it hadn't been for my Army courses I wouldn't have had 'sandbag' stacking 101' 'foxhole digging for dummies' 'advanced napalm concoctions' 'bridge blowing for fun and profit' and other useful stuff.

One dark night I got a knock on my hooch door (Vietnam, '64) and it was some army Sgt who'd flown halfway across Vietnam because he somehow heard that I had most of the Army course books, and specifically the one on the portable flamethrower. What he needed was the formula for how to melt napalm down so's it could be used in one. They had a bunch of the flamethrowers but no fuel. He remembered that in Korea they'd cooked napalm until it was liquid and used that, but he didn't have the formula for how to cut it, cook it and stay alive. I did. (One used a 55-gal. drum with a fire under it and the lowest ranking and most expendable troop to stir it.)

Another time a Sergeant wanted ME personally to come out to a bridge and evaluate it for demolition. I'd never fired off anything bigger than a cherry bomb but I had the Special Forces course book on how much of what explosive it took to cut X amount of concrete. I thought I'd just give him the formula but it didn't quite work out that way. I soon found myself measuring a bridge support out in nowhere.

For an air force guy I had a lot of fun, and without all these correspondence courses it wouldn't have happened.

While in Vietnam we weren't totally taking these courses for career improvement. The five of us at our little location were desperate for defensive smarts . . . we were living with a bunch of army admin. types who didn't know much about such mundane things as foxhole digging and sandbag stacking. In fact, the sandbags at the army compound guard gate were stacked like bricks . . . one row on top of another. A fact is that a .30 caliber rifle round can penetrate 30 inches of loose dirt
. . . and one sandbag's width is just about useless after it starts leaking out.

So, the five of us commenced taking all the USMC and US Army (and some ECI) correspondence courses we could because the field manuals for whatever subject came with the course. Those field manuals were vital and we couldn't find them anywhere in the army domain locally. Each of us took a different set of subjects and I was the so-called training manager. Shortly, even with the delays in mail delivery back then, I had accumulated a whole bookshelf of training and field manuals of all sorts of interesting subjects.

For instance our little group knew that if you dug a foxhole that you needed a burrow in it called a 'grenade sump'. Like if someone rolls one into your hole then it'll drop into this slanted burrow and blow up in the dirt. We learned how to string concertina wire. We learned how to lay trip wires for flares. All this was to set up defenses for our little radar station which was literally out in the open at the end of the dirt airfield. If we didn't do it, it wasn't going to get done because the local army people sure as hell couldn't help us. They had typewriters for weapons.

We got interested in these things and began taking courses for fun too. I took some chaplain counseling courses; useless but interesting. I took psychological warfare courses. It was either this or drink when off duty and this became not only healthier but more practical.

These Guys

The military has a senior officer course called, 'The Industrial College of the Armed Forces'. It's usually reserved for Lt. Cols. and up, but available by correspondence for majors (with special permission.) I was a captain. So, I got my AF Wing Commander at Perrin to endorse me and was off and running on that. Went through the one-year course in six months and nailed that on my record. Before I was eligible for major I'd completed all the career courses up through full colonel level by correspondence, knowing full well no one was going to invite me to attend in residence and this was my only edge at a promotion board hearing. I still have a stack of 'diplomas' and 'course completion certificates' in a footlocker.

F-106 TACTICAL EMPLOYMENT EVALUATION
ADC/ADWC PROJECT 68-12
USAF INTERCEPTOR WEAPONS SCHOOL 1968
Sent to me by Deryl Sadler
By Lt. Col. Robert W. Stonestreet, USAF (Ret.)

In the fall of 1967 the war in Vietnam was reaching its peak. The air war in North Vietnam was going full blast under the code name "Rolling Thunder." Some classic air battles were being fought between USAF F-105s/F-4s, Navy/Marine F-4s and North Vietnamese MiG-17s, MiG-19s and MiG-21s in and around the Hanoi/Haiphong area. The North Vietnamese were using Surface-to-Air missiles (SAMs), as well as very effectively using ground radar for controlling their fighters. The Americans were also using radar control when possible through ground radar systems, airborne systems (USAF EC-121s and Navy E-2Bs) and naval surface ship radar. The overall scenario was very much like a classic air defense battle that the Aerospace Defense Command (ADC) had been training for over the past fifteen to twenty years.

Through the first six months of 1967 the Americans had enjoyed an approximately 5 to 1 "kill ratio" over the North Vietnamese. In August the North Vietnamese introduced new tactics that turned the tide in their favor. The MiGs, utilizing ground radar control, would initially stay at low altitude until abeam of the US fighters, thus avoiding detection by the fighter's radar. Then they would position themselves above and behind the American strike force and make a diving attack with "Atoll" infrared missiles, fire and keep going, utilizing hit and run tactics! The results of this new tactic from August 1967 until the end of February 1968 were five MiG-21s lost and eighteen U.S. aircraft lost. Needless to say, the Pentagon got very concerned.

In January of 1968 the commander of Aerospace Defense Command (ADC), Lt. Gen. Arthur C. Agan, invited several USAF general officers to attend a Senior Officer Course at the USAF Interceptor Weapons School (IWS) located at Tyndall AFB, Florida, home of the USAF Air Defense Weapons Center. Among those who attended were General Bruce K. Holloway, Vice Chief of Staff of the Air Force and Major General George B. Simler, Director of Operations, HQ USAF. The course was usually tailored to the amount of time the attendees had available, but normally consisted of classroom presentations and a minimum of one flight in the F-106. General's Holloway and Simler were both very impressed with the performance of the

F-106. They were especially impressed with the capability of flying at high speed at minimum altitude, finding a fighter size target (T-33) with radar at 30,000 feet, "locking on" with radar, conducting a "snap-up" simulated firing attack (pull up into a steep climb) and go past the target in a supersonic climb. General Simler asked if the F-106 could fly from Northern Thailand to the Hanoi area at minimum altitude, fight for five minutes in afterburner and return home without air-to-air refueling. On paper it could be done. Apparently Generals Holloway, Agan and Simler discussed the F-106 capabilities and decided that it could possibly handle the MiG problem in Southeast Asia. Shortly after these talks the Air Defense Weapons Center (ADWC) Commander, Colonel Thomas D. DeJarnette, was called to ADC Headquarters for a conference with Gen. Agan.

Col. DeJarnette returned to Tyndall AFB on a Friday night and called a special meeting Saturday morning with Lt. Col. Mark Oliphant, IWS Commander, Major Jim Jordan, Operations Officer, Major Tom Wotring, F-106 Flight Commander and me. At that time I was the Supervisor of the "Tactics Research and Development Section" at IWS. Col. DeJarnette's instructions to us were to form an F-106 squadron (on paper initially), handpick the pilots and key personnel from any ADC resources, determine what modifications to the F-106 would be needed, determine aircrew training requirements (based on the air war as it existed in Vietnam), set up a training program, train the aircrews and be ready to move to Southeast Asia as soon as possible. Naturally, the whole scenario was fascinating to us, to form an outfit very similar to the "Flying Tigers" (American Volunteer Group) of World War II fame. We didn't waste any time getting started on what would be known officially as ADC/ADWC Project 68-12, "F-106 Tactical Employment Evaluation." The whole thing was highly classified and this new program was to be conducted so as to have minimum impact on the normal school activities.

I might mention here that IWS had added "fighter versus fighter" training, both academic and flying, to the curriculum in 1965 for the F-101, F-102 and F-106 aircrews, so we were not starting from scratch. Out of flying school, I went through F-86 training at Nellis AFB and then to the 4th Fighter Wing in Korea, so I developed the course myself. In addition to the classroom work, if I remember correctly, each student flew five demonstration flights and five applied tactics flights and we labeled it Air Combat Training (ACT). ADC pilots, as well as others were being sent to Vietnam at that time with a minimum of fighter versus fighter training. Major John Boyd of "Energy-

Maneuverability Theory" fame was stationed at Eglin AFB at this time. I made a trip over to Eglin and talked to Major Boyd about doing E-M comparison charts for us. He was kind enough to develop E-M charts on F-101/F-102/F-106 versus the MiGs for our academic course. The F-106 looked very good versus the MiG-21. In addition to this, I participated in a tactics development working group called "Project Blue Racer" at the Fighter Weapons School at Nellis AFB in 1965. We were told that Tactical Air Command was not allowed to do any fighter versus fighter training at that time. I was also one of the IWS pilots that participated in a project called "Have Doughnut" at Nellis AFB flying the F-102 against the MiG-17.

The first thing we did was to organize the squadron and to start selecting the aircrews, on paper of course. We selected them based mostly on first hand knowledge of the capabilities of those pilots who had attended the F-106 course at IWS over the past few years. We decided from the start to utilize airborne radar control to the fullest extent possible through the EC-121 Early Warning and Control aircraft, the type aircraft (BIG EYE) that were already operating in Southeast Asia. Major Deryl Sadler, supervisor of the IWS Ground Environment (Ground Control Intercept) Section of the school, and his staff were part of the team. We then started a training program, both flying and academic. One thing high on our list was to interview any and all Vietnam veteran pilots we could contact to learn as much as possible about the military situation, tactics, enemy capabilities, etc. Major Sadler sent Captain Grady Cook to Southeast Asia to gather first hand information on the EC-121 aircraft operations and capabilities. We picked the brains of numerous F-4 and F-105 aircrews who had returned from combat tours in Southeast Asia. On March 24, 1968 Majors Jim Jordan, Danny Schuyler, Tom Wotring and I went to Nellis AFB for project "Have Drill" to participate in some special training related to the war in Southeast Asia. We got the opportunity to fly the F-106 in simulated combat against a MiG-21. The training program began to take shape in a way that as close as possible simulated the actual air war situation in Vietnam.

It was determined immediately that the F-106 would need either a built-in gun or gun pod, for close-in fighting, and a bubble canopy for better visibility. These would be the major modifications desired and the hardest things to accomplish in a short time period. The training program would consist of F-101s acting as a strike force (similar to F-105s on a bombing mission), F-102s and F-106s acting as escort for the strike force and all operating under radar control from an EC-121. F-104s out of Homestead AFB, Florida acted as MiG-21s or the "aggressor squadron." They were small, hard to see visually and the engine gave off very little smoke. The F-104s operated out of Tyndall during the test program so that the aircrews could brief and debrief together. On some missions the F-102s acted as MiG-17s/19s. The EC-121s operated over Georgia and Alabama where the terrain was rugged and somewhat similar to North Vietnam and resulted in significant ground clutter on the controller's radarscope. Several new techniques and procedures for controlling aircraft were developed under these trying conditions and some adopted by the Air Force.

Of major importance were the tactics employed. During the in-between years, post Korea and pre-Vietnam, the tacticians were convinced that there wouldn't be any more close-in "dogfighting" as in the past, that future air combat would be fought with air to air missiles. As we learned in Vietnam they were only partially right. The necessity of getting in close to make a positive visual identification resulted in a close-in fight and normally too close for air-to-air missiles to function successfully. In our training it was required that a positive visual identification be made before engagement. We had developed identification/engagement tactics in the fall of 1965 with the Fighter Weapons School at Nellis AFB, during the "Blue Racer" project. Basically, it was two aircraft approximately one mile apart in trail, the first would make an identification and the second was already "locked on" and ready to fire if declared hostile. I understand that the tactics developed during the "Blue Racer" project were used to some extent in Southeast Asia.

We were in the final stages of planning, organizing and initiating the project when President Lyndon Johnson announced a "bombing halt" effective April 1, 1968 for the northern part of North Vietnam, which included the Hanoi/Haiphong area. This completely changed the air war situation as far as air-to-air combat was concerned and thus eliminated the need for a specially trained F-106 unit. However, Gen. Agan decided to continue the project with the objectives basically the same, except for the deployment to Southeast Asia, and with a plan to eventually rotate all F-106 squadrons through this training.

During the next several weeks over 600 sorties were flown using ten different types of aircraft. Different tactics were tried, primarily with priority on protecting the strike force from attack. The attacking F-104s (as MiG-21s) were completely free to try different tactics also. Initially, they were usually successful in getting through, but as the F-106 crews gained experience, they got better and better at preventing the F-104s from reaching the strike force. It was quite an advantage having excellent radar control from the EC-121 in addition to search radar in the fighter itself. The F-104s were also vectored in to the strike force by ground radar control. As time went on the F-106s could prevent the F-104s from reaching the strike force nearly every time. A project report was issued in the summer of 1968 entitled ADC/ADWC Project 68-12, "F-106 Tactical Employment Evaluation."

When I departed IWS for F-4 school and Vietnam in June 1969, arrangements were being made to invite Marine and Navy squadrons to rotate through the training against the F-106s instead of the F-104s and they accepted. Major Ed Woelfel was running the program during this time. At a reunion a few years ago Ed Woelfel told me about a briefing for the Joint Chiefs of Staff and Lt. Randy Cunningham, the U.S. Navy Vietnam Ace, was present. Lt. Cunningham was asked what he attributed his success against the MiGs to and he said "the training I received at Tyndall AFB against the F-106s." Ed said he was called to Washington, D.C. the next day to brief the USAF Chief of Staff on the Tyndall program. I believe this might have been the original "aggressor squadron" concept, before either "Red Flag" or "Top Gun" was developed.

Lt. Col. Robert W. Stonestreet
USAF (Ret.)

These Guys

TOP SECRET - "Need to Know"
By Deryl Sadler

In Jan. of '68 General Agan, then CO of ADC, came down to Tyndall and a limited group of IWS people were locked in the room with him. He explained a test program he wanted us to run and it would be TS 'need to know' for both the aircrews and the controllers.

Basically he wanted to pair the F106A and the EC121D and see if they could work as an effective team in a combat environment, i.e., air to air dogfighting. This meant several things . . . could the 121 work effectively over land, could it really detect the targets via raw radar, could it provide close control for the fighters. Up until then the answer had been an emphatic NO on all of those.

I, as the lead controller, explained that none of our four instructors knew squat about the 121 and had never seen the inside of one . . . and why didn't he go get his experienced crews involved. The good general explained that was exactly why we were going to do this task for him, we didn't know squat about the 121 and would go into the test with no preconceived notions or experiences.

Somewhat less than enthusiastic about our new role . . . and also unable to discuss it outside our group . . . we flew down to McCoy to see what we could see. Timmerman was the CO. He was also less than enthusiastic about turning over an airplane to people who didn't know crap about it. He was further incensed that we wouldn't whisper in his ear anything about the project. He had a flaming letter from Agan to give us whatever we wanted, when we wanted it and no questions. He was mad.

And so we commenced teaching ourselves how to work that beast. We asked a lot of questions. We learned that the radar techs had all the answers we needed, more than the ops folds. Our four controllers wound up being two because one couldn't fly and the other was an Aussie exchange officer. We flew 7 days a week and gradually learned that a) yes, the radar did work over land, b) we could use it without the IFF very well, c) we could do close control very well on raw radar (blip was 9 degrees wide, and that's BIG), d) we could detect the enemy aircraft out at 150 miles ON THE DECK and without IFF, (something that Connie people repeatedly said couldn't be done), we were dangerous.

Equally improved were our 106 pilots who learned to shoot maneuvering live drones with deadly accuracy due to clipped fuses in the missiles, thereby making them 'point and shoot' bullets. Our research led to the eventual addition of a Gatling gun and removal of the bar at the top of the canopy in place of a clear canopy. There were other interesting things such as an odd maneuver only available with the big delta wind of the 106 . . . it would do a sort of an in-place 'flip' and suddenly be on the tail of an aggressor that had gotten into the six o'clock position . . . something that the S. Korean F-5's learned about to their dismay in an exercise. The Six was undoubtedly the best air to air fighter available until the F-15 came on board but was never acknowledged as such because of the ADC role.

We used F-104s out of Homestead as MiGs and they were not to turn on their IFF for mission purposes, simulating real MiGs under close control who didn't need that luxury. These were controlled from the heavy radar at Tyndall which had super coverage out across the swamps. Their tactics could be anything of their own devising and their favorite was to scale toward our attacking force on the deck, and then do a snap-up into the formation. Most of the dogfights were at mach-plus and the sonic booms beat the hell out of the Florida peninsula for three solid months, even to the point of blowing out all the windows in the downtown section of Sop choppy. Fortunately, that was on a Sunday and no one was hurt by flying glass.

We lost two excellent pilots, my good friends, who were killed during the test phase, while under my control. The plane was never recovered as it went straight down into the Florida swamps and the hole filled in with water instantly.

What we learned was written up, tucked away, and almost completely discarded except for the Six mods which were eventually incorporated. None of our 121 missions were above 2,000 feet and many were at 500 if not a tad lower. None were over water and none were with IFF on. If we could see it, it was hostile unless we were told otherwise. We learned how to use the inversion layer to augment our coverage and distance and it was almost a requirement to have that layer to bounce the radar. If you were below it, you could see above it and under it. If you were above it, you were screwed, and guess what SEA was fraught with . . . inversions. We could repeatedly see our fighters taking off from Tyndall at 100-150 miles and assume control of them right away; same with our simulated MiGs. We'd catch them as soon as they entered coverage and commence an attack, frequently in 'look-down' mode for the fighter.

We deployed to Korea to exercise with the S. Korean F-105s and surprised them. We deployed to the NW USA to take advantage of mountainous terrain and that too was successful.

We reluctantly considered our test a success and knew what we were going to be asked to do. By now our augmentation crews from McCoy were standard people we'd name, requested: two radar techs, a radio tech and a weapons tech. The flight crew was immaterial so long as they knew how to drive and navigate, a point that caused some friction now and then.

The flight crew considered themselves in charge of the mission prior to colliding with our group. When we laid out the track, requested hard turns, set the mission altitude and even the engine RPM, some of these people got more than a bit testy. We'd found that regardless of the so-called 'constant speed generators', the radar worked best at 2300 RPM, not the 2100 RPM that the pilot normally liked for best flight speed and operation. And you should have seen them squeak about dropping down on the deck over the Okeefenokee Swamp, sometimes considerably under 500'. A typical mission only lasted about twenty minutes, but that twenty minutes clipping treetops sure got their attention. One indignant pilot said he was writing this whole thing up and turning it in to Flight Safety, etc. That was his last flight with us and we never heard from him again. Still other Connie pilots were doing what they dreamed of, scalding across the trees and having excitement for once, and begged to stay on our project.

When and if we deployed to SEA, we had a short list of whom we wanted to drive our plane. The enlisted crew really had no choice . . . they were drafted . . . and our two IWS controllers had no choice . . . we were all there was until we could train some other people . . . rapidly, we hoped, because sure as there's water in the river, we, our 106 crews, and our plane were going very shortly. Agan wanted to prove that ADC had a mission other than surveillance.

I mentioned 'our plane'. That was another story. We were supported with flight crews from Otis, McClellan and McCoy during all this. Our back-end crew was from McCoy and the two controllers from Tyndall IWS. Col Timmerman gave us the hangar queen of his fleet, as we learned from our EM. Those radar techs rebuilt that bird to THEIR specs, inserted some non-reg homemade gear of theirs on the circuits, and that one bird was really spiffy radar and radio-wise. Sure, we flew on three engines a hell of a lot but the mission came first . . . unless we got down to two engines which never happened.

When we went on the NW deployment our crew plus one McCoy controller that we trusted showed up at McClellan per orders to pick up a flight crew and an airplane. We would fly up to WA state and work with Sixes at McChord whilst hiding in valleys and such. Could we do this in mountainous terrain? We didn't really know.

I went to see the squadron commander, a full colonel whose name I forget now, and he was downright aggravated that this MAJOR . . . had the gall to come in and say he was ready for his airplane. What airplane? I told him if he didn't know, I couldn't tell him. The conversation went, appropriately enough, downhill at mach three from that point on. Suffice it to say he was red in the face and approaching a stroke.

He sends me out of the room and calls ADC. After a long time he calls me back in and reads me the riot act and informs me that HE will be the pilot and HE will damn well find out what this is all about. He wasn't speaking softly. I asked for a 0700 takeoff the next morning, my EM worked all night on the assigned bird, and Ray Cobb and I showed up at 0600 and walked up the ramp. Whereupon we were told that we'd missed the mission briefing which was at 0500 and where the hell had we been.

I told the good colonel there was no mission briefing and that we'd file in the air, something he'd have known if he hadn't thrown me out of his office the afternoon before. He was not a happy camper at all. I gave him the coordinates where I wanted to be and told him that we'd pick up the mission altitude upon arrival. He comes back to the rear where we're merrily working on the radar and tweaking scopes during the drive to Seattle. This tells him absolutely nothing and he's really unhappy now.

When we arrive in the area I call the Air Defense Sector and they scramble our fighters and we establish contact. I put them on CAP while we descend our bird to find a mission altitude, looking for the inversion layer. It was LOW that day, and when I finally found it we were scraping treetops again. The sounds from the cockpit were overwhelming so I turned the intercom off and told the tech to listen to it.

Our fighters descended into a long valley over 100 miles away in the intercept area over land, and we had continuous contact, both radio and radar, due to the inversion, so we ran some head-on intercepts that were successful, then gave the pilot permission to climb and head west, go over the ocean so we could look back at the fighters over land. By now the deleted invectives from the cockpit are really loud. The colonel is going to have heads, mine first, when we land.

About this time the radar goes out so we called our birds in and perched them on our wings so we could have a Kodak moment with snow-covered Mt. Olympia in the background. Oops . . . forgot to notify the pilot and suddenly he sees two Sixes on his wingtips and to him that's a near miss; now he's really, really steamed.

We cancelled the rest of the day and all the way home he lectured me about protocol and safety. When we landed we both made our separate reports to CINC ADC and I awaited orders to return to Tyndall, or Leavenworth, whichever was to be ordained.

Turned out that neither was ordained; the CO was NOT our pilot the next mission, we didn't hear from him the rest of the week and all went quite well from then on. I went to his office to give him an interim report as I departed and thank him for the squadrons' participation, and he wouldn't see me. Guess he was too overcome by emotion.

What saved our asses? That was one of the bombing halts over N. Vietnam. So we were relegated to training up some follow-on crews to learn what we'd learned and soon we at IWS sort of went our separate ways to schools and other assignments and this deployment never did gel except for the Six getting a lot of combat mods installed. Clear canopy, guns, etc.

We always wondered if anyone really read the report except for the 106 part. On the Connie side we'd mentioned a whole slew of improvements . . . remove the useless height-finder from the roof was one, better ball-bearings in the radar so we could do an area sweep with it instead of waiting on a complete rotation, data link for secure comm. or fighter control (and we'd practiced an early version of this successfully), and finally we recommended ball turrets and waist gunners. Surely THAT should have brought an angry comment from somewhere, but it didn't.

What it did do was years later, '74 up at Boeing when AWACS was in its infancy, someone at ADC actually released money for a study on a self-defense system "based on an earlier test project with the EC-121." So I guess someone finally read it and thought it was a serious recommendation!

This article was sent to me by Lt. Colonel Deryl L. Sadler, Tyndall AFB, Panama City, Fla. Lt. Colonel Sadler was in the 4757th Air Defense Squadron. He and his crew taught themselves how to work the "beast" he writes about, during Jan. of '68.

SURVIVAL SCHOOLS
By Deryl Sadler

From: dlsad@comcast.net
To: clara19126@msn.com
Subject: Re: F-15 incident
Date: Sat, 20 Sep 2008 17:11:21 -0700

There was an old axiom left over from Wars 1 and 2. "Try never to leave a perfectly good airplane, but when it stops working, make it quick!"
I was duly impressed with this when going through both survival schools, water and ground. The water survival was at Tyndall just a few miles from where I worked at the time. It was more or less in the swamps and beach area. Besides camping out in the snake-infested brush we also got to be dragged around by a parachute through a muddy field, dropped off a tower blindfolded and allowed to find our way from under a wet parachute, taught to paddle an inflatable dingy (useless exercise) and did some three parasailing adventures. Two low level, one high level. At a signal from the boat you'd cut loose and merrily float down into the sting-ray, snake and turtle infested waters. Lordy but that was fun! Also we did a night dump just so we could see how that worked. Clambering into a dingy whilst soaking wet and then finding land that wasn't occupied by some sort of hostile vermin was part of that game.
Then a few years later I got to do this at Spokane on the one that featured prisoner of war training. And oh yes, we were made extremely uncomfortable. Hikes through the woods (again avoiding hostile vermin), dining out on weeds and bark, playing escape and evasion, prisoner interrogation, night-time navigation in deep woods with a scout compass and once again, parachute training.
Part of this one was being hooked into your harness and then to a rope. Rope goes up over a two-story beam with a pulley on it. End of rope is in the hands of a two-striper that didn't care for officers and was probably miffed at being assigned away from civilization anyway. We jump off a ramp and are swinging wildly back and forth and at some inconvenient position this airman is going to turn loose of the rope and we'll do our 'practice fall and roll' from howsomever we happen to hit the earth. Unfortunately this dipwick waited until I was at the top of my swing and turned loose. You guessed it, I dropped straight down like a rock, flat on my back. None of this 'tuck and roll' nonsense for me.

So while I'm lying there debating on how best to kill this trooper I'm grabbed and put on a board and hauled to the clinic for Xrays. Turns out nothing is broken so they give me some pills and the next day I'm hauling a 50 lb pack up and down mountains whilst 'escaping'. The buddy student assigned with me has to put my pack on and off because I can't bend over. At all. But I'm the senior officer in the class by a wide margin and far the oldest at 41, and the rest of them are very early 20s if that. Damned if I'll give up and wash back a class. Besides not being too young I wasn't too bright either, thinking back on it.

Anyway, to cut the long story short, I would have had few qualms about departing a failed airplane and taking my chances somewhere far from an explosion. I grew up with vermin and while not at home with them, could at least tolerate them for a while. Much better than burn therapy. I recall several heroes swearing that they'd ride the plane down and take their chances rather than step out in the cold air. Yup, you do that.

Another story in the year 2007 about something other than the cold war, by a cold war warrior who is always thinking about the whole picture of war, but his thinking leads him back to those days of the iron curtain, and the way the world was then.

MY PLAN FOR DESERT STORM II
By Deryl Sadler

As another USAF retiree friend just said, "Next stop, Iran."
My plan for Desert Storm II was a bit simpler than what happened. Could be adapted for Iran I'm sure. I thought we ought to make concentric circles about ten miles apart out from Baghdad. Then starting at the outermost one we'd drop a tactical nuke on it. Each day we'd move one ring closer but not necessarily in a line. When they decided to surrender we'd quit. No fuss, no muss, no big buildup of troops, minimum expenditure in fuel, weapons and manpower. Probably take half a dozen missions is all.
One of the plans I worked on in the late '60s was similar. It was a logistical study of how many missions it would take with F-100 aircraft carrying tactical nukes to make a cleared no-man's land across Vietnam. Would have probably been a whole lot less messy than what they finally did with Agent Orange.
Agent Orange, by the way, was so called because of the identifying orange stripe around the 55-gallon drum holding the stuff. I forget all the details exactly but there were also agents 'blue', 'yellow', 'green' and so on for about 13 different defoliant concoctions which were later grouped under the heading of Agent Orange. The defoliant operation went on from something like 1960 through 1972 and even for two years in Korea; really started good in Vietnam in January of '65 with the Ranch Hand missions using C-130s as sprayers.
I was never quite sure what there was in Korea that needed defoliating but that's just my lack of geographical knowledge. I'm sure they must have a jungle or two there somewhere.

I thought it was all rocks.

Here is another kind person who offered his help in obtaining my brother's papers from USAFSS.[The Editor]

Subj: YOUR BROTHER AT SAMPSON AFB
Date: 11/15/02 8:54:13 AM Pacific Standard Time
From: Scanlon . . .
From: To: IdaReedBlanford@aol.com

I too trained in that frigid place from Oct 54 thru Dec 54. It is a long story but I ended up in the British army as a musician. Attended the Band Masters School at Kneller Hall in London; later served as Band Master of the Regimental Band of H.M. Black Watch in Scotland. Was commissioned a Captain and Director of Music Regimental Band of the Royal Artillery Corps then named Director of Music Regimental Band of H.M. Scots Guard at Wellington Barracks, London. Retired August 1992 and returned to the U.S. with my wife and children. Wife passed away in 1999 and I reside here in Charlottesville, VA where I teach arranging, etc. and guest conduct from time to time. You might be able to obtain your brothers records from the USAF records center and since you have his service number it should be easy. Their address can be found on the official website of the U.S. Air Force. Good luck in your Quest. LT.C. M.J.P. Scanlon, Scots Guard (Ret.)

These Guys

CHRISTMAS OPS TEMPO: *As told to me by Bob Schiesser, USNS Grasp Principle Port Engineer, Norfolk, VA*

The President has authorized the Department of Defense to assist Santa with the Twelve Days of Christmas. Status of acquisitions follows:

Day 1 - Partridge in a pear tree: The Army and Air Force are in the process of deciding whose area of responsibility Day 1 falls under. Since the partridge is a bird, the Air Force believes it should have the lead. The Army, however, feels trees are part of the land component command's area of responsibility. After three months of discussion and repeated Ops Deps tank sessions, a $1M study has been commissioned to decide who should lead this joint program.

Day 2 - Two turtle doves: Since doves are birds, the Air Force claims responsibility. However, turtles are amphibious, so the Navy-Marine Corps team feels it should take the lead. Initial studies have shown that turtles and doves may have interoperability problems. Terms of reference are being coordinated for a four-year, $10M DARPA study.

Day 3 - Three French Hens: At State Department instigation, the Senate Committee on Foreign Affairs has blocked off-shore purchase of hens, from the French or anyone else. A $6M program is being developed to find an acceptable domestic alternative.

Day 4 - Four Calling Birds: Source selection has been completed, with the contract awarded to AT&T. However, the award is being challenged by a small disadvantaged business.

Day 5 - Five Golden Rings: No available rings meet MILSPEC for gold plating. A three-year, $5M accelerated development program has been initiated.

Day 6 - Six Geese a-Laying: The six geese have been acquired. However, the shells of their eggs seem to be very fragile. It might have been a mistake to build the production facility on a nuclear waste dump at former Air Force base that was closed under BRAC.

Day 7 - Seven Swans a-Swimming: fourteen swans have been killed trying to get through the Navy SEAL training program. The program has been put on hold while the training procedures are reviewed to determine why the washout rate is so high.

Day 8 - Eight Maids a-Milking: The entire class of maids a milking training program at Aberdeen is involved in a sexual harassment suit against the Army. The program has been put on hold pending resolution of the lawsuit.

Day 9 - Nine Ladies Dancing: Recruitment of the ladies dancing has been halted by a lawsuit from the "Don't Ask, Don't Tell Association." Members claim they have a right to dance and wear women's clothing as long as they're off duty.

Day 10 - Ten Lords a-Leaping: The ten lords have been abducted by terrorists. Congress has approved $2M in funding to conduct a rescue operation. Army Special Forces and a USMC MEU(SOC) are conducting a "NEO-off" competition for the right to rescue.

Day 11 - Eleven Pipers Piping: The pipe contractor delivered the pipes on time. However, he thought DoD wanted smoking pipes. DoD lost the claim due to defective specifications. A $22M dollar retrofit program is in process to bring the pipes into spec.

Day 12 - Twelve Drummers Drumming: Due to cutbacks only six billets are available for drumming drummers. DoD is in the process of coordinating an RFP to obtain the six additional drummers by outsourcing; however, funds will not be available until FY 09.

As a result of the above-mentioned programmatic delays, and due to a high OPTEMPO that requires diversion of modernization funds to support current readiness. Christmas is hereby postponed until further notice.

# # #

Subj: FW: HOW TO BAKE A CHICKEN
Date: 11/7/02 7:51:24 AM Pacific Standard Time
From: Port Engineer, USNS Sioux, MSC (Military Sealift Command) DoD/DoN
To: IdaReedBlanford

How about this at the same time as your Rum Cake recipe?

From: Hieber, Ray
Sent: Thursday, November 07, 2002 7:29 AM
To: Burke, John; Scroggins, Pete; Anamosa, John; Hetzer, Robert; Mills, John; Schumacher, Joe; Palihnich, Ivo; Cornelius, Clarence; Leoncio, Orlando; Schiesser, Robert
Subject: HOW TO BAKE A CHICKEN

When I found this recipe I thought it was perfect for people, like me, who just are not sure how to tell when poultry is cooked thoroughly, but not dried out. Give this a try.

BAKED STUFFED CHICKEN

6-7 lb. chicken
1 cup melted butter
1 cup stuffing
1 cup uncooked popcorn
salt/pepper to taste

Preheat oven to 350 degrees. Brush chicken well with melted butter, salt and pepper. Fill cavity with stuffing and popcorn. Place in baking pan with the neck end toward the back of the oven.

Listen for popping sounds. When the chicken's ass blows the oven door open and the chicken flies across the room, it's done.

These Guys

This is one of the notices that I sent out, looking for someone who may have known my brother at his last post, the 6901st (or other places).

Subj: Hi, this is Trish (Noland) Schiesser
Date: 10/26/02 3:36:23 PM Pacific Daylight Time

Would it be possible for you to pass the word that I am looking for anyone who remembers SSGT Phil Noland, USAFSS, when he was at Ft. Meade (maybe approx. 57-58) or San Angelo or Goodfellow or Japan, Middle East (TUSLOG Det 3) 1960-61, Supv. Head for "C" Flt. under Capt. Dodi Aspell. Phil was 202xx. "He took the place of one of the best in the business," according to Dodi.
Phil eventually went to 6901st Zweibrucken prox. 62 - Jan. 64, where he became mentally ill after a three day TDY to London in July 1963.
If anyone even knew him or has photos or has even heard his name, would appreciate an e-mail at: Clara19126@msn.com.

Respectfully, Trish Schiesser, Phil's sister.

JACK WOOD, Karamursel, Turkey
by Trish Schiesser and Jack Wood

I'd like to acknowledge receiving my Charlie Flight photo signed by Phil, my brother in USAFSS at Karamursel, TUSLOG Det.3, Supervisory Head of Charlie Flight, to Jack Wood, who was also in Charlie Flight at the time my brother, SSGT Phil Noland was Supv. Head for Captain Dodi Aspell.

Also, Jack appears in "Body of Secrets: Anatomy of the Ultra Secret National Security Agency," James Bamford's book, on page 155, which states: "Among the very few Westerners to have listened to the world's first manned space mission as it was happening" was Karamursel intercept operator Jack Wood. "Our mission," he said, "was the number one mission in the world - to monitor the Russian manned space program. After nearly forty years, I still remember the excitement of hearing Yuri Gagarin's voice over my headset. . . . We were all tuned in for that historic moment. Loose translation: 'I see you and hear you well, OK'."

The Russians had some trouble with the spacecraft's reentry, but after ten minutes the parts broke away that were giving them trouble and the spacecraft steadied and the landing was successful.

Thank you, Jack Wood, for noticing my request on the Karamursel site and paying attention to my call for help and sending the photograph, with everybody's signatures on the back of it, and my brother in the first row, squatting, third from the left. What a surprise it was for me, for you were one of the first who had discovered my brother by going into your "treasure trove" of memories of your time in the USAFSS and bringing forth a jewel for me.

May God bless you, all of your life,

Trish (Noland) Schiesser

Jack Wood, I just learned, in 2007, passed away several years ago. I sent my condolences to the KAS site on the Internet and they were received by the webmaster, Pete Johnson, and he said he would pass the word.
T.S. [The Editor]

The Air Force tried to tell their cold war servicemen that there was no place such as the 6901st Zweibrucken, nor any other "spying" type organizations under the auspices of the United State Air Force Security Service. Hence this article.

SURREAL OR TONGUE IN CHEEK - By Trish Schiesser

I remember when we were at Wright Pat back in the fifties and my brother tried to convince me he had some kind of admin role, but he spent a lot of time in that circular test area (I don't remember the technological name, word, sorry) but one sat in THE SEAT and rotated around the room, face flattening out like rubber, eventually, body taking G forces. I wonder how fast a human could go at that point in time. The only reason I think he might have been there was because he seemed to be "holding" back what he did on any given day. He had a Ford 500 Fairlane, a 1957, and he'd had it for awhile, called it his, "black beauty," and someone sideswiped it and did some nasty damage to his pride and joy. We all heard the crash - Mom/Phil/Doll, me - wondering what the heck was going on as I'd been listening to the Bobwhites outside the Air Force housing window. Still in my granny gown I flew down the stairs and followed Phil and Mom and Doll, we looked like a pack of Indians (no prejudice meant) following the leader. Phil saw the damage and there he stood, in the middle of the street, in his jockey shorts, jumping up and down doing a mighty angry dance.

I wonder what he was doing there at Wright Pat, that's what he called it, and so did we in order to keep up with his lingo and not appear stupid. Now I know he was in the USAFSS, even then, because when he received his "second" discharge papers "they" said he'd been in the USAFSS for 12 years, so many months and so many days. That is how long he served. I wish I could ask him questions today, but he isn't here and he wasn't there and there was no such place. This is all according to the USAFSS. Oh, yeah, and he supposedly didn't go to Cheyenne after that either, 'cause no one ever went there - there was nothing but isolation and no USAFSS, and though I don't remember seeing him again until November 1959 when our little half-sister, Ellen Lucille Ruvituso, (yes, there is a Mafia), a Mongoloid, was born and we stood together in the hospital as her godparents, lest she should die, but she didn't die for seven months and he wasn't at the funeral and I wish I hadn't been either.

I wonder where he wasn't at the time, since there never was a USAFSS and he probably was in limbo because he wasn't anywhere in my mind. I do know that he loved that job that was never there and I know the 6901st didn't exist so he couldn't have lost his mind and disappeared because there was no place to disappear to, was there? After that non-happening I do know that he had a beautiful mind. "They" say his writings were surreal, after that, but then how would "they" know - they weren't there. He remembered some things, though, because his non-existent handsome face lit up when a special non-plane flew over the cuckoo's nest (our mother's house, actually).

 He had turned towards me and his knowing hazel/brown eyes shadowed, quickly, which wasn't supposed to be left in there, but I caught it. I caught it! And, I didn't have the notion to ask him about his un-world, nor the one he was left in by the USAFSS.

Phil's sister.

I was a young girl when Phil was at Wright Patterson AFB but I do remember all these things happening, and while researching for this book, the "story" that was going around was that these places never existed, so therefore how could many of the "guys" in this book have been there - so this was the way we wrote for awhile, until these places became existent. [The Editor]

A RANGER'S WORDS - By Trish Schiesser

I just talked to a guy whose name is Frank. He bought my husband's 1977 MG. Frank was in the Army during VN. He won't write a story for me.

"I've put all that behind me and I don't like to talk about it, but I will tell ya that I signed up for a second tour over there and didn't get to go.

"My father was in the navy on tin cans during WWII. His ship had just left Pearl Harbor on 7 Dec 1941 - before the bombing."

"Lucky man, your father," I said.

"Yeah.

"Back to me? I was a Ranger. Yeah, I jumped.

"Ya know, I could go to the VA and sit in a group and tell stories and get $3000.00 but I don't do it. I don't want to remember. I did my part.

"I enlisted in the Army at the age of seventeen, before I got drafted. I was one of the few who wanted to go to Vietnam. I wanted to do what needed to be done.

"I did what I had to do - and no, I'm not going to talk about it - no National Guard for me, and now I just go about my business, knowing I served.

"Wish they wouldn't have taken our brown berets away from us, though. That wasn't right. I still have mine at home. Taking those away was like a slap in the face. I don't know what idiot decided on that one. They shoulda done it the other way around. Well, it's over and done with, and that's that."

We said our goody-bye and I watched him get into the little ol' MG and drive up the street and around the corner and out of sight.

I couldn't get him to tell stories, but I did get him to talk a little bit. Given more time, who knows what he may have told me.

JOHNNY CASH
By Trish Schiesser

At the risk of repeating many stories about Johnny Cash, all I can say is:

Johnny Cash returned to Keesler AFB in '56, from a tour with the USAFSS, of which he was a member, in Bremerhaven, and performed at the Airman's club at Keesler.

Johnny was a Radio Intercept Operator at Landsberg AFB. Read Johnny's own account of his USAFSS experience in his biography, "Cash," (written with Patrick Carr), Harper Paperbacks 1997.

All of you must remember Johnny Cash, and that he served his country well, as you all did.

He has passed on, joining his wife June Carter Cash. May they rest easily and sing much in the skies of the wild blue yonder.

DUGWAY-BENDER GESTALT TESTS

Date: 10/30/02 08:53:38 PM
Name: Trish
E-mail: USAFSS Club (USAFSS Lite)
Subj: DODTRANSCRIPTS: Cold War

I'm reading an Oct. 09, 2002 Briefing on Cold War-era Chemical and Biological Warfare Tests: Identified as Project 112. There were 134 tests planned under this project of which 46 tests did take place. If anyone wants a copy please e-mail me and I'll forward. Question: What is/are irradiated BG spores? Interesting reading. I'm not finished yet. Thank you. Trish

I received no answer to this e-mail.

Name: Bill Yunkun
Subject: Re: DODTRANSCRIPTS . . . Cold War

Information about those "Dugway" tests is all over the net. An example is at:
http://www.deploymentlink.osd.mil/current_issues/shad/shad_intro.shtml

Some of us were stationed east of Dugway during the tests. The prevailing winds might have carried and dispersed air born spores to D.C., the U.K., Europe, Turkey, Pakistan, Nam, the Pl. and back to CONUS before we could take cover. Rashes, diminished performance, and the urge to go to the bathroom in the middle of the night have been identified by the CDC as precursors to the full blown onset of Dugway Syndrome.

I have since read in my brother's papers through the FOIA, that he was tested for "Bender Gestalt" which coincides with The Dugway Syndrome. These "spores" were spread among our servicemen, by our Government, as a test for germ warfare and such. Even today, our servicemen are fighting for Veteran's Hospital rights and a confirmation to having been exposed to these tests.

These Guys

This is some "chat" from the former Bravenet forum of USAFSS Lite. They, and myself, chat about the Fulda Gap. And about the fact that one of them bought a giant TV for his misses.

FULDA GAP
By Trish Schiesser (and others)

"Snoopy" (that was me)

If the Soviet Union was to attack the west by ground they would have come thru the Fulda Gap and would have been met with "Tactical Nuclear Weapons" according to war plans. That was the only way to stop or slow the advance.

Replying to:

Again, Happy Kwanza season, EW. My son, Sgt., USA was at Fulda Gap oh, about I don't know how many years ago - - just before the wall came down and when it came down, he and the guy across the borderline exchanged hats, etc., and Whit (my son) brought his mom home a piece of the wall. He has had stereo after stereo, one after the other. I miss him so much. He lives in KY. But, then I think I've told his story before. He had a TS clearance - nuclear weapons. He'll be 43 in April if he survives those winter storms as he 18 wheels it up and down the east coast, and the west coast. Gawd, I though my new 34" t.v. was big. It's about time you did something nice for that fine lady of yours. ☺ Trish

Replying to:

First thing me and 20 other AF warriors did when we showed up at the Oh-Wurst was get an apartment off base. Then I bought a German AF/FM/SW stereo to listen to some folk singer named Bob Dylan. He sounded like he gargled with broken glass and napalm. If Dylan or Joan Baez became boring, there was always Hillbilly Gasthaus on AM. Get enough of that, and we could get 5 digit Russ. WX on wouldya believe . . . FM? And during the winter, there was clear-text Russ. tank traffic, again on FM apparently coming thru the Fulda Gap. Hell, the guys at Hof could have stayed in their bunks and copied the traffic. Trying to remember, but I think the Russ. stuff

was from the 12th Guards Tank Army. Spiffy stuff on a $100 Kraut home stereo system. EW
Replying to:

I know at Sunny Zwei we ran millions of lines thru the good old IBM 1410 daily. One of my duties was to remove the "chat" on its way to DIRNSA.

Phil
6901SCG

USAFSS COMMAND EMBLEM

From the Internet and Ed #2 of USAFSS-Lite:
By Trish Schiesser

Some time ago I had asked what the USAFSS Command Emblem Symbolism meant. I've found the answer. Ed #2 of USAFSS-Lite, I think it was you who gave me some info. Here goes:
The USAF Security Service was established on 20 October 1948 at Arlington Hall Station, Virginia. HQ USAFSS moved to newly constructed HQ building 2000 the 1st week of August 1953.
Some time ago I had asked what the USAFSS Command Emblem Symbolisim meant. I've found the answer.

The USAFSS Command Emblem Symbolizes the command mission. It consists of a shield divided equally into quarters by a vertical and horizontal line and identifying cross. Significant of the command's worldwide influence, the first quarter is blue, thereon a green sphere with yellow land markings. Pertinent to transmission, the second quarter is red, there on a yellow lightning streak. Significant of the United States Air Force, the third quarter is yellow, thereon a blue half wing. Symbolic of protection and security, the fourth quarter is blue, thereon over a sword with point to base (hilt and pommel yellow), a white shield thereon a yellow flame shaded red. The emblem was approved by Headquarters USAF in August 1952.

THE OTHER THREE:

The USAFSS was re-designated as the Electronic Security Command on 1 August 1979.
On a field of blue, a silver shield bearing a chess piece is displayed over a blade of lightning, and identifying scroll is unfurled underneath. The blue field, as the dominant color, represents ESC's Air Force subordination to preserve the link with the Air Force Security Service emblem, whose principal color was blue, and symbolizes the valor and loyalty of the men and women of the command. The lightning blade of the sword is drawn from the USAFSS emblem to preserve tradition and to represent the identification with electronics. Connecting the bolt to a sword hilt suggests its transformation into a weapon, much as the more passive mission of USAFSS evolved into the active role with which ESC is charged. Immediate readiness

of response is also embodied in the lightning bolt sword. The silver shield has its origin in the USAFSS emblem, denoting now, as then, both defense and the security resulting from that defense. The chess piece - a black knight - conveys several meanings. Classic deception as embodied in the Trojan horse is suggested. The color black takes meaning from the rule of chess that black moves second; black's tactics are therefore counter moves, representing ESC countermeasures missions. The knight is a powerful chess man; he strikes from unexpected quarter and is the only piece able to strike while obstructed. He employs elegant rather than brute force. All these attributes combine to symbolize C3 Countermeasures and the move/countermove nature of electromagnetic warfare.

The Electronic Security Command was re-designated as the Air Force Intelligence Command on 1 October 1991. The emblem of the Air Force Intelligence Command is symbolic of its diverse missions. The knight chess piece had its origin in the ESC emblem and conveys classic deception as embodied in the Trojan horse. It is a powerful chess man; he strikes from unexpected quarter and is the only piece able to strike while obstructed. The shield had its origin in the USAFSS emblem, denoting now, as then, both defense and the security resulting from that defense. It is separated into four quadrants to symbolize the Command's worldwide mission of support. The double-edged sword refers to the military role of the Air Force. It signifies the readiness of AFIC to electronic in both defensive and offensive operations to ensure the security of the nation.

The Air Force Intelligence Command was re-designated to the Air Intelligence Agency on 1 October 1993. Blue and yellow are the Air Force colors. Blue alludes to the sky, the primary theater of Air Force operations. Yellow refers to the sun and the excellence required of Air Force personnel. The globe signifies the intelligence the agency provides to the Air Force Global Reach-Global Power Mission.. The key represents the Agency's efforts to unlock its protagonist's secrets. The teeth on the sword symbolize the disciplines of intelligence gathering - SIGINT, HUMINT, IMAGERY, and MASINT. The chess reflects counter-intelligence and the ability to use intelligence information in a variety of ways. The compass rose symbolizes intelligence operations reaching the four corners of the earth and the uses of satellite information gathering.

For further information go to:
http://www.aia.af.mil/aia/homepages/ho/hisshld.cfm
Credit is given to www.silentwarriors.com/usafss.htm and Ed Watts, ex-USAFSS.

NOTE: The USAFSS command emblem is shown on the back cover.

FROM AN EX-USAFSS GUY (#1)
By Jim Stallings

The gentleman who referred Jim Stallings to the editor shall remain anonymous. He also does not know Stallings, personally. This piece is taken from several e-mails I received from Stallings. Although I am not sure why Stallings wrote the things he wrote (he said he was teasing in one of his e-mails to me which I have chosen not to print.) I felt that his information was pertinent, not only to the era in which said research was being done, but what I, as an author/editor received on a daily basis. This man's e-mails are far from being the worst treatment I received while researching, though he had me frightened for a moment - but I'd been through far worse and I felt, after all, though he was a bit misguided with his teasing, that he's a decent guy. Serving at the 6901st was a more than arduous job and many men eventually suffered a great deal from the isolation of the work, and went "south" like my brother. This guy apologized to me. Here are his e-mails. I am indebted to you, Jim. T.S.

Anonymous referred me to you. I found him by accident trying to learn about the status of Parkbrau beer. His book excerpts took me immediately back to my mixed emotions of being in Germany 40 years ago.

I was stationed at the 6901st from Feb 1960 to March 1963. I was an E-3 airman second-class, so didn't hang with NCOs. I don't remember your brother, S/Sgt Phil Noland, but his picture may bring him back for me.

I remember a S/Sgt John Burns and a S/Sgt Steve Vaughn who were killed in a car accident. *(Editor's note: I had been researching for some buddies my brother had lost but don't know if these were the right men).*

I was 19 when I got to Zweibrucken. The Air Force was a diversion for me after a childish year of college, and getting to Germany was my enlistment goal. Once there I was just a lost little boy alone in a large new strange world. I was too immature to grasp it fully, gather it all in, know it intimately, love it for itself. I was more interested in what every 19 year old, anywhere, is. Despite this, I appreciate now that I had the time most do not, to do and see things that I now cherish, but failed to experience things I now regret.

I was a 20250, radio intercept analyst. I wanted to be a pilot, but couldn't pass the vision test. I opted for navigator. Vision problem again. I decided on air traffic control. No openings. How about electronics? I was surprised - I was color-blind. Sorry, electronics is out if you can't distinguish red from green. What's left? Photography school or this radio intercept analysis thing. Which will get me overseas? The radio school. I'll take it. Highest grade at Goodfellow, AFB, TX security service tech school could get his (I don't remember any women attendees) pick of the world-wide assignments available to graduates. I placed second. There were five choice Germany spots open, naturally, so that I might not have to work so hard. I took one of the German assignments.

I was ordered [sounds officious, huh?] to Darmstadt. I got off the Air Force bus at Zweibrucken. At first I thought, all right! Headquarters. Later I discovered that the stations under the 6901st, such as Darmstadt, got the promotions. A friend who was a kind of doofus and not very bright went to Darmstadt and got his third stripe which was a rarity in the Air Force Security Service in a first enlistment. I regretted (again) being at the 6901st. Also, it seemed to me there was a more intimate relationship with the "enemy" or more "realness" when you could be near the radio actually copying the traffic he sent, than reading it on paper.

The radio intercept operators were so good, I understood, that they could copy the Morse code, and ID the station by the way the operator created letters, or "his hand." The intercept operators could read a book while copying the traffic.

Usually the messages intercepted were just testing equipment and atmospheric quality. "ASA DE [this is] RET QSA II" [How do you read me?] The response often was "Guhor" [good] or "QSA 5" [1 to 5, five being the best.] A question mark in Morse code is dit dit dah dah dit dit. The Russians would send a "?" as if it were IMI which is dit dit then dah dah then dit dit. So we copied it as it sounded.

There were three character Q-signals, and they are international shorthand used then as now by everyone sending Morse.

We intercepted different equipment. There was both manual and automatic Morse. There was teletype. There was voice. There was radar that could be intercepted and identified with an oscilloscope. The Morse transmissions could be shown on an oscilloscope and matched to other oscilloscope patterns to identify the operator and his station.

We could not discuss our work with others in the building that did not have the need to know. Our discarded paper was placed in tall paper "burn bags" and they were incinerated in the basement every day. The chimney had a steel grate to catch any partially burned paper and to avoid, I suppose, an incursion through the chimney. I pulled the dirty burn bag detail once. Afterwards I blew my nose and I saw "top secret" on the handkerchief: a lame joke.

Those who were 20250's maintained histories of soviet and eastern bloc country military radio stations and their connected radar positions. When I was debriefed before leaving the 6901st, I was told I couldn't talk about what I did for 20 years, as I recall the number, although it may have been 10 years. We were closely related to the British, with CHQ, at the time and shared information. One such sharing was a widely disseminated classified monthly report. In it I once wrote, and had supervisory approval, that such and such Russian military station was no longer in place as there had been no intercepted communication from it for some time. The British replied in the monthly report that they had heard the station during this period.

My area of specialization (but, hey, I was only 19) was the Moscow and Oral and Smiles area. Being involved in my small way was tantalizing. It was a deathly serious matter. But, I guess at my age, death was remote and could not captivate my attention or interest for long intervals.

Last week I met a Russian in Castle Rock, CO who lives in Aurora, CO. He said that he was originally from the Black Sea area. He mentioned the town. I said, near Odessa? Yes. Near Tbilisi? Yes. Woe, it was forty years ago that those cities were important to me. Tbilisi contained a town completely American in every detail. Only English was spoken. It was a Russian spy training area, we were told. *(Jim Stallings note: I believe these training camps are being/ or have been demolished).*

Once we intercepted a voice message from one of the eastern bloc countries where the operator said WWIII would start at 7:00 tomorrow! I was scared. I had no way to let my family know. The tape of the transmission was played over and over again by the language experts at the 6901st. Flash messages were sent to the States. Finally, the language guys decided the operator was drunk and WWIII was going to be started by his wife when he got home.

We would fly aircraft straight toward E. Germany and sometimes we'd penetrate the border, which lit up the E. German radar stations. We could learn the radio and radar networks that way.

One of the preconditions for war, we understood, was a complete radio shut down followed by coming back up with new call signs and frequencies. Keeping track of communications was partially to be alert to this. Once Czechoslovakia went silent and then returned. A couple of E-4 airmen first class figured it out in a couple of months.

Most of the Soviet and their satellite countries used three letter call signs. We had a slide rule with letters. If we had a partial call sign, we could often get one missing letter using the slide rule.

One aggressive Captain at the 6901st implemented what was called a "Bull Moose" program, which was the above-mentioned flight of U.S. aircraft into the "enemy" countries, and we'd track the radar that lit up. He was a bundle of energy and seemed always to be in a hurry the few times I encountered him.

In the Security Service we never referred to an enemy. We were instructed to refer to "potential enemy." But a common expression was, "my job is so secret that only the Russian's know what I do." Everyone knew who the "enemy" was.

NSA analysts Martin and Mitchell defected to the Russians during my time at the 6901st. We were told not to mention their names outside the two Security Service buildings we worked in. It was a serious matter. Any discussion by us might imply some truth to anything they said to the Russians. It turns out they gave away - confirmed is more likely - a great deal of what we did.

We were shown Russian diplomatic license plates to report if we saw them - supposing that if we saw them they were not where they should be. It was understood that the enemy had spies in the neighborhood.

Classified information was stamped with Classified, Secret, or Top Secret. There was a second word following the classification. We were never to utter outside the buildings the second word with the classification. I once said them both together just as naturally as I might say my own name, outside the building to a colleague. Nothing was said of it. But, I felt an embarrassment for it for many years.

After about a year and a half I transferred to a rack of ten teletypes, which were connected to U.S. military sites in Europe and the mid-east. It was a mechanical job, but there was an exhilaration of handling the rapid pace of managing the machines and the paper and tape that they spit out.

A normal crew was five guys. Olin Hightower, a fine black fellow who now reminds me of the black DI in Officer and a Gentleman, and I were proud that we could do the same job with no other help.

I am proud to say I may be one of the first Americans to own a Mercedes. A 1951 150S as I recall . . . four on the floor . . . convertible . . . leather seats . . . and real wood trim. Wanted to bring it home, but it was deteriorating. It would have cost a fortune to maintain in 1963. I walked away from it. The Air Force wrote several times asking what I wanted to do with it. I ignored them.

Sorry for the length,
Jim Stallings.

FROM AN EX-USAFSS GUY (#2)
By Jim Stallings

I looked at the picture of Phil, but I do not remember meeting him. Sorry.

By the way, I have made a few corrections to my long e-mail for accuracy in case your research would not have caught them. These errors were caused by my too careless use of "spell checker."

"Good AFG, TX" should have been, of course, Goodfellow AFB, San Angelo, TX.

"We were closely related to the British, with CHQ. . . ." CHQ should have been GCHQ. (Editor's note: GCHQ stands for: Originally, British Government Code and Cypher School, but was renamed Government Communications Headquarters in an effort to hide its activities.)

"My area of specialization . . . was Moscow and Oral and Smiles area." This should have been Orel and Smolensk.

"Classified information was stamped with Classified, Secret, and Top Secret." This should have been, "Confidential, Secret, and Top Secret."

Olin Hightower who I worked with in the teletype room reminds me of the black actor Lou Gossett.

Whew. I feel better now.

Good luck with your book.

Jim Stallings

FROM AN EX-USAFSS GUY (#3)
By Jim Stallings

A couple of names you might contact for their insight and experiences at the 6901st.

Ernie S. and Ray W., GA. They are my age.

Ernie had a better connection, I suspect, with the intelligence work we did by virtue of the department, men and superiors he worked with. Ray, a good friend, reminds me of a studious type and may have been more "committed and involved" in his work. Besides, Ray worked in a different section, and may have had a job much different from mine which may add to your research. (Jim Stallings note: I never contacted the above men - fresh out of time)

I telephoned Ray out of the blue one day after not talking with him for 20 years. He owned a . . . store in . . . and when he answered the phone, I asked, "Do you have any Dockers pants 36 x 32?"

He immediately said, "Is this Jim Stallings?"

Cool. He remembered my size.

I called Ernie a few years ago. He had always been my idol and image of a girl-getter. He was a man's man and a lady's man, to boot. An envious combination shared by a very few fellows anywhere. He was a handsome blond southerner with a crew cut like mine, and a likeable personality. He was a soft-spoken guy with a magical false bashfulness that is so endearing, and made him approachable and seem more like guys like me, than he really was. As a southerner, he expected to be liked. I, by contrast, expected to be un-liked and ignored.

He once bragged that he and a friend spent the night with a German mother and her daughter! We (or maybe just I) walked around wide-eyed and preoccupied in delicious salacious thought for days. I was very immature, but I could define fun. But, I have learned that some men (or boys) receive a greater sense of self-respect and stature among men, only when they can demonstrate that a female (presumed by the hearer to be pretty) is interested in them. The encounter may not make any sense and may have important contradictory details from those related.

The Army troops had class B passes which meant they had to be on base before midnight for bed check, and the Air Force had class A passes which meant they could go anywhere within 250 miles of the post as long as they showed up for work. The relevance, so goes the story, is the Army would get the German girls drunk, and the Air Force guys (or guy, for all I knew) would take them home.

Whenever Ernie was late for work on Sunday mornings, he always told S/Sgt Vaughn that Mass took longer than usual. He would always have a smile trying to break out on his face as if to show Sgt. Vaughn that the excuse offered as real, may just only be a joke. Ernie was probably not a Catholic or a church goer or near a church anywhere in Europe in the previous 12 months or even on base the night before. But it always worked to assuage the Sgt's anger from Ernie's being temporarily AWOL. We always laughed, and knew that that excuse, even if original with us, would not buy us anything from Sgt. Vaughn. Only Ernie could get away with it. Sergeants can be envious, too, and recognized a treasure when they saw him.

When I telephoned Ernie, he said that he remembered me after all those 20-30 years. We exchanged Christmas cards once, he sending me one first to my surprise and delight (I am a quintessential hero worshiper), but we had little in common then as now, and let the renewed contact remain both an oddity and something never again to be satisfying. One cannot really capture anything from the past. Our appetites change, and the menu does not make us salivate looking over our shoulder at the back of it. And when I look in the mirror, it may be as well to remember Ernie as I did, than how I might now.

There may be closer relationships, less superficial ones, those mutually shared that are strong enough to endure changes. Seeing Ray might be less traumatic for me today than seeing a potential balding and overweight Ernie.
Jim Stallings

FROM AN EX-USAFSS GUY (4)
By Jim Stallings

Trish:

Writing now about my days at the 6901st brings me a melancholy that is hard to shake. I don't like the feeling. It is like experiencing a tragedy.

I ought to be happy describing my time there, like describing a vacation, but I am not. Yet, as I remember those times, I can manage a smile. The melancholy was directly connected, I thought, to some past experiences, but the feeling actually may come from simply by recalling the 40 years ago, when I was 20, gradually brings closer to consciousness the sad nearness of 70.

By the way, the late comedian Brother Dave was the rage in the early 60s among guys at the 6901st and apparently at other places in the AF. When I was being discharged and at Maguire AFB in Trenton, NJ in March 1963, I briefly met a guy in the AF and we quickly found ourselves quoting parts of Bro Dave's comedy album featuring nonsense about Julius Cesar. "If you say so." And he say (snapping his fingers), 'So?' "Teeth, hair and eyeballs all over the highway," which talk show host Neal Boortz (a military brat) still says today. "I know what's in every book in every library in the world. Words." All said with a southern accent. Spoken like a southern minister, "Little David [of Goliath fame] searched [pronounced: surry-ched] in the round about there of, and BEHOLD! He found a flat, slick, slimy river rock, and he taken it (which is southern for took) and placed in his blue suede shoe tongue [of his slingshot] . . ." "The giant said to little David, 'I'm gonna hit you on the head so hard you're gonna hum like a ten-penny finishing nail hit with a greasy ball-peen hammer.'" Ha ha hahaha. Funny stuff. "The rocket ship traveled at 186,000 MPH-straight up. The guy inside looked at the Instruments as seriously as you can look at things like that and said, 'Oh my God.' And a little voice came back, 'Yes?'" I was pleased to see Bro Dave as a presenter at an Academy Awards (probably in the 70s) shortly before I learned of his death.

A new guy at the 6901st was called a "jeep."

A guy referred to his girlfriend as his "hammer" or as Ernie pronounced it, "hammah."

I learned to play pinochle at the 6901st. My parent's played it for years when I was a kid. I remember playing with my customary partner, a black guy named Charles from Washington, D.C. We called him "CW" . . . for the code for Morse transmissions or "cw" which means, I guess, continuous wave.

CW was a naturally likeable guy. A guy's always learning. He came to my bunk one day while I was reading. He sat down and said, "Jim, we haven't talked for a while so I thought, we need to spend some time together." I would tell him to get away from me. Don't misunderstand; we weren't gay. CW was just practicing, I think, being personable, and social conversation. I liked him a lot; one of my favorite people. Have never been able to contact him. He loved pinochle as much as I did. He would drink bourbon or something while we played foursomes in the barracks and get drunk. But I could never tell he was dead drunk. One night he got up from the table to go to the latrine down the hall. He didn't come back. I opened the double doors at the entrance to the large bay of bunks at the end of the barracks. He was sprawled out on the floor in the hallway, passed out cold. The funniest thing I ever saw.

He once left for the latrine as we were dealing the next hand. We dealt him the most perfect pinochle hand he would ever in his life hope to see. When he sat back down and started picking up his cards, he didn't demonstrate a trace of elation that his cards should have produced - a cool customer. Then we started the bidding. I went first and bid the minimum, and the others added the minimum raise. CW added the minimum; the bidding kept going around the table getting higher and higher. We had arranged ahead of time that CW would not get the bid. Finally, the bidding was so rich, CW passed and bitched for five minutes that despite his perfect hand he still couldn't get the bid. We laughed a long time after we told him what we did. He laughed with us, but more out of relief, I suspect. Of course, there was poker but that was more serious, and I always was too nervous of screwing up like a dork, to enjoy it. Pinochle was more fun and required longer periods of concentration and personal skill and strategy, I thought. CW and I developed the style when taking the last trick of just holding our last card next to our stomach face up on the table saying "bring 'em to papa," or something stupid like that - just to demonstrate that we had the skill to know - in case the others didn't - the last and valuable trick was ours.

We also developed the aggressive style when we unexpectedly trumped a valuable trick, of standing up immediately and slapping our card loudly on top of the other cards with some natural profanity, I suppose. Great charisma, great fun, always produced big grins or laughter from all.

CW and I once went together downtown to Zweibrucken looking for girls. When we got to a carnival that was in town, he started acting odd. I asked him what was going on. He wasn't a prude, but he surprised me by asking about our being together under the circumstances which included his being black. I was stunned. That hadn't even occurred to me. He was a good guy and friend - I enjoyed his company. I told him that I didn't feel that way about him at all. I was not unmindful, however, of the current state of affairs among black and whites in Americans.

We actually picked up a couple of dirty (as in actually dirt) waifs at a bus stop in Kaiserslautern later that night. They acted a bit goofy. I still feel sorry for them. They said that they were runaways from (Communist) East Germany. That made us a bit cautious. Later, I left CW alone with one of the girls in the back seat of my car as I walked under a full moon in a sparse wood with the other girl. CW apologized later.

"No sweat," the current phrase of the day.

We couldn't get rid of the girls. They drove back with us to Zweibrucken. We looked for a place to put them. Everything was closed. The girl I was attached to kept asking, "What will we make while you're at work?" Huh? Make? Why, we can't pay you anything. Hell, you're a derelict, I thought to myself, but probably have more money than I do. It turns out she meant, "What will we DO while you are at work?" I could almost cry now from the sadness of such a question addressed to such a loser as I from an apparently simple girl as she. God, I hate myself for not helping them more than I did. It was as if I was so much smarter, so much more secure, so much more mature than she. Unlike these two girls, I at least had a family here in Germany with the AF and at home. (But, unlike me, she spoke two languages.) I was naïve, and while genuinely concerned for them, also, a bit too sensitive. I also imagined then the realistically tangled web our relationship could become.

I still use that expression today: "What will we MAKE tonight?" It has become a sort of inside "thing" (I hate to say joke) with a friend of mine who knows the story. The expression still saddens me.

We dumped the girls somewhere in Zweibrucken very late at night and returned to the post. I am still embarrassed by it, and feel so sorry for the predicament of those two girls. For me it was a sad and touching experience. Growing up in rural America, I had never experienced such simple desperation, and yet they seemed to be oblivious to their plight - like lost little unwanted puppies left beside some country road. Maybe their oblivion was a blessing of youth or just a brighter, freer comparison to their life in East Germany.

I have often wondered if, on the other hand, if they were more than they appeared to be - being from East Germany.

There was a one-time friend, Richard R. Anderson. When he got drunk he always wanted to rent a car and drive to Frankfurt. I thought, how stupid. He got stopped drunk by MPs on the way to Frankfurt one night. He got the car in a ditch and couldn't get the VW out. After the squadron commander got through with him, Anderson henceforth referred to himself as Richard "Example R." Anderson. He always had a city-like-wise guy way of speaking, but was a funny guy when he wasn't drunk. He worked as a Russian linguist.

I almost got into trouble with him. I rented the damn car because I had a license and wasn't drunk. The Captain wanted to know why I gave him the keys. Because he demanded them and had paid for the car and so it was his. Driving it drunk then became his problem not mine. Drunk he was no longer a funny guy; he was threatening and dangerous, so when he started demanding the keys, he got 'em pretty quick. But, I got away from him.

Sorry.

This writing is therapeutic for me.

Jim Stallings

FROM AN EX-USAFSS GUY (#5)
By Jim Stallings

Subj: Daughter
Date: 5/15/03 2:52:33 PM Pacific Daylight Time
From: jvspa6240@sbcglobal.net
To: IdaReedBlanford@aol.com

Sorry for the loss of your daughter, and her shortened life with you. You dealt with it wonderfully for her and you.

My father who lost my sister to leukemia in 1955, said that death of one's own child is the worst thing to happen to a person. It turns out to be the most sensitive thing I ever heard of him saying. He and my mother had eight kids, I being the oldest.

Raymond C. Waits lives in Thomasville, GA now and is 65. I am 62 with DOB of 6-2-40. Ernie Sowell is probably 63. I found four listings for Ernest L. Sowell in Hernando, MS. Two showed an age of 85, which is not my Ernie.

Jim Stallings

I would suppose Jim was looking for former USAFSS buddies and couldn't find them. I didn't want to leave this e-mail out of his writings, because it shows him as a kind fellow.

FROM AN EX-USAFSS GUY (#6)
By Jim Stallings

I live in Sikeston, MO, 150 miles on a nearly straight line between both Memphis and St. Louis on Interstate 55.

I'm a CPA, and still working - that's not retired.

I have always wanted to be a writer of fiction but lack the creativity and persistence. I have maybe fifty books on writing. On my desk right now is Henry James' "The Future of the Novel," which includes his famous, "The Art of Fiction," essay.

I told a high school teacher friend of mine yesterday that I was looking forward to James' Impression of Gustave Flaubert as I had read it, three years ago, the best fiction ever, "Madam Bovary." "You're kidding?" said my friend laughing, so much for sharing anything about Henry James, with her.

I am not very smart, so when I read Henry James I have to read it slowly and almost out loud so as to comprehend (or to ignore) all the modifying and unpunctuated phrases he adds in the style of the day.

Jim Stallings

(Editor's Note: I managed to find my e-mail answer to Jim's comments about Henry James. Here it is. T.S.)

Anyone who is tackling Henry James has to either be extra-smart or stupid as the day is long!!!! I mean this with hilarity! OF COURSE YOU WOULD READ JAMES' WORKS SLOWLY otherwise you'd go insane! He is a fabulous writer (I do believe he's dead, so you should refer to him as he was . . .) When I was studying James I likened him to Faulkner, only in the respect that they both are wordy and seem to talk in the round, constantly, at least James did. They both drove me batty, but as one matures one sees the light.

Ahhh, "Madam Bovary" Flaubert did an excellent job with Emma. She certainly did not figure her married life would be so boring, did she? I felt horrified when she shoved the poison into her mouth - but today, I have to say that I can understand why she did what she did to herself; especially after all my grief for my daughter.

As for reading James' criticism of Flaubert's "Madam Bovary," I should think it would be a good, short read.

Do you have James' THE CRITICAL MUSE: Selected Literary Criticism by Penguin Classics? It's a good one. Buy it if you don't have it, since you are interested. Or, go to the library. It's not an expensive book.

Oh, and the book: THE NOVEL by James Michener is a grand book, although I am not a fan of his, THE NOVEL is excellent. You really should read it before anything else.

Hugs, and this has been most interesting, Jim. Thanks, Trish.

FROM AN EX-USAFSS GUY (#7)
By Jim Stallings

(Editor's Note: I have chosen not to include the e-mail that Jim refers to as "teasing." This particular e-mail placed Jim in an unflattering light and did actually give me a bit of fear, for a moment (nothing that I would feel today because of my increased exposure to those who were threatening to me, and those who were/are kind.) Jim wrote it trying to scare me and said he could be the FBI or something to that effect. The object of this book is not to gain revenge but to enlighten. This is the last e-mail I received from Jim. Jim, if you read this, I HATE teasing. My brother teased me when I was a little girl. But your teasing, and some others' throughout my research for this book (and the next book to come) has taught me to be more understanding of the weirdness that can come forth from some of you guys and to learn to take it with a grain of salt.

In 1962 the 6901st had a softball team that included, I suppose, some of the Army guys stationed at Zweibrucken. I remember attending a game on the post at 6901st the day Marilyn Monroe died. It was a shocker, and they announced her death, I think, over the loudspeaker. Portable radios weren't that ubiquitous.

    The coach of the softball team was an aggressive Air Force Captain who I recall taught our hitters at the 6901st a technique he called the "G-neck." The batter held the bat normally with both hands together but up near the label - a large choking up as we might say - near the center of the bat where the label is.

    The principal of the G-neck was that with that grip the hitter could either bunt or hit away. Despite cutting the bat nearly in half by holding it so far up on the handle, he demonstrated, to the surprise of his team, the ability of the ordinary hitter to actually hit the ball over the fence. Softballs are as hard as a baseball.

    The G-neck then was a tactic that could confuse and surprise the defense which would come in for what looked like a bunt. Our team used it to great advantage as I recall in one game at home, and the coach, the Captain, came laughing and jumping on players for the perfect execution of the G-neck.

    The foundation and hallmark of memory however were our pitchers. One was tall and thin whose face, right now in my mind's eye might pass for a shorter version of Ted Williams. He was blazing speed. His delivery was almost a straight arm windmill of a delivery and extremely accurate.

    The teams often played double-headers.

The other fellow was a great contrast. He was a perfect - if seen from the distance of the stands - perfect Peter Ustinoff. His delivery was more traditional, in my view, in that his arm was bent rather than straight. His pitching style was much slower but the ball could not find a straight course to the plate. He could throw more curves than an author of a detective story. His change of pace, or change-up, was a thing of delight. The opposing team's hitter always provided a comedy show for us. This Peter Ustinoff pitcher would throw his normal delivery but as his hand reached his right leg, he would slap his hand against his leg, which propelled the ball out of his hand sending it with only the remaining energy left. The batter seeing the arm whirling speedily would swing in anticipation of a fast-ball, but would always be ten feet before the ball reached the plate.

The contrast was funny to us, also. If Ustinov started, the batters would adjust to his speed. In the second game the whirlwind speedball guy pitched, and his speed actually scared good hitters so much they would actually jump back out of the way of a pitch right down the middle.

The field was down the street from our barracks, which were at the end of the street furthest from the main entrance. One would walk past the Rod and Gun club, past the softball field on the left and then the chow hall on the right leaving the last familiar destination, the theater further on ahead, and on the left and the BX on the right separated by a large snack bar/cafeteria.

The working buildings (two of them) were across the road and behind the barracks. The Squadron HQ was across the street from our two barracks. On the main floor was a TV room on the right of the entrance and on the left was the First Sergeant and Squadron Commander. An entrance as I recall from the outside of the main floor was the lady who would do our laundry for us. Upstairs was another TV room. That was where I learned to play pinochle. It was on the second floor the leaders (none over E-4, airman first class as I recall) collected our KP dues every payday, usually a long line. My last Christmas there they gave the German ladies a bonus for Christmas. I was "short," not much time left on my assigned time at the 6901st and discharge from the AF. But, I had remembered or imagined some slight or slights from the German ladies, and refused to pay the bonus. I had to pull KP, of course, but I didn't care. I washed pots and pans quite a lot. I remember joking that my boots had dental cavities from all the garbage that got on them. It was a diversion, I figured.

The commander of the 6901st as I recall was a Colonel Hartzog. I could be wrong as it was forty years ago. One day there was a problem involving Warsaw, Poland. I cannot remember the details. I was working on the third floor with the teletypes at the time. Colonel Hartzog (won't guarantee the name) appeared at my elbow on one of the teletypes. He spoke and I typed. The exchange between the distant station and 6901st went on for fifteen minutes. It is noteworthy that I didn't type all that well, but I kept up with his dictation and what I typed could be seen on the paper in front of us like, well, a typewriter.

My nickname on the teletypes was "Mazie," meaning nothing whatsoever.

Sgt. Burn (E-5) was a short, big bellied guy who ran one of the shifts in our intelligence section - which included the teletypes. He was a no-nonsense guy.

Sgt. Steve Vaughn another E-5 ran another shift.

I have a few pictures of the 6901st which include me, and a lot of pictures of the guys at Goodfellow AFB.

As we entered our working buildings we walked up a short flight of stairs to face a little guard station actually built out into the hallway. You could get your badge then. Most were yellow and black affairs with a picture. The officers and the communication guys on the fourth floor had green badges. I got a green badge when I started working in the teletype room.

As we got to the top of the first flight of stairs and stood facing the guard station, we could turn to our right and enter my favorite place, a snack bar. Some stand up stations to eat and drink and visit - a normal cafeteria-style line to buy food and drink. It was a fairly small room. But as you reached the end there was a German lady who fixed the toast and I was fascinated with watching her quickly butter each slice. Getting started in that snack bar was the first and essential order of the day.

Across the way, as I recall, past the working buildings was the Army medical building: dentist, doctors, etc.

When we got to the 6901st our first two weeks, I guess, maybe a month, was spent walking guard duty around and through the building wearing a .45 caliber pistol which was surprisingly heavy. Loaded? I don't remember.

Once I got so drunk in Zweibrucken, I could barely walk. I ended up walking back to base the long way which was a curving road up the hill toward the Canadian Base - although not to it - that wound around to Turene Kaserene. Another friend of mine has a slightly different name for it, but I think mine is right. For my own benefit, I checked that out of curiosity. Anyway, the back way to 6901st got you on a road that led to

Homberg, a little town that we avoided on May 1, because there were reportedly so many communists there who might or did harass American forces.

I fell down the incline at the roadside. I may have rolled twenty feet, and crawled back up the embankment to the road and a German guy on a motor scooter (not a motorcycle) saw me, and gave me a ride to the base the right way, which was back to town and then up the shorter route. I got off his motor scooter and for his courtesy I gave him everything in my pocket. I hoped as I stumbled to the barracks - he couldn't take me past the guard station at the entrance - that I hadn't given away keys to my locker.

One day the order came out that nobody could have a footlocker, only wall lockers. I didn't obey that order because it was inconvenient and nobody had actually come for the footlocker. I had some good excuse. Shortly thereafter, the Squadron Commander appeared in the large bay of double bunks that were at each end of the corridors. We were alone. I moved to attention looking at him. He looked at me. We were at a Mexican Stand off. He finally ordered me to call the place to attention. Dolt! I forgot about that part - but hell we were alone and there was nobody to call to attention. Small excuse. He inquired why I still had a footlocker. I explained. I got a 14-2 for my disobedience. Two hours of extra duty for two weeks. But I still got my only medal - a conduct medal.

One of my roommates in the bay I was assigned to was Bill Gurley (his real name). Everyone should remember Bill Gurley; a very effeminate guy. He would stand in front of his wall locker and without a trace of embarrassment or awareness of his actions would switch his weight from one leg to the other and throw his hip out each time saying, "I don't have anything to wear." Nobody ever laughed at this to my knowledge; but it was so funny. We knew homosexuals, of course, didn't worry about them, and didn't assign them to high station they command today. Bill Gurley had his friends, too, and they were not as ostentatious as he was. I don't think Bill was gay, frankly. But, wow.

The label we attached to new guys was "jeep." It was another word for rookie or recruit or whatever. One big ole guy, a Swede, as I recall, picked on me a lot, until one day I said to him, "Don't mess with me jeep." He stopped. I was relieved, and the ease with which he stopped, I right this minute suspect, was because I misinterpreted his comments, as you have mine, a good natured teasing.

I apologize for the teasing. I am in the Sikeston, MO telephone book. I am just an ordinary guy. Non-threatening, but I can imagine from the

Internet, anything is possible. I too quickly get to the teasing and being personal.
>I have intruded on you, and for that I regret.
>I will not contact you again.
>Good luck.

Jim Stallings.

Good luck to you, too, Jim Stallings. T.S.

These Guys

The pictures mentioned in this piece are unavailable, but I felt the information about them priceless, therefore I included this piece in this book. [The Editor]

ZWEIBRUCKEN PICTURES
By Steve

Subj: Zweibrucken pics
Date: 12/15/02 6:42:51 AM Pacific Standard Time
From: Steve
To: IdaReedBlanford

Hi Trish,

I wandered into a file that holds some photos of Zwei I found on the internet a couple years ago and did not use on my website. I'd have to do some work to find the origin of the site or sites. Thought I'd attach the photos for you and add few words. Perhaps the photos will help you have a better "feel" for Sunny Zwei.

[3.jpg and dtown.jpg] - These two are the old bombed out city hall. I think the locals called it a castle (Schloss) but am not sure anymore. Heard it housed the SS during the war. Pattons tanks sat up on the hill to the south of town (by Canadian airbase) and leveled most of Zwei. The old "city hall" sat on a triangular Platz and I recall eating in two Gasthauser (taverns) located on the platz.

[7.jpg] - The manicured orchard that sloped steeply to the west was behind the 6901 barracks and HQS office. I often saw tiny deer (Reybock) eating the fallen fruit.

[aerial.jpg] - View looking north. The Kreuzberg Kaserne and the 6901 are on the northern hill in the top center/center left.

[barracks.jpg] - Looking westward from 6901 barracks toward army barracks. The windy road [Amerika Strasse] that ran up the hill straightened out heading north and ran behind those snowy army barracks. Directly to the west (behind the army barracks) and abutting that unseen road (Amerika Strasse) to the west were the two 6901 SCG Ops Buildings.

[ops 1 and ops 2.jpgs] - There were two secure 6901 Operations Bldgs. surrounded by barbed wire and connected by an enclosed walkway/elevated hallway. They were oriented parallel (and N/S) to Amerika Strasse. The Ops 2 photo shows what looks like a large chimney on the end. It housed an incinerator for classified docs.

Air Police guarded the Ops Bldgs and a picture ID badge was required for entry. In the Ops 1.jpg the upper (northern) most building is partially visible. The 6901 mailroom was located in the basement at the upper end and is not visible.

[road.jpg] - The road straight ahead was extremely steep and unpaved and was a shortcut downtown if you were on foot. At the bottom it ran past the odiferous hops emanating from the Parkbrauerei.

[Uphill.jpg] I walked, drove and thumbed up that windy street darn near daily to reach Ops and the barracks.

Steve

Since this book has no photographs, many of these photos can be found on www.6901.org. Steve was very helpful in showing me what Zweibrucken looked like, and his comments about it, because this was the last base my brother, Phil, was located before he disappeared in Jan. 1964 after a 3 day TDY to London, coming back from that TDY a very different man - a broken man - "all washed up," as he put it in some of his hospital papers I hold. Steve was one of the "good" guys who optioned to "help" me discover where my brother had served, rather than lead me on a wild goose chase, as some from the USAFSS Lite website did. I am very thankful to Steve for giving me a picture of where the 6901st or better known as the 690wurst was located. Steve, I thank you for this wonderful treat. (The Editor).

HAPPIER YOUNG MEN
Part of a Memoir by James F. Swain

I was a product of growing up in the 1940s and 50s. Radio programs were a major medium in those days and neighborhood movie theaters provided the ultimate escape from reality with their folio of black and white films. The movies of the 40s had a great deal to do with shaping my views of action and adventure. Film stories about the desert always intrigued me. Neighborhood theaters, unlike the movie houses of the large cities, were not owned by the major Hollywood studios, profit and economy factors often dictated the showing of reruns, films that were anywhere from two to ten years old. I worked as an usher at a local theater after school during the week and full time during the weekends. The theater owners would schedule genre marathons during certain weeks that would include horror classics, action/adventure flicks, war movies and so forth. For example, one could view "Gunga Din," "Lives of the Bengal Lancers," "Beau Gueste," and "Four Feathers" all in one week. All of these classic films had war or the military as their general theme. This prelude is mentioned, for some years later, I would be stationed near a desert and be part and parcel of a special military mission.

I enlisted in the United States Air Force in 1955. After basic training, appropriate aptitude testing, and technical school I was to be assigned worldwide as a Morse Intercept Radio Operator. The Cold War was in its' prime time, and later I would work with analysts, linguists and other specially trained personnel in satisfying the mission requirements of the United States Air Force Security Service. The USAF Security Service was America's post war answer to Blechley Park in Britain. We were communication spies, code breakers, all very young and very talented. The command had appropriate airborne missions as well, daring and dangerous and deserve special mention under a separate cover. Security Service units were in some cases geographically remote and if located on a major air base, detached from the main base and self contained.

It was early spring in 1957 and I was stationed in Tripoli, Libya. This was Wheelus Air Base and at that time, the Americans were guests of the King of Libya. Wheelus was one of several post WWII bases located in North Africa. Moammar Gadafi was a very young Libyan then whom, in later years, would expel the American Forces in Libya after deposing the King. Tripoli was one of two capital cities in Libya, the other being Benghazi, south of

Tripoli. Within a fifty mile radius of Tripoli, there did exist the ruins of several ancient Roman cities and they still remain today. The cities of Leptus Magna and Sabratha are two of the ancient ruins and are notably famous primarily due their magnificent condition and defiance of the sands of time.

Tripoli hosted a very special breed of Italian. Tripolatania, as the city was referred to in Roman days, was the home of Italians whose genealogy spanned back to the days of Roman Conquerors. Picture a middle-eastern capital city with a cadre of Italians who practiced western culture including Catholicism, smack in the middle of Tripoli, a city predominately Arab and Mosques towering everywhere. They were proud, not large in numbers, and fostered western style living within the confines of a third world Arab nation. These Italians, in time, would be forced to leave their ancestral homeland pursuant to Gadhafi's orders to make Libya a pure Arab State.

What a history lesson for me! I would occasionally visit the downtown Tripoli area, via horse and carriage no less, and while away some afternoons at a café, movie house or simply wander around town. The coffee shops, movie theaters and restaurants were primarily operated by Italians however one could barter with an Arab at a local bazaar featuring clothing, antique goods and the like. I managed to complete some conversational Italian courses at the base and those classes came to my linguistic aid on several occasions. The British had several Army posts in and around Tripoli. The Brits, like us, bartered for military posts with various North African countries immediately following the war.

The British leased a cinema house located in the center of Tripoli. The theater offered MWR for the soldiers and Americans were welcome. Being a movie buff, I attended several movies, mostly European with English subtitles. One afternoon I viewed an Italian film entitled "Scandal in Sorrento." I was most impressed with the fiery young actress who had the lead and was superbly gorgeous. After the film, I studied the credits carefully and determined her name to be: "Sophia Loren." After seeing her, Cyd Charise, Rhonda Flemming and Jeannie Crain moved down one notch on my all time "Beauty List." During barracks conversations I would mention her name but no one knew who she was. Every GI had a Pin up Girl and make no mistake about mine . . . "Sophia." She had made some Hollywood films at the time, but not being in the States, I had missed them.

These Guys

I have always managed to be in the right place at the right time and Tripoli, Libya was no exception. Providence was about to bestow exciting news for this nineteen-year-old code breaker. Rumors flourished around Wheelus Field that John Wayne, Rossano Brazzi and Sophia Loren were in Libya and filming a picture. The very mention of Sophia Loren was like receiving a hormone shot. My God was it true and if so, where were they filming? My investigative prowess took command, and after many inquiries I learned that portions of the picture were being filmed at Leptus Magna. Leptus Magna was less than thirty miles from the Air Base. Through further curiosity, I learned the film's title "Legend of the Lost." Getting to the shooting location would be a difficult task and there was no schedule for the cast to visit the Air Base. Curiously enough, the Base Commander was married to Ella Raines who was the feminine interest in the film "Tall in the Saddle" with John Wayne. Perhaps they all got together at the Officers Club at one point.

I met with and conversed with one of my fellow GI's soon after learning about the film. After some fifty years I cannot recall his name. He was an interesting fellow, who attended a university in the Midwest and had ventured to receive a degree in Zoology. He was an analyst and had received permission to build and staff a small zoo near our communications compound during his off time. I will refer to him as "Jack" to compensate for my memory loss. Jack made frequent trips to the perimeter of the Libyan Desert. He had trapped a gazelle, desert falcon and other critters and displayed them in his small zoo. During one conversation I told him I was a movie enthusiast and further related the filming of "Legend of the Lost" at Leptus Magna. Jack told me that he made frequent visits to check on his traps on the desert outskirts near Leptus Magna, and that I was welcome to join him on his next trip.

Some days later, Jack and I headed out of the Air Base toward the desert. He had commandeered a jeep from the Base motor pool with proper authorization due to his zoo keeping which benefitted morale and recreation. As we drove southwest along the Libyan Desert we talked of his creature interest and efforts and of my obsession to meet Sophia Loren. Around noontime we approached the outskirts of Leptus Magna. We parked the jeep and followed on foot a cadre of men to the ancient ruins. A couple of vehicles with motion picture cameras and boom microphones could be seen in the distance.

As we continued to walk on, we came to a staging area that housed props and about twenty or thirty men. It was then that I spotted a grotto like ruin and low and behold, there was Sophia lunching with Roassano Brazzi. Before being asked to leave, I cocked the shutter of my Agfa camera, aimed at the lunch area and snapped a black and white still. Jack and I were politely asked to leave again and we honored that request. Jack said: "Did you get her picture" and I replied: "I sure as hell did!" I had Sophia's photograph safely locked in the chamber of my camera! I was elated and can only liken the experience to having your first ice cream!

Jack had traps to check on the way back to the base and he talked of his love of animals and in my young foolish prime, spoke of Sophia. I had the still photo developed and the beautiful Miss Loren with her pristine smile, imaged out perfectly. The photo is a great conversation piece and who is to say that I didn't lunch with Sophia Loren!

To Jack Lemon and Walter Matthau, bless their souls, I send a message of competitive spirit and can honestly state: "We saw her first!" A delightful afternoon that we were privileged to view Sophia Loren made us "Happier Young Men!"

RE: 6901st SCG ZWEIBRUCKEN
By Bill Tarin

This e-mail is in answer to my questions of Bill Tarin, former USAFSS who served at the 6901st Zweibrucken and Karamursel, Turkey.

Trish,

Just remember that it was 45 years ago that I was in Zweibrucken (July 1962 to July 1964) and remembering details is not easy anymore.

Also, I believe that the unit in Misawa, Japan was the 6920th, but am not sure. The location in Turkey where I was stationed was Karamursel for three years during 1971 through 1973. I had my wife and daughter there (she was born three months before we went to Karamursel) and our two sons who were born in Turkey, one at Ankara, and the other at Izmir, both in US military hospitals, but because of their birth in Turkey, they both have dual citizenships. Our daughter Beth now lives in Council Bluffs, Iowa, the oldest son Mike lives in Parker, Colorado, and the youngest son Joe is now deceased, having passed on at age 24 in 1997 of complications of diabetes. I may have told you all that before.

As I recall, the correct designation was 6901st Special Communications Group. Also, as I recall, there was a sister organization in the Far East that was also a Special Communications Group, but I do not remember what it was called. It was 69xx something. I believe it was in Misawa, Japan. All units under the USAF Security Service were designated as 69xx something, with a few exceptions in certain areas of the world and many of those had a 69xx designation that was hidden to the public, most likely so that it would not be associated with USAF Security Service. For example, in Turkey where I served also, the units there were TUSLOG Det. xx some number. TUSLOG Det. is Turkish US Logistics Detachment, as I remember it. But the unit where I served had a 69xx number that most people did not know about. I served in another place like that earlier in another country.

The 6901st was responsible for activity in the European Theater and I believe also the Mid East and Near East. Most Security Service units in the European Theater were directly responsible to the 6901st (for example, the 6911th in Darmstadt, Germany) which in turn the 6901st was responsible to

HQ USAF Security Service in San Antonio, Texas. There were also links in responsibility to NSA, but I do not remember the details. So much time has gone by and I cannot remember all details.

USAF Security Service is a major command in the Air Force, such as Strategic Air Command, Tactical Air Command, Military Transport Service, and others. Many names and designations have changed over the years, but those few I just mentioned were the names back before the 80's. I have not kept up with the name changes. The name of the USAFSS has been changed, and I would have to look up what it is now called.

There was no airfield at the 6901st itself. It was a very small US Army base and was a German base during WWII. Across town in Zweibrucken was the Canadian Air Force Base, and that had the only airfield that I knew of. Ramstein Air Force Base was the main US Air Base for us.

I worked in an office up on the top floor of one of the buildings and worked a night shift the whole time I was there. I did not get to know very many people in the buildings due to my night hours and most other guys worked during the day while I was sleeping. The office I was in processed computer printouts and I, along with about four other guys, did the proofreading of the printouts and corrected those printouts by keypunching corrections and rerunning the program on the mainframe so that the information would be correct for the guys working during the day shift. I worked from 10 p.m. until I finished for the night, usually anywhere from 2 a.m. to 6 a.m., depending on the corrections that had to be made. I worked a consistent four nights on and four nights off for the whole two years that I was there. My circle of friends was probably about 12-20 people due to the strange hours I was assigned to work.

I am sorry I do not have a lot of details about the base, but I hope that what I have given you will help. The more I tell you, the more that comes back to me. I do remember that base as being a major part of my life, and at times I really enjoyed it there and at other times I wanted to get out of there.

Best to you,
Bill

WILLIAM TARIN - Knew of Phil
By William Tarin

From: Trish Schiesser
Sent: Thursday, June 23, 2005 3:14 PM
To: Bill Tarin
Subject: 6901st

Bill,

My name is Trish Schiesser. I am an honorary member of 6901st. I saw your name and message there. Do you happen to remember a S/SGT (holding a temp T/SGT) Phil Noland at 6901st. He was there July 62-Jan 64. He was a 20270 (analyst) and I believe worked under Halvorsen.
If you know of him or knew him would you kindly answer this e-mail: Clara19126@msn.com.

Thank you, and thank you for your fine service at the 6901st.

Don Levesque will vouch for me if you have any questions about me.

God Bless,
Trish Schiesser

From: "William M. Tarin"
To: "Trish Schiesser"
Sent: Thursday, June 23, 2005 2:37 PM
Subject: RE: 6901st

Trish,

The name Phil Noland sounds familiar and I think I vaguely remember him. Since he was a higher rank than me at the time, I probably knew only the name because I do not remember working with him. I worked with a T/Sgt Darling and one other T/Sgt most of my time there. I arrived at the 6901st from San Angelo as an E-3 in July 62 and left as an E-4 (temp E-5) in July 64 enroute to Shemya, Alaska. Most of the guys I knew there were the same rank as me. I also recall the name Halvorsen, but am not sure who he was.

Sorry I could not be of further assistance. That was a very long time ago, and the memory cells do not work as well as they once did. I can picture a lot of the guys I knew, but only kept up with one for several years.

From: Trish Schiesser
Sent;   Saturday, October 15, 2005 12:01 PM
To: William M. Tarin
Subject: RE: 6901st

Bill,

How wonderful to know that you, at least, knew Phil. You arrived at the same time I believe and Phil left (disappeared) Jan 09, 1964, only to show up at our mother's home in NY, very mentally ill. He had left 6901st and gone on a 3 day TDY to London in July 1963 and came back suffering some kind of mental illness - or maybe something was "given" to him. His papers say something about Bender Gestalt, which I have since looked up on the Internet, and the AF also diagnosed him as paranoid/schizophrenic. Now, how this happened to a serviceman serving his country in "excellence" in every way, up until the 3 day TDY to London, is beyond my thinking. The AF tried to drum him out of the service by making some charges, but they did not stick, and our mother went to the Pentagon and the White House and had the AF's ruling overturned to an Honorable discharge, full benefits, etc. But, he lived a broken man till his death in 1986, when he was killed by a NY taxi cab running him down. He was 55 then. Still a young man.
I thank you from the bottom of my heart in letting me know that you vaguely remember him. Your memory serves to tell me there really was a 6901st, as the AF likes us to believe there was no such place. Baloney, I say!

God Bless You,
Trish

These Guys

From: "William M. Tarin
To: "Trish Schiesser"
Sent: Saturday, October 15, 2005 5:43 PM

Trish

Thank you for writing again. Yes, there really was a 6901st. That is a place I will never forget. Had many fond memories there and grew to like almost everyone I knew there, even those of higher rank. I worked rotating shift work there and spent most of my time in a very small office. I now remember a TSgt Snell (or Schnell) who I worked with. Never heard what happened to him. I still cannot remember Halvorsen, except for the name and do not remember what rank he was. I also remember a female Captain there, which was kind of unusual back then. Do not remember her name.

Forty years ago is a long time, but I certainly vaguely remember Phil Noland. I lived in the 2nd floor of the barracks where the Orderly room was until I made E-4, then got moved to a barracks near the entrance gate down by the chow hall. Went from an open bay area to a 6 man room. I was a 20250 and may remember him slightly from the association of our AFSC.

Now that you mention the incident of the TDY, which happened while I was still there, seems like I vaguely remember something about that, but am not real sure. The problem of course is our different ranks. I arrived there as an E-3 and left an E-5. Most guys associated with others approximately their same rank, and TSgt's and above were generally ignored, and kind of feared, unless working with someone of higher rank. That was just the nature of the beast then.

How are you related to him or know him? You never mentioned. I have pictures of some of the buildings at the base, but have never taken the time to scan them into my computer. That is one of my long, long list of projects that I have wanted to work on for some time. I will keep your email address and if I do manage to scan those pictures in, I will send you some of the better ones if you like. Photography was a lot different then.
Bill

Since these e-mails were written, I wrote to Bill that Phil Noland was my brother. [The Editor] And, Bill remembered some more of what it was like the night Phil came back from the 3-day TDY to London, a changed and "broken" man.

This was generously sent to me by A/1c Ray M. Thomson, AF18410468 - Radio Traffic Analyst Aide - serving during the Cold War at the USAFSS 6910th 50'S GROUP. You may find other interesting bits of history on http://www.raymack.com.

OUR SECRET COLD WAR
By Ray Thomson

I remember it like it was last year, but it is really over 55 years ago now . . . A bunch of very non-military college-age kids were serving in the United States Air Force Security Service (USAFSS). Our unit was the 6910th Security Group, based at a former German air base just outside the beautiful little Bavarian town of Landsberg am/Lech. Our daily jobs were part of an Air Force intelligence mission and highly classified. Although far from home and in the land of a former enemy, most of us privately gave thanks that we were not with our USAFSS counterparts in *Korea*; we knew we had a plum assignment in Bavaria. We spent our spare time chasing German frauleins, drinking German beer, snapping our German cameras, traveling throughout Western Europe, and dreaming about getting out at the end of our 4-year enlistment.

On the other hand, we were all very serious about our jobs, part of a large intelligence gathering enterprise. Because of the sensitive nature of our jobs, we were forbidden to take leave in the border area near the Iron Curtain, but listening to Russian radio signals *across* that border was our job. The truth is, we were hand picked for our jobs. Not that we knew *anything* about what we were getting into, but many of us had college degrees or other aptitudes that filtered us into the USAFSS. We received on-the-job training in communications intelligence (COMINT) at Brooks AFB in San Antonio, Texas. We were then sent worldwide to work in a *secret* part of the Cold War. USAFSS units were stationed from Alaska to Korea, and from Scotland to North Africa . . .

Yeah, we were kind of a smart-alec bunch of kids, but we did our jobs well. Our work became most serious when the Russians made some move or change in their military operations - changes we were often the first to detect. These changes were usually preceded by changes in the Russians' radio call signs - call signs which we were often the first to detect; call signs which we spent *months* tying to specific military units (ground and air), thus defining their military organizations, or "order of battle." *The Russians changed their call signs because they knew we were listening and that the change would confuse our monitoring efforts.* (Of course, the Allies did the same thing.) Usually these changes turned out to be military training or maneuvers, but the Allies always had to treat them as the real thing - *perhaps an invasion of Europe.* Our monitoring could bring all Allied Forces to a silent alert. *Soon their monitors knew that we knew - this was the secret cold war.*

One of our 6910th buddies, Jim Duffy, tells of an incident in 1954 while he was CQ. The Teletype began to rattle and he was chilled to see a traffic analysis report from the Far East that a flight of IL-28 bombers had left the Kamchatka Peninsula and were heading for the Aleutians! Jim said, "I thought it was probably a mistake, but remembering the Pearl Harbor fiasco, I called the USAFE Headquarters in Wiesbaden and the alert began worldwide. Well, it was the best alert scramble the 6910th ever had, but I soon discovered that some *nitwit* was sending "practice traffic," and forgot to slug the header with 'PRACTICE TRAFFIC!' Of course it was very embarrassing to report my miscue, and I was kidded for weeks, in the squadron. However, I later got a letter of commendation from the 'old man' and the Department of Defense in D.C. Even though it was a mistake, I had followed 'alert procedures' to the letter, and the high command recognized I had done the right thing. Of course, most of us knew nothing about this incident until Duffy told his story at our first reunion.

These were the days we earned our stripes. We were called to duty (often rousted out of bed) at the first hint of a call sign change, and worked around the clock until the crisis was over. (Or, if an alert were ever the real thing, until we were told to burn our records and evacuate!) We worked at wall-sized maps of the USSR, labeled TOP SECRET. These "alerts" called for urgent and coordinated efforts by all sections, beginning with the Radio Intercept Operators who listened to the cacophony of static and radio signals in Morse code and copied them down with unbelievable accuracy, using typewriters equipped with the Cyrillic alphabet. Then there were the Crypto Analysts, who dealt with the complexities of encoded messages and call signs. There were also airmen trained as Russian Language Analysts, whose job was to translate clear text and voice messages. We had Radio Direction Finding (RDF) Operators who tried to fix the positions of the Russian transmitters. Finally, there were the Radio Traffic Analysts, whose job was to learn as much as they could from the "headers" of the messages, i.e., the parts of the message that were not encrypted. All of our jobs depended, to some degree, on mistakes made by the Russian radio operators. All military operators are taught rigorous rules of "radio discipline" designed to prevent such mistakes, but they do happen, and can reveal information the enemy should know.

Secrecy was all-important in our highly sensitive work. We were warned regularly, in security lectures we were required to attend, that we could not *describe or discuss our work in any way, with friends or family.* In fact, we were strictly forbidden to discuss our work with *each other* outside the secure buildings where we worked. Even within our secure compounds, the various sections where we were assigned were isolated from each other. So, even though we might bunk together, at the office we had no contact with buddies in another section unless we had a "need to know." To my knowledge, among those I knew, we were faithful in observing all these security rules; when we returned to civilian life we continued this secrecy about our jobs, although our friends and families sometimes thought we made too much of our "secret jobs."

I especially remember one security lecture, while in training at Brooks AFB that made a lasting impression on me. One morning at breakfast, we were shocked to read in the newspaper ("The San Antonio Light") a story about our training at Brooks. *The story pretty well told exactly what we were being trained for in our "secret compound" on the base!* Knowing this story would undermine the security lectures we were receiving, the CO called a meeting of everyone as soon as we reached the office. His message to us went something like this:

"We know the newspaper has this story and runs it periodically--it sells newspapers! *You bought one, didn't you?* We have taught you that the elements of this story are certainly no secret to our enemies, they know of your jobs and your training and they are training their operators to defeat your efforts! We are training our communications personnel to protect our communications from *their* analysts! *What our enemies don't know - NOW HEAR THIS! - is how successful we are!* Do you see that if you *brag* about your "secret work" or *hint* at "the importance of your job," or *say anything at all*-you may infer something about the success of our efforts?; that, gentlemen, is why the only way to have security is simply to never, never say anything about your jobs, to anyone."

So, did we help keep the Russian bear at bay? Yes, certainly, but I never knew any specifics about the successes or failures of our efforts. The fact is, as "worker bees" in a huge intelligence organization, we were never told the ultimate value of the information that we gathered. *Why? because we did not have "the need to know."*

Well, here we are 50 years later, and I'm writing this bit of personal history about my "secret job." Why? Because the work we did in the early 1950's has little bearing on the world of COMINT today; because the means, methods, and technology that we used *(Morse code for goodness sake!)* are now so outmoded as to be only a page in COMINT history. *Why, we worked with card files, not computers!* Because we have been superceded by five decades of COMINT gathering secrets that I know nothing about; because much of our early work has now been declassified and is the subject of numerous books, movies and "discussions" on the internet about what we did and how we did it, so long ago. Because I know there were some *who lost their lives* in the intelligence war; USAFSS airmen who flew secret airborne monitoring missions (SIGINT) against the Russians and were shot down. I'm especially proud that *their* story is *finally* being told. Because I've relished remembering and reliving my experiences with a great group of former 6910th airmen that I organized on the Internet, THE USAFSS 6910TH 50'S GROUP. Our association includes our webpage (http://www.usafss6910th.org maintained by webmaster *Marvin Mobley*), a Yahoo e-mail-list (hosted by myself), newsletters, and *two great* reunions in 2000 and 2002 (planned and hosted by *Bill Purser*). And *finally* because, in my dotage, I have longed to share something of what we did with my family and friends and to say that we took great pride in doing it well. The USAFSS motto was "Freedom Through Vigilance." I'm certain I speak for all those I knew when I say, "We would do it again in a heartbeat if called on."

A/1c Ray M. Thompson, AF18410468 - Radio Traffic Analyst Aide
raymackt@comcast.net
http://www.raymack.com
Version 6 - November 2005

Notations: 1 A Master Sgt. Jim Schuman, who had served in Korea, was assigned to our section. He told us of working with Korean translators so near the front that, on one occasion, they were over run and had to be evacuated by air. Later, in a special base parade Sgt. Schuman was awarded a medal for his service in Korea.

2 Why, didn't we know the story, although we were there? Because we "didn't have the need to know."

3 We love to tell this story: one of the Radio Intercept Operators at Landsberg AFB was a guy named Johnny Cash. And, yes, he was the *Johnny Cash* destined to become a C&W super star. Read Johnny's own account of his USAFSS experiences in his biography "Cash," (written with Patrick Carr), Harper Paperbooks 1997.

4 I recommend *Body of Secrets,* by James Bamford, Doubleday 2001

5 Try these in Google: USAFSS, AIA, COMINT, SIGINT, ELINT

6 Read *The Price of Vigilance*, by a member of USAFSS, Larry Tart; Ballantine Books 2001. It's been a privilege to have Larry in our USAFSS 6910th 50's Group mail list.

7 Newsletter No. 4 - September 2000, USAFSS 6910th 50's Group, 142 pages, published by Ray M. Thompson.

These Guys

This is in answer to an article I wrote on the NEW USAFSS CLUB site when "they" were being friendly to me. It includes a reply from EW. The e-mail subject: Re: 6901 SCG. Every effort has been made to contact the writer of this article, but to no avail. I feel that it is important to the nation to read what he wrote and so I'll call him, EW or anonymous.

I was researching for anything my brother, a SSGT at 6901st Zweibrucken, may have been involved in. [The Editor]

LOW VISIBILITY TDY ASSIGNMENTS
By EW or Anonymous

Replying to:

How many of us guys back then 'volunteered' for those low visibility TDY assignments from Peshawar, Hof, London, Templehof, Chicksands, Bremerhaven, Kirknewton, Bodo, Frankfurt, Crete, Trab, and other unpublished sites, except to dodge the only option available for refusing orders - 'volunteering' for a rice paddy in Nam? Why does it seem that the AF is only now denying the existence of a first rate operational analysis and think tank like 6901st SCG? It could have pulled the plausible deniability thing almost any time after about 1973, when it stopped tasking the USAFSS to make clandestine personnel drops from unmarked a/c over Riga, Tallinn, Batumi, Makhachkala, and who knows how many other LZ's. Jumping from an aircraft was not enjoyable when the jumper received minimal mission training, carried 75 pounds of first gen. satellite burst comm. gear, an M-2, K-rations, and a #$@% cyanide pill. He had to take it on faith that friendlies would meet him and that egress would be by NATO sub or mule. It did not help that our own people tested our loyalty with Eastern Bloc girls trained to exploit any weakness, then report it back to the brass. A white buddy was caught like that and got booted out with a BCD. The only cover an African-American like me could use in country was to say I was a guest lecturer in Marxian studies at Patrice Lamumba University. Just how long would that excuse work? I was better suited to lay pipe than spy. My so-called TDY training in the UK was a farce. The two night jumps Art Vukovick, Dick Smith and I made over Severodvinsk and Tura will never be acknowledged by any agency in the U.S. Government. Dick's bones may still be rotting under a pile of rocks next to that pork rendering plant at Tura. Bastard GRU tied him up, shot him in the back of the head, then drank vodka until sunrise. Vuki and I managed to get out, but we could never recall exactly how. There were several hops in an old DeHaviland and the case officer later said the ground people spoke Urdu. I took to drink for a few years, but hooked up with the Savior. Vuki died two years back while in a duck blind over to his farm near Minot. Guys like him and me do not want recognition for our service. It was just a job and is all in the past. But what has happened at this late stage of life that the brass and ticket punchers have chosen now as the time to deny places like Zwei ever existed? Next thing you know, they will deny Valley Forge, Nam, and the Pueblo. Sounds like BS from Orwell's Ministry of Truth. Give us a #$@% break.

9/13/02 11:43:12 PM

# # #

These Guys

The USNS Spica (AFS-9) was a stores ship taken out of commission on January 26, 2008. Her keel was laid in England on April 1, 1965. Originally named the Tarbatness, it was a British Royal Fleet Auxiliary during the cold war. She was brought into the United States Naval Service Fleet in 1981 and renamed Spica. At one time, she hung off the shores of Vietnam providing provisions to other ships which were in dire need. Below you will read "A little note . . ." by its final master.

A LITTLE NOTE FROM USNS SPICA'S FINAL VOYAGE
By Capt. Keith Walzak, final master, USNS Spica

At 0700, on 24 January 2008, USNS Spica let go of its last line in Norfolk.
On the pier, was no one.
No banners, no flags, no dignitaries, no media.
The men who let the lines go, got into their cars and drove away.
Spica headed down the river, past Grasp and Grapple asleep at their berths.
Maybe they blinked as the Spica rode past. Maybe they just dreamt it.
Still further down the river, they rode past Big Horn, at BAE Shipyard.

Maybe the Big Horn said, "I can't come out to play," and back to sleep it went.

As Spica passed Craney Island, she noticed that the oilers weren't too thirsty because no one was there at the piers.
Still further, as Spica rode past Naval Station Norfolk, her little sister, USNS Saturn, was just waking up, for another days work.

Maybe they spoke. Maybe Spica said, "I'm not that old. My captain will be 51 tomorrow, and I am three years younger than he is."

Maybe Saturn responded, "We are young in spirit, and still willing to work."

Maybe Spica responded, "So true. Be well sister, I'll see you in a year."

Still further down the river, Spica passed all the ships of the fleet, many of which she had fed over the years, some since their birth, as ships.
Not one looked over, not one said goodbye, or thanks for your service.
Maybe they didn't notice her.
But that is how it has always been. Just as MSC, (Military Sealift Command) has always been. Our pride and our ships' pride lie in jobs well done. No one

ever says how cool it is to pass over a pallet of cheese, or hundreds of dozens of eggs. But every slice and every egg finds a home in the belly of a Sailor. Looking back, only once, over her quarter, Spica said goodbye to Norfolk for the last time. The seas were calm. Maybe a final way of saying thanks for the service, from the river itself.
One more day in the North Atlantic, in January.

Maybe the sea said, "You are still only a small ship, compared to me. I want you to remember me when you go to sleep, for the last time."

High seas and winds and snow pushed the Spica, but maybe she thought, "For my crew, once more, I will keep them safe."

At Midnite, she looked down the mouth of the Delaware River. Her high freeboard, provided a lee for her last pilot.
Only a few more hours to go.
Up the river, back and forth she rode. Never before had she seen these waters. Maybe she started to fret.
Into the Basin. Her final berth. Dozens of ex-Navy vessels surrounded her. They were all different.

Not the sleek hulls she remembered feeding and supplying, over the years. They were ghostly. Maybe she was afraid. Maybe she thought, "I have nothing to give these ghosts. I have nothing in common with them."

Maybe she was very afraid. Maybe she thought, "I shouldn't have to go out like this. I am still a wonderful, capable ship."

Until the very end, she held it together, for her last crew. First Line.
Finished with the Wheel. Finally, her last "FINISHED WITH ENGINES."
With all her lines fast on the pier, maybe she knew it was over.
But maybe she looked around and couldn't believe it when she saw, USNS Mohawk, USNS El Paso, USNS Joshua Humphreys.

And maybe, just maybe, if ships can remember, like us old sailors, they told sea stories to each other, and maybe they all started with, "Remember when we served the Fleet?"
Farewell Spica. You served us well.

I had been e-mailing back and forth with Ed Watts, an ex-USAFSS person. Ed said that he had been really busy: "I am here doing work trying to get the Camp in shape to begin a new season. (The camp gives underprivileged kids a 10 day camping experience in a rustic setting, we run four sessions a summer for kids 8-12 years old and also a more rustic experience for kids 13-15 years old in what we call our Pioneer Camp) and my wife and I recently spent twenty two days in South America; however I have not forgotten that you want other stories too, and will try to think of some that can be printed . . . Ed. When the kids see me, some of them sing the song: a horse is a horse unless of course the horse is Mr. Ed!" My answer to Ed, was: "Ed, you have made me happy today. Just when things look dark, up comes another person to make my day. (My first child, a daughter, was dying of breast cancer at the time, May 23, 2002 and she died July 19, 2002) I'll tell you a secret: I refer to Ed Leonard as Mr. Ed, because he is as kind and good as a character in my story, "Ida's Ride." "How grand that the underprivileged children you share your life with love you as Mr. Ed!"

ELITISTS
By Ed Watts

I don't know if this would fit in but it is a funny incident while I was in Security Service.

One night I was running an operation where we had to have messages to Headquarters (and other places which I don't know whether they are still classified or not) within ten minutes or so. I had an Airman who worked for me who could cut you in half with just a word. The Officer in Charge that night was a Major who had just been transferred into Security Service recently with practically no experience in such operations. At that time we were one of the first to secure carbonless carbon paper and I was handwriting messages to go to the Comm. Center for transmission. The first time I sent the Airman in to the Major for his sign-off he kept looking around for books for, in his words, Standing Operating Procedures, and then came to me and asked, here are the SOPs? I told him that with an operation like this, we had no real SOP as each was somewhat different, so he just signed off on the first message. When I sent up the second message, the Major read the first page, the white copy, and then read the second page, the yellow copy as I remember, and then looked up at the Airman and said, Airman, these messages read almost the same! The Airman looked at him, put his hands on his hips and with that sharp tongue replied, "They should Sir, they are carbons!!" The Major came out to me, placed his hand on my shoulder where I was seated and said, "Watts, how long have you been running these operations?" I replied, "Two years, Sir." He then gave me a knowing look and simply responded, "You write 'em and I'll just sign 'em."

Ed also wrote:
Trish, you know I am there for support when you feel the need, and I hope the others will understand your pain during this critical time. I think most of those here would say the same. As far as writing for the book, I know we have some really talented folks out there who can spin a yarn and make their feeling known very well indeed. As Trish says, she doesn't want you to reveal any secrets, just reflect the tone of our days in Cold War USAFSS. Sounds like it could be a good project to me. Of course, it needs to come second to her family at this time, but it could help her keep it together during this time of stress too. Besides, it feels kind of good to write once in a while, don ya think?
Hang in there Trish
edwatts@mindspring.com

Bravenet Web Services 11/17/02

This is the newspaper article which was published in the Monterey newspaper that was requested by Trish and others. I'm not sure of the date, but I believe it was either in July or September 1955 when I was at Army Language School. (I was a little lax about dating some stuff back then because I thought I would remember it . . . guess what???)

SCHOOL GIVES "NO COMMENT" TO MOSCOW SPY CHARGE
By Ed Watts

Associated press - Moscow - Top Army Language School spokesmen took an attitude of "no comment" on assertions the Associated Press said were published in Moscow that the Army Language School and Syracuse University "were busy training subversive agents for the U.S. Air Force." An AP dispatch from Moscow said the Soviet Defense Ministry which Marshall Georgi Zhukov heads had issued a new warning against new "spies." The dispatch said a full page in a Soviet publication, "Soviet Fleet," cautions the Russian people to be watchful for spies of the Foreign Intelligence Services. The Soviet paper was quoted further as saying such "spies resort to the dirtiest methods to gather information." Both Army Language School and Syracuse University were credited with training such "spies" by the Russian assertions according to AP. (ALS name was subsequently changed to Defense Language Institute - also, I tried hard not to resort to "dirty methods" as I was careful to take a shower every day!).

Ed Watts

Thank you Ed, for your humor on the situation. [The Editor]

This article was sent to me by Bill Person who received it from Ken Mays. Thank you, Bill, for making me aware of another fine story and a God bless you to Bill Weaver who made it through . . . and a fond remembrance of Jim Zwayer who didn't. . . .

SR-71 BREAKUP
By Bill Weaver

Among professional aviators, there's a well-worn saying: Flying is simply hours of boredom punctuated by moments of stark terror. And yet, I don't recall too many periods of boredom during my 30-year career with Lockheed, most of which was spent as a test pilot.

By far, the most memorable flight occurred on Jan. 25, 1996. Jim Zwayer, a Lockheed flight test reconnaissance and navigation systems specialist, and I were evaluating those systems on an SR-71 Blackbird test from Edwards AFB, Calif. We also were investigating procedures designed to reduce trim drag and improve high-Mach cruise performance. The latter involved flying with the center-of-gravity (CG) located further aft than normal, which reduced the Blackbird's longitudinal stability.

We took off from Edwards at 11:20 and completed the mission's first leg without incident. After refueling from a KC-135 tanker, we turned eastbound, accelerated to a Mach 3.2 cruise speed and climbed to 78,000 ft., our initial cruise-climb altitude.

Several minutes into cruise, the right engine inlet's automatic control system malfunctioned, requiring a switch to manual control. The SR-71's inlet configuration was automatically adjusted during supersonic flight to decelerate air flow in the duct, slowing it to subsonic speed before reaching the engine's face. This was accomplished by the inlet's center-body spike translating aft, and by modulating the inlet's forward bypass doors. Normally, these actions were scheduled automatically as a function of Mach number, positioning the normal shock wave (where air flow becomes subsonic) inside the inlet to ensure optimum engine performance.

Without proper scheduling, disturbances inside the inlet could result in the shock wave being expelled forward - a phenomenon known as an "inlet unstart." That causes an instantaneous loss of engine thrust, explosive banging noises and violent yawing of the aircraft - like being in a train wreck.

Unstarts were not uncommon at that time in the SR-71's development, but a properly functioning system would recapture the shock wave and restore normal operation.

On the planned test profile, we entered a programmed 35 degree bank turn to the right. An immediate unstart occurred on the right engine, forcing the aircraft to roll further right and start to pitch up. I jammed the control stick as far left and forward as it would go. No response. I instantly knew we were in for a wild ride.

I attempted to tell Jim what was happening and to stay with the airplane until we reached a lower speed and altitude. I didn't think the chances of surviving an ejection at Mach 3.18 and 78,800 ft. were very good. However, G-forces built up so rapidly that my words came out garbled and unintelligible, as confirmed later by the cockpit recorder.

The cumulative effects of system malfunctions, reduced longitudinal stability, increased angle-of-attack in the turn, supersonic speed, high altitude and other factors imposed forces on the airframe that exceeded flight control authority and the Stability Augmentation System's ability to restore control.

Everything seemed to unfold in slow motion. I learned later the time from event onset to catastrophic departure from controlled flight was only 2-3 seconds. Still trying to communicate with Jim, I blacked out, succumbing to extremely high g-forces. The SR-71 then literally disintegrated around us. From that point, I was just along for the ride.

My next recollection was a hazy thought that I was having a bad dream. Maybe I'll wake up and get out of this mess, I mused. Gradually regaining consciousness, I realized this was no dream; it had really happened. That also was disturbing, because I could not have survived what had just happened. Therefore, I must be dead. Since I didn't feel bad - just a detached sense of euphoria - I decided being dead wasn't so bad after all.

AS FULL AWARENESS took hold, I realized I was not dead, but had somehow separated from the airplane. I had no idea how this could have happened; I hadn't initiated an ejection. The sound of rushing air and what sounded like straps flapping in the wind confirmed I was falling, but I couldn't see anything. My pressure suit's face plate had frozen over and I was staring at a layer of ice.

The pressure suit was inflated, so I knew an emergency oxygen cylinder in the seat kit attached to my parachute harness was functioning. It not only supplied breathing oxygen, but also pressurized the suit, preventing my blood from boiling at extremely high altitudes. I didn't appreciate it at the time, but the suit's pressurization had also provided physical protection from intense buffeting and G-forces. That inflated suit had become my own escape capsule.

My next concern was about stability and tumbling. Air density at high altitude is insufficient to resist a body's tumbling motions, and centrifugal forces high enough to cause physical injury could develop quickly. For that reason, the SR-71's parachute system was designed to automatically deploy a small-diameter stabilizing chute shortly after ejection and seat separation. Since I had not intentionally activated the ejection system - and assuming all automatic functions depended on a proper ejection sequence - it occurred to me the stabilizing chute may not have deployed.

However, I quickly determined I was falling vertically and not tumbling. The little chute must have deployed and was doing its job. Next concern: the main parachute, which was designed to open automatically at 15,000 ft. Again, I had no assurance the automatic-opening function would work.

I couldn't ascertain my altitude because I still couldn't see through the iced-up face plate. There was no way to know how long I had been blacked-out, or how far I had fallen. I felt for the manual-activation D-ring on my chute harness, but with the suit inflated and my hands numbed by cold, I couldn't locate it. I decided I'd better open the face plate, try to estimate my height above the ground then locate that "D" ring. Just as I reached for the face plate, I felt the reassuring sudden deceleration of main-chute deployment.

I raised the frozen face plate and discovered its up-latch was broken. Using one hand to hold that plate up, I was descending through a clear, winter sky with unlimited visibility. I was greatly relieved to see Jim's parachute coming down about a quarter of a mile away. I didn't think either of us could have survived the aircraft's breakup, so seeing Jim had also escaped lifted my spirits incredibly.

I could also see burning wreckage on the ground a few miles from where we would land. The terrain didn't look at all inviting - a desolate, high plateau dotted with patches of snow and no signs of habitation.

I tried to rotate the parachute and look in other directions. But with one hand devoted to keeping the face plate up and both hands numb from high-altitude, subfreezing temperatures, I couldn't manipulate the risers enough to turn. Before the breakup, we'd started a turn in the New Mexico-Colorado-Oklahoma-Texas border region. The SR-71 had a turning radius of about 100 miles at that speed and altitude, so I wasn't even sure what state we were going to land in. But because it was about 3:00 p.m., I was certain we would be spending the night out here.

At about 300 ft. above the ground, I yanked the seat kit's release handle and made sure it was still tied to me by a long lanyard. Releasing the heavy kit ensured I wouldn't land with it attached to my derriere, which could break a leg or cause other injuries. I then tried to recall what survival items were in that kit, as well as techniques I had been taught in survival training.

Looking down, I was startled to see a fairly large animal - perhaps an antelope - directly under me. Evidently, it was just as startled as I was because it literally took off in a cloud of dust.

My first-ever parachute landing was pretty smooth. I landed on fairly soft ground, managing to avoid rocks, cacti and antelopes. My chute was still billowing in the wind, though. I struggled to collapse it with one hand, holding the still-frozen face plate up with the other.

"Can I help you?" a voice said.

Was I hearing things? I must be hallucinating. Then I looked up and saw a guy walking toward me, wearing a cowboy hat. A helicopter was idling a short distance behind him. If I had been at Edwards and told the search-and-rescue unit that I was going to bail out over the Rogers Dry Lake at a particular time of day, a crew couldn't have gotten to me as fast as that cowboy-pilot had.

The gentleman was Albert Mitchell, Jr., owner of a huge cattle ranch in northeastern New Mexico. I had landed about 1.5 miles from his ranch house - and from a hangar for his two-place Hughes helicopter. Amazed to see him, I replied I was having a little trouble with my chute. He walked over and collapsed the canopy, anchoring it with several rocks. He had seen Jim and me floating down and had radioed the New Mexico Highway Patrol, the Air Force and the nearest hospital.

Extracting myself from the parachute harness, I discovered the source of those flapping-strap noises heard on the way down. My seat belt and shoulder harness were still draped around me, attached and latched. The lap belt had been shredded on each side of my hips, where the straps had fed through knurled adjustment rollers. The shoulder harness had shredded in a similar manner across my back. The ejection seat had never left the airplane; I had been ripped out of it by the extreme forces, seat belt and shoulder harness still fastened.

I also noted that one of the two lines that supplied oxygen to my pressure suit had come loose, and the other was barely hanging on. If that second line had become detached at high altitude, the deflated pressure suit wouldn't have provided any protection. I knew an oxygen supply was critical for breathing and suit-pressurization, but didn't appreciate how much physical protection an inflated pressure suit could provide. That the suit could withstand forces sufficient to disintegrate an airplane and shred heavy nylon seat belts, yet leave me with only a few bruises and minor whiplash was impressive. I truly appreciated having my own little escape capsule.

After helping me with the chute, Mitchell said he'd check on Jim. He climbed into his helicopter, flew a short distance away and returned about 10 minutes later with devastating news: Jim was dead. Apparently, he had suffered a broken neck during the aircraft's disintegration and was killed instantly. Mitchell said his ranch foreman would soon arrive to watch over Jim's body until the authorities arrived.

I asked to see Jim and, after verifying there was nothing more that could be done, agreed to let Mitchell fly me to the Tucumcari hospital, about 60 miles to the south.

I have vivid memories of that helicopter flight, as well, I didn't know much about rotorcraft, but I knew a lot about "red lines," and Mitchell kept the speed at or above red line all the way. The little helicopter vibrated and shook a lot more than I thought it should have. I tried to reassure the cowboy-pilot I was feeling OK; there was no need to rush. But since he'd notified the hospital staff that we were inbound, he insisted we get there as soon as possible. I couldn't help but think how ironic it would be to have survived one disaster only to be done in by the helicopter that had come to my rescue.

However, we made it to the hospital safely - and quickly. Soon, I was able to contact Lockheed's flight test office at Edwards. The test team there had been notified initially about the loss of radio and radar contact then told the aircraft had been lost. They also knew what our flight conditions had been at the time, and assumed no one could have survived. I briefly explained what had happened, describing in fairly accurate detail the flight conditions prior to breakup.

The next day, our flight profile was duplicated on the SR-71 flight simulator at Beale AFB, California. The outcome was identical. Steps were immediately taken to prevent a recurrence of our accident. Testing at a CG aft of normal limits was discontinued, and trim-drag issues were subsequently resolved via aerodynamic means. The inlet control system was continuously improved and, with subsequent development of the Digital Automatic Flight and Inlet Control System, inlet unstarts became rare.

Investigation of our accident revealed that the nose section of the aircraft had broken off aft of the rear cockpit and crashed about 10 miles from the main wreckage. Parts were scattered over an area approximately 15 miles long and 10 miles wide. Extremely high air loads and G-forces, both positive and negative, had literally ripped Jim and me from the airplane. Unbelievably good luck is the only explanation for my escaping relatively unscathed from that disintegrating aircraft.

Two weeks after the accident, I was back in an SR-71, flying the first sortie on a brand-new bird at Lockheed's Palmdale, California assembly and test facility. It was my first flight since the accident, so a flight test engineer in the back seat was probably a little apprehensive about my state of mind and confidence. As we roared down the runway and lifted off, I heard an anxious voice over the intercom. "Bill! Bill! Are you there?" "Yeah, George, what's the matter?" "Thank God! I thought you might have left." The rear cockpit of the SR-71 has no forward visibility - only a small window on each side -

and George couldn't see me. A big red light on the master-warning panel in the rear cockpit had illuminated just as we rotated, stating, "Pilot Ejected." Fortunately, the cause was a misadjusted micro-switch, not my departure. Bill Weaver flight tested all models of the Mach-2, F-104 Starfighter and the entire family of Mach 3+Blackbirds - the A-12, YF-12 and SR71. He subsequently was assigned to Lockheed's L-1011 project as an engineering test pilot, became the company's chief pilot and retired as Division Manager of Commercial Flying Operations. He still flies Orbital Sciences Corporation's L-1011, which has been modified to carry a Pegasus satellite-launch vehicle (AW&ST Aug. 25, 2003, p. 56). An FAA Designated Engineering Representative Flight Test Pilot, he's also involved in various aircraft-modification projects, conducting certification flight tests.

"For those who fly . . . or long to."

Ken Mays

These Guys

This is an article in the Mekong Express Mail - The Thailand Laos Cambodia Brotherhood, Inc., by Bob Wheatley. I want to thank Bob for his permission to print this personally vivid and important article. Copyright, September, 2003.

LISTENING TO THE RED CHINESE PILOTS AT RAMASUN STATION
By Bob Wheatley

When I arrived at Ramasun Station in December, 1967, based on the images in the news footage I'd seen coming out of Nam, I was expecting to see tin roof hooches and dirt streets and outdoor latrines. Instead, Ramasun Station was way beyond anything I might have envisioned in my wildest dreams. It looked almost like some apartment complex back in the States, and it really seemed out of place here in this remote site. Stepping off the shuttle bus from Udorn in the blazing late morning sun, I just stared in amazement for a moment. "So this would be my home for the next twelve months . . . Not bad! Not bad at all!" I thought. "How had I managed to get so damned lucky?"

The site, located at the fringes of the small town Nong Soong, was situated a dozen klicks or so south of the city of Udon Thani, just off the Friendship Highway. The 7th Radio Research Field Station, as it was otherwise known, was an Army post, run by the Army Security Agency. I and the other airmen who were stationed there were part of an Air Force detachment of the 6922nd Security Wing. We were given separate living quarters from the Army troops. I was pleasantly surprised to find that all of the barracks were really quite nice concrete block air-conditioned buildings, a far cry from the hooches I'd seen when I landed at the Udorn Air Base! In fact, all of the buildings on post were air-conditioned. "What luxury!" I thought. Air conditioning was something we would have killed for on my previous tour on Okinawa! I'm almost ashamed to mention the tennis courts, swimming pool, bowling alley and the indoor theater. I understand a few months before my arrival, Ramasun Station had been just a tent city. As they say, "Timing is everything!"

The barracks, like the native homes I'd seen on the bus trip from Udorn, were built on pylons several feet off the ground. And aside from keeping the bottom floor dry during Monsoon, I'm sure it helped to keep out the snakes as well. All the streets on post were paved in concrete and had streetlights to make for safe walking at night. It was important to be able to see where you were stepping, as it was not uncommon for the Cobras and "Two Steppers" to crawl out onto the pavement to warm themselves in the cool of the night. In fact, I understand Ramasun's call sign, "Cobra7" derived from the hundreds of cobras which the construction crews had uncovered when clearing the site for construction of the new facilities. In keeping with the Cobra 7 image, in the headquarters building stood a huge seven or eight foot tall carved wood King Cobra, hood flared, reared up and ready to strike. It presented quite an imposing figure, and it certainly commanded one's attention upon entering the HQ building.

Most of the area on the post was occupied by huge antenna arrays. Their presence, I thought, sure must have given away the purpose of the post, even though our mission was supposed to be Top Secret. The outside perimeter was bounded by a tall chain-link fence, topped with barbed wire, to keep out whatever and whomever lurked beyond. We were issued M-16s (on paper), but I was somewhat disappointed to find they were to be kept in the armory and distributed only in the event of an attack. Of course, the MPs on post were constantly armed, as were the Thai Army perimeter guards. But I couldn't help but wonder if, in case of a concerted attack, "would it be too late by the time we were able to get to our weapons?" Things would happen later in my tour there to reinforce those concerns, but that is a whole "nother story."

Security was very tight though. The Thai guards at the gate closely eyed everyone who entered the post and checked ID's. The radio compound where we worked was inside a chain link fence enclosure, nested inside a second chain link fence, both topped by barbed wire. Guard towers were positioned all around the place, and it looked like a maximum-security prison. There was only one way in or out. To get inside and to leave, we had to pass through a chain link "tunnel" to the guard station. There we would stop and show both our badges and our faces to the guard on duty; then and only then, would we be allowed in or out of the gates. The rooms inside the operations building were somewhat small and were crammed to the gills with state-of-the-art radio gear and encryption equipment. For obvious security reasons, there were no windows at all in the building, and I wondered if the post were attacked, would we inside even know it in time to react to save ourselves? Fortunately, we never had to find that out, although we were put on full "alert" at least once during my stay, when the Udorn Air Base up the road was attacked by NVA sappers.

Inside ops, there were facilities for monitoring radio transmissions, both voice and Morse, of all the direct or indirect participants in the war. In the Mandarin Voice Intercept Section our primary target was Chi-Com civilian and military air transport. I spent most of my time at the console of my R-390A Collins receiver, listening for transmissions from the IL-18 Coots, daily making their way from Beijing down to Hanoi, carrying diplomats, advisors, troops and arms to aid the North. We continually searched the HF band for enemy traffic. Upon recognizing a target, a reel to reel tape was started to record the intercept, and a hand written translation was generated "on the fly." A more complete typewritten transcript was generated from the tapes, after the fact, which the Intel analysts used to compile a "big picture" view of enemy capability and intent.

The mission was carried out 24 hours a day, seven days a week. To provide constant coverage, each flight worked rotating shifts, three day shifts on, then one day off, then three swings and a day off, then three midnight shifts, followed by four whole days off. Then the cycle would repeat. The four consecutive days off gave us the opportunity to play tourist and see more of Thailand than we otherwise would have. We took full advantage of it, visiting many attractions in the region. The down side was, the ever changing shifts kept our bodies off balance, and we never really had a chance to get used to any one schedule. But rotating the shifts was a way of spreading the misery around evenly. Day shifts were the most active, followed by swings. But mid-shifts seemed excruciatingly long.

After about 8:00 or 9:00 PM, the Chinese went off the air. The day's flights had all landed well before that time, as the Chinese were loath to fly at night. Communications after that were extremely rare. Mid shift ran from 2300 to 0700 hours. On mids, we were left to endlessly scan the HF band listening to mostly static, guzzling cup after cup of the bitter black brew that we kept cooking on the hotplate. We passed time by making entries in the shift logbook, with frequent references to our "bleeding" eyeballs. The intended purpose of the shift log was to pass along any important happenings to the next shift, but on mids it was treated more as a "dear diary," a place to "publish" our poetry and prose. Finally, about 0600 the Chi-coms would come back on air and begin establishing contact with one another again. Then we'd be pretty busy the remainder of the shift.

In their position reports, the Chi-com aircraft we monitored referred to their navigational beacons and ground stations by encoded "trinomes" presumably so we wouldn't know their positions when they made their navigational reports to their ground controllers. On a monthly basis, all of the trinomes were changed in an attempt to throw us off track. It was all quite a futile effort for them. After listening to their transmissions for a time, we became familiar with the operator's voices, and we could easily identify each one when we heard them. Combining the voice ID with our knowledge of their navigational routes, which never changed, we were able to break out all of the new trinomes within a couple of hours of the changeover. Similarly, I'm told that the "ditty boppers" in the Morse intercept section could ID the enemy Morse operators by the unique quirks in the way each one sent code.

As a shift supervisor, I was responsible for about fifteen men on my shift in the voice intercept section. Most things we listened in on were pretty routine -- aircraft position reports, high altitude weather conditions, ETAs, and so-on. But occasionally something more significant was intercepted, and it fell to me to determine what was routine and what merited reporting immediately to the intelligence analyst. If important enough, a "FLASH PRIORITY" message could be generated that would be in the hands of the President within three minutes from anywhere in the world.

At least one such FLASH report had been generated from one of our stations in Taiwan. It detailed the shoot down of one of our stations in Taiwan. It detailed the shoot down of one of our airborne reconnaissance platforms by a Chinese MiG-21 over the china mainland. The "ACRP" (Airborne Communications Reconnaissance Platform) had two flights daily originating out of Taiwan, one out of Taipei at the north end of the island, and one out of Tainan, further south. They'd make a course for the mainland and fly the length of Eastern China, gathering intelligence as they proceeded up and down the coast. Then they'd return to base at the end of the day.

Along the way, our various ground stations within VHF range would listen in on the Chi-com fighter squadrons as they'd scramble and rise up to meet the recon planes. It was a game of "cat and mouse" to the pilots involved. When our recon planes would come over a given fighter squadron's sphere of coverage, the MiGs would scramble and follow along below until the next squadron up the coast would take over the chase. But the practical ceiling of the MiG 21 was below that of our reconnaissance planes, and generally speaking, the MiGs were no real threat to them, simply escorting and keeping close watch on the ACRP.

This occasion was the fatal exception to that rule. The MiG pilot had made a "zoom climb" to the highest altitude he could make. At the moment he topped out, he released his air to air rockets. The linguist in Taiwan listening in on the fighter pilot reported that he'd heard him say, "P'a gao er shih ch'ien . . . Fa she le!" (wait . . .), then excitedly, "Wo ding-le-ta-de pigu! Wo ding-le-ta-de pigu!" Translation: "Climbing to twenty-thousand (meters) . . . Rockets fired!" (wait . . .) "I fixed his ass! I fixed his ass!" The meaning of that transmission was dismayingly clear. The "game" had become deadly serious! The account of what had happened was instantly passed to us via encrypted teletype transmission. All of our listening posts were instructed to listen for reference to the shoot down by any of the Chinese ground stations we monitored.

As word of the shoot down passed around, the mood in the radio ops room took on the air of a funeral. I would liken it to the moment America learned of the Challenger Space Shuttle disaster. Some of those on board that plane were guys with whom we'd attended language school. And all were fellow airmen -- brothers, whether we knew them or not. Were it not for the "luck of the draw," any one of us could have been aboard that flight. Everyone in the room was stunned. We never learned if there were any survivors among the crew of the aircraft. I suspect not -- but we never heard any more on the matter, for we did not have "the need to know."

But not everything was so serious at Ramasun. Off duty time was pretty laid back. Even if it was rear echelon, to the best of my recollection, we never had to fall out for reveille and roll call, nor did we have the parade drills and inspections we'd had in other places. I'd been stationed prior to my arrival in SEA. Aside from monthly "Commander's Calls," as long as we showed up for our scheduled duty shift on time, our time was pretty much our own. At Commander's Call, we were given updates on the status of the war, the latest developments in air weaponry (to remind us we were, after all, still in the Air Force), and any items of interest regarding day to day operations of the Detachment. And of course, there were the obligatory scare films they showed us to educate and hopefully make us aware and wary of the dangers of VD.

To sum it up, quite in contrast to my early misgivings, my tour at Ramasun Station turned out to be a "piece of cake" compared to that of many others -- especially with regard to the living conditions. It all seemed so incongruous with wartime! Not that I wanted to trade places, but I actually felt somewhat guilty, knowing there were others who were eating out of cans and sleeping in snake and leech infested swamps, while so many of us were living the "easy life."

Indeed, my feelings regarding my service at Ramasun had always been somewhat ambivalent. For many years after returning Stateside, I felt almost as if I had no right to grieve the war-at least not as much right as my brothers in arms, who had returned with missing or paralyzed limbs or blinded eyes, or those who had tasted that singular moment of pure, distilled, mutual terror, when you look into the eyes of the enemy, and take his life, before he can take yours . . . "Why not me?" I asked myself. "Why was I so fortunate, when so many others were not?" I've learned these are questions almost universally asked among survivors of war, especially by those who escaped physically unscathed. But like all wars, that war touched every one of its participants, whether front line or rear echelon, in the most profound ways. The wounds that I and many others like me brought home are simply the ones unseen, the ones for which no Purple Heart is ever awarded.

My association with the TLCB has helped to change those ambivalent feelings. I've come to appreciate, regardless of where we were stationed or what our AFSC or MOS, all of our efforts were of vital importance to the war effort. Were it not so, we would never have been there. I am proud of my service and thankful for the opportunity to have served at "Cobra 7."

Email from Robert E. Wheatley, Tuesday, October 25, 2005
Re: Permission to use article, "Listening to the Red Chinese pilots at Ramasun Station" in the Mekong Express Mail, Volume 4, Issue 3 Copyright Sept 2003.

CAPTURE OF THE PUEBLO
By Robert E. Wheatley

Hello Trish,

I would be honored to have you use the article in your book. All I ask is that you let me know when the book is available, so I can obtain a copy of it for my collection.

As a matter of fact, I have another recollection of Ramasun Station that might interest you. It is my account of the day the Pueblo intelligence ship was taken by the North Koreans in international waters in the Sea of Japan. I was on duty the day that occurred, January 23, 1968. Again, we were apprised of the situation in near real time by FLASH priority message. The news absolutely sickened me. Below is an excerpt from my memoir, recounting the story.

Indeed, Communications Intelligence could be a very dangerous game, depending upon your assignment. I was on duty at Ramasun the day the Pueblo intelligence ship was captured off the coast of Korea by the North Koreans. We were kept abreast of the goings on that day in the Sea of Japan by FLASH priority messages, and we were advised to listen for any reference to it by any of our targets. However, our primary targets in the Mandarin Voice Intercept section were the Chinese IL-18 transports, carrying diplomatic passengers and weapons and ammunition from Beijing down to Hanoi. Secondary targets were the ubiquitous ancient AN-2 biplanes, which ran the shorter transport hops within China and sometimes across the border into North Vietnam.

We searched the communications bands with all the focus we could muster that day, slowly tweaking the tuning dial, straining, listening for any communication that might give any clue. To our disappointment, we never heard any reference to the Pueblo from any of our targets. I remember the growing knot in the pit of my stomach over the course of that duty shift as the situation remorselessly deteriorated and it became ever more apparent the ship would be taken by force. We knew those guys were doomed to death or capture. Oh, for just any scrap of information that might help save them! They were sitting ducks out there alone on the high seas, practically defenseless, doing a job very similar to what I and my men were doing, only in a much more dangerous environment. They too were our brothers in COMINT, though we had never met.

While the ship was being raked with 50-caliber machine gun fire and taking multiple rounds from North Korean 3-inch guns, the men of Pueblo desperately but unsuccessfully attempted to burn or dump overboard the more than 1 ton of classified documents that had been stowed aboard the ship. The aircraft carrier USS Enterprise, the most powerful warship in the world at the time, was located some 500 miles to the south, just 45 minutes away by air. In spite of prior assurances the Pueblo would be rescued in the event of just such an emergency, no order was ever issued to launch the Enterprise warplanes against the North Korean gunboats. But if we had means to save those men and the ship and all the classified information and equipment aboard, why in the world would we choose not to do so?

I am certain the men of Enterprise would have loved nothing better than to enter the fray and kick some Communist ass! But the Vietnam War was but a hot spot in the overall Cold War with the Communists. Having his hands full with Vietnam, LBJ was reluctant to chance opening a new hot spot in Korea. Once again, military men were just pawns in this game and were all too readily expendable. Worse yet, the rest of us were asked to stand by, listen and "watch" it happen, impotent to do anything, because the orders to intervene would never be issued!

I kept hoping against hope somehow we would receive a last minute message the North Koreans had been repelled and the Pueblo saved. It was not to be. One of the crew was killed during the shelling, when a North Korean 3-inch shell came through the hull of the ship and hit him in the abdomen, cutting him completely in two. However, the immediate concern of those in high places was that the men of the Pueblo would not be able to destroy all sensitive information and equipment before being boarded by the North Koreans. Indeed, for years afterward, the crew would be stigmatized by innuendo and outright allegation that they had failed in their duty to protect the secrecy of the mission - that it would have been far better for them to go down with the ship and die, taking their secrets with them. That concept in itself was not at all surprising to me, for it was just as I and my own men had been taught in our Air Force Security Service training.

During and in the immediate aftermath of the incident, all our "ears" at Ramasun were tuned to pick up any scrap of information that might help our analysts gauge the magnitude of the damage to national security resulting from the event. As it turned out, the capture of the Pueblo was a huge intelligence coup for the Communists. Apparently, the North Koreans didn't fully appreciate what they had, but the Soviets certainly did, and they were quick to move in to take over the operation, going through the ship with a fine-tooth comb. The men of the Pueblo were held prisoner under extremely harsh conditions, enduring many beatings, torture sessions and brutal interrogations before finally being repatriated nearly a year later. I can only thank God or fate that I was never required to make such a sacrifice for my country.

Bob Wheatley, "Air Force Lingy" Silent Warrior ~ Secret War
Sergeant, USAF Security Service
Shift Supervisor/Mandarin Linguist
Detachment 4, 6922 Security Wing
Ramasun Station, 7th Radio Research Field Station - Call Sign "Cobra 7"
Nong Soong/Udorn Thailand, 1967-1968
Personal Quotation: Someday the sands of my life's hourglass will have run finally their course. Then the true measure of my life's worth will be the impressions I have made, for good or ill, on the hearts and minds of those whose lives I have touched during my sojourn here.

NO HERO'S WELCOME: *from the Memoirs of Sgt. Robert Wheatley, USAF Security Service - Chapter Six*

Our "Secret War" and the fall of Lima Site-85
By Robert Wheatley

America absolutely ruled the skies over Southeast Asia - "air superiority" was the term used to describe it. In South Vietnam, we were virtually unopposed in the air. Of course, in the North there were the MiG's and AAA and Russian built SAM's (surface to air missiles) to contend with, especially in the heavily defended areas around Hanoi and Haiphong. The SAM's were deadly, and many of our pilots who flew out of Thailand were shot down by them, and were taken prisoner by the North Vietnamese. Most of them spent the remainder of the war, languishing in the "Hanoi Hilton" or in the other POW camps around Hanoi. There, they endured frequent beatings and torture, both physical and mental. Their ordeal has been the subject of many books.

But aside from taking a vigorous defensive posture against the air strikes in the North, the communists that year also redoubled their offensive efforts against our air bases. They knew full well where the strikes were originating, and they would try their damnedest to stop them, or at least slow them down. The air base at Danang in South Vietnam became known as "Rocket City," because of the frequent rocket attacks there. But attacks against American bases were not limited to South Vietnam alone. Our installations in Thailand, Laos and Cambodia were also targets. Isolated, as we were at Ramasun, it was fortunate for us, the Communists weren't as interested in us as they were in the air bases and radar installations.

Lima Site 85 was a radar navigational site located inside the borders of Laos. It provided pinpoint navigation data for our Thai based planes that were making the bombing runs over Hanoi. It gave them all-weather capability and allowed precision bombing under otherwise impossible conditions. As part of the agreements of the Geneva Convention of 1962, Laos was officially taking a neutral stance in the war. For this reason and because of the American public's opposition to expansion of the war outside of South Vietnam, this site and others inside Laos were considered Top Secret. Yes, that's right. We were actually attempting to fight a war, even though our hands had been figuratively tied behind our backs! Incredibly enough, there were then many, and still are some, who would have us apologize for that!

The men working there were mostly Air Force personnel, volunteers, who had been given leave from their "official" duties to be hired by the civilian high-tech firm that had developed the "cutting-edge" radar equipment in use there. They had been "sanitized," or as we called it, "sheep dipped." Posing as civilians, they were required to wear civilian clothes exclusively while in Laos. They were not allowed to carry military arms, which would, of course, give away the fact that they were military personnel. The men and their families were sworn to secrecy. Three crews worked the site and rotated in and out of LS-85 at five-day intervals from Udorn via helicopter. At any given time there were fifteen or so Americans on the site. Although, Top Secret, the North Vietnamese knew of the site's existence, and they were well aware of its significance, they wanted badly to eliminate it, for it was a tremendously valuable asset to us, and it was much more than just a "thorn in the side" to them.

The location had been chosen for its inaccessibility and for the clear radar view it provided. In a bold, almost audacious move, it had been positioned atop a karst mountain, Phou Pha Thi, or "Sacred Mountain," in Northern Laos. It was located a scant thirty miles from North Vietnam's borders, and was less than 150 miles from Hanoi. The summit was more than a mile high, and the sides of the mountain were very nearly vertical, making a ground based assault almost impossible. But, that same rugged terrain was a two edged sword, for it would make escape from the site via the ground route equally difficult.

On January 12th, 1968, seventeen days before the beginning of the Tet Offensive, the North Vietnamese sent in several Russian-built AN-2 biplanes in an attempt to destroy it. The scene was one right out of World War I! Beginning the attack at 1:20 PM, they made three bombing and strafing runs at the site, injuring three Lao soldiers and one US technician. Some on the scene reported the concussions from the blasts felt like those of 250 pound bombs. While it appears to have been within the capability of the large AN-2 biplanes to carry such a load, later analysis showed the "bombs" they dropped were not 250 pounders. Instead, they had dropped 120 mm mortars through tubes in the floor of the aircraft. "Rube Goldberg" fashion, they had been rigged to be armed by the air stream as they fell, another throwback to

WW I technology. Additionally, a number of Soviet 57 mm unguided rockets and machine gun fire had been hurled against the summit of Phu Pha Thi.

In spite of all that, very little actual damage was done to the site's radar equipment in the attack. The fruit of their undeniably courageous attempt was only one antenna temporarily disabled. In return, their planes were shot out of the sky for their effort. One was downed, crashing into a ridge after being hit by intense ground fire on its second bombing pass at the summit. Another, in a surrealistic dogfight between a World War I biplane and a modern jet powered aircraft, was dispatched by a sharpshooter, armed with an assault rifle, while hanging out the door of an Air America (read that "CIA") Huey helicopter. The enemy AN-2 pilots and crew were all killed in the crashes.

The account of the incident by the North Vietnamese was surprisingly similar to our own. The following excerpt from the book "Air War over North Viet Nam" a history of the Vietnamese Peoples' Air Force 1949-1977 by Toperczer, tells the story from the enemy's viewpoint.

"Four AN-2s took off from Gia Lam at 1143 hours on 12 January. Each was armed with a pair of UB-16-57 unguided rocket pods and three 12.7 mm machine guns. One aborted leaving three to continue the attack. They approached Pha Thi at lunch time and making three passes hit the mountain top site with rockets and machine gun fire. On the return leg of the mission the AN-2s that had received hits were flying very low through the valleys and the hilly terrain when they collided in mid-air. Both aircraft crashed resulting in the loss of Phan Nhu Can, a very experienced AN-2 pilot. The third AN-2 hit a mountain side and was destroyed. For the loss of three aircraft and crews, the TACAN site sustained only light damage and remained in operation."

All in all, it was a pitiful attempt by the NVA at the use of air power. And they certainly didn't get much return on their investment of three planes and their crews. But what the North Vietnamese lacked in air power, they made up for in manpower. For human life there was a cheap commodity, and they seemed to be ready and willing to spend as much of it as was necessary to achieve their ends. I find it interesting to note, the primary lament in Toperczer's account of the incident was not so much the loss of human life, as the loss of Phan Nhu Can, "a very experienced AN-2 pilot." In fact, the tenacity of the North Vietnamese in building and rebuilding The Ho Chi Minh Trail in Laos always reminded me of the ants whose hills I used to kick down when I was a kid. No matter how much devastation was wreaked, no matter how many of them you stomped, a hundred or a thousand more emerged from the burrows to replace every one you killed. Just worker ants with no sense of self, only of community, they were driven by a single minded purpose - to build and rebuild what had been knocked down, no matter what the cost to the individual.

In spite of the enemy's lack of success in the January air attack, the fact they even attempted it was ominous. It was indeed predictive that more attacks on Phu Pha Thi were to follow. The North Vietnamese had sacrificed several of the precious few aircraft in their small air defense fleet. That should have been a clear indication of how determined they were to take out Site 85. Undeterred, in February, North Vietnam began massing a large force inside of Laos and commenced construction of a road that would enable them to bring in heavy artillery. All of these activities were well known to us at Ramasun and Udorn, and reports of the enemy's progress were being sent regularly from the US embassy in Vientiane to the State Department back in the US. The implications were fully appreciated by Major General Secord, who was responsible for defense of the installation. Unfortunately, his repeated impassioned pleas for more support for the site's defense via preemptive air strikes on the road were met with lukewarm responses from 7th Air Force and the Vientiane US Embassy. I quote here from Secord's book, "Honored and Betrayed":

"Naturally, I requested 7th Air Force support as soon as we spotted the road. Our goal was to whack 'em hard whenever they cranked up a tractor, to obliterate the construction in the early stages and make it crystal clear that we would simply not tolerate a road in the area. Since the NVA was basically a "road-bound" army with no aerial support, this would preclude any movement of heavy artillery to the site and basically end the battle before it could start. However, the response from 7th Air Force was underwhelming."

"I'm sorry, Mr. Secord, we have higher-priority targets," the strike coordinator told me-- not once, but several times.

"I finally replied, you cannot expect us to hold this site unless you give us sufficient tac air to prevent the completion of the road."

"Well, Mr. Secord, what would you have us do-assign a whole wing to your operation?"

"If necessary, yes sir!"

"For the duration of the war?"

"If that's what it takes, you're right!"

"Well, I'm sorry; we just have higher-priority targets."

"Long weeks passed; more calls. A few strikes were authorized, but the road crept further and further, like a cancer, toward Phou Pha Thi. We'd knock off a bulldozer or tractor and another would arrive the next day to take its place. Burned-out "Cats" littered its shoulder, like locust skins, but the road kept coming."

In fact, this half hearted response by 7th Air Force had its roots in decisions made at the highest echelons of our government. The following excerpt is from a telegram from the Vientiane embassy to Department of State, dated February 20, 1968.

"A specific and immediate area of high concern is Site 85, a guerrilla base and command post in northern Sam Neua province, which has been the target of concentrated enemy pressure for several months. The USAF installed its TSQ-81 navigational device there last fall."

"Recommendation: That you discuss Ambassador Sullivan's request urgently with the Joint Chiefs with a view to getting a sufficiently high priority for air support operations in Laos to meet his requirements."

In a telegram dated 27 February, the State Department responded that Sullivan's request had been discussed by the Joint Chiefs and his recommendations had been relayed to the Department of Defense. But the issue of dedicating air resources to Laos was fundamental and "requires resolution at the highest level." The communiqué further stated that the question was being considered by none other than the Secretary of Defense himself, Robert S. McNamara.

In their "infinite wisdom," rather than expending the resources necessary to defend the site and taking a chance our military presence in Laos be revealed, our political leaders, had decided on an alternative plan. Taking into consideration the enemy's rate of advancement, our best intelligence estimates reported the site could not be held beyond March 10th. But because the facility was so vital to the mission, it was decided by "powers that be" in the Administration to keep it in operation until it became apparent that it was about to fall. Then the men would be air extracted out and the equipment destroyed - or so the plan went. Of course, this superbly crafted "plan" begs the questions, "If the site was so damned vital to the mission, why then would we sit back and allow it to be taken by the enemy, without doing everything in our power to prevent it?" And secondly, "What would we do to replace this purportedly all important facility, after allowing the enemy to take it?" (It never was replaced, to the best of my knowledge.)

It seems apparent that those in charge were so frightened at the prospect of our "Secret War" being revealed to the public, they were not thinking beyond the ends of their noses. Our presence and activities on the ground in Laos would be kept from the public at all costs! For once revealed, the backlash would surely exact a heavy political toll on the Johnson Administration. This is just one shining example of how the battle of wills between the Administration and the anti war faction at home further endangered the lives of those of us on the ground in Southeast Asia. Would that our enemies had been only half as concerned about revealing their presence in Laos to the world as our leaders were of ours!

By early March, the enemy had amassed a ground force around the area, between five and seven battalions in strength. Sure enough, heavy artillery and mortar shelling began on the evening of March 10th and continued throughout the night. But unlike the air attack in January, this attack was devastating. According to survivors, major damage had been inflicted very early in the shelling. This came as somewhat of a surprise to us, for our weapons experts had underestimated the accuracy of their guns. Was this attributable to poor intelligence or was it due to a certain amount of arrogance on our part? Perhaps it was a little of both.

At first light on the 11th, a rescue attempt was made to extract the men from the doomed site. The rescue was only partly successful. Five of the sixteen men on site at the time were picked up by Search and Rescue choppers, manned by the dedicated men of the ARRS, "Air Rescue and Recovery Service," flying out of Udorn. Under heavy enemy fire, and disregarding their own safety, they swooped into the site in a desperate attempt to save the men trapped there. One of the five picked up was killed aboard the chopper during the rescue, a victim of the intense ground fire. While lifting off amidst a storm of hot flying lead, a round came crashing through the thin skin of the aircraft, ripping into the body of one of the men just rescued. In spite of desperate efforts to save him, he was dead before the chopper touched down again at Udorn. The other four were returned to Udorn in shock, but alive.

Eight were reported dead on the site. For reasons unknown (possibly because they had little faith they would be rescued) they had apparently attempted to escape down the back of the mountain, instead of meeting at the rendezvous point where the choppers were to pick them up. It was a fatal mistake! Having reached a narrow ledge fifty feet or so below the summit, the desperate men found they had nowhere to go. Meanwhile, unknown to them, an enemy suicide squad, one of a couple dozen men, had managed to scale the back of the mountain and surprised them, huddled there together on the narrow ledge. The enemy squad was part of a unit believed to have been specially trained for the mission by Russian "Spetznatz" Special Forces. Trapped like rats with no path of escape, the men of LS-85 went down on the spot and died violently amidst exploding grenades and a hail of Communist bullets that ripped their flesh.

It's safe to say, those men who died that day on that remote, lonely spot in Laos were not "blood and guts," battle hardened combat soldiers. They were inadequately armed or entirely unarmed REMF's - technicians, men trained to watch and interpret blips on RADAR screens, to maintain the high tech equipment, and to help direct the bombing strikes against the enemy's stronghold. They were ill prepared to engage in such a battle with well trained and well armed elite enemy special forces. To the NVA, it must have been like shooting fish in a barrel, little more than an execution. Three of the bodies were later recovered from the ledge, and the other five, never recovered, were presumed to have fallen over the sheer 2,000 foot precipice. Three of the sixteen remained unaccounted for, presumed dead, but reported to their families as "Missing in Action." For years afterward, persistent reports kept surfacing of one or more Americans having been captured from LS-85 by the NVA.

On the morning of the 12th, as I marked my 22nd birthday, F-4 Phantoms out of Udorn were sent in to drop Napalm on Lima Site 85 to ensure that nothing of any value was left for the enemy to exploit. As it turned out, the target was too small, situated atop a karst mountain in difficult terrain for the fast moving F4's to be effective. Not one of the bombs or napalm canisters dropped hit the mountain top. Follow-up flights of A1 Skyraider propeller driven attack planes were sent in to finish the job. When the A1's were done, the destruction of Site 85 was complete. It was feared by some that one or more of the MIA's might have been still hiding in the rubble of the site when the Nape was dropped, but that, as far as I know, is pure conjecture.

Search planes had been sent in to look for possible survivors, but none were ever found. Even after the destruction of the site, the area around Phu Pha Thi was still crawling with enemy forces. One of the search planes, an A1E, piloted by Captain Donald Elliot Westbrook, was shot down near the site on the morning of the 13th by enemy fire. Rubble from the crash of his plane was seen strewn over a large area in the mountainous terrain. No signal beacon had been activated and no voice contact was made with him. His body was never recovered.

Perhaps the most tragic part of this whole story is that we knew it was coming and yet, did nothing until it was too little, too late. As though frozen in place, we watched, literally for months, while an accident took place in slow motion before our eyes. It was an accident that might well have been prevented. Yet through our inaction, it became inevitable. I quote from a telegram from the Vientians US embassy to the US State Department in Washington, DC, dated March 11th, 1968. Reporting on the attack, it read in part, *"We will, of course, continue reports as information comes in. At first glance, however, it appears we may have pushed our luck one day too long in attempting to keep this facility in operation."* And from a follow up communiqué, dated March 27, from Ambassador Sullivan in Vientiane to General Momyer at the State Department, *"We made clear from the very beginning that this site could not be defended against a determined and superior enemy force. We gave regular and accurate estimates of its progressive deterioration, and as early as Feb. 26, advised you that it could probably not be held beyond March 10. Therefore, its fall should have come as no surprise to anyone."*

Who was ultimately responsible for this tragedy? I believe the American people were at least indirectly responsible. And perhaps we'll never really know for sure where the direct responsibility lies. I'm sure there is plenty of blame to go around. The communiqué above from Ambassador Sullivan to General Momyer gives us an idea of the kind of finger pointing that must have gone on in high places in its aftermath.

And what of the men of LS-85? What did they think of it all? The attack was no surprise to them. They were certainly aware of the situation that was developing. They had access to the same intelligence information regarding their situation that we had at Udorn and Ramasun Station and the Vientiane Embassy. In fact, the sites own radar equipment was being used to track enemy movements. They could easily see what was happening, as the enemy forces tightened the ring of death around Phou Pha Thi. What must have gone through their minds in those last weeks and days? Did they have any faith that they would be rescued in time? They were told they would be! Did they think the enemy would abort their mission? Of course not! They knew full well the gravity of the situation, yet continued with rotations, allowing themselves to be ferried into the site, despite the imminent danger. Why would anyone do such a seemingly suicidal thing? It was simply their duty - what they had been trained to do! Those brave men of Site 85 died unquestioning, to the end faithfully carrying out that duty to their country. And in return for their devotion, they were betrayed by the nation they had served. But as with all military men, "Theirs was not to reason why; theirs was but to do or die . . ."

And die they did. I hope that one last day of operation was worth the lives of these patriots.

May Their Souls Rest in Peace

Lt. Col. Clarence Finlay Blanton
MSGT James Henry Calfee
SSGT James Woodrow Davis
SSGT Henry Gerald Gish
TSGT Willis Rozelle Hall
TSGT Herbert Arthur Kirk
TSGT Melvin Arnold Holland
SGT David Stanley Price
TSGT Patrick Lee Shannon
TSGT Donald Kenneth Springsteadah
SSGT Don Franklin Worley
CMSGT Richard Etchberger

There were so many people that need never have died,
There were so many tears that need never have been cried,

These Guys

There were politicians who stood there and lied,
It was hard to know who was on our side.

The rattle of gunfire and the sergeant's yell,
Hit the ground men as the mortars fell,
Caught in the crossfire with no place to hide,
Can anyone tell us who is on our side?

We ask for support but it never arrives,
Our commanders tell us that their hands are tied,
The help we were promised hasn't materialized,
Does anyone know who is on our side?

Now there's a lot more men that needn't have died,
And there's a lot more tears that need never have been cried,
All of these men were filled with pride,
It's true that no one was on their side.

Demoralized dejected and wondering what for,
What are we doing in this stinking war,
We are serving our country with honour and pride,
It's only the men fighting with you that are on your side.

We should always remember and never forget,
The war we could have won if we'd only been let,
Remember our fallen service men with honour and pride,
Remember all the men that need never have died.

Paul Filer, Jan. 2001
For America's Vietnam Vets

The "plan" to do nothing but keep those men there until the last minute was fatally flawed. But because of the politics of that war, our choices were limited. There was very little we could have done, other than to pull them out sooner. That is exactly what we should have done. As Ambassador Sullivan's message to General Momyer implied, it would have been impossible for us to send in enough US ground troops in secret to defend the site against such a large enemy force, even if we'd had them available. (We did not.) For the defense of the site, we'd had to rely on about 100 troops from the Thai Special Forces, and on bands of several hundred Laotian freedom fighters of the Hmong people. The Hmong irregulars were led by Lao General Van Pao. Though the Thais and Van Pao's troops were uncommonly dedicated, brave and fierce fighters, they had to finally retreat in the face of the overwhelming odds the NVA had arrayed against them. They had wisely pulled back to live and fight another day. But what about using air strikes? In fact, increasingly intense air strikes were employed in the last few weeks before the fall of LS-85. But the kind of massive air strikes needed (strikes on the scale of those concurrently being successfully used at the siege of Khe Sanh) could not likely be kept secret.

Our hands had been tied by the American people and by the politicians at the highest levels. Although at that very moment, the enemy was losing the battle for Khe Sanh and other major battles in South Vietnam, here in Laos, he had the advantage. And he knew it full well; for he was not operating under such constraints as were we. We were not supposed to have US military personnel in Laos, and their presence there would be covered up and vigorously denied by our government, and by the Royal Lao government, at every turn. Officially, those men never existed! On the other hand, Ho Chi-Minh did not have to "ask permission" from anyone to do what was necessary to win. His people would not dare question his decisions. Nor did he worry about the Geneva Convention or Laos' supposed neutrality. Ho Chi-Minh was not forced to fight a "Secret War." Furthermore, he had as many conscript as were needed to draft for military service, worker ants - ones who would not, indeed could not say, "Hell no! We won't go!"

From Bob Wheatley - Re: Reprint Permission: In my memoir I have written about other repercussions of the capture of Pueblo, affecting the overall Cold War and specific incidents that took place in Thailand while I was there. Below is a chapter that might interest you.

SITTING DUCKS, SAPPERS, AND ARTIFICIAL BOUNDARIES
By Bob Wheatley

First, a note to me, from Bob.

Hello again Trish,

You certainly have my permission to use my write-up on my recollections of the Pueblo Incident - Bamford has used my account of the Chinese MiG incident in his book, "Body of Secrets."

Like you, I believe Bucher and his men were given a raw deal. They became scapegoats for an intelligence disaster of unprecedented proportion. It was a disaster that might well have been prevented, had a much embattled Administration had the gumption to do what was right and engage the North Koreans. But it seems the easier thing to do at the time was to just let it happen and not have to deal with a renewed armed conflict in Korea. I don't know for certain, but I believe Bucher was probably understanding orders to scuttle the ship, rather than let it be taken. Perhaps LBJ was banking on him blindly following those orders. But Bucher's loyalty and human compassion for his men got in the way of that. God rest his soul.
With regard to Johnson, we now know he was reaching the end of his political rope by that time, and he probably had little will to put up a fight, even if he had deemed it the right thing to do. To compound his problems, a week after the Pueblo was taken the infamous '68 Tet Offensive would commence in Vietnam - the proverbial last straw for him, I think. It was only two months later that LBJ figuratively threw in the towel and announced he would not seek or accept his party's nomination for the Presidency in the next election. I can tell you from a personal standpoint, his symbolic "surrender" was little encouragement for those of us who were already there, fully engaged in the war against the Communists that were attempting to dominate the world.

Nineteen-Sixty-Eight will be remembered by many in the intelligence community as a year of betrayals, missteps and intelligence disasters of unprecedented scope. They were incidents which would hold repercussions for national security far beyond the events themselves, impacting many lives and other events, which at first glance, may have seemed completely unrelated at the time.

One warm July evening that year some of my fellow airmen were killed and wounded in an attack on the Udorn Air Base, just up the road from us. A mere "harassment raid" it was officially called, though I'm sure it was just a little more than harassment to those wounded and to the families of those who were killed. In that raid, one of the Thai perimeter guards was killed, cut down by machine gun fire. Four Americans were wounded, one of them fatally, by an exploding satchel charge detonated by one of the sappers.

Their primary target was a C-141 Starlifter transport. In this case, it was one being used as a medical evacuation plane. I remember having seen it sitting parked on the base a day or two before the attack. I took particular note of it, only because it was so unusual to see one there. It was reported to the press the raiders must have mistaken it for a B-52 bomber.

That story may have satisfied the press corps, but I found it absurd, as the two aircraft look nothing alike. Besides, there were no B-52's stationed at Udorn. B-52's were considered especially "high value assets" and they were invariably stationed in places they were least vulnerable to attack. There were none at all stationed in Vietnam, and in Thailand they were stationed only at Utapao Air Base far to the south, just outside of Bangkok.

Did the Starlifter just happen to be the biggest, easiest target available at Udorn at the time? Was it simply a target of opportunity, or did the raiders know exactly what its mission was and specifically target it for that reason? After all, this was a war - one they were fighting to win! For them, there were no boundaries and no "rules of engagement." Any target was fair game!

The raid began at about 10:20 PM. The happenings on the scene that night were related to me by a member of the flight line crew there. He had seen the whole thing, watching from a ditch where he'd taken cover when the shooting started. Unarmed and defenseless, he had no choice but to hide and hope to survive it.

The C-141 had been sitting on the taxiway, awaiting arrival of a flight from Vientiane, which was carrying two just recovered American POW's. They were Major Fred N. Thompson an F-100 pilot shot down on March 20th that year, and Major James F. Low, an F-4D pilot, who had been shot down December 16th the previous year. The men had been released by the North Vietnamese in some kind of propaganda move. Some say it was part of a prisoner exchange deal with the US. At any rate, their return was shrouded in secrecy.

As part of the requirement for their release, the North Vietnamese had apparently insisted they be immediately airlifted out without further stops in country. Instead, the US plan called for them to be routed through Udorn. Upon landing at Udorn, they would then be immediately airlifted out to a hospital in the Philippines by the Starlifter's med-evac crew. Speculation is that particular Udorn attack was purely in retaliation for the US reneging on its part of the prisoner exchange deal.

Based on the timing, that theory seems to make sense. But if true, it raises another question. How did the North Vietnamese know far enough in advance to move troops across the Mekong, into Thailand and into position for the attack? I believe much of their intelligence was being passed to them by the Soviets and Chi-coms. We knew they listened in on our communications, just as we were listening in on theirs. We depended heavily upon our encryption technology to protect our most sensitive communications.

Of course, our encryption methodology had been compromised by that time, by virtue of the capture of the KW-7 encryption equipment on the Pueblo intelligence ship in January. Unfortunately, we had mistakenly assumed the code was still secure, because in addition to having the equipment, one needed the vital encryption key, which was constantly being changed. Hindsight being twenty-twenty, we know now that was a wrong assumption.

Only years later was it learned a spy in the Pentagon had been regularly passing the code key to the Soviets. Naval Chief Petty Officer, John Walker, a cryptographic technician, supplied the encryption key lists to the Soviets from early 1968 until the time he was finally arrested in 1985. Unknown to us at the time, those key lists, together with capture of the equipment on Pueblo, had made our Top Secret encrypted transmissions easily readable by the enemy.

In the words of former KGB chief, Oleg Kalugin, "I was John Walker's supervisor. When he came into the Soviet embassy [in late 1967] he produced immediately very convincing proof of his great value." [After capture of Pueblo] "His access to cryptographic material [the code key lists] allowed us to read all US secret communications."

Based upon Kalugin's statements, the Soviets were almost certainly aware of every detail of the released POW's planned itinerary well in advance. Astonishingly enough, after his arrest in 1985, Walker still called himself a patriot. He rationalized his betrayal, saying he "knew" the Soviets would not risk passing that intelligence to the North Vietnamese, and therefore, with respect to the Vietnam War, his espionage was, in his words, "doing no real harm."

Indeed the Soviets themselves deny having passed to the North Vietnamese, intelligence obtained by their decryption of our secure communications. Retired KGB officer Boris Solomatin states, "The handing over to the Vietnamese, in any form of information or data, which we got from Walker, was contrary to our own interests, because it could lead to his being exposed, and to run the risk of this would be silly."

Still, I have often wondered about the timing of that raid on Udorn. Certainly, armed with the right intelligence from the Soviets, the North Vietnamese would be able to have their sappers in place and ready for the attack when the time came. In spite of the Soviet denials, I still have to wonder whether the timing of that particular attack with respect to the POW's return was something more than mere coincidence. Was it more fallout from the Pueblo Incident?

At any rate, the precise moment the Vientiane flight touched down on the runway, the attack commenced. The main assault was concentrated primarily on the C-141, though I also learned from another source that at least one unexploded satchel charge was later recovered from the intake on one of the parked F-4 Phantoms.

When it became apparent they were under attack, the commander of the C-141, Captain Robert Shultz, and his flight engineer, Tech Sgt. Paul Yonkie dove for cover - too late to escape injury. In a blinding flash that lit up the night, white-hot shrapnel from an exploding grenade or satchel charge invaded Sgt. Yonkie's chest and abdomen, and Captain Shultz's hands and wrists were slashed to the bone by shards of flying metal.

Newspaper reports afterward put the number of attackers at about ten. I suspect there may have been considerably more than that, as the battle went on for thirty minutes or more on base before they could be driven back. And the fighting continued throughout the night in the glare of the flares illuminating the paddies in the surrounding area.

It was rumored arming of the flight line personnel at the air base was initially delayed, because the First Sergeant, who had possession of the key to the weapons lockers was off base when the attack occurred. Fortunately, several minutes into the assault, someone else was finally found to open the lockers and distribute the weapons and ammo clips. Under the circumstances, it was fortunate we didn't suffer more casualties than we did.

When word of the ongoing attack on the nearby air base reached us at Ramasun Station, we were put on full alert. To put it mildly, it was a somewhat disconcerting sight - two armed MPs *inside* the operations building, stationed facing the only door, with weapons at the ready, locked and loaded. Under ordinary circumstances, even MPs were never allowed inside the inner-sanctum of the Top-Secret operations center where we worked. The significance of their presence there was immediately apparent to me. It could only mean we were under imminent threat of attack. My blood ran cold.

To this day, it's difficult for me to reconcile why the rest of us were not immediately issued weapons with an attack under way just a few miles up the road, and at least the threat of attack at our own station. Actually I can, but the conclusions are disturbing. I would have felt at least a little better about the situation that night had I and my men been allowed to carry our own M-16's and not have to entrust our security entirely to armed guards, however well trained and dedicated!

True enough, we were technicians and linguists, not trained as combat troops. But in other wars, even technicians and linguists had been provided means of self-defense! We each had been trained in the use of the M-16, and we had been required to qualify with live ammo, before being shipped overseas. Furthermore, we had all been officially assigned a weapon and were required to sign for it upon arrival at our duty stations in country. Yet, while

I was there at least, we were never drilled on what to do, nor told where to retrieve those weapons in case of attack. I never touched an M-16 while I was there. We were simply informed, "They're in the armory." They probably were, but I had serious doubts we would be allowed to actually use them when the time came.

Today I have to ask myself, "Was it all just for show-something with which "powers that be" could cover themselves in case of a major loss of life due to hostile action in Thailand? Was it a measure of deniability for those who were calling the shots in this war, and a means of hopefully silencing angry bereaved families back home?"

As shift supervisor, I should have at least been made aware where the weapons lockers were located and given the means to quickly open them if we did indeed come under attack. I was not. Unarmed as we were, if the enemy were to breach our perimeter defenses and overrun the post, we would have been "sitting ducks," much the same as the poor hapless men of LS-85 had been. Some loss of life is inevitable and expected in war. We all knew and accepted that. But some of it is unnecessary and is preventable. I kept thinking it was another tragedy waiting to happen. And had it happened, it may have been swept under the rug, just as the LS-85 incident had been.

The operations compound at Ramasun Station was situated very near the perimeter of the post. Once inside the wire, it would take the enemy raiders only seconds to cover the distance to the ops building. If the building was stormed, the two guards at the entrance might take out a lot of enemy troops, but in the face of a concerted rush by an enemy suicide unit, they almost certainly would have been overwhelmed. Still, we inside the building were supposed to remain unarmed at our radio receivers, carry on with the mission, and pretend nothing unusual was going on outside - just as the men of LS-85 had continued to man their RADAR and communications equipment to the last.

Indeed, in the event the post was overrun, in the last moments we would likely have been preoccupied, feverishly destroying equipment and classified documents and too busy to participate in our own defense! In our Security Service training we'd had it drummed into our heads we were to take care of classified information FIRST at any cost! Our personal safety was a last concern.

This very policy is in sync with another possible, much more sinister reason we in the ops compound were not allowed to carry arms. I did not know it at the time, but I have since learned some disturbing facts from one in a position to know. An MP who had been stationed there at Ramasun, states there were always contingency plans - standing orders among the MP force that no one in the compound was to be taken alive if the post were in danger of being overrun by the enemy.

On condition of anonymity in a letter to me he writes, "The MP's were told no one at Ops was to be taken alive if we were overrun. Ops would be the final point of defense. We were told before Ops would be overrun the Air Force would be sent in to destroy it and the remaining personnel!"

It's a chilling thought to me, if it is indeed true. Now I have to wonder, were the armed MP's I saw at the door of the ops building that night there to dispatch *us*, rather than to defend us from the enemy? In the event things did not go well outside the building, would they have turned their weapons on us? My mind recoils from such a prospect. It's too incredible, too distasteful to accept, yet I have to wonder. Certainly, if this scenario was true, arming those of us in the operations center would have made their task much more difficult, in fact impossible to carry out.

As for possible air strikes, I knew then, and it's a well documented historical fact, Lima Site 85 had been destroyed just months earlier by a Napalm strike by our own aircraft out of Udorn. Though the nape was dropped on site-85 *after* the enemy had taken it, it doesn't require too much of a stretch of the imagination to believe they might have preemptively done the same at Ramasun Station, if the situation had warranted.

After all, there was at least some evidence that three of the men at LS-85 had been taken alive and made prisoners by the enemy. Like us, they were men who held Top Secret security clearances, and were in possession of vital information of great potential value to enemy intelligence. And we were fully aware the Communists had ways of making even the strongest, most well indoctrinated man talk.

Certainly, what had happened earlier in the year at LS-85 and in the Sea of Japan were "lessons learned" for those calling the shots in this war. They would want to ensure they did not make the same mistakes again, would they not? They would want to avoid another intelligence disaster like the "Pueblo Incident" and the loss of Lima Site-85. They would take all steps necessary to see to it Ramasun Station's personnel not be captured alive by the enemy!

Our post was but eleven kilometers from Udorn, a mere heartbeat away by air. Within minutes after orders were issued, aircraft could be scrambled, and the post where we served would no longer exist. All that would remain is smoldering rubble. Ramasun Station would be obliterated from the landscape in a smoky, billowing orange fireball, and we who served there would be wiped out with it!

Of course, on an intellectual level we in Security Service understood going in, we were all expendable to protect the security of "the mission." We had been told as much, many times over. It was an integral part of our Security Service training and indoctrination. In fact, I remember on more than one occasion in classroom security training sessions, we had been told that at least some of our operatives inside Laos had been issued cyanide capsules and were under orders to commit suicide, if they were in imminent danger of being captured. Still, at the time, I don't think any of us wanted to truly believe in our "heart of hearts" we might actually be purposely sacrificed in order to prevent our live capture. That was the stuff of spy novels!

After all, we were *American* boys! Uncle Sam had invested literally millions of dollars and years in the training of each of us. "Surely, we are of too much value to them alive for them to actually do such a thing!" At least we all consoled ourselves with that rationalization. It was a source of comfort and means of making the possible consequences of what we were involved in less intimidating in our minds.

I am a good deal older and wiser now, and I realize we were perhaps naïve and overly optimistic in allowing ourselves to believe that at the time. But the young are by definition, naïve and by nature, optimistic. Back then, not one of us, I'm sure, truly believed in our hearts we were ever going to die. That sort of thing only happens to others. But the undeniable hard reality remains: preserving the secrecy of "the mission" was *everything!*

In all fairness, good conscience compels me to add, it remains in serious question in my own mind whether American pilots would have actually carried out any such orders to destroy one of our own installations, especially if they knew in advance the purpose of the strikes would be to take out our own troops. The whole premise is surely repugnant to anyone who served on our side, as it is to me.

But knowing the missteps and betrayals exemplified in the capture of Pueblo and the loss of LS-85 earlier that year, one has to wonder how far our government might actually have gone to protect its secrets. What "knee-jerk" reactions might result from the disastrous loss of the Pueblo and Lima Site 85? What deceptions and new betrayals might be possible? What sacrifices might be asked of us in the name of national security?

Back at the air base, after the flight line was finally secured, both Yonkie and Shultz were stabilized and immediately evacuated to the hospital at Clark Air Base in Manila. There, Captain Shultz would recover from his wounds. But after putting up a valiant struggle to live, Sgt. Yonkie finally succumbed to his injuries weeks later. He was but 34 years old, and I understand he left behind a grieving wife and three young daughters. A so-called "REMF" as defined by some, his only mission was to help airlift out our wounded, and he surely didn't expect, nor deserve to die in such a way. But then, neither did any of the more than 58,200 American casualties of that war whose names cover that massive wall in Washington, DC.

The morning after the attack, I heard that Yonkie and Shultz had been seriously wounded and were air evacuated out, but I didn't learn the particulars of their eventual fates until many years later, after I'd returned stateside. In the days following the attack there was of course much talk amongst us about it in the ops center, and I learned from the Intel analyst, at least one of the raiders killed in that fatal raid had been confirmed a Captain in the North Vietnamese Army. At least one other raider, who had been captured alive, was also NVA.

His live capture was a stroke of good luck for our side, and a very unfortunate one for him. He was exhaustively interrogated, before finally being handed over to the Thai authorities for further questioning. Talk in the intelligence community was, his would be a fate far worse than death. He would pray to die before the Thais were through with him. In fact, newspaper reports stated the sapper had died in the hospital from wounds suffered during the attack on the air base. He may have died in the hospital, but I suspect it may not have been from wounds inflicted in the attack.

Admittedly, much of these ramblings represent only speculation on what *might* or *could* have taken place that night at Ramasun, had the enemy chosen to hit us. In any case, we spent a restless, uneasy night waiting there in the windowless radio room, anticipating an attack that thankfully never came. After that incident, I never slept quite as soundly or as comfortable at night on post. "Yes, there damned sure IS a war going on, and it is here!" Moreover, I was left with little confidence I and my men would be given the means with which to defend ourselves if, and when the need arose. I felt closer than ever to the men of USS Pueblo and Lima Site-85.

These and countless other demonstrable acts of aggression by the North Vietnamese Army in Thailand, Laos and Cambodia certainly confirmed in my own mind the validity of the Domino Theory, a theory that is much pooh-poohed by many today to validate their own anti-war stance back then. The "Domino Theory" proposed other nations of the region would fall under Communist control if South Vietnam were to fall. I insist it was not just some unfounded fear, despite arguments to the contrary.

The Communist sympathizers and revisionists of history, who would characterize North Vietnam's part in the war as simply a struggle to unite the two halves of their own country, are dead wrong! There is absolutely no doubt North Vietnam was actively promoting and directly aiding the Communist insurgents in Thailand, Laos, and Cambodia, as well as the Viet Cong in South Vietnam. In the larger picture of the global Cold War, the North Vietnamese were receiving massive aid from the Chinese and Soviet Communists, who would have loved nothing better than to see their brand of oppressive government spread around the world. These are all things to which I can attest from first-hand knowledge.

The live capture of the Udorn sapper had been a rare opportunity to glean intelligence on their operations. Usually in the raids on Thai bases, aside from the ones who sacrificed themselves as human bombs with satchel charges strapped to their bodies, most of the raiders would get away. After a brief firefight, they'd disengage, melt back into the rain forest and retreat beyond the borders to find refuge in Laos or Cambodia, where our troops and planes were not supposed to follow.

The Communist forces that were invading South Vietnam were using the sanctuary of Cambodia and Laos in the same way. These "no man's lands" were key factors in perpetuating the Vietnam War and thereby determining its final outcome. This point cannot be overly emphasized! By their own admission to the North Vietnamese, Laos and Cambodia were absolutely crucial to their success in South Vietnam.

The restriction of not being able to openly send our ground troops into those areas in meaningful numbers was the main factor which enabled the North to keep the ground war in the South alive, year after bloody year. Because we were never allowed to eliminate the Communists' places of refuge, logistical supply, and training and staging of troops, the war persisted, like some throbbing abscessed tooth. The American people gradually grew increasingly opposed to an ongoing conflict, which seemed to have no end in sight. As time went on, more of the mainstream began to add their own voices to the voices of the radicals, who for their own reasons had opposed the war from the beginning.

That public fatigue with the war is what would eventually allow the American people to look the other way, as our political leaders finally pulled the rug out from under the South, ending all U.S, support for them. It's what would allow America to look the other way and ignore the mass murder that would take place in Cambodia under the Pol Pot regime, a debacle so horrific it shocked and embarrassed even the North Vietnamese, and the countless atrocities that would be carried out in Laos by the Pathet Lao.

I quote again, a telegram from the Vientiane embassy to the Department of State in Washington, dated March 16, 1968. It clearly illustrates the growing sense by our Lao allies that America lacked the will to do what was necessary to help them protect themselves in the face of determined Communist aggression.

"As we enter the last few weeks of dry season without visible reduction of North Vietnamese presence or activities, Lao are bracing themselves for another series of enemy attacks. This time there is somewhat less sense of panic than in February and a more careful measuring of circumstances. However, there is also an underlying worry and

fatalism, which reflects a broad scale of uncertainties. Chief among these is apparent inability of friendly forces in South Vietnam to reassert initiative, especially in countryside and marks of diminishing support for war in the United States."

Yes, we did send missions into Laos, trying our best to fight and win a "Secret War." But they were much less extensive and less effective than they might otherwise have been, because of their necessarily clandestine nature. That secrecy was a necessity imposed upon us by a recalcitrant American public and the politicians. For our involvement in an officially "neutral" Laos would have been an escalation unacceptable to the anti-war protesters back home! And any news of Americans involved in a shooting war in Thailand certainly would not have been well received by them either. But then, those who were protesting in the streets at home were not the ones sitting in a jungle, halfway around the world, risking life and limb for their country, were they? Better we should let the Communists escape to regroup, re-supply and return in a few days or weeks and do it all again!

Far from helping us, the protesters back home were virtually cutting our legs from under us! Because of political expedience, we on the ground outside the borders of South Vietnam were to be kept unarmed and defenseless. And theater wide, we were to be bound by ridiculous "rules of engagement" and expected to observe artificial boundaries our enemies were not obliged to observe. It was absolute insanity, a completely, indefensibly *asinine* way to fight a war - one that just would not allow us to win!

See Bob Wheatley's personal Vietnam War web site: - http://www.Viet-REMF.net for more stories and information.

These Guys

This Preface, and Acknowledgment is a partial Brief History of the Air Intelligence Agency and its Predecessor Organizations from A Continuing Legacy: USAFSS to AIA, 1948- 2000, by Dr. Dennis F. Casey and MSgt Gabriel G. Marshall and published by the Air Intelligence Agency History Office, San Antonio, TX. This came to me via http://www.Silent.Warriors.com/Wheelock.htm, to each, I give credit. I feel that their words describe, best, the continuing legacy of the USAFSS - AIA, 1948- 2000.

USAFSS to AIA - 1948 - 2000
By Dr. Casey and MSgt Marshall

The Air Intelligence Agency's rich and colorful heritage began nearly fifty-two years ago and encompasses much of the Cold War. Indeed, the activities and many accomplishments of the United States Air Force Security Service, later the Electronic Security Command, and for a brief time the Air Force Intelligence Command contributed importantly to the history of the United States during this period which was replete with the threat of nuclear confrontation with our primary opponent, the Soviet Union. As scholars look back on this period and try to explain its major trends and developments, as well as its frustrations and the chasm that separated the two super powers, the role of air intelligence will surely be seen as a defining influence.

As the Air Intelligence Agency steps forward into the 21st century and carries out its mission of information operations it is worth a moment to reflect on where the command was, where it has been and what it has achieved. This publication outlines briefly the command's first 52 years as the Air Force's air intelligence arm and chronicles many of the important contributions which have provided for the continued security of the United States. We wish to recognize the superb support provided by the 690th Information Systems Squadron Visual Production Flight and the Headquarters Air Intelligence Agency Public Affairs Office. To Jim Pierson and Mary Holub and the others who endeavored tirelessly over the years to record this exciting and important story, and to Juan Jimenz whose assistance and advice were invaluable, we express our special thanks.

The Foreword: In this fast-paced environment of the 21st century, driven as it often is by seemingly constantly changing information age technologies, it is fundamentally important to pause occasionally and reflect on where the Air Intelligence Agency (AIA) has been. Even in the autumn of 1947, when Colonel Richard P. Klocko began lying the groundwork for a separate Air

Force organization devoted to special information, change was everywhere. Unprecedented accuracy and speed in communications, the unleashing of the atomic age, and the advent of a bipolar world heralded much of this change. The Air Force Security Group established on 23 June 1948, underwent a significant metamorphosis and became the United States Air Force Security Service (USAFSS) on 20 October 1948, before even five months had passed. Not quite two years later USAFSS personnel found themselves headed into a new conflict when on 25 June 1950 North Korean ground forces crossed the 38th parallel into South Korea. The Cold War had suddenly heated up. Today's AIA is a fused intelligence organization serving as a critical part of the air operations arm of the United States. Its mission continues to change as it endeavors to provide its many customers with current, readily usable and focused information products and services. AIA's personnel accomplish this complex mission of information operations with a high degree of professionalism and effectiveness. They participate directly in combat operations and capitalize upon new and promising technologies, adapting them to current as well as perceived needs. In so doing AIA defines and sharpens the Air Force Core Competency of information operations. Today's AIA warriors, backed by a rich 52-year heritage, look forward to the challenges of the future and stand ready to defend the United States and its people, its interests and its allies in the 21st century.

This Foreword signed by: Bruce A. Wright, Major General, USAF
Commander, Air Intelligence Agency

This is a short story by Vince Wuwert, Sgt., USAFSS about his time serving his country.

THE GOOD AND THE BAD
By Vince Wuwert

My comments about serving with the United States Air Force Security Service Command back during the late 60's can be separated into two categories, the good and the bad.

The good part of my service was the travel. My first tour was in England with the 6950th Security Group in Bedfordshire. We had an "elephant cage" as an antenna. Best intelligence gathering piece of equipment that existed in those days. We had a mission at Chicksands that is classified to this date, some 32 years later. The Cold War was at its height in those days. Our mission at Chicksands was exciting, and down right interesting during the 1967 Israeli vs. Arabs war.

We were close to London from Bedfordshire. All the touristy stops were included every time I went to "the smoke." I still have a few dozen color snapshots of my days in England. The people I met and worked with were the ones that made it all bearable. They were the best. Had a roommate at Chicksands who was one of those "funny type drunks," never had a harsh word for him or from him. The local pub keepers knew him by his first name by the time his tour was completed. He loved his Watney's Brown beer served up at room temperature at the Black Swan Pub in Shefford.

I met a guy, from Pennsylvania who was a voice intercept operator. He knew Russian at the level of a junior high school student; funny guy, weird. He would ask if I wanted a box of popcorn when we went to the base theater to see a new movie. I'd always oblige and pay for it but he would always include a one liner like, "thanks for paying for my popcorn. Now what color of popcorn do YOU want?" We had to work a swing shift on Christmas Day of 1967. He showed up appearing to be Mr. Air Force - spit shined shoes, neatly starched fatigues and wearing a Santa Claus red hat. Most of the guys got a kick out of it, but his section supervisor, said it was not Air Force issue so he had to remove it.

The bad things about serving in Security Service came when I was reassigned to Detachment Four of the 6922nd Security Wing, out of Clark AFB in the Philippines. The base location was in North East Thailand. It was in 1968 & 69 when the war was so actively being pursued in Vietnam. My base site was eight miles south from the town of Udorn Thani, the provincial capital.

We worked in a building that had no windows, and was guarded night and day by armed guards in two story towers. The facility was totally air conditioned, but it also had its bad aspects. The field mice from the surrounding rice paddies would make their way into the building through the floor trenches which housed the coaxial cables for the antennas and power lines. We'd trap them in a small wire box, send them to the Army electronics maintenance room, and watch as they were dumped into a GI butt can and electrocuted with a field generator phone pack power source. We even had mice in our barracks from time to time. And the barracks were totally sealed and air conditioned. Cement cinder block construction. How they got in is beyond my understanding.

One time one of the guys on my flight in Thailand, came down with contagious hepatitis and every one got an injection of 5cc of Gamma Globulin; getting that injection in your butt felt like being stung by a dozen bees. It hurt big time. But it also saved us all from being infected. When guys would go to sit down after receiving one of those injections of gamma globulin, we would sort of ease our butts into a chair. No matter how gently you tried to avoid pressure on your back side, it always hurt.

Once in a while we would hear by the window rattling the roar of an Air Force RF4-C jet fighter plane making a low level approach to the run way in Udorn. They would make their approaches so low I swear you could see the pilots, and loud? They were awesomely loud.

One time I got the crap scared out of me. I was at the Ramasun Station NCO club with a few buddies after a swing shift. It was about one in the morning. We were sitting out on the patio enjoying a few cold beers, when suddenly we heard small arms fire. Everyone got up at once. Since the club was only about one hundred meters from the perimeter of the base we all thought the worst, except me: I walked over to a door on the opposite side of where we were sitting, and looked out at the guard tower. More small arms fire came from the tower and I turned and ran to the opposite side of the patio only to see about ten guys trying to get through a door made for only one. The nearest protective bunker was about twenty-five meters from the door and they were all headed towards it. About two minutes after we had all made it to the bunker, some guy comes from the NCO club and happily announces, "Hey you dumb shits. It was the Thai perimeter guard. He was shooting at some dogs." We all came out. Good training for us to make it to the bunker in time, but it was all for nothing. No attack. And the Thai guard missed the dog. It didn't help my confidence in the security of the base.

The worst thing about Security Service, without a doubt, was coming home. I got on a flight back to the USA from Bangkok's Don Muang AFB and headed for Travis AFB in California. We stopped at Kadena AFB in Okinawa, and then were supposed to fly non stop to Travis. It didn't happen that way. We had to stop at Elmendorf AFB in Alaska - emergency landing, oil leak in one of the engines of the aircraft. I began to wonder if after all this crap I had been through in Thailand, if I was going to make it home safely. But we landed safely.

After being separated from the Air Force at Travis, a buddy and I decided to tour San Francisco for a day. We hit all the high spots. Fisherman's Warf, the boat tour of San Francisco Bay and a trip through China Town after a short ride on one of the famous San Francisco Trolleys. When we finally made it to the San Francisco Airport we encountered a young woman probably in her mid twenties, hippy girl with long straight hair. Dressed like a tramp. Saw the Vietnamese Service Ribbons on our Air Force uniforms and snottily referred to us as "baby killers." That has always sat in my mind, distastefully. Down inside my soul I can rationalize away the idea that I had never killed babies in Vietnam when I was stationed in Thailand. I never fired a weapon at anyone and never directed artillery fire at anyone. I never dropped bombs on any village, but yet I was referred to as a baby killer. My only connection to all of that is that I did indeed provide information to people who did drop bombs, fired weapons and fired artillery that might have killed innocent babies and civilians but I have come to the conclusion that Vietnam was a time in my life when my skills were needed. I did my duty. Just like all the guys who were 'in country'. If some of my information I collected while working for Security Service in Thailand, caused the death of innocents or enemy in Vietnam, then I did my duty. It was damn war. And like my relatives who were in combat in WWII, it was my turn to serve. I have never lost an instant of sleep knowing I was part of a system that "might have caused" the death of other human beings. I just never gave a damn.

Perhaps the best way for me to express my over all feelings about my years of service during the Cold War, would be to quote the dear gentleman from Stratford-upon-Avon. Mr. Shakespeare said it best in his play "Henry V." He wrote in Act IV and scene III, "We few, we happy few, we band of brothers, for he today that sheds his blood with me shall be my brother be he never so vile this day shall gentle his condition. And gentlemen in England, now abed shall think themselves accursed they were not here, and hold their man hoods cheap, whiles any speaks that fought with us upon Saint Crispin's day."

I have been to the Vietnam Veterans Memorial Wall in our nations Capital. I have seen the names of Security Service brethren who died aboard the EC-47 aircraft known as Baron-52. There are other names of my brethren who are known but to God, who lost their lives while conducting unarmed reconnaissance flights over European territories. They served. They did so in silence. They did so unprotected. And they upheld the finest tradition of the United States Air Force. They gave the "last full measure of devotion" as President Lincoln once said. I am proud to be associated with these people.

And for all of us who served those many years and finally collected a pension from the Dept. of Defense, I salute you. God Bless you, my brothers. We served with honor. We served in Silence. We were, Silent Warriors!

Vince Wuwert USAF/SS 1965-69 Service at 6950th SG, England
                                         Det. 4, 6922nd SW Ramasun Station
                                         Udorn Province Thailand

These Guys

This is an e-mail from Vince Wuwert, Ret. USAFSS, in answer to one I sent to him about writing THESE GUYS . . .

THOSE DITS AND DAHS . . .
By Vince Wuwert

Trish,
Keep it . . . work on it. It's good; very good; like I said a long time ago. I wish we could have an evening together; just you and me, and the spirit of Phil, your brother. I would tell you much about USAF Security Service. What happened to all those dits and dahs that those Rooskie operators in Mocbaw sent to my ears. Are they still embedded in my memory some place? Sometimes, when I am alone, and it's quiet, I can hear the tone, the dits and dahs . . . the static . . . the background cursing of airmen who are "working a - freq" and trying to snatch a bit of good "shit" to report to guys like Phil. At times, thirty-five years later, I yearn to hear it all again, and realize, I am protecting America by stealing their signals. I grew up in those days. I never forgot. I've tried. It never goes away. We made history. But no one cared. You care . . . so don't quit. Phil will honor your life in a very special way if you continue. Keep it up. You are one cool lady.
I almost could feel the cool droplets of fog at Chicksands; only being able to see two feet in front of myself. Listening for voices of men going to the mess hall from the operations building, so dark, like being inside an ice cube. It's zero visibility wherever you look. Oh, how I loved it. I loved it more than life itself. We made history. Please record it for us and then tell the world about us by writing about it.

Sgt. Vince Wuwert

Go Trish . . . and Go Navy . . . victorious over Army . . . big time!

"Ahh, Vince, Go Navy it is, as my husband was in the Navy, and so was our first daughter, BUT I have a son in the Army, and a daughter who was in the Army Reserves. So, it's a split decision." T.S. [The Editor]

TYPING 101 - THE AF WAY
By Vince Wuwert

This is in answer to my e-mail to Vince. My part is: So, once again, masked man, you have taught me something else!!! What else can you tell me about the typing class you took? Thanks ever so much, Sarge. Trish

When Vince told me about "typing 101" it became clear to me why my brother, Phil, took typing at the University of Alabama, Tuscaloosa, Alabama when I KNEW he'd been typing, swiftly, for many, many years, and had taught me to type on his Royal non-electric portable typewriter. Here goes Vince's reply:

Trish,
I can tell you tons, they started us out in Tech school at Keesler AFB in late Nov. of 65 with a paper key board, and the instructor would sit up front and say "J" dit dah dah dah "U" dity dah, and we went from there, each new letter we learned on the paper key board had Morse code to go with it, so when we learned the fingering for the typed letter it also had a "code" sequence to go with it. We did all the letters and all the alphabet and code at the same time. But when I got on the line in England, I saw guys sitting near me with their lean-back GI chairs take their Royal special standards and tip them towards their laps and hack ditties with the middle fingers of each hand. NEVER used the entire two hands for code, you just pecked at it in sort of a rhythm, only time I used both hands, while at my position console, was when I serviced a piece of traffic, meaning: The case notation, the call signs, the frequency on short wave, the time, and my personal sign, which in England was //WD.
I had no trouble typing in college when I returned to UT in 1969, none at all. My Royal Electric was fabulous, although I DID use a small portable manual typewriter that my dad's girlfriend gave to me.
I wish Phil were still alive, dang could we ever e-mail a lot of really good stories betwixt us; any more questions? I'll be glad to add to your knowledge of AF typing classes. They taught us efficiently, and it stayed with me to this day; no lie GI.
Nippon

CHECK OUT RECONNAISSANCE FLIGHTS AND SINO-AMERICAN RELATIONS
By Vince Wuwert

The above title is available on Google.

Trish,
When you read the paragraph titled . . . (and it's the first paragraph) Jump to the Documents . . . read carefully where it says that "NSA operated US Air Force aircraft near the Chinese territory . . . and to collect radar and other intelligence . . ." (that summarizes my mission in Thailand . . .)

SR-71 "Incursion" flights along the chink border with NVN and Laos . . . our guys at Det. 4, 6922nd Security Wing USAFSS were quite busy at those times. . . .

The chinks would track them . . . and we gleaned all sorts of radar intelligence from their "plottings . . ." and to think . . . one of the SR-71's that did that over flight is in a museum in Dayton Ohio (not far from me) small world ain't it?

Vince

Sgt. Vince Wuwert was a "ditty bopper" in Thailand at Det.4, 6922nd Security Wing USAFSS during the cold war. He also served at Chicksands, England.

This piece contains two e-mails from Vince Wuwert to the Editor, Trish Schiesser. Somehow I had asked a question which stimulated his mind, and here are the answers, which make fascinating reading.

CHINA
By Vince Wuwert

We were watching them very carefully in the 60's. Chairman Mao was in the midst of the Great Cultural Revolution if you might recall. The chink ops used to send at the end of their traffic, stuff like this: MW MW MW 235 53.EE. Which meant MW=Mao's words, and the numbers related to pages and paragraphs - the ops wanted to stay sharp on what Chairman Mao's thoughts said - they thought it was a message from God. (But, more of this later.)

Anything that went short wave and from China, we copied. At Ramasun it was mainly Air Force mission; that is radar stations and related networks. The ops were very sloppy. They sent cut numbers and other characters in Code I never understood. I think our NSA feedback for some nets sucked. Like the "WOB" once every three weeks, the entire net changed call signs and day and night frequencies. We had to find them. They had a regular rotation, "rota" schedule and we should have been waiting at the next "rota" frequency but we were supplied nothing. We had to find it, and it was hideous, but the only way we could find them was to search a certain range of frequencies and hope he'd show up at five till the hour for his five minute WX broadcast, and the simplex responses from all the outstations. Believe me, all the guys in the AF unit earned the Vietnamese Service ribbon, for supporting the mission in Vietnam, just for finding the "WOB" each month. We used to cuss that net something awful. It was so frustrating - just awful.

Now, for more on MW - Mao's words. A reference to a page and paragraph from Mao's little red book he wrote titled: THE THOUGHTS OF CHAIRMAN MAO. The chink ops wanted to stay abreast of what Mao's Word said. They quoted him constantly in their traffic suffixes. They thought Mao was a God.

I wish I could describe how I truly felt physically when we had to find that weather case titled The WOB. It was a pain. It truly was. There were other occasions when the Army ditty boppers would find the net control. Pass along the frequency and call sign. We'd check it out and wait for him at five till the hour. The WOB operator was sloppy with his code sending. So much of his ditties were run together. Cut numbers. No breaks between number groups of five numbers. Nothing was in any type of organized format being sent. It was one very long sentence and you had to know your stuff to know where to break off a group, hit the space bar, or carriage return to start a new line. Two other things that helped an operator to identify the WOB net control. Not only was the operator sloppy, the signal came in "five by" most of the time, and his net control call sign was a mixture of two to three numbers and one letter; always a total of four to the call signs.

Once we'd recovered all his outstation call signs, the night and day frequencies, and were able to read the traffic, it was another routine net to copy, and somewhat of a "gravy" mission. You copied him at five till the hour and his transmission lasted perhaps six minutes. And then there was the Mao's word transmission chatter at the end of the traffic after the net control had received the QSL's from the outstations. The rest of the hour you could "search for a target" or just relax. The weather net was very important. Even though the US had satellites that covered weather in the SEA region, there is nothing like an on the ground spotter telling you the weather and giving you a rather accurate prediction from the enemy's side. One must remember in those days, good weather conditions allowed accurate interdiction of the Ho Chi Minh trail through Laos and Cambodia and clear skies over "downtown" meant the usual day for the citizens of Hanoi would include a "rain of bombs" courtesy of the US and Naval aircraft.

Give me the Russian ditty boppers any time. They were organized. Well disciplined network wise. Clean code. Always on time when they were on scheduled missions.

All my guys who sat "racks" as ditty boppers at Ramasun and Chicksands in the UK, have my respect forever. When it came to a "hot mission" they were the best. We saved a lot of lives with the intelligence we gathered. And in the case of Ramasun, we were always on the spot, when Da Nang's 6924th Security Squadron operations area would get a VC mortar attack. We picked up their missions in addition to ours. Some times the guys at Ramasun would laugh and essentially make fun of the guys at Da Nang after we had dropped their mission to them when the AICP had ended. We'd laugh about the scenario of "sitting there copying a ground VC target and KABOOM, hey what happened to the walls in the building? They ain't there anymore, and then wonder who would get out of the building the fastest to get into the sand bagged bunkers. Would there be enough room? And were we going to die?" A sobering scenario for sure.

Odd. You ask a simple question and I pour out another story, Trish. You stimulated my memory. I guess that's okay.

Sawadee krup,
Vince

These Guys

This is an e-mail from Vince to me [The Editor] where he lets it all hang out.

"GO TO HELL"
By Vince Wuwert

Subj: Re: (no subject)
Date: 10/10/02 5:16:50 PM Pacific Daylight Time
From   VAWuwert
To: IdaReedBlanford

Trish,

I watched guys like Phil . . . those I worked with at Chicksands with the 6950th and in Thailand with Det.4. They would look over all the crap we intercepted and pick out some stuff and circle it, then report on it. I watched them lots of times. Phil was an analyst right? That's an AFSC of 202x0.
Sometimes they would have a bunch of 202's standing behind us at our positions. They were looking for a specific piece of information that might be passed by one of the mission targets.
I was once told that our "stuff" was so good at deciphering Rooskies codes, etc. that we could break their most difficult complex codes in 24 hours. Nowadays it would probably take about five minutes, with computers.
Us guys at Chicksands woke up Lyndon B. Johnson a couple of times. I used to be a real liberal when it came to the Kennedy's. I loved Bobby. I actually felt a loss when he got his head blown off by Sirhan.
Strange coincidence about him and his brother JFK; in 1963 when he was assassinated in Dallas . . . I was in a library at U of Toledo and came out to go to marching band practice about 3:30 pm. Place was a mad house. Went up to the Student Union and watched Walter Cronkite dishing out all the bad news.
In 1968 I had just returned from the library on base at Ramasun where I had been catching up on some news from the state side newspapers like the NY Times and LA Times, etc., I was in the barracks ten minutes when this guy came walking through and said they had shot Kennedy. I told him, hey numb nuts, he died in 63, where you been? He told me they had shot him in LA at a rally in a hotel. Next day he died.
I was really upset . . . until years later I found out what a crook he really was . . . and his brother Teddy is the worst one of the bunch. He gets away with that shit . . . like manslaughter of Mary Jo Kopecchnie at Chappaquidick

because he is a Kennedy. I always refer to him as the only murderer in the US Senate. If Kennedy endorses it, it must be bad for the country. His old man, old Joe Kennedy was a bootlegger and made millions during Prohibition. Invested in it and became a multi millionaire. Asshole!

I liked JFK until I read that he had been cheatin' on Jackie and doinking Marilyn Monroe too. When Joe Dimaggio died they quoted him as saying he was glad that Bobby had been assassinated. He said they screwed up Marilyn something awful . . . he hated them too . . . and a great baseball hero like Joe D . . . if he hates something it must be wrong.

I admired what you have said about Phil. He did indeed do his duty for his country and did it with honor and for them to screw him over so badly is reprehensible. But that's the way the military is. They only have a conscience when the American public blows a gasket. Ask Mrs. Rose Bucher . . . her husband Lt. Commander Lloyd M. Bucher and his crew were held for a year in captivity in N. Korea after their ship the USS Pueblo was hijacked on the high seas. She wrote letters, visited Congressmen and finally got in to see LBJ himself. She virtually got the entire crew released less one crew member who was killed in the hijacking, Seaman Duane Hodges, by her tireless actions. The Pueblo if you will remember, was a floating "collection vessel." They were sampling and collecting anything the N. Koreans sent including radar paintings and morse and non-morse communications, and other ELINT and COMMINT (source was a classified briefing at Goodfellow AFB in 1968). Believe me . . . Phil was good . . . or they wouldn't have allowed him to re-enlist so many times . . . they needed him.

Like I said, stay away from Teddy if you meet him. And don't get into a car with him.

I think the last few years of my life have been the happiest. The reunion in England two years ago . . . meeting you, and our many discussions and e-mails, etc. I wish I had a sister like you. Believe me, I think you and I are fighters, and our foe has been 'dysfunctionalism.' Dysfunctional families especially. Best advice I ever got about how to handle feuding family members is to just tell them to "go to Hell!" Can't always do that. It's not always wise, but it certainly reflects my feelings about a lot of them. So I just have very little to do with most of my family, cousins, etc. I am cordial, usually meeting at a funeral, sad huh? I feel more love for kids I went to high school with than my own family. I guess kids you grew up with accepted you with unconditional love so to speak. Lots of kids I know, and I still see from time to time, felt that way. They could have robbed a bank or been married

six times and have a dozen illegitimate kids and I'd still care about them. Life is goofy sometimes, but that's what makes it so beautiful.
Hey, take care of the back, kid. Hope the MD's can help you with some meds. You got a ton of stuff to publish. If you don't get better I'll come out there to where you live and surprise ya, and rattle your cage . . . me, and your mate, Strider, will straighten you around to the right way.
Oh, by the way, I have NEVER peed on anyone's grave. I have heard that so much in life though, "I'll pee on your grave when you're dead." Usually it's the other way around, some one else pees on yours . . . aaahhh . . . ain't life gooooddddd? Yeah, a laugh a minute, depending upon how you look at it.
Cheers, and Sawadee Krup
Vince

I asked an ex-USAFSS fellow what it was like while serving and doing his job as a "ditty bopper" during the cold war. Here are two stories, just about the same, as he updated one, and I thought both were good, so I have placed them together for this book. T.S.[The Editor]

FROM MY DAYS AT CHICKSANDS
By Vince Wuwert

Trish,

Here goes . . . I'll see if I can remember how I had to "service" my traffic, that means, ID all the stuff pertinent to an intercepted message from my days at Chicksands with the 6950th.

RTAY00106/RBOH DE UPU//8095M/0645Z/WD

Think I have it all correct, now that I read it - shit - some of this shit just never leaves me. Sometimes when I am alone and it's really quiet, I swear, I can hear a transmitter, and one of those Rooskies calling up RBOH. RBOH was the call sign of an outstation - think it was Uralask, south and east of Moscow a few hundred k's.

RBOH had a transmitter that made it sound like it was transmitting in a bucket of water - sort of a burbling bubbly sound - it's hard to describe, but we knew him when we heard him. It was definitely from net RTAY00106. Bill Person makes reference to these type of notations in his book titled: CRITIC MAKERS.

QRU BT QRU BT SK EE   //1743Z
                        //wd

ANOTHER VERSION OF "MY DAYS AT CHICKSANDS"
By Vince Wuwert

What happened to all those dits and dahs that those Rooskie operators in Mocbaw sent to my ears? Are they still embedded in my memory some place? Sometimes, when I am alone, and it's quiet, I can hear them - the tone, the dits and dahs - the static - the background cursing of airmen who are "working a freq" and trying to snatch a bit of good shit to report to guys like your Phil, the Analyst. [The Editor's brother.]

At times, thirty-five years later, I yearn to hear it all again and realize I was protecting America by stealing their signals. I grew up in those days. I've never forgotten. I've tried. It never goes away. We made history! But no one cared. You care. So, don't quit. Phil will honor your life in a very special way if you continue. Keep it up. You are one cool lady.

I can almost feel the cool droplets of fog at Chicksands (England); only being able to see two feet in front of myself; listening for voices of men going to the mess hall from their operations building - so dark - like being inside an ice cube. It was zero visibility wherever you looked. Oh, how I loved it. I loved it more than life itself.

We made history. Please record it for us and tell the world about us by writing about it.

Vince Wuwert, USAFSS SGT. (Ret.)

This is an e-mail to the [Editor] early on, about SSGT Phil Noland, Editor's brother.

WUWERT RE: PHIL, 20270
By Vince Wuwert

Subj: Re: (no subject)
Date: 12/14/02 3:12:18 PM Pacific Standard Time
From   VAWuwert
To: Ida . . .

Trish,

I will advise my buddy about the book you just mentioned. The 20270 means, as far as I can remember, "202" = analyst career category, "7" is level of training and proficiency. He was a "7" level and was probably at that time a TSGT? Perhaps? and I don't know what the "0" means . . . but I think it denotes a specific type of analysis . . . like COMINT analysis or perhaps "ELINT" . . . NOT SURE. I was a ditty bopper remember. I copied the code and your brother deciphered a lot of it, depending upon what the "traffic" was . . . you are correct with the GS-15 stuff . . . perhaps he was noted at that level for a particular mission he was doing . . . (mission=job) special sort of duty that may or may not have been done "on station" at the 6901st. Will advise my buddy also that "ferret missions" were run out of 6901st in Germany. Dang . . . you are one heck of a research lady . . . keep up the good work.
Vince

The GS-15 is incorrect; it is SO G-15/6901stSCG/1963, which I was later informed by the FOIA is a Good Conduct Medal with two bronze loops. Unusual for anyone at the 6901st to receive any recognition.

RAMASUN STATION, THAILAND
By Vince Wuwert

Subj: Re: (no subject)
Date: 12/14/02 4:16:46 PM Pacific Standard Time
From: VAWuwert
To: IdaReedBlanford

When I was at Ramasun Station, they had a fixed location . . . us at Ramasun . . . in which it was called "Homespun" meaning you were to search a frequency spectrum and try to identify unknown targets, "Transmitters," not previously ID'd. Trouble was, we had a narrow Azimuth to cover, and our frequencies were often clogged with 'printer shit' and other ELINT signals not decipherable by manual morse ops. Hated it, worst waste of time; more AF make-work shit.
Vince
PS met Larry Tart at Chicksands at the reunion in 2000. Fascinating guy. Carries a piece of a C-130 USAFS aircraft, shot down over Russia. Everyone perished. Of course, the Russian sons of bitches denied any knowledge, until we got permission to go in and pick up the pieces. He kept one.
Vince

Larry Tart wrote a book about the shoot down of the above mentioned aircraft. It is excellent and if you haven't read it, go to your local bookstore and it will be there: It is entitled: THE PRICE OF VIGILANCE. You'll never forget it, once you read it. (The Editor).

A PART OF AN E-MAIL FROM VAWUWERT, ABOUT ENGLAND.
By Vince Wuwert

When I was stationed in England, I bought a bicycle. Narrow wheels, narrow handle bars, three speed, and I just got on it one lovely summer day and rode out the upper gate of Chicksands. I must have ridden about five miles. I took pictures of some old churches, and a lot of "thatch roofed" homes.

Actually, the picture from Chicksands of the Priory isn't very good. I have one that is bigger than an 8 ½ by 11 full color. I purchased it at the reunion. It's a side view, which overlooks the lawn tennis area of the grounds.

In London and in Cambridge I couldn't keep myself from just staring at those old buildings and churches - especially Cambridge. It was history I was observing. History that my senior English class teacher talked about and now I was standing before it.

Mind the lorry,

Vince

THANK YOU FOR YOUR SERVICE
By Vince Wuwert

Subj: Re: Hi Vince, it's Trish
Date: 12/31/02 3:20:45 AM Pacific Standard Time
From: VAWuwert . . .
To: IdaReedBlanford . . .

Trish,
Please forgive me if I sounded a bit apprehensive when you stated you were coming to interview me. Come any time. I'm privileged to meet you and will answer "any" questions you may have.
More later.
Happy New Year. I hope it's better than 2002 was for you. And on behalf of all the guys from Security Service, we thank you for your service to our country on our behalf.

Sgt. Vince Wuwert   Veteran   AF 15740029

Actually, the pleasure is all mine - doing "These Guys" has been a most rewarding, edifying experience that I know God has led me to do. The answers to my questions and the stories submitted are wondrous and I will never forget you guys for helping me out as much as you have. [The Editor].

This book is YOUR book, guys.

Some information about my brother's AFSC 20270, and information on the SR-71.

Subj: FW: Re: A Little Help
Date: 12/15/02 4:10:07 PM Pacific Standard Time
From:
To: VAWuwert

Vince,
Hope the message below helps your friend.

The AFSC 20270 is what I was.

202=Communications Analyst
   7=skill level (you had 3 level, 5 level, 7 level, and 9 level)
    0=additional shred out of AFSC (in this case - nothing)
George.

Original Message
Sent 12/15/2002 5:06:21 PM
Subj: Re: A little help

Thanks, Dick.
Think that should suffice, and no beans were spilled.
I sort of suspected that's what it was, but never really got involved
in that aspect of the work.

George

Original Message
Sent 12/15/2002 f:18:21 PM
Subject: Re: A little help

George,
Ferret missions were normally run by allies. They were sent into the sensitive area to elicit some form of reaction. They normally flew routes which would, by their nature provoke the opposition to do something like turn on a particular piece of equipment. Our job (ground site and airborne when we

were flying at the same time) was to provide our own special brand of oversight and protection.

Dick

Subj: Fwd: FW: Re: A Little Help
Date: 12/15/02 6:08:44 PM Pacific Standard Time
From: VAWuwert
To: IdaReedBlanford

Trish,
The last paragraph mimicks your information per Larry Tarts book. When I was in Thailand, in 68&69, the same type of operation was done via usage of the SR-71. And monitored by "ground" ops. It would incur (violate is a better word) the Chink airspace, and the chinks would "turn on" certain equipment. Of course they would want their HQ's to know what they were "tracking," so they manual morsed all of it back to net control. And of course, yours truly and all his buddies were "listening" actively on those dates that we had a 'SENIOR CROWN' in the area. The "freq's" lit up like a Christmas tree. Only real excitement we would have other than the attack in July of 1968 on the air base in Udorn.

I have pictures of an actual SR-71 that flew in that area of the world during the time I was in USAFSS and copying my missions at Ramasun station. We got some very good shit on the enemy. Very good. Trust me. But like I have always held . . . it was our duty. We did it because we were trained. Never dreamed it would be of such major intelligence importance, but it was.

By the by . . . I am now a member of a rather exclusive veterans organization. The TLC-Brotherhood. The only qualification is that you served on active duty in Thailand, Laos, or Cambodia. I qualify. Got all my membership stuff the other day including a neat patch. Gotta find a location on my Veetnam Vets Camo uniform.
God love ya and Strider, to! (Editor's Note: Strider is aka for my husband, Bob).
My last Christmas with the post office. Yaaaahooooooo!
Sgt. Vince Wuwert

Subj: Cold War
Date: 3/19/03 9:34:01 Pacific Standard Time
From: VAWuwert
To: IdaReedBlanford

Dear Trish,
Thanks for the remarks about the Cold War medal. You earned it. You earned it because the support from the depth of your heart has been with all of us, men and women, all branches all around the world who served under the constant threat of a Soviet assault.
Now, we are facing a new type of enemy. One who will kill in the name of Allah, and other strange names for God.
When I was a teenager . . . I used to laugh at guys in the military. I was ignorant. Young. Arrogant. No more do I begrudge military people who sacrifice so many miles from home, and sacrifices which might take their lives. They are heroes to me. And you know how I love to march with heroes.
I am so fortunate. I've grown up and served the greatest nation on the face of the Earth, and enjoyed its liberty. I helped preserve that liberty in a small way. I sacrificed too. And so have you. Some times I think you have forfeited unwillingly so much for the sake of displaying your writing talents. But it takes "guts." And guts are what count now days, and you have an ample supply of character too. That's all that is needed.
I want to encourage you again, to keep up the good work. It will pay off some day.
Some times I sit back and day dream. Oh, how I wish I could live it all again . . . my youth, my military service. But as the old TV commercial used to expound, "You only go around once in life." I have no regrets. Save for two. Marrying Satan's sister the first time, and ever returning to Toledo. But you make the best of the time and the situations that you encounter.
God Bless the troops . . . from President Bush on down. They will do an honorable job of kicking the shit out of Iraq's tyrants. If we can bring liberty to Iraq, then I am all for it. Liberty . . . isn't that what Phil [Editor's brother] was also trying to defend those many years? I think he would say that it's a job that has to be done.
He rests from his labors and disappointments of life now; beneath American soil, beside American military men and women, a fitting place to be for an

eternity; beside brother military troops. Rank means nothing when you are dead, but the service he rendered will always be remembered.
We'll get Bin Laden, and it will be like George W. Bush said, "Dead or Alive" ... preferably dead.
Cheers kid,
Stuff on the way to your house soon.
Vince

Vince had sent me a Cole War Victory Commemorative Medal, Ribbon and Pin as a gift. I keep it on my desk, not ever very far away from me, as a reminder of what you guys deserve, a REAL medal for having fought the Cold War, and doing such a splendid job, keeping America safe.

Subj: Re: THESE GUYS - MAO'S WORDS
Date: 8/11/03 3:36:46 PM Pacific Daylight Time
From: VAWuwert
To: IdaReedBlanford

Trish,

ADP - AERODROME TRAFFIC (Copied that stuff at Chicksands.) Ever hear of Aeroflot Airlines? The Rooskies kept excellent records. They recorded back to Mockba all the landings and take offs throughout the country. If they went to war then Aeroflot was automatically a part of the Rooskie Air Force. Get my drift? We needed to keep an eye on that and the Rooskies told us everything. MW - "Mao's Word" used to have our slant eyed Chinks send that. They used to read Mao's little red book while they weren't sending traffic (this was back in the late 60s during the Great Leap forward and the Cultural Revolution . . . both total failures) . . . and they liked it so much they exchanged all those brilliant phrases between stations. One would send . . . MW . . . 345 (meaning a page and a line or paragraph.)
BT - end of transmission.
SK EE - Keying by a target operator, means end of transmission, signing off, all that sort of stuff.
A guy I knew when I was in Thailand who was a "voice intercept op" specialized in Chinese. One time he said he was recording a transmission and it was of an old man, passing traffic, and he always ended each transmission with "Chairman Mao will live ten thousand times ten thousand years." One time he said the old man messed up. He ended his transmission with "chairman Mao will live a thousand years." He said he never heard the guy again.
Any more questions?
Vincenzo

IF YOU HAVE ANY QUESTIONS
By Vince Wuwert

Subj: Re: THESE GUYS
Date: 8/11/03 3:55:24 PM Pacific Daylight Time
From: VAWuwert
To: IdaReedBlanford

Trish,

No kiddin,' if you have any questions, just ask.
Before I die, I'm going to put down on paper just exactly what I did in the AF for 3 years six months and four days. And why I had a Top Secret Clearance.
One time I got to talking, some what in depth, with my older brother . . . about radios . . . and antennas, like we used at Chicksands and in the Far East at Thailand. He had the blankest look on his face when I tried to explain what I did, and this is a very intelligent man who thinks his freedoms come from the US Congress, and not preserved by American fighting men and women. He's a liberal Democrat. Get the picture?
This is the same brother who has not once had the decency to tell a veteran of any war, let alone his own brother, ME, thanks for serving our nation. I guess he got pissed off at me when I told him that the guy who was leading the Massacre at Mai Lai, Lt. Calley, remember him?, he said the guy should be shot by firing squad, and I told him the guy should get the Congressional Medal of Honor, for eliminating a big bunch of potential GI killers. During that war, kids would often toss a grenade at a passing convoy of trucks, and women were the worst. The VC used all sorts of pathetic ways to kill us.
By the way, speaking of killing children, how did you like how the 101st Airborne units that killed Quasay and Ursay Hussein? Both of them had multiple bullet wounds, and one had a head shot, which our forces believed was self inflicted. Real heroes weren't they? Responsible for hundreds of Iraqi citizens being slaughtered for no reason; both were pathetic sociopathic wretches, killed without conscience, and then preached, "May Allah be praised by these deaths" - sickening bastards - I hope we get the old man and hang him by his balls in the middle of Baghdad and let the Iraqi citizens see their hero, kind of like Mussolini and his whore at the end of WWII. The Italians shot them, then hung them from a light pole near a petrol station.

Oh, well, I suppose I have made you so sick you won't be able to eat dinner in a couple of hours, right?
Keep in touch, kid,
Vince

Vince did not make me sick. I kind of knew all these things, and the things to come from THESE GUYS who were giving me all they could possibly give . . . in the only way they could give it. (The Editor)

These Guys

Subj: Re: USAF Security Service - Plaine de Jars Area
Date: 9/12/03 12:15:27 AM Eastern Daylight Time
From: IdaReedBlanford
To: VAWuwert

Yes, he, Bill Person, crashed in a T-28 in the Plaine de Jars area, I believe. I'm not looking at notes. I'd have to look up date - 1965 maybe.

Plain of Jars . . . in Laos . . . yeah I recall seeing it notated on a huge map on a wall in the compound at Ramasun Station in Thailand. Not a good place to crash. God bless him . . . got out alive.

One time some guy wrote some really cute shit on a map. (Excuse my French). Those maps were floor to ceiling covered with clear Plexi glass so we could make "special notations and plots," get my drift? Well one time, some guy wrote, Charlie Chink, and had an arrow pointed towards the area on the map of SE China, then a bit lower was "Luke the Gook" and an arrow pointing to Hanoi and down lower was "slimey slope" with an arrow pointing into the heart of Thailand and then some one had printed, "Fuck them all." All this on a highly classified map. No one ever erased it. It was an unspoken morale booster.

The guys in the Army section at Ramasun used to copy Laotian guerillas Morse Code x-missions as well as Laotian voice transmissions both military and civilian. The Lao's would oft times use a field hand crank generator to service enough electrical juice to make a transmission, or a small transmitter powered by flash light batteries. Easy to stow. Would cover a distance of perhaps five miles at most, but us Americans had the electronic equipment to "listen" to those transmissions from a hundred miles away. We were gooooooood!

Wish you the best as you encounter the guy who knew Phil. Hope he opens up. You know how to push the right buttons with people.

Got errands to run. Still mourning the passing of Johnny Cash, but us old ditty boppers don't live forever!

Vince

Subj: Gen. Custer
Date: 9/12/03 6:42:29 AM Pacific Daylight Time
From: VAWuwert
To: IdaReedBlanford

During the Monroe County Fair parade in 2002 my guys from Vietnam Veterans #142 marched down main street Monroe. When we got to the corner upon which Gen. Custer stands astride his horse we did our "column left" and came to a halt. Every one did a left face, and we rendered "Present Arms" to Gen. Custer.

Afterwards, I asked why we had done that. No answer. I then made the mistake of saying, "Why should we be doing a present arms to a guy who lost his last battle?" A couple of guys chuckled but I don't think I made any friends amongst US Army veterans.

Like I said, no air cover. He would have won if the Wright brothers could have advised him.

Vince

Here one can see the funny side of Vince Wuwert! I can picture him now, his fat ol' stogie in his mouth, ditty bopping and thinking up this kind of stuff! Or, did it just come out of his mouth, naturally.

These Guys

An e-mail from me to Vince and Vince's answer. Vince has become a very good buddy to me and he's a good ol' Sarge who served his country well.

Subj: (no subject)
Date: 12/22/2003 4:44:52 AM Pacific Standard Time
From: VAWuwert
To: IdaReedBlanford

Trish: You learned plenty while there and you DID plenty while you were there - don't forget that, my dear Vince.

Vince: Actually, I thought my time with USAF in England was a waste of my life, until I encountered you.
I had no idea so many former USAF-SS people were writing books about their experiences. Believe me, going to work at midnight, and listening to static and ditty dits, for 8 hours or trying to find "Ivan's nephew" whom we hadn't heard in weeks, can be a pain. A professional ditty bopper will find him eventually. Electronic equipment helps. Antennas - Receivers. Good maintenance.
I never gave a thought to the importance of my work. We just did it. I can still hear the voices of guys copying long range bombers going over the North pole. They had a mode of panic in their voices. They would yell at their receivers as if "Ivan" could answer their insults and barbs.
The actions of NCO's was professional, directing operators, copying code. Discipline was paramount. If you failed to pick up a signal then you might lose the target. We prevailed in our coverage, and that is one of the reasons the Cold War remained cold.
Odd, I'd leave the area to walk down the hill to the mess hall for AM chow after a session like that, and observe the serenity of the surrounding rolling hills of Bedfordshire and see the mist in the trees and along the ground. It was so peaceful. No one ever knew there was such panic inside the building I had just left. But better to be vigilant and prepared and to know your enemies' next move in advance. So I guess my service was worthwhile.
On another note; my older brother gave me three volumes of a work written by some guy about the History of the British Empire. In the text which covers 1776-2000, there is mention of WWII, but no mention of Bletchley Park, Chicksands or any other intercept sites. Or Enigma codes, or any reference what so ever in the history. Those working in Secret during the war

helped for the most part to save their arses . . . and not even so much as a paragraph in the history books. Some times I hate being a veteran. If we don't write about ourselves, no one else does.

Vince

SECURITY BREACH AT CHICKSANDS
By Vince Wuwert

Subj: Re: (no subject)
Date: 1/4/2004 7:00:34 PM Pacific Standard Time
From: IdaReedBlanford
To: VAWuwert

In a message dated 1/4/2004 5:14:10 PM Pacific Standard Time, VAWuwert writes:

Did I ever tell you of the "security breach at Chicksands?" Happened about 1967. Some new guy was doing "guard duty" inside the compound. There were places beyond the guard shack where Red Badge (no security clearance) people could go but only if escorted and in some cases blindfolded.
Well these Blokes tell the young airman that they need to go to the power generator at the rear of the building. You're supposed to take them outside . . . and walk around the building. He didn't. He just said, "Oh we can take a short cut through the building." He walked three Blokes down the ramp past highly classified maps, and Lord only knows how much equipment they saw . . . the place went bananas. The SP's collared him and all the Blokes pronto. The Blokes were put into seclusion/isolation inside the building under an armed guard for hours until a guy from British Intelligence service from Whitehall (London) could come up and interview them. Debrief them so to speak . . . and then have them sign a security oath never to disclose what they had seen; the airman? Never saw or heard about him after that; like he vanished into thin air.
The usual procedure is to remove them from the Security Service . . . jail them . . . and charge them with a low level espionage violation. And then have the kid plead guilty and then dishonorably discharge him. All because he wanted to save a few minutes for the Blokes and just didn't think.
Another time, some guys were messing around in ops, and a guy took a rubber stamp that read Secret (Codeword) and stamped his fatigue shirt on the back. He had to leave ops out of uniform, no fatigue shirt. It ended up in the incinerator.

Sawadee Krup,
Vince

Vince, your third graph here, sounds like what "they" tried on my brother, but our mother caught them at it and solved everything. Thank God! T.S.

SURMISES ABOUT PHIL
By Vince Wuwert

This is an e-mail about Vince's suppositions about my brother, Phil.

Subj: Phil Noland
Date: 1/29/2004 2:39:18 AM Pacific Standard Time
From: VAWuwert
To: IdaReedBlanford

Trish,
If Phil was in San Angelo, he was at Goodfellow AFB. It had a Security Service unit there at one time. It was the training base for 292x2s (non-morse intercept ops. They intercepted non-morse signals, translated via HF and VHF waves) and also it had a 202 - analysts school. Probably other units also, related to the mission of Security Service that I didn't know about.
I was there in 1968 as part of the two T program. You did two tours overseas, with one being a long tour (more than eighteen months) and the second "tour" was a year. I served twenty-two months at Chicksands then went to Goodfellow for a seminar, school, and military bearing instructions. Far as I am concerned it was a waste of money, but it was the first time since basic training that I was treated decently by NCOs. It was nice to be told you were the "cream of the crop" in Security Service as operators.
It was a two week TDY thing. We had a stand by inspection the second day we were there . . . (Inspection was on a Saturday morning and you were free until Monday morning) . . . The stand-by was a joke too. You stood by your bunk in the squad bay, all neat and spit and polished and the NCO walked through and never spoke to anyone and never looked at anything, and then got to the end of the room and said we were dismissed - easiest inspection I ever encountered, and the rest of the two weeks was classes until 1600 hrs. The rest of the time was ours.
We got a briefing from Brig. General Stapleton. (I recall seeing him at Chicksands in 1967. He was a full bird colonel then and had an aide who was a captain. He had been nominated for his first star at that time, and eventually retired as a two star general). Anyway, I recall them sealing off the room. And about thirty guys sat back, and this guy takes off his coat and tosses it aside and sits on the desk and says, "Now tell me what it was like at

your last base," eventually guys started talking about missions, and the way they were treated by NCOs and Officers, etc. I told him he could take the Sq. C.O. a Major McKenzie and fire him because he was a useless chicken shit jerk. Stapleton made a note of it.

It was all very interesting. I recall going to a rodeo there, and also to paying a visit to a local "Shakey's Pizza parlor." A big deal for me then.

From about 30 guys in attendance in that class then, I don't think there were any re-enlistments. That's also the base where I "stole" the neatest ash tray. It was all glass. And in the bottom of it was the full color traditional Security Service Crest. Got it at the NCO club. Got it home and dropped it in the sink and it ended up in the trash.

San Angelo is out in the middle of nowhere. It was at one time during WWII a pilot school. The runways are still used and in 1968, they were used by student pilots at other bases in Texas. Texas used to be loaded with AFB and Army bases. LBJ got them situated there when he was in Congress.

Gulfport Mississippi was interesting. I used to hop a bus in Biloxi and go over to the movie theater there. As I recall it was just off highway #90 in Gulfport and showed first run films in a very nice theater. I know there is a naval station there, but am unaware there might be anything connected to USAF security service there. They had a couple nice beaches there, but I think the beaches are now located about a half mile inland after several hurricanes have hit there. Same way in Biloxi.

My first trip "downtown" in Biloxi was interesting. First time I had ever seen blue-green water (Gulf of Mexico) and as I rode in a bus along the beach on #90, I saw the bow section of a freight type ship on the side of the road. It had washed ashore during one of the hurricanes in the late 50s so they just chopped it up a bit and converted it to a restaurant.

Only hotel on the beach side of the road that I can recall was a Holiday Inn. That's all changed now.

I once heard a story about the son of the famous news reporter . . . Walter Winchell . . . his son was stationed at Keesler during the War, and died from food poisoning. The food was ingested on the base. If you could have seen how the food was prepared, like I did on KP for a week in Nov. of 65, you'd understand.

I would love to see all of the paper work that you have from the DoD about Phil . . . but you probably know more about details than I do. I think I told you, the only thing I got back from the FOIA people concerning my military record was a list of all the units I was in, nothing was said about the nature of my training, other than the school squadron (3411th). Keesler AFB was a hard time for me, and a lot of guys; shitty town, but New Orleans was only 50 miles West. I never got a leave until I got orders for England. I'd been gone from Toledo from Sept. of 65 until March of 66. I saw a photo of myself taken in my old house where I grew up. I looked so young and THIN. None of my civilian clothes fit me after basic and tech school, so I spent a lot of time in uniform. I wore fatigues at home.

Somewhere in my piles of junk, I have a lot of pictures, mostly black and whites, of the base and a few guys I knew then. One guy I met in basic was from Chillicothe Ohio, down by the Ohio River. We hit it off pretty nicely and did a lot of things together when we were off duty. He was like me, a nice guy, wasn't a womanizer, but he drank too much. It got him into a bit of trouble. Last I heard from him again, he was going to San Angelo, for non-morse training. I got to Chicksands and I heard from him again, he said he had gotten orders to come to the 6950th and was anxious to see me. Never heard from him again. Tried to find him - he has a rather common name too - name was Jon E. Smith.

Another guy I met at Keesler was Ron Catania. He was a second generation Italian. He loved his pastas and pizza's. We used to hit an Italian place in Biloxi on Sat. nights. He went to Chicksands with me, but I rarely saw him. He was on a different flight and his work hours were just the opposite of mine. Nice guy. I've tried to find him too, but no dice. All I can remember is that he was from the Boston area.

It's now 0430. There is a fire in a house three doors down. Guy fell asleep on his couch while smoking. Lots of smoke and water damage. Guy had been in and out of jail. Didn't learn much, did he? But the fire trucks awoke us and I can't get back to sleep. So, I write.

There are more personal writings in this e-mail, which I, the editor, felt did not contribute to the situations at hand, so I deleted them, but remember them, and the man who wrote them to me, a very special person, who loved his AF and serving his country.

Subj: Re: Bill's Book
Date: 1/29/2004 8:13:23 PM Pacific Standard Time
From: IdaReedBlanford
To: VAWuwert

In a message dated 1/29/2004 3:19:35 PM Pacific Standard Time, VAWuwert writes:

His book says on the inside blank flap in the front "To Vincent Wuwert, my comrade in labyrinth, Bill Person." I had a hard time putting his book down. So much of what he has written is classified and I was shocked, but his intro was very good. I was also unaware of the Oath of Secrecy I swore at Keesler, just before my deployment overseas the first time was for 30 years, if that is true then I can say what I want. I'll try to query him some time about that exact issue.
He mentioned the deployment of Russian Long Range Bombers. We used to track them from Chicksands . . . they'd send back traffic to their bases in NW Russia, and we'd steal their plots and then plot them on a map. They were using the same code rotas they used in the early 50s . . . they never knew "we knew," that is, why I once wrote to you, we helped wake up the President of the United States, Santa Claus and all his elves on a couple of occasions . . . the planes were headed over the N pole and one time they hit the radar "trip wires" of the DEW line in northern Canada.
We'd be busy as hell at Chicksands, then you'd finish your tour and head for the barn (barracks or mess hall or airman's club for a drink) and the rest of the world never knew the danger.
I'm anxious to "dig into" Person's book. Did you have anything to do with the editing and re-writes, etc? [Editor's note: No, I did not.] It's as if he is bringing out stuff I knew was "on the table or the console" at the Sands. Very cool so far and I just started reading.
Sawadee Krup,
Cheerio, mind the gap and watch out for the lorry,
Vince

These Guys

RADIO CAROLINE
By Vince Wuwert

When I was stationed in England in the late 60's with the USAF Security Service I was a Morse Intercept Operator assigned to Baker Flight at the 6950th Security Group. My midnight shifts could be boring until the assigned targets went on duty around 0400 Zulu. A few of the guys would dial their receivers down to the Broadcast band to tune in a British Pirate radio station called Radio Caroline. It was a converted fishing trawler, anchored in the North Sea off the East Coast of England and their British disc jockeys played rock and roll. And Rock and roll trumps short wave static every time! This particular evening it was Oldies night. For nearly an hour I listened to Doo Wop, some Big Band pieces by the Glenn Miller Orchestra, and some Elvis Presley hits. They even sneaked in a couple of Beatles hits from a mere four years previous. It was glorious!

As the Oldies Hour wound down the announcer stated that the sign-off recording would be by the American vocalist Johnny Mathis, titled, MISTY. My high school sweetheart and I danced to that very recording by Mathis, at my Senior Prom. It was fabulous. The soft smooth hushed tones of Johnny Mathis expressing how "misty" he got "just holding her hand." As I felt myself drifting through nostalgia heaven, I thought about that young lady back in the states I had escorted to my prom. Holding her around the waist and gazing into her eyes as we danced. It made me feel as if she were next to me that very moment.

Suddenly, I felt a hand on my shoulder and moved to see the Five Chevrons of my TSGT section NCO. His voice had an air of anger as he said, "Airman Wuwert. You're not listening to the broadcast band are you?" I faced him and remarked, "Sergeant Romiti I wouldn't think of such a thing." He looked me in the eye and said, "Airman, if I catch you on the broadcast band, and not searching for your mission targets, I'll send you to meet with Senior Master Sergeant San Miguel, (the Mission Supervisor of Baker Flight), and I guarantee he will find extra duty for you to do after this shift, like clean the incinerator and latrines for five hours."

I responded in a military manner. "Yes Sarge. You can rest assured I wouldn't want to trouble the Mission Supervisor, nor clean latrines or the incinerator. No sir. Not me. You can depend upon me Sarge." As he walked away I slowly turned my Hammurlund SP-600 receiver knob slowly to my assigned range of frequencies. Then I let out a long, soft sigh of relief at not getting caught.

During the remaining four hours of the shift my mind drifted from time to time back to my high school prom in Toledo, Ohio in June of 1963, dancing and wondering whatever became of that young lady.

So wherever you are (name withheld), thanks for the memories. You were worth the trouble and the risk of getting caught.

Every effort has been made to find the men mentioned in this piece, to no avail, so I mention their names in fond memory. VAW

These Guys

KEESLER AFB
By Vince Wuwert

Trish,
In technical school, the 3380th Technical Training Center, at Keesler AFB, in Biloxi, MS, I was in the 3411th School squadron.
We had guys on my shift (noon until 6 p.m. school hours) who were being trained to repair computers of the day in the late 60's, aircraft radio repair (jets and other avionics used in Vietnam Fighter planes mostly, i.e. RF4's, F-102's, F105's, etc.) Ground radio repair, i.e. ditty bop short wave receivers like me, Air Craft ground control, operators, microwave transmission and reception repair.
It was a heck of a time. Each squadron at that base had about 200-250 guys spread over three shifts or school times, i.e., A shift 0600 to noon, B shift 1200-1800 and C shift from 1800 to 2400. Eventually they went to a twenty-four hour basis, with several schools doing instruction from midnight to 0600, big demand at that time was for ditty boppers, and radar and aircraft radio repair guys. Those latter two schools were very long, eighteen months, mine was only sixteen weeks.
In Ditty bop school they also taught Flare-9, which was the big elephant cage direction finding apparatus procedures, they taught you how to get a "fix" on a target, the new way, with the ultra sensitive antenna like the one they had at Chicksands, San Vito, Karamursel, Ramasun, Clark AB, and Misawa and at Elmendorf, Alaska.
But the basic need to graduate from any of the ditty bop schools was typing. I used to watch ops at Chicksands, who knew their mission targets so well that they could copy a target sending Morse code at about 10-15 groups per minute with the middle finger of one hand and smoke a cigarette with the other, and when the ash got a bit too long they'd flick it into the key bay, and the ashes would get on the keys and eventually get imbedded in the copy paper. One of our flight clerks, who handled the raw copy and had to separate six ply paper, with five sets of carbon paper to separate from the copy would tell us he could smell cigarettes on the paper. I used to tell him he was nuts, but he was telling me the truth.
Sometimes I wake up in the middle of the night, 0200 or so, and I can hear a Russian sending a call sign . . . U U F UUF UUF DE U R G GA IMI . . . then I wake up and realize it's just a nightmare. I can still hear the clatter of typewriters and at times I can hear one of our NCO's at Chicksands typing

away behind me across an aisle, where the guys had the long range Russian Bomber missions, and those bombers would be headed toward the N. Pole and going over "the top" to trip the D.E.W. line radar, and we had them about fifty miles out from their bases. They told us everything; their altitude; range from base; radio freqs, but we never knew if they were just screwing with us or not, i.e., if they had nukes on board or what? And, I can hear the guys yelling out call signs and saying this, blankety blank, changed freqs., and call signs, but I know his transmitter. The guy's a jerk, real slow herky jerky code, and another guy would yell out a different freq. and say, "I got him, I got him," and then they'd ring up the DF section in ops and get fixes on them. We were all over those guys, and those weenies didn't know we were listening to everything.

I can still picture the Wing Commander, Colonel (full bird that is) Christy, standing in the ops room, reading the plexi glass map plots, wearing only his flight suit, his flight cap, and bedroom slippers, watching at 0300 the entire scenario, because they were headed towards the N. Pole. Once in awhile the old man (Colonel Christy) would actually come down and stand behind a lot of the ops and watch them copy it right off the line, live copy, guys would say, "Excuse me Colonel" and then push him aside as they moved to another position console to give verbal information to another op. It was exciting and scary and to think we did this, guys like Phil, too, we did this for you, and all Americans, while your were snug in your beds, resting yourselves for another hectic day of life, and not realizing the Rooskies are coming and maybe this time "it's the real thing."

Now you know why we were called "Silent Warriors."

Vince

These Guys

Here are two quotes sent to Vince Wuwert and in turn sent to me by e-mail re: Laos: quiet and Laos: AA flak.

LAOS: QUIET and LAOS: AA FLAK
By Vince Wuwert

Trish,
Here is the quote from my buddy who lives in New York State. He flew as crew, ditty bopper, on an EC-47 with Det. 3, 6994the Security Squadron.

"No, never had the pleasure of flying over the Royal Kingdom. Lee Heying, might have. And John O'Meara and I flew seven flights out of Pleliku. Pleiku had the Laos coverage. Also a mean area along the DMZ & slightly North of it. I flew one of those DMZ flights. You got double credit for those. Never brought my flight paperwork back to Tan San Nhout, with me. Lost credit for the whole seven flights. The night flights over Laos could be hairy. The gooks would drag an AA gun captured from the 'frogs' at Dien Bien phu, to the top of an 8,000 ft. mountain. Wait for slow birds like the C-47's and open up. I never experienced flak at night. But I was told that it was tough on the underwear."
Dusty Mosier, Det. 3 6994th Security Squadron Pleiku SVN 1967.

Vince

LAOS: AA FLAK

"Vince you can quote me . . . only if you use the derogatory term 'frogs.'"
You realize my information about where the AA guns came from was only hearsay from the boys who were PCS at Pleiku.
It's a shame Johnny O'Meara is gone. He was in a plane that got the ass-end of it shot, over Laos. He also told me stories of being able to read a newspaper from the light of the AA flak explosions. Each op on a two man radio flight that is . . . were seated by a window in the midsection of the plane. Of course once the planes were shot at all the outside/inside lights were extinguished. Hence anything outside really got your attention. Hopefully one of these reunions, crazy Lee Heying will attend and you will get some really good stories.

"Further, but not needed is a PS reference to his application to get employment at Air America at the Udorn RTAFB in Udorn. (Read Air America=CIA) I applied in early 1969 or late '68, don't recall . . . and I was rejected. I still have the rejection letter some place. I want to hang it on my wall if I ever get a house again . . . and can have an "office" area . . . it will look nice next to my two College Degrees and my case of my three military medals from the AF. . . ."

Vince

Subj: USS PUEBLO
Date: 1/30/2004 8:04:11 AM Pacific Standard Time
From: VAWuwert
To: IdaReedBlanford, jay-j@mindspring.com, gnrogers99@yahoo.com, dan1945us@yahoo.com

Dear Trish and Ray,

A significant day in history for anyone associated with the US Navy. Commander Lloyd M. Bucher passed away yesterday. Bucher, you might recall, was the commander of an AGER, a floating intelligence collection vessel, when it was hijacked upon the high seas 20 miles off shore from N. Korea in 1968.

He and his remaining crew suffered horribly at the hands of North Korea in a prison. Torture, beatings and malnutrition were suffered by all the crew.

My buddy from Chicksands, who served on Dog Flight as a "202" analyst, at the same time I was there back in the late 60s, now resides in retirement in his home town of Pueblo, Colorado. He told me about a reunion the survivors of USS Pueblo were having there and sent me a lot of information about it from his local newspaper. He also sent me their web site address.

The web site was quite interesting and eventually as I looked over its pages I saw an official USS PUEBLO patch that had been worn on the jackets of the men. I inquired to the webmaster and purchased a couple of them, authentic in every detail, after explaining to him that I too, was a member of the intelligence collection family and would be honored to have one of their patches for my personal collection. I requested two.

He acknowledged my request and sent me a hand written note that they would be on the way soon. I sent him the $10 fee he requested (they normally went for $15 each) and waited. About a month later I got a handwritten letter from Mrs. Rose Bucher, apologizing for the delay. I've kept it.

Oh yes, the USS PUEBLO patch quickly went into active service. It is sewn on one of the pockets of my Camo blouse of my Vietnam Veterans of America uniform. I've gotten a couple of inquiries from folks wondering why I am wearing it. Am I a former member of the crew? I simply explain that I wear it as a way to honor fellow intelligence collection/and crew members of the Pueblo, and also to remind people that the USS PUEBLO is STILL

a commissioned vessel of the US Navy and we demand its intact return. I'll keep that patch until I die.
"Eternal Father strong to save whose arms have quelled the boundless wave, o hear us when we call to thee for those in peril on the sea. . ."

Vince

Subj: USS PUEBLO II
Date: 1/30/2004 8:15:52 AM Pacific Standard Time
From: VAWuwert
To: IdaReedBlanford

Dear Trish,

Don't recall if I have mentioned this to you before, about the Pueblo.
It was January of 1968 and I had a day off from my shift schedule at Chicksands and decided to go to London for the day. There was snow on the ground and it was quite cold.
I remember arriving at the train station in Bedford and seeing the headline on a newspaper stand near the platform gate. I bought a copy of the London paper, and the headline read, US Spy Ship Captured by N. Korea. I was shocked! The cold weather made me feel even colder as I sat in a compartment and read every word.
Lots of military guys remember where they were when Kennedy died, and all that sort of stuff, but I recall where I was when it was made public that the Pueblo had been captured. I have been curious about it ever since.
The story I wrote to you earlier about contact with Mrs. Bucher is true. I still have the letter somewhere. I'll have to send her a note of sympathy. I'm sure she would appreciate some kind words from a fellow intelligence collection family member.
As far as I am concerned, Lloyd M. Bucher should have gotten the Congressional Medal of Honor. He led his men in a manner consistent with the highest tradition of the US Navy, and it was far beyond the call of duty. His crew should have all been awarded the Navy Cross for their suffering in captivity.
And I hope all those Admirals who wanted to Court Martial him for losing his ship rot in hell.
God is love,
Vince

Amen to that, Vince. [The Editor]

HONORABLE SERVICEMEN
By Vince Wuwert

Subj: (no subject)
Date: 1/30/2004 9:51:03 AM Pacific Standard Time
From: VAWuwert
To: IdaReedBlanford

Dear Trish,

Today is January 30th of 2004. I observe my final day as an employee of the US Postal service. When I started active service in July of 1969, Richard Nixon was President of the USA. As I finish, the President of the USA is GW Bush, a Republican also. And, as in 1969, our nation is at war, and daily counting its war dead. And as in 1969, I am saddened to learn of the losses of American troops in both Vietnam and in Iraq.
As President Kennedy once said, "The price of freedom is high, but Americans have always paid it."
I am honored to say that I have served to preserve freedom but am saddened that my brother and sisters in arms have lost their lives.
Today, January 30th of 2004, twenty-three stand as a nation, as the most powerful nation on the face of the Earth. We have the highest standard of living, and the strongest defense in the history of mankind to defend it.
We have not, as a nation, always been right, but we have always and will always, be the nation that loves freedom and is openly and intensely in love with it. It is freedom that brought about the greatest inventions in the history of mankind, like flight, the electric light bulb, and space flight to name a few. Along the way we have lost brothers and sisters. I recall the shock of being made aware that friends of mine had been lost in war. But this nation is the offspring of war. If it hadn't been for the Minute Men throughout the Revolutionary War, we would still be eating "steak and kidney pies" and we would be bearing allegiance to King George III.
Too often Americans see July 4th as a day of fun and frivolity. To me it brings memories of my childhood friends who served in the Cold War and in Vietnam. In a special way I love them dearly. Perhaps when all of time is over and my work on Earth is done and the Roll is called up yonder, I'll be reunited with them.
To those of you who think your time on Earth has been useless, it hasn't.

I now light up the best of Cuban Cigars . . . and enjoy my favorite adult beverage . . . and thank God almighty for freedom, America, and Seagram's 7.
God Bless America. And may God Bless all who have served our nation with HONOR!
Vince

Vince Wuwert was and still is an honorable serviceman to his country.

Subj: When the roll is called up Yonder I'll be there
Date: 1/30/2004 9:58:04 AM Pacific Standard Time
From: VAWuwert
To: IdaReedBlanford

Trish,
Some sad and tearful remembrances.
When the Roll is called up Yonder is an old Gospel Hymn. When they do my funeral, if anyone is in attendance, I want them to play that old hymn.
I am sad this final day of my USPS career. But yet happy. I have seen the best of both worlds. The good and the bad.
But I only need to focus upon myself. I have "Miles to go before I sleep, miles to go . . ." wrote Mr. Frost.
I thank you for your friendship and your encouragement. You have been a charming friend. I appreciate beyond words . . . your words . . . and your life. . . .
May as the ditty boppers of my Chinese ditty bopper enemy said in 1968 . . . "May you live ten thousand times ten thousand years . . ."
God love ya Trish. Thanks so much and I look forward to reading your brilliant works.

I love ya kid. Good luck to you. And God love ya in a very special way!!!
Sawadee Krup,
Vince

THE RUSSIANS ARE COMING
By Vince Wuwert

My friend, George Williams from Pueblo, Colorado sent me via the Internet a video of the Russian Long Range Bomber TU-95. It was fascinating. These are the type bombers whose manual Morse transmissions we used to copy when I was in operations at Chicksands back in the late 60's.

The video was taken from inside one of the aircraft (which the author was able to view). It showed the Crew Members dressed in their heavy flight suits, wearing their skull cap type head cover, with their "gomer" goggles atop their heads. Inside the aircraft was a scene reminiscent of a WWII B-17 bomber. The bulkheads were green, with bundles of wires attached, traversing forward and aft.

The navigator had few modern avionics and he was using a slide rule to make mathematical calculations relative to their air speed, wind drift, and fuel consumption, etc. The Radio operator wasn't much better equipped either. And I could have sworn I saw a Morse key attached to a shelf beneath an HF radio receiver. And this was filmed in the 80's.

The film showed pictures of the flight deck which looked more akin to a flying telephone booth; very cramped. The air to air refueling boom was located directly on the center line of the fuselage nose and a profile of the aircraft from the outside gave it a view that reminded me of a woodpecker - long narrow beak. During their mission they refueled from a large four engine jet cargo plane specially equipped to carry aviation fuel.

There were no audio comments made about the mission and the video eventually took a quick change towards ending when the two F-16's showed up on their port side, and cruised with them less than a quarter mile away. Guess it was time to go home when those aircraft showed up and most likely they had penetrated Canadian air space as the F-16's had the familiar RCAF markings on their fuselage.

As I watched the video I had thoughts of those few shifts I mentioned, at Chicksands, back in the late 60's. Sometimes on swing shifts and extending into a midnight shift the guys covering long range Russian bombers would be very busy. At that time the Russians still used manual Morse transmissions to communicate with their home bases as they tested the D.E.W. line "over the pole" by penetrating Canadian air space. The Morse intercept operators on Baker flight would be very involved tracking them. A call sign would come through the ether and guys knew the bad guys were on their way over the pole. I remember hearing an operator start whacking away at his typewriter and loudly responding to the Direction Finding operator at another location in the ops building. The operator would make sure he had the proper frequency for his long range mission network and then hit the call button. I'd hear all sorts of things being said. But watching them work was a treat for me. There were no holds barred. This was personal. And it was National security at stake; serious business.

"Yeah, this is Mike 19," the ditty bopper would say sternly. "I have a guy sending numbers at 8255 and he's my Baker four two beam. Can you hear him? That's him right there. He's next to that chirpy bastard sending letters. Yeah! There's that puke! All numbers. Call sign is Julie six niner tango. Got it? He's calling right now. Stay on his butt. Yeah . . . there he goes again. Can we get a fix?" Less than a minute later the operator would get a read out of the azimuth of the target from our unit and also from the unit at San Vito.

The operator would often have company too. When other aircraft were up and calling the home base, other ops would be listening and getting involved in the same "dance." Call signs, requests for DF read outs and the constant over the shoulder reaches by the analysts tearing off the six ply chatter roll sheets and scurrying into the Mission Supervisor's office to extract information from the copy and to plot the location of the aircraft on a huge map. Sometimes the analysts would put on a headset with a microphone mouth piece added to it and look right over the shoulder of a ditty bopper to relay the information to the tracking map in the Mission Supervisor's office.

When the tracking got too far over the pole for the other DF location to pick up a signal, then we'd rely on the encryption traffic the Long Range Bomber radio Operators would send back to base. In the event the bombers went past a certain point on our huge maps it resulted in a Critic report directly to a facility in the States. There were times, when the First Lieutenant, who was our Baker Flight Commander, would come out onto the floor and he too would be part of the "dance," by standing behind the operators and watch the traffic being intercepted. It was not unusual to see the base commander, show up, half asleep wearing his bedroom slippers, flight suit and sit inside the Mission Supervisor's office and watch the unfolding drama. Was this going to be the real thing? A real bombing run to attack the U.S.? Or was it just another game?

I can still hear the clatter and tapity tap of the typewriters as the Ditty boppers slammed their fingers into those keys . . . the guys yelling at each other as they garnered call signs and picked up frequency changes. If a guy lost a target transmission, by going QSY, then all heck broke loose. Guys were cursing some of the filthiest things imaginable. But to me it was okay, because it was aimed at the Cold War enemy. I once watched a guy go through half a pack of cigarettes during a four hour period copying those targets. And it was common to see NCO's sort of "conduct" the operational "dance," telling the guys to monitor a certain frequency range, checking back and forth with the analysts when a new call sign popped up. It was nerve wracking. And it's likely our unit woke up Lyndon B. Johnson with the intelligence we had recovered and indirectly the interceptor wings across northern Canada and in Alaska at Elmendorf, AFB, and of course dear old Santa and his elves!

I can still recall hearing one of the guys hacking ditties sent by these long range bombers and referring to them as bastards and yelling other choice obscenities at their R-390 HF receivers. No one ever ordered them to cease that type of language. The mission was more important. And as the shift wore on and we finally realized it was just a routine exercise by "Ivan the ass," and his flight of bombers, the cigarette smoke would clear and the clickety clack tap tap of the M-80 mills would become only an echo in my mind.

It was a time when heart beats accelerated but cool heads and professionalism amongst operators, analysts, and Mission commanders prevailed. I remember one guy finished off the transmission of a bomber radio op by calling him a bastard and yelling at his receiver and saying . . . "I had you by the balls the entire time you Rooskie son of a bitch!" And with that he pushed his chair back from his console and typewriter, threw his head set into his typewriter - it was over - and we won. Freedom was defended by the Silent Warriors once again.

Those were the days of long ago at Chicksands. And you never knew we were working. Hope you all slept well that night. Das v Danya Comrades.

REMEMBRANCES OF A DITTY BOPPER
By Vince Wuwert

The noises, conversations, anxious moments of concern in the operations room, while we tracked an F-105 straying over South China air space after visiting "down town" Hanoi; the joy of hearing the clickety clack of our Royal Standard typewriters, as we tracked the SR-71 over N. Vietnam, and Chinese air space; the stinky smell of cigarette smoke filling the room, while analysts walked by and pulled chatter roll six ply from our "mills." And I can still hear the profane, back hills southern twang voice of a ditty bopper from West Virginia, who kept screaming obscenities at his short wave receiver and referring to his "target" on frequency forty-three fifty-five kilo cycles as a slant eyed bastard. And then taking the cigar stub from the corner of his mouth and snuffing the ashes out across the face of the receiver. And then there was the guy who had a terrible case of intestinal flatulence. He silently and stealthily nauseated all six of us guys with his gas passing. But he never missed copying one single ditty.

Seeing small charts of information on our consoles, encased in plastic sleeves with notations made with grease pencils to change frequencies and call signs and the little notes at the bottom that would change from day to day that said, "Fuck this place. I'm short! Forty-six days left in the war!"

It was so long ago but yet at times it seems as if it was this morning.

I suppose I am holding back. But sometimes I just don't want to look back, but yet I knew full well years ago in Thailand what all our guys were doing was very important.

I think I'll take a break from my memory room and go into Udorn to the Chai Porn Hotel for a nice Kobe steak dinner, a couple of San Miguel beers and a good cigar. Then I can stroll down the main road and smell the stench of an open klong, hear the high pitched horns of the "Lao Lao buses," or find a nice open air restaurant and sit at a table alone while enjoying a nice strong sweet tea and watching the motorbikes, the samolars, and the Suzy Wong's go by. And perhaps try to put out of my mind the sound of an RF4-C jet taking off from Udorn heading north and east to visit the sons of Ho Chi Minh along the trail through Western Vietnam and Eastern Laos and hope that the driver and the REO in the rear seat return unscathed.

Sawadee Krup, Nippon

THE SECRET WAR WEAPON IN THAILAND
By Vince Wuwert

Ramasun Station: The Secret War weapon in Thailand.

When I arrived at Ramasun Station in late April of 1968 it was hot, dusty and dirty. Our first briefing upon landing at Udorn Royal Thai Air Base was from a Staff Sergeant who lectured us for one minute about VD growing on the walls of the strip clubs that were strung out for a mile down the road running from the south side of Udorn, to just north of the village of Kom Kring.

We lodged in a western style hotel overnight and the next day five other USAF airmen and myself were driven to Ramasun Station about eight miles south of Udorn Thani, and it was in the middle of rice paddies and carved out land for barracks buildings, antennas and support facilities.

My first time in operations at Ramasun, which was home to the Army Security Agency's 7th Radio Research Field Station and Detachment 4 of the 6922nd Security Group was a real let down. We had typewriters with keys that stuck, headsets that appeared to have been purchased at a garage sale. Outside, were the antenna's fixed towers, so many feet in the air, to sixty feet tall, from which were strung configurations of wires which made up long wire antennas, rhombics, sloping V's and some configurations that looked like a wall of diagonally placed wires strung between two large towers and making absolutely no sense as to how they were going to be used. They were unconventional looking to say the least and when the early morning dew on all the wires had the sun shine on them they appeared to be apparatuses from outer space.

Inside the ops building rooms, the walls contained Plexiglas covered maps all of South East Asia, including Thailand, Cambodia, Laos, North and South Vietnam and most of South East China. At the top of each one were letters four inches high which spelled out SECRET.

My mission and that of Able Flight of Det. 4, was to intercept Morse Signals sent by selected countries' forces. Most of the time the Comint and Sigint we intercepted was routine, but occasionally there was the "hot Scooby" that the enemy sent in the open. Stuff like airfields being closed for "technical reasons" or perhaps a radar station sending Morse signals from a radar site that was tracking USAF and US Navy Fighter jets as they attacked Hanoi, Haiphong, and other targets in Laos. When the enemy started "chatting" that they had our planes on their radar scopes, they were giving us vital information, every time they sent a ditty dah dit, we knew about it.

Most shifts at Ramasun were boring. Occasionally a target network would decide to change all their call signs, and go from a four digit-letter sign to perhaps a trinome and then they would pull the big dump on us changing not only call signs, but frequencies. Some times the ditty boppers, which are technically known as Morse Intercept Operators, would take days to search a High Frequency radio short wave range to find a familiar target, and then working either simplex or perhaps duplex, (duplex sending on one frequency and the outstations sending back to their net control on another frequency) they pulled every trick in the book to confuse us. Sometimes it would take a month to find and recover the entire network. The new call signs of all the outstations, the net control stations' new call sign and the day frequency and the night frequency's, with short wave the day time transmission frequencies were higher up the frequency dial and the night frequencies were lower. That's because in the day time, HF signals go farther and can be received much easier by a network if they are of shorter, thus higher, frequencies; the night time, vice versa.

Sometimes a ditty bopper really had it made if he covered a single network that only transmitted at five minutes before the hour, twenty four hours a day. The only major problem is that the "Chi-com" Operators used their version of a "bug" keying device and they were very sloppy. The sent Morse code numbers that were "cut" and they often ran their transmissions of numbers without any break in their groupings. It was a pain in the butt trying to copy them on most occasions but it was a mission that had to be done and our guys at Det. 4 did it in a professional manner.

THIS WAS TO BE CONTINUED, BUT NEVER WAS, HOWEVER THIS EDITOR THOUGHT IT TO BE FILLED WITH INTERESTING INFORMATION, SO PRINTED WHAT SHE HAD. (TS)

NCOs
By Vince Wuwert

Subj: NCOs
Date: 2/1/2004 8:59:55 AM Pacific Standard Time
From: VAWuwert
To: IdaReedBlanford

hahahahahahahah!!!! I guess you guys did feel like shootin' some of those hated NCOs. Tell me about the NCOs (since my brother was one) and don't spare the rod, laddy. Trish

NCOs? To be honest with you . . . some of them I liked. Really. And as in the war movies, etc., I would have walked in front of them to take a bullet or to protect them in some way, they were leaders. They could motivate you without destroying your spirit. They could lead you and not make you feel as if you were a dog being led to a food bowl.

They were all business on flight duty, but friendly and in some rare instances they would take an interest in your life, goals, and your past.

We had one in Thailand by the name of George Stephens. His rank was . . . as we said then . . . Prick First Class! Actually he was a Technical Sergeant. He was a hard ass. No one liked him. We all kept our distance. We didn't socialize with him and he didn't socialize with airmen. They were beneath him. He would threaten you with extra duty, and support from other NCOs if you rebuffed him. He chewed tobacco. He condemned us guys who smoked MJ, or cigarettes or cigars as dirty tobacco users. His uniform fatigues were a bit in need of laundering and sewing. He usually wore a baseball cap that was light blue and had two large script "SS" on the front. SS simply meant Security Service. He was a soft ball player for the command soft ball team, guys organized to play ball representing the entire world wide command. He tried to mix his meager abilities of leadership with his enthusiasm of baseball by constantly shouting orders and belittling the airmen when things didn't come across as he expected.

On one occasion at Ramasun in the ops room, he told me to roll down to a certain frequency and pick up a "target" sending numbers. I rolled to that freq . . . and couldn't pick up anything. He kept shouting . . . "copy him . . . copy him . . . he's going right now." He neglected to take into consideration that not all the consoles in the room were wired with the exact same antennas. His was probably pointing in a different direction from mine. As the time came for me to pick up an hourly target, I rolled to my freq and my "mission target" was transmitting. I started my copy and he jumped from his control seat and walked up to me yelling and cursing and asking why I wasn't copying "his" target . . . and I stopped typing, pulled my headsets off and told him I had heard nothing at his "alleged" frequency, and my assigned mission was active and I was copying it. He said he didn't give a fuck what my mission was and he was going to "run me off the island." I never spoke to him again for the remaining three months I was assigned to the unit. When I'd see him on flight I'd ignore him. I figured it was best to keep my distance. I also used to fire up one of my rum soaked crooked cigars. They stunk to high heaven. When I'd see him in my immediate area I'd draw a couple of big drafts and blow out the smoke. It was like trying to kill pesky flies with the billowing blue smoke.

Concerning the aforementioned NCO, I went to see the "Old Man" about him. The Det. 4 Commander was a Captain by the name of Gary Engler. I asked him if he could manage to remove me from flight and put me on days as a paper shuffler and pencil pusher. I told him about the incident and also told him that guys like Stephens are the reason the USAF would not get a reenlistment from me. The guy scared me. Well, Captain Engler, sat me down and told me he was well aware from other complaints from guys about this NCO. But he denied my request to be removed from flight and said my work on the SR-71 copy and a few other things had brought very important intelligence to the 6922nd Security Wing (the HQ located at Clark AFB in the PI) He said, "your personal sign is W.E. isn't it?" I answered, "Yes." I was shocked that he was able to pin point my work. It was the only time in over three years of overseas duty that anyone in authority had complimented me on my work. I stayed on flight, and as I said previously, I kept my distance. I knew quite well how some overzealous NCO with a little bit of authority could "fuck over" someone. I didn't want to be in that category. I just wanted to do my time and go home.

There was another NCO, with the last name of Goldberg. We called him the Mouse. When he put on his chintzy looking Army headsets the ear piece adjustment rods stuck out a bit from his head and his round face and pouchy nose made him look like a mouse, thus the name. He was a jerk. Single and shacking up down town. His "tealock" appeared to have come from the same class of rodents he did. He was subtle with his abuse. He was always defending how great the USAF was. And we kept telling him from the airmen's point of view, that guys like him were too stupid to make it on the outside that was why they were USAF "lifers." He would bristle.

One time he got on a couple of guys with extra duty like clean up and running stupid errands. He was also a bit abusive to guys when they were down town and was with his "tea lock." So, one of the guys inquired if we might all put about ten baht into a "kitty" and hire a Lout song taow driver to kill him down town. They were serious. Although I had the baht ready, and willing to pay out, I figured they'd catch us all for sure. I managed to talk the other airmen out of the idea, saying "it's a great idea, but they will catch us, so is it worth killing this ass hole, and then having to spend 30 years in Leavenworth?"

I had a little guy Staff Sergeant at Chicksands who was my section supervisor for a few months. Little guy could hack ditties really well . . . he kept his proficiency even though he became a non-com. He took an interest in my work and queried me often about how some of the Russian operators would send, and could I tell the difference in style of transmission . . . and were they sloppy with their transmissions . . . or did they ask for traffic to be repeated, etc., he was a good guy. His name escapes me. He smoked like a chimney. Always had a cigarette on his lips in the corner of his mouth. One time he was so busy, slapping his typewriter that the weed in the corner of his mouth had a rather extended ash dangling. I had been sitting next to him copying the same type mission and had just finished when I saw the ash fall on the pant leg of 1505's. I reached over and brushed it away . . . the ash had just started to burn through. Got it just in time. He looked over at me straight faced, never said thanks, but jest kept going. Hitting the carriage return and slapping the keys. I could see the line meter on his R-390 receiver jumping around like it was leaning against an electrical charge . . . he was busy . . . and as I got up to empty my ash tray into a nearby "buttcan" he looked over and gave me the quick thumbs up gesture. He wrote a nice APR on me. (Airman's Proficiency Report) I have it some where. I heard a few years ago that he did his twenty years and was living in the Washington, DC area and working for a firm which sends "couriers" carrying classified information around town. The type guys who have a strong chain handcuffed to their wrists, which are attached to a brief case, locked so tightly it would require three keys to open it, and carrying a "piece" beneath their jackets. He's one of the few NCOs that I wish even to this day, I could meet and greet.

Most of the NCOs I encountered, who were on flight, were jerks. On occasion, as described above, I'd encounter one who put mission duty ahead of personality and the USAF. They gave their best and they did it for themselves first . . . and then the USAF.

I was always fascinated by NCOs who dressed in uniforms that were so sharp, meaning neat, pressed, starched, and fitted neatly, but who never seemed to do any work. They had GI haircuts and everything about them was neat and clean, but they never did anything. They had spit shined shoes all the time. They reminded me of my USAF recruiter in Toledo. Those recruiter guys won't get the attention of a prospective recruit looking like a slob.

There were a couple of NCOs on flight at Chicksands that you could laugh with and exchange insults and know you weren't going to face extra duty. They would often announce that any PTAR error would be met with a good ass kicking at the end of the shift.

Subj: NCOs-continued
Date: 2/1/2004 9:52:18 AM Pacific Standard Time
From: VAWuwert
To: IdaReedBlanford

Trish, sorry for the abrupt stoppage of my e-mail about NCOs. My computer went wacko for a few minutes. Couldn't type anymore.
I'll continue:

A good ass kicking essentially met a mild chewing out for making an error on your daily log of target assignments. We'd often respond to his "ass kickin" statement, by asking if "he made a mistake could we kick HIS ass?"
When I was in training at Keesler in 1965, I did a week of KP. We'd start at -0400 and usually end at 2300. Very long days. The NCO in charge of the mess hall KP was a Staff Sgt. Not a bad guy but he loved to bitch about cleanliness. He had to show every guy how to do his job . . . from guys mopping floors at all times . . . all the way up to the guys washing the dishes in the "clipper rooms."
One time between meals we were caught sleeping on a clearing table in the dish washing "clipper room." I had probably logged some serious Z's for about half an hour when numb nuts NCO comes in and awakens me and a couple of guys, with his shouting and threats. I think we broke a dozen plates that shift, just tossing them across the room if they came through the "hot" dryer with food caked on them.
One time in the latrine at the mess hall at Keesler, the urinal contained a huge palmetto bug. It looked like a cockroach on steroids. It was huge. As I went into the latrine another guy was coming out and he said, "don't use the urinal," I laughed and told him I had to "P" big time. I should have heeded his advice. I came out and said, "What the hell was that?" Some one said, "Seasoning for tomorrows roast beef."
On another occasion this same mess hall NCO told us guys who were working on the serving line beside civilian KP to not take any shit from the foreign troops, especially those from Vietnam. We had guys from Vietnam and other NATO nations (enlisted) eating in our mess halls. So one time I'm on a serving line, and these Vietnamese guys come through . . . they get served and nearly devour all the white rice we have set aside for them . . . a few minutes later one of them comes back with an empty plate and says, "Lice? You have moe lice?" And the civvies KP, who was born and raised in

Dixie and hated anything and anyone from outside Mississippi, and especially Asians, says, "Rice? You mean rice, right? Do you see any rice on that serving table boy? If there isn't any on the serving table, then (and his volume went up about ten notches) there isn't anymore god dam rice you slant eyed jack ass - now get the fuck out of here or I'll beat the shit out of you with my spatula." I held my laughter. On another occasion some student leader came through the chow line with a cigarette in his mouth. This same civvies KP guy got all over him, verbal abuse about his stupidity and he said, "You come through my fucking mess line with a cigarette in your mouth boy and I'll step around this table and rip your lips off - what the fuck is wrong with you? And you're a student leader, you're a red rope, you God dam dumb ass!" There was no smoking permitted along the serving line and it was strictly enforced. On those two occasions, I must say, were the only times I enjoyed being around a local civilian and working beside him.

The analyst type NCOs I had very little contact with them. They were usually very polite and would "ask politely" if we could monitor a certain frequency a little more often than was assigned to us, and they would say, "We're expecting a closure for 'technical reasons' at this particular aerodrome, etc., and if it gets passed in traffic, would you give us a buzz right away?" When they asked stuff like that, I'd be on the alert, the entire 8 hour shift. One time some airman first class analyst stepped into our section and demanded a certain type of traffic be given to him pronto if it came across. He wasn't vulgar, just condescending. "Do you think you can do that?" He was out of hearing distance when I turned my swivel chair towards him and gave him the middle finger, and said, "Fuck you," rather softly. But a lot of guys saw me and laughed, and oh yeah, he didn't get his information. It had been picked up by a later Morse Intercept operator on a different shift flight.

Generally the NCOs in the 202, 203 classifications were a bit more above the mental standard of human beings. NCOs that were former Morse ops usually were within the Cro-Magnon man status, scraped their knuckles when they walked by, know what I mean?

From what you have said about Phil, he seems like the type of guy who if he came to some of my guys, he'd tell us what he needed and a small tid bit of "why" he needed and "ask" us to be on alert. I probably would have had NO problems with him.

Take care, kid. Sorry my e-mails are so long, but you got me going, and the more I wrote, the more I recalled. And speaking of recruiters earlier, I live only five blocks from the second floor walk up office of my recruiter in 1965.

The building is still in tact. But the lower floor is no longer occupied by a retail store. I think about signing those papers of enlistment, every time I drive by. Changed my life and for the most part, it changed it for good.
Vince

TRUE RUSSIAN STORY FROM CHICKSANDS
By Vince Wuwert

From: VAWuwert@aol.com
To: Clara19126@msn.com
Sent: Tuesday, August 02, 2005 12:29 PM

Trish,
True story from Chicksands.
Back in the late 60s the CCCP (Soviet Union) and the Warsaw Pact nations (the opposite of NATO) included all the Iron countries' forces, like Rumania, Czechoslovakia, East Germany, Poland, all those places.
Up until the demise of the Soviet Union in the 80s (thank you Ronald Reagan!) they held maneuvers in the summer and the winter.
We used to monitor all their Air to Air communications like bombers to ground bases, etc., most of it was voice - Russian. Well anyway, my old Buddy, (I only knew the guy for a year and when I left Chicksands I never heard from him), Bill Cook, a Russian linguist voice intercept operator at Chicksands told me he had been copying the air to air combat frequency of the Russian AF fighters, MiG's.
He told me he was copying this one guy who with their tracking on a board nearby, showed him over Poland somewhere - the transmission went something like this:
All in Russian, of course!

This is Zebra one. Am at altitude fifteen thousand and am preparing to execute ninety degree left turn on course three six zero, (due north). New course will be two seven zero.
Second voice: This is zebra alpha two, am at altitude fifteen thousand and am at course three six zero and preparing to execute ninety degree right turn to course zero nine zero right turn to course.
This is Zebra alpha two executing right turn now.
This is Zebra one executing left turn now.
My buddy, Bill said he had his reel to reel tape recorder going, and all he heard was a blood curdling god awful scream - two of them.

A totally true story. A few days later in Stars and Stripes, there was a story about a plane crash during Warsaw Pact maneuvers, attributed to mechanical difficulties, and only one plane was mentioned . . . lying Rooskie bastards.
Vince

THE BATTLEFIELD
By Vince Wuwert

The air is thick, too heavy with humidity to inhale. The stench of dead VC is around me. This battlefield has the light wisp of gun powder and cordite filling my nostrils. An arm moves. Is my enemy dead? Or still with a breath of life in him?
I look him over and he smiles. His eyes are a soft brown. His face is crusted with blood - blood from his wounds inflicted by me. His hand opens and he has no weapon.

A medic arrives and looks at his wounds. "This guy will bleed out in a moment or two. He's hit in his chest and bleeding all over the place. Too much damage to repair in the field," he says softly.

I never knew that man I killed, that day, upon the battlefield. He was my age. His weapon was dirty, a sign of lengthy travel through jungle and fields looking for me, looking for me to be his next target. But my training has been superior and I have avoided his bullets.

The battlefield that day was a whirlwind of death. Like the chariot of fire which took Elijah up to Heaven. My chariot that day was my feet. My fire was the napalm dropped from the sky upon my enemy. Today my bullets and napalm brought death and carnage upon the battlefield. My enemy is now destroyed. The enemy troop has my hand in his palm. He smiles as he moves his lips. He gurgles. No longer is he my enemy - now a dead body. No soul within - an empty shell.

But as life has moved forward and that battlefield left behind, my soul seems to be oozing from my body. The leakage of caring cannot be stopped by an occasional meeting with a counselor, or with alcohol. I did my duty they tell me. A duty in war can be a task of mundane repetition like washing laundry, peeling potatoes, or loading a magazine with two dozen rounds. Lock and load is the command. I lock and load every day of my life since the "Nam."

My friends now have their names on a Wall. I walked past that black Wall a long time ago and I see the battlefield again. Their battlefield is gone. They have returned to eternal rest and they are forever young. But I have to adjust to the tortures of unexplained memories of people dying, bleeding, being maimed for life. I was lucky, my mind is whole, my life has been filled with many blessings, but deep within me is the gnawing question, why wasn't it me?

Is the battlefield still in the "Nam?" or did I bring it home and now it lives within my mind? They say Freedom is not free. And that Peace has a price. But I say insanity is not a savior. For days when I walk through the mist shrouded valleys of Virginia's Blue Ridge I am at peace. I had fought to stay alive. I survived as did my best buddy in the "Nam."

On Christmas one year my buddy called me and cried for an hour. Telling me his battlefield still lives and thrives within his soul. No pills or talking has helped him. He lives, but yet he is dead; dead and still breathing, a paradox of pain, the twisting of fate. The alcohol he consumes and the pills he ingests fail him each day.

The battlefield is quiet now. Villagers walked through it while carrying their bags of rice or walking beside their beast of burden stacked high with their crops for sale in the market place of a nearby village. The valley in the "Nam" often is shrouded in mist, much like the Blue Ridge. But unlike the "Nam," the Blue Ridge is free and the Au Shau is still in bondage and pain.

My friends, today, tell me my time in the "Nam" was in vain. I tell them they are fools and that God sent me for a reason and He has never failed me, and that I will not question His reasoning.

My buddy is now resting beneath the quiet bluegrass covered soil of Kentucky. His torture is finished. His mind is at rest. His soul is now free. The troop plays Taps as the Honor Guard folds Old Glory. The Captain turns to present it to his widow. A lady of grace and a loving mate for my buddy for all those years of his torture. His children cry softly. His wife utters a soft "thank you," as the Captain recites, "This flag is given to you on behalf of a grateful nation for his service to the United States Army and on behalf of the President of the United States his Commander in Chief."

When I draw my last breath will I see that battlefield again? Will I see that little brown man with his blood caked face looking deeply into my eyes as he held out his hand and touched me? Will I smell the cordite? Will I hear the moans of the dying? Will I trip over a discarded rifle, or slip walking over expended bullet casings? Will I retch when I see the blood spattered tall grass and smell the guts of dead GI's? Will I recall the taste of salt as my sweaty face drips moisture from my forehead?

Is Hell for only the Commies and heaven only for the defenders of freedom? Will my back ache from carrying a fifty caliber across paddies and fields? Will I see it again? Will I hear the crackling radio calls of "Two Lima six this is Two Lima one, over?" the voices of guys calling in artillery rounds. Will I see the battle shredded trees that remind me of shucking corn on our back porch on the farm in the Blue Ridge?

The battlefield is a memory. Memories, I have learned, only embrace in love, or cause you to vomit, if you feed them.

I feed only the good memories. The battlefield needs no nourishment.
2005

With all of Wuwert's knowledge, this is a piece of fiction based on fact. And a good piece of fiction it is. [The Editor]

I know you "guys" know this is YOUR book, but I couldn't pass up the chance to allow two "gals" in here, after all, they "served" with you, so hope you don't mind - here goes.[The Editor]

ELMENDORF AFB, ANCHORAGE
By Jeri Xieques

Hey Gurfren,
Dunno if this is something you would want to use . . . it could have happened anywhere I suppose, but it just happened to have happened at a USAFSS site. To me!

I was Secretary to the Chief of the Operations Division at the 6981st Radio Group Mobile at Elmendorf AFB, in Anchorage, in the early 60s, one of two females in the entire outfit. In those days, women hadn't begun to see the military as a career option; we were all housewives, nurses, school teachers, or secretaries. At the 81st, little red-haired Doris was the Commander's Secretary, and I was the blonde back in Ops.

Sometime during 1962, the Ops Division hosted a Conference, with Operations officers from D.C., Shemya, Northeast Cape, and other locations attending. The place had been spiffed up all shiny-clean because we really wanted to make a good impression on our visitors.

The first day of the conference, the men were all gathered in the conference room, and as was the custom in those days, I was asked to bring in coffee. (Women's Lib hadn't been heard of yet!) Since our small office coffee pot was waaay too small to serve the entire group, Captain Marin, one of our own Ops Officers, told me I could run upstairs and fill the coffee cups from one of the large coffee urns that served the guys up there. So I dutifully piled several cups onto a cafeteria tray and proceeded upstairs.

As I approached the door to the upstairs room, my knees began to shake and my tummy suddenly got butterflies. You see, I knew that behind that door there was something like 200 or more guys, one of the "tricks," the day shift. I had never been in there before.

These Guys

I was all of 22 or 23 years old then, married to an airman downstairs in Admin, but still fairly naïve and a little bit shy. A lot shy when it came to walking into a roomful of 200 plus guys.

With a big gulp, I managed to push the buzzer to request entrance into the room; the door was opened, and I walked in. "Teetered in" might be a more apt description. In those days, secretaries dressed up, and in my high heeled pumps, wearing my slim skirt and dressy blouse, I felt very conspicuous. The low hum of quiet chatter in the large room fell silent as my presence became known.

Of course, the coffee service was halfway across the room . . . they couldn't have put it by the door, now could they? As I made my wobbly way to my destination, I felt 400 plus eyes on me. Not daring to look at anyone, I kept my own two eyes on the coffee area just ahead of me.

Having reached the table with the large coffee urn, I filled all the cups on my tray, and was then faced with making the return trip back to the door and safety! The distance seemed to have doubled in length, and I felt as though I were nothing but "T and A." Those 200 plus eyes seemed to have turned to 400 before I got out of there. I shook so badly that I sloshed coffee all over the tray! If any of those cups contained more than half a cupful by the time I reached the Conference Room, I'll be surprised.

Our guests were properly appreciative of the coffee they received, and Captain Marin seemed to have a particularly mischievous grin on his face as he thanked me. He asked, "Did you have any problems," and I replied brightly, "Oh no!" I think he knew why there was as much coffee on the tray as there was in the cups . . . and why there was a little bit, more pink, in my cheeks than usual. By the second day of the conference, we had made arrangements to bring one of the large urns downstairs to serve the visitors.

And I never went upstairs again!

Jeri

And now allow me to print one of the final stories for this book; I call it:

BATTLE OF TODAY
By an Air Force Reservist

Bill Person introduces this piece.
This will bring some tears. Very sad, indeed . . . May God continue to bless the United States Marine Corps and all who have given in service to our nation. [No matter which war or conflict.]

Gentlemen,

I just wanted to share with all of you my most recent Air Force Reserve trip. As most of you know, I have decided to go back into the Air Force Reserves as a part time reservist and after six months of training, I have recently been promoted to Lieutenant Colonel and have been fully mission qualified as an Aircraft Commander of a KC-135R stratotanker aircraft.

On Friday of last week, my crew and I were tasked with a mission to provide air refueling support in order to tanker six F-16's over to Incirlik Air Base in Turkey. We were then to tanker back to the states, six more F-16's that were due maintenance. It started out as a fairly standard mission -- one that I have done many times as an active duty Captain in my former jet -- the KC-10A extender.

We dragged the F-16's to Moron Air Base in Spain where we spent the night and then finished the first part of our mission the next day by successfully delivering them to Incirlik. When I got on the ground in Turkey, I received a message to call the Tanker Airlift Control Center that my mission would change. Instead of tankering the F-16's that were due maintenance, I was cut new orders to fly to Kuwait City and pick up twenty-two "HR's" and return them to Dover Air Force Base in Delaware.

It had been a while since I had heard of the term "HR" used, and as I pondered what the acronym could possibly stand for, it dawned on me that it stood for human remains. There were twenty-two fallen comrades who had just been killed in the most recent attacks in Fallujah and Baghdad, Iraq over the last week.

I immediately alerted the crew of the mission change and although they were exhausted due to an ocean crossing, the time change and minimum round time in Spain for crew rest, we all agreed that it was more important to get these men back to their families as soon as possible.

We were scheduled to crew rest in Incirlik, Turkey for the evening and start the mission the next day. Instead, we decided to extend/continue our day and fly to Kuwait in order to pick up our precious cargo. While on the flight over to Kuwait, I knew that there were protocol procedures for accepting and caring for human remains, however, in my 13 years of active duty service, I never once had to refer to this regulation.

As I read the regulation on the flight over, I felt prepared and ready to do the mission. My game plan was to pick up the Human Remains and turn around to fly to Mildenhal Air Base in England, spend the night, and then fly back the next day. This was the quickest way to get them home, considering the maximum crew duty day that I could subject my crew to legally and physically. I really pushed them to the limits but no one complained at all.

I thought that I was prepared for the acceptance of three men until we landed at Kuwait International. I taxied the jet over to a staging area where the honor guard was waiting to load our soldiers. I stopped the jet and the entire crew was required to stay on board. We opened the cargo door, and according to procedure, I had the crew line up in the back of the aircraft in formation and stand at attention. As the cargo loader brought up the first pallet of caskets, I ordered the crew to "Present Arms." Normally, we would snap a salute at this command, however, when you are dealing with a fallen soldier, the salute is a slow 3 second pace to position. As I stood there and finally saw the first four of twenty-two caskets draped with the American Flags, the reality had hit me. As the Marine Corps honor guard delivered the first pallet on board, I then ordered the crew to "Order Arms," where they rendered an equally slow 3 second return to the attention position. I then commanded the crew to assume an at ease position and directed them to properly place the pallet. The protocol requires that the caskets are to be loaded so when it comes time to exit the aircraft, they will go head first. We did this same procedure for each and every pallet until we could not fit any more.

I felt a deep pit in my stomach when there were more caskets to be brought home and they would have to wait for the next jet to come through. I tried to do everything in my power to bring more home, but I had no more space on board. When we were finally loaded, with our precious cargo and fueled for the trip back to England, a Marine Corps Colonel from first battalion came on board our jet in order to talk to us. I gathered the crew to listen to him and his words of wisdom.

He introduced himself and said that it is the motto of the Marines to leave no man behind and it makes their job easier knowing that there were men like us to help them complete this task. He was the most expeditious manner possible. He then said, "Major Zarnik, these are MY MARINES and I am giving them to you. Please take great care of them as I know you will." I responded with telling him that they are my highest priority and that although this was one of the saddest days of my life, we are all up for the challenge and will go above and beyond to take care of your Marines, "Semper Fi, Sir." A smile came on his face and he responded with a loud and thunderous, "Ooo Rah!" He then asked me to please pass along to the families that these men were extremely brave and had made the ultimate sacrifice for their country and that we appreciate and empathize with what they are going through at this time of their grievance. With that, he departed the jet and we were on our way to England. [Many cold war and "hot" war veterans deserved this type of homecoming, but were held back by secrets and a vow of secrecy they took, about all that they did for our country, so they were not welcomed home and are just now receiving information that has been declassified, and they are allowed to talk about it, (some do, some don't), too late for some of them for they have been killed or have killed themselves, and their relatives have no idea why.] (Editor's comment.)

I had a lot of time to think about the men that I had the privilege to carry. I had a chance to read the manifest on each and every one of them. I read about their religious preferences, their marital status, the injuries that were their cause of death. All of them were under age 27 with most in the 18-24 range. Most of them had wives and children. They had all been killed by an "IED" which I can only deduce as an incendiary explosive device like rocket propelled grenades; mostly fatal head injuries and injuries to the chest area. I could not even imagine the bravery that they must have displayed and the agony suffered in this God Forsaken War. My respect and admiration for these men and what they are doing to help others in a foreign land is beyond calculation. I know that they are all with God now and in a better place.

The stop in Mildenhal was uneventful and then we pressed on to Dover where we would meet the receiving Marine Corps honor guard. When we arrived, we applied the same procedures in reverse. The head of each casket was to come out first. This was a sign of respect rather than defeat. As the honor guard carried each and every American flag covered casket off of the jet, they delivered them to awaiting families with military hearses. I was extremely impressed with how diligent the Honor Guard had performed the seemingly endless task of delivering each of the caskets to the family without fail and with precision. There was not a dry eye on our crew or in the crowd. The Chaplain then said a prayer followed by a speech from Lt. Col. Klaus of the second Battalion. In his speech, he also reiterated similar condolences to the families as the Colonel from First Battalion back in Kuwait.

I then went out to speak with the families as I felt it was my duty to help console them in this difficult time. Although I would probably be one of the last military contacts that they would have for a while, the military tends to take care of its own. I wanted to make sure that they did not feel abandoned and more than that appreciated for their ultimate sacrifice. It was the most difficult thing that I have ever done in my life. I listened to the stories of each and every one that I had come in contact with and they all displayed a sense of pride during an obviously difficult time. The Marine Corps had obviously prepared their families well for this potential outcome.

So, why do I write this story to you all? I just wanted to put a little personal attention to the numbers that you hear about and see in the media. It is almost like we are desensitized by all of the "numbers" of our fallen comrades coming out of Iraq. I heard one commentator say that "it is just a number." Are you kidding me? These are our American Soldiers not numbers! It is truly a sad situation that I hope will end soon. Please hug and embrace your loved ones a little closer and know that there are men out there that are defending you and trying to make this a better world. Please pray for their families and when you hear the latest statistics and numbers of our soldiers killed in combat, please remember this story. It is the only way that I know to more personalize these figures and have them truly mean something to us all.

Thanks for all of your support for me and my family as I take on this new role in completing my Air Force Career and supporting our country. I greatly appreciate all of your comments, gestures and may God bless America, us all, and especially the United States Marine Corps.
Semper Fi!

This letter stands for what our service members in the cold war should have had, but no one knew what they were doing because of all the secret intelligence that was going on. They couldn't talk about what they were doing, to their families, friends, or even to the men working next to them. There was no welcoming home for them, just a debriefing that reiterated they'd better keep their mouths shut. And, while I'm at it, they were not considered Veterans and have had, to this day problems obtaining medical attention.
I say to these cold war warriors, keep on keepin' on, guys. (The Editor).

These Guys

This is the last entry in THESE GUYS.... I deem it appropriate for all of you who have contributed to this book, and/or served in the USAFSS or Vietnam. May God bless all of you, for you have served your country in a great time of need, and you have done it well. I give you a hand salute and a well-done, and if I were in this Congress of the United States you would have had your Cold Medal a long time ago. Thank you to all of you Silent Warriors, those who made it back and those who did not, but I am sure are looking over all of us at this very minute. The Cold War 1945-1991, [The Editor]

LIFE'S CLOCK
By Bill Person

Mortal men have a mortal time
That spans this earthly life,
And bears the times of good and woe
Of happiness and strife.

The treasures that are earned
Are seen in the ones that care
And had a part while he lived
And lovingly they did share.

For the clock of life is wound but once
And no man can truly say
When the hands will point to that time
On the very hour of his last day

There is no magic crystal ball,
No formula to guide along the way.
To journey here, or venture there
We can only do our best and pray.

We should revel in this gift of life,
To spread cheer and joy to everyone.
There's enough sadness to endure in our time
Before our life's work is done.

These Guys

The winding's done, the tics begun
The days they trickle fast
Let it be said, he made a mark
When the final day is past.

Let there be no sadness
When remembering him at his best
And celebrate his days of living.
When at last he's laid to rest.

THE END